CompTIA® Security+ SY0-501 Cert Guide
Fourth Edition

David L. Prowse

800 East 96th Street
Indianapolis, Indiana 46240 USA

CompTIA® Security+ SY0-501 Cert Guide Fourth Edition

ISBN-13: 978-0-7897-5899-6
ISBN-10: 0-7897-5899-7

Library of Congress Control Number: 2017951236

Printed in the United States of America

1 17

Trademarks

Editor-in-Chief
Mark Taub

Product Line Manager
Brett Bartow

Acquisitions Editor
Michelle Newcomb

Development Editor
Eleanor Bru

Managing Editor
Sandra Schroeder

Senior Project Editor
Tonya Simpson

Copy Editor
Bill McManus

Indexer
Ken Johnson

Proofreader
Paula Lowell

Technical Editor
Chris Crayton

Publishing Coordinator
Vanessa Evans

Cover Designer
Chuti Prasertsith

Compositor
Studio Galou

Warning and Disclaimer

Special Sales

Contents at a Glance

Elements Available Online

View Recommended Resources

Real-World Scenarios

Table of Contents

About the Author

David L. Prowse is an author, technologist, and technical trainer. He has penned a dozen books for Pearson Education, including the well-received *CompTIA A+ Exam Cram*. He also develops video content, including the *CompTIA A+ LiveLessons* video course. Over the past two decades he has taught CompTIA A+, Network+, and Security+ certification courses, both in the classroom and via the Internet. David has 20 years of experience in the IT field and loves to share that experience with his readers, watchers, and students.

He runs the website www.davidlprowse.com in support of his books and videos.

Acknowledgments

It takes a lot of amazing people to publish a book. Special thanks go to Eleanor Bru, Chris Crayton, Michelle Newcomb, and all the other people at Pearson (and beyond) who helped make this book a reality. I appreciate everything you do!

About the Technical Reviewer

Chris Crayton (MCSE) is an author, technical consultant, and trainer. In the past, he has worked as a computer technology and networking instructor, information security director, network administrator, network engineer, and PC specialist. Chris has authored several print and online books on PC repair, CompTIA A+, CompTIA Security+, and Microsoft Windows. He has also served as technical editor and content contributor on numerous technical titles for several leading publishing companies. Chris holds numerous industry certifications, has been recognized with many professional teaching awards, and has served as a state-level SkillsUSA competition judge.

We Want to Hear from You!

As the reader of this book, *you* are our most important critic and commentator. We value your opinion and want to know what we're doing right, what we could do better, what areas you'd like to see us publish in, and any other words of wisdom you're willing to pass our way.

We welcome your comments. You can email or write to let us know what you did or didn't like about this book—as well as what we can do to make our books better.

Please note that we cannot help you with technical problems related to the topic of this book.

When you write, please be sure to include this book's title and author as well as your name and email address. We will carefully review your comments and share them with the author and editors who worked on the book.

Email: feedback@pearsonitcertification.com

Mail: Pearson IT Certification
ATTN: Reader Feedback
800 East 96th Street
Indianapolis, IN 46240 USA

Reader Services

Register your copy of *CompTIA Security+ SY0-501 Cert Guide* at www.pearsonitcertification.com for convenient access to downloads, updates, and corrections as they become available. To start the registration process, go to www.pearsonitcertification.com/register and log in or create an account.* Enter the product ISBN 9780789758996 and click Submit. When the process is complete, you will find any available bonus content under Registered Products.

*Be sure to check the box that you would like to hear from us to receive exclusive discounts on future editions of this product.

CompTIA

Becoming a CompTIA Certified IT Professional is Easy

It's also the best way to reach greater professional opportunities and rewards.

Why Get CompTIA Certified?

Growing Demand

Labor estimates predict some technology fields will experience growth of over 20% by the year 2020.* CompTIA certification qualifies the skills required to join this workforce.

Higher Salaries

IT professionals with certifications on their resume command better jobs, earn higher salaries and have more doors open to new multi-industry opportunities.

Verified Strengths

91% of hiring managers indicate CompTIA certifications are valuable in validating IT expertise, making certification the best way to demonstrate your competency and knowledge to employers.**

Universal Skills

CompTIA certifications are vendor neutral—which means that certified professionals can proficiently work with an extensive variety of hardware and software found in most organizations.

Learn more about what the exam covers by reviewing the following:

- Exam objectives for key study points.

- Sample questions for a general overview of what to expect on the exam and examples of question format.

- Visit online forums, like LinkedIn, to see what other IT professionals say about CompTIA exams.

Purchase a voucher at a Pearson VUE testing center or at CompTIAstore.com.

- Register for your exam at a Pearson VUE testing center:

- Visit pearsonvue.com/CompTIA to find the closest testing center to you.

- Schedule the exam online. You will be required to enter your voucher number or provide payment information at registration.

- Take your certification exam.

Congratulations on your CompTIA certification!

- Make sure to add your certification to your resume.

- Check out the CompTIA Certification Roadmap to plan your next career move.

Learn more: **Certification.CompTIA.org/securityplus**

* Source: CompTIA 9th Annual Information Security Trends study: 500 U.S. IT and Business Executives Responsible for Security
** Source: CompTIA Employer Perceptions of IT Training and Certification

Introduction

Welcome to the *CompTIA Security+ SY0-501 Cert Guide*. The CompTIA Security+ Certification is widely accepted as the first security certification you should attempt to attain in your information technology (IT) career. The CompTIA Security+ Certification is designed to be a vendor-neutral exam that measures your knowledge of industry-standard technologies and methodologies. It acts as a great stepping stone to other vendor-specific certifications and careers. I developed this book to be something you can study from for the exam and keep on your bookshelf for later use as a security resource.

I'd like to note that it's unfeasible to cover all security concepts in depth in a single book. However, the Security+ exam objectives are looking for a basic level of computer, networking, and organizational security knowledge. Keep this in mind while reading through this text, and remember that the main goal of this text is to help you pass the Security+ exam, not to be the master of all security. Not just yet at least!

Good luck as you prepare to take the CompTIA Security+ exam. As you read through this book, you will be building an impenetrable castle of knowledge, culminating in hands-on familiarity and the know-how to pass the exam.

> **IMPORTANT NOTE**   The first thing you should do before you start reading Chapter 1, "Introduction to Security," is check my website for errata and updated information, and mark those new items in the book. Go to www.davidlprowse.com and then the Security+ section. On my site you will also find videos, bonus test questions, and other additional content. And, of course, you can contact me directly at my website to ask me questions about the book.

Goals and Methods

The number one goal of this book is to help you pass the SY0-501 version of the CompTIA Security+ Certification Exam. To that effect, I have filled this book and practice exams with more than 600 questions/answers and explanations in total, including three 80-question practice exams. One of the exams is printed at the end of the book, and all exams are located in Pearson Test Prep practice test software in a custom test environment. These tests are geared to check your knowledge and ready you for the real exam.

The CompTIA Security+ Certification exam involves familiarity with computer security theory and hands-on know-how. To aid you in mastering and understanding the Security+ Certification objectives, this book uses the following methods:

- **Opening topics list:** This defines the topics to be covered in the chapter.

- **Topical coverage:** The heart of the chapter. Explains the topics from a theory-based standpoint, as well as from a hands-on perspective. This includes in-depth descriptions, tables, and figures that are geared to build your knowledge so that you can pass the exam. The chapters are broken down into two to three topics each.

- **Key Topics:** The Key Topic icons indicate important figures, tables, and lists of information that you should know for the exam. They are interspersed throughout the chapter and are listed in table format at the end of the chapter.

- **Key Terms:** Key terms without definitions are listed at the end of each chapter. See whether you can define them, and then check your work against the complete key term definitions in the glossary.

- **Real-World Scenarios:** Included in the supplemental online material are real-world scenarios for each chapter. These offer the reader insightful questions and problems to solve. The questions are often open-ended, and can have several different solutions. The online material gives one or more possible solutions and then points to video-based solutions and simulation exercises online to further reinforce the concepts. Refer to these real-world scenarios at the end of each chapter.

- **Review Questions:** These quizzes, and answers with explanations, are meant to gauge your knowledge of the subjects. If an answer to a question doesn't come readily to you, be sure to review that portion of the chapter. The review questions are also available online.

- **Practice Exams:** There is one practice exam printed at the end of the book, and additional exams included in the Pearson Test Prep practice test software. These test your knowledge and skills in a realistic testing environment. Take these after you have read through the entire book. Master one, then move on to the next. Take any available bonus exams last.

Another goal of this book is to offer support for you, the reader. Again, if you have questions or suggestions, please contact me through my website: www.davidlprowse. com. I try my best to answer your queries as soon as possible.

Who Should Read This Book?

This book is for anyone who wants to start or advance a career in computer security. Readers of this book can range from persons taking a Security+ course to individuals already in the field who want to keep their skills sharp, or perhaps retain their job due to a company policy mandating they take the Security+ exam. Some information assurance professionals who work for the Department of Defense or have privileged access to DoD systems are required to become Security+ certified as per DoD directive 8570.1.

This book is also designed for people who plan on taking additional security-related certifications after the CompTIA Security+ exam. The book is designed in such a way to offer an easy transition to future certification studies.

Although not a prerequisite, it is recommended that CompTIA Security+ candidates have at least two years of IT administration experience with an emphasis on security. The CompTIA Network+ certification is also recommended as a prerequisite. Before you begin your Security+ studies, it is expected that you understand computer topics such as how to install operating systems and applications, and networking topics such as how to configure IP, what a VLAN is, and so on. The focus of this book is to show how to secure these technologies and protect against possible exploits and attacks. Generally, for people looking to enter the IT field, the CompTIA Security+ certification is attained after the A+ and Network+ certifications.

CompTIA Security+ Exam Topics

If you haven't downloaded the Security+ certification exam objectives, do it now from CompTIA's website: https://certification.comptia.org/. Save the PDF file and print it out as well. It's a big document—review it carefully. Use the exam objectives list and acronyms list to aid in your studies while you use this book.

The following two tables are excerpts from the exam objectives document. Table I-1 lists the CompTIA Security+ domains and each domain's percentage of the exam.

Table I-1   CompTIA Security+ Exam Domains

Domain	Exam Topic	% of Exam
1.0	Threats, Attacks and Vulnerabilities	21%
2.0	Technologies and Tools	22%
3.0	Architecture and Design	15%
4.0	Identity and Access Management	16%
5.0	Risk Management	14%
6.0	Cryptography and PKI	12%

The Security+ domains are then further broken down into individual objectives. To achieve better flow and to present the topics in more of a building-block approach, I rearranged the concepts defined in the objectives. This approach is designed especially for people who are new to the computer security field.

Table I-2 lists the CompTIA Security+ exam objectives and their related chapters in this book. It does not list the bullets and sub-bullets for each objective.

> **NOTE**   Chapter 19 gives strategies for taking the exam and therefore does not map to any specific objectives.

Table I-2   CompTIA Security+ Exam Objectives

Objective	Chapter(s)
1.1 Given a scenario, analyze indicators of compromise and determine the type of malware.	2, 13
1.2 Compare and contrast types of attacks.	7, 9, 14, 17
1.3 Explain threat actor types and attributes.	1, 17
1.4 Explain penetration testing concepts.	12
1.5 Explain vulnerability scanning concepts.	12
1.6 Explain the impact associated with types of vulnerabilities.	5, 12
2.1 Install and configure network components, both hardware- and software-based, to support organizational security.	6, 8, 10, 13, 15
2.2 Given a scenario, use appropriate software tools to assess the security posture of an organization.	13, 14, 18
2.3 Given a scenario, troubleshoot common security issues.	10, 11, 17
2.4 Given a scenario, analyze and interpret output from security technologies.	3, 4, 8
2.5 Given a scenario, deploy mobile devices securely.	3, 6, 9
2.6 Given a scenario, implement secure protocols.	6, 7, 13
3.1 Explain use cases and purpose for frameworks, best practices and secure configuration guides.	12, 18
3.2 Given a scenario, implement secure network architecture concepts.	6, 7, 9, 10, 13
3.3 Given a scenario, implement secure systems design.	3, 4
3.4 Explain the importance of secure staging deployment concepts.	5, 12
3.5 Explain the security implications of embedded systems.	3, 4, 18
3.6 Summarize secure application development and deployment concepts.	5
3.7 Summarize cloud and virtualization concepts.	4, 6
3.8 Explain how resiliency and automation strategies reduce risk.	12, 16
3.9 Explain the importance of physical security controls.	10

Objective	Chapter(s)
4.1 Compare and contrast identity and access management concepts.	10
4.2 Given a scenario, install and configure identity and access services.	10
4.3 Given a scenario, implement identity and access management controls.	10, 11
4.4 Given a scenario, differentiate common account management practices.	11
5.1 Explain the importance of policies, plans and procedures related to organizational security.	18
5.2 Summarize business impact analysis concepts.	16
5.3 Explain risk management processes and concepts.	12, 18
5.4 Given a scenario, follow incident response procedures.	18
5.5 Summarize basic concepts of forensics.	18
5.6 Explain disaster recovery and continuity of operation concepts.	16
5.7 Compare and contrast various types of controls.	1, 12
5.8 Given a scenario, carry out data security and privacy practices.	18
6.1 Compare and contrast basic concepts of cryptography.	14
6.2 Explain cryptography algorithms and their basic characteristics.	14
6.3 Given a scenario, install and configure wireless security settings.	9, 10
6.4 Given a scenario, implement public key infrastructure.	15

Companion Website

Register this book to get access to the Pearson Test Prep practice test software and other study materials plus additional bonus content. Check this site regularly for new and updated postings written by the author that provide further insight into the more troublesome topics on the exam. Be sure to check the box that you would like to hear from us to receive updates and exclusive discounts on future editions of this product or related products.

To access this companion website, follow these steps:

1. Go to www.pearsonitcertification.com/register and log in or create a new account.

2. On your Account page, tap or click the **Registered Products** tab, and then tap or click the **Register Another Product** link.

3. Enter this book's ISBN (9780789758996).

4. Answer the challenge question as proof of book ownership.

5. Tap or click the **Access Bonus Content** link for this book to go to the page where your downloadable content is available.

Please note that many of our companion content files can be very large, especially image and video files.

If you are unable to locate the files for this title by following the preceding steps, please visit http://www.pearsonitcertification.com/contact and select the "Site Problems/Comments" option. Our customer service representatives will assist you.

Pearson Test Prep Practice Test Software

As noted previously, this book comes complete with the Pearson Test Prep practice test software containing three full exams. These practice tests are available to you either online or as an offline Windows application. To access the practice exams that were developed with this book, please see the instructions in the card inserted in the sleeve in the back of the book. This card includes a unique access code that enables you to activate your exams in the Pearson Test Prep software.

> **NOTE**   The cardboard sleeve in the back of this book includes a piece of paper. The paper lists the activation code for the practice exams associated with this book. Do not lose the activation code. On the opposite side of the paper from the activation code is a unique, one-time-use coupon code for the purchase of the Premium Edition eBook and Practice Test.

Accessing the Pearson Test Prep Software Online

The online version of this software can be used on any device with a browser and connectivity to the Internet including desktop machines, tablets, and smartphones. To start using your practice exams online, simply follow these steps:

1. Go to www.PearsonTestPrep.com and select **Pearson IT Certification** as your product group.

2. Enter your email/password for your account. If you do not have an account on PearsonITCertification.com or CiscoPress.com, you will need to establish one by going to PearsonITCertification.com/join.

3. On the My Products tab, tap or click the **Activate New Product** button.

4. Enter this book's activation code and click **Activate**.

5. The product will now be listed on your My Products tab. Tap or click the **Exams** button to launch the exam settings screen and start your exam.

Accessing the Pearson Test Prep Software Offline

If you wish to study offline, you can download and install the Windows version of the Pearson Test Prep software. There is a download link for this software on the book's companion website, or you can just enter this link in your browser:

http://www.pearsonitcertification.com/content/downloads/pcpt/engine.zip

To access the book's companion website and the software, simply follow these steps:

1. Register your book by going to http://www.pearsonitcertification.com/register and entering the ISBN: **9780789758996**.

2. Respond to the challenge questions.

3. Go to your account page and select the **Registered Products** tab.

4. Click the **Access Bonus Content** link under the product listing.

5. Click the **Install Pearson Test Prep Desktop Version** link under the Practice Exams section of the page to download the software.

6. Once the software finishes downloading, unzip all the files on your computer.

7. Double-click the application file to start the installation, and follow the onscreen instructions to complete the registration.

8. Once the installation is complete, launch the application and click the **Activate Exam** button on the My Products tab.

9. Click the **Activate a Product** button in the Activate Product Wizard.

10. Enter the unique access code found on the card in the sleeve in the back of your book and click the **Activate** button.

11. Click **Next** and then the **Finish** button to download the exam data to your application.

12. You can now start using the practice exams by selecting the product and clicking the **Open Exam** button to open the exam settings screen.

Note that the offline and online versions will synch together, so saved exams and grade results recorded on one version will be available to you on the other as well.

Customizing Your Exams

Once you are in the exam settings screen, you can choose to take exams in one of three modes:

- Study Mode
- Practice Exam Mode
- Flash Card Mode

Study Mode allows you to fully customize your exams and review answers as you are taking the exam. This is typically the mode you would use first to assess your knowledge and identify information gaps. Practice Exam Mode locks certain customization options, as it is presenting a realistic exam experience. Use this mode when you are preparing to test your exam readiness. Flash Card Mode strips out the answers and presents you with only the question stem. This mode is great for late-stage preparation when you really want to challenge yourself to provide answers without the benefit of seeing multiple-choice options. This mode will not provide the detailed score reports that the other two modes will, so it should not be used if you are trying to identify knowledge gaps.

In addition to these three modes, you will be able to select the source of your questions. You can choose to take exams that cover all of the chapters or you can narrow your selection to just a single chapter or the chapters that make up specific parts in the book. All chapters are selected by default. If you want to narrow your focus to individual chapters, simply deselect all the chapters then select only those on which you wish to focus in the Objectives area.

You can also select the exam banks on which to focus. Each exam bank comes complete with a full exam of questions that cover topics in every chapter. The exam printed in the book is available to you as well as two additional exams of unique questions. You can have the test engine serve up exams from all banks or just from one individual bank by selecting the desired banks in the exam bank area.

There are several other customizations you can make to your exam from the exam settings screen, such as the time of the exam, the number of questions served up, whether to randomize questions and answers, whether to show the number of correct answers for multiple-answer questions, or whether to serve up only specific types of questions. You can also create custom test banks by selecting only questions that you have marked or questions on which you have added notes.

Updating Your Exams

If you are using the online version of the Pearson Test Prep software, you should always have access to the latest version of the software as well as the exam data. If you are using the Windows desktop version, every time you launch the software, it will check to see if there are any updates to your exam data and automatically download any changes that were made since the last time you used the software. This requires that you are connected to the Internet at the time you launch the software.

Sometimes, due to many factors, the exam data may not fully download when you activate your exam. If you find that figures or exhibits are missing, you may need to manually update your exams.

To update a particular exam you have already activated and downloaded, simply select the **Tools** tab and click the **Update Products** button. Again, this is only an issue with the desktop Windows application.

If you wish to check for updates to the Pearson Test Prep exam engine software, Windows desktop version, simply select the **Tools** tab and click the **Update Application** button. This will ensure you are running the latest version of the software engine.

Premium Edition eBook and Practice Tests

This book also includes an exclusive offer for 70 percent off the Premium Edition eBook and Practice Tests edition of this title. Please see the coupon code included with the cardboard sleeve for information on how to purchase the Premium Edition.

This chapter covers the following subjects:

- **Security 101:** School is in session. This section discusses some of the basic principles of information security such as CIA and AAA, some basic threats, and various ways to mitigate those threats.

- **Think Like a Hacker:** "To know your Enemy, you must become your Enemy" (Sun Tzu). However, sometimes the hacker is your adversary, sometimes not. This section describes the various hats worn in the hacker society, as well as the other actors on the security stage and their attributes.

- **Threat Actor Types and Attributes:** From script kiddies to hacktivists to nation states, the stage is filled with different individuals and entities you will defend against. Their motives might be pure, they might not—this section describes the other attackers you should know.

CHAPTER 1

Introduction to Security

Welcome! Before we launch into heavy-duty security, I'd like to go over some foundation-level security concepts. I recommend that everyone read this chapter, but if you are a seasoned professional, you might opt to scan or skip it. For those of you new to the IT security field, this chapter (and the rest of the book) acts as the basis of your IT sleuthing career.

It is so important in today's organizations to protect information and information systems from unauthorized access and to prevent the modification, disruption, or destruction of data unless it is approved by the organization. That in a nutshell is **information security**. Companies consider it so important that many IT directors have transformed into full-fledged executives—chief information officer (CIO), chief security officer (CSO), or chief technology officer (CTO). But let's not get ahead of ourselves! This book is for persons wanting to embark on, or continue along, the path as a security administrator. Many other names are given to that particular position, but we'll stick with that one for the sake of continuity throughout this book.

This entire book is all about information security; it's about locating risks and vulnerabilities to your information, and eliminating those risks, or at least reducing them to a point acceptable to your organization.

This first chapter talks about some basic fundamental security concepts and teaches you to think like a hacker but act like an administrator.

Let's begin!

Foundation Topics

Security 101

The first thing we need to get out of the way is that nothing is ever completely or truly secure. People might give clever definitions of something that could be completely secure, but it is a utopia—something that can be imagined but never achieved. There is always a way around or through any security precaution that we construct.

Now that it's understood that there is no perfect scenario, we can move on to some security basics that can help to build a solid foundation upon which proper mitigating of security risks can begin.

The CIA of Computer Security

No, we're not talking about the acronym associated with national security, but computers can indeed be the victim of covert operations. To defend against the worst, IT people attempt to adhere to three core principles of information security: confidentiality, integrity, and availability. Collectively, these three are known as the CIA triad as illustrated in Figure 1-1.

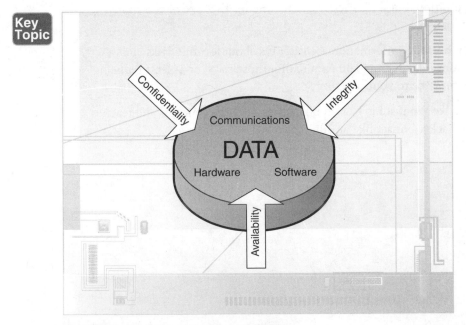

Figure 1-1 The CIA of Computer Security

By employing the concepts of confidentiality, integrity, and availability to its data, an organization can properly secure its hardware, software, and communications. Let's discuss each of the three items of the CIA triad in a little more depth.

- **Confidentiality:** This concept centers on preventing the disclosure of information to unauthorized persons. For the public it signifies Social Security numbers (or other country-specific identification), driver's license information, bank accounts and passwords, and so on. For organizations this can include all the preceding information, but it actually denotes the confidentiality of data. To make data confidential, the organization must work hard to make sure that it can be accessed only by authorized individuals. This book spends a good amount of time discussing and showing how to accomplish this. For example, when you use a credit card number at a store or online, the number should be encrypted with a strong cipher so that the card number cannot be compromised. Next time you buy something over the Internet, take a look at how the credit card number is being kept confidential. As a security professional, confidentiality should be your number one goal. In keeping data confidential, you remove threats, absorb vulnerabilities, and reduce risk.

- **Integrity:** This means that data has not been tampered with. Authorization is necessary before data can be modified in any way; this is done to protect the data's integrity. For example, if a person were to delete a required file, either maliciously or inadvertently, the integrity of that file will have been violated. There should have been permissions in place to stop the person from deleting the file. Here's a tip for you: Some organizations do not delete data—ever!

- **Availability:** Securing computers and networks can be a strain on resources. Availability means that data is obtainable regardless of how information is stored, accessed, or protected. It also means that data should be available regardless of the malicious attack that might be perpetrated on it.

These three principles should be applied when dealing with the security of hardware, software, or communications. They should be foremost in the mind of a security administrator.

Another acronym to live by is the AAA of computer security: authentication, authorization, and accounting.

- **Authentication:** When a person's identity is established with proof and confirmed by a system. Typically, this requires a digital identity of some sort, a username/password, biometric data, or other authentication scheme.

- **Authorization:** When a user is given access to certain data or areas of a building. Authorization happens after authentication and can be determined in several ways, including permissions, access control lists, time-of-day restrictions, and other login and physical restrictions.

- **Accounting:** The tracking of data, computer usage, and network resources. Often it means logging, auditing, and monitoring of the data and resources. Accountability is quickly becoming more important in today's secure networks. Part of this concept is the burden of proof. You as the security person must provide proof if you believe that someone committed an unauthorized action. When you have indisputable proof of something users have done and they cannot deny it, it is known as **non-repudiation**.

This AAA concept should also be applied to any security plan you develop. But it goes further than this. There are authentication protocols based on the concept of AAA such as RADIUS and TACACS+, which we cover in more depth in Chapter 10, "Physical Security and Authentication Models." Because of this, AAA is also referred to as a protocol. The details of AAA are set in stone within several RFC documents that can be downloaded from the following link: http://tools.ietf.org/wg/aaa/.

The Basics of Information Security

Information security is the act of protecting data and information systems from unauthorized access, unlawful modification and disruption, disclosure, corruption, and destruction. We discuss how to implement information security throughout the entire book, but for now let's talk about several basic types of threats you need to be aware of to be an effective security administrator:

- **Malicious software:** Known as malware, this includes computer viruses, worms, Trojan horses, spyware, rootkits, adware, ransomware, crypto-malware, and other types of unwanted software. Everyone has heard of a scenario in which a user's computer was compromised to some extent due to malicious software.

- **Unauthorized access:** Access to computer resources and data without consent of the owner. It might include approaching the system, trespassing, communicating, storing and retrieving data, intercepting data, or any other methods that would interfere with a computer's normal work. Access to data must be controlled to ensure privacy. Improper administrative access falls into this category as well.

- **System failure:** Computer crashes or individual application failure. This can happen due to several reasons, including user error, malicious activity, or hardware failure.

- **Social engineering:** The act of manipulating users into revealing confidential information or performing other actions detrimental to the users. Almost everyone gets e-mails nowadays from unknown entities making false claims or asking for personal information (or money!); this is one example of social engineering.

Many information security technologies and concepts can protect against, or help recover from, the preceding threats. The question is, does your organization have the resources to implement them? Even on a low budget the answer is usually "yes." It all starts with planning, which is effectively free.

In general, a security administrator should create a proactive security plan that usually starts with the implementation of security controls. When creating the security plan, some IT professionals divide the plan into three categories of controls as follows:

- **Physical:** Things such as alarm systems, surveillance cameras, locks, ID cards, security guards, and so on.

- **Technical:** Items such as smart cards, access control lists (ACLs), encryption, and network authentication.

- **Administrative:** Various policies and procedures, security awareness training, contingency planning, and disaster recovery plans (DRPs). Administrative controls can also be broken down into two subsections: procedural controls and legal/regulatory controls.

NOTE   We'll expand on these and other security controls in Chapter 12, "Vulnerability and Risk Assessment."

These information security controls are used to protect the confidentiality, integrity, and availability, or "CIA" of data.

More specifically, several ways to prevent and help recover from the previous threats include

- **User awareness:** The wiser the user, the less chance of security breaches. Employee training and education, easily accessible and understandable policies, security awareness e-mails, and online security resources all help to provide user awareness. These methods can help to protect from all the threats mentioned previously. Although it can only go so far while remaining cost-effective and productive, educating the user can be an excellent method when attempting to protect against security attacks.

- **Authentication:** Verifying a person's identity helps to protect against unauthorized access. Authentication is a preventative measure that can be broken down into five categories:

    — Something the user knows; for example, a password or PIN

    — Something the user has; for example, a smart card or other security token

— Something the user is; for example, the biometric reading of a fingerprint or retina scan

— Something a user does; for example, voice recognition or a written signature

— Somewhere a user is; for example, a GPS-tracked individual, or when a system is authenticated through geographic location

■ **Anti-malware software:** Anti-malware protects a computer from the various forms of malware and, if necessary, detects and removes them. Types include antivirus and anti-spyware software. Well-known examples include programs from Symantec and McAfee, as well as Microsoft's Windows Defender. Nowadays, a lot of the software named "antivirus" can protect against spyware and other types of malware as well.

■ **Data backups:** Backups won't stop damage to data, but they can enable you to recover data after an attack or other compromise, or system failure. From programs such as Windows Backup and Restore, Windows File History, and Bacula to enterprise-level programs such as Veritas Backup Exec and the various cloud-based solutions, data backup is an important part of security. Note that fault-tolerant methods such as RAID 1, 5, 6, and 10 are good preventative measures against hardware failure but *might* not offer protection from data corruption or erasure. For more information on RAID, see Chapter 16, "Redundancy and Disaster Recovery."

■ **Encryption:** This involves changing information using an algorithm (known as a cipher) to make that information unreadable to anyone except users who possess the proper "key." Examples of this include wireless sessions encrypted with Advanced Encryption Standard (AES), web pages encrypted with HTTP Secure (HTTPS), and e-mails encrypted with Secure/Multipurpose Internet Mail Extensions (S/MIME) or Pretty Good Privacy (PGP).

■ **Data removal:** Proper data removal goes far beyond file deletion or the formatting of digital media. The problem with file deletion/formatting is data *remanence*, or the residue, left behind, from which re-creation of files can be accomplished by some less-than-reputable people with smart tools. Companies typically employ one of three options when met with the prospect of data removal: clearing, purging (also known as sanitizing), and destruction. We talk more about these in Chapter 18, "Policies and Procedures."

By combining a well-thought-out security plan with strong individual security methods, a security professional can effectively stop threats before they become realities, or at the least, in worst-case scenarios, recover from them quickly and efficiently. The strongest security plans take many or all of these methods and combine them in a layering strategy known as **defense in depth**, which can be defined as the building up and layering of security measures that protect data throughout the entire life cycle starting from inception, on through usage, storage, and network transfer, and finally to disposal.

Think Like a Hacker

I'm not condoning any malicious activity, but to think like a hacker, you have to understand the hacker. A good hacker understands the mind of a security administrator, making computer and network security a difficult proposition. But the converse is true as well—the smart security person is aware of hackers and their methods.

So, ask yourself, why do people decide to become hackers? In the minds of some malicious individuals, it may simply be because users are there to be taken advantage of! Another common answer is greed—in this case the act of hacking for illegal monetary gain. Other attackers have an agenda, or believe in a cause. Some want to get free access to movies and music. Finally, some just want to cause mayhem and anarchy. Consider this when you secure your organization's computers—they just might be a target! Of course, people use different names to classify these types of individuals: hacker, cracker, cyber-criminal, and so on. It doesn't matter what you call them, but the accepted term in most network security circles is hacker—which we will use throughout this book.

Now consider this: Not all hackers are malicious. That's right! There are different types of hackers. Various names are used by different organizations, but some of the common labels include the following:

- **White hats:** These people are non-malicious; for example, an IT person who attempts to "hack" into a computer system before it goes live to test the system. Generally, the person attempting the hack has a contractual agreement with the owner of the resource to be hacked. White hats often are involved in something known as ethical hacking. An **ethical hacker** is an expert at breaking into systems and can attack systems on behalf of the system's owner and with the owner's consent. The ethical hacker uses penetration testing and intrusion testing to attempt to gain access to a target network or system.

- **Black hats:** These are malicious individuals who attempt to break into computers and computer networks *without* authorization. Black hats are the ones who attempt identity theft, piracy, credit card fraud, and so on. Penalties for this type of activity are severe, and black hats know it; keep this in mind if and when you come into contact with one of these seedy individuals—they can be brutal, especially when cornered. Of course, many vendors try to make the term "black hat" into something cuter and less dangerous. But for the purposes of this book and your job security, we need to speak plainly, so here we will consider a black hat to be a malicious individual.

- **Gray hats:** These are possibly the most inexplicable people on the planet. They are individuals who do not have any affiliation with a company but risk breaking the law by attempting to hack a system and then notify the administrator of the system that they were successful in doing so—just to let them know! Not to do anything malicious (other than breaking in…). Some gray hats offer to fix security vulnerabilities at a price, but these types are also known as green hats or mercenaries.

- **Blue hats:** These are individuals who are asked to attempt to hack into a system by an organization, but the organization does not employ them. The organization relies on the fact that the person simply enjoys hacking into systems. Usually, this type of scenario occurs when testing systems.

- **Elite:** Elite hackers are the ones who first find out about vulnerabilities. Only 1 out of an estimated 10,000 hackers wears the Elite hat—and I say that figuratively. The credit for their discoveries is usually appropriated by someone else more interested in fame. Many of these types of individuals don't usually care about "credit due" and are more interested in anonymity—perhaps a wise choice. You do not want to get on an Elite hacker's bad side; they could crumple most networks and programs within hours if they so desired.

I mentioned before that no system is truly secure (and I use the term "system" loosely). Hackers know this and count on it. There's always a way to circumnavigate a defense. It's a constant battle in which administrators and attackers are consistently building and breaking down better and better mouse traps. The scales are always tipping back and forth; a hacker develops a way to break into a system, then an administrator finds a way to block that attack, then the hacker looks for an alternative method, and so on. This seems to reek of the chicken and the egg—which came first? Answer: You have to take it on a case-by-case basis. The last few sentences of banter are there for one reason—to convince you that you need to be on your toes; that you need to review logs often; that you need to employ as many security precautions as possible; that you need to keep abreast of the latest attacks and ways to mitigate risk; and that you must never underestimate the power and resilience of a hacker.

Threat Actor Types and Attributes

The security arena has other types of personas as well. It's important to understand the types of attackers that you might encounter and their characteristics and personality traits. Keep in mind that these "actors" can find ways to access systems and networks just by searching the Internet. So, some attacks can be perpetrated by people with little knowledge of computers and technology. Other actors have increased knowledge—and with knowledge comes power—the type of power you want to be ready for in advance. However, all levels of attackers can be dangerous. Let's describe several of the actors now.

The first of these personas is the **script kiddie**. This is an unsophisticated individual with little or no skills when it comes to technology. The person uses code that was written by others and is freely accessible on the Internet. For example, a script kiddie might copy a malicious PHP script directly from one website to another; only the knowledge of "copy and paste" is required. It's a derogatory term that is often associated with juveniles. Though the processes they use are simple, script kiddies can knowingly (and even unwittingly) inflict incredible amounts of damage to insecure systems. These people almost never have internal knowledge of a system and typically have a limited amount of resources, so the amount, sophistication, and extent of their attacks is constrained. They are often thrill-seekers and are motivated by a need to increase their reputation in the script-kiddie world.

Next is the **hacktivist**—a combination of the terms *hack* and *activist*. As with the term *hacker*, the name of hacktivist is often applied to different kinds of activities; from hacking for social change, to hacking to promote political agendas, to full-blown cyberterrorism. Due to the ambiguity of the term, a hacktivist could be inside the company or attack from the outside and will have a varying amount of resources and funding. However, the hacktivist is usually far more competent than a script kiddie.

Cyber-criminals might work on their own, or they might be part of **organized crime**—a centralized enterprise run by people motivated mainly by money. Individuals who are part of an organized crime group are often well-funded and can have a high level of sophistication.

Individuals might also carry out cyberattacks for governments and nation states. In this case, a government—and its processes—is known as an **advanced persistent threat (APT)**, though this term can also refer to the set of computer-attacking processes themselves. Often, an APT entity has the highest level of resources, including open-source intelligence (OSINT) *and* covert sources of intelligence. This, coupled with extreme motivation, makes the APT one of the most dangerous foes.

Companies should be prepared for insiders and competitors as well. In fact, they might be one and the same. An inside threat can be one of the deadliest to servers and networks, especially if the person is a systems administrator or has security clearance at the organization.

You should know these actors and their motivations, but in the end, it doesn't matter too much what you call the attacker. Be ready to prevent the basic attacks and the advanced attacks and treat them all with respect.

> **NOTE**   For the bulk of this book I will simply use the term *attacker* to represent any individual or group that perpetrates an attack on any type of technology.

Chapter Review Activities

Use the features in this section to study and review the topics in this chapter.

Review Key Topics

Review the most important topics in the chapter, noted with the Key Topic icon in the outer margin of the page. Table 1-1 lists a reference of these key topics and the page number on which each is found.

Table 1-1   Key Topics for Chapter 1

Key Topic Element	Description	Page Number
Figure 1-1	The CIA of computer security	4
Bulleted list	Definitions of confidentiality, integrity, and availability	5
Bulleted list	Definitions of authentication, authorization, and accounting	5

Define Key Terms

Define the following key terms from this chapter, and check your answers in the glossary:

information security, confidentiality, integrity, availability, authentication, authorization, accounting, non-repudiation, defense in depth, white hat, ethical hacker, black hat, script kiddie, hacktivist, organized crime, advanced persistent threat (APT)

Review Questions

Answer the following review questions. Check your answers with the correct answers that follow.

1. In information security, what are the three main goals? (Select the three best answers.)

   A. Auditing

   B. Integrity

   C. Non-repudiation

   D. Confidentiality

   E. Risk Assessment

   F. Availability

2. To protect against malicious attacks, what should you think like?

   A. Hacker

   B. Network admin

   C. Spoofer

   D. Auditor

3. Tom sends out many e-mails containing secure information to other companies. What concept should be implemented to prove that Tom did indeed send the e-mails?

   A. Authenticity

   B. Non-repudiation

   C. Confidentiality

   D. Integrity

4. Which of the following does the *A* in CIA stand for when it comes to IT security? (Select the best answer.)

   A. Accountability

   B. Assessment

   C. Availability

   D. Auditing

5. Which of the following is the greatest risk when it comes to removable storage?

   A. Integrity of data

   B. Availability of data

   C. Confidentiality of data

   D. Accountability of data

6. When it comes to information security, what is the *I* in CIA?

   A. Insurrection

   B. Information

   C. Indigestion

   D. Integrity

7. You are developing a security plan for your organization. Which of the following is an example of a physical control?

   A. Password

   B. DRP

   C. ID card

   D. Encryption

8. A user receives an e-mail but the e-mail client software says that the digital signature is invalid and the sender of the e-mail cannot be verified. The would-be recipient is concerned about which of the following concepts?

   A. Confidentiality

   B. Integrity

   C. Remediation

   D. Availability

9. Cloud environments often reuse the same physical hardware (such as hard drives) for multiple customers. These hard drives are used and reused when customer virtual machines are created and deleted over time. What security concern does this bring up implications for?

   A. Availability of virtual machines

   B. Integrity of data

   C. Data confidentiality

   D. Hardware integrity

10. Which of the following individuals uses code with little knowledge of how it works?

    A. Hacktivist

    B. Script kiddie

    C. APT

    D. Insider

11. When is a system completely secure?

    A. When it is updated

    B. When it is assessed for vulnerabilities

    C. When all anomalies have been removed

    D. Never

Answers and Explanations

1. **B, D, and F.** Confidentiality, integrity, and availability (known as CIA, the CIA triad, and the security triangle) are the three main goals when it comes to information security. Another goal within information security is accountability.

2. **A.** To protect against malicious attacks, think like a hacker. Then, protect and secure like a network security administrator.

3. **B.** You should use non-repudiation to prevent Tom from denying that he sent the e-mails.

4. **C.** Availability is what the *A* in CIA stands for, as in "the availability of data." Together the acronym stands for confidentiality, integrity, and availability. Although accountability is important and is often included as a fourth component of the CIA triad, it is not the best answer. Assessment and auditing are both important concepts when checking for vulnerabilities and reviewing and logging, but they are not considered to be part of the CIA triad.

5. **C.** For removable storage, the confidentiality of data is the greatest risk because removable storage can easily be removed from the building and shared with others. Although the other factors of the CIA triad are important, any theft of removable storage can destroy the confidentiality of data, and that makes it the greatest risk.

6. **D.** The *I* in CIA stands for integrity. The acronym CIA stands for confidentiality, integrity, and availability. Accountability is also a core principle of information security.

7. **C.** An ID card is an example of a physical security control. Passwords and encryption are examples of technical controls. A disaster recovery plan (DRP) is an example of an administrative control.

8. **B.** The recipient should be concerned about the integrity of the message. If the e-mail client application cannot verify the digital signature of the sender of the e-mail, then there is a chance that the e-mail either was intercepted or is coming from a separate dangerous source. Remember, integrity means the reliability of the data, and whether or not it has been modified or compromised by a third party before arriving at its final destination.

9. **C.** There is a concern about data confidentiality with cloud computing because multiple customers are sharing physical hard drive space. A good portion of customers run their cloud-based systems in virtual machines. Some virtual machines could run on the very same hard drive (or very same array of hard drives). If one of the customers had the notion, he could attempt to break through the barriers between virtual machines, which if not secured properly, would not be very difficult to do.

10. **B.** A script kiddie uses code and probably doesn't understand how it works and what the repercussions will be. Other actors such as hackers, hacktivists, insiders, and so on will usually have a higher level of sophistication when it comes to technology. An advanced persistent threat (APT) is a group of technical processes or the entity that implements those processes. An APT is just that—advanced—and is on the other side of the spectrum from the script kiddie.

11. **D.** A system can never truly be completely secure. The scales are always tipping back and forth; a hacker develops a way to break into a system, then an administrator finds a way to block that attack, and then the hacker looks for an alternative method. It goes on and on; be ready to wage the eternal battle!

This chapter covers the following subjects:

- **Malicious Software Types:** This portion of the chapter helps you to differentiate between the various malicious software threats you should be aware of for the exam, including viruses, worms, Trojans, ransomware, spam, and more.

- **Delivery of Malware:** Here we discuss how malware finds its way to computer systems. Malware can be delivered via websites, e-mail, removable media, third-party applications, and botnets.

- **Preventing and Troubleshooting Malware:** Finally, we discuss how to defend against malware threats in a proactive way, and how to fix problems that do occur in the case that threats have already manifested themselves. This is the most important section of this chapter; study it carefully!

Simply stated, the most important part of a computer is the data. The data must be available, yet secured in such a way so that it can't be tampered with. Computer systems security is all about the security threats that can compromise an operating system and the data held within. Threats such as viruses, Trojans, spyware, and other malicious software are extremely prevalent in today's society, and so, this chapter is an important part of the book. Applications that can help to secure your computers against malware threats include antivirus programs, anti-spyware applications, or combination anti-malware programs. By implementing these security applications and ensuring that they are updated regularly, you can stave off the majority of malicious software attacks that can target a computer system.

CHAPTER 2

Computer Systems Security Part I

To combat the various security threats that can occur on a computer system, we first need to classify them. Then we need to define how these threats can be delivered to the target computer. Afterward we can discuss how to prevent security threats from happening and troubleshoot them if they do occur. Let's start with the most common computer threat and probably the most deadly— malicious software.

Foundation Topics

Malicious Software Types

Malicious software, or **malware**, is software designed to infiltrate a computer system and possibly damage it without the user's knowledge or consent. Malware is a broad term used by computer professionals to include viruses, worms, Trojan horses, spyware, rootkits, adware, and other types of undesirable software.

Of course, we don't want malware to infect our computer system, but to defend against it we first need to define it and categorize it. Then we can put preventative measures into place. It's also important to locate and remove/quarantine malware from a computer system in the case that it does manifest itself.

For the exam, you need to know about several types of malware. Over the past several years, an emphasis shift from viruses to other types of malware, such as spyware and ransomware, has occurred. Most people know about viruses and have some kind of antivirus software running. However, many people are still confused about the various other types of malware, how they occur, and how to protect against them. Because of this, computer professionals spend a lot of time fixing malware issues (that are not virus related) and training users on how to protect against them in the future. However, viruses are still a valid foe; let's start by discussing them.

Viruses

A computer **virus** is code that runs on a computer without the user's knowledge; it infects the computer when the code is accessed and executed. For viruses to do their dirty work, they first need to be executed by the user in some way. A virus also has reproductive capability and can spread copies of itself throughout the computer—if it is first executed, by the user or otherwise. By infecting files accessed by other computers, the virus can spread to those other systems as well. The problem is that computers can't call in sick on Monday; they need to be up and running as much as possible, more than your average human.

One well-known example of a virus is the Love Bug. Originating in 2000, this virus would arrive by an e-mail titled "I love you" with an attachment named love-letter-for-you.txt.vbs, or one of several other permutations of this fictitious love. Some users would be tricked into thinking this was a text file, but the extension was actually .vbs, short for Visual Basic script. This virus deleted files, sent usernames and passwords to its creator, infected 15 million computers, and supposedly caused $5 billion in damage. Educate your users on how to screen their e-mail!

NOTE   Throughout this book I typically give older examples of malware and attacks, ones that have been defeated or at least reduced heavily. There are always new malicious attacks being developed. It is up to you to keep on top of those threats. A couple of quick Internet searches will provide you with several threat blogs and anti-malware applications that you can use to keep up to date on the latest attacks. I also highly recommend visiting on a regular basis the Common Vulnerabilities and Exposures (CVE) feed from MITRE: https://cve.mitre.org/cve/.

You might encounter several different types of viruses:

Key Topic

- **Boot sector:** Initially loads into the first sector of the hard drive; when the computer boots, the virus then loads into memory.

- **Macro:** Usually placed in documents and e-mailed to users in the hopes that the users will open the document, thus executing the virus.

- **Program:** Infects executable files.

- **Encrypted:** Uses a simple cipher to encrypt itself. The virus consists of an encrypted copy of the virus code (to help avoid detection) and a small decryption module. Different encrypting keys can be used for each file to be infected, but usually there is only one decrypting code.

- **Polymorphic:** Builds on the concept of an encrypted virus, but the decrypting module is modified with each infection. So, it can change every time it is executed in an attempt to avoid antivirus detection.

- **Metamorphic:** Similar to polymorphic but rewrites itself completely each time it is going to infect a new file in a further attempt to avoid detection.

- **Stealth:** Uses various techniques to go unnoticed by antivirus programs.

- **Armored:** Protects itself from antivirus programs by tricking the program into thinking that it is located in a different place from where it actually resides. Essentially, it has a layer of protection that it can use against the person who tries to analyze it; it will thwart attempts by analysts to examine its code.

- **Multipartite:** A hybrid of boot and program viruses that attacks the boot sector or system files first and then attacks the other files on the system.

Sometimes, what appears to be a virus really isn't. That is the case with a *virus hoax*. A virus hoax is when a user gets a message warning that the computer is infected by a nonexistent virus. It might appear within an e-mail or as a pop-up on a website. This is a ploy to try to get unsuspecting users to pay for tech support that isn't needed. It could also be a method for con artists to access people's computers remotely. We'll talk more about hoaxes in Chapter 17, "Social Engineering, User Education, and Facilities Security."

Worms

A **worm** is much like a virus except that it self-replicates, whereas a virus does not. It does this in an attempt to spread to other computers. Worms take advantage of security holes in operating systems and applications, including backdoors, which we discuss later. They look for other systems on the network or through the Internet that are running the same applications and replicate to those other systems. With worms, the user doesn't need to access and execute the malware. A virus needs some sort of carrier to get it where it wants to go and needs explicit instructions to be executed, or it must be executed by the user. The worm does not need this carrier or explicit instructions to be executed.

A well-known example of a worm is Nimda (*admin* backward), which propagated automatically through the Internet in 22 minutes in 2001, causing widespread damage. It spread through network shares, mass e-mailing, and operating system vulnerabilities.

Sometimes, the worm does not carry a payload, meaning that in and of itself, it does not contain code that can harm a computer. It may or may not include other malware, but even if it doesn't, it can cause general disruption of network traffic and computer operations because of the very nature of its self-replicating abilities.

Trojan Horses

Trojan horses, or simply Trojans, appear to perform desirable functions but are actually performing malicious functions behind the scenes. These are not technically viruses and can easily be downloaded without being noticed. They can also be transferred to a computer by way of removable media, especially USB flash drives. One example of a Trojan is a file that is contained within a downloaded program such as a key generator—known as a "keygen" used with pirated software—or another executable. If users complain about slow system performance and numerous antivirus alerts, and they recently installed a questionable program from the Internet or from a USB flash drive, their computers could be infected by a Trojan.

Remote access Trojans (RATs) are the most common type of Trojan, examples of which include Back Orifice, NetBus, and SubSeven; their capability to allow an attacker higher administration privileges than those of the owner of the system makes them quite dangerous. The software effectively acts as a remote administration tool, which happens to be another name for the RAT acronym. These programs have the capability to scan for unprotected hosts and make all kinds of changes to a host when connected. They are not *necessarily* designed to be used maliciously, but are easy for an average person to download and manipulate computers with. Worse, when a target computer is controlled by an attacker, it could easily become a robot, or simply a *bot*, carrying out the plans of the attacker on command. We'll discuss bots later in this chapter.

RATs can also be coded in PHP (or other languages) to allow remote access to websites. An example of this is the web shell, which has many permutations. It allows an attacker to remotely configure a web server without the user's consent. Quite often, the attacker will have cracked the FTP password in order to upload the RAT.

RATs are often used to persistently target a specific entity such as a government or a specific corporation. One example of this is the PlugX RAT. Malicious software such as this is known as an advanced persistent threat (APT). Groups that have vast resources at their disposal might make use of these APTs to carry out objectives against large-scale adversaries. APT groups could take the form of large hacker factions, and even some corporations and governments around the globe.

Ransomware

Some less than reputable persons use a particularly devious malware known as **ransomware**—a type of malware that restricts access to a computer system and demands that a ransom be paid. Also known as crypto-malware, it encrypts files and/or locks the system. It then informs the user that in order to decrypt the files, or unlock the computer to regain access to the files, a payment would have to be made to one of several banking services, often overseas. It often propagates as a

Trojan or worm, and usually makes use of encryption to cause the user's files to be inaccessible. This usage of encryption is also known as cryptoviral extortion. One example of this is CryptoLocker. This ransomware Trojan encrypts certain files on the computer's drives using an RSA public key. (The counterpart private key is stored on the malware creator's server.) Though the Trojan can be easily defeated by being either quarantined or removed, the files remain encrypted, and are nearly impossible to decrypt (given the strength of the RSA key). Payment is often required in voucher form, or in the form of a cryptocurrency such as Bitcoin. Ransomware attacks grew steadily for several years until 2013 when CryptoLocker (and other similar ransomware Trojans) appeared—now hundreds of thousands of computers worldwide are affected each year.

> **NOTE** Sometimes a user will inadvertently access a fraudulent website (or pop-up site) that says that all the user's files have been encrypted and payment is required to decrypt them; some imposing government-like logo will accompany the statement. But many of these sites don't actually encrypt the user's files. In this case, we are talking about plain old extortion with no real damage done to the computer or files. These types of sites can be blocked by pop-up blockers, phishing filters, and the user's common sense when clicking searched-for links.

Spyware

Spyware is a type of malicious software either downloaded unwittingly from a website or installed along with some other third-party software. Usually, this malware collects information about the user without the user's consent. Spyware could be as simple as a piece of code that logs what websites you access, or go as far as a program that records your keystrokes (known as a keylogger). Spyware is also associated with advertising (those pop-ups that just won't go away!), and is sometimes related to malicious advertising, or *malvertising*—the use of Internet-based advertising (legitimate and illegitimate) to distribute malicious software.

Spyware can possibly change the computer configuration without any user interaction; for example, redirecting a browser to access websites other than those wanted. **Adware** usually falls into the realm of spyware because it pops up advertisements based on what it has learned from spying on the user. **Grayware** is another general term that describes applications that are behaving improperly but without serious consequences. It is associated with spyware, adware, and joke programs. Very funny…not.

One example (of many) of spyware is the Internet Optimizer, which redirects Internet Explorer error pages out to other websites' advertising pages. Spyware can even be taken to the next level and be coded in such a way to hijack a person's computer. Going beyond this, spyware can be used for cyber-espionage, as was the case with Red October—which was installed to users' computers when they unwittingly were redirected to websites with special PHP pages that exploited a Java flaw, causing the download of the malware.

Rootkits

A **rootkit** is a type of software designed to gain administrator-level control over a computer system without being detected. The term is a combination of the words "root" (meaning the root user in a Unix/Linux system or administrator in a Windows system) and "kit" (meaning software kit). Usually, the purpose of a rootkit is to perform malicious operations on a target computer at a later date without the knowledge of the administrators or users of that computer. A rootkit is a variation on the virus that attempts to dig in to the lower levels of the operating system— components of the OS that start up before any anti-malware services come into play. Rootkits can target the UEFI/BIOS, boot loader, kernel, and more. An example of a boot loader rootkit is the Evil Maid Attack; this attack can extract the encryption keys of a full disk encryption system, which we discuss more later. Another (more current) example is the Alureon rootkit, which affects the master boot record (MBR) and low-level system drivers (such as atapi.sys). This particular rootkit was distributed by a botnet, and affected over 200,000 (known) Microsoft operating systems.

Rootkits are difficult to detect because they are activated before the operating system has fully booted. A rootkit might install hidden files, hidden processes, and hidden user accounts. Because rootkits can be installed in hardware or software, they can intercept data from network connections, keyboards, and so on.

Fileless Malware

Malware doesn't have to reside on the hard drive of a computer. It can also reside within RAM (and possibly other locations). Fileless malware—also known as non-malware—functions without putting malicious executables within the file system, and instead works in a memory-based environment. Sound potent? It can be, but the attacker will usually need to have remote access to the system—via SSH, a RAT, or otherwise—in order to deploy the malware. The term "fileless" is somewhat of a misnomer because the attack may actually contain files. The systems affected, such as ATMs, often suffer from weak endpoint security, and the organization that owns those systems might also have ineffective access control policies.

Spam

Have you ever received an e-mail asking you to send money to some strange person in some faraway country? Or an e-mail offering extremely cheap Rolex watches? Or the next best penny stock? All of these are examples of spam. **Spam** is the abuse of electronic messaging systems such as e-mail, texting, social media, broadcast media, instant messaging, and so on. Spammers send unsolicited bulk messages indiscriminately, usually without benefit to the actual spammer, because the majority of spam is either deflected or ignored. Companies with questionable ethics condone this type of marketing (usually set up as a pyramid scheme) so that the people at the top of the marketing chain can benefit; however, it's usually not worthwhile for the actual person who sends out spam.

The most common form of spam is e-mail spam, which is one of the worst banes of network administrators. Spam can clog up resources and possibly cause a type of denial-of-service to an e-mail server if there is enough of it. It can also mislead users, in an attempt at social engineering. And the bulk of network-based viruses are transferred through spam e-mails. Yikes! The worst type of spamming is when a person uses another organization's e-mail server to send the spam. Obviously illegal, it could also create legal issues for the organization that owns the e-mail server.

A derivative of spam, called *spim* (spam over instant messaging), is the abuse of instant messaging systems, chat rooms, and chat functions in games specifically. It is also known as messaging spam, or IM spam.

Summary of Malware Threats

Table 2-1 summarizes the malware threats discussed up to this point.

Key Topic

Table 2-1 Summary of Malware Threats

Malware Threat	Definition	Example
Virus	Code that runs on a computer without the user's knowledge; it infects the computer when the code is accessed and executed.	Love Bug virus Ex: love-letter-for-you.txt.vbs
Worm	Similar to viruses except that it self-replicates, whereas a virus does not.	Nimda Propagated through network shares and mass e-mailing
Trojan horse	Appears to perform desired functions but actually is performing malicious functions behind the scenes.	Remote access Trojan Ex: PlugX

Malware Threat	Definition	Example
Ransomware	Malware that restricts access to computer files and demands a ransom be paid by the user.	Often propagated via a Trojan Ex: CryptoLocker
Spyware	Malicious software either downloaded unwittingly from a website or installed along with some other third-party software.	Internet Optimizer (a.k.a. DyFuCA)
Rootkit	Software designed to gain administrator-level control over a computer system without being detected. Can target the UEFI/BIOS, boot loader, and kernel.	Boot loader rootkits Ex: Evil Maid Attack, Alureon
Spam	The abuse of electronic messaging systems such as e-mail, broadcast media, and instant messaging.	Identity theft e-mails (phishing) Lottery scam e-mails

Delivery of Malware

Malware is not sentient (…not yet) and can't just appear out of thin air; it needs to be transported and delivered to a computer or installed on a computer system in some manner. This can be done in several ways. The simplest way would be for attackers to gain physical access to an unprotected computer and perform their malicious work locally. But because it can be difficult to obtain physical access, this can be done in other ways, as shown in the upcoming sections. Some of these methods can also be used by an attacker to simply gain access to a computer, make modifications, and so on, in addition to delivering the malware.

The method that a threat uses to access a target is known as a **threat vector**. Collectively, the means by which an attacker gains access to a computer in order to deliver malicious software is known as an **attack vector**. Probably the most common attack vector is via software.

Via Software, Messaging, and Media

Malware can be delivered via software in many ways. A person who e-mails a zipped file might not even know that malware also exists in that file. The recipients of the e-mail will have no idea that the extra malware exists unless they have software to scan their e-mail attachments for it. Malware could also be delivered via FTP. Because FTP servers are inherently insecure, it's easier than you might think to upload insidious files and other software. Malware is often found among peer-to-peer (P2P) networks and bit torrents. Great care should be taken by users who use these technologies. Malware can also be embedded within, and distributed by, websites through the use of corrupting code or bad downloads. Malware can even be distributed by advertisements. And of course, removable media can victimize a computer as well. Optical discs, USB flash drives, memory cards, and connected devices such as smartphones can easily be manipulated to automatically run malware when they are inserted into the computer. (This is when AutoPlay/AutoRun is not your friend!) The removable media could also have hidden viruses or worms and possibly logic bombs (discussed later) configured to set that malware off at specific times.

Potential attackers also rely on user error. For example, if a user is attempting to access a website but types the incorrect domain name by mistake, the user could be redirected to an altogether unwanted website, possibly malicious in nature. This type of attack is known as **typosquatting** or URL hijacking. *URL* stands for uniform resource locator, which is the web address that begins with http or https. The potential attacker counts on the fact that millions of typos are performed in web browsers every day. These attackers "squat" on similar (but not exact) domain names. Once the user is at the new and incorrect site, the system becomes an easy target for spyware and other forms of malware. Some browsers come with built-in security such as anti-phishing tools and the ability to auto-check websites that are entered, but the best way to protect against this is to train users to be careful when typing domain names.

> **NOTE**   Speaking of what a user types, some attackers will make use of a keylogger to record everything that the user types on the keyboard. This tool could be hardware or software-based, and is often used by security professionals as well. More about keyloggers appears in Chapter 13, "Monitoring and Auditing."

Another way to propagate malware is to employ automation and web attack-based software "kits," also known as exploit kits. Exploit kits are designed to run on web servers and are usually found in the form of PHP scripts. They target client computers' software vulnerabilities that often exist within web browsers. One example of an exploit kit is the Blackhole exploit kit. This is used (and purchased) by potential attackers to distribute malware to computers that meet particular criteria, while the entire process is logged and documented.

> **NOTE**   The automating of cyber-crime, and the software used to do so, is collectively referred to as *crimeware*.

Botnets and Zombies

I know what you are thinking—the names of these attacks and delivery methods are getting a bit ridiculous. But bear with me; they make sense and are deadly serious. Allow me to explain—malware can be distributed throughout the Internet by a group of compromised computers, known as a **botnet**, and controlled by a master computer (where the attacker resides). The individual compromised computers in the botnet are called **zombies**. This is because they are unaware of the malware that has been installed on them. This can occur in several ways, including automated distribution of the malware from one zombie computer to another. Now imagine if all the zombie computers had a specific virus or other type of attack loaded, and a logic bomb (defined a bit later) was also installed, ready to set off the malware at a specific time. If this were done to hundreds or thousands of computers, a synchronized attack of great proportions could be enacted on just about any target. Often, this is known as a distributed denial-of-service, or DDoS, attack, and is usually perpetuated on a particularly popular server, one that serves many requests. If a computer on your network is continually scanning other systems on the network, is communicating with an unknown server, and/or has hundreds of outbound connections to various websites, chances are the computer is part of a botnet.

But botnets can be used for more than just taking down a single target. They can also be used to fraudulently obtain wealth. One example of this type of botnet is the ZeroAccess botnet. It is based on Trojan malware that affects various Microsoft operating systems, and is used to mine Bitcoins or perpetuate click fraud. It is hidden from many antivirus programs through the use of a rootkit (infecting the MBR). In 2012 it was estimated that the botnet consisted of up to 10 million computers. You can imagine the sheer power of a botnet such as this, and the amount of revenue it can bring in per month. Every couple of months you can read about another botnet mastermind who has been brought to justice—only to be replaced by another entrepreneur.

Active Interception

Active interception normally includes a computer placed between the sender and the receiver to capture and possibly modify information. If a person can eavesdrop on your computer's data session, then that data can be stolen, modified, or exploited in other ways. Examples of this include session theft and man-in-the-middle (MITM) attacks. For more information on these attacks, see the section titled "Malicious Attacks" in Chapter 7, "Networking Protocols and Threats."

Privilege Escalation

Privilege escalation is the act of exploiting a bug or design flaw in a software or firmware application to gain access to resources that normally would've been protected from an application or user. This results in a user gaining additional privileges, more than were originally intended by the developer of the application; for example, if a regular user gains administrative control, or if a particular user can read another user's e-mail without authorization.

Backdoors

Backdoors are used in computer programs to bypass normal authentication and other security mechanisms in place. Originally, backdoors were used by developers as a legitimate way of accessing an application, but soon after they were implemented by attackers who would use backdoors to make changes to operating systems, websites, and network devices. Or the attacker would create a completely new application that would act as a backdoor, for example Back Orifice, which enables a user to control a Windows computer from a remote location. Often, it is installed via a Trojan horse; this particular one is known as a remote access Trojan, or RAT, as previously mentioned. Some worms install backdoors on computers so that remote spammers can send junk e-mail from the infected computers, or so an attacker can attempt privilege escalation. Unfortunately, there isn't much that can be done about backdoors aside from updating or patching the system infected and keeping on top of updates. However, if network administrators were to find out about a new backdoor, they should inform the manufacturer of the device or the application as soon as possible. Backdoors are less common nowadays, because their practice is usually discouraged by software manufacturers and by makers of network devices.

Logic Bombs

A **logic bomb** is code that has, in some way, been inserted into software; it is meant to initiate one of many types of malicious functions when specific criteria are met. Logic bombs blur the line between malware and a malware delivery system. They are indeed unwanted software but are intended to activate viruses, worms, or Trojans at a specific time. Trojans set off on a certain date are also referred to as **time bombs**. The logic bomb ticks away until the correct time, date, and other parameters have been met. So, some of the worst bombs do not incorporate an explosion whatsoever. The logic bomb could be contained within a virus or loaded separately. Logic bombs are more common in the movies than they are in real life, but they do happen, and with grave consequences; but more often than not, they are detected before they are set off. If you, as a systems administrator, suspect that you have found a logic bomb, or a portion of the code of a logic bomb, you should notify your superior immediately and check your organization's policies to see if you should take any other actions. Action could include placing network disaster recovery processes on standby; notifying the software vendor; and closely managing usage of the software, including, perhaps, withdrawing it from service until the threat is mitigated. Logic bombs are the evil cousin of the Easter egg.

Easter eggs historically have been a platonic extra that was added to an OS or application as a sort of joke; often, it was missed by quality control and subsequently released by the manufacturer of the software. An older example of an Easter egg is the capability to force a win in Windows XP's Solitaire by pressing the Alt+Shift+2 keys simultaneously. Easter eggs are not normally documented (being tossed in last minute by humorous programmers) and are meant to be harmless, but nowadays they are not allowed by responsible software companies and are thoroughly scanned for. Because an Easter egg (and who knows what else) can possibly slip past quality control, and because of the growing concerns about malware in general, many companies have adopted the idea of Trustworthy Computing, which is a newer concept that sets standards for how software is designed, coded, and checked for quality control. Sadly, as far as software goes, the Easter egg's day has passed.

Preventing and Troubleshooting Malware

Now that we know the types of malware, and the ways that they can be delivered to a computer, let's talk about how to stop them before they happen, and how to troubleshoot them if they do happen. Unfortunately, given the number of computers you will work on, they *will* happen.

If a system is affected by malware, it might be sluggish in its response time or display unwanted pop-ups and incorrect home pages; or applications (and maybe even the whole system) could lock up or shut down unexpectedly. Often, malware uses CPU and memory resources directly or behind the scenes, causing the system to run slower than usual. In general, a technician should look for erratic behavior from the computer, as if it had a mind of its own! Let's go over viruses and spyware, look at how to prevent them, and finally discuss how to troubleshoot them if they do occur.

Preventing and Troubleshooting Viruses

We can do several things to protect a computer system from viruses. First, every computer should have a strong endpoint protection platform—meaning that antivirus software should be running on it. There are many providers of antivirus protection, plus manufacturers of operating systems often bundle AV software with the OS or offer free downloads. Second, the AV software should be updated, which means that the software requires a current license; this is renewed yearly with most providers. When updating, be sure to update the AV engine *and* the definitions if you are doing it manually. Otherwise, set the AV software to automatically update at periodic intervals, for example, every day or every week. It's a good idea to schedule regular full scans of the system within the AV software.

As long as the definitions have been updated, antivirus systems usually locate viruses along with other malware such as worms and Trojans. However, these systems usually do not locate logic bombs, rootkits, and botnet activity. In lieu of this, keep in mind that AV software is important, but it is not a cure-all.

Next, we want to make sure that the computer has the latest updates available. This goes for the operating system *and* applications. Backdoors into operating systems and other applications are not uncommon, and the OS manufacturers often release fixes for these breaches of security. Windows offers the Windows Update program. This should be enabled, and you should either check for updates periodically or set the system to check for updates automatically. It might be that your organization has rules governing how Windows Update functions. If so, configure Automatic Updates according to your company's policy.

It's also important to make sure that a firewall is available, enabled, and updated. A firewall closes all the inbound ports to your computer—or network—in an attempt to block intruders. For instance, Windows Firewall is a built-in software-based feature included in Windows. This is illustrated in Figure 2-1. You can see that the firewall in the figure is enabled for private and guest/public networks. Always verify functionality of the endpoint firewall!

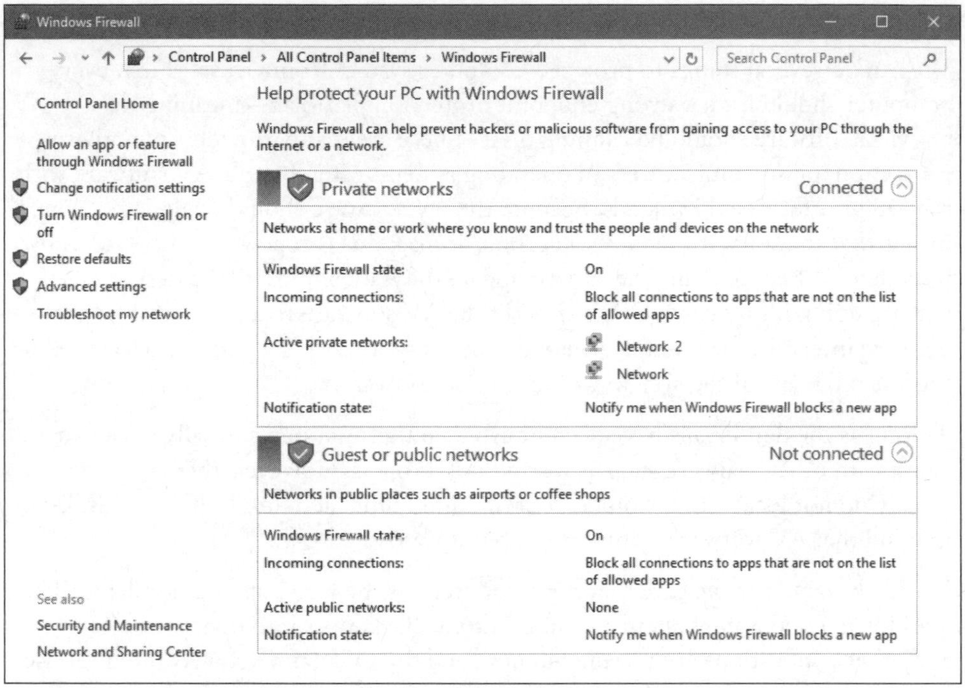

Figure 2-1 Windows Firewall in Windows 10

You might also have a hardware-based firewall; for example, one that is included in a small office/home office (SOHO) router. By using both, you have two layers of protection from various attacks that might include a payload with malware. Keep in mind that you might need to set exceptions for programs that need to access the Internet. This can be done by the program, or the port used by the protocol, and can be configured to enable specific applications to communicate through the firewall while keeping the rest of the ports closed.

Another way to help prevent viruses is to use what I call "separation of OS and data." This method calls for two hard drives. The operating system is installed to the C: drive, and the data is stored on the D: drive (or whatever letter you use for the second drive). This compartmentalizes the system and data, making it more difficult for viruses to spread and easier to isolate them when scanning. It also enables easy reinstallation without having to back up data! A less expensive way to accomplish this is by using two partitions on the same drive.

NOTE There are viruses that can affect other types of operating systems as well. Android, iOS, and other desktop systems such as macOS and Linux are all susceptible, although historically have not been targeted as much as Windows systems.

Encryption is one excellent way to protect data that would otherwise be compromised (or lost) due to virus activity on a computer. Windows operating systems make use of the Encrypting File System (EFS), which can encrypt files on an individual basis. When a file is encrypted in this manner, the filename shows up green in color within Windows Explorer or File Explorer. It prevents clear-text access, and defies modification in most cases. Encryption of this type probably won't prevent viruses from occurring, but it can help to protect individual files from being compromised. We'll talk more about encryption in Chapter 14, "Encryption and Hashing Concepts," and Chapter 15, "PKI and Encryption Protocols."

Finally, educate users as to how viruses can infect a system. Instruct them on how to screen their e-mails, and tell them not to open unknown attachments. Show them how to scan removable media before copying files to their computer, or set up the computer to scan removable media automatically. Sometimes user education works; sometimes it doesn't. One way to make user education more effective is to have a technical trainer educate your users, instead of doing it yourself. Or, consider creating interactive online learning tutorials. These methods can provide for a more engaging learning environment.

By using all of these techniques, virus infection can be severely reduced. However, if a computer is infected by a virus, you want to know what to look for so that you can "cure" the computer.

Here are some typical symptoms of viruses:

- Computer runs slower than usual.
- Computer locks up frequently or stops responding altogether.
- Computer restarts on its own or crashes frequently.
- Hard drives, optical drive, and applications are not accessible or don't work properly.
- Strange sounds occur.
- You receive unusual error messages.
- Display or print distortion occurs.
- New icons appear or old icons (and applications) disappear.
- There is a double extension on a file attached to an e-mail that was opened; for example: .txt.vbs or .txt.exe.
- Antivirus programs will not run or can't be installed.
- Files have been corrupted or folders are created automatically.
- System Restore capabilities are removed or disabled.

Here is a recommended procedure for the removal of malware in general:

1. Identify malware symptoms.

2. Quarantine infected systems.

3. Disable System Restore (in Windows).

4. Remediate infected systems:

   a. Update anti-malware software.

   b. Use scan and removal techniques (for example, Safe Mode and preinstallation environments).

5. Schedule scans and run updates.

6. Enable System Restore and create a restore point (in Windows).

7. Educate end users.

Before making any changes to the computer, make sure that you back up critical data and verify that the latest updates have been installed to the OS and the AV software. Then perform a thorough scan of the system using the AV software's scan utility; if allowed by the software, run the scan in Safe Mode. Another option is to move the affected drive to a "clean machine," a computer that is not connected to any network, and is used solely for the purpose of scanning for malware. This can be done by using a USB converter kit or a removable drive system, or by slaving the affected drive to another hard drive port of the other computer. Then, run the AV software on that clean machine to scan that drive. PC repair shops use this isolated clean machine concept.

Hopefully, the AV software finds and quarantines the virus on the system. In the case that the AV software's scan does not find the issue, or if the AV software has been infected and won't run, you can try using a free online scanner.

In rare cases, you might need to delete individual files and remove Registry entries. This might be the only solution when a new virus has infected a system and there is no antivirus definition released. Instructions on how to remove viruses in this manner can be found on AV software manufacturers' websites.

When it comes to boot sector viruses, your AV software is still the best bet. The AV software might use a bootable USB flash drive or bootable disc to accomplish scanning of the boot sector, or it might have boot shielding built in. Some UEFI/BIOS programs have the capability to scan the boot sector of the hard drive at startup; this might need to be enabled in the UEFI/BIOS setup first. You can also use recovery environments and the command-line to repair the boot sector.

Another possibility is to use freely downloadable Linux-based tools and Live Linux discs such as Knoppix, which can be used to boot and repair the computer.

Keep in mind that the recovery environments and other command-line methods might not fix the problem; they might render the hard drive inoperable depending on the type of virus. So, it is best to first use the AV software's various utilities that you have purchased for the system.

Preventing and Troubleshooting Worms and Trojans

Worms and Trojans can be prevented and troubleshot in the same manner as viruses. There are free online scanners for Trojans, but in most cases, standard AV software scans for worms and Trojans in addition to viruses (and perhaps other malware as well). Usually, AV software can easily detect remote access Trojans, which were mentioned previously in the chapter, either by detecting the attacker's actual application or by detecting any .exe files that are part of the application and are used at the victim computer.

Prevention is a matter of maintenance, and careful user interaction with the computer. Keeping the AV software up to date is important once again, but even more important becomes the user's ability to use the computer properly—to navigate only to legitimate websites and to screen e-mail carefully.

Troubleshooting these types of malware is done in basically the same way as with viruses. The malware should be quarantined and/or removed if at all possible with AV software or with advanced techniques mentioned in the previous section. The same prevention and troubleshooting techniques apply to ransomware because it is often delivered in the form of a Trojan.

Preventing and Troubleshooting Spyware

Preventing spyware works in much the same manner as preventing viruses when it comes to updating the operating system and using a firewall. Also, because spyware is as common as viruses, antivirus companies and OS manufacturers add anti-spyware components to their software. Here are a few more things you can do to protect your computer in the hopes of preventing spyware:

- Use (or download) and update built-in anti-spyware programs such as Windows Defender. Be sure to keep the anti-spyware software updated.

- Adjust web browser security settings. For example, disable (or limit) cookies, create and configure trusted zones, turn on phishing filters, restrict unwanted websites, turn on automatic website checking, disable scripting (such as JavaScript and ActiveX), and have the browser clear all cache on exit. All of these things can help to filter out fraudulent online requests for usernames, passwords, and credit card information, which is also known as web-page spoofing. Higher security settings can also help to fend off session hijacking, which is the act of taking control of a user session after obtaining or generating an authentication ID. We'll talk more about web browser security in Chapter 5, "Application Security."

- Uninstall unnecessary applications and turn off superfluous services (for example, Remote Desktop services or FTP if they are not used).

- Educate users on how to surf the web safely. User education is actually the number one method of preventing malware! Access only sites believed to be safe, and download only programs from reputable websites. Don't click OK or Agree to close a window; instead press Alt+F4 on the keyboard to close that window, or use the Task Manager to close out of applications. Be wary of file-sharing websites and the content stored on those sites. Be careful of e-mails with links to downloadable software that could be malicious.

- Consider technologies that discourage spyware. For example, use a browser that is less susceptible to spyware, and consider using virtual machines.

- Verify the security of sites you visit by checking the certificate, or by simply looking for HTTPS in the URL.

Here are some common symptoms of spyware:

- The web browser's default home page has been modified.

- A particular website comes up every time you perform a search.

- Excessive pop-up windows appear.

- The network adapter's activity LED blinks frequently when the computer shouldn't be transmitting data.

- The firewall and antivirus programs turn off automatically.

- New programs, icons, and favorites appear.

- Odd problems occur within windows (slow system, applications behaving strangely, and such).

- The Java console appears randomly.

To troubleshoot and repair systems infected with spyware, first disconnect the system from the Internet (or simply from the local area network). Then, try uninstalling the program from the Control Panel or Settings area of the operating system. Some of the less malicious spyware programs can be fully uninstalled without any residual damage. Be sure to reboot the computer afterward and verify that the spyware was actually uninstalled! Next, scan your system with the AV software to remove any viruses that might have infested the system, which might get in the way of a successful spyware removal. Again, in Windows, do this in the recovery environment (for example, Safe Mode) if the AV software offers that option.

NOTE   In some cases, Safe Mode is not enough, and you need to boot off of a disc or USB flash drive with a bootable OS or kernel (Knoppix, for example) and then rerun the scans.

Next, scan the computer with the anti-spyware software of your choice in an attempt to quarantine and remove the spyware. You can use other programs to remove malware, but be careful with these programs because you will probably need to modify the Registry. Remove only that which is part of the infection.

Finally, you need to make sure that the malware will not re-emerge on your system. To do this, check your home page setting in your browser, verify that your HOSTS file hasn't been hijacked (located in C:\WINDOWS\system32\drivers\etc), and make sure that unwanted websites haven't been added to the Trusted Sites within the browser.

Badware

Viruses, spyware, and other types of malware are sometimes lumped into the term *badware*. Although all the aforementioned attacks are indeed malicious, some types of badware are not malicious in their intent, but the user loses a certain amount of control when they utilize them. An example of this is a shopping toolbar that aids in the shopping process, but simultaneously records where the person was shopping and what was bought, and sends that information back to the badware's main server without the user's knowledge or consent. Another example is where a user installs a particular program that is legitimate except for the fact that it installs another program (possibly spyware or scareware) without the user's consent. In a nutshell, badware is software that does things you do not want it to do, often without your consent. The best way for a user to protect against badware in general is to be careful what is installed on the computer, and to only install software from legitimate, authentic entities, while being wary of any unknown removable media before connecting it to the computer.

Preventing and Troubleshooting Rootkits

A successfully installed rootkit enables unauthorized users to gain access to a system and act as the root or administrator user. Rootkits are copied to a computer as a binary file; this binary file can be detected by signature-based and heuristic-based antivirus programs, which we discuss in Chapter 3, "Computer Systems Security Part II." However, after the rootkit is executed, it can be difficult to detect. This is because most rootkits are collections of programs working together that can make many modifications to the system. When subversion of the operating system takes place, the OS can't be trusted, and it is difficult to tell if your antivirus programs run properly, or if any of your other efforts have any effect. Although security software manufacturers are attempting to detect running rootkits, it is doubtful that they will be successful. The best way to identify a rootkit is to use removable media (a USB flash drive or a special rescue disc) to boot the computer. This way, the operating system is not running, and therefore the rootkit is not running, making it much easier to detect by the external media.

Sometimes, rootkits will hide in the MBR. Often, operating system manufacturers recommend scrubbing the MBR (rewriting it, for example, within System Recovery Options or other recovery environment) and then scanning with antivirus software. This depends on the type of rootkit. The use of GPT in lieu of MBR helps to discourage rootkits. I suggest using GPT whenever possible.

Unfortunately, because of the difficulty involved in removing a rootkit, the best way to combat rootkits is to reinstall all software (or re-image the system). Generally, a PC technician, upon detecting a rootkit, will do just that, because it usually takes less time than attempting to fix all the rootkit issues, plus it can verify that the rootkit has been removed completely.

Preventing and Troubleshooting Spam

The Internet needs to be conserved, just like our environment. Might sound crazy, but it's true. There is only so much space to store information, and only so much bandwidth that can be used to transfer data. It is estimated that spam causes billions of dollars in fraud, damage, lost productivity, and so on every year; besides botnets and P2P networks, it's one of the biggest gobblers of Internet resources. The worst part is that most spammers do not bear the burden of the costs involved; someone else usually does. So the key is to block as much spam as possible, report those who do it, and train your users. Here are several ways to implement anti-spam security controls and, hopefully, reduce spam:

- **Use a spam firewall/filter:** This can be purchased as software for the server or as a hardware-based appliance. These appliances monitor spam activity and create and update whitelists and blacklists, all of which can be downloaded to the appliance automatically. Network administrators should also block any e-mails that include attachments that do not comply with company rules. For example, some companies enable only .zip, .txt, .doc, and .docx to go through their e-mail attachment filter (or .zips only). If your company uses a web-hosting company for its website and for e-mail, that company likely has many spam filtering options. And on the client side, you can configure Outlook and other mail programs to a higher level of security against spam; this is usually in the Junk Email Options area, as shown in Figure 2-2. Spam filters can also be installed on individual clients. Many popular antivirus suites have built-in spam filtering. Make sure it is enabled! Just as an example, my personal e-mail account (which I try to keep private) has a filter at the web hosting company, plus my anti-malware software package filters the e-mails, and Outlook is set to High in the Junk Email Options page, and of course, I still get at least several spams to my inbox every single day!

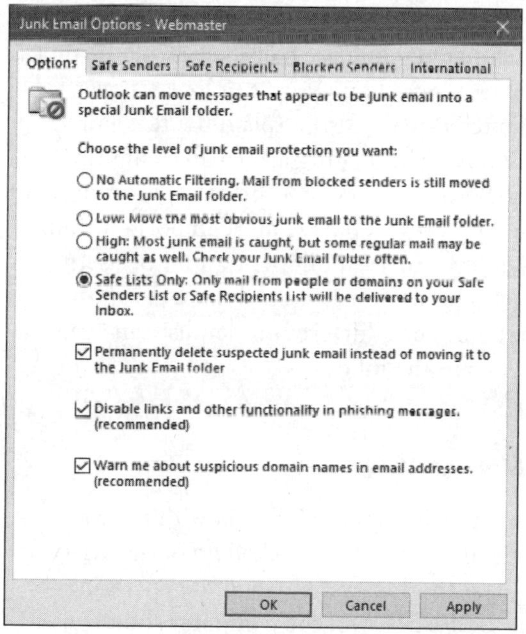

Figure 2-2   Outlook Junk Email Options Set at Highest Level of Security

- **Close open mail relays:** SMTP servers can be configured as **open mail relays,** which enables anyone on the Internet to send e-mail through the SMTP server. Although this is desirable to customers of the company that runs the SMTP server, it is not desirable to the company to have a completely open mail relay. So, open mail relays should either be closed or configured in such a way that only customers and properly authenticated users can use them. Open mail relays are also known as *SMTP open relays.*

- **Remove e-mail address links from the company website:** Replace these with online forms (for example, secure PHP forms) that enable a person to contact the company but not see any company e-mail addresses. Use a separate advertising e-mail address for any literature or ads. Consider changing this often; marketing people might already do this as a form of tracking leads. Taking it to the next level, consider an e-mail service.

- **Use whitelists and blacklists:** Whitelists are safe lists of e-mail addresses or entire e-mail domains that are trusted, whereas blacklists are lists of e-mail addresses or e-mail domains that are not trusted. These lists can be set up on e-mail servers, e-mail appliances, and within mail client programs such as Outlook.

- **Train your users:** Have them create and use a free e-mail address whenever they post to forums, tech support portals, and newsgroups, and instruct them not to use their company e-mail for anything except company-related purposes. Make sure that they screen their e-mail carefully; this is also known as e-mail vetting. E-mail with attachments should be considered volatile unless the user knows exactly where it comes from. Train your employees never to make a purchase from an unsolicited e-mail. Also, explain the reasoning behind using blind carbon copy (BCC) when sending an e-mail to multiple users. Let's not beat around the bush; we all know that this is the most difficult thing to ask of a company and its employees who have more important things to do. However, some companies enforce this as policy and monitor users' e-mail habits. Some companies have a policy in place in which users must create a "safe" list. This means that only the addresses on that list can send e-mail to the user and have it show up in the inbox.

You Can't Save Every Computer from Malware!

On a final and sad note, sometimes computers become so infected with malware that they cannot be saved. In this case, the data should be backed up (if necessary by removing the hard drive and slaving it to another system), and the operating system and applications reinstalled. The UEFI/BIOS of the computer should also be flashed. After the reinstall, the system should be thoroughly checked to make sure that there were no residual effects and that the system's hard drive performs properly.

Summary of Malware Prevention Techniques

Table 2-2 summarizes the malware prevention techniques discussed up to this point.

Key Topic

Table 2-2   Summary of Malware Prevention Techniques

Malware Threat	Prevention Techniques
Virus	Run and update antivirus software.
	Scan the entire system periodically.
	Update the operating system.
	Use a firewall.
Worm	Run and update antivirus software.
	Scan the entire system periodically.
Trojan horse	Run and update antivirus software.
	Scan the entire system periodically.
	Run a Trojan scan periodically.
Spyware	Run and update anti-spyware software.
	Scan the entire system periodically.
	Adjust web browser settings.
	Consider technologies that discourage spyware.
Rootkit	Run and update antivirus software.
	Use rootkit detector programs.
Spam	Use a spam filter.
	Configure whitelists and blacklists.
	Close open mail relays.
	Train your users.

Chapter Summary

Computer security threats can be delivered by way of software or within an e-mail, via zombie computers that are part of a botnet, by using exploit kits, and through backdoors and the act of privilege escalation. The idea is that the attacker wants to either render the computer useless or gain administrative access to it. The reason, more often than not, is that the attacker wants confidential information, such as company secrets, credit card numbers, or even classified government information. But it could also be that the attacker simply wants to create havoc.

Whatever the reason, be sure to know the warning signs for the various types of malware you might encounter: from virus-caused lockups and restarts to spyware-caused web browser modifications. If malware does infect a computer, be sure to implement the proper removal procedure; either the one listed in this chapter, or one that is provided to you by your organization's written policies.

However, prevention is the key to a productive business environment. Understand the prevention techniques for viruses, worms, Trojans, spyware, and ransomware. Review those methods periodically to make sure that you are implementing the best and most up to date strategies possible. I say it often: "An ounce of prevention is worth a pound of cure" to quote Benjamin Franklin. This is one instance where just a little bit of time spent securing systems and educating users could save an organization hours—possibly days—and perhaps a whole lot of money in the process.

Chapter Review Activities

Use the features in this section to study and review the topics in this chapter.

Review Key Topics

Review the most important topics in the chapter, noted with the Key Topic icon in the outer margin of the page. Table 2-3 lists a reference of these key topics and the page number on which each is found.

Table 2-3   Key Topics for Chapter 2

Key Topic Element	Description	Page Number
Bulleted list	Types of viruses	20
Table 2-1	Summary of malware threats	25
Numbered list	Malware removal procedure	34
Table 2-2	Summary of malware prevention techniques	41

Define Key Terms

Define the following key terms from this chapter, and check your answers in the glossary:

malware, virus, worm, Trojan horse, remote access Trojan (RAT), ransomware, spyware, adware, grayware, rootkit, spam, threat vector, attack vector, typosquatting, botnet, zombie, active interception, privilege escalation, backdoors, logic bomb, time bomb, open mail relay

Complete the Real-World Scenarios

Complete the Real-World Scenarios found on the companion website (www.pearsonitcertification.com/title/9780789758996). You will find a PDF containing the scenario and questions, and also supporting videos and simulations.

Review Questions

Answer the following review questions. Check your answers with the correct answers that follow.

1. A group of compromised computers that have software installed by a worm or Trojan is known as which of the following?

    A. Botnet

    B. Virus

    C. Rootkit

    D. Zombie

2. Which of the following computer security threats can be updated automatically and remotely? (Select the best answer.)

    A. Virus

    B. Worm

    C. Zombie

    D. Malware

3. You have been given the task of scanning for viruses on a PC. What is the best of the following methods?

    A. Recovery environment

    B. Dual-boot into Linux

    C. Command Prompt only

    D. Boot into Windows normally

4. Which of the following is a common symptom of spyware?

    A. Infected files

    B. Computer shuts down

    C. Applications freeze

    D. Pop-up windows

5. Dan is a network administrator. One day he notices that his DHCP server is flooded with information. He analyzes it and finds that the information is coming from more than 50 computers on the network. Which of the following is the most likely reason?

   A. Virus

   B. Worm

   C. Zombie

   D. PHP script

6. Which of the following is not an example of malicious software?

   A. Rootkits

   B. Spyware

   C. Viruses

   D. Browser

7. Which type of attack uses more than one computer?

   A. Virus

   B. DoS

   C. Worm

   D. DDoS

8. What is a malicious attack that executes at the same time every week?

   A. Virus

   B. Worm

   C. Ransomware

   D. Logic bomb

9. Which of these is a true statement concerning active interception?

   A. When a computer is put between a sender and receiver

   B. When a person overhears a conversation

   C. When a person looks through files

   D. When a person hardens an operating system

10. Which of the following types of scanners can locate a rootkit on a computer?

    A. Image scanner

    B. Barcode scanner

    C. Malware scanner

    D. Adware scanner

11. Which type of malware does not require a user to execute a program to distribute the software?

    A. Worm

    B. Virus

    C. Trojan horse

    D. Stealth

12. Whitelisting, blacklisting, and closing open relays are all mitigation techniques addressing what kind of threat?

    A. Spyware

    B. Spam

    C. Viruses

    D. Botnets

13. How do most network-based viruses spread?

    A. By optical disc

    B. Through e-mail

    C. By USB flash drive

    D. By instant messages

14. Which of the following defines the difference between a Trojan horse and a worm? (Select the best answer.)

    A. Worms self-replicate but Trojan horses do not.

    B. The two are the same.

    C. Worms are sent via e-mail; Trojan horses are not.

    D. Trojan horses are malicious attacks; worms are not.

15. Which of the following types of viruses hides its code to mask itself?

   A. Stealth virus

   B. Polymorphic virus

   C. Worm

   D. Armored virus

16. Which of the following types of malware appears to the user as legitimate but actually enables unauthorized access to the user's computer?

   A. Worm

   B. Virus

   C. Trojan

   D. Spam

17. Which of the following would be considered detrimental effects of a virus hoax? (Select the two best answers.)

   A. Technical support resources are consumed by increased user calls.

   B. Users are at risk for identity theft.

   C. Users are tricked into changing the system configuration.

   D. The e-mail server capacity is consumed by message traffic.

18. One of your co-workers complains of very slow system performance and says that a lot of antivirus messages are being displayed. The user admits to recently installing pirated software and downloading and installing an illegal keygen to activate the software. What type of malware has affected the user's computer?

   A. Worm

   B. Logic bomb

   C. Spyware

   D. Trojan

19. A user complains that they were browsing the Internet when the computer started acting erratically and crashed. You reboot the computer and notice that performance is very slow. In addition, after running a netstat command you notice literally hundreds of outbound connections to various websites, many of which are well-known sites. Which of the following has happened?

    A. The computer is infected with spyware.

    B. The computer is infected with a virus.

    C. The computer is now part of a botnet.

    D. The computer is now infected with a rootkit.

20. One of your users was not being careful when browsing the Internet. The user was redirected to a warez site where a number of pop-ups appeared. After clicking one pop-up by accident, a drive-by download of unwanted software occurred. What does the download most likely contain?

    A. Spyware

    B. DDoS

    C. Smurf

    D. Backdoor

    E. Logic bomb

21. You are the network administrator for a small organization without much in the way of security policies. While analyzing your servers' performance you find various chain messages have been received by the company. Which type of security control should you implement to fix the problem?

    A. Antivirus

    B. Anti-spyware

    C. Host-based firewalls

    D. Anti-spam

22. You are the security administrator for your organization and have just completed a routine server audit. You did not notice any abnormal activity. However, another network security analyst finds connections to unauthorized ports from outside the organization's network. Using security tools, the analyst finds hidden processes that are running on the server. Which of the following has most likely been installed on the server?

    A. Spam

    B. Rootkit

    C. Backdoor

    D. Logic bomb

    E. Ransomware

Answers and Explanations

1. **A.** A botnet is a group of compromised computers, usually working together, with malware that was installed by a worm or a Trojan horse. An individual computer within a botnet is referred to as a zombie (among other things). A virus is code that can infect a computer's files. A rootkit is a type of software designed to gain administrator-level access to a system.

2. **C.** Zombies (also known as zombie computers) are systems that have been compromised without the knowledge of the owner. A prerequisite is the computer must be connected to the Internet so that the hacker or malicious attack can make its way to the computer and be controlled remotely. Multiple zombies working in concert often form a botnet. See the section "Delivery of Malware" earlier in this chapter for more information.

3. **A.** You should use a recovery environment. Most often, this would be the one built into Windows. Many manufacturers suggest using this, and more specifically Safe Mode. However, it could also be a Linux rescue disc or flash drive. That's not a true dual-boot though. An actual dual-boot is when Windows and Linux are both installed to the hard drive. Command Prompt only is not enough, nor is it necessary for some virus scanning scenarios. Booting into Windows normally is tantamount to doing nothing. Remember to use a recovery environment when scanning for viruses.

4. **D.** Pop-up windows are common to spyware. The rest of the answers are more common symptoms of viruses.

5. **B.** A worm is most likely the reason that the server is being bombarded with information by the clients; perhaps it is perpetuated by a botnet. Because worms self-replicate, the damage can quickly become critical.

6. **D.** A web browser (for example, Internet Explorer) is the only one listed that is not an example of malicious software. Although a browser can be compromised in a variety of ways by malicious software, the application itself is not the malware.

7. **D.** A DDoS, or distributed denial-of-service, attack uses multiple computers to make its attack, usually perpetuated on a server. None of the other answers use multiple computers.

8. **D.** A logic bomb is a malicious attack that executes at a specific time. Viruses normally execute when a user inadvertently runs them. Worms can self-replicate at will. Ransomware is a type of malware that restricts access to files (or entire systems) and demands a ransom be paid.

9. **A.** Active interception normally includes a computer placed between the sender and the receiver to capture information. All other statements concerning active interception are false. If a person overhears a conversation it can be considered eavesdropping. When a person looks through files it could be normal or malicious. When a person hardens an operating system, that person is making it more secure. We discuss these concepts as we progress through the book.

10. **C.** Malware scanners can locate rootkits and other types of malware. These types of scanners are often found in anti-malware software from manufacturers such as McAfee, Symantec, and so on. Adware scanners (often free) can scan for only adware. Always have some kind of anti-malware software running on live client computers!

11. **A.** Worms self-replicate and do not require a user to execute a program to distribute the software across networks. All the other answers do require user intervention. Stealth refers to a type of virus.

12. **B.** Closing open relays, whitelisting, and blacklisting are all mitigation techniques that address spam. Spam e-mail is a serious problem for all companies and must be filtered as much as possible.

13. **B.** E-mail is the number one reason why network-based viruses spread. All a person needs to do is double-click the attachment within the e-mail, and the virus will do its thing, which is most likely to spread through the user's address book. Removable media such as optical discs and USB flash drives can spread viruses but are not nearly as common as e-mail. A virus can also spread if it was incorporated into a link within an instant message, or as an attachment to the IM. This is definitely something to protect against, but not quite as common as e-mail-based viruses, especially in larger organizations' networks.

14. **A.** The primary difference between a Trojan horse and a worm is that worms will self-replicate without any user intervention; Trojan horses do not self-replicate.

15. **D.** An armored virus attempts to make disassembly difficult for an antivirus software program. It thwarts attempts at code examination. Stealth viruses attempt to avoid detection by antivirus software altogether. Polymorphic viruses change every time they run. Worms are not viruses.

16. **C.** A Trojan, or a Trojan horse, appears to be legitimate and looks like it'll perform desirable functions, but in reality is designed to enable unauthorized access to the user's computer.

17. **A and C.** Because a virus can affect many users, technical support resources can be consumed by an increase in user phone calls. This can be detrimental to the company because all companies have a limited number of technical support personnel. Another detrimental effect is that unwitting users may be tricked into changing some of their computer system configurations. The key term in the question is "virus hoax." The technical support team might also be inundated by support e-mails from users, but not to the point where the e-mail server capacity is consumed. If the e-mail server is consumed by message traffic, that would be a detrimental effect caused by the person who sent the virus and by the virus itself but not necessarily by the hoax. Although users may be at risk for identity theft, it is not one of the most detrimental effects of the virus hoax.

18. **D.** A Trojan was probably installed (unknown to the user) as part of the keygen package. Illegal downloads often contain malware of this nature. At this point, the computer is compromised. Not only is it infected, but malicious individuals might be able to remotely access it.

19. **C.** The computer is probably now part of a botnet. The reason the system is running slowly is probably due to the fact that there are hundreds of outbound connections to various websites. This is a solid sign of a computer that has become part of a botnet. Spyware, viruses, and rootkits might make the computer run slowly, but they will not create hundreds of outbound connections.

20. **A.** Of the answers listed, the download most likely contains spyware. It could contain other types of malware as well, such as viruses, Trojans, worms, and so on. The rest of the answers are types of network attacks and methods of accessing the computer to drop a malware payload. A DDoS is a distributed denial-of-service attack, which uses many computers to attack a single target. Smurf is an example of a DDoS. We'll talk more about these in Chapter 7. Backdoors are vulnerabilities in code that can allow a hacker (or even the programmer) administrative access to an operating system. Logic bombs are ways of delivering malware; they are based on timing.

21. **D.** The chain messages are e-mails (similar to the archaic chain *letter*) that are being spammed on the network. Therefore, anti-spam security controls need to be implemented. This would be a type of preventive control. Antivirus programs find and quarantine viruses, worms, and Trojans, but unless they are part of an AV suite of software, they will not check e-mail. Anti-spyware tools will attempt to prevent spyware from being installed on the computer. Host-based firewalls block attacks from coming through specific ports, but will

not catch spam messages. However, a HIDS (host-based intrusion detection system) could possibly detect spam, and a HIPS (host-based intrusion prevention system) might even prevent or quarantine it. We'll discuss host-based firewalls, HIDS, and HIPS more in Chapter 3.

22. **B.** Most likely, a rootkit was installed. These can evade many routine scans, so there is no fault here. It's just that more in-depth analysis was required to find the rootkit. The hidden processes are the main indicator of the rootkit. Spam is simply harassment by e-mail (and other messaging systems), to put it nicely. Backdoors are programmed ways to bypass security of an operating system. A logic bomb is code that defines when a particular type of malware will execute. Ransomware is when a computer is operationally held hostage; files are not retrievable by the user (because they have been encrypted) until a ransom is paid. It's important to run in-depth scans periodically. They can be time consuming, but they can uncover many threats and vulnerabilities that would otherwise go unnoticed. We'll discuss these types of scans more in Chapters 12 and 13.

This chapter covers the following subjects:

- **Implementing Security Applications:** In this section, you learn how to select, install, and configure security applications such as personal firewalls, antivirus programs, and host-based intrusion detection systems. You'll be able to distinguish between the various tools and decide which is best for the different situations you'll see in the field.

- **Securing Computer Hardware and Peripherals:** Here we delve into the physical: how to protect a computer's hardware, UEFI/BIOS, wireless devices, and peripherals such as USB devices.

- **Securing Mobile Devices:** In this section, we will discuss how to protect mobile devices and the data they contain. By using screenlocks, encryption, remote wipe utilities, good BYOD policies, and more, we can protect devices from malicious attack, theft, and data loss.

CHAPTER 3

Computer Systems Security Part II

In the previous chapter we discussed malicious software, which is one of the biggest threats to computer systems' security. But it doesn't stop there; your computer can be accessed in other ways, including via the UEFI/BIOS and by external devices. And "computer" doesn't just mean that desktop computer at a user's desk. It also means laptops, tablets, and smartphones—actually any other systems or devices that have processing power and an operating system. These threats can be eliminated by implementing proper configuration of the UEFI/BIOS, and providing for security applications on every one of your client computers on the network—be they desktop computers, laptops, mobile devices, or IoT devices.

Foundation Topics

Implementing Security Applications

In the previous chapter, we discussed endpoint protection platforms; namely anti-malware suites. These application suites usually have antivirus, anti-spyware, and anti-spam components. Often, they also have a built-in firewall, known as a personal firewall. And perhaps the application suite also has a built-in *intrusion detection system (IDS)*, a piece of software that monitors and analyzes the system in an attempt to detect malicious activities. The type of IDS that a client computer would have is a **host-based intrusion detection system (HIDS)**. But there are other types of standalone software firewalls and HIDSs; we cover these in just a bit. Another type of built-in security is the pop-up blocker. Integrated into web browsers and web browser add-ons, pop-up blockers help users avoid websites that could be malicious. Let's discuss these security applications in a little more depth, starting with personal firewalls.

Personal Software Firewalls

Personal firewalls are applications that protect an individual computer from unwanted Internet traffic. They do so by way of a set of rules and policies.

Some personal firewalls (also known as host-based firewalls) prompt the user for permission to enable particular applications to access the Internet. In addition, some personal firewalls have the capability to detect intrusions to a computer and block those intrusions; this is a basic form of a HIDS that we talk more about in the next section.

Examples of software-based personal firewalls include the following:

- **Windows Firewall:** Built into Windows, the basic version is accessible from the Control Panel or by typing `firewall.cpl` in the Run prompt or Command Prompt. The advanced version, Windows Firewall with Advanced Security, can be accessed by typing `wf.msc` in the Run prompt or Command Prompt. This advanced version enables a user to perform more in-depth configurations such as custom rules.

- **ZoneAlarm:** Originally a free product that is still available (see the following link), this was purchased by Check Point and is now also offered as part of a suite of security applications. Go to https://www.zonealarm.com/software/ free-firewall/.

- **PF (packet filter) and IPFW (IP Firewall):** PF is the command-line-based firewall built into OS X version 10.10 and higher and macOS. Its predecessor, IPFW, was available in OS X through 10.9 but was deprecated in 10.7. Some OS X versions and macOS also include a graphical firewall titled "Firewall." PF and IPFW are also used in FreeBSD.

- **iptables:** Used in Linux systems. Is used to configure the tables provided by the Linux kernel firewall and its rules. Can be extended upon using various configuration tools and third-party add-ons.

Anti-malware application suites from Symantec, McAfee, Kaspersky, and so on include personal firewalls as well. This has become a common trend, and you can expect to see personal firewall applications built into most anti-malware application suites in the future.

Because they are software, and because of the ever-increasing level of Internet attacks, personal firewalls should be updated often, and in many cases it is preferable to have them auto-update, although this depends on your organization's policies.

As software, a personal firewall can utilize some of the computer's resources. In the late 1990s and early 2000s, there were some complaints that particular anti-malware suites used too much CPU power and RAM, sometimes to the point of crashing the computer; in some cases this was because of the resources used by the firewall. Today, some anti-malware suites still run better than others, depending on the scenario. So, a smart systems administrator selects an endpoint protection platform that has a small footprint, and one that works best with the organization's operating systems and applications. Some organizations opt not to use personal firewalls on client computers and instead focus more on network-based firewalls and other security precautions. The choice of whether to use personal firewalls, network-based firewalls, or both can vary but careful analysis should be performed before a decision is made. For example, take an organization that accepts credit card payments over the phone and performs the transactions over the Internet. The individual computers that are used to carry out the transactions need to have a personal firewall installed with the proper ports filtered in order to comply with financial regulations.

Personal firewalls (like any software application) can also be the victim of attack. If worms or other malware compromise a system, the firewall could be affected. This just reinforces the concept that antivirus suites should be updated often; daily updates would be the optimal solution.

A common scenario for security in small offices and home offices is to have a four-port SOHO router/firewall protecting the network and updated personal firewalls on every client computer. This combination provides two levels of protection for the average user. This defense layering approach is normally adequate for smaller networks, but larger networks usually concentrate more on the network firewall(s) and network-based IDS(s) than on personal firewalls, although it is common to see both levels of firewall security in larger networks as well.

Host-Based Intrusion Detection Systems

Let's start by talking about intrusion detection systems (IDSs) in general. An IDS is used to monitor an individual computer system or a network, or a portion of a network, and analyze data that passes through to identify incidents, attacks, and so forth. You should be aware of two types of IDSs for the exam:

- **Host-based intrusion detection system (HIDS):** Loaded on an individual computer, it analyzes and monitors what happens inside that computer—for example, whether any changes have been made to file integrity. A HIDS is installed directly within an operating system, so it is not considered to be an "inline" device, unlike other network-based IDS solutions. One of the advantages of using a HIDS is that it can interpret encrypted traffic. Disadvantages include its purchase price, its resource-intensive operation, and its default local storage of the HIDS object database; if something happens to the computer, the database will be unavailable.

- **Network intrusion detection system (NIDS):** Can be loaded on the computer, or can be a standalone appliance, but it checks all the packets that pass through the network interfaces, enabling it to "see" more than just one computer; because of this, a NIDS is considered to be an "inline" device.

Advantages include the fact that it is less expensive and less resource intensive, and an entire network can be scanned for malicious activity as opposed to just one computer. Of course, the disadvantage is that a NIDS cannot monitor for things that happen within an operating system. For more information about NIDS solutions, see the section "NIDS Versus NIPS" in Chapter 8, "Network Perimeter Security."

Following are two main types of monitoring that an IDS can carry out:

- **Statistical anomaly:** It establishes a performance baseline based on normal network traffic evaluations, and then compares current network traffic activity with the baseline to detect whether it is within baseline parameters. If the sampled traffic is outside baseline parameters, an alarm is triggered and sent to the administrator.

- **Signature-based:** Network traffic is analyzed for predetermined attack patterns, which arc known as *signatures*. These signatures are stored in a database that must be updated regularly to have effect. Many attacks today have their own distinct signatures. However, only the specific attack that matches the signature will be detected. Malicious activity with a slightly different signature might be missed.

For more information about the various types of monitoring methodologies, see the section "Monitoring Methodologies" in Chapter 13, "Monitoring and Auditing."

IDS solutions need to be accurate and updated often to avoid the misidentification of legitimate traffic or, worse, the misidentification of attacks. Following are two main types of misidentification you need to know for the exam:

- **False positive:** The IDS identifies legitimate activity as something malicious.

- **False negative:** The IDS identifies an attack as legitimate activity. For example, if the IDS does not have a particular attack's signature in its database, the IDS will most likely not detect the attack, believing it to be legitimate, and the attack will run its course without any IDS warnings.

Some antivirus application suites have basic HIDS functionality, but true HIDS solutions are individual and separate applications that monitor log files, check for file integrity, monitor policies, detect rootkits, and alert the administrator in real time of any changes to the host. This is all done in an effort to detect malicious activity such as spamming, zombie/botnet activity, identity theft, keystroke logging, and so on. Three examples of HIDS applications include the following:

- **Trend Micro OSSEC** (https://ossec.github.io/index.html): A free solution with versions for several platforms.

- **Verisys** (www.ionx.co.uk/products/verisys): A commercial HIDS file integrity monitoring solution for Windows.

- **Tripwire** (https://www.tripwire.com/products/tripwire-file-integrity-monitoring/): Another commercial HIDS solution.

There are several compliance regulations that require the type of file integrity monitoring that a HIDS can provide, including PCI DSS and NIST 800-53. When selecting a HIDS, make sure it meets the criteria of any compliance regulations that your organization must adhere to.

It is important to protect the HIDS database because this can be a target for attackers. It should either be encrypted, stored on some sort of read-only memory, or stored outside the system.

If an IDS observes an incident, it notifies the systems or network administrator so that she might quarantine and fix the problem. However, over time, the need for prevention has become more desirable, and so *intrusion prevention systems (IPSs)* and intrusion detection and prevention systems (IDPSs) were developed. For the local computer system, this is known as host-based IPS, or HIPS. These not only detect incidents and attacks, but also attempt to prevent them from doing any real damage to the computer or to the network. Once again, typical companies such as McAfee and Symantec (and the aforementioned HIDS/HIPS providers) offer host-based intrusion prevention systems. There are also downloadable implementations for Linux that prevent malicious code from executing, such as Security-Enhanced Linux (SELinux). It is a set of kernel modifications originally developed by the National Security Agency (NSA) but was released to the open source community for download. We talk more about this in Chapter 11, "Access Control Methods and Models."

A security administrator can review the logs of a host-based IDS at any time. However, if the computer has been shut down, the administrator will not be able to review information pertaining to system processes and network processes, nor information stored in memory, because all those items are volatile. HIDS logs that refer to archived storage, the MBR (or GPT), the system disk, e-mail, and so on will still be available for review. By reviewing the logs of a HIDS, a security administrator can find out if the computer has been compromised by malware, or if it is communicating with a botnet.

Pop-Up Blockers

For a website to generate revenue, a webmaster often advertises other products and services, charging fees to the organization that creates these products and services. The only way that an organization can continually advertise on the website is if it is positive it will get a certain amount of click-through response for its ads. However, web users quickly learn to define which windows are advertisements and which aren't. So advertisers need to constantly create new and exciting ways to advertise their products. The traditional JavaScript-based pop-up window doesn't do as good of a job as it used to because many web browsers have built-in pop-up blockers, but you still see tons of them on the Internet, perhaps in other formats such as Flash. They can take their toll on user productivity—and can be detrimental to the user's computer. For example, some pop-up ads, if clicked, force the user to go to one or more separate websites that could have harmful code. Or worse yet, the pop-up itself could have malicious code built in; perhaps the Close button within the ad launches some other process altogether.

Some attackers create entire websites with malicious pop-ups just to infect as many computers as they can. You might ask: "Why take advantage of users?" Some attackers might answer: "Because they are there to be taken advantage of!" Not that I condone this behavior, but this mentality is infectious, making pop-ups and all their cousins common; so, systems administrators should try their best to block pop-ups. One way to do this is with a **pop-up blocker**. These can be either enabled on or added to most web browsers.

One of the problems with pop-up blocking is that it might block content that is not an advertisement but instead is integral to the actual website. For example, I used to run a bulletin board system that has the capability to let users know that they have new private messages from other users; one of the options is for this alert to show up as a pop-up window. Because so many users do not see this alert, and instead get a message from the browser that says "Pop-up blocked" or something similar, which can look sort of suspicious to the user, I decided to turn off that functionality and instead let the main login page of the website (and e-mails) notify the user of new messages. This type of philosophy should be taken into account by webmasters when they define what the purpose of their website will be. Proper website functionality should be integrated directly into the actual web page, because most users ignore pop-ups or consider them malicious and attempt to close them, or block them, if they weren't otherwise blocked automatically by their browser.

When dealing with the previously listed applications and add-ons, pop-up blocking is known as **ad filtering**, but this can be taken to another level, known as content filtering. **Content filters** block external files that use JavaScript or images from loading into the browser. Content filtering continues to become more and more important as advertisers become more and more clever. Most newer web browser versions offer some kind of filtering, plus proxy-based programs such as Squid can filter content (among other things) for multiple computers. For more about proxy servers, see the section "Firewalls and Network Security" in Chapter 8.

Of course, advertisers have devised some new tricks in an attempt to get past the pop-up blockers and content filters: flash-based pop-ups, pop-*under* ads, dynamic HTML (DHTML) hover ads, and so on. Advertisers continue to battle for ad space with smart new ad types, so systems administrators should be prepared to update their clients' web browsers and browser add-ons on a regular basis.

Data Loss Prevention Systems

Data loss prevention (DLP) is a concept that refers to the monitoring of data in use, data in motion, and data at rest. A DLP system performs content inspection and is designed to prevent unauthorized use of data as well as prevent the leakage of data outside the computer (or network) that it resides in. DLP systems can be software or hardware-based solutions and come in three varieties:

- **Endpoint DLP systems:** These systems run on an individual computer and are usually software-based. They monitor data in use, such as e-mail communications, and can control what information flows between various users. These systems can also be used to inspect the content of USB-based mass-storage devices or block those devices from being accessed altogether by creating rules within the software.

- **Network DLP systems:** These can be software- or hardware-based solutions and are often installed on the perimeter of the network. They inspect data that is in motion.

- **Storage DLP systems:** These are typically installed in data centers or server rooms as software that inspects data at rest.

Cloud-based DLP solutions are offered by most cloud providers to protect against data breaches and misuse of data. These often integrate with software, infrastructure, and platform services, and can include any of the systems mentioned previously. Cloud-based DLP is necessary for companies that have increased bring your own device (BYOD) usage (discussed later in the chapter), and that store data and operate infrastructure within the cloud.

As with HIDS solutions, DLP solutions must be accurate and updated to reduce the number of false positives and false negatives. Most systems alert the security administrator in the case that there was a possibility of data leakage. However, it is up to the administrator to determine whether the threat was real.

Securing Computer Hardware and Peripherals

Now that the operating system is better secured, let's talk about securing computer hardware, the BIOS, and external peripheral devices.

There is a plethora of devices that can be connected to a computer system, such as USB flash drives, external SATA hard drives, and optical discs, just to mention a few. What if you want to stop people from using USB connections and USB-connected devices on the computer—without using a DLP solution? Well, there's the underlying firmware without which our computer could not run; I'm speaking of the BIOS, which can secure these ports and devices. However, the BIOS must be secured as well!

> **NOTE**   While firmware implementations such as UEFI replace, or work in conjunction with, the BIOS in many new computers, manufacturers still tend to refer to the firmware as the BIOS. For simplicity in this book I normally use the term "BIOS" to refer to both the BIOS and the UEFI. However, if a particular technology works in the UEFI only, it will be described as such.

Securing the BIOS

The BIOS can be the victim of malicious attacks; for mischievous persons, it can also act as the gateway to the rest of the system. Protect it! Otherwise, your computer might not boot—or worse. Following are a few ways to do so:

- **Flash the BIOS:** *Flashing* is a term that describes the updating of the BIOS. By updating the BIOS to the latest version, you can avoid possible exploits and BIOS errors that might occur. An updated BIOS (and newer motherboard) can also better protect from electromagnetic interference (EMI) and electromagnetic pulses (EMP). All new motherboards issue at least one new BIOS version within the first six months of the motherboard's release. Normally, you would flash the BIOS first before making any changes to the BIOS configurations.

- **Use a BIOS password:** The password that blocks unwanted persons from gaining access to the BIOS is the supervisor password. Don't confuse it with the user password (or power-on password) employed so that the BIOS can verify a user's identity before accessing the operating system. Both of these are shown in Figure 3-1. Because some computers' BIOS password can be cleared by opening the computer (and either removing the battery or changing the BIOS jumper), some organizations opt to use locking cables or a similar locking device that deters a person from opening the computer.

Key Topic

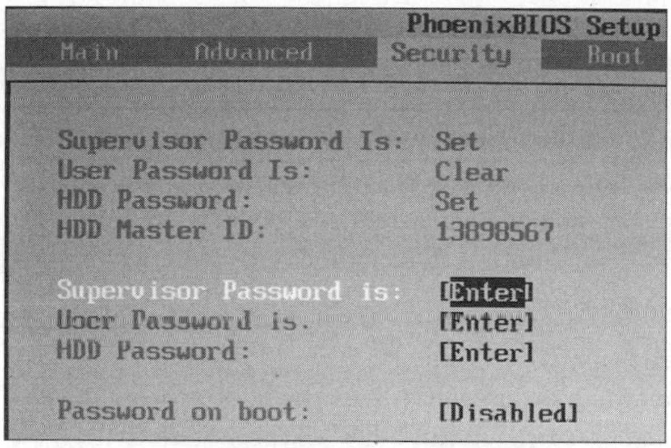

```
                              PhoenixBIOS Setup
    Main        Advanced      Security        Boot

    Supervisor Password Is:   Set
    User Password Is:         Clear
    HDD Password:             Set
    HDD Master ID:            13898567

    Supervisor Password is:   [Enter]
    User Password is:         [Enter]
    HDD Password:             [Enter]

    Password on boot:         [Disabled]
```

Figure 3-1   BIOS and Drive Lock Passwords

On a semi-related note, many laptops come equipped with *drive lock* technology; this might simply be referred to as an HDD password or other similar name. If enabled, it prompts the user to enter a password for the hard drive when the computer is first booted. If the user of the computer doesn't know the password for the hard drive, the drive locks and the OS does not boot. An eight-digit or similar hard drive ID can associate the laptop with the hard drive installed (refer to Figure 3-1). On most systems this password is clear by default, but if the password is set and forgotten, it can usually be reset within the BIOS. Some laptops come with documentation clearly stating the default BIOS and drive lock passwords—change them as part of the initial configuration of the computer.

- **Configure the BIOS boot order:** Set up the BIOS to reduce the risk of infiltration. For example, change the BIOS boot order (boot device priority) so that it looks for a hard drive first and not any type of removable media.

- **Disable external ports and devices:** If a company policy requires it, disable removable media including the optical drives, eSATA ports, and USB ports.

- **Enable the secure boot option:** UEFI 2.3.1 and higher offer an option called secure boot. This can secure the boot process of the computer by preventing unsigned—or improperly signed—device drivers and OS loaders. Implementing this may or may not be possible depending on the type of hardware used by your organization. Review hardware documentation and device drivers, and more importantly test the configuration, before implementing this option.

Today's UEFI-based systems use a **root of trust**, which is code—usually embedded in hardware in the form of a trusted platform module (TPM)—that incorporates encryption in the form of a public key. For a system with secure boot enabled to start up properly, kernel-based operating system drivers must present private keys that match the root of trust's public key. This process can prevent a system from being booted by undesirable OSes that can reside on flash drives or elsewhere, and prevent OSes that have been tampered with from booting. This tampering might occur in-house, or previously while in transit through the manufacturing supply chain.

Secure boot, also known as trusted boot, is an excellent method for protecting the boot process. However, if something occurs that causes the boot process to fail, we won't know because that data is stored in the UEFI of the system that failed to boot. More importantly, we want to be sure that secure boot is working properly. Enter the **measured boot** option. Measured boot takes measurements of each step of the secure boot process. It signs them, stores them, and sends those measurements to an external source, such as a remote attestation service. A trusted, external, third-party system is required for **attestation**—meaning verification of the integrity of the computer in question has been corroborated. Basically, the remote attestation service compares the measurements with known good values. From this information, the remote service can *attest* to the fact that the boot process is indeed secure—or has failed to meet the requirements.

Securing Storage Devices

The storage device is known to be a common failure point because many storage devices have moving parts or use removable media. Storage devices also can pose security risks because usually they are external from a computer system and are possibly located in an insecure area. Also, keeping track of removable media can be difficult. Some of the solutions to this include physical security, encryption, and policies that govern the use and storage of removable media. This section discusses removable storage devices, such as discs and external USB drives, network attached storage (NAS), and whole disk encryption. Hardware security modules take hardware-based encryption to the next level—we also discuss the basics of how these HSMs operate.

Removable Storage

Removable storage, or removable media, includes optical discs, USB devices, eSATA devices, and even floppy disks in some cases. A network administrator can prevent access to removable media from within the BIOS and within the operating system policies. In many companies, all removable media is blocked except for specifically necessary devices, which are approved on a case-by-case basis. Users should be trained on the proper usage of removable media and should *not* be allowed to take any data home with them. Users who sometimes work from home should do so via a virtual private network (VPN) connection to keep the data confidential, yet accessible.

USB devices must be carefully considered. They are small but can transport a lot of data. These devices can be the victim of attacks and can act as the delivery mechanism for attacks to a computer. For example, a USB flash drive might have data files or entire virtual operating systems that can be exploited by viruses and worms. Also, an attacker can install a special type of virus or worm onto the flash drive that is executed when the flash drive is connected to the computer; in this scenario the computer is the target for the malware. Organizations must decide whether to allow USB devices to be used. Organizational policies should state that USB sticks should not be carried from one department to another without proper security procedures in place. Operating system group policies can be implemented to enforce which users are allowed to use USB devices. As mentioned earlier, the BIOS can also disable the use of USB devices on a local computer. Finally, the data on a USB device can be encrypted with various programs—for example, Windows BitLocker—on the software side, or you might opt to purchase a secure USB flash drive, such as one by IronKey (http://www.ironkey.com/en-US/).

USB flash drives can easily be considered inherently insecure devices. It's the nature of the beast, so to speak. As such, a security administrator needs to implement **removable media controls** governing the usage of USB sticks and other removable media. These should include but are not limited to: USB lockdown in the BIOS and OS; limited use of USB devices; scanning of media devices for malware; encryption of data; monitoring of connected systems; and auditing of removable media. In addition, the reuse and disposal of removable media should be carefully managed—destruction of media might be necessary. Finally, a security administrator should be instrumental in writing policies for the company that dictate how these controls are implemented and educate users about these policies and maintain their awareness over time.

Network Attached Storage

Network attached storage (NAS) is a storage device that connects directly to your Ethernet network. Basic home and office NAS devices usually contain two hard drives, enabling you to set up RAID 1 mirroring, which protects your data if one drive fails. A more advanced example of NAS would be a device that looks more like a computer and might house up to 32 drives and contain terabytes of data. Possibly hot-swappable, these drives can be physically replaced, and the data can be rebuilt in a short amount of time. However, when it comes to RAID arrays, what we desire is **high availability**—meaning continuously operational for extended periods of time—in the neighborhood of 99.9% average uptime or higher.

A NAS device might be part of a larger storage area network (SAN); therefore, network security should also be considered when implementing any type of NAS. For more information on network security, see Chapters 6 through 9. To protect a single NAS device, consider data encryption, authentication, and constant secure logging of the device.

Whole Disk Encryption

Encryption is a huge component of today's computer security. By encrypting information, the data is rearranged in such a way that only the persons with proper authentication can read it. To encrypt an entire hard drive, you either need a **self-encrypting drive (SED)** or some kind of full disk encryption (FDE) software. ("Disk," though not accurate in some cases, is the commonly used term here.) Several types of FDE software are currently available on the market; one developed by Microsoft is called BitLocker—available in the elite editions of several newer versions of Windows. Full disk encryption software can encrypt the entire disk, which, after complete, is transparent to the user. Following are some requirements for encrypting an entire drive:

- Trusted platform module (TPM)—A chip residing on the motherboard that stores the encrypted keys. (This is part of the concept mentioned previously known as the root of trust.)

  or

- An external USB key to store the encrypted keys.

  and

- A hard drive with two volumes, preferably created during the installation of Windows. One volume is for the operating system (most likely C:) that will be encrypted; the other is the active volume that remains unencrypted so that the computer can boot. If a second volume needs to be created, the BitLocker Drive Preparation Tool can be of assistance and can be downloaded from the Microsoft Download Center.

BitLocker software is based on the Advanced Encryption Standard (AES) and can use 128-bit and 256-bit keys. Keep in mind that a drive encrypted with BitLocker usually suffers in performance compared to a nonencrypted drive and could have a shorter shelf life as well.

In the appropriate Windows version/edition, BitLocker security settings can be accessed via the following steps:

Step 1.   Navigate to the Run prompt.

Step 2.   Type `gpedit.msc` and press Enter.

Step 3.   In the Group Policy Editor window, navigate to Computer Configuration > Administrative Templates > Windows Components > BitLocker Drive Encryption.

Figure 3-2 shows the BitLocker configuration settings window.

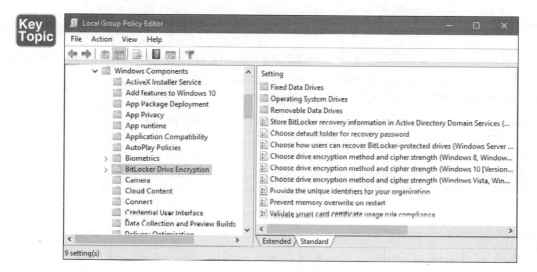

Figure 3-2   BitLocker Configuration Settings Window

NOTE   For more information about BitLocker and how to use it, see the following link.

https://technet.microsoft.com/en-us/library/hh831713(v-ws.11).aspx

Although it can be a lot of work to implement, double encryption can be a very successful technique when it comes to securing files. For example, a hard drive encrypted with BitLocker could also use EFS to encrypt individual files. This way, files that are copied to external media will remain encrypted, even though they don't reside on the drive using whole disk encryption.

Hardware Security Modules

Hardware security modules (HSMs) are physical devices that act as secure cryptoprocessors. This means that they are used for encryption during secure login/authentication processes, during digital signings of data, and for payment security systems. The beauty of a hardware-based encryption device such as an HSM (or a TPM) is that it is faster than software encryption.

HSMs can be found in adapter card form, as devices that plug into a computer via USB, and as network-attached devices. They are generally tamper-proof, giving a high level of physical security. They can also be used in high-availability clustered environments because they work independently of other computer systems and are used solely to calculate the data required for encryption keys. However, many of these devices require some kind of management software to be installed on the computer they are connected to. Some manufacturers offer this software as part of the purchase, but others do not, forcing the purchaser to build the management software themselves. Due to this lack of management software, and the cost involved in general, HSMs have seen slower deployment with some organizations. This concept also holds true for hardware-based drive encryption solutions.

Often, HSMs are involved in the generation, storage, and archiving of encrypted key pairs such as the ones used in Secure Sockets Layer (SSL) sessions online, public key cryptography, and public key infrastructures (PKIs), which we discuss more in Chapter 14, "Encryption and Hashing Concepts," and Chapter 15, "PKI and Encryption Protocols."

Securing Wireless Peripherals

In today's "hassle-free" world of peripherals, there are a ton of wireless devices in use. Unfortunately, because wireless signals are generally spread spectrum, they can be more easily intercepted than wired signals. Some wireless peripherals, such as keyboards and mice, can have their keystrokes and clicks captured with the most basic of attacks. To protect against this, some manufacturers offer encrypted wireless device solutions, with AES being one of the most common encryption protocols used. Wireless displays use technologies such as Wi-Fi Direct (WiDi) that is backward compatible with standard Wi-Fi technologies. As such, these displays should make connections using WPA2 and AES. Wi-Fi-enabled cameras and SD/microSD cards should be configured in a similar manner. The same goes with external storage devices, printers, and multi-function devices. The bottom line is this: Any peripheral that connects in a wireless fashion needs to have proper authentication put in place (such as WPA2) and strong encryption (such as AES-256 or higher). Also keep in mind that newer types of authentication and encryption become available occasionally. Remember to periodically check whether your wireless security schemes are up to date.

Securing Mobile Devices

Unfortunately, smartphones and tablets (and other mobile devices) can be the victims of attack as well. Attackers might choose to abuse your service or use your device as part of a larger scale attack, and possibly to gain access to your account information.

Though mobile devices can be considered "computers," and most of the information mentioned in this chapter and the previous chapter applies to them as well, there are some other things we should consider specifically for the mobile device.

Users of mobile devices should be careful who they give their phone number to, and should avoid listing their phone number on any websites, especially when purchasing products. Train your users not to follow any links sent by e-mail or by text messages if these are unsolicited. (If there is any doubt in the user's mind, then it is best to ignore the communication.) Explain the issues with much of the downloadable software, such as games and ringtones, to your users. Use a locking code/password/gesture that's hard to guess; this locks the mobile device after a specific amount of time has lapsed. Use complex passwords when necessary; for example, if required by company policy.

In general, mobile operating system software must be updated just like desktop computer software. Keep these devices up to date, and there will be less of a chance that they will be affected by viruses and other malware. You can encrypt data in several ways, and some organizations have policies that specify how data will be encrypted. More good general tips are available at the following National Cyber Awareness System (NCAS) and U.S. Computer Emergency Readiness Team (US-CERT) website links. Make your users aware of them.

- https://www.us-cert.gov/ncas
- https://www.us-cert.gov/ncas/tips/ST05-017.html

It should be noted that some organizations will use the term "portable electronic device," which refers to any portable device that can store and record data and transmit text, images, video, and audio data. Devices in the portable electronic device (PED) category include laptops, media players, e-readers, gaming devices, cell phones, pagers, radios, audio devices, fitness devices, and so on. However, for this book we are most concerned with smartphones and tablets and refer to them as mobile devices.

Let's discuss some of the attacks and other concerns for mobile devices, as well as ways to prevent these things from happening, and how to recover from them if they do occur.

Malware

It's not just Windows that you have to worry about when it comes to malware. Every operating system is vulnerable, some less than others. Historically, in the mobile device marketplace, Android has proven to be somewhat of a stomping ground for malware; for example, the GinMaster Trojan steals confidential information from the Android device and sends it to a remote website. Viruses, worms, rootkits, and other types of malware are commonly found in the Android OS, and are sometimes found in iOS and other mobile device operating systems.

As with desktop operating systems, mobile operating systems should be updated to the newest version possible (or the point release for the version installed). AV software can also be used. Newer models of mobile devices come with built-in security programs. These programs should be updated regularly, and configured for optimal security. Care should be taken when tapping links within e-mails, texts, or social media networks. Personal or organizational information should never be shared on social networks, and should usually not be stored on the mobile device.

NOTE Social engineering attacks are also quite common on mobile devices. Techniques such as hoaxes, pretexting, phishing, and many more are commonplace. We'll discuss how to combat social engineering in general within Chapter 17, "Social Engineering, User Education, and Facilities Security."

Botnet Activity

Mobile devices can be part of botnets—just like desktop computers. Because they are more easily accessible than desktop computers at this point, they make up a big part of some of today's botnets. A mobile device can take part in the launching of distributed denial-of-service (DDoS) attacks, or inadvertently join in with a click fraud outfit, or could be part of a scam to get users of other mobile devices to send premium-rate Short Message Service (SMS) messages. And that's just the beginning. Methods for preventing a mobile device from joining a botnet (without the user's knowledge) are similar to those mentioned previously concerning malware. Great care should be taken when downloading applications. The user should make sure the apps are from a legitimate source. Also, rooting (or jailbreaking) the mobile device is not recommended. The programs used in conjunction with rooting the device are often malicious, or are closely aligned with other malicious programs. In addition, a mobile device with custom firmware, also known as custom ROM, is more susceptible to root access from would-be attackers and botnets. Not to mention that over-the-air (OTA) firmware updates might not work anymore. If it appears that a device has become part of a botnet, that device should be wiped, either by a hard reset or other means.

SIM Cloning and Carrier Unlocking

Another attack on smartphones is SIM cloning (also known as phone cloning), which allows two phones to utilize the same service and allows an attacker to gain access to all phone data. V1 SIM cards had a weak algorithm that made SIM cloning possible (with some expertise). However, V2 cards and higher are much more difficult (if not impossible) to clone due to a stronger algorithm on the chip. Users and administrators should be aware of the version of SIM card being used and update it (or the entire smartphone) if necessary.

There are techniques available to unlock a smartphone from its carrier. Users should be advised against this, and a security administrator should create and implement policies that make unlocking the SIM card difficult, if not impossible. Unlocking the phone—making it SIM-free—effectively takes it off the grid and makes it difficult to track and manage. When the SIM is wiped, the International Mobile Subscriber Identity (IMSI) is lost and afterward the user cannot be recognized. However, the security administrator can attempt to blacklist the smartphone through its provider using the International Mobile Equipment Identity (IMEI), electronic serial number (ESN), or Mobile Equipment Identifier (MEID). The ID used will vary depending on the type and age of smartphone. Regardless, as a security administrator, you would rather avoid that tactic altogether because the damage has already been done; so, protection of the SIM becomes vital.

Wireless Attacks

Anytime a cell phone or smartphone connects, it uses some type of wireless service. Whether it's 4G, 3G, GSM, Wi-Fi, infrared, RFID, or Bluetooth, security implications exist. To minimize risks, the best solution is to turn off the particular service when not in use, use airplane mode, or simply turn the mobile device off altogether if it is not being used.

Bluetooth is especially vulnerable to virus attacks, as well as bluejacking and bluesnarfing.

Bluejacking is the sending of unsolicited messages to Bluetooth-enabled devices such as mobile phones. Bluejacking can be stopped by setting the affected Bluetooth device to "undiscoverable" or by turning off Bluetooth altogether.

Bluesnarfing is the unauthorized access of information from a wireless device through a Bluetooth connection. Generally, bluesnarfing is the theft of data (calendar information, phonebook contacts, and so on). Ways of discouraging bluesnarfing include using a pairing key that is not easy to guess; for example, stay away from 0000 or similar default Bluetooth pairing keys! Otherwise, Bluetooth devices should be set to "undiscoverable" (only after legitimate Bluetooth devices have been set up, of course), or Bluetooth can be turned off altogether.

For more information about Bluetooth vulnerabilities (and other wireless attacks in general), see the section "Securing Wireless Networks" in Chapter 9, "Securing Network Media and Devices."

Wi-Fi has many vulnerabilities as well. Not only should mobile devices connect in a secure, encrypted fashion, but also the security administrator needs to keep a sharp eye on the current CVEs, and the available updates and patches for those vulnerabilities. For example, there was a flaw in the programming of a well-known Wi-Fi System on Chip (SoC). The firmware had a vulnerability that could result in buffer overflows, which could then be exploited by an attacker—connecting remotely via Wi-Fi—ultimately allowing the execution of their own code. Sometimes SoCs are not properly vetted for vulnerabilities and so security administrators must be ready to patch at a moment's notice—and this applies not only to smartphones and other typical mobile devices, but also to just about any devices in the Internet of Things (IoT) that have built-in Wi-Fi connections.

Theft

More than 100 mobile devices end up missing (often stolen) every minute. Let me repeat—every minute! You can imagine the variety of reasons why this is. The worst attack that can be perpetuated on a smartphone or tablet is theft. The theft of a mobile device means the possible loss of important data and personal information. There are a few ways to protect against this loss of data, and recover from the theft of a mobile device if it does happen.

First, mobile devices in an organization should utilize data encryption. The stronger the encryption, the more difficult it is for a thief to decode and use the data on the device. If at all possible, use *full device encryption*, similar to Windows BitLocker. The actual conversations on phones can also be encrypted. Voice encryption can protect the confidentiality of spoken conversations and can be implemented with a special microSD chip (preferably) or with software.

Mobile devices should also be set up for GPS tracking so that they can be tracked if they are lost or stolen. The quicker a device can be located, the less risk of data loss, especially if it is encrypted. However, GPS tracking can also be a security vulnerability for the device and possibly the user if an attacker knows how to track the phone.

The beauty of mobile devices is in their inherent portability—that and the ability to track SIM cards. Administrators of mobile devices should consider remote *lockout* programs. If a device is lost or stolen, the admin can lock the device, disallowing a would-be attacker access. In addition, the device can be configured to use the "three strikes and you're out" rule, meaning that if a user tries to be authenticated to the device and is unsuccessful after three attempts, the user is locked out. Taking it to the next level, if the data is extremely sensitive, you might want to consider a remote wipe program. If the mobile device is reported as lost or stolen, these programs can remove all data from the phone in a bit by bit process, making it difficult (if not impossible) to recover. This is known as *sanitizing* the phone remotely. Of course, a solid backup strategy should be in place before a data sanitizing or remote wipe solution is implemented.

Screen locks, complex passwords, and taking care when connecting to wireless networks are also important. Though a screen lock won't deter the knowledgeable attacker, it will usually deter the average person who, for example, finds a stray phone sitting in a coffee shop, mall, or other public location. User training should be implemented when users first receive their device. Though many organizations don't take the time to do this, it is a great way to show users how to secure their device, while checking whether their encryption, GPS tracking, and other features are working properly. They can also be trained on how to inform your organization and local law enforcement in the case that a device is lost or stolen, effectively reducing the risk of data loss by allowing you to find the device faster or mitigate the problem in other ways.

NOTE   In the case of theft, the two best ways to protect against the loss of confidential or sensitive information are encryption and a remote wipe program.

Application Security

Let's speak more about the applications' security on mobile devices. We've already mentioned that applications should (usually) be updated to the latest version, and discussed the importance of proper user interaction; but let's delve a bit deeper and talk about ways to encrypt data that is transferred through applications.

Encryption is one of the best ways to ensure that data is secured and that applications work properly without interference from potential attackers. However, a security administrator should consider whole device encryption, which encrypts the internal memory and any removable (SD) cards. Sometimes an admin might forget about one or the other. Then there is data in transit; data that is on the move between a client and a server. Most applications for mobile devices communicate with a server of some sort; for example, when a person uses a web browser, an e-mail client, a contacts database, or actual "apps" that work independently of a browser, but operate in a similar manner, meaning that they ultimately connect to a server. Weather apps, games, social media apps, and so on all fall into this category.

Let's consider the web browser, for instance. A mobile device will connect to websites in a very similar manner as a desktop computer. Basic websites will use a Hypertext Transfer Protocol (HTTP) connection. But websites that require any type of personally identifiable information (PII) will use HTTP Secure (HTTPS). This can then utilize one of several types of encryption, such as Transport Layer Security (TLS).

NOTE   We'll discuss HTTPS, TLS, and many other security protocols in more depth within Chapter 5 and Chapter 15.

Whatever the security protocol, the important point here is that the server connected to makes use of a database that stores encryption keys. The key (or a portion thereof) is sent to the client device and is agreed upon (handshaking occurs) so that the transfer of data, especially private information, is encrypted and protected. Often, HTTPS pages are used to aid in the process of authentication— the confirmation of a person's (or computer's) identity, typically with the help of a username/password combination. Examples of this include when you log in to your account with a bank or with a shopping portal.

One of the important roles for the server is key management—the creation, storage, usage, and retirement of encryption keys. Proper key management (and the regular updating of keys) is a security administrator's primary concern. Generally, an organization will purchase a master key algorithm from a third-party company such as VeriSign. That company informs the organization if a key has become compromised and needs to be revoked. These third parties might also take part in credential management (the managing of usernames, passwords, PINs, and other passcodes, usually stored within a secure database) to make things a bit easier for the security administrator. It depends on the size of the organization and its budget. This gets quite in-depth, as you can imagine. For now, realize that a mobile device is an easy target. Therefore, applications (especially third-party apps) should be scrutinized to make sure they are using a solid encryption plan when personal information is transferred back and forth. Of course, we'll get more into encryption and key management in Chapters 14 and 15.

Authentication to servers and other networks (and all their applications) can get even more complicated when the concept of transitive trust is implemented. Effectively, a transitive trust is when two networks (or more) have a relationship such that users logging in to one network get access to data on the other. In days gone by, these types of trusts were created automatically between different sections of networks. However, it was quickly realized that this type of transitivity was insecure, allowing users (and potential attackers) access to other networks that they shouldn't have had access to in the first place. There's a larger looming threat here as well. The **transitive trust** is based on the transitive property in mathematics, which states that if A is equal to B, and B is equal to C, then A is automatically equal to C. Put into computer terms: if the New York network trusts the California network, and the California network trusts the Hong Kong network, then the New York network automatically trusts the Hong Kong network. You can imagine the security concerns here, as well as the domino effect that could occur. So, organizations will usually prefer the non-transitive trust, where users need to be authenticated to each network separately, and therefore are limited to the applications (and data) they have access to on a per-network basis.

To further restrict users, and increase application security, **application whitelisting** is often used. This means that a list of approved applications is created by the administrator and that the user can work with only those applications, and no others. This is often done within a computer policy and can be made more manageable by utilizing a mobile device management system (which we will detail a bit later). Users often only need access to several apps: phone, e-mail, contacts, and web browser. These applications would make up the whitelist, and if a user tried to use other apps, they would be denied, or at the very least, would be prompted for additional user credentials. If a user needed access to another app, such as the camera, the security administrator would weigh the security concerns (GPS, links to social media, and so on) and decide whether to add the app to the whitelist. Whitelisting can also be helpful when dealing with apps that utilize OAuth; a common mechanism used by social media companies to permit users to share account information with third-party applications and websites. Contrast the concept of application whitelisting with **application blacklisting**—the denial of individual applications—a common method used when working with e-mail, and by antivirus and HIDS programs.

The messaging app is a particularly devious gateway for attackers. SMS and MMS are vulnerable to malware, and unwary users of mobile devices are especially susceptible to Trojans and phishing via SMS texts. One way to prevent this is to install mobile anti-malware in the form of one mobile security suite or another. This endpoint protection platform needs to be updated and is best controlled from a mobile device management (MDM) solution. Another way is to block messaging apps altogether or to use company-approved messaging apps. This option depends on what type of mobile environment you are allowing. It will work for some mobile environments where the IT department has more control over devices, but probably not for BYOD.

If your organization uses a mobile payment method, it is important to understand that the applications that control these payment methods and the devices they run on can have several vulnerabilities. These include weak passwords (for the mobile device and for the payment app), user error, and phishing. Not only that, the technology itself is inherently insecure given the mobility of the device. Users should be educated about not using their mobile devices for payment while making a public Wi-Fi connection. They should also be taught how to properly and discreetly use payment apps. And of course, they should be instructed on how to avoid loss or theft of a mobile device, and what to do if loss or theft occurs. As the security administrator, you should consider using an external reader for payment transactions on mobile devices and teaching users to keep the reader separate from the mobile device when not in use.

Geotagging (also written as geo-tagging) is another application concern. Photos, videos, websites, messages, and much more can be geotagged. Geotagging is the adding of data to the content in question, helping users to gather location-specific information. For example, if a user wanted to take a picture of their favorite store at the mall and help friends to find it, the user could geotag the picture. However, this requires that the smartphone (or other mobile device) have GPS installed and running. This then means that the user's smartphone can be physically located and tracked. Depending on the applications running, this could pose a security threat. In a corporate environment, the security administrator will often choose to disable geotagging features. There are several privacy implications when it comes to geotagging. One of the most dangerous is the fact that many users don't even know that they are geotagging their media when they do so—some of the applications are that transparent. For people in the company such as executives (who might carry a wealth of confidential information), this is the type of feature that should be disabled. If a potential attacker can track an executive, then the attacker can find out where the executive lives, determine when the executive is in the office, and determine the location of clients, all of which can help the attacker to commit corporate espionage. When it comes down to it, the usage of GPS in general should be examined carefully, weighing the benefits against the possible vulnerabilities. This includes GPS derivatives such as GPS tagging, geofencing, and geolocation. (We'll discuss those terms in more depth in Chapter 9.) Many executives and other employees use their mobile devices at work, which brings up many security concerns besides GPS. Collectively these are known as BYOD concerns and are described in the following section.

BYOD Concerns

Around 2011, organizations began to allow employees to bring their own mobile devices into work and connect them to the organization's network (for work purposes only, of course). This "bring your own device" concept has since grown into a more popular method of computing for many organizations. It is enticing from a budgeting standpoint, but can be very difficult on the security administrator, and possibly on the user as well.

NOTE   Companies may implement similar strategies, such as choose your own device (CYOD), where employees select a device from a company-approved list, or corporate owned, personally enabled (COPE), where employees are supplied a phone by the company that can also be used for personal activities. For simplicity, I refer to these collectively as BYOD unless CYOD or COPE needs to be addressed specifically.

In order to have a successful BYOD implementation, the key is to implement **storage segmentation**—a clear separation of organizational and personal information, applications, and other content. It must be unmistakable where the data ownership line occurs. For networks with a lot of users, consider third-party offerings from companies that make use of **mobile device management (MDM)** platforms. These are centralized software solutions that can control, configure, update, and secure remote mobile devices such as Android, iOS, BlackBerry, and so on, all from one administrative console. The MDM software can be run from a server within the organization, or administered within the cloud. It makes the job of a mobile IT security administrator at least manageable. From the central location, the security administrator can carry out the tasks of application management, content management, and patch management. The admin can also set up more secure levels of mobile device access control. *Access control* is the methodology used to allow access to computer systems. (More on access control in Chapter 11.) For larger organizations, MDM software makes it easy for an admin to view inventory control, such as how many devices are active for each of the mobile operating systems used. It also makes it simpler to track assets, such as the devices themselves, and the types of data each contains. In addition, MDM software makes it less complicated to disable unused features on multiple devices at once, thereby increasing the efficiency of the devices, reducing their footprint, and ultimately making them more secure. For instance, an employee who happens to have both a smartphone and a tablet capable of making cellular calls doesn't necessarily need the latter. The admin could disable the tablet's cellular capability, which would increase battery efficiency as well as security for that device. Insecure user configurations such as rooting and jailbreaking can be blocked from MDM, as can **sideloading**— the art of loading third-party apps from a location outside of the official application store for that device. Note that sideloading can occur in several ways: by direct Internet connection (usually disabled by default); by connecting to a second mobile device via USB OTG (USB On-The-Go) or Bluetooth; by copying apps directly from a microSD card; or via tethering to a PC or Mac. Finally, application control becomes easier as well. Applications can be installed, uninstalled, updated, and secured from that central location. Even devices' removable storage (often USB-based) can be manipulated—as long as the removable storage is currently connected to the device.

User acceptance of BYOD is mixed in its reactions. Some employees like the idea of using their own device (which they might not have been allowed to use at work previously) and not having to train on a separate work computer. However, some employees believe that BYOD is just a way to move computing costs from the company to the user, and the level of trust is low. Around 2013, studies showed that the *perception* of BYOD (and MDM solutions) varied. Approximately 40 percent of users believe that their employer can see personal information on their mobile devices. This brings up a variety of legal concerns, such as the right to privacy. Companies that offer BYOD MDM solutions counter this by drawing a clear line in the sand, defining exactly what employers can see (for example, corporate e-mail) and what they can't see (such as personal texts). In general, these companies try to protect the privacy of the individual. Many organizations will write clear privacy policies that define, if necessary, selective wipes of secure corporate data while protecting personal data. As of the writing of this book, the technology is not perfect, and there will be some debate over time as to its long-term viability.

Part of the debate includes some additional concerns; for example, additional legal concerns exist about such things as employee misconduct and fraud. As of the writing of this book, legal precedents are being set, and the general consensus is gravitating toward a separation of personal and organizational data. Anything found that could possibly implicate an employee of wrongdoing would have to be found in the organizational portion of the data. From a forensics point of view, however, and because the device can't be split in two, if any potential wrongdoing is investigated, the device would need to be confiscated for analysis.

Most employees (of all age groups) are also concerned with how on-board devices (such as the on-board camera) can be used against them with or without their knowledge. Companies that offer BYOD solutions tend to refer to the camera (and photos/video taken) as part of the personal area of the device. However, those same companies will include GPS location as something the company can see, but this can be linked to a corporate login, with GPS tracking the user only when the user is logged in. Onboarding and offboarding in general are another concern. Essentially, *onboarding* is when the security administrator takes control of the device temporarily to configure it, update it, and perhaps monitor it, and *offboarding* is when the security administrator relinquishes control of the device when finished with it. It brings up some questions for the employee: When does it happen? How long does it last? How will my device be affected? Are there any architectural/infrastructural concerns? For example, will the BYOD solution change the core files of my device? Will an update done by a person when at home render the device inactive the next day at work? That's just the tip of the iceberg when it comes to questions and concerns about BYOD. The best course of action is for an organization to set firm policies about all of these topics.

Policies that need to be instituted include an acceptable use policy, a data ownership policy, and a support ownership policy. In essence, these define what a user is allowed to do with the device (during work hours), who owns what data and how that data is separated, and under what scenarios the organization takes care of technical support for the device as opposed to the user. We'll talk more about policies such as these in Chapter 18.

To help secure the mobile devices in a BYOD enterprise environment, some third-party providers offer: embedded certificate authority for managing devices and user identify; sophisticated posture monitoring and automated policy workflow so non-compliant devices do not get enterprise access; and certificate-based security to secure e-mail and reduce the chance of data loss.

Table 3-1 summarizes the mobile security techniques we covered in this section. With a mixture of user adherence to corporate policies, the workplace respecting the user's right to privacy, and a strong security plan, BYOD can be a success.

Key Topic

Table 3-1 Summary of Mobile Device Security

Mobile Device Security Topic	Countermeasure
Malware	Update device to latest version (or point release for the current version).
	Use security suites and AV software. Enable them if preloaded on the device and update regularly.
	Train users to carefully screen e-mail and selectively access websites.
	Be careful of social networks and third-party apps.
Botnets & DDoS	Download apps from a legitimate source. If BYOD is in place, use company-approved apps.
	Refrain from "rooting" or "jailbreaking" the device.
	Have data backed up in case the device becomes part of a botnet and has to be wiped.
SIM cloning	Use V2 and newer cards with strong encryption algorithms.
Wireless attacks	Use a strong password for the wireless network.
	Turn off unnecessary wireless features such as mobile hotspot, tethering, and so on.
	Disable Bluetooth if not in use for long periods of time (also conserves battery).
	Set device to undiscoverable.
Theft	Utilize data and voice encryption (especially in BYOD implementations).
	Implement lockout, remote locator, and remote wipe programs.
	Limit the amount of confidential information stored on the device.
	Use screen locks and complex passwords.

Mobile Device Security Topic	Countermeasure
Application security	Use encryption from reputable providers.
	Use anti-malware endpoint protection platforms.
	Utilize non-transitive trusts between networks and apps.
	White-list applications.
	Disable geotagging.
BYOD concerns	Implement storage segmentation.
	Utilize an MDM solution.
	Create and implement clear policies that the organization and user must adhere to.
	Consider CYOD or COPE as opposed to the traditional BYOD method.

Chapter Summary

A good security administrator is proactive. Preventing the threats discussed in this chapter requires updating systems and applications, and possibly redesigning networks and systems from the ground up. It also means using firewalls, host-based intrusion detection systems (HIDSs), and data loss prevention (DLP) systems. It requires in-depth configuration of applications, filtering, and secure policies. And of course, this all signifies a need for user training.

Software is not the only place to increase security. Hardware can be physically protected, and firmware such as the BIOS should be secured as well. As mentioned, the most important thing to a company (technologically speaking) is its data. So, the securing of all types of storage devices, especially removable storage, is paramount. This can be done in a physical manner and in a logical manner by utilizing hardware security modules (HSMs) and encryption, respectively.

A computer is a computer. It doesn't matter if it's a PC from 1986 or a mobile device from this year. All computers need to be secured using the same principles and policies. However, historically mobile devices have tended to fall through the cracks. So, companies have really started gearing up the security for these devices. In most organizations it is not feasible to stop a person from bringing their smartphone into work. Some organizations have decided to embrace this practice and benefit from it with a policy of bringing in your own device (BYOD) to be used for work purposes in addition to personal. While this creates a whole slew of new security considerations, some organizations are implementing BYOD and CYOD successfully by creating a well-defined demarcation point between the user's data and the organization's. By instituting this concept, along with a mobile device management (MDM) solution and strong policies for theft, wireless attacks, and application security, mobile devices can survive and thrive in the enterprise or small office, yet remain safe and accessible for personal use.

Many of the topics we discussed in this chapter, such as encryption and policies, will be covered in more depth as we progress throughout the book. You will find that the upcoming chapters tend to build upon this and the previous chapter. Be sure to review these chapters carefully before continuing with the book.

Chapter Review Activities

Use the features in this section to study and review the topics in this chapter.

Review Key Topics

Review the most important topics in the chapter, noted with the Key Topic icon in the outer margin of the page. Table 3-2 lists a reference of these key topics and the page number on which each is found.

Table 3-2   Key Topics for Chapter 3

Key Topic Element	Description	Page Number
Figure 3-1	BIOS and drive lock passwords	61
Figure 3-2	BitLocker configuration settings window	65
Table 3-1	Summary of mobile device security	77

Define Key Terms

Define the following key terms from this chapter, and check your answers in the glossary:

host-based intrusion detection system (HIDS), personal firewall, pop-up blocker, ad filtering, content filters, root of trust, measured boot, attestation, removable media controls, high availability, self-encrypting drive (SED), hardware security module (HSM), bluejacking, bluesnarfing, transitive trust, application whitelisting, application blacklisting, storage segmentation, mobile device management (MDM), sideloading

Complete the Real-World Scenarios

Complete the Real-World Scenarios found on the companion website (www.pearsonitcertification.com/title/9780789758996). You will find a PDF containing the scenario and questions, and also supporting videos and simulations.

Review Questions

Answer the following review questions. Check your answers with the correct answers that follow.

1. What are some of the drawbacks to using a HIDS instead of a NIDS on a server? (Select the two best answers.)

    A. A HIDS may use a lot of resources, which can slow server performance.

    B. A HIDS cannot detect operating system attacks.

    C. A HIDS has a low level of detection of operating system attacks.

    D. A HIDS cannot detect network attacks.

2. What are two ways to secure the computer within the BIOS? (Select the two best answers.)

    A. Configure a supervisor password.

    B. Turn on BIOS shadowing.

    C. Flash the BIOS.

    D. Set the hard drive first in the boot order.

3. What are the two ways in which you can stop employees from using USB flash drives? (Select the two best answers.)

    A. Utilize RBAC.

    B. Disable USB devices in the BIOS.

    C. Disable the USB root hub.

    D. Enable MAC filtering.

4. Which of the following are Bluetooth threats? (Select the two best answers.)

    A. Bluesnarfing

    B. Blue bearding

    C. Bluejacking

    D. Distributed denial-of-service

5. To mitigate risks when users access company e-mail with their smartphone, what security policy should be implemented?

    A. Data connection capabilities should be disabled.

    B. A password should be set on the smartphone.

    C. Smartphone data should be encrypted.

    D. Smartphones should be only for company use.

6. Your manager wants you to implement a type of intrusion detection system (IDS) that can be matched to certain types of traffic patterns. What kind of IDS is this?

    A. Anomaly-based IDS

    B. Signature-based IDS

    C. Behavior-based IDS

    D. Heuristic-based IDS

7. You are the security administrator for your organization. You want to ensure the confidentiality of data on mobile devices. What is the best solution?

    A. Device encryption

    B. Remote wipe

    C. Screen locks

    D. AV software

8. You are tasked with implementing a solution that encrypts the CEO's laptop. However, you are not allowed to purchase additional hardware or software. Which of the following solutions should you implement?

    A. HSM

    B. TPM

    C. HIDS

    D. USB encryption

9. A smartphone has been lost. You need to ensure 100% that no data can be retrieved from it. What should you do?

    A. Remote wipe

    B. GPS tracking

    C. Implement encryption

    D. Turn on screen locks

10. Which of the following is a concern based on a user taking pictures with a smartphone?

   A. Application whitelisting

   B. Geotagging

   C. BYOD

   D. MDM

11. A smartphone is an easy target for theft. Which of the following are the *best* methods to protect the confidential data on the device? (Select the two best answers.)

   A. Remote wipe

   B. E-mail password

   C. GPS

   D. Tethering

   E. Encryption

   F. Screen lock

12. Carl is the security administrator for a transportation company. Which of the following should he encrypt to protect the data on a smartphone? (Select the two best answers.)

   A. Public keys

   B. Internal memory

   C. Master boot record (MBR)

   D. Steganographic images

   E. Removable memory cards

13. Which of the following is an advantage of implementing individual file encryption on a hard drive that already uses whole disk encryption?

   A. Individually encrypted files will remain encrypted if they are copied to external drives.

   B. It reduces the processing overhead necessary to access encrypted files.

   C. NTFS permissions remain intact when files are copied to an external drive.

   D. Double encryption doubles the bit strength of the encrypted file.

14. You oversee compliance with financial regulations for credit card transactions. You need to block out certain ports on the individual computers that do these transactions. What should you implement to best achieve your goal?

    A. HIPS

    B. Antivirus updates

    C. Host-based firewall

    D. NIDS

15. Which of the following would most likely be considered for DLP?

    A. Proxy server

    B. Print server

    C. USB mass storage device

    D. Application server content

Answers and Explanations

1.   A and D. Host-based intrusion detection systems (HIDSs) run within the operating system of a computer. Because of this, they can slow a computer's performance. Most HIDS do not detect network attacks well (if at all). However, a HIDS can detect operating system attacks and will usually have a high level of detection for those attacks.

2.   A and D. Configuring a supervisor password in the BIOS disallows any other user to enter the BIOS and make changes. Setting the hard drive first in the BIOS boot order disables any other devices from being booted off, including floppy drives, optical drives, and USB flash drives. BIOS shadowing doesn't have anything to do with computer security, and although flashing the BIOS may include some security updates, it's not the best answer.

3.   B and C. By disabling all USB devices in the BIOS, a user cannot use his flash drive. Also, the user cannot use the device if you disable the USB root hub within the operating system. RBAC, which stands for role-based access control, defines access to networks by the person's role in the organization (we will cover this more later in the book). MAC filtering is a method of filtering out computers when they attempt to access the network (using the MAC addresses of those computers).

4. **A and C.** Bluesnarfing and bluejacking are the names of a couple of Bluetooth threats. Another attack could be aimed at a Bluetooth device's discovery mode. To date there is no such thing as blue bearding, and a distributed denial-of-service attack uses multiple computers to attack one host.

5. **B.** A password should be set on the phone, and the phone should lock after a set period of time. When the user wants to use the phone again, the user should be prompted for a password. Disabling the data connection altogether would make access to e-mail impossible on the smartphone. Smartphone encryption of data is possible, but it could use a lot of processing power that may make it unfeasible. Whether the smartphone is used only for company use is up to the policies of the company.

6. **B.** When using an IDS, particular types of traffic patterns refer to signature-based IDS.

7. **A.** Device encryption is the best solution listed to protect the confidentiality of data. By encrypting the data, it makes it much more difficult for a malicious person to make use of the data. Screen locks are a good idea but are much easier to get past than encryption. Antivirus software will not stop an attacker from getting to the data once the mobile device has been stolen. Remote sanitization (remote wipe) doesn't keep the data confidential; it removes it altogether! While this could be considered a type of confidentiality, it would only be so if a good backup plan was instituted. Regardless, the best answer with confidentiality in mind is encryption. For example, if the device was simply lost, and was later found, it could be reused (as long as it wasn't tampered with). But if the device was sanitized, it would have to be reloaded and reconfigured before being used again.

8. **B.** A TPM, or trusted platform module, is a chip that resides on the motherboard of the laptop. It generates cryptographic keys that allow the entire disk to be encrypted, as in full disk encryption (FDE). Hardware security modules (HSMs) and USB encryption require additional hardware. A host-based intrusion detection system requires either additional software or hardware.

9. **A.** If the device has been lost and you need to be 100% sure that data cannot be retrieved from it, then you should remotely sanitize (or remotely "wipe") the device. This removes all data to the point where it cannot be reconstructed by normal means. GPS tracking might find the device, but as time is spent tracking and acquiring the device, the data could be stolen. Encryption is a good idea, but over time encryption can be deciphered. Screen locks can be easily circumvented.

10. **B.** Geotagging is a concern based on a user taking pictures with a mobile device such as a smartphone. This is because the act of geotagging utilizes GPS, which can give away the location of the user. Application whitelisting is when there is an approved list of applications for use by mobile devices. Usually implemented as a policy, if the mobile device attempts to open an app that is not on the list, the process will fail, or the system will ask for proof of administrative identity. BYOD stands for bring your own device, a technological concept where organizations allow employees to bring their personal mobile devices to work and use them for work purposes. MDM stands for mobile device management, a system that enables a security administrator to configure, update, and secure multiple mobile devices from a central location.

11. **A and E.** Remote wipe and encryption are the best methods to protect a stolen device's confidential or sensitive information. GPS can help to locate a device, but it can also be a security vulnerability in general; this will depend on the scenario in which the mobile device is used. Passwords should never be e-mailed and should not be associated with e-mail. Tethering is when a mobile device is connected to another computer (usually via USB) so that the other computer can share Internet access, or other similar sharing functionality in one direction or the other. This is great as far as functionality goes, but more often than not can be a security vulnerability. Screen locks are a decent method of reducing the chance of login by the average person, but they are not much of a deterrent for the persistent attacker.

12. **B and E.** When encrypting a smartphone, the security administrator should encrypt internal memory and any long-term storage such as removable media cards. The admin must remember that data can be stored on both. Public keys are already encrypted; it is part of their inherent nature. Smartphones don't necessarily use an MBR the way Windows computers do, but regardless, if the internal memory has been encrypted, any boot sector should be secured. Images based on steganography, by their very nature, are encrypted through obfuscation. It is different from typical data encryption, but it's a type of cryptography nonetheless.

13. **A.** By implementing individual file encryption (such as EFS) on files that are stored on a disk encrypted with whole disk encryption, the files will remain encrypted (through EFS) even if they are copied to a separate drive that does not use whole disk encryption. However, running two types of encryption will usually *increase* processing overhead, not reduce it. NTFS permissions aren't relevant here; however, if files are copied to an external drive, those files by default lose their NTFS permissions and inherit new permissions from the parent folder on the new drive. We'll discuss NTFS permissions more

in Chapter 11. We shouldn't call this *double* encryption—rather, the files are encrypted twice separately. The bit strength is not cumulative in this example, but there are two layers of encryption, which is an example of defense in depth and security layering.

14. **C.** To meet regulations, a properly configured host-based firewall will be required on the computers that will be transacting business by credit card over the Internet. All of the other answers—antivirus updates, NIDS, and HIPS—are good ideas to secure the system (and/or network), but they do not address the core issue of filtering ports, which is the primary purpose of the firewall. Also, a network-based firewall will often not be secure enough to meet regulations, thus the need for the extra layer of protection on the individual computers.

15. **C.** Of the answers listed, the USB mass storage device would be the most likely asset to be considered for data loss prevention (DLP). It's the only device listed in the answers that should have any real organizational data! A proxy server temporarily caches such data as HTTP and FTP. A print server forwards printed documents to the correct printer (again the data is usually held temporarily). An application server contains programs, but usually doesn't store organizational data files. It's the devices and computers that store actual company data files that we are primarily concerned with.

This chapter covers the following subjects:

- **Hardening Operating Systems:** This section details what you need to know to make your operating system strong as steel. Patches and hotfixes are vital. Reducing the attack surface is just as important, which can be done by disabling unnecessary services and uninstalling extraneous programs. Group policies, security templates, and baselining put on the finishing touches to attain that "bulletproof" system.

- **Virtualization Technology:** This section delves into virtual machines and other virtual implementations with an eye on applying real-world virtualization scenarios.

Imagine a computer with a freshly installed server operating system (OS) placed on the Internet or in a DMZ that went live without any updating, service packs, or hotfixes. How long do you think it would take for this computer to be compromised? A week? Sooner? It depends on the size and popularity of the organization, but it won't take long for a nonhardened server to be compromised. And it's not just servers! Workstations, routers, switches: You name it; they all need to be updated regularly, or they *will* fall victim to attack. By updating systems frequently and by employing other methods such as group policies and baselining, we are *hardening* the system, making it tough enough to withstand the pounding that it will probably take from today's technology...and society.

OS Hardening and Virtualization

Another way to create a secure environment is to run operating systems *virtually*. Virtual systems allow for a high degree of security, portability, and ease of use. However, they are resource-intensive, so a balance needs to be found, and virtualization needs to be used according to the level of resources in an organization. Of course, these systems need to be maintained and updated (hardened) as well.

By utilizing virtualization properly and by implementing an intelligent update plan, operating systems and the relationships between operating systems can be more secure and last a long time.

Foundation Topics

Hardening Operating Systems

An operating system that has been installed out-of-the-box is inherently insecure. This can be attributed to several things, including initial code issues and backdoors, the age of the product, and the fact that most systems start off with a basic and insecure set of rules and policies. How many times have you heard of a default OS installation where the controlling user account was easily accessible and had a basic password, or no password at all? Although these types of oversights are constantly being improved upon, making an out-of-the-box experience more pleasant, new applications and new technologies offer new security implications as well. So regardless of the product, we must try to protect it after the installation is complete.

Hardening of the OS is the act of configuring an OS securely, updating it, creating rules and policies to help govern the system in a secure manner, and removing unnecessary applications and services. This is done to minimize OS exposure to threats and to mitigate possible risk.

Quick tip: There is no such thing as a "bulletproof" system as I alluded to in the beginning of the chapter. That's why I placed the term in quotation marks.

Remember, no system can ever truly be 100% secure. So, although it is impossible to reduce risk to zero, I'll show some methods that can enable you to diminish current and future risk to an acceptable level.

This section demonstrates how to harden the OS through the use of patches and patch management, hotfixes, group policies, security templates, and configuration baselines. We then discuss a little bit about how to secure the file system and hard drives. But first, let's discuss how to analyze the system and decide which applications and services are unnecessary, and then remove them.

Removing Unnecessary Applications and Services

Unnecessary applications and services use valuable hard drive space and processing power. More importantly, they can be vulnerabilities to an operating system. That's why many organizations implement the concept of **least functionality**. This is when an organization configures computers and other information systems to provide only the essential functions. Using this method, a security administrator will restrict applications, services, ports, and protocols. This control—called CM-7—is described in more detail by the NIST at the following link:

https://nvd.nist.gov/800-53/Rev4/control/CM-7

The United States Department of Defense describes this concept in DoD instruction 8551.01:

http://www.dtic.mil/whs/directives/corres/pdf/855101p.pdf

It's this mindset that can help protect systems from threats that are aimed at insecure applications and services. For example, instant messaging programs can be dangerous. They might be fun for the user but usually are not productive in the workplace (to put it nicely); and from a security viewpoint, they often have backdoors that are easily accessible to attackers. Unless they are required by tech support, they should be discouraged and/or disallowed by rules and policies. Be proactive when it comes to these types of programs. If a user can't install an IM program to a computer, then you will never have to remove it from that system. However, if you do have to remove an application like this, be sure to remove all traces that it ever existed. That is just one example of many, but it can be applied to most superfluous programs.

Another group of programs you should watch out for are remote control programs. Applications that enable remote control of a computer should be avoided if possible. For example, Remote Desktop Connection is a commonly used Windows-based remote control program. By default, this program uses inbound port 3389, which is well known to attackers—an obvious security threat. Consider using a different port if the program is necessary, and if not, make sure that the program's associated service is turned off and disabled. Check if any related services need to be disabled as well. Then verify that their inbound ports are no longer functional, and that they are closed and secured. Confirm that any shares created by an application are disabled as well. Basically, remove all instances of the application or, if necessary, re-image the computer!

Personally, I use a *lot* of programs. But over time, some of them fall by the wayside and are replaced by better or newer programs. The best procedure is to check a system periodically for any unnecessary programs. For example, in Windows we can look at the list of installed programs by going to the Control Panel > Programs > Programs and Features, as shown in Figure 4-1. You can see a whopping 83.4 GB of installed programs, and the system in the figure is only a year old.

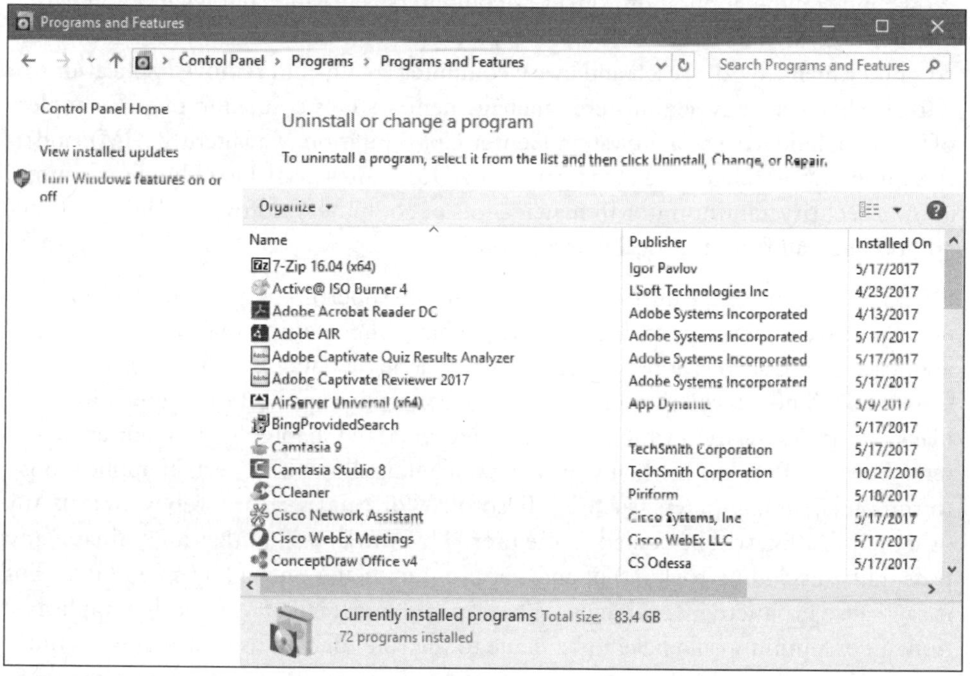

Figure 4-1   Windows Programs and Features Window

Notice in the figure that Camtasia Studio 8 and Camtasia 9 are installed. Because version 8 is an older version, a person might consider removing it. This can be done by right-clicking the application and selecting Uninstall. However, you must con-sider wisely. In this case, the program is required for *backward compatibility* because some of the older projects cannot be upgraded to a newer version of the program.

Programs such as this can use up valuable hard drive space, so if they are not neces-sary, it makes sense to remove them to conserve hard drive space. This becomes more important when you deal with audio/video departments that use big applica-tions such as Camtasia, or Pro Tools, or Premiere Pro. The applications are always battling for hard drive space, and it can get ugly! Not only that, but many applications place a piece of themselves in the Notification Area in Windows. So, a part of the program is actually running behind the scenes using processor/RAM resources. If the application is necessary, there are often ways to eliminate it from the Notification Area, either by right-clicking it and accessing its properties, or by turning it off with a configuration program such as the Task Manager or Msconfig.

Consider also that an app like this might also attempt to communicate with the Internet to download updates, or for other reasons. It makes this issue not only a resource problem, but also a security concern, so it should be removed if it is unused. Only software deemed necessary should be installed in the future.

Now, uninstalling applications on a few computers is feasible, but what if you have a larger network? Say, one with 1,000 computers? You can't expect yourself or your computer techs to go to each and every computer locally and remove applications. That's when centrally administered management systems come into play. Examples of these include Microsoft's System Center Configuration Manager (SCCM), and the variety of mobile device management (MDM) suites available. These programs allow a security administrator to manage lots of computers' software, configurations, and policies, all from the local workstation.

Of course, it can still be difficult to remove all the superfluous applications from every end-user computer on the network. What's important to realize here is that applications are at their most dangerous when actually being used by a person. Given this mindset, you should consider the concept of application whitelisting and blacklisting. Application whitelisting, as mentioned in Chapter 3, "Computer Systems Security Part II," is when you set a policy that allows only certain applications to run on client computers (such as Microsoft Word and a secure web browser). Any other application will be denied to the user. This works well in that it eliminates any possibility (excluding hacking) of another program being opened by an end user, but it can cause productivity problems. When an end user really *needs* another application, an exception would have to be made to the rule for that user, which takes time, and possibly permission from management. **Application blacklisting**, on the other hand, is when individual applications are disallowed. This can be a more useful (and more efficient) solution if your end users work with, and frequently add, a lot of applications. In this scenario, an individual application (say a social media or chat program) is disabled across the network. This and whitelisting are often performed from centralized management systems mentioned previously, and through the use of policies, which we discuss more later in this chapter (and later in the book).

Removing applications is a great way to reduce the attack surface and increase performance on computers. But the underlying services are even more important. Services are used by applications and the OS. They, too, can be a burden on system resources and pose security concerns. Examine Figure 4-2 and note the highlighted service.

Key Topic

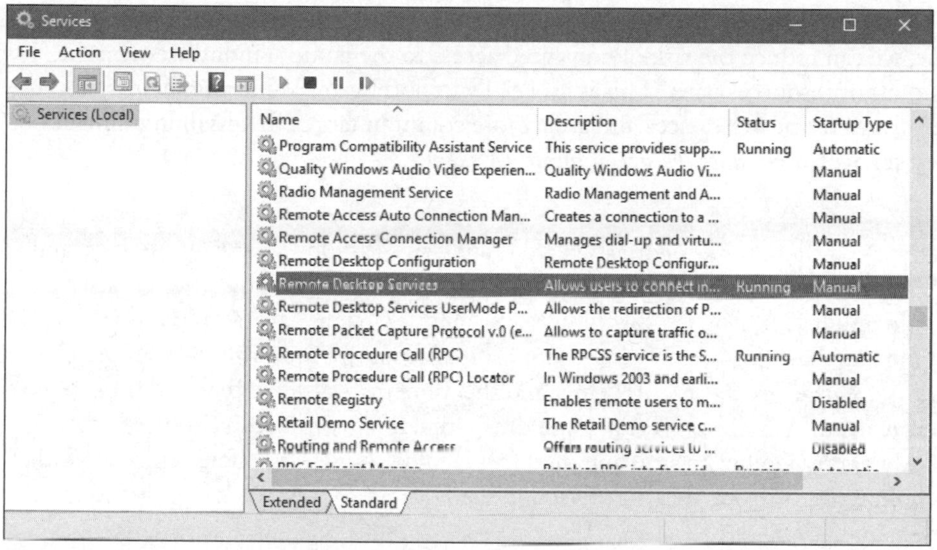

Figure 4-2 Services Window of a Windows Computer

The highlighted service is Remote Desktop Services. You can see in the figure that it is currently running. If it is not necessary, we would want to stop it and disable it. To do so, just right-click the service, select Properties, click the Stop button, click Apply, and change the Startup Type drop-down menu to the Disabled option, as shown in Figure 4-3.

Key Topic

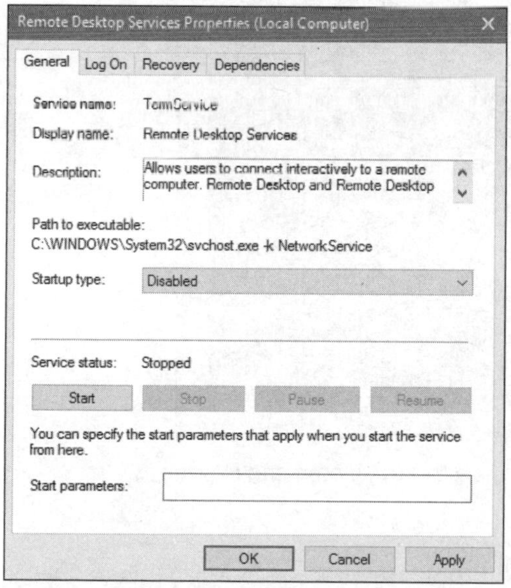

Figure 4-3 Remote Desktop Services Properties Dialog Box

This should be done for all unnecessary services. By disabling services such as this one, we can reduce the risk of unwanted access to the computer and we trim the amount of resources used. This is especially important on Windows servers, because they run a lot more services and are a more common target. By disabling unnecessary services, we *reduce the size of the attack surface*.

> **NOTE** Even though it is deprecated, you might see Windows XP running here and there. A system such as this might have the Telnet service running, which is a serious vulnerability. Normally, I wouldn't use Windows XP as an example given its age (and the fact that Microsoft will not support it anymore), but in this case I must because of the insecure nature of Telnet and the numerous systems that will probably continue to run Windows XP for some time—regardless of the multitude of warnings. Always remember to stop and disable Telnet if you see it. Then, replace it with a secure program/protocol such as Secure Shell (SSH). Finally, consider updating to a newer operating system!

Services can be started and stopped in the Windows Command Prompt with the `net start` and `net stop` commands, as well as by using the `sc` command. Examples of this are shown in Figure 4-4.

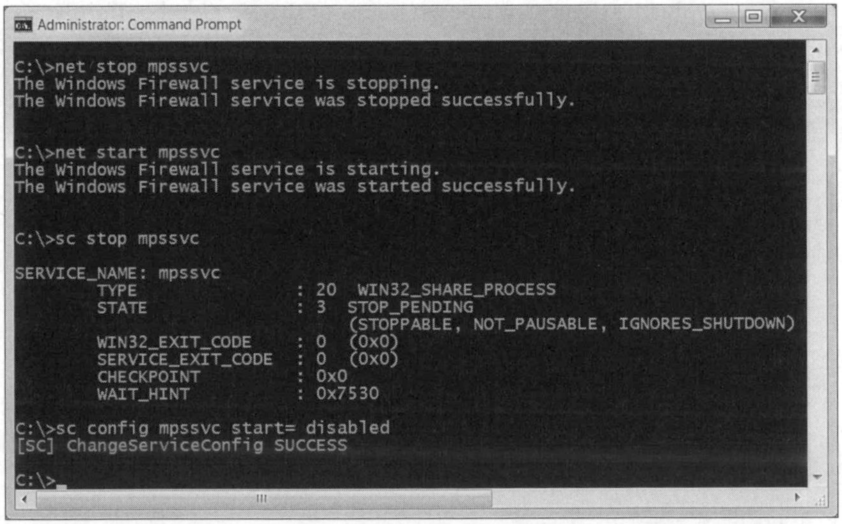

Figure 4-4 Stopping and Disabling a Service in the Windows Command Prompt

> **NOTE** You will need to run the Command Prompt in elevated mode (as an administrator) to execute these commands.

In Figure 4-4 we have stopped and started the Windows Firewall service (which uses the service name mpssvc) by invoking the `net stop` and `net start` commands. Then, we used the `sc` command to stop the same service with the `sc stop mpssvc` syntax. It shows that the service stoppage was pending, but as you can see from Figure 4-5, it indeed stopped (and right away, I might add). Finally, we used a derivative of the `sc` command to *disable* the service, so that it won't start again when the system is restarted. This syntax is

```
sc config mpssvc start= disabled
```

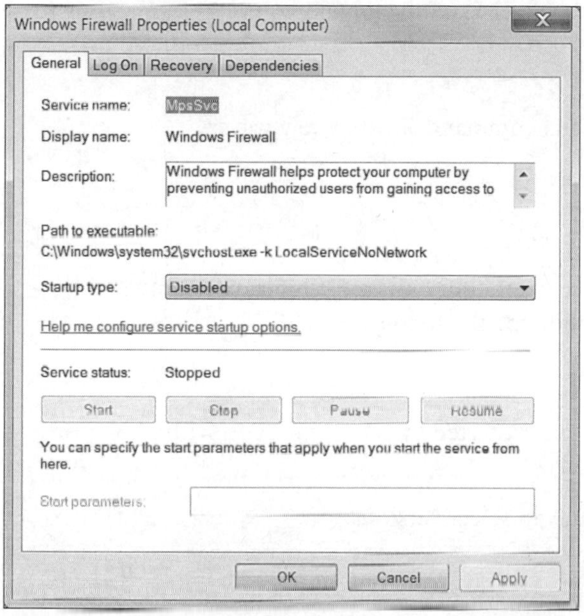

Figure 4-5 Windows Firewall Properties Dialog Box

Note that there is a space after the equal sign, which is necessary for the command to work properly. Figure 4-5 shows the GUI representation of the Windows Firewall service.

You can see in the figure that the service is disabled and stopped. This is a good place to find out the name of a service if you are not sure. Or, you could use the `sc query` command.

In Linux, you can start, stop, and restart services in a variety of ways. Because there are many variants of Linux, how you perform these actions varies in the different GUIs that are available. So, in this book I usually stick with the command-line, which is generally the same across the board. You'll probably want to display a list of services (and their status) in the command-line first. For example, in Ubuntu you can do this by typing the following:

```
service --status-all
```

For a list of upstart jobs with their status, use the following syntax:

```
initctl list
```

> **NOTE** In Linux, if you are not logged in as an administrator (and even sometimes if you are), you will need to type `sudo` before a command, and be prepared to enter an administrator password. Be ready to use `sudo` often.

Services can be stopped in the Linux command-line in a few ways:

- By typing the following syntax:

  ```
  /etc/init.d/<service> stop
  ```

  where <service> is the service name. For example, if you are running an Apache web server, you would type the following:

  ```
  /etc/init.d/apache2 stop
  ```

  Services can also be started and restarted by replacing `stop` with `start` or `restart`.

- By typing the following syntax in select versions:

  ```
  service <service> stop
  ```

Some services require a different set of syntax. For example, Telnet can be deactivated in Red Hat by typing `chkconfig telnet off`. Check the MAN pages within the command-line or online for your particular version of Linux to obtain exact syntax and any previous commands that need to be issued. Or use a generic Linux online MAN page; for example: http://linux.die.net/man/1/telnet.

In macOS/OS X Server, services can be stopped in the command line by using the following syntax:

```
sudo serveradmin stop <service>
```

However, this may not work on macOS or OS X *client*. For example, in 10.9 Mavericks you would simply quit processes either by using the Activity Monitor or by using the `kill` command in the Terminal.

> **NOTE**   Ending the underlying process is sometimes necessary in an OS when the
> service can't be stopped. To end processes in Windows, use the Task Manager or the
> `taskkill` command. The `taskkill` command can be used in conjunction with the
> executable name of the task or the process ID (PID) number. Numbers associated
> with processes can be found with the `tasklist` command. In Linux, use the `kill`
> command to end an individual process. To find out all process IDs currently run-
> ning, use the syntax `ps aux | less`. (Ctrl+Z can break you out of commands such
> as this if necessary.) On mobile devices, the equivalent would be a force quit.
>
> Let's not forget about mobile devices. You might need to force stop or completely
> uninstall apps from Android or iOS. Be ready to do so and lock them down from a
> centralized MDM.

Table 4-1 summarizes the various ways to stop services in operating systems.

Key Topic

Table 4-1   Summary of Ways to Stop Services

Operating System	Procedure to Stop Service
Windows	Access `services.msc` from the Run prompt.
	Use the `net stop <servicename>` command in the Command Prompt.
	Use the `sc stop <servicename>` command in the Command Prompt.
Linux	Use the syntax `/etc/init.d/<servicename> stop`.
	Use the syntax `service <servicename> stop` (in select versions).
	Use the syntax `chkconfig <servicename> off` (in select versions).
macOS/OS X	Use the `kill` command to end processes. Also works in Linux. In Windows, this is the `taskkill` command.

Windows Update, Patches, and Hotfixes

To be considered secure, operating systems should have support for multilevel security, and be able to meet government requirements. An operating system that meets
these criteria is known as a **Trusted Operating System (TOS)**. Examples of certified Trusted Operating Systems include Windows 7, OS X 10.6, FreeBSD (with the
TrustedBSD extensions), and Red Hat Enterprise Server. To be considered a TOS,
the manufacturer of the system must have strong policies concerning updates and
patching.

Even without being a TOS, operating systems should be updated regularly. For example, Microsoft recognizes the deficiencies in an OS, and possible exploits that could occur, and releases patches to increase OS performance and protect the system.

Before updating, the first thing to do is to find out the version number, build number, and the patch level. For example, in Windows you can find out this information by opening the System Information tool (open the Run prompt and type `msinfo32.exe`). It will be listed directly in the System Summary. You could also use the `winver` command. In addition, you can use the `systeminfo` command in the Command Prompt (a *great* information gatherer!) or simply the `ver` command.

Then, you should check your organization's policies to see what level a system should be updated to. You should also test updates and patches on systems located on a clean, dedicated, testing network before going live with an update.

Windows uses the Windows Update program to manage updates to the system. Versions before Windows 10 include this feature in the Control Panel. It can also be accessed by typing `wuapp.exe` in the Run prompt. In Windows 10 it is located in the Settings section, or can be opened by typing `ms-settings:windowsupdate` in the Run prompt.

Updates are divided into different categories:

- **Security update:** A broadly released fix for a product-specific security-related vulnerability. Security vulnerabilities are rated based on their severity, which is indicated in the Microsoft Security Bulletin as critical, important, moderate, or low.

- **Critical update:** A broadly released fix for a specific problem addressing a critical, non-security–related bug.

- **Service pack:** A tested, cumulative *set* of hotfixes, security updates, critical updates, and updates, as well as additional fixes for problems found internally since the release of the product. Service packs might also contain a limited number of customer-requested design changes or features. Note that Windows 7 and Windows Server 2008 R2 are the last of the Microsoft operating systems to use service packs. If possible, the testing of service packs should be done offline (with physical media). Disconnect the computer from the network by disabling the network adapter before initiating the SP upgrade.

- **Windows update:** Recommended update to fix a noncritical problem certain users might encounter; also adds features and updates to features bundled into Windows.

- **Driver update:** Updated device driver for installed hardware. It's important to verify that any drivers installed will be compatible with a system. A security administrator should be aware of the potential to modify drivers through the use of driver shimming (the adding of a small library that intercepts API calls) and driver refactoring (the restructuring of driver code). By default, shims are not supposed to be used to resolve compatibility issues with device drivers, but it's impossible to foresee the types of malicious code that may present itself in the future. So, a security administrator should be careful when updating drivers by making sure that the drivers are signed properly and first testing them on a closed system.

There are various options for the installation of Windows updates, including automatic install, defer updates to a future date, download with option to install, manual check for updates, and never check for updates. The types available to you will differ depending on the version of Windows. Automatic install is usually frowned upon by businesses, especially in the enterprise. Generally, you as the administrator want to specify what is updated, when it is updated, and to which computers it is updated. This eliminates problems such as patch level mismatch and network usage issues.

In some cases, your organization might opt to turn off Windows Update altogether. Depending on your version of Windows, this may or may not be possible within the Windows Update program. However, your organization might go a step further and specify that the Windows Update *service* be stopped and disabled, thereby disabling updates. This can be done in the Services console window (Run > services.msc) or from the Command Prompt with one of the methods discussed earlier in the chapter—the service name for Windows Update is wuauserv.

Patches and Hotfixes

The best place to obtain patches and hotfixes is from the manufacturer's website. The terms *patches* and *hotfixes* are often used interchangeably. Windows updates are made up of hotfixes. Originally, a **hotfix** was defined as a single problem-fixing patch to an individual OS or application installed live while the system was up and running and without needing a reboot. However, this term has changed over time and varies from vendor to vendor. (Vendors may even use both terms to describe the same thing.) For example, if you run the systeminfo command in the Command Prompt of a Windows computer, you see a list of hotfixes similar to Figure 4-6. They can be identified with the letters *KB* followed by seven numbers. Hotfixes can be single patches to individual applications, or might affect the entire system.

Key Topic

```
C:\WINDOWS\system32\cmd.exe
Time Zone:                 (UTC-05:00) Eastern Time (US & Canada)
Total Physical Memory:     16,286 MB
Available Physical Memory: 13,895 MB
Virtual Memory: Max Size:  18,718 MB
Virtual Memory: Available: 15,786 MB
Virtual Memory: In Use:    2,932 MB
Page File Location(s):     C:\pagefile.sys
Domain:                    WORKGROUP
Logon Server:              \\AV-EDITOR
Hotfix(s):                 4 Hotfix(s) Installed.
                           [01]: KB3194623
                           [02]: KB3199986
                           [03]: KB3202790
                           [04]: KB3200970
Network Card(s):           2 NIC(s) Installed.
                           [01]: Intel(R) Ethernet Connection (2) I21
8-V
                                 Connection Name: dpro42
                                 DHCP Enabled:    No
```

Figure 4-6 Running the `systeminfo` Command in Windows

On the other side of the spectrum, a gaming company might define hotfixes as a "hot" change to the server with no downtime, and no client download is necessary. The organization releases these if they are critical, instead of waiting for a full patch version. The gaming world commonly uses the terms *patch version*, *point release*, or *maintenance release* to describe a group of file updates to a particular gaming version. For example, a game might start at version 1 and later release an update known as 1.17. The .17 is the point release. (This could be any number, depending on the amount of code rewrites.) Later, the game might release 1.32, in which .32 is the point release, again otherwise referred to as the patch version. This is common with other programs as well. For example, the aforementioned Camtasia program that is running on the computer shown in Figure 4-1 is version 9.0.4. The second dot (.4) represents very small changes to the program, whereas a patch version called 9.1 would be a larger change, and 10.0 would be a completely new version of the software. This concept also applies to blogging applications and forums (otherwise known as bulletin boards). As new threats are discovered (and they are extremely common in the blogging world), new patch versions are released. They should be downloaded by the administrator, tested, and installed without delay. Admins should keep in touch with their software manufacturers, either through phone or e-mail, or by frequenting their web pages. This keeps the admin "in the know" when it comes to the latest updates. And this applies to server and client operating systems, server add-ons such as Microsoft Exchange or SQL Server, Office programs, web browsers, and the plethora of third-party programs that an organization might use. Your job just got a bit busier!

Of course, we are usually not concerned with updating games in the working world; they should be removed from a computer if they are found (unless perhaps you work for a gaming company). But multimedia software such as Camtasia is prevalent in some companies, and web-based software such as bulletin-board systems are also common and susceptible to attack.

Patches generally carry the connotation of a small fix in the mind of the user or system administrator, so larger patches are often referred to as software updates, service packs, or something similar. However, if you were asked to fix a single security issue on a computer, a patch would be the solution you would want. For example, there are various Trojans that attack older versions of Microsoft Office for Mac. To counter these, Microsoft released a specific patch for those versions of Office for Mac that disallows remote access by the Trojans.

Before installing an individual patch, you should determine if it perhaps was already installed as part of a group update. For example, you might read that a particular version of macOS or OS X had a patch released for iTunes, and being an enthusiastic iTunes user, you might consider installing the patch. But you should first find out the version of the OS you are running—it might already include the patch. To find this information, simply click the Apple menu and then click About This Mac.

Remember: All systems need to be patched at some point. It doesn't matter if they are Windows, Mac, Linux, Unix, Android, iOS, hardware appliances, kiosks, automotive computers…need I go on?

Unfortunately, sometimes patches are designed poorly, and although they might fix one problem, they could possibly create another, which is a form of software regression. Because you never know exactly what a patch to a system might do, or how it might react or interact with other systems, it is wise to incorporate patch management.

Patch Management

It is not wise to go running around the network randomly updating computers, not to say that you would do so! Patching, like any other process, should be managed properly. **Patch management** is the planning, testing, implementing, and auditing of patches. Now, these four steps are ones that I use; other companies might have a slightly different patch management strategy, but each of the four concepts should be included:

Key Topic

- **Planning:** Before actually doing anything, a plan should be set into motion. The first thing that needs to be decided is whether the patch is necessary and whether it is compatible with other systems. Microsoft Baseline Security Analyzer (MBSA) is one example of a program that can identify security misconfigurations on the computers in your network, letting you know whether patching is needed. If the patch is deemed necessary, the plan should consist of a way to test the patch in a "clean" network on clean systems, how and when the patch will be implemented, and how the patch will be checked after it is installed.

- **Testing:** Before automating the deployment of a patch among a thousand computers, it makes sense to test it on a single system or small group of systems first. These systems should be reserved for testing purposes only and should not be used by "civilians" or regular users on the network. I know, this is asking a lot, especially given the amount of resources some companies have. But the more you can push for at least a single testing system that is not a part of the main network, the less you will be to blame if a failure occurs!

- **Implementing:** If the test is successful, the patch should be deployed to all the necessary systems. In many cases this is done in the evening or over the weekend for larger updates. Patches can be deployed automatically using software such as Microsoft's SCCM and third-party patch management tools.

- **Auditing:** When the implementation is complete, the systems (or at least a sample of systems) should be audited; first, to make sure the patch has taken hold properly, and second, to check for any changes or failures due to the patch. SCCM and third-party tools can be used in this endeavor.

NOTE   The concept of patch management, in combination with other application/ OS hardening techniques, is collectively referred to as *configuration management*.

There are also Linux-based and Mac-based programs and services developed to help manage patching and the auditing of patches. Red Hat has services to help sys admins with all the RPMs they need to download and install, which can become a mountain of work quickly! And for those people who run GPL Linux, there are third-party services as well. A network with a lot of mobile devices benefits greatly from the use of a MDM platform. But even with all these tools at an organization's disposal, sometimes, patch management is just too much for one person, or for an entire IT department, and an organization might opt to contract that work out.

Group Policies, Security Templates, and Configuration Baselines

Although they are important tasks, removing applications, disabling services, patching, hotfixing, and installing service packs are not the only ways to harden an operating system. Administrative privileges should be used sparingly, and policies should be in place to enforce your organization's rules. A **Group Policy** is used in Microsoft and other computing environments to govern user and computer accounts through a set of rules. Built-in or administrator-designed security templates can be applied to these to configure many rules at one time—creating a "secure configuration." Afterward, configuration baselines should be initiated to measure server and network activity.

To access the Group Policy in Windows, go to the Run prompt and type `gpedit.msc`. This should display the Local Group Policy Editor console window. Figure 4-7 shows a typical example of this on a Windows client.

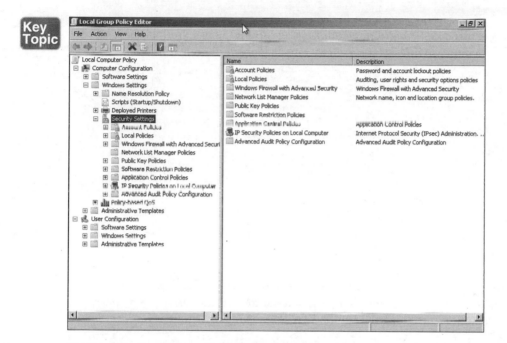

Figure 4-7 Local Group Policy Editor in Windows

Although there are many configuration changes you can make, this figure focuses on the computer's security settings that can be accessed by navigating to Local Computer Policy > Computer Configuration > Windows Settings > Security Settings. From here you can make changes to the password policies (for example, how long a password lasts before having to be changed), account lockout policies, public key policies, and so on. We talk about these different types of policies and the best way to apply them in future chapters. The Group Policy Editor in Figure 4-7 is known as the Local Group Policy Editor and only governs that particular machine and the local users of that machine. It is a basic version of the Group Policy Editor used by Windows Server domain controllers that have Active Directory loaded.

It is also from here that you can add security templates as well. **Security templates** are groups of policies that can be loaded in one procedure; they are commonly used in corporate environments. Different security templates have different security levels. These can be installed by right-clicking Security Settings and selecting Import

Policy. This brings up the Import Policy From window. This technique of adding a policy template becomes much more important on Windows Server computers. Figure 4-8 shows an example of the Import Policy From window in Windows Server.

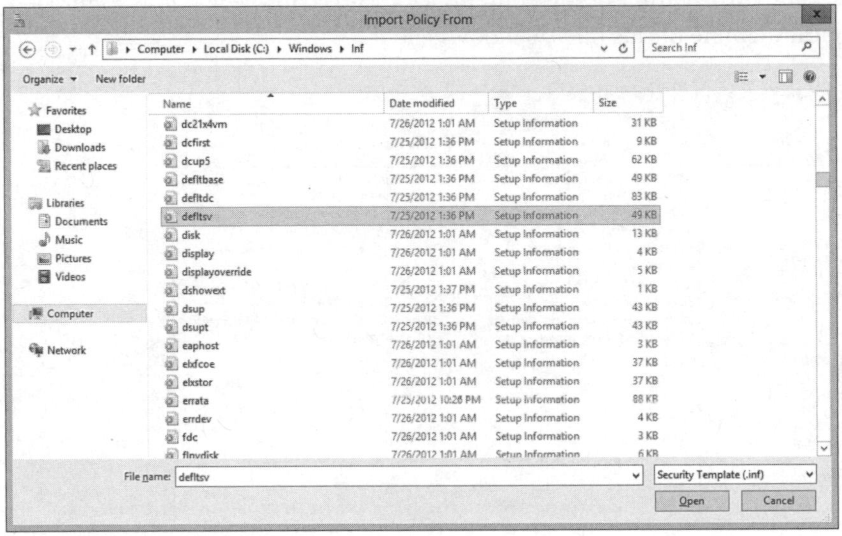

Figure 4-8   Windows Server Import Policy From Window

There are three main security templates in Windows Server: defltbase.inf (uncommon), defltsv.inf (used on regular servers), and defltdc.inf (used in domain controllers). By default, these templates are stored in %systemroot%\inf (among a lot of other .inf files).

Select the policy you desire and click Open. That establishes the policy on the server. It's actually many policies that are written to many locations of the entire Local Security Policy window. Often, these policy templates are applied to organizational units on a domain controller. But they can be used for other types of systems and policies as well.

NOTE   Policies are imported in the same manner in Server 2003, but the names are different. For example, the file securedc.inf is an information file filled with policy configurations more secure than the default you would find in a Windows Server 2003 domain controller that runs Active Directory. And hisecdc.inf is even more secure, perhaps too secure and limiting for some organizations. Server Templates for Server 2003 are generally stored in %systemroot%\Security\templates. I normally don't cover Server 2003 because it is not supported by Microsoft any longer, but you just might see it in the field!

In Windows Server you can modify policies, and add templates, directly from Server Manager > Security Configuration Wizard as well. If you save templates here, they are saved as .xml files instead of .inf files.

Group Policies are loaded with different Group Policy objects (GPOs). By configuring as many of these GPOs as possible, you implement OS hardening, ultimately establishing host-based security for your organization's workstations.

Baselining is the process of measuring changes in networking, hardware, software, and so on. Creating a baseline consists of selecting something to measure and measuring it consistently for a period of time. For example, I might want to know what the average hourly data transfer is to and from a server. There are many ways to measure this, but I could possibly use a protocol analyzer to find out how many packets cross through the server's network adapter. This could be run for 1 hour (during business hours, of course) every day for 2 weeks. Selecting different hours for each day would add more randomness to the final results. By averaging the results together, we get a baseline. Then we can compare future measurements of the server to the baseline. This can help us to define what the standard load of our server is and the requirements our server needs on a consistent basis. It can also help when installing additional computers on the network. The term *baselining* is most often used to refer to monitoring network performance, but it actually can be used to describe just about any type of performance monitoring. Baselining and benchmarking are extremely important when testing equipment and when monitoring already installed devices.

Any baseline deviation should be investigated right away. In most organizations, the baselines exist. The problem is that they are not audited and analyzed often enough by security administrators, causing deviations to go unnoticed until it is too late. Baselining becomes even more vital when dealing with a real-time operating system (RTOS). These systems require near 100% uptime and lightning-fast response with zero latency. Be sure to monitor these carefully and often. We discuss baselining further in Chapter 13, "Monitoring and Auditing."

Hardening File Systems and Hard Drives

You want more? I promise *more*. The rest of the book constantly refers to more advanced and in-depth ways to harden a computer system. But for this chapter, let's conclude this section by giving a few tips on hardening a hard drive and the file system it houses.

First, the file system used dictates a certain level of security. On Microsoft computers, the best option is to use NTFS, which is more secure, enables logging (oh so important), supports encryption, and has support for a much larger maximum partition size and larger file sizes. Just about the only place where FAT32 and NTFS are on a level playing field is that they support the same amount of file formats. So, by far, NTFS is the best option. If a volume uses FAT or FAT32, it can be *converted* to NTFS using the following command:

```
convert volume /FS:NTFS
```

For example, if I want to convert a USB flash drive named M: to NTFS, the syntax would be

```
convert M: /FS:NTFS
```

There are additional options for the `convert` command. To see these, simply type `convert /?` in the Command Prompt. NTFS enables for file-level security and tracks permissions within access control lists (ACLs), which are a necessity in today's environment. Most systems today already use NTFS, but you never know about flash-based and other removable media. A quick `chkdsk` command in the Command Prompt or right-clicking the drive in the GUI and selecting Properties can tell you what type of file system it runs.

Generally, the best file system for Linux systems is ext4. It allows for the best and most configurable security. To find out the file system used by your version of Linux, use the `fdisk -l` command or `df -T` command.

System files and folders by default are hidden from view to protect a Windows system, but you never know. To permanently configure the system to not show hidden files and folders, navigate to the File Explorer (or Folder) Options dialog box. Then select the View tab, and under Hidden Files and Folders select the Don't Show Hidden Files, Folders, or Drives radio button. To configure the system to hide protected system files, select the Hide Protected Operating System Files checkbox, located below the radio button previously mentioned. This disables the ability to view such files and folders as bootmgr and pagefile.sys. You might also need to secure a system by turning off file sharing, which in most versions of Windows can be done within the Network and Sharing Center.

In the past, I have made a bold statement: "Hard disks *will* fail." But it's all too true. It's not a matter of *if*; it's a matter of *when*. By maintaining and hardening the hard disk with various hard disk utilities, we attempt to stave off that dark day as long as possible. You can implement several strategies when maintaining and hardening a hard disk:

- **Remove temporary files:** Temporary files and older files can clog up a hard disk, cause a decrease in performance, and pose a security threat. It is recommended that Disk Cleanup or a similar program be used. Policies can be configured (or written) to run Disk Cleanup every day or at logoff for all the computers on the network.

- **Periodically check system files:** Every once in a while, it's a good idea to verify the integrity of operating system files. A file integrity check can be done in the following ways:

  — With the chkdsk command in Windows. This examines the disk and provides a report. It can also fix some errors with the /F option.

  — With the SFC (System File Checker) command in Windows. This utility checks and, if necessary, replaces protected system files. It can be used to fix problems in the OS, and in other applications such as Internet Explorer. A typical command you might type is SFC /scannow. Use this if chkdsk is not successful at making repairs.

  — With the fsck command in Linux. This command is used to check and repair a Linux file system. The synopsis of the syntax is fsck [-sAVRTNP][-C [fd]][-t fstype][filesys ...][--] [fs-specific-options]. More information about this command can be found at the corresponding MAN page for fsck. A derivative, e2fsck, is used to check a Linux ext2fs (second extended file system). Also, open source data integrity tools can be downloaded for Linux such as Tripwire.

- **Defragment drives:** Applications and files on hard drives become fragmented over time. For a server, this could be a disaster, because the server cannot serve requests in a timely fashion if the drive is too thoroughly fragmented. Defragmenting the drive can be done with Microsoft's Disk Defragmenter, with the command-line defrag command, or with other third-party programs.

- **Back up data:** Backing up data is critical for a company. It is not enough to rely on a fault-tolerant array. Individual files or the entire system can be backed up to another set of hard drives, to optical discs, to tape, or to the cloud. Microsoft domain controllers' Active Directory databases are particularly susceptible to attack; the System State for these operating systems should be backed up, in case that the server fails and the Active Directory needs to be recovered in the future.

- **Use restoration techniques:** In Windows, restore points should be created on a regular basis for servers and workstations. The System Restore utility (rstrui.exe) can fix issues caused by defective hardware or software by reverting back to an earlier time. Registry changes made by hardware or software are reversed in an attempt to force the computer to work the way it did previously. Restore points can be created manually and are also created automatically by the OS before new applications, service packs, or hardware are installed. macOS and OS X use the Time Machine utility, which works in a similar manner. Though there is no similar tool in Linux, a user can back up the ~/home directory to a separate partition. When these contents are decompressed to a new install, most of the Linux system and settings will have been restored. Another option in general is to use imaging (cloning) software. Remember that these techniques do not necessarily back up data, and that the data should be treated as a separate entity that needs to be backed up regularly.

- **Consider whole disk encryption:** Finally, whole disk encryption can be used to secure the contents of the drive, making it harder for attackers to obtain and interpret its contents.

A recommendation I give to all my students and readers is to separate the OS from the data physically. If you can have each on a separate hard drive, it can make things a bit easier just in case the OS is infected with malware (or otherwise fails). The hard drive that the OS inhabits can be completely wiped and reinstalled without worrying about data loss, and applications can always be reloaded. Of course, settings should be backed up (or stored on the second drive). If a second drive isn't available, consider configuring the one hard drive as two partitions, one for the OS (or system) and one for the data. By doing this, and keeping a well-maintained computer, you are effectively hardening the OS.

Key Topic

Keeping a Well-Maintained Computer

This is an excerpt of an article I wrote that I give to all my customers and students. By maintaining the workstation or server, you are hardening it as well. I break it down into six steps (and one optional step):

Step 1. **Use a surge protector or UPS:** Make sure the computer and other equipment connect to a surge protector, or better yet a UPS if you are concerned about power loss.

Step 2. **Update the BIOS and/or UEFI:** Flashing the BIOS isn't always necessary; check the manufacturer's website for your motherboard to see if an update is needed.

Step 3. **Update the OS:** For Windows, this includes any combination hotfixes (and possibly SPs) and any Windows Updates beyond that, and setting Windows to alert if there are any new updates. For Linux and macOS/OS X, it means simply updating the system to the latest version and installing individual patches as necessary.

Step 4. **Update anti-malware:** This includes making sure that there is a current license for the anti-malware (antivirus and anti-spyware) and verifying that updates are turned on and the software is regularly scanning the system.

Step 5. **Update the firewall:** Be sure to have some kind of firewall installed and enabled; then update it. If it is Windows Firewall, updates should happen automatically through Windows Update. However, if you have a SOHO router with a built-in firewall, or other firewall device, you need to update the device's ROM by downloading the latest image from the manufacturer's website.

Step 6.   **Maintain the disks:** This means running a disk cleanup program regularly and checking to see whether the hard disk needs to be defragmented from once a week to once a month depending on the amount of usage. It also means creating restore points, doing computer backups, or using third-party backup or drive imaging software.

Step 7.   **(Optional) Create an image of the system:** After all your configurations and hardening of the OS are complete, you might consider creating an image of the system. Imaging the system is like taking a snapshot of the entire system partition. That information is saved as one large file, or a set of compressed files that can be saved anywhere. It's kind of like system restore but at another level. The beauty of this is that you can reinstall the entire image if your system fails or is compromised, quickly and efficiently, with very little configuration necessary—only the latest security and AV updates since the image was created need be applied. Of course, most imaging software has a price tag involved, but it can be well worth it if you are concerned about the time it would take to get your system back up and running in the event of a failure. This is the basis for standardized images in many organizations. By applying mandated security configurations, updates, and so on, and then taking an image of the system, you can create a snapshot in time that you can easily revert to if necessary, while being confident that a certain level of security is already embedded into the image.

NOTE   To clean out a system regularly, consider re-imaging it, or if a mobile device, resetting it. This takes care of any pesky malware by deleting everything and reinstalling to the point in time of the image, or to factory condition. While you will have to do some reconfigurations, the system will also run much faster because it has been completely cleaned out.

Virtualization Technology

Let's define virtualization. **Virtualization** is the creation of a virtual entity, as opposed to a true or actual entity. The most common type of entity created through virtualization is the virtual machine—usually housing an OS. In this section we discuss types of virtualization, identify their purposes, and define some of the various virtual applications.

Types of Virtualization and Their Purposes

Many types of virtualization exist, from network and storage to hardware and software. The CompTIA Security+ exam focuses mostly on virtual machine software. The **virtual machines (VMs)** created by this software run operating systems or individual applications. The virtual operating system—also known as a guest or a virtual desktop environment (VDE)—is designed to run *inside* a real OS. So, the beauty behind this is that you can run multiple various operating systems simultaneously from just one PC. This has great advantages for programmers, developers, and systems administrators, and can facilitate a great testing environment. Security researchers in particular utilize virtual machines so they can execute and test malware without risk to an actual OS and the hardware it resides on. Nowadays, many VMs are also used in live production environments. Plus, an entire OS can be dropped onto a DVD or even a flash drive and transported where you want to go.

Of course, there are drawbacks. Processor and RAM resources and hard drive space are eaten up by virtual machines. And hardware compatibility can pose some problems as well. Also, if the physical computer that houses the virtual OS fails, the virtual OS will go offline immediately. All other virtual computers that run on that physical system will also go offline. There is added administration as well. Some technicians forget that virtual machines need to be updated with the latest service packs and patches just like regular operating systems. Many organizations have policies that define standardized virtual images, especially for servers. As I alluded to earlier, the main benefit of having a standardized server image is that mandated security configurations will have been made to the OS from the beginning—creating a template, so to speak. This includes a defined set of security updates, service packs, patches, and so on, as dictated by organizational policy. So, when you load up a new instance of the image, a lot of the configuration work will already have been done, and just the latest updates to the OS and AV software need to be applied. This image can be used in a virtual environment, or copied to a physical hard drive as well. For example, you might have a server farm that includes two physical Windows Server systems and four virtual Windows Server systems, each running different tasks. It stands to reason that you will be working with new images from time to time as you need to replace servers or add them. By creating a standardized image once, and using it many times afterward, you can save yourself a lot of configuration time in the long run.

Virtual machines can be broken down into two categories:

- **System virtual machine:** A complete platform meant to take the place of an entire computer, enabling you to run an entire OS virtually.

- **Process virtual machine:** Designed to run a single application, such as a virtual web browser.

Whichever VM you select, the VM cannot cross the software boundaries set in place. For example, a virus might infect a computer when executed and spread to other files in the OS. However, a virus executed in a VM will spread through the VM but not affect the underlying *actual* OS. So, this provides a secure platform to run tests, analyze malware, and so on...and creates an *isolated* system. If there are adverse effects to the VM, those effects (and the VM) can be compartmentalized to stop the spread of those effects. This is all because the virtual machine inhabits a separate area of the hard drive from the actual OS. This enables us to isolate network services and roles that a virtual server might play on the network.

Virtual machines are, for all intents and purposes, emulators. The terms *emulation*, *simulation*, and *virtualization* are often used interchangeably. Emulators can also be web-based; for example, an emulator of a SOHO router's firmware that you can access online. You might also have heard of much older emulators such as Basilisk, or the DOSBox, or a RAM drive, but nowadays, anything that runs an OS virtually is generally referred to as a virtual machine or virtual appliance.

A *virtual appliance* is a virtual machine image designed to run on virtualization platforms; it can refer to an entire OS image or an individual application image. Generally, companies such as VMware refer to the images as virtual appliances, and companies such as Microsoft refer to images as virtual machines. One example of a virtual appliance that runs a single app is a virtual browser. VMware developed a virtual browser appliance that protects the underlying OS from malware installations from malicious websites. If the website succeeds in its attempt to install the malware to the virtual browser, the browser can be deleted and either a new one can be created or an older saved version of the virtual browser can be brought online!

Other examples of virtualization include the virtual private network (VPN), which is covered in Chapter 10, "Physical Security and Authentication Models," and virtual desktop infrastructure (VDI) and virtual local area network (VLAN), which are covered in Chapter 6, "Network Design Elements."

Hypervisor

Most virtual machine software is designed specifically to host more than one VM. A byproduct is the intention that all VMs are able to communicate with each other quickly and efficiently. This concept is summed up by the term **hypervisor**. A hypervisor allows multiple virtual operating systems (guests) to run at the same time on a single computer. It is also known as a virtual machine manager (VMM). The term *hypervisor* is often used ambiguously. This is due to confusion concerning the two different types of hypervisors:

Key Topic

- **Type 1–Native:** The hypervisor runs directly on the host computer's hardware. Because of this it is also known as "bare metal." Examples of this include VMware vCenter and vSphere, Citrix XenServer, and Microsoft Hyper-V. Hyper-V can be installed as a standalone product, known as Microsoft Hyper-V Server, or it can be installed as a role within a standard installation of Windows Server 2008 (R2) or higher. Either way, the hypervisor runs independently and accesses hardware directly, making both versions of Windows Server Hyper-V Type 1 hypervisors.

- **Type 2–Hosted:** This means that the hypervisor runs within (or "on top of") the operating system. Guest operating systems run within the hypervisor. Compared to Type 1, guests are one level removed from the hardware and therefore run less efficiently. Examples of this include VirtualBox, Windows Virtual PC (for Windows 7), Hyper-V (for Windows 8 and higher), and VMware Workstation.

Generally, Type 1 is a much faster and much more efficient solution than Type 2. It is also more elastic, meaning that environments using Type 1 hypervisors can usually respond to quickly changing business needs by adjusting the supply of resources as necessary. Because of this elasticity and efficiency, Type 1 hypervisors are the kind used by web-hosting companies and by companies that offer cloud computing solutions such as infrastructure as a service (IaaS). It makes sense, too. If you have ever run a powerful operating system such as Windows Server within a Type 2 hypervisor such as VirtualBox, you will have noticed that a ton of resources are being used that are taken from the hosting operating system. It is not nearly as efficient as running the hosted OS within a Type 1 environment. However, keep in mind that the hardware/software requirements for a Type 1 hypervisor are more stringent and more costly. Because of this, some developing and testing environments use Type 2–based virtual software.

Another type of virtualization you should be familiar with is **application containerization**. This allows an organization to deploy and run distributed applications without launching a whole virtual machine. It is a more efficient way of using the resources of the hosting system, plus it is more portable. However, there is a lack of isolation from the hosting OS, which can lead to security threats potentially having easier access to the hosting system.

Securing Virtual Machines

In general, the security of a virtual machine operating system is the equivalent to that of a physical machine OS. The VM should be updated to the latest service pack. If you have multiple VMs, especially ones that will interact with each other, make sure they are updated in the same manner. This will help to ensure patch compatibility between the VMs. A VM should have the newest AV definitions, perhaps have a personal firewall, have strong passwords, and so on. However, there are several things to watch out for that, if not addressed, could cause all your work compartmentalizing operating systems to go down the drain. This includes considerations for the virtual machine OS as well as the controlling virtual machine software.

First, make sure you are using current and updated virtual machine software. Update to the latest patch for the software you are using (for example, the latest version of Oracle VirtualBox). Configure any applicable security settings or options in the virtual machine software. Once this is done, you can go ahead and create your virtual machines, keeping in mind the concept of standardized imaging mentioned earlier.

Next, keep an eye out for network shares and other connections between the virtual machine and the physical machine, or between two VMs. Normally, malicious software cannot travel between a VM and another VM or a physical machine as long as they are properly separated. But if active network shares are between the two—creating the potential for a directory traversal vulnerability—then malware could spread from one system to the other.

If a network share is needed, map it, use it, and then disconnect it when you are finished. If you need network shares between two VMs, document what they are and which systems (and users) connect to them. Review the shares often to see whether they are still necessary. Be careful with VMs that use a *bridged* or similar network connection, instead of network address translation (NAT). This method connects directly with other physical systems on the network, and can allow for malware and attacks to traverse the "bridge" so to speak.

Any of these things can lead to a failure of the VM's isolation. Consequently, if a user (or malware) breaks out of a virtual machine and is able to interact with the host operating system, it is known as **virtual machine escape**. Vulnerabilities to virtual hosting software include buffer overflows, remote code execution, and directory traversals. Just another reason for the security administrator to keep on top of the latest CVEs and close those unnecessary network shares and connections.

Going further, if a virtual host is attached to a network attached storage (NAS) device or to a storage area network (SAN), it is recommended to segment the storage devices off the LAN either physically or with a secure VLAN. Regardless of where the virtual host is located, secure it with a strong firewall and disallow unprotected file transfer protocols such as FTP and Telnet.

Consider disabling any unnecessary hardware from within the virtual machine such as optical drives, USB ports, and so on. If some type of removable media is necessary, enable the device, make use of it, and then disable it immediately after finishing. Also, devices can be disabled from the virtual machine software itself. The boot priority in the virtual BIOS should also be configured so that the hard drive is booted from first, and not any removable media or network connection (unless necessary in your environment).

Due to the fact that VMs use a lot of physical resources of the computer, a compromised VM can be a threat in the form of a denial-of-service attack. To mitigate this, set a limit on the amount of resources any particular VM can utilize, and periodically monitor the usage of VMs. However, be careful of monitoring VMs. Most virtual software offers the ability to monitor the various VMs from the main host, but this feature can also be exploited. Be sure to limit monitoring, enable it only for authorized users, and disable it whenever not necessary.

Speaking of resources, the more VMs you have, the more important resource conservation becomes. Also, the more VMs that are created over time, the harder they are to manage. This can lead to **virtualization sprawl**. VM sprawl is when there are too many VMs for an administrator to manage properly. To help reduce the problem, a security administrator might create an organized library of virtual machine images. The admin might also use a virtual machine lifecycle management (VMLM) tool. This can help to enforce how VMs are created, used, deployed, and archived.

Finally, be sure to protect the raw virtual disk file. A disaster on the raw virtual disk can be tantamount to physical disk disaster. Look into setting permissions as to who can access the folder where the VM files are stored. If your virtual machine software supports logging and/or auditing, consider implementing it so that you can see exactly who started and stopped the virtual machine, and when. Otherwise, you can audit the folder where the VM files are located. Finally, consider making a copy of the virtual machine or virtual disk file—also known as a *snapshot* or *checkpoint*—encrypting the VM disk file, and digitally signing the VM and validating that signature prior to usage.

NOTE   Enterprise-level virtual software such as Hyper-V and VMware vCenter/vSphere takes security to a whole new level. Much more planning and configuration is necessary for these applications. It's not necessary to know for the Security+ exam, but if you want to gather more information on securing Hyper-V, see the following link:

https://technet.microsoft.com/en-us/library/dd569113.aspx

For more information on how to use and secure VMware, see the following link:

https://www.vmware.com/products/vsphere.html#resources

Table 4-2 summarizes the various ways to protect virtual machines and their hosts.

Key Topic

Table 4-2 Summary of Methods to Secure Virtual Machines

VM Security Topics	Security Methods
Virtualization updating	Update and patch the virtualization software.
	Configure security settings on the host.
	Update and patch the VM operating system and applications.
Virtual networking security and virtual escape protection	Remove unnecessary network shares between the VMs and the host.
	Review the latest CVEs for virtual hosting software to avoid virtual machine escape.
	Remove unnecessary *bridged* connections to the VM.
	Use a secure VLAN if necessary.
Disable unnecessary hardware	Disable optical drives.
	Disable USB ports.
	Configure the virtual BIOS boot priority for hard drive first.
Monitor and protect the VM	Limit the amount of resources used by a VM.
	Monitor the resource usage of the VM.
	Reduce VM sprawl by creating a library of VM images and using a VMLM tool.
	Protect the virtual machine files by setting permissions, logging, and auditing.
	Secure the virtual machine files by encrypting and digitally signing.

One last comment: A VM should be as secure as possible, but in general, because the hosting computer is in a controlling position, it is likely to be more easily exploited, and a compromise to the hosting computer probably means a compromise to any guest operating systems it contains. Therefore, if possible, the host should be even more secure than the VMs it controls. So, harden your heart, harden the VM, and make the hosting OS solid as a rock.

Chapter Summary

This chapter focused on the hardening of operating systems and the securing of virtual operating systems. Out-of-the-box operating systems can often be insecure for a variety of reasons and need to be *hardened* to meet your organization's policies,

Trusted Operating System (TOS) compliance, and government regulations. But in general, they need to be hardened so that they are more difficult to compromise.

The process of hardening an operating system includes: removing unnecessary services and applications; whitelisting and blacklisting applications; using anti-malware applications; configuring personal software-based firewalls; updating and patching (as well as managing those patches); using group policies, security templates, and baselining; utilizing a secure file system and performing preventive maintenance on hard drives; and in general, keeping a well-maintained computer.

Well, that's a lot of work, especially for one person. That makes the use of *automation* very important. Automate your work whenever you can through the use of templates, the imaging of systems, and by using specific workflow methods. These things, in conjunction with well-written policies, can help you (or your team) to get work done faster and more efficiently.

One great way to be more efficient (and possibly more secure) is by using *virtualization*, the creation of a virtual machine or other emulator that runs in a virtual environment, instead of requiring its own physical computer. It renders dual-booting pretty much unnecessary, and can offer a lot of options when it comes to compartmentalization and portability. The virtual machine runs in a hypervisor—either Type 1, which is also known as bare metal, or Type 2, which is hosted. Type 1 is faster and more efficient, but usually more expensive and requires greater administrative skill. Regardless of the type you use, the hypervisor, and the virtual machines it contains, needs to be secured.

The hosting operating system, if there is one, should be hardened appropriately. The security administrator should update the virtual machine software to the latest version and configure applicable security settings for it. Individual virtual machines should have their virtual BIOS secured, and the virtual machine itself should be hardened the same way a regular, or *non-virtual*, operating system would be. (That clarification is important, because many organizations today have more virtual servers than non-virtual servers! The term *regular* becomes inaccurate in some scenarios.) Unnecessary hardware should be disabled, and network connections should be *very* carefully planned and monitored. In addition, the administrator should consider setting limits on the resources a virtual machine can consume, monitor the virtual machine (and its files), and protect the virtual machine through file permissions and encryption. And of course, *all* virtual systems should be tested thoroughly before being placed into production. It's the implementation of security control testing that will ensure compatibility between VMs and virtual hosting software, reduce the chances of exploitation, and offer greater efficiency and less downtime in the long run.

Chapter 4 builds on Chapters 2 and 3. Most of the methods mentioned during Chapters 2 and 3 are expected to be implemented in addition to the practices listed in this chapter. By combining them with the software protection techniques we will cover in Chapter 5, "Application Security," you will end up with a quite secure computer system.

Chapter Review Activities

Use the features in this section to study and review the topics in this chapter.

Review Key Topics

Review the most important topics in the chapter, noted with the Key Topic icon in the outer margin of the page. Table 4-3 lists a reference of these key topics and the page number on which each is found.

Key Topic

Table 4-3   Key Topics for Chapter 4

Key Topic Element	Description	Page Number
Figure 4-2	Services window of a Windows Computer	93
Figure 4-3	Remote Desktop Services Properties dialog box	93
Figure 4-4	Stopping and disabling a service in the Windows Command Prompt	94
Table 4-1	Summary of ways to stop services	97
Bulleted list	Windows Update categories	98
Figure 4-6	systeminfo command in Windows	100
Bulleted list	Patch management four steps	101
Figure 4-7	Local Group Policy Editor in Windows	103
Figure 4-8	Windows Server Import Policy From window	104
Bulleted list	Maintaining and hardening a hard disk	106
Step list	Keeping a well-maintained computer	108
Bulleted list	Types of hypervisors	112
Table 4-2	Summary of methods to secure VMs	115

Define Key Terms

Define the following key terms from this chapter, and check your answers in the glossary:

hardening, least functionality, application blacklisting, Trusted Operating System (TOS), hotfix, patch, patch management, Group Policy, security template, baselining, virtualization, virtual machine (VM), hypervisor, application containerization, virtual machine escape, virtualization sprawl

Complete the Real-World Scenarios

Complete the Real-World Scenarios found on the companion website (www.pearsonitcertification.com/title/9780789758996). You will find a PDF containing the scenario and questions, and also supporting videos and simulations.

Review Questions

Answer the following review questions. Check your answers with the correct answers that follow.

1. Virtualization technology is often implemented as operating systems and applications that run in software. Often, it is implemented as a virtual machine. Of the following, which can be a security benefit when using virtualization?

    A. Patching a computer will patch all virtual machines running on the computer.

    B. If one virtual machine is compromised, none of the other virtual machines can be compromised.

    C. If a virtual machine is compromised, the adverse effects can be compartmentalized.

    D. Virtual machines cannot be affected by hacking techniques.

2. Eric wants to install an isolated operating system. What is the best tool to use?

    A. Virtualization

    B. UAC

    C. HIDS

    D. NIDS

3. Where would you turn off file sharing in Windows?

    A. Control Panel

    B. Local Area Connection

    C. Network and Sharing Center

    D. Firewall properties

4. Which option enables you to hide the bootmgr file?

    A. Enable Hide Protected Operating System Files

    B. Enable Show Hidden Files and Folders

    C. Disable Hide Protected Operating System Files

    D. Remove the -R Attribute

5. Which of the following should be implemented to harden an operating system? (Select the two best answers.)

    A. Install the latest updates.

    B. Install Windows Defender.

    C. Install a virtual operating system.

    D. Execute PHP scripts.

6. What is the best (most secure) file system to use in Windows?

    A. FAT

    B. NTFS

    C. DFS

    D. FAT32

7. A customer's SD card uses FAT32 as its file system. What file system can you upgrade it to when using the convert command?

    A. NTFS

    B. HPFS

    C. ext4

    D. NFS

8. Which of the following is not an advantage of NTFS over FAT32?

   A. NTFS supports file encryption.

   B. NTFS supports larger file sizes.

   C. NTFS supports larger volumes.

   D. NTFS supports more file formats.

9. What is the deadliest risk of a virtual computer?

   A. If a virtual computer fails, all other virtual computers immediately go offline.

   B. If a virtual computer fails, the physical server goes offline.

   C. If the physical server fails, all other physical servers immediately go offline.

   D. If the physical server fails, all the virtual computers immediately go offline.

10. Virtualized browsers can protect the OS that they are installed within from which of the following?

    A. DDoS attacks against the underlying OS

    B. Phishing and spam attacks

    C. Man-in-the-middle attacks

    D. Malware installation from Internet websites

11. Which of the following needs to be backed up on a domain controller to recover Active Directory?

    A. User data

    B. System files

    C. Operating system

    D. System State

12. Which of the following should you implement to fix a single security issue on the computer?

    A. Service pack

    B. Support website

    C. Patch

    D. Baseline

13. An administrator wants to reduce the size of the attack surface of a Windows Server. Which of the following is the best answer to accomplish this?

    A. Update antivirus software.

    B. Install updates.

    C. Disable unnecessary services.

    D. Install network intrusion detection systems.

14. Which of the following is a security reason to implement virtualization in your network?

    A. To isolate network services and roles

    B. To analyze network traffic

    C. To add network services at lower costs

    D. To centralize patch management

15. Which of the following is one example of verifying new software changes on a test system?

    A. Application hardening

    B. Virtualization

    C. Patch management

    D. HIDS

16. You have been tasked with protecting an operating system from malicious software. What should you do? (Select the two best answers.)

    A. Disable the DLP.

    B. Update the HIPS signatures.

    C. Install a perimeter firewall.

    D. Disable unused services.

    E. Update the NIDS signatures.

17. You are attempting to establish host-based security for your organization's workstations. Which of the following is the *best* way to do this?

    A. Implement OS hardening by applying GPOs.

    B. Implement database hardening by applying vendor guidelines.

    C. Implement web server hardening by restricting service accounts.

    D. Implement firewall rules to restrict access.

18. In Windows, which of the following commands will *not* show the version number?

   A. `Systeminfo`

   B. `Wf.msc`

   C. `Winver`

   D. `Msinfo32.exe`

19. During an audit of your servers, you have noticed that most servers have large amounts of free disk space and have low memory utilization. Which of the following statements will be correct if you migrate some of the servers to a virtual environment?

   A. You might end up spending more on licensing, but less on hardware and equipment.

   B. You will need to deploy load balancing and clustering.

   C. Your baselining tasks will become simpler.

   D. Servers will encounter latency and lowered throughput issues.

Answers and Explanations

1. **C.** By using a virtual machine (which is one example of a virtual instance), any ill effects can be compartmentalized to that particular virtual machine, usually without any ill effects to the main operating system on the computer. Patching a computer does not automatically patch virtual machines existing on the computer. Other virtual machines can be compromised, especially if nothing is done about the problem. Finally, virtual machines can definitely be affected by hacking techniques. Be sure to secure them!

2. **A.** Virtualization enables a person to install operating systems (or applications) in an isolated area of the computer's hard drive, separate from the computer's main operating system.

3. **C.** The Network and Sharing Center is where you can disable file sharing in Windows. It can be accessed indirectly from the Control Panel as well. By disabling file sharing, you disallow any (normal) connections to data on the computer. This can be very useful for computers with confidential information, such as an executive's laptop or a developer's computer.

4. **A.** To hide bootmgr, you either need to click the radio button for Don't Show Hidden Files, Folders, or Drives or enable the Hide Protected Operating System Files checkbox.

5. **A and B.** Two ways to harden an operating system include installing the latest updates and installing Windows Defender. However, virtualization is a separate concept altogether; it can be used to create a compartmentalized OS, but needs to be secured and hardened just like any other OS. PHP scripts will generally not be used to harden an operating system. In fact, they can be vulnerabilities to websites and other applications.

6. **B.** NTFS is the most secure file system for use with today's Windows. FAT and FAT32 are older file systems, and DFS is the distributed file system used in more advanced networking.

7. **A.** The convert command is used to upgrade FAT and FAT32 volumes to the more secure NTFS without loss of data. HPFS is the High Performance File System developed by IBM and is not used by Windows. ext4 is the fourth extended filesystem used by Linux. NFS is the Network File System, something you would see in a storage area network.

8. **D.** NTFS and FAT32 support the same number of file formats, so this is not an advantage of NTFS. However, NTFS supports file encryption, larger file sizes, and larger volumes, making it more advantageous in general in comparison to FAT32, and is capable of higher levels of security, most especially down to the file level.

9. **D.** The biggest risk of running a virtual computer is that it will go offline immediately if the server that it is housed on fails. All other virtual computers on that particular server will also go offline immediately.

10. **D.** The beauty of a virtualized browser is that regardless of whether a virus or other malware damages it, the underlying operating system will remain unharmed. The virtual browser can be deleted and a new one can be created; or if the old virtual browser was backed up before the malware attack, it can be restored. This concept applies to entire virtual operating systems as well, if configured properly.

11. **D.** The System State needs to be backed up on a domain controller to recover the Active Directory database in the future. The System State includes user data and system files but does not include the entire operating system. If a server fails, the operating system would have to be reinstalled, and then the System State would need to be restored. Consider backing up the system state in the command-line—see the following TechNet link for more: https://technet.microsoft.com/en-us/library/cc753201(v=ws.11).aspx.

12. **C.** A patch can fix a single security issue on a computer. A service pack addresses many issues and rewrites many files on a computer; it may be overkill to use a service pack when only a patch is necessary. Also, only older Windows operating

systems (for example, Windows 7 and Windows Server 2008 R2 and previous) use service packs. You might obtain the patch from a support website. A baseline can measure a server or a network and obtain averages of usage.

13. **C.** Often, operating system manufacturers such as Microsoft refer to the attack surface as all the services that run on the operating system. By conducting an analysis of which services are necessary and which are unnecessary, an administrator can find out which ones need to be disabled, thereby reducing the attack surface. Updates, service packs, antivirus software, and network intrusion detection systems (NIDSs) are good tools to use to secure an individual computer and the network but do not help to reduce the size of the attack surface of the operating system.

14. **A.** Virtualization of computer servers enables a network administrator to isolate the various network services and roles that a server may play. Analyzing network traffic would have to do more with assessing risk and vulnerability and monitoring and auditing. Adding network services at lower costs deals more with budgeting than with virtualization, although, virtualization can be less expensive. Centralizing patch management has to do with hardening the operating systems on the network scale.

15. **C.** Patch management is an example of verifying any new changes in software on a test system (or live systems for that matter). Verifying the changes (testing) is the second step of the standard patch management strategy. Application hardening might include updating systems, patching them, and so on, but to be accurate, this question is looking for that particular second step of patch management. Virtualization is the creating of logical OS images within a working operating system. HIDS stands for host-based intrusion detection system, which attempts to detect malicious activity on a computer.

16. **B and D.** Updating the host-based intrusion prevention system is important. Without the latest signatures, the HIPS will not be at its best when it comes to protecting against malware. Also, disabling unused services will reduce the attack surface of the OS, which in turn makes it more difficult for attacks to access the system and run malicious code. Disabling the data loss prevention (DLP) device would not aid the situation, and it would probably cause data leakage from the computer. Installing a perimeter firewall won't block malicious software from entering the individual computer. A personal firewall would better reduce the attack surface of the computer, but it is still not meant as an anti-malware tool. Updating the NIDS signatures will help the entire network, but might not help the individual computer. In this question, we want to focus in on the individual computer, not the network. In fact, given the scenario of the question, you do not even know if a network exists.

17. A. The best way to establish host-based security for your organization's work-stations is to implement GPOs (Group Policy objects). When done properly from a server, this can harden the operating systems in your network, and you can do it from a central location without having to configure each computer locally. It is the only answer that deals with the client operating systems. The other answers deal with database and web servers, and firewalls that protect the entire network.

18. B. Of the answers listed, the only one that will not show the version number is `wf.msc`. That brings up the Windows Firewall with Advanced Security. All of the other answers will display the version number in Windows.

19. A. If you migrate some of these low-resource servers to a virtual environment (a very smart thing to do), you could end up spending more on licensing, but less on hardware, due to the very nature of virtualization. In fact, the goal is to have the gains of hardware savings outweigh the losses of licensing. Load balancing and clustering deals with an OS utilizing the hardware of multiple servers. This will not be the case when you go virtual, nor would it have been the case anyway, because clustering and load balancing is used in environments where the server is very resource-intensive. Baselining, unfortunately, will remain the same; you should analyze all of your servers regularly, whether they are physical or virtual. These particular servers should not encounter latency or lowered throughput because they are low-resource servers in the first place. If, however, you considered placing into a virtual environment a Windows Server that supports 5,000 users, you should definitely expect latency.

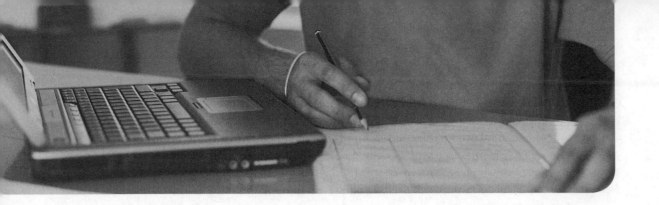

This chapter covers the following subjects:

- **Securing the Browser:** What is a computer without a web browser? Some might answer "worthless." Well, a compromised browser is worse than no browser at all. The web browser must be secured to have a productive and enjoyable web experience.

- **Securing Other Applications:** Organizations use many applications, and they each have their own group of security vulnerabilities. In this section, we spend a little time on common applications such as Microsoft Office and demonstrate how to make those applications safe.

- **Secure Programming:** Programmers use many techniques when validating and verifying the security of their code. This important section covers a few basic concepts of programming security such as system testing, secure code review, and fuzzing.

Browser security should be at the top of any security administrator's list. It's another example of inherently insecure software "out of the box." Browsers are becoming more secure as time goes on, but new malware always presents a challenge—as mentioned in Chapter 1, "Introduction to Security," the scales are always tipping back and forth.

CHAPTER 5

Application Security

Most browsers have plenty of built-in options that you can enable to make them more secure, and third-party programs can help in this endeavor as well. This chapter covers web browsers in a generic fashion; most of the concepts we cover can be applied to just about any browser. However, users don't just work with web browsers. They use office applications frequently as well, so these should be secured, too. Also, other applications, such as the command-line, though a great tool, can be a target. Back office applications such as the ones that supply database information and e-mail are also vulnerable and should be hardened accordingly. And finally, any applications that are being developed within your dominion should be reviewed carefully for bugs.

Be sure to secure any application used or developed on your network. It takes only one vulnerable application to compromise the security of your network.

Let's start with discussing how to secure web browsers.

Foundation Topics

Securing the Browser

There is a great debate as to which web browser to use. It doesn't matter too much to me, because as a security guy I am going to spend a decent amount of time securing whatever it is that is in use. However, each does have advantages, and one might work better than the other depending on the environment. So, if you are in charge of implementing a browser solution, be sure to plan for performance *and* security right from the start. I do make some standard recommendations to customers, students, and readers when it comes to planning and configuring browser security. Let's discuss a few of those now.

The first recommendation is to *not* use the very latest version of a browser. (Same advice I always give for any application, it seems.) Let the people at the top of the marketing pyramid, the innovators, mess around with the "latest and greatest;" let those people find out about the issues, backdoors, and whatever other problems a new application might have; at worst, let their computer crash! For the average user, and especially for a fast-paced organization, the browser needs to be rock-solid; these organizations will not tolerate any downtime. I always allow for some time to pass before fully embracing and recommending software. The reason I bring this up is because most companies share the same view and implement this line of thinking as a company policy. They don't want to be caught in a situation where they spent a lot of time and money installing something that is not compatible with their systems.

NOTE   Some browsers update automatically by default. While this is a nice feature that can prevent threats from exploiting known vulnerabilities, it might not correspond to your organization's policies. This feature would have to be disabled in the browser's settings or within a computer policy so that the update can be deferred until it is deemed appropriate for all systems involved.

The next recommendation is to consider what type of computer, or computers, will be running the browser. Generally, Macs run Safari. Linux computers run Firefox. Edge and Internet Explorer (IE) are common in the Windows market, but Firefox and Google Chrome work well on Windows computers, too. Some applications such as Microsoft Office are, by default, linked to the Microsoft web browser, so it is wise to consider other applications that are in use when deciding on a browser. Another important point is whether you will be centrally managing multiple client computers' browsers. Edge and IE can be centrally managed through the use of Group Policy objects (GPOs) on a domain. I'll show a quick demonstration of this later in the chapter.

When planning what browser to use, consider how quickly the browser companies fix vulnerabilities. Some are better than others and some browsers are considered to be more secure than others in general. It should also be noted that some sites recommend—or in some cases *require*—a specific browser to be used. This is a "security feature" of those websites and should be investigated before implementing other browsers in your organization.

When it comes to functionality, most browsers work well enough, but one browser might fare better for the specific purposes of an individual or group. By combining the functions a user or group requires in a browser, along with the security needed, you should come up with the right choice. You should remember that the web browser was not originally intended to do all the things it now does. In many cases, it acts as a shell for all kinds of other things that run inside of it. This trend will most likely continue. That means more new versions of browsers, more patching, and more secure code to protect those browsers. Anyway, I think that's enough yappin' about browsers—we'll cover some actual security techniques in just a little bit.

General Browser Security Procedures

First, some general procedures should be implemented regardless of the browser your organization uses. These concepts can be applied to desktop browsers as well as mobile browsers.

- Implement policies.

- Train your users.

- Use a proxy and content filter.

- Secure against malicious code.

Each of these is discussed in more detail in the following sections.

Implement Policies

The policy could be hand-written, configured at the browser, implemented within the computer operating system, or better yet, configured on a server centrally. Policies can be configured to manage add-ons, and disallow access to websites known to be malicious, have Flash content, or use a lot of bandwidth. As an example, Figure 5-1 shows the Local Group Policy of a Windows 10 computer focusing on the settings of the two Microsoft browsers. You can open the Local Group Policy Editor by going to Run and typing gpedit.msc. Then navigate to

User Configuration > Administrative Templates > Windows Components

From there, depending on which browser you want to modify security settings for, you can access Internet Explorer (especially the Security Features subsection) or Microsoft Edge.

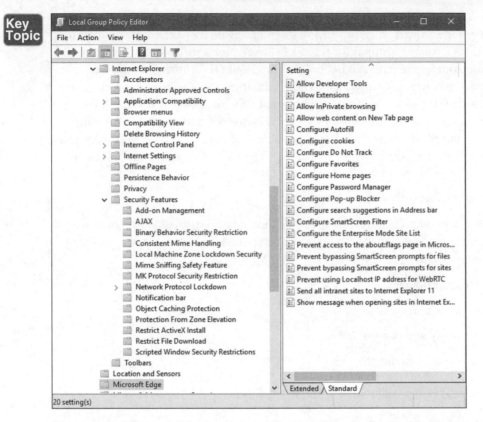

Figure 5-1 Microsoft Edge and Internet Explorer Security Features in the Local Computer Policy

In the figure, you can see that the folder containing the Microsoft Edge policy settings is opened and that there are many settings that can be configured. The figure also shows Internet Explorer open at the top of the window. As you can see, there are many folders and consequently many more security settings for IE.

Of course, literally hundreds of settings can be changed for Internet Explorer. You can also modify Internet Explorer Maintenance Security by navigating to

User Configuration > Windows Settings > Internet Explorer Maintenance > Security

An example of this in Windows 7 is shown in Figure 5-2. The Security Zones and Content Ratings object was double-clicked to show the dialog box of the same name, which allows you to customize the Internet security zones of the browser. Some versions of Windows will not enable you to access the Local Computer Policy; however, most security features can be configured directly within the browser in the case that you don't have access to those features in the OS.

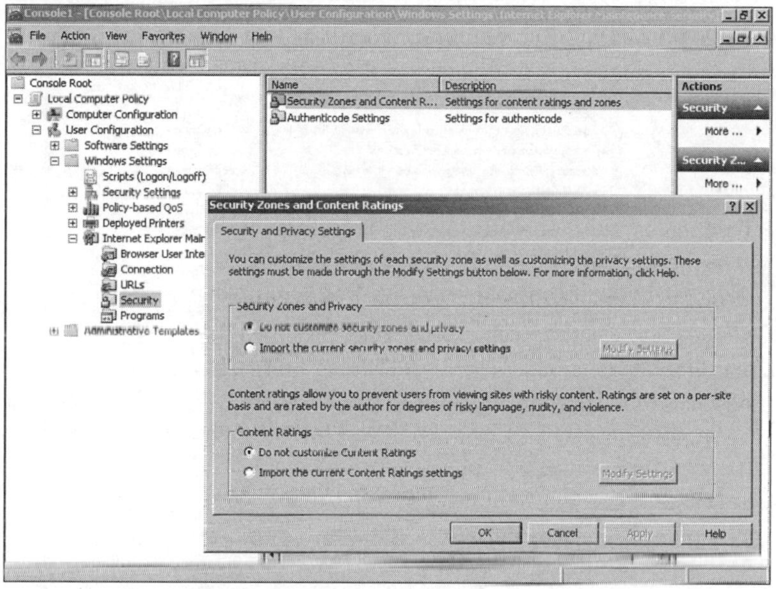

Figure 5-2   Internet Explorer Maintenance Security in the Local Computer Policy

NOTE   These are just examples. I use Windows 10 and Windows 7 as examples here because the chances are that you will see plenty of those systems over the lifespan of the CompTIA Security+ Certification (and most likely beyond). However, you never know what operating systems and browser an organization will use in the future, so keep an open mind.

Now, you wouldn't want to configure these policy settings on many more than a few computers individually. If you have multiple computers that need their IE security policies updated, consider using a template (described in Chapter 4, "OS Hardening and Virtualization"), or if you have a domain controller, consider making the changes from that central location. From there, much more in-depth security can be configured and deployed to the IE browsers within multiple computers. An example of the IE policies, as managed from a domain controller, is shown in Figure 5-3.

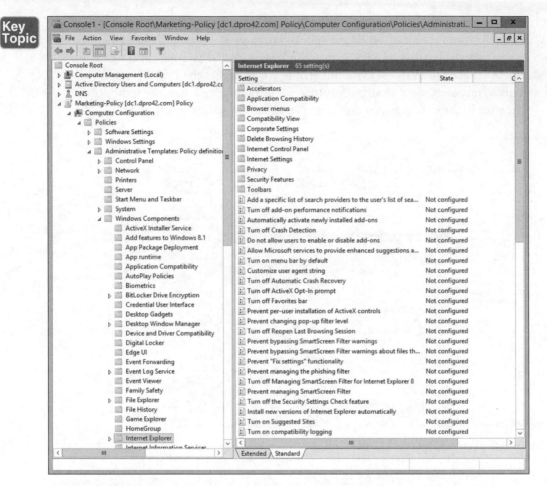

Figure 5-3 Internet Explorer Policies in the Marketing-Policy GPO

For this, I set up a Windows Server as a domain controller (controlling the domain dpro42.com), created an organizational unit (OU) named Marketing, and then created a Group Policy object named Marketing-Policy that I added to a Microsoft Management Console (MMC). From that policy, the Internet Explorer settings, which can affect all computers within the Marketing OU, can be accessed by navigating to

Computer Configuration > Policies > Administrative Templates > Windows Components > Internet Explorer

From here we can configure trusted and non-trusted sites, zones, and advanced security features in one shot for all the computers in the OU. A real time-saver!

NOTE   You should also learn about viewing and managing group policies with the Group Policy Management Console (GPMC). In Windows Server 2012 R2 and higher, you can access this by going to Administrative Tools > Group Policy Management or by going to Run and typing gpmc.msc. It can also be added to an MMC.

Train Your Users

User training is important to determine which websites to access, how to use search engines, and what to do if pop-ups appear on the screen. The more users you can reach with your wisdom, the better! Onsite training classes, webinars, and downloadable screencasts all work great. Or if your organization doesn't have those kinds of resources, consider writing a web article to this effect — make it engaging and interesting, yet educational.

For example, explain to users the value of pressing Alt+F4 to close pop-up windows instead of clicking No or an X. Pop-ups could be coded in such a way that No actually means Yes, and the close-out X actually means "take me to more annoying websites!" Alt+F4 is a hard-coded shortcut key that *usually* closes applications. If that doesn't work, explain that applications can be closed by ending the task or process, force stopping, or force quitting, depending on the OS being used.

Another example is to show users how to determine if their communications are secure on the web. Just looking for HTTPS in the address bar isn't necessarily enough. A browser might show a green background in the address bar if the website uses a proper encryption certificate. Some browsers use a padlock in the locked position to show it is secure. To find out the specific security employed by the website to protect the session, click, or right-click, the padlock icon and select More Information or Connection, or something to that effect (depending on the browser). This will show the encryption type and certificate being used. We'll talk more about these concepts in Chapter 14, "Encryption and Hashing Concepts," and Chapter 15, "PKI and Encryption Protocols."

Use a Proxy and Content Filter

HTTP proxies (known as proxy servers) act as a go-between for the clients on the network and the Internet. Simply stated, they cache website information for the clients, reducing the number of requests that need to be forwarded to the actual corresponding web server on the Internet. This is done to save time, make more efficient use of bandwidth, and help to secure the client connections. By using a content filter in combination with this, specific websites can be filtered out, especially ones that can potentially be malicious, or ones that can be a waste of man-hours, such as peer-to-peer (P2P) websites/servers. I know—I'm such a buzzkill. But these filtering devices are common in today's networks; we talk more about them in Chapter 8, "Network Perimeter Security." For now, it is important to know how to connect to them with a browser. Remember that the proxy server is a mediator between the client and the Internet, and as such the client's web browser must be configured to connect to them. You can either have the browser automatically detect a proxy server or (and this is more common) configure it statically. Figure 5-4 shows a typical example of a connection to a proxy server.

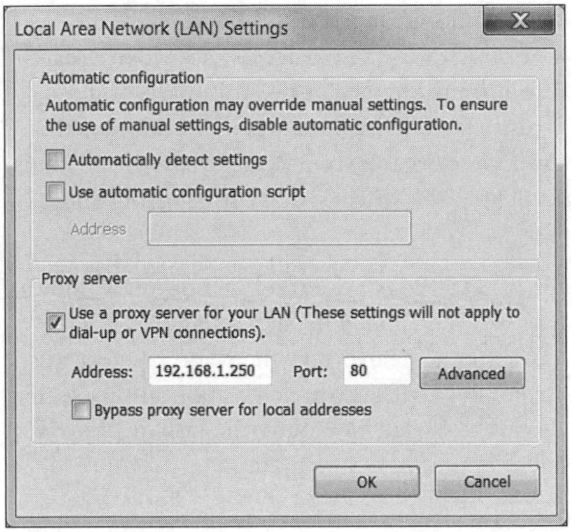

Figure 5-4   A Proxy Server Connection Within a Browser's Settings

This setting can also be configured within an organizational unit's Group Policy object on the domain controller. This way, it can be configured one time but affect all the computers within the particular OU.

Of course, any fancy networking configuration such as this can be used for evil purposes as well. The malicious individual can utilize various malware to write their own proxy configuration to the client operating system, thereby redirecting the unsuspecting user to potentially malevolent websites. So as a security administrator you should know how to enable a legitimate proxy connection used by your organization, but also know how to disable an illegitimate proxy connection used by attackers.

NOTE   When checking for improper proxy connections, a security admin should also check the hosts file for good measure. It is located in %systemroot%\System32\Drivers\etc.

Secure Against Malicious Code

Depending on your company's policies and procedures, you might need to configure a higher level of security concerning ActiveX controls, Java, JavaScript, Flash media, phishing, and much more. We discuss these more as we progress through the chapter.

Web Browser Concerns and Security Methods

There are many ways to make a web browser more secure. Be warned, though, that the more a browser is secured, the less functional it becomes. For the average company, the best solution is to find a happy medium between functionality and security. However, if you are working in an enterprise environment or mission-critical environment, then you will need to lean much farther toward security.

Basic Browser Security

The first thing that you should do is to update the browser—that is, if company policy permits it. Remember to use the patch management strategy discussed earlier in the book. You might also want to halt or *defer* future updates until you are ready to implement them across the entire network.

Next, install pop-up blocking and other ad-blocking solutions. Many antivirus suites have pop-up blocking tools. There are also third-party solutions that act as add-ons to the browser. And of course, newer versions of web browsers will block some pop-ups on their own.

After that, consider security zones if your browser supports them. You can set the security level for the Internet and intranet zones, and specify trusted sites and restricted sites. In addition, you can set custom levels for security; for example, disable ActiveX controls and plug-ins, turn the scripting of Java applets on and off, and much more.

NOTE   For step-by-step demonstrations concerning web browser security, see my online real-world scenarios and corresponding videos that accompany this book.

As for mobile devices, another way to keep the browser secure, as well as the entire system, is to avoid jailbreaking or rooting the device. If the device has been misconfigured in this way, it is easier for attackers to assault the web browser and, ultimately, subjugate the system.

Cookies

Cookies can also pose a security threat. **Cookies** are text files placed on the client computer that store information about it, which could include your computer's browsing habits and possibly user credentials. The latter are sometimes referred to as *persistent* cookies, used so that a person doesn't have to log in to a website every time. By adjusting cookie settings, you can either accept all cookies, deny all cookies, or select one of several options in between. A high cookie security setting will usually block cookies that save information that can be used to contact the user, and cookies that do not have a privacy policy.

You can also override any automatic cookie handling that might occur by configuring the prompt option. This way, a user will be prompted when a website attempts to create a cookie. For example, in Figure 5-5 my website www.davidlprowse.com was accessed. The site automatically tried to create a cookie due to the bulletin board system code. The browser sees this, stops it before it occurs, and verifies with the user whether to accept it. This particular cookie is harmless, so in this case I would accept it. There is a learning curve for users when it comes to knowing which cookies to accept. I guarantee that once or twice they will block a cookie that subsequently blocks functionality of the website. In some cases, an organization deals with too many websites that have too many cookies, so this particular security configuration is not an option.

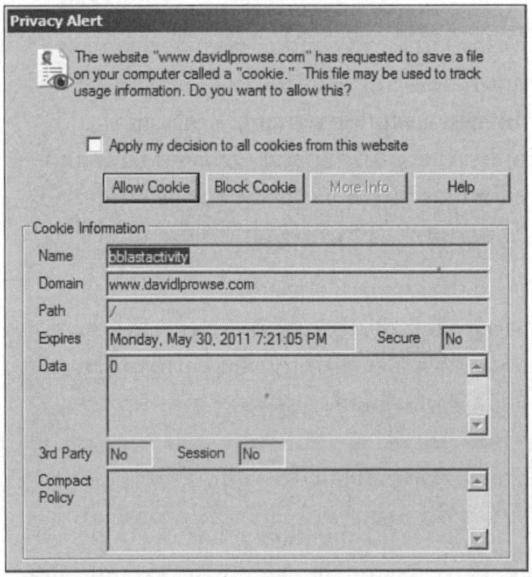

Figure 5-5   Cookie Privacy Alert

Tracking cookies are used by spyware to collect information about a web user's activities. Cookies can also be the target for various attacks; namely, session cookies are used when an attacker attempts to hijack a session. There are several types of session hijacking. One common type is cross-site scripting (also known as XSS), which is when the attacker manipulates a client computer into executing code considered trusted as if it came from the server the client was connected to. In this way, the attacker can acquire the client computer's session cookie (allowing the attacker to steal sensitive information) or exploit the computer in other ways. We cover more about XSS later in this chapter, and more about session hijacking in Chapter 7, "Networking Protocols and Threats."

LSOs

Another concept similar to cookies is **locally shared objects (LSOs)**, also called Flash cookies. These are data that Adobe Flash-based websites store on users' computers, especially for Flash games. The privacy concern is that LSOs are used by a variety of websites to collect information about users' browsing habits. However, LSOs can be disabled via the Flash Player Settings Manager (a.k.a. Local Settings Manager) in most of today's operating systems. LSOs can also be deleted entirely with third-party software, or by accessing the user's profile folder in Windows. For example, in Windows, a typical path would be

C:\Users\[*Your Profile*]\AppData\Roaming\Macromedia\Flash Player\#SharedObjects\[*variable folder name*]

Add-ons

You can enable and disable add-on programs for your browser in the settings or the add-ons management utility. But be wary with add-ons. Many companies will disallow them entirely because they can be a risk to the browser and possibly to the entire system or even the network. For example, in Figure 5-6, the Shockwave Flash Object ActiveX control is selected on a computer running IE. There are scenarios where this control could cause the browser to close or perhaps cause the system to crash; it can be turned off by clicking Disable toward the bottom of the window. Many add-ons are ActiveX controls, and ActiveX could also be turned off altogether in the advanced settings of the web browser. Depending on the add-on and the situation, other ways to fix the problem include updating Flash and upgrading the browser.

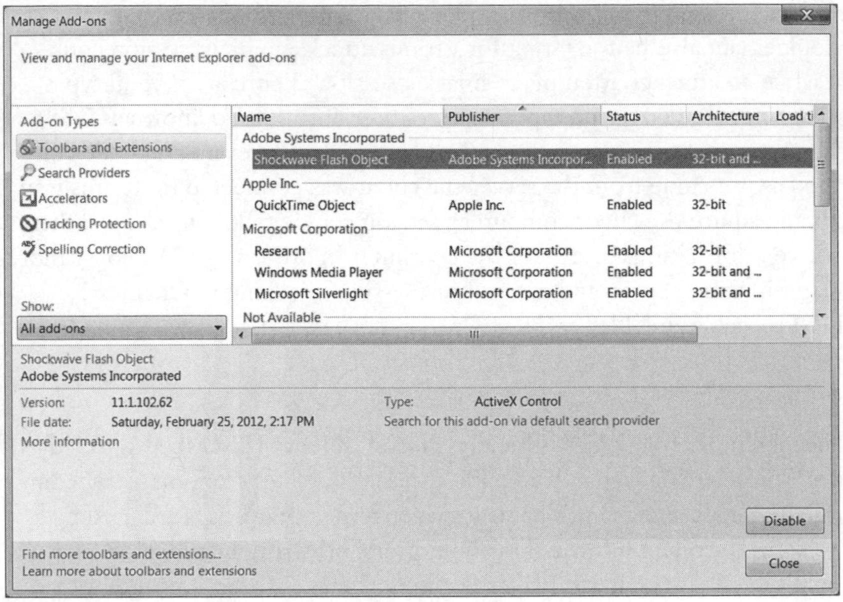

Figure 5-6 Managing Add-ons

ActiveX controls are small program building blocks used to allow a web browser to execute a program. They are similar to Java applets; however, Java applets can run on any platform, whereas ActiveX can run only on Internet Explorer (and Windows operating systems). You can see how a downloadable, executable ActiveX control or Java applet from a suspect website could possibly contain viruses, spyware, or worse. These are known as *malicious add-ons*—Flash scripts especially can be a security threat. Generally, you can disable undesirable scripts from either the advanced settings or by creating a custom security level or zone. If a particular script technology cannot be disabled within the browser, consider using a different browser, or a content filtering solution.

Advanced Browser Security

If you need to configure advanced settings in a browser, locate the settings or options section—this is usually found by clicking the three lines or three dots in the upper-right corner of the web browser. Then, locate the advanced settings. If you are using a Microsoft-based browser in Windows, you might also opt to go to the Control Panel (in icons mode), click Internet Options, and then select the Advanced tab of the Internet Properties dialog box.

Temporary browser files can contain lots of personally identifiable information (PII). You should consider automatically flushing the temp files from a system every day. For example, a hotel that offers Internet access as a service for guests might enable this function. This way, the histories of users are erased when they close the browser. On a related note, salespeople, field technicians, and other remote users should be trained to delete temporary files, cookies, and passwords when they are using computers on the road. In general, most companies discourage the saving of passwords by the browser. Some organizations make it a policy to disable that option. If you do save passwords, it would be wise to enter a master password. This way, when saved passwords are necessary, the browser will ask for only the master password, and you don't have to type or remember all the others. Use a password quality meter (for example, www.passwordmeter.com) to tell you how strong the password is. Personally, I don't recommend allowing any web browser to store passwords. Period. But, your organization's policies may differ in this respect. You might also consider a secure third-party password vault for your users, but this comes with a whole new set of concerns. Choose wisely!

A company might also use the advanced settings of a browser to specify the minimum version of SSL or TLS that is allowed for secure connections. Some organizations also disable third-party browser extensions altogether from the advanced settings.

You might also consider connecting through a VPN or running your browser within a virtual machine. These methods can help to protect your identity and protect the browser as well.

Of course, this section has only scraped the surface, but it gives you an idea of some of the ways to secure a web browser. Take a look at the various browsers available they are usually free—and spend some time getting to know the security settings for each. Remember to implement Group Policies from a server (domain controller) to adjust the security settings of a browser for many computers across the network. It saves time and is therefore more efficient.

In Chapter 4 we mentioned that removing applications that aren't used is important. But removing web browsers can be difficult, if not downright impossible, and should be avoided. Web browsers become one with the operating system, especially so in the case of Edge/IE and Windows. So, great care should be taken when planning whether to use a new browser—because it might be difficult to get rid of later on.

Keep in mind that the technology world is changing quickly, especially when it comes to the Internet, browsing, web browsers, and attacks. Be sure to periodically review your security policies for web browsing and keep up to date with the latest browser functionality, updates, security settings, and malicious attacks.

One last comment on browsers: sometimes a higher level of security can cause a browser to fail to connect to some websites. If a user cannot connect to a site, consider checking the various security settings such as trusted sites, cookies, and so on. If necessary, reduce the security level temporarily so that the user can access the site.

Securing Other Applications

Typical users shouldn't have access to any applications other than the ones they specifically need. For instance, would you want a typical user to have full control over the Command Prompt or PowerShell in Windows? The answer is: Doubtful. Protective measures should be put into place to make sure the typical user does *not* have access.

One way to do this is to use **User Account Control (UAC)** on qualifying Windows operating systems. UAC is a security component of Windows Vista and newer, and Windows Server 2008 and newer. It keeps every user (besides the actual Administrator account) in standard user mode instead of as an administrator with full administrative rights—even if the person is a member of the administrators group. It is meant to prevent unauthorized access and avoid user error in the form of accidental changes. A user attempting to execute commands in the Command Prompt and PowerShell will be blocked and will be asked for credentials before continuing. This applies to other applications within Windows as well.

Another way to deny access to applications is to create a policy. For example, on a Windows Server, you can do this in two ways. The first way is to disallow access to specific applications; this policy is called Don't Run Specified Windows Applications (a form of application blacklisting). However, the list could be longer than Florida, so another possibility would be to configure the Run Only Specified Windows Applications policy (a form of application whitelisting), as shown in Figure 5-7. This and the previously mentioned policy are adjacent to each other and can be found at the following path in Windows Server:

Policy (in this case we use the Marketing-Policy again) > User Configuration > Policies > Administrative Templates > System

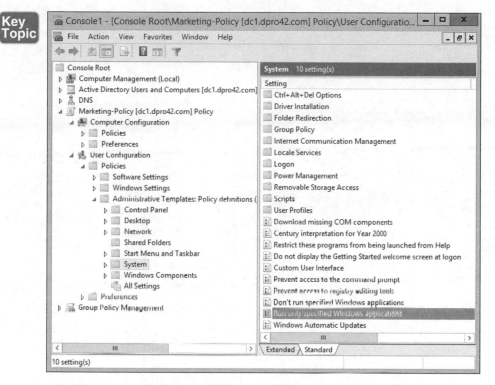

Figure 5-7   Run Only Specified Windows Applications Policy

When double-clicked, the policy opens and you can enable it and specify one or more applications that are allowed. All other applications will be denied to the user (if the user is logged on to the domain and is a member of the Marketing OU to which the policy is applied). Maybe you as the systems administrator decide that the marketing people should be using only Microsoft Word—a rather narrow view, but let's use that just for the sake of argument. All you need to do is click the Enabled radio button, click the Show button, and in the Show Contents window add the application; in this case, Word, which is winword.exe. An example of this is shown in Figure 5-8.

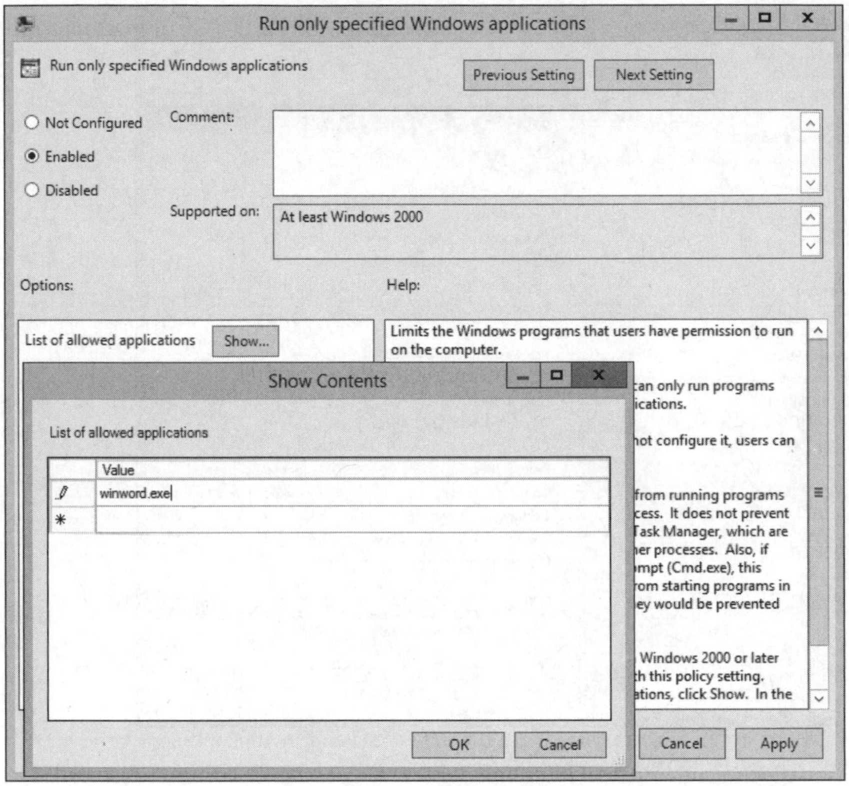

Figure 5-8 Adding a Single Allowed Application

This is in-depth stuff, and the CompTIA Security+ exam *probably* won't test you on exact procedures for this, but you should be aware that there are various ways to disallow access to just about anything you can think of. Of course, when it comes to Windows Server, the more practice you can get the better—for the exam, and for the real world.

For applications that users *are* allowed to work with, they should be secured accordingly. In general, applications should be updated, patched, or have the appropriate service packs installed. This is collectively known as *application patch management*, and is an overall part of the configuration management of an organization's software environment. Table 5-1 shows some common applications and some simple safeguards that can be implemented for them.

Table 5-1 Common Applications and Safeguards

Application Name	Safeguards
Outlook	Install the latest Office update or service pack. (This applies to all Office suite applications.)
	Keep Office up to date with Windows Update. (This also applies to all Office suite applications.)
	Consider an upgrade to a newer version of Office, if the currently used one is no longer supported.
	Increase the junk e-mail security level or use a whitelist.
	Read messages in plain text instead of HTML.
	Enable attachment blocking.
	Use a version that enables Object Model Guard functionality, or download it for older versions.
	Password protect any .PST files.
	Use strong passwords for Microsoft accounts if using web-based Outlook applications.
	Use encryption: Consider encrypting the authentication scheme, and possibly other traffic, including message traffic between Outlook clients and Exchange servers. Consider a digital certificate. Secure Password Authentication (SPA) can be used to secure the login, and S/MIME and PGP/GPG can be used to secure actual e-mail transmissions. Or, in the case of web-based e-mail, use SSL or TLS for encryption.
Word	Consider using passwords for opening or modifying documents.
	Use read only or comments only (tracking changes) settings.
	Consider using a digital certificate to seal the document.
Excel	Use password protection on worksheets.
	Set macro security levels.
	Consider Excel encryption.

Mobile apps should be secured as well. You might want to disable GPS to protect a mobile app, or the mobile device in general. You should also consider strong passwords for e-mail accounts and accounts to "app stores" and similar shopping portals. Watch for security updates for the mobile apps your organization uses.

We also need to give some thought to back office applications that run on servers. Database software, e-mail server software, and other back office "server" software needs to be hardened and secured as well. High-level server application examples from Microsoft include SQL Server and Exchange Server—and let's not forget FTP servers and web servers. These applications have their own set of configuration requirements and might be insecure out-of-the-box. For instance, a database server, FTP server, or other similar server will often have its own separate administrator account with a blank password by default. It is common knowledge what the names of these administrative user accounts are, and if they haven't been secured, hacking the system becomes mere child's play. Be sure to rename accounts (and disable unnecessary accounts) and configure strong passwords, just the way you would in an operating system.

One other thing to watch for in general is consolidation. Some organizations, in an attempt to save money, will merge several back office systems onto one computer. While this is good for the budget, and uses a small amount of resources, it opens the floodgates for attack. The more services a server has running, the more open doorways that exist to that system—and, the more possible ways that the server can fail. The most important services should be compartmentalized physically or virtually in order to reduce the size of the attack surface, and lower the total amount of threats to an individual system. We'll discuss servers more in Chapter 6, "Network Design Elements."

Organizations use many applications specific to their type of business. Stay on top of the various vendors that supply your organization with updates and new versions of software. Always test what effects one new piece of software will have on the rest of your installed software before implementation.

So far in this chapter we have discussed browser software, server-based applications, and other apps such as Microsoft Office. But that just scratches the surface. Whatever the application you use, attempt to secure it by planning how it will be utilized and deployed, updating it, and configuring it. Access the manufacturer's website for more information on how to secure the specific applications you use. Just remember that users (and other administrators) still need to work with the program. Don't make it so secure that a user gets locked out!

Secure Programming

We mentioned several times that many applications are inherently insecure out-of-the-box. But this problem can be limited with the implementation of secure programming or **secure coding concepts**. Secure coding concepts can be defined as the best practices used during software development in an effort to increase the security of the application being built—they *harden* the code of the application. In this section we cover several types of secure coding concepts used by programmers, some of the vulnerabilities programmers should watch out for, and how to defend against them.

Software Development Life Cycle

To properly develop a secure application, the developer has to scrutinize it at every turn, and from every angle, throughout the life of the project. Over time, this idea manifested itself into the concept known as the **software development life cycle (SDLC)**—an organized process of planning, developing, testing, deploying, and maintaining systems and applications, and the various methodologies used to do so. A common SDLC model used by companies is the **waterfall model**. Using this model the SDLC is broken down into several sequential phases. Here's an example of an SDLC's phases based on the waterfall model:

1. **Planning and analysis.** Goals are determined, needs are assessed, and high-level planning is accomplished.

2. **Software/systems design.** The design of the system or application is defined and diagrammed in detail.

3. **Implementation.** The code for the project is written.

4. **Testing.** The system or application is checked thoroughly in a testing environment.

5. **Integration.** If multiple systems are involved, the application should be tested in conjunction with those systems.

6. **Deployment.** The system or application is put into production and is now available to end users.

7. **Maintenance.** Software is monitored and updated throughout the rest of its life cycle. If there are many versions and configurations. version control is implemented to keep everything organized.

This is a basic example of the phases in an SDLC methodology. This one actually builds on the original waterfall model but it is quite similar. However, it could be more or less complicated depending on the number of systems, the project goals, and the organization involved.

NOTE   The SDLC is also referred to as: software development process, *systems* development lifecycle, or *application* development life cycle. CompTIA uses the term *software* development life cycle in its Security+ objectives, but be ready for slightly different terms based on the same concept.

While variations of the waterfall model are commonplace, an organization might opt to use a different model, such as the V-shaped model, which stresses more testing, or rapid application development (RAD), which puts more emphasis on process and less emphasis on planning. Then there is the **agile model**, which breaks work into small increments and is designed to be more adaptive to change. The agile model has become more and more popular since 2001. It focuses on customer satisfaction, cooperation between developers and business people, face-to-face conversation, simplicity, and quick adjustments to change.

The increasing popularity of the agile model led to DevOps, and subsequently, the practice of secure DevOps. DevOps is a portmanteau of the terms *software development* and *information technology operations*. It emphasizes the collaboration of those two departments so that the coding, testing, and releasing of software can happen more efficiently—and hopefully, more securely. DevOps is similar to continuous delivery—which focuses on automation and quick execution—but from an organizational standpoint is broader and supports greater collaboration. A secure DevOps environment should include the following concepts: secure provisioning and deprovisioning of software, services, and infrastructure; security automation; continuous integration; baselining; infrastructure as code; and *immutable* systems. Immutable means unchanging over time. From a systems and infrastructure viewpoint it means that software and services are replaced instead of being changed. Rapid, efficient deployment of new applications is at the core of DevOps and it is one of the main tasks of all groups involved.

Core SDLC and DevOps Principles

The terms and models discussed in the previous section can be confusing at times because they are similar, and because there are gray areas between them that overlap. So, if you are ever confused while working in the field, it's good to think back to the core fundamentals of security. From a larger perspective, a programmer/ systems developer and the security administrator should always keep the CIA concept in mind:

- **Maintaining confidentiality:** Only allowing users access to data to which they have permission

- **Preserving integrity:** Ensuring data is not tampered with or altered

- **Protecting availability:** Ensuring systems and data are accessible to authorized users when necessary

The CIA concepts are important when doing a **secure code review**, which can be defined as an in-depth code inspection procedure. It is often included by organizations as part of the testing phase of the SDLC but is usually conducted before other tests such as fuzzing or penetration tests, which we discuss more later in this chapter.

In general, quality assurance policies and procedures should be implemented while developing and testing code. This will vary from one organization to the next, but generally includes procedures that have been developed by a team, a set of checks and balances, and a large amount of documentation. By checking the documentation within a project, a developer can save a lot of time, while keeping the project more secure.

From a larger perspective, an organization might implement modeling as part of its software quality assurance program. By modeling, or simulating, a system or application, it can be tested, verified, validated, and finally accredited as acceptable for a specific purpose.

One secure and structured approach that organizations take is called threat modeling. **Threat modeling** enables you to prioritize threats to an application, based on their potential impact. This modeling process includes identifying assets to the system or application, uncovering vulnerabilities, identifying threats, documenting threats, and rating those threats according to their potential impact. The more risk, the higher the rating. Threat modeling is often incorporated into the SDLC during the design, testing, and deployment phases.

Some other very important security principles that should be incorporated into the SDLC include

- **Principle of least privilege:** Applications should be coded and run in such a way as to maintain the principle of least privilege. Users should only have access to what they need. Processes should run with only the bare minimum access needed to complete their functions. However, this can be coupled with separation of privilege, where access to objects depends on more than one condition (for example, authentication plus an encrypted key).

- **Principle of defense in depth:** The more security controls the better. The layering of defense in secure coding may take the form of validation, encryption, auditing, special authentication techniques, and so on.

- **Applications should never trust user input:** Input should be validated carefully.

- **Minimize the attack surface area:** Every additional feature that a programmer adds to an application increases the size of the attack surface and increases risk. Unnecessary functions should be removed, and necessary functions should require authorization.

- **Establish secure defaults:** Out-of-the-box offerings should be as secure as possible. If possible, user password complexity and password aging default policies should be configured by the programmer, not the user. Permissions should default to no access and should be granted only as they are needed.

- **Provide for authenticity and integrity:** For example, when deploying applications and scripts, use *code signing* in the form of a cryptographic hash with verifiable checksum for validation. A digital signature will verify the author and/or the version of the code—that is, if the corresponding private key is secured properly.

- **Fail securely:** At times, applications will fail. How they fail determines their security. Failure exceptions might show the programming language that was used to build the application, or worse, lead to access holes. Error handling/ exception handling code should be checked thoroughly so that a malicious user can't find out any additional information about the system. These error-handling methods are sometimes referred to technically as pseudocodes. For example, to handle a program exception, a properly written pseudocode will basically state (in spoken English): "If a program module crashes, then restart the program module."

- **Fix security issues correctly:** Once found, security vulnerabilities should be thoroughly tested, documented, and understood. Patches should be developed to fix the problem, but not cause other issues or application regression.

There are some other concepts to consider. First is *obfuscation*, which is the complicating of source code to make it more difficult for people to understand. This is done to conceal its purpose in order to prevent tampering and/or reverse engineering. It is an example of security through obscurity. Other examples of security through obscurity include code camouflaging and steganography, both of which might be used to hide the true code being used. Another important concept is *code checking*, which involves limiting the reuse of code to that which has been approved for use, and removing dead code. It's also vital to incorporate good memory management techniques. Finally, be very careful when using third-party libraries and software development kits (SDKs), and test them thoroughly before using them within a live application.

For the Security+ exam, the most important of the SDLC phases are maintenance and testing. In the maintenance phase, which doesn't end until the software is removed from all computers, an application needs to be updated accordingly, corrected when it fails, and constantly monitored. We discuss more about monitoring in Chapter 13, "Monitoring and Auditing." In the testing phase, a programmer (or team of programmers and other employees) checks for bugs and errors in a variety of ways. It's imperative that you know some of the vulnerabilities and attacks to a system or application, and how to fix them and protect against them. The best way to prevent these attacks is to test and review code.

Programming Testing Methods

Let's discuss the testing methods and techniques that can be implemented to seek out programming vulnerabilities and help prevent attacks from happening.

Programmers have various ways to test their code, including system testing, input validation, and fuzzing. By using a combination of these testing techniques during the testing phase of the SDLC, there is a much higher probability of a secure application as the end result.

White-box and Black-box Testing

System testing is generally broken down into two categories: black-box and white-box. **Black-box testing** utilizes people who do not know the system. These people (or programs, if automated) test the functionality of the system. Specific knowledge of the system code, and programming knowledge in general, is not required. The tester does not know about the system's internal structure and is often given limited information about what the application or system is supposed to do. In black-box testing, one of the most common goals is to crash the program. If a user is able to crash the program by entering improper input, the programmer has probably neglected to thoroughly check the error-handling code and/or input validation.

On the other side of the spectrum, **white-box testing** (also known as transparent testing) is a way of testing the internal workings of the application or system. Testers must have programming knowledge and are given detailed information about the design of the system. They are given login details, production documentation, and source code. System testers might use a combination of fuzzing (covered shortly), data flow testing, and other techniques such as stress testing, penetration testing, and sandboxes. *Stress testing* is usually done on real-time operating systems, mission-critical systems, and software, and checks if they have the robustness and availability required by the organization. A *penetration test* is a method of evaluating a system's security by simulating one or more attacks on that system. We speak more about penetration testing in Chapter 12, "Vulnerability and Risk Assessment." A **sandbox** is a term applied to when a web script (or other code) runs in its own environment (often a virtual environment) for the express purpose of not interfering with other processes, often for testing. Sandboxing technology is frequently used to test unverified applications for malware, malignant code, and possible errors such as buffer overflows.

A third category that has become more common of late is *gray-box testing*, where the tester has internal knowledge of the system from which to create tests but conducts the tests the way a black-box tester would—at the user level.

Compile-Time Errors Versus Runtime Errors

Programmers and developers need to test for potential compile-time errors and runtime errors. Compile time refers to the duration of time during which the statements written in any programming language are checked for errors. *Compile-time errors* might include syntax errors in the code and type-checking errors. A programmer can check these without actually "running" the program, and instead checks it in the compile stage when it is converted into machine code.

A *runtime error* is a program error that occurs while the program is running. The term is often used in contrast to other types of program errors, such as syntax errors and compile-time errors. Runtime errors might include running out of memory, invalid memory address access, invalid parameter value, or buffer overflows/dereferencing a null pointer (to name a few), all of which can only be discovered by running the program as a user. Another potential runtime error can occur if there is an attempt to divide by zero. These types of errors result in a software exception. Software and hardware exceptions need to be handled properly. Consequently, **structured exception handling (SEH)** is a mechanism used to handle both types of exceptions. It enables the programmer to have complete control over how exceptions are handled and provides support for debugging.

Code issues and errors that occur in either compile time or run time could lead to vulnerabilities in the software. However, it's the runtime environment that we are more interested in from a security perspective, because that more often is where the attacker will attempt to exploit software and websites.

Input Validation

Input validation is very important for website design and application development. **Input validation**, or data validation, is a process that ensures the correct usage of data—it checks the data that is inputted by users into web forms and other similar web elements. If data is not validated correctly, it can lead to various security vulnerabilities including sensitive data exposure and the possibility of data corruption. You can validate data in many ways, from coded data checks and consistency checks to spelling and grammar checks, and so on. Whatever data is being dealt with, it should be checked to make sure it is being entered correctly and won't create or take advantage of a security flaw. If validated properly, bad data and malformed data will be rejected. Input validation should be done both on the client side and, more importantly, on the server side. Let's look at an example next.

If an organization has a web page with a PHP-based contact form, the data entered by the visitor should be checked for errors, or maliciously typed input. The following is a piece of PHP code contained within a common contact form:

```
else if (!preg_match('/^[A-Za-z0-9.-]+$/', $domain))
 {
```

```
// character not valid in domain part
$isValid = false;
}
```

This is a part of a larger piece of code that is checking the entire e-mail address a user enters into a form field. This particular snippet of code checks to make sure the user is not trying to enter a backslash in the domain name portion of the e-mail address. This is not allowed in e-mail addresses and could be detrimental if used maliciously. Note in the first line within the brackets it says A-Za-z0-9.-, which is telling the system what characters are allowed. Uppercase and lowercase letters, numbers, periods, and dashes are allowed, but other characters such as backslashes, dollar signs, and so on are not allowed. Those other characters would be interpreted by the form's supporting PHP files as illegitimate data and would not be passed on through the system. The user would receive an error, which is a part of client-side validation. But, the more a PHP form is programmed to check for errors, the more it is possible to have additional security holes. Therefore, server-side validation is even more important. Any data that *is* passed on by the PHP form should be checked at the server as well. In fact, an attacker might not even be using the form in question, and might be attacking the URL of the web page in some other manner. This can be checked at the server within the database software, or through other means. By the way, the concept of combining client-side and server-side validation also goes for pages that utilize JavaScript.

This is just one basic example, but as mentioned previously, input validation is the key to preventing attacks such as SQL injection and XSS. All form fields should be tested for good input validation code, both on the client side and the server side. By combining the two, and checking every access attempt, you develop complete mediation of requests.

NOTE   Using input validation is one way to prevent *sensitive data exposure*, which occurs when an application does not adequately protect PII. This can also be prevented by the following: making sure that inputted data is never stored or transmitted in clear text; using strong encryption and securing key generation and storage; using HTTPS for authentication; and using a salt, which is random data used to strengthen hashed passwords. Salts are covered in more detail in Chapter 14.

Static and Dynamic Code Analysis

Static code analysis is a type of debugging that is carried out by examining the code *without* executing the program. This can be done by scrutinizing code visually, or with the aid of specific automated tools—static code analyzers—based on the language being used. Static code analysis can help to reveal major issues with code that could even lead to disasters. While this is an important phase of testing, it should always be followed by some type of dynamic analysis—for example, fuzz testing. This is when the program is actually executed while it is being tested. It is meant to locate minor defects in code and vulnerabilities. The combination of static and dynamic analysis by an organization is sometimes referred to as glass-box testing, which is another name for white-box testing.

Fuzz Testing

Fuzz testing (also known as fuzzing or dynamic analysis) is another smart concept. This is where random data is inputted into a computer program in an attempt to find vulnerabilities. This is often done without knowledge of the source code of the program. The program to be tested is run, has data inputted to it, and is monitored for exceptions such as crashes. This can be done with applications and operating systems. It is commonly used to check file parsers within applications such as Microsoft Word, and network parsers that are used by protocols such as DHCP. Fuzz testing can uncover full system failures, memory leaks, and error-handling issues. Fuzzing is usually automated (a program that checks a program) and can be as simple as sending a random set of bits to be inputted to the software. However, designing the inputs that cause the software to fail can be a tricky business, and often a myriad of variations of code needs to be tried to find vulnerabilities. Once the fuzz test is complete, the results are analyzed, the code is reviewed and made stronger, and vulnerabilities that were found are removed. The stronger the fuzz test, the better the chances that the program will not be susceptible to exploits.

As a final word on this, once code is properly tested and approved, it should be reused whenever possible. This helps to avoid "re-creating the wheel" and avoids common mistakes that a programmer might make that others might have already fixed. Just remember, code reuse is only applicable if the code is up to date and approved for use.

Programming Vulnerabilities and Attacks

Let's discuss some program code vulnerabilities and the attacks that exploit them. This section gives specific ways to mitigate these risks during application development, hopefully preventing these threats and attacks from becoming realities.

NOTE   This is a rather short section, and covers a topic that we could fill several books with. It is not a seminar on how to program, but rather a concise description of programmed attack methods, and some defenses against them. The Security+ objectives do not go into great detail concerning these methods, but CompTIA does expect you to have a broad and basic understanding.

Backdoors

To begin, applications should be analyzed for backdoors. As mentioned in Chapter 2, "Computer Systems Security Part I," backdoors are used in computer programs to bypass normal authentication and other security mechanisms in place. These can be avoided by updating the operating system and applications and firmware on devices, and especially by carefully checking the code of the program. If the system is not updated, a malicious person could take all kinds of actions via the backdoor. For example, a software developer who works for a company could install code through a backdoor that reactivates the user account after it was disabled (for whatever reason—termination, end of consulting period, and so on). This is done through the use of a logic bomb (in addition to the backdoor) and could be deadly once the software developer has access again. To reiterate, make sure the OS is updated, and consider job rotation, where programmers check each other's work.

Memory/Buffer Vulnerabilities

Memory and buffer vulnerabilities are common. There are several types of these, but perhaps most important is the buffer overflow. A **buffer overflow** is when a process stores data outside the memory that the developer intended. This could cause erratic behavior in the application, especially if the memory already had other data in it. Stacks and heaps are data structures that can be affected by buffer overflows. The stack is a key data structure necessary for the exchange of data between procedures. The heap contains data items whose size can be altered during execution. Value types are stored in a stack, whereas reference types are stored in a heap. An ethical coder will try to keep these running efficiently. An unethical coder wanting to create a program vulnerability could, for example, omit input validation, which could allow a buffer overflow to affect heaps and stacks, which in turn could adversely affect the application or the operating system in question.

Let's say a programmer allows for 16 bytes in a string variable. This won't be a problem normally. However, if the programmer failed to verify that *no more than* 16 bytes could be copied over to the variable, that would create a vulnerability that an attacker could exploit with a buffer overflow attack. The buffer overflow can also be initiated by certain inputs. For example, corrupting the stack with no-operation (no-op, NOP, or NOOP) machine instructions, which when used in large numbers can start a NOP slide, can ultimately lead to the execution of unwanted arbitrary code, or lead to a denial-of-service (DoS) on the affected computer.

All this can be prevented by patching the system or application in question, making sure that the OS uses data execution prevention, and utilizing bounds checking, which is a programmatic method of detecting whether a particular variable is within design bounds before it is allowed to be used. It can also be prevented by using correct code, checking code carefully, and using the right programming language for the job in question (the right tool for the right job, yes?). Without getting too much into the programming side of things, special values called "canaries" are used to protect against buffer overflows.

On a semi-related note, **integer overflows** are when arithmetic operations attempt to create a numeric value that is too big for the available memory space. This creates a *wrap* and can cause resets and undefined behavior in programming languages such as C and C++. The security ramification is that the integer overflow can violate the program's default behavior and possibly lead to a buffer overflow. This can be prevented or avoided by making overflows trigger an exception condition, or by using a model for automatically eliminating integer overflow, such as the CERT As-if Infinitely Ranged (AIR) integer model. More can be learned about this model at the following link:

http://www.cert.org/secure-coding/tools/integral-security.cfm

Then there are memory leaks. A **memory leak** is a type of resource leak caused when a program does not release memory properly. The lack of freed-up memory can reduce the performance of a computer, especially in systems with shared memory or limited memory. A kernel-level leak can lead to serious system stability issues. The memory leak might happen on its own due to poor programming, or it could be that code resides in the application that is vulnerable, and is later exploited by an attacker who sends specific packets to the system over the network. This type of error is more common in languages such as C or C++ that have no automatic garbage collection, but it could happen in any programming language. There are several memory debuggers that can be used to check for leaks. However, it is recommended that garbage collection libraries be added to C, C++, or other programming language, to check for potential memory leaks.

Another potential memory-related issue deals with pointer dereferencing—for example, the null pointer dereference. Pointer dereferencing is common in programming; when you want to access data (say, an integer) in memory, dereferencing the pointer would retrieve different data from a different section of memory (perhaps a different integer). Programs that contain a **null pointer dereference** generate memory fault errors (memory leaks). A null pointer dereference occurs when the program dereferences a pointer that it expects to be valid, but is null, which can cause the application to exit, or the system to crash. From a programmatical standpoint, the main way to prevent this is meticulous coding. Programmers can use special memory error analysis tools to enable error detection for a null pointer deference. Once identified, the programmer can correct the code that may be causing the error(s). But this concept can be used to attack systems over the network by initiating IP address to hostname resolutions—ones that the attacker hopes will fail—causing a return null. What this all means is that the network needs to be protected from attackers attempting this (and many other) programmatical and memory-based attacks via a network connection. We'll discuss how to do that in Chapters 6 through 9.

NOTE For more information on null pointer dereferencing (and many other software weaknesses), see the Common Weakness Enumeration portion of MITRE: https://cwe.mitre.org/. Add that site to your favorites!

A programmer may make use of **address space layout randomization (ASLR)** to help prevent the exploitation of memory corruption vulnerabilities. It randomly arranges the different address spaces used by a program (or process). This can aid in protecting mobile devices (and other systems) from exploits caused by memory-management problems. While there are exploits to ASLR (such as side-channel attacks) that can bypass it and de-randomize how the address space is arranged, many systems employ some version of ASLR.

Arbitrary Code Execution/Remote Code Execution

Arbitrary code execution is when an attacker obtains control of a target computer through some sort of vulnerability, thus gaining the power to execute commands on that remote computer at will. Programs that are designed to exploit software bugs or other vulnerabilities are often called arbitrary code execution exploits. These types of exploits inject "shellcode" to allow the attacker to run arbitrary commands on the remote computer. This type of attack is also known as **remote code execution (RCE)** and can potentially allow the attacker to take full control of the remote computer and turn it into a zombie.

RCE commands can be sent to the target computer using the URL of a browser, or by using the Netcat service, among other methods. To defend against this, applications should be updated, or if the application is being developed by your organization, it should be checked with fuzz testing and strong input validation (client side and server side) as part of the testing stage of the SDLC. If you have PHP running on a web server, it can be set to disable remote execution of configurations. A web server (or other server) can also be configured to block access from specific hosts.

NOTE RCE is also very common with web browsers. All browsers have been affected at some point, though some instances are more publicized than others. To see proof of this, access the Internet and search for the Common Vulnerabilities and Exposures (CVE) list for each type of web browser.

XSS and XSRF

Two web application vulnerabilities to watch out for include **cross-site scripting (XSS)** and **cross-site request forgery (XSRF)**.

XSS holes are vulnerabilities that can be exploited with a type of code injection. Code injection is the exploitation of a computer programming bug or flaw by inserting and processing invalid information—it is used to change how the program executes data. In the case of an XSS attack, an attacker inserts malicious scripts into a web page in the hopes of gaining elevated privileges and access to session cookies and other information stored by a user's web browser. This code (often Java-Script) is usually injected from a separate "attack site." It can also manifest itself as an embedded JavaScript image tag, header manipulation (as in manipulated HTTP response headers), or other HTML embedded image object within e-mails (that are web-based). The XSS attack can be defeated by programmers through the use of output encoding (JavaScript escaping, CSS escaping, and URL encoding), by preventing the use of HTML tags, and by input validation: for example, checking forms and confirming that input from users does not contain hypertext. On the user side, the possibility of this attack's success can be reduced by increasing cookie security and by disabling scripts in the ways mentioned in the first section of this chapter, "Securing the Browser." If XSS attacks by e-mail are a concern, the user could opt to set his e-mail client to text only.

The XSS attack exploits the trust a user's browser has in a website. The converse of this, the XSRF attack, exploits the trust that a website has in a user's browser. In this attack (also known as a one-click attack), the user's browser is compromised and transmits unauthorized commands to the website. The chances of this attack can be reduced by requiring tokens on web pages that contain forms, special authentication techniques (possibly encrypted), scanning .XML files (which could contain the code required for unauthorized access), and submitting cookies twice instead of once, while verifying that both cookie submissions match.

More Code Injection Examples

Other examples of code injection include SQL injection, XML injection, and LDAP injection. Let's discuss these briefly now.

Databases are just as vulnerable as web servers. The most common kind of database is the relational database, which is administered by a relational database management system (RDBMS). These systems are usually written in the Structured Query Language (SQL). An example of a SQL database is Microsoft's SQL Server (pronounced "sequel"); it can act as the back end for a program written in Visual Basic or Visual C++. Another example is MySQL, a free, open source relational database often used in conjunction with websites that employ PHP pages. One concern with SQL is the SQL injection attack, which occurs in databases, ASP.NET applications, and blogging software (such as WordPress) that use MySQL as a back end. In these attacks user input in web forms is not filtered correctly and is executed improperly, with the end result of gaining access to resources or changing data. For example, the login form for a web page that uses a SQL back end (such as a WordPress login page) can be insecure, especially if the front-end application is not updated. An attacker will attempt to access the database (from a form or in a variety of other ways), query the database, find out a user, and then inject code to the password portion of the SQL code—perhaps something as simple as x = x. This will allow any password for the user account to be used. If the login script was written properly (and validated properly), it should deflect this injected code. But if not, or if the application being used is not updated, it could be susceptible. It can be defended against by constraining user input, filtering user input, and using stored procedures such as input validating forms. Used to save memory, a *stored procedure* is a subroutine in an RDBMS that is typically implemented as a data-validation or access-control mechanism which includes several SQL statements in one procedure that can be accessed by multiple applications.

When using relational databases such as SQL and MySQL, a programmer works with the concept of *normalization*, which is the ability to avoid or reduce data redundancies and anomalies—a core concept within relational DBs. There are, however, other databases that work within the principle of de-normalization, and don't use SQL (or use code in addition to SQL). Known as NoSQL databases, they offer a different mechanism for retrieving data than their relational database counterparts. These are commonly found in data warehouses and virtual systems provided by cloud-based services. While they are usually resistant to SQL injection, there are NoSQL injection attacks as well. Because of the type of programming used in NoSQL, the potential impact of a NoSQL injection attack can be greater than that of a SQL injection attack. An example of a NoSQL injection attack is the JavaScript Object Notation (JSON) injection attack. But, NoSQL databases are also vulnerable to brute-force attacks (cracking of passwords) and connection pollution (a combination of XSS and code injection techniques). Methods to protect against NoSQL injection are similar to the methods mentioned for SQL injection. However, because NoSQL databases are often used within cloud services, a security administrator for a company might not have much control over the level of security that is implemented. In these cases, careful scrutiny of the service-level agreement (SLA) between the company and the cloud provider is imperative.

LDAP injection is similar to SQL injection, again using a web form input box to gain access, or by exploiting weak LDAP lookup configurations. The Lightweight Directory Access Protocol is a protocol used to maintain a directory of information such as user accounts, or other types of objects. The best way to protect against this (and all code injection techniques for that matter) is to incorporate strong input validation.

XML injection attacks can compromise the logic of XML (Extensible Markup Language) applications—for example, XML structures that contain the code for users. It can be used to create new users and possibly obtain administrative access. This can be tested for by attempting to insert XML metacharacters such as single and double quotes. It can be prevented by filtering *in* allowed characters (for example, A–Z only). This is an example of "default deny" where only what you explicitly filter in is permitted; everything else is forbidden.

One thing to remember is that when attackers utilize code injecting techniques, they are adding their own code to existing code, or are inserting their own code into a form. A variant of this is command injection, which doesn't utilize new code; instead, an attacker executes system-level commands on a vulnerable application or OS. The attacker might enter the command (and other syntax) into an HTML form field or other web-based form to gain access to a web server's password files.

NOTE   Though not completely related, another type of injection attack is DLL injection. This is when code is run within the address space of another process by forcing it to load a dynamic link library (DLL). Ultimately, this can influence the behavior of a program that was not originally intended. It can be uncovered through penetration testing, which we will discuss more in Chapter 12.

Once again, the best way to defend against code injection/command injection techniques in general is by implementing input validation during the development, testing, and maintenance phases of the SDLC.

Directory Traversal

Directory traversal, or the ../ (dot dot slash) attack, is a method of accessing unauthorized parent (or worse, root) directories. It is often used on web servers that have PHP files and are Linux or UNIX-based, but it can also be perpetrated on Microsoft operating systems (in which case it would be ..\ or the "dot dot backslash" attack). It is designed to get access to files such as ones that contain passwords. This can be prevented by updating the OS, or by checking the code of files for vulnerabilities, otherwise known as fuzzing. For example, a PHP file on a Linux-based web server might have a vulnerable `if` or `include` statement, which when attacked properly could give the attacker access to higher directories and the passwd file.

Zero Day Attack

A **zero day attack** is an attack executed on a vulnerability in software, before that vulnerability is known to the creator of the software, and before the developer can create a patch to fix the vulnerability. It's not a specific attack, but rather a group of attacks including viruses, Trojans, buffer overflow attacks, and so on. These attacks can cause damage even after the creator knows of the vulnerability, because it may take time to release a patch to prevent the attacks and fix damage caused by them. It can be discovered by thorough analysis and fuzz testing.

Zero day attacks can be prevented by using newer operating systems that have protection mechanisms and by updating those operating systems. They can also be prevented by using multiple layers of firewalls and by using whitelisting, which only allows known good applications to run. Collectively, these preventive methods are referred to as zero day protection.

Table 5-2 summarizes the programming vulnerabilities/attacks we have covered in this section.

Table 5-2 Summary of Programming Vulnerabilities and Attacks

Vulnerability	Description
Backdoor	Placed by programmers, knowingly or inadvertently, to bypass normal authentication, and other security mechanisms in place.
Buffer overflow	When a process stores data outside the memory that the developer intended.
Remote code execution (RCE)	When an attacker obtains control of a target computer through some sort of vulnerability, gaining the power to execute commands on that remote computer.
Cross-site scripting (XSS)	Exploits the trust a user's browser has in a website through code injection, often in web forms.
Cross-site request forgery (XSRF)	Exploits the trust that a website has in a user's browser, which becomes compromised and transmits unauthorized commands to the website.
Code injection	When user input in database web forms is not filtered correctly and is executed improperly. SQL injection is a very common example.
Directory traversal	A method of accessing unauthorized parent (or worse, root) directories.
Zero day	A group of attacks executed on vulnerabilities in software before those vulnerabilities are known to the creator.

The CompTIA Security+ exam objectives don't expect you to be a programmer, but they do expect you to have a basic knowledge of programming languages and methodologies so that you can help to secure applications effectively. I recommend a basic knowledge of programming languages used to build applications, such as Visual Basic, C++, C#, Java, and Python, as well as web-based programming languages such as HTML, ASP, and PHP, plus knowledge of database programming languages such as SQL. This foundation knowledge will help you not only on the exam, but also as a security administrator when you have to act as a liaison to the programming team, or if you are actually involved in testing an application.

Chapter Summary

Without applications, a computer doesn't do much for the user. Unfortunately, applications are often the most vulnerable part of a system. The fact that there are so many of them and that they come from so many sources can make it difficult to implement effective application security. This chapter gave a foundation of methods you can use to protect your programs.

The key with most organizations is to limit the number of applications that are used. The fewer applications, the easier they are to secure and, most likely, the more productive users will be. We mentioned the whitelisting and blacklisting of applications in this chapter and in Chapter 4, and those methods can be very effective. However, there are some applications that users cannot do without. One example is the web browser. Edge, Internet Explorer, Firefox, Chrome, and Safari are very widely used. For mobile devices, Safari, Chrome, and the Android browser are common. One general rule for browsers is to watch out for the latest version. You should be on top of security updates for the current version you are using, but always test a new version of a browser very carefully before implementing it.

In general, browser security precautions include implementing policies, training your users, using proxy and content filters, and securing against malicious code. Beyond that, different browsers have their own specific methods of security. For instance, each has its own methods for managing cookies, working with trusted sites, using add-ons, turning off ActiveX and JavaScript, and watching for properly encrypted sessions. Use these and other methods mentioned in the chapter to thoroughly secure the browsers on your client computers.

Other applications can be secured by implementing User Account Control (UAC), whitelisting applications through policy, using strong password protection, and encrypting data and traffic.

As a security administrator, you usually work with applications that have already been developed for you. But sometimes, you might dabble in some development yourself. If this is the case, you should adhere to the principles of secure programming discussed in this chapter. The software development life cycle (SDLC) gives you a methodical process of planning, developing, testing, deploying, and maintaining your systems and applications, while maintaining the confidentiality, preserving the integrity, and protecting the availability of your data. Principles you should invoke include least privilege, defense in depth, minimizing the attack surface, and failing securely.

To really make the most of the SDLC, you should test thoroughly, or at least verify that your programmers have done so. Black-box and white-box testing, sandboxing, fuzzing, and input validation checks are excellent methods for testing code and preventing programming vulnerabilities and attacks such as the use of backdoors, buffer overflows, remote code execution, code injection, directory traversal, and zero day attacks.

Learn as much as you can about web browsers, and other commonly used applications such as the Microsoft Office suite, so that you can be better prepared to protect them. Build your knowledge about programming techniques, including high-level languages such as Visual Basic and C++, and web-based languages including HTML and PHP. By combining the knowledge of a systems administrator and a programmer, you will have the best chance of securing your systems and applications.

Chapter Review Activities

Use the features in this section to study and review the topics in this chapter.

Review Key Topics

Review the most important topics in the chapter, noted with the Key Topic icon in the outer margin of the page. Table 5-3 lists a reference of these key topics and the page number on which each is found.

Table 5-3 Key Topics for Chapter 5

Key Topic Element	Description	Page Number
Figure 5-1	Microsoft Edge and Internet Explorer security features in the Local Computer Policy	130
Figure 5-3	Internet Explorer policies in the Marketing-Policy GPO	132
Figure 5-4	A proxy server connection within a browser's settings	134
Figure 5-7	Run Only Specified Windows Applications policy	141
Bulleted list	Important security principles to incorporate into the SDLC	147
Table 5-2	Summary of programming vulnerabilities and attacks	159

Define Key Terms

Define the following key terms from this chapter, and check your answers in the glossary:

cookies, locally shared object (LSO), User Account Control (UAC), secure coding concepts, software development life cycle (SDLC), waterfall model, agile model, secure code review, threat modeling, black-box testing, white-box testing, sandbox, structured exception handling (SEH), input validation, fuzz testing, buffer overflow, integer overflow, memory leak, null pointer dereference, address space layout randomization (ASLR), remote code execution (RCE), cross-site scripting (XSS), cross-site request forgery (XSRF), directory traversal, zero day attack

Complete the Real-World Scenarios

Complete the Real-World Scenarios found on the companion website (www.pearsonitcertification.com/title/9780789758996). You will find a PDF containing the scenario and questions, and also supporting videos and simulations.

Review Questions

Answer the following review questions. Check your answers with the correct answers that follow.

1. What key combination should be used to close a pop-up window?

   A. Windows+R

   B. Ctrl+Shift+Esc

   C. Ctrl+Alt+Del

   D. Alt+F4

2. Which protocol can be used to secure the e-mail login from an Outlook client using POP3 and SMTP?

   A. SMTP

   B. SPA

   C. SAP

   D. Exchange

3. What are two ways to secure a Microsoft-based web browser? (Select the two best answers.)

   A. Set the Internet zone's security level to High.

   B. Disable the pop-up blocker.

   C. Disable ActiveX controls.

   D. Add malicious sites to the Trusted Sites zone.

4. Heaps and stacks can be affected by which of the following attacks?

   A. Buffer overflows

   B. Rootkits

   C. SQL injection

   D. Cross-site scripting

5. As part of your user awareness training, you recommend that users remove which of the following when they finish accessing the Internet?

   A. Instant messaging

   B. Cookies

   C. Group policies

   D. Temporary files

6. Which statement best applies to the term *Java applet*?

   A. It decreases the usability of web-enabled systems.

   B. It is a programming language.

   C. A web browser must have the capability to run Java applets.

   D. It uses digital signatures for authentication.

7. Which of the following concepts can ease administration but can be the victim of a malicious attack?

   A. Zombies

   B. Backdoors

   C. Buffer overflow

   D. Group Policy

8. In an attempt to collect information about a user's activities, which of the following will be used by spyware?

   A. Tracking cookie

   B. Session cookie

   C. Shopping cart

   D. Persistent cookie

9. What is it known as when a web script runs in its own environment and does not interfere with other processes?

   A. Quarantine

   B. Honeynet

   C. Sandbox

   D. VPN

10. How can you train a user to easily determine whether a web page has a valid security certificate? (Select the best answer.)

    A. Have the user contact the webmaster.

    B. Have the user check for HTTPS://.

    C. Have the user click the padlock in the browser and verify the certificate.

    D. Have the user call the ISP.

11. To code applications in a secure manner, what is the best practice to use?

    A. Cross-site scripting

    B. Flash version 3

    C. Input validation

    D. HTML version 5

12. An organization hires you to test an application that you have limited knowledge of. You are given a login to the application but do not have access to source code. What type of test are you running?

    A. White-box

    B. Gray-box

    C. Black-box

    D. SDLC

13. You check the application log of your web server and see that someone attempted unsuccessfully to enter the text below into an HTML form field. Which attack was attempted?

`test; etc/passwd`

- **A.** SQL injection
- **B.** Code injection
- **C.** Command injection
- **D.** Buffer overflow

14. An attacker takes advantage of a vulnerability in programming that allows the attacker to copy more than 16 bytes to a standard 16-byte variable. Which attack is being initiated?

- **A.** Directory traversal
- **B.** Command injection
- **C.** XSS
- **D.** Buffer overflow
- **E.** Zero day attack

15. What's the best way to prevent SQL injection attacks on web applications?

- **A.** Input validation
- **B.** Host-based firewall
- **C.** Add HTTPS pages
- **D.** Update the web server

16. Which of the following attacks uses a JavaScript image tag in an e-mail?

- **A.** SQL injection
- **B.** Cross-site scripting
- **C.** Cross-site request forgery
- **D.** Directory traversal
- **E.** Null pointer dereference

17. Which of the following should occur first when developing software?

- **A.** Fuzzing
- **B.** Penetration testing
- **C.** Secure code review
- **D.** Patch management

18. You are the security administrator for a multimedia development company. Users are constantly searching the Internet for media, information, graphics, and so on. You receive complaints from several users about unwanted windows appearing on their displays. What should you do?

    A. Install antivirus software.

    B. Install pop-up blockers.

    C. Install screensavers.

    D. Install a host-based firewall.

19. You have analyzed what you expect to be malicious code. The results show that JavaScript is being utilized to send random data to a separate service on the same computer. What attack has occurred?

    A. DoS

    B. SQL injection

    C. LDAP injection

    D. Buffer overflow

20. Which of the following best describes a protective countermeasure for SQL injection?

    A. Validating user input within web-based applications

    B. Installing an IDS to monitor the network

    C. Eliminating XSS vulnerabilities

    D. Implementing a firewall server between the Internet and the database server

21. You have implemented a security technique where an automated system generates random input data to test an application. What have you put into practice?

    A. XSRF

    B. Fuzzing

    C. Hardening

    D. Input validation

22. Many third-party programs have security settings disabled by default. What should you as the security administrator do before deploying new software?

   A. Network penetration testing

   B. Input validation

   C. Application whitelisting

   D. Application hardening

23. Which of the following will allow the triggering of a security alert because of a tracking cookie?

   A. Anti-spyware application

   B. Anti-spam software

   C. Network-based firewall

   D. Host-based firewall

24. Your organization's servers and applications are being audited. One of the IT auditors tests an application as an authenticated user. Which of the following testing methods is being used?

   A. White-box

   B. Penetration testing

   C. Black-box

   D. Gray-box

25. Which of the following encompasses application patch management?

   A. Policy management

   B. Fuzzing

   C. Configuration management

   D. Virtualization

Answers and Explanations

1.   **D.** Alt+F4 is the key combination that is used to close an active window. Sometimes it is okay to click the X, but malware creators are getting smarter all the time; the X could be a ruse.

2. **B.** SPA (Secure Password Authentication) is a Microsoft protocol used to authenticate e-mail clients. S/MIME and PGP can be used to secure the actual e-mail transmissions.

3. **A and C.** By increasing the Internet zone security level to High, you employ the maximum safeguards for that zone. ActiveX controls can be used for malicious purposes; disabling them makes it so that they do not show up in the browser. Disabling a pop-up blocker and adding malicious sites to the Trusted Sites zone would make a Microsoft-based web browser (such as Internet Explorer) less secure.

4. **A.** Heaps and stacks are data structures that can be affected by buffer overflows. Value types are stored in a stack, whereas reference types are stored in a heap. An ethical coder will try to keep these running efficiently. An unethical coder will attempt to use a buffer overflow to affect heaps and stacks, which in turn could affect the application in question or the operating system. The buffer overflow might be initiated by certain inputs and can be prevented by bounds checking.

5. **B.** The best answer is cookies, which can be used for authentication and session tracking and can be read as plain text. They can be used by spyware and can track people without their permission. It is also wise to delete temporary Internet files as opposed to temporary files.

6. **C.** To run Java applets, a web browser must have that option enabled. Java increases the usability of web-enabled systems, and Java is a programming language. It does not use digital signatures for authentication.

7. **B.** Backdoors were originally created to ease administration. However, attackers quickly found that they could use these backdoors for a malicious attack.

8. **A.** A tracking cookie will be used, or misused, by spyware in an attempt to access a user's activities. Tracking cookies are also known as browser cookies or HTTP cookies, or simply cookies. Shopping carts take advantage of cookies to keep the shopping cart reliable.

9. **C.** When a web script runs in its own environment for the express purpose of not interfering with other processes, it is known as running in a sandbox. Often, the sandbox will be used to create sample scripts before they are actually implemented. Quarantining is a method used to isolate viruses. A honeynet is a collection of servers used to attract attackers and isolate them in an area where they can do no damage. VPN is short for virtual private network, which enables the connection of two hosts from remote networks.

10. **C.** In general, the user should click the padlock in the browser; this will show the certificate information. Often, the address bar will have different colors as the background; for example, green usually means that the certificate is valid, whereas red or pink indicates a problem. Or, you might have to click the name of the website listed in the address bar just before where it says HTTPS to find out the validity of the certificate. Contacting the webmaster and calling the ISP are time-consuming, not easily done, and not something that an end user should do. Although HTTPS:// can tell a person that the browser is now using Hypertext Transfer Protocol Secure, it does not necessarily determine whether the certificate is valid.

11. **C.** Input validation is the best practice to use when coding applications. This is important when creating web applications or web pages that require information to be inputted by the user.

12. **B.** A gray-box test is when you are given limited information about the system you are testing. Black-box testers are not given logins, source code, or anything else, though they may know the functionality of the system. White-box testers are given logins, source code, documentation, and more. SDLC stands for software development life cycle, of which these types of tests are just a part.

13. **C.** In this case a command was entered, and the attacker was attempting to gain access to the password file within the /etc directory. If the attacker tried to inject code, he would not use commands, but rather PHP, ASP, or another language. SQL injections are usually run on databases, not web servers' HTML forms. Buffer overflows have to do with memory and how applications utilize it.

14. **D.** A buffer overflow can be initiated when a string variable is not programmed correctly—for example, if the variable allows for more than the standard amount of bytes. Directory traversal is when an attacker uses commands and code to access unauthorized parent directories. Command injection is when commands and command syntax are entered into an application or OS. XSS or cross-site scripting is when code is injected into a website form to obtain information and unauthorized access. Zero day attacks are ones that are not known to hardware/software manufacturers when they are launched.

15. **A.** Input validation is the best way to prevent SQL injection attacks on web servers and database servers (or combinations of the two). Host-based firewalls aid in preventing network attacks but not necessarily coded attacks of this type. HTTPS pages initiate a secure transfer of data, but they don't necessarily lock out attackers who plan on using SQL injection. Updating the web server is a good idea, but will have little if any effect on the forms that are written by the web programmer.

16. **B.** Cross-site scripting (XSS) can be initiated on web forms or through e-mail. It often uses JavaScript to accomplish its means. SQL injection is when code (SQL based) is inserted into forms or databases. Cross-site request forgery (XSRF) is when a user's browser sends unauthorized commands to a website, without the user's consent. Directory traversal is when an attacker attempts to gain access to higher directories in an OS. A null pointer dereference is a memory dereference that can result in a memory fault error.

17. **C.** Of the listed answers, secure code review should happen first in the SDLC. It should be followed by fuzzing and penetration testing, in that order. Patch management is a recurring theme until the software meets the end of its life cycle.

18. **B.** The windows that are being displayed are most likely pop-ups. Standard pop-up blockers will prevent most of these. Antivirus software of itself does not have pop-up blocking technology but might be combined in a suite of anti-malware software that does have pop-up blocking capability. Screensavers won't affect the users' web sessions. Host-based firewalls are a good idea and will prevent attacks, but since a firewall will allow the connections that users make to websites, it cannot stop pop-ups.

19. **D.** Buffer overflows can be initiated by sending random data to other services on a computer. While JavaScript is commonly used in XSS attacks, it can also be used to create a buffer overflow. DoS stands for denial-of-service, which is when a computer sends many packets to a server or other important system in the hope of making that system fail. SQL and LDAP injection do not use JavaScript.

20. **A.** Input validation is extremely important when it comes to secure programming. To prevent SQL injection attacks, be sure that the developers have thoroughly tested the web page by validating user input. An IDS can help to detect network attacks, but is not going to help prevent SQL injection. Eliminating XSS vulnerabilities might just happen to help with all types of code injection, but you can't be sure. You should validate inputs specifically for each attack. A firewall may stop some network-based attacks, but not coded attacks.

21. **B.** Fuzzing (or fuzz testing) is when a person, or more commonly an automated system, enters random data into a form or application in an effort to test it. XSRF (cross-site request forgery, also abbreviated as CSRF) is an exploit of a website where unauthorized commands are issued from a trusted user. Hardening is the act of securing an operating system or application. Input validation is when forms and other web pages are checked to make sure that they will filter inputted data properly, and is used in conjunction with fuzzing.

22. **D.** You should employ application hardening. This means updating the application, configuring strong passwords, applying policies if necessary, and in general, configuring the settings of the application securely. Network penetration testing is when a group of tools is used to see if a host has open ports or other vulnerabilities. Input validation is when the code of a form is checked to make sure it filters user input correctly. Application whitelisting is when only specific applications are allowed to be run, usually enforced by computer policy.

23. **A.** Anti-spyware can be used to trigger security alerts in case a user's web browser accesses a web page that includes a tracking cookie. Anti-spam software can possibly trigger alerts when an e-mail appears to be spam (or simply move it to a junk folder automatically). Firewalls can be configured to send alerts to security administrators, but usually they concern an IP address that attempted to gain access to the network.

24. **D.** This would be an example of gray-box testing. The IT auditor is not an employee of the company (which is often a requirement for white-box testing) but rather an outside consultant. Being an outside consultant, the IT auditor should not be given confidential details of the system to be tested. However, the auditor was given a real login, so the auditor cannot be employing black-box testing. Penetration testing might be occurring in this scenario as well—this is when an auditor, or other security expert, tests servers' network connections for vulnerabilities. But the scenario only states that the auditor is testing an application.

25. **C.** Configuration management encompasses application patch management and other ways of hardening an OS or application. Policy management is considered separate because it can be used to harden or *soften* a system; plus, it is best done at a server—affecting many systems at once. Fuzzing (or fuzz testing) is the act of providing random data to a computer program, testing it in an automated fashion. Virtualization is the term used to refer to any virtual computing platform.

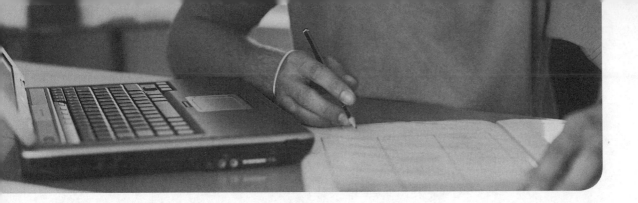

This chapter covers the following subjects:

- **Network Design:** This section discusses network design elements such as switches and routers, and how to protect those devices from attack. It also talks about network address translation, private versus public IP addresses, and the private IP ranges. You then learn about network zones and interconnections—for example, intranets and extranets, demilitarized zones, LANs, and WANs. Finally, you learn how to defend against attacks on your virtual local area networks, IP subnets, and telephony devices.

- **Cloud Security and Server Defense:** As time moves forward, more and more organizations transfer some or all of their server and network resources to the cloud. This creates many potential hazards and vulnerabilities that must be addressed by the security administrator and by the cloud provider. Top among these concerns are the servers, where all data is stored and accessed. Servers of all types should be hardened and protected from a variety of attacks in an effort to keep the integrity of data from being compromised. However, data must also be available. And so, the security administrator must strike a balance of security and availability. In this section, we'll discuss cloud-based threats as well as server vulnerabilities, and how to combat them effectively.

Up until now we have focused on the individual computer system. Let's expand our security perimeter to now include networks. Network design is extremely important in a secure computing environment. The elements that you include in your design can help to defend against many different types of network attacks. Being able to identify these network threats is the next step in securing your network. If you apply the strategies and defense mechanisms included in this chapter, you should be able to stave off most network-based assaults. The security of the servers and network infrastructure of an organization is the job of the security administrator, but with the inclusion of the cloud the areas of responsibility might vary. This depends on how much of the cloud is provided by a third party, and how much of the cloud is held privately within the organization's domain. Whether dealing with cloud providers, onsite cloud-based resources, locally owned servers and networks, or a mixture of all of them, the security administrator has a lot of duties and must understand not only security but how computer networking really functions. To save time and be more efficient, this chapter and the following three chapters assume that you have a working knowledge of networks and that you have the CompTIA Network+ certification or commensurate experience. Hereafter, this book will work within that mindset and will refer directly to the security side of things as it progresses. So, put on your networking hat and let's begin with network design.

CHAPTER 6

Network Design Elements

Network Design

Proper network design is critical for the security of your network, servers, and client computers. You need to protect your network devices so that they and the clients that they connect together will be less subject to attack. Implementing network address translation and properly employing standard private IP ranges can further protect all the computers in a standard network. A thorough knowledge of network zones—for example, local area networks and demilitarized zones—is also important when designing a secure network. Finally, by utilizing subnetworks, virtual local area networks (VLANs), network access control, and secure telephony devices, you can put the final touches on your network design.

We start with a quick review of the OSI model, which most of the topics in Chapters 6 through Chapter 9 (and beyond) relate to. This is not a full discourse on the OSI model, which is a prerequisite concept for the Security+ exam, but should help to stimulate your brain and help get you thinking from an "OSI" point of view.

The OSI Model

The Open Systems Interconnection (OSI) reference model was created and ratified by the International Organization for Standardization (ISO), and is represented in the United States by the American National Standards Institute (ANSI). This model was created to do the following:

- Explain network communications between hosts on the LAN or WAN.

- Present a categorization system for communication protocol suites (such as TCP/IP).

- Show how different protocol suites can communicate with each other.

Remember, network communications existed before the OSI model was created. This model is an abstract way of categorizing the communications that already exist. The model was devised to help engineers understand what is happening with communication protocols behind the scenes. It is broken down into seven layers, as shown in Table 6-1. They are listed numerically, which would be considered from the bottom up.

Table 6-1 OSI Model Layers

Layer #	Name	Usage	Unit of Measurement
Layer 1	Physical layer	Physical and electrical medium for data transfer.	Bits
Layer 2	Data link layer	Establishes, maintains, and decides how data transfer is accomplished over the physical layer.	Frames
Layer 3	Network layer	Dedicated to routing and switching information between different hosts, networks, and internetworks.	Packets
Layer 4	Transport layer	Manages and ensures error-free transmission of messages between hosts through logical addressing and port assignment (connection-oriented). Also manages streaming connections, where n number of errors are permitted (connectionless).	Segments (TCP) Datagrams (UDP)
Layer 5	Session layer	Governs the establishment, termination, and synchronization of sessions within the OS over the network and between hosts.	Messages
Layer 6	Presentation layer	Translates the data format from sender to receiver and provides mechanisms for code conversion, data compression, and file encryption.	Messages
Layer 7	Application layer	Where message creation begins. End-user protocols such as FTP, HTTP, and SMTP work on this layer.	Messages

NOTE The "units of measurement" in the table are also referred to as protocol data units, or PDUs.

We could fill a book on the OSI model, but again, understanding this model is a prerequisite for the Security+ exam, so it will not be covered in depth here. However, at the very least you should know the layers, their order, and their basic descriptions. In Chapter 7, "Networking Protocols and Threats," we will apply different protocols to their respective OSI layers.

If you feel you need to brush up on the OSI model more, then consider computer networking books (for example, Network+ textbooks), online articles, and networking training classes.

> **NOTE**   For a short primer about the OSI model and its layers, see the following link:
>
> http://www.davidlprowse.com/articles/?p=905
>
> Also, consider one of the many CompTIA Network+ books available, or see the following links:
>
> http://www.cisco.com/cpress/cc/td/cpress/fund/ith/ith01gb.htm#xtocid166844
>
> https://support.microsoft.com/en-us/help/103884

> **NOTE**   You'll also see the TCP/IP model (a.k.a. Internet protocol suite). This is similar to the OSI model with slightly different names for the layers: application, transport, Internet, and link. Compared to the OSI model, it disregards much of the physical layer, and the application layer equates to the OSI's application, presentation, and session layers.

Network Devices

Let's begin with the network devices common on today's networks. Central connecting devices such as switches need to be secured and monitored; it makes sense because these devices connect all the computers on your local area network. Attacks aimed at these devices could bring down the entire LAN. And of course, routers are extremely important when interconnecting LANs and subnets. Because many routers have visible IP addresses on the Internet, you should expand your line of thinking to include the act of securing these devices from attackers that might come from outside and *inside* your network. It is more common that attackers will be situated outside your network, but you never know!

Switch

Ethernet switching was developed in 1996 and quickly took hold as the preferred method of networking, taking the place of deprecated devices such as hubs and older-style bridges. This is due to the switch's improvement in the areas of data transfer and security. A switch is a central connecting device to which all computers on the network can connect. The switch regenerates the signal it receives and (by default) sends the signal to the correct individual computer. It does this by mapping computers' MAC addresses to their corresponding physical port. This can effectively make every port an individual entity, thus securing the network, and exponentially increasing data throughput. Switches employ a matrix of copper wiring instead of the standard trunk circuit, and intelligence to pass information to the correct port. The CompTIA Security+ exam focuses on layer 2 and layer 3 switches. Layer 2 switches deal with MAC addresses only. But layer 3 switches work with MAC addresses *and* IP addresses. Most of the attacks we discuss are layer 2 based, but not all. Be ready to secure on both layers.

Although the switch is an excellent star-based topological solution, some security implications are still involved with it. These include but are not limited to the following:

Key Topic

- **MAC flooding:** Switches have memory set aside to store the MAC address to the port translation table, known as the Content Addressable Memory table, or **CAM table**. A MAC flood can send numerous packets to the switch, each of which has a different source MAC address, in an attempt to use up the memory on the switch. If this is successful, the switch changes state to what is known as **fail-open mode**. At this point, the switch broadcasts data on all ports the way a hub does. This means two things: First, that network bandwidth will be dramatically reduced, and second, that a mischievous person could now use a protocol analyzer, running in promiscuous mode, to capture data from any other computer on the network. Yikes!

  Some switches are equipped with the capability to shut down a particular port if it receives a certain amount of packets with different source MAC addresses. For example, Cisco switches use port security, which can act as a flood guard (among many other things). This restricts a port by limiting and identifying MAC addresses of the computers permitted to access that port. A Cisco switch defines three categories of secure MAC addresses as part of a policy on the switch. Other providers have like policies that can be implemented. Other ways to secure against MAC flooding and constrain connectivity include using network access control (NAC) and 802.1X-compliant devices, dynamic VLANs, and network intrusion detection systems (NIDSs), and consistently monitoring the network. We speak more to these concepts later in this chapter and in future chapters.

- **MAC spoofing:** MAC spoofing is when an attacker masks the MAC address of their computer's network adapter with another number. This can allow a user to disguise their computer as another system on, or off, the network, thus fooling a switch and possibly gaining access. Cisco's port security feature and NAC systems or other application layer solutions can help to prevent this, but in the case of an insider attempting this, a router should also be configured to only accept a certain amount of static MAC addresses. This attack can be enhanced by initiating a *DHCP starvation attack*, which works by broadcasting DHCP requests with spoofed MAC addresses, which can ultimately exhaust the address space available to DHCP servers. To help prevent against this, enable DHCP snooping. Also, close off any untrusted switch interfaces—meaning, ones that connect outside the network or firewall. Finally, another related attack is *ARP spoofing*, which is when an attacker can make a system appear as the destination host sought by the sender, with obvious repercussions. This can be prevented by: reducing the time an entry stays in the ARP cache—on the switch and on the clients; checking/removing static ARP entries; using dynamic ARP inspection; and also using the aforementioned DHCP snooping.

> **NOTE**   When making changes to Cisco switches, or any other switches, always remember to save (and back up) the appropriate config files. Keep a log of what changes were applied to which backup files.

- **Physical tampering:** Some switches have a dedicated management port. If this is accessible, a person could perpetuate a variety of attacks on the network. Even if a single port of the switch is accessible, a person could attempt the aforementioned MAC flooding attack and move on from there. In addition, if a person were to get physical access to the switch, that person could attempt *looping*, which is when both ends of a network cable are connected to the same switch; or, when two cascading switches are connected to each other with two patch cables instead of just one. Plus, the potential for inadvertent looping grows with each additional switch. To avoid cable loops, consider a hierarchical switched environment; for instance, one where all LAN switches connect to a the "master" switch, also known as an aggregation switch. Some switches come with the ability to enable loop protection within the firmware. For example, you should enable the **Spanning Tree Protocol (STP)**—that is, if it isn't enabled by default. STP—as well as Rapid STP and multiple STP—builds a logical loop-free topology for the Ethernet network and can recognize and bypass improper connections. However, it's preferable to prevent the problem from physically happening in the first place. So, remember that the switch needs to be physically secured, most likely in a server room with some type of access control system, and all switches should be checked for internal cable loops. It sounds so simple, but it is commonly overlooked by many companies. Also, disable any unused ports on the switch, if the switch has that capability. Finally, employ good cable management: label ports and cables and organize patch cables as necessary.

Bridge

A bridge is used to separate a physical LAN (or WLAN) into two logical networks, or to connect two networks together. You do this by physically connecting the device to both sections of the network. The device will then seek out MAC addresses on both sides and keep that information stored in a table. If a person on one side of the bridge wants to communicate on the network, the bridge will decide whether the information should cross to the other side. This eliminates some broadcasting. A bridge often resides on the data link layer. Note that since the advent of switching, bridges have become much less commonplace. However, you may see them connecting two network sections together. That said, security becomes vital. For example, in a wireless bridged environment, you might opt for an IPsec tunnel between devices. However, if you find yourself in a bridged environment, then you should probably consider a newer, more secure solution.

Router

A router connects two or more networks to form an internetwork. Routers are used in LANs, in WANs, and on the Internet. This device routes data from one location to another, usually by way of the IP address and IP network numbers. Routers function on the Network layer of the OSI model.

Routers come in several forms: SOHO routers, those four-port devices used in homes and small offices to connect to the Internet; servers, which can be configured for routing if they have multiple network adapters and the proper software; and, most commonly, black-box devices such as Cisco routers. Routers are intelligent and even have their own operating system; for example, Cisco routers use IOS (Internetwork Operating System). Often, a DMZ will be set up within a router, especially SOHO router devices; we speak more about the DMZ later in this chapter.

Routers can be the victim of denial-of-service attacks, malware intrusions, and other attacks (covered in more depth later in this chapter) and can spread these attacks and malware to other sections of the network. Routers can be protected from these attacks in the following ways:

- **Secure router configuration:** Most routers are inherently insecure out-of-the-box. This means that they might have a blank default password, easily guessable username, known IP addresses, default routing tables, and so on. The first line of defense is to configure the username and password so that it is hard to guess and hard to crack. This means very complex passwords. Go through all possible default configurations and lock them down before putting the router on a live network.

- **Firewalls:** Firewalls protect against and filter out unwanted traffic. A firewall can be an individual device or can be added to a router. For example, most

SOHO routers have a firewall built in, and Cisco Integrated Services Routers (ISR) include the Cisco IOS Firewall. Regular routers, and routers with firewall functionality, have the ability to block certain kinds of traffic. For example, if ICMP has been blocked, then you would not be able to ping the router. You can find more information on firewalls in Chapter 8, "Network Perimeter Security."

- **Intrusion prevention systems (IPSs):** An IPS will not only detect but also prevent directed attacks, botnet attacks, malware, and other forms of attacks. An IPS can be installed as a network-based solution or on a particular computer and some routers. More information on network-based IPS (and IDS) solutions can be found in Chapter 8.

- **Secure VPN connectivity:** Instead of connecting directly to a router, virtual private networks enable for secure connections utilizing IPsec and SSL. Secure VPN connectivity can be implemented with SOHO routers (for smaller organizations), VPN concentrators (for larger organizations), advanced routers like ones offered by Cisco, or with a Windows Server. You can find more information about VPNs in Chapter 10, "Physical Security and Authentication Models."

- **Content filtering:** Content filtering blocks or restricts access to certain websites. This provides protection from malicious websites. Content filtering can be installed as a server, as an appliance (for example, a web security gateway), or on some routers. You can find more information about content filters in Chapter 8.

- **Access control lists (ACLs):** Access control lists enable or deny traffic. These can be implemented on a router and within firewalls; in some cases the two will be the same physical device. For example, an ACL can be configured to deny any connections by computers that have IP addresses outside the network number. ACLs are instrumental in blocking *IP spoofing* attacks. You can find more information about ACLs in Chapter 11, "Access Control Methods and Models."

NOTE   The CompTIA Security+ objectives also refer to the channel service unit (CSU) and data service unit (DSU). These two devices—often combined as a CSU/DSU—are within the realm of data communications equipment (DCE). They connect data terminal equipment (DTE) such as a router to a digital circuit such as a T-1. Today, the functionality of these devices (or device) is often incorporated into a router in the form of a WAN interface card (WIC) or otherwise. Cable and DSL modems are also considered to be CSU/DSUs. It's important to update the firmware on these devices periodically and replace old hardware with new devices.

Network Address Translation, and Private Versus Public IP

Network address translation (NAT) is the process of changing an IP address while it is in transit across a router. This is usually implemented so that one larger address space (private) can be remapped to another address space, or single IP address (public). In this case it is known as network masquerading, or IP masquerading, and was originally implemented to alleviate the problem of IPv4 address exhaustion. Today, NAT provides a level of protection in IPv4 networks by hiding a person's private internal IPv4 address—known as the *firewall effect*. Basic routers only allow for basic NAT, which is IPv4 *address*-translation-only. But more advanced routers allow for PAT, or **port address translation**, which translates both IPv4 addresses and port numbers. Commonly, a NAT implementation on a firewall hides an entire private network of IPv4 addresses (for example, the 192.168.1.0 network) behind a single publicly displayed IPv4 address. Many SOHO routers, servers, and more advanced routers offer this technology to protect a company's computers on the LAN. Generally, when an individual computer attempts to communicate through the router, **static NAT** is employed, meaning that the single private IPv4 address will translate to a single public IPv4 address. This is also called **one-to-one mapping**.

It is also important to know the difference between private and public addresses. A private address is one not displayed directly to the Internet and is normally behind a firewall (or NAT-enabled device). Typically, these are addresses that a SOHO router or DHCP server would assign automatically to clients. A list of reserved private IPv4 ranges is shown in Table 6-2. Public addresses are addresses displayed directly to the Internet; they are addresses that anyone can possibly connect to around the world. Most addresses besides the private ones listed in Table 6-2 are considered public addresses. Figure 6-1 shows an example of a router/firewall implementing NAT. The router's public address is 207.172.15.50, and its private address is 10.0.0.1. Computers to the left of the router are on the LAN, and all their IP addresses are private, protected by NAT, which occurs at the router. Servers on the Internet (within the cloud) have public IPv4 addresses (for example, 208.96.234.193) so that they can be accessed by anyone on the Internet.

Table 6-2 Private IPv4 Ranges (as Assigned by the IANA)

IP Class	Assigned Range
Class A	10.0.0.0–10.255.255.255
Class B	172.16.0.0–172.31.255.255
Class C	192.168.0.0–192.168.255.255

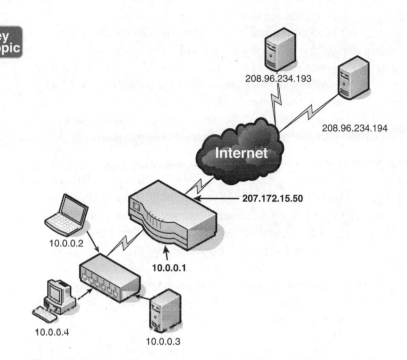

208.96.234.193

208.96.234.194

Internet

207.172.15.50

10.0.0.2

10.0.0.1

10.0.0.4

10.0.0.3

Figure 6-1 Example of Public and Private IPv4 Addresses

Keep in mind that most internal networks—meaning LANs—are either subnetted or are classless in nature. It's important to know the private IP ranges and their classes, but just remember that classless is very common, especially in larger networks.

You should also know the categories of IPv6 addresses. Table 6-3 provides a review of these types. Keep in mind that the standard "private" range for IPv6 is FE80::/10, which spans addresses that start with FE80, FE90, FEA0, and FEB0. This is the default reserved range of IPv6 addresses that computers on a LAN (and behind a firewall) will be assigned from.

Table 6-3 Types of IPv6 Addresses

IPv6 Type	Address Range	Purpose
Unicast	Global unicast starts at 2000 Link-local ::1 and FE80::/10	Address assigned to one interface of one host.
Anycast	Structured like unicast addresses	Address assigned to a group of interfaces on multiple nodes. Packets are delivered to the "first" interface only.
Multicast	FF00::/8	Address assigned to a group of interfaces on multiple nodes. Packets are delivered to all interfaces.

There are risks involved with IPv6 auto-configured addresses. Once a computer is physically connected to a network, it can easily obtain an IPv6 address without any user interaction and begin communicating with other hosts on the network, perhaps in an insecure manner. To avoid this, consider using 802.1X authentication, which stops IPv6 traffic until the host is authenticated to the network. You can read more on 802.1X in Chapter 10. Also, consider using encrypted tunnels, and network adapters that are certified for secure wired and/or wireless transmissions.

A last word about IP security—both IPv4 and IPv6 have security issues, and both have various ways that they can be secured. Don't be fooled; both types of IP networks need to be designed with security in mind. For example, IPv6 has IPsec support built in, but that might not be the best method of security for your organization. IPv4 also can make use of IPsec, and in that aspect can be just as secure as IPv6, but the support isn't built in, so you might choose to implement alternative security methods for IPv4. Many networks use both protocols, and though one is working in a secure manner, that doesn't mean the other protocol is protected. Remember to design both types of IP networks to address all security concerns, and test them thoroughly on multiple platforms.

Network Zones and Interconnections

When designing your network, think about all the pieces of the network and all the connections your network might make to other networks. Are you in charge of a single local area network? Or are you responsible for more than one local area network that perhaps form a wide area network? What kind of, and how many Internet connections do you have? Will you have servers that need to be accessed by users on the Internet? Is the cloud or virtualization involved? And will you need to share information with company employees who work from home or with other organizations, while securing that information from the average user on the Internet? The more interconnections and network zones that you have, the more security risk you are taking on. Keep this in mind as you read through the section.

LAN Versus WAN

A local area network, or LAN, is a group of networked computers contained in a small space such as a small office, a school, or one or two close-knit buildings. Generally, the computers in the LAN are all assigned private IP addresses and are behind a firewall. Although computers on a LAN do not have to connect to the Internet, they usually do, but do so via a router that acts as an IP proxy and employs NAT. (NAT is far more common on IPv4 networks, but not unheard of on

IPv6 networks.) It is important to secure computers on the LAN by placing them behind the router, assigning private IP addresses if necessary, and verifying that anti-malware programs are installed.

A wide area network, or WAN, is one or more LANs connected together. The big difference between a LAN and a WAN is that a WAN covers a larger geographic area. This implies that the services of a telecommunications or data communications provider are necessary. The security implications of a WAN are great; the more connections your network has, the more likely attacks will become. All connections should be monitored and firewalled if possible. Consider that there might be connections to other states or countries...and, to the biggest WAN of them all—the Internet.

Internet

The Internet is the worldwide interconnection of individual computers and computer networks. Because it is a public arena, anyone on the Internet can possibly be a target, or an attacker. All types of sessions on the Internet should be protected at all times. For example, voice calls should be done within a protected VoIP system; data sessions should be protected by being run within a virtual private network; and so on. Individual computers should be protected by firewalls and anti-malware programs. Networks should be protected by firewalls as well. But what about systems that need to access the LAN and also need to be accessed by clients on the Internet? Well, one option is to create an area that is not quite the LAN, and not quite the Internet; this is a demilitarized zone, or DMZ.

Demilitarized Zone (DMZ)

In computer security, a **demilitarized zone (DMZ)** is a special area of the network (sometimes loosely referred to as a subnetwork) that houses servers that host information accessed by clients or other networks on the Internet. Some of these servers might include web, FTP, mail, and database computers. It's important that each server is configured with the proper default gateway IP address so that users on the Internet can access it. These servers might also be accessible to clients on the LAN in addition to serving the Internet. There are several ways to set up a DMZ; a common way is the **3-leg perimeter** DMZ, as shown in Figure 6-2. Notice the third "leg" that branches off the firewall to the right. This leads to a special switch that has WWW and FTP servers connected to it. Also note that the DMZ is on a different IP network than the LAN, although both the LAN and DMZ are private IP network numbers.

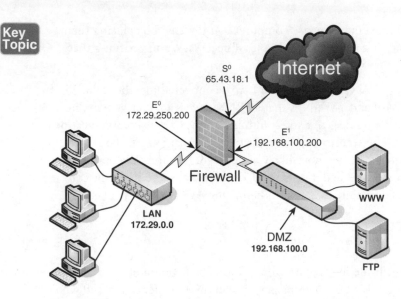

Figure 6-2   3-Leg Perimeter DMZ

The firewall can (and usually will) be configured in a secure fashion on the DMZ connection (192.168.100.200) and an even more secure fashion on the LAN connection (172.29.250.200). The DMZ connection in Figure 6-2 needs to have only inbound ports 80 (WWW) and 21 (FTP) open; all other ports can be closed, thus filtering inbound traffic. The LAN connection can be completely shielded on the inbound side. Although DMZs can be created logically, they are most often found as physical implementations. There are several other implementations of a DMZ. For example, a DMZ can be set up with two firewalls that surround it, also known as a **back-to-back perimeter** network configuration; in this case the DMZ would be located between the LAN and the Internet. A DMZ might also be set up within a router, especially in small organizations that use basic SOHO router devices. It all depends on the network architecture and security concerns of the organization.

Intranets and Extranets

Intranets and extranets are implemented so that a company (or companies) can share its data using all the features and benefits of the Internet, while keeping that data secure within the organization, select organizations, and specific users. In the case of an intranet, only one company is involved; it could be as simple as an internal company website, or a more advanced architecture of servers, operational systems, and networks that deploy tools, applications, and, of course, data. In the case of an extranet, multiple companies can be involved, or an organization can opt to share its data and resources with users who are not part of the organization(s). This sharing is done via the Internet, but again, is secured so that only particular people and organizations can connect.

Whether you have an intranet or an extranet, security is a major concern. Proper authentication schemes should be implemented to ensure that only the appropriate users can access data and resources. Only certain types of information should be stored on an intranet or extranet. Confidential, secret, and top secret information should not be hosted within an intranet or extranet. Finally, the deployment of a firewall(s) should be thoroughly planned out in advance. An example of a company that hosts an intranet and an extranet is shown in Figure 6-3. Note that data commuters from Company A can access the intranet because they work for the company. Also note that Company B can access the extranet, but not the intranet. In this example, the company (Company A) has created two DMZs, one for its intranet and one for its extranet. Of course, it is possible to set this up using only one DMZ, but the access control lists on the firewall and other devices would have to be planned and monitored more carefully. If possible, separating the data into two distinct physical locations will have several benefits, namely, being more secure; although, it will cost more money to do so. This all depends on the acceptable risk level of the organization and its budget!

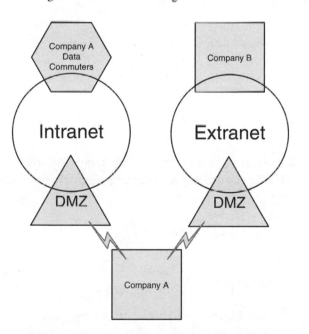

Figure 6-3   Example of an Intranet and an Extranet

Network Access Control (NAC)

In this chapter, we have mentioned several types of networking technologies and design elements. But whichever you choose to use, it needs to be controlled in a secure fashion. **Network access control (NAC)** does this by setting the rules by which connections to a network are governed. Computers attempting to connect to a network are denied access unless they comply with rules pertaining to levels of antivirus protection, system updates, and so on...effectively weeding out those who would perpetuate malicious attacks. The client computer continues to be denied until it has been properly updated, which in some cases can be taken care of by the NAC solution automatically. This often requires some kind of preinstalled software (an agent) on the client computer, or the computer is scanned by the NAC solution remotely—which would be known as agentless. When agents are used, there is usually a posture or health check at the host or the endpoint. Often this is tied into role-based access. There are two types of agents: persistent and dissolvable. Persistent agents are installed on the target device and can be used over and over again. Dissolvable agents provide for one-time authentication and are then deleted. Agentless NAC systems are also available but they offer less control and fewer inspection capabilities.

Some companies (such as Cisco) offer hardware-based NAC solutions, whereas other organizations offer paid software-based NAC solutions and free ones such as PacketFence (https://packetfence.org), which is open source.

The IEEE 802.1X standard, known as port-based network access control, or PNAC, is a basic form of NAC that enables the establishment of authenticated point-to-point connections, but NAC has grown to include software; 802.1X is now considered a subset of NAC. See the section "Authentication Models and Components" in Chapter 10 for more information about IEEE 802.1X.

Subnetting

Subnetting is the act of creating subnetworks logically through the manipulation of IP addresses. These subnetworks are distinct portions of a single IP network.

Subnetting is implemented for a few reasons:

- It increases security by compartmentalizing the network.
- It is a more efficient use of IP address space.
- It reduces broadcast traffic and collisions.

To illustrate the first bullet point, examine Figure 6-4. This shows a simple diagram of two subnets within the 192.168.50.0 IPv4 network using the subnet mask 255.255.255.240; this would also be known as 192.168.50.0/28 in CIDR notation (covered shortly). You can see that the subnets are divided; this implies that traffic is isolated—it cannot travel from one subnet to another without a route set up specifically for that purpose. So, computers within Subnet ID 2 can communicate with each other by default, and computers within Subnet ID 8 can communicate with each other, but computers on Subnet 2 *cannot* communicate with computers on Subnet 8, and vice versa.

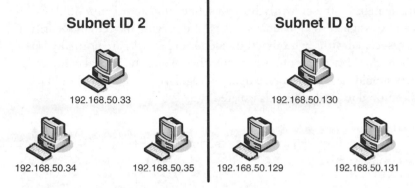

Subnet ID 2

192.168.50.33

192.168.50.34   192.168.50.35

Subnet ID 8

192.168.50.130

192.168.50.129   192.168.50.131

Figure 6-4   Example of a Subnetted Network

As a security precaution, using subnet 0 (zero) is discouraged, and instead a network administrator should start with subnet 1, which in the preceding example would be 192.168.50.16. This avoids any possible confusion regarding the actual network number (192.168.50.0) and its subnets. If a network administrator were to use the first subnet and then inadvertently use a default subnet mask (such as 255.255.255.0), this would create a security vulnerability—the hosts on that subnet would have access to more of the network than they normally should. This kind of mistake is common when using the first subnet and is the main reason it is discouraged.

Another common example of an organization subnetting its network is to take what would normally be a Class A network (with the 255.0.0.0 subnet mask) and make it classless by changing the subnet mask to, for example, 255.255.255.224. This is called *classless interdomain routing*, or CIDR, which is based on variable-length subnet masking (VLSM). For instance, we could use 10.7.7.0 as the network number. Normally, it would simply be referred to as the 10 network if it was Class A. But the subnet mask 255.255.255.224 makes it *function* as a subnetted Class C network, which effectively makes it classless. In CIDR notation this would be written out as 10.7.7.0/27, because there are 27 masked bits in the subnet mask. The subnet mask's "224" is the key. When we calculate this, we find that we can have 30 usable hosts per subnet on the 10.7.7.0 network. The first range of hosts would be 10.7.7.1– 10.7.7.30, the second range would be 10.7.7.33–10.7.7.62, and so on. A host with the IP address 10.7.7.38 would not be able to communicate (by default) with a host using the IP address 10.7.7.15 because they are on two separate subnets.

NOTE   You can check the preceding statements by searching for and using a free online *subnetting calculator*. I highly recommend you practice this!

When compartmentalizing the network through subnetting, an organization's departments can be assigned to individual subnets, and varying degrees of security policies can be associated with each subnet. Incidents and attacks are normally isolated to the subnet that they occur on. Any router that makes the logical connections for subnets should have its firmware updated regularly, and traffic should be occasionally monitored to verify that it is isolated.

NOTE   For a short primer about subnetting, see the following link: www.davidlprowse.com/articles/?p=1185

Virtual Local Area Network (VLAN)

A VLAN is implemented to segment the network, reduce collisions, organize the network, boost performance, and, hopefully, increase security. A device such as a switch can control the VLAN. Like subnetting, a VLAN compartmentalizes the network and can isolate traffic. But unlike subnetting, a VLAN can be set up in a physical manner; an example of this would be the port-based VLAN, as shown in Figure 6-5. In this example, each group of computers such as Classroom 1 has its own VLAN; however, computers in the VLAN can be located anywhere on the *physical* network. For example, Staff computers could be located in several physical areas in the building, but regardless of where they are located, they are associated with the Staff VLAN because of the physical port they connect to. Due to this, it is important to place physical network jacks in secure locations for VLANs that have access to confidential data.

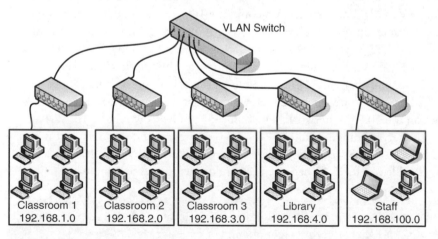

Figure 6-5   Example of a VLAN

There are also logical types of VLANs, such as the protocol-based VLAN and the MAC address–based VLAN, that have a whole separate set of security precautions, but those precautions go beyond the scope of the CompTIA Security+ exam.

The most common standard associated with VLANs is IEEE 802.1Q, which modifies Ethernet frames by "tagging" them with the appropriate VLAN information, based on which VLAN the Ethernet frame should be directed to.

VLANs restrict access to network resources, but this can be bypassed through the use of **VLAN hopping**. VLAN hopping can be divided into two categories, as shown in Table 6-4.

Key Topic

Table 6-4   Types of VLAN Hopping

VLAN Hopping Method	How It Works	How to Defend
Switch spoofing	The attacking computer must be capable of speaking the tagging and trunking protocols used by the VLAN trunking switch to imitate the switch. If successful, traffic for one or more VLANs is then accessible to the attacking computer.	Put unplugged ports on the switch into an unused VLAN. Statically configure the switch ports in charge of passing tagged frames to be trunks and to explicitly forward specific tags. Disable Dynamic Trunking Protocol (DTP) if necessary. Avoid using default VLAN names such as VLAN or VLAN1.
Double tagging	In a double-tagging attack, an attacking host attaches two VLAN tags to the frames it transmits. The first, proper header is stripped off by the first switch the frame encounters, and the frame is then forwarded. The second, false header is then visible to the second switch that the frame encounters.	Upgrade firmware or software. Pick an unused VLAN as the default VLAN (also known as a native VLAN) for all trunks, and do not use it for any other intent. Consider redesigning the VLAN if multiple 802.1Q switches are used.

MAC flooding attacks can also be perpetuated on a VLAN, but because the flood of packets will be constrained to an individual VLAN, VLAN hopping will not be possible as a result of a MAC flood.

VLANs can also be the victims of ARP attacks, brute-force attacks, spanning-tree attacks, and other attacks, all of which we discuss in later chapters.

> **NOTE**   So far, the virtual LANs we have discussed use physical switches to make the connectivity between computers. However, in a completely virtualized environment—one where all of the operating systems are virtual—it is possible to use a virtual switch to connect the systems together. In this case, everything is virtual, from the servers to the network infrastructure. It is often used in testing environments, and gives new meaning to the term "virtual LAN."

Telephony

Telephony aims at providing voice communication for your users and requires various equipment to accomplish this goal. Older devices such as modems can be the victim of an attack, but nowadays computers are also heavily involved in telephony; this is known as computer telephony integration, or CTI. What does this mean for you, the security administrator? Well, for one thing, special telephones and servers require particular security, for a whole new level of attacks and ways of targeting this equipment. The telephone, regardless of what type, is still one of the primary communication methods and therefore needs to be up and running all the time.

Modems

In networking environments such as a network operations center (NOC) or server room, modems are still used by network administrators to connect to servers and networking equipment via dial-up lines. Often, this is a redundant, worst-case scenario implementation—sometimes, it is the default way for admins to access and configure their networking equipment. In some cases, this is done without any authentication, and to make matters worse, sometimes admins use Telnet to configure their equipment. Of course, this is insecure, to say the least. A modem can be the victim of **war-dialing**, which is the act of scanning telephone numbers by dialing them one at a time. Computers usually pick up on the first ring, and the war-dialing system makes a note of that and adds that number to the list. Besides the obvious social annoyance this could create, a hacker would then use the list to attempt to access computer networks. Now think back to the system that has no authentication scheme in place!

So to protect modem connections, a network admin should 1) use the callback feature in the modem software and set it to call the person back at a preset phone number; 2) use some type of username/password authentication scheme and select only strong passwords because war-dialers will most likely try password guessing; and 3) use dial-up modems sparingly, only in secure locations, and try to keep the modem's phone number secret. And by the way, a quick word on Telnet: it is not secure and should be substituted with SSH or another, more secure way of configuring a remote device.

For the typical user who still uses a modem on a client computer, set the modem to not answer incoming calls, and be sure not to use any remote control software on the system that houses the modem. Finally, consider upgrading to a faster and more secure Internet access solution!

PBX Equipment

A private branch exchange (PBX) makes all of an organization's internal phone connections and also provides connectivity to the public switched telephone network (PSTN). Originally, PBXs were simple devices, but as time progressed they incorporated many new features and along the way became more of a security concern. For example, an attacker might attempt to exploit a PBX to obtain free long distance service or to employ social engineering to obtain information from people at the organization that owns the PBX. To secure a standard PBX, make sure it is in a secure room (server room, locked wiring closet, and so on); usually it should be mounted to the wall but could be fixed to the floor as well. Also, change passwords regularly, and only allow authorized maintenance; log any authorized maintenance done as well. PBX computers often have a remote port (basically a built-in modem or other device) for monitoring and maintenance; ensure that this port is not exploited and that only authorized personnel know how to access it. Today's PBX devices might act as computer-telephony integration servers on the network, and/or might incorporate VoIP, which is also known as an IP-PBX.

VoIP

Voice over Internet Protocol (VoIP) is a broad term that deals with the transmission of voice data over IP networks such as the Internet. It is used by organizations and in homes. In an organization, IP phones can be the victim of attacks much like individual computers can. In addition, VoIP servers can be exploited the same way that other servers can; for example, by way of denial-of-service attacks. When securing VoIP servers—also known as VoIP gateways or *media gateways*—security administrators should implement many of the same precautions that they would make for more traditional servers, such as file servers and FTP servers. Some VoIP solutions, especially for home use, use the Session Initiation Protocol (SIP), which can be exploited by man-in-the-middle (MITM) attacks. To help reduce risk, VoIP systems should be updated regularly and use encryption and an authentication scheme.

Another concern with VoIP is *availability*. If there are multiple types of network traffic competing for bandwidth, you could use the Quality of Service (QoS) configuration to prioritize traffic on a router, and to ultimately increase the availability of IP telephony. We could talk about VoIP for days, but luckily for you, the exam requires that you have only a basic understanding of what VoIP is and how to protect it in a general sense. Most of the ways that you will mitigate risk on a VoIP system are the same as you would for other server systems, and these are covered later in this chapter as well as in Chapter 7.

Cloud Security and Server Defense

Historically, the "cloud" was just a name for the Internet—anything beyond your network that you as a user couldn't see. Technically speaking, the cloud was the area of the telephone company's infrastructure—it was everything between one organization's demarcation point and the demarcation point of another organization. It included central offices, switching offices, telephone poles, circuit switching devices, packet assemblers/disassemblers (PADs), packet switching exchanges (PSEs), and so on. In fact, all these things, and much more, are still part of the "cloud," in the technical sense. Back in the day, this term was used only by telecommunications professionals and network engineers.

Today, the "cloud" has a somewhat different meaning. Almost everyone has heard of it and probably used it to some extent. It is used heavily in marketing, and the meaning is less technical and more service-oriented than it used to be. It takes the place of most intranets and extranets that had existed for decades before its emergence.

We talked about basic computer protection in Chapter 2, "Computer Systems Security Part I," the hardening of operating systems (including virtual operating systems) in Chapter 4, "OS Hardening and Virtualization," and secure programming in Chapter 5, "Application Security." In this section, we'll build on those knowledge sets and describe some server defense. I place servers in this section of the chapter because they are at the heart of networking. Servers control the sending and receiving of all kinds of data over the network, including FTP and websites, e-mail and text messaging, and data stored as single files and in database format. A great many of these servers are now in the cloud, with more moving there every day. And the cloud, however an organization connects to it, is all about networking. So, the cloud, virtualization, and servers in general are all thoroughly intertwined.

Cloud Computing

Cloud computing can be defined as a way of offering on-demand services that extend the capabilities of a person's computer or an organization's network. These might be free services, such as personal browser-based e-mail from various providers, or they could be offered on a pay-per-use basis, such as services that offer data access, data storage, infrastructure, and online gaming. A network connection of some sort is required to make the connection to the "cloud" and gain access to these services in real time.

Some of the benefits to an organization using cloud-based services include lowered cost, less administration and maintenance, more reliability, increased scalability, and possible increased performance. A basic example of a cloud-based service would be browser-based e-mail. A small business with few employees definitely needs e-mail, but it can't afford the costs of an e-mail server and perhaps does not want to have its own hosted domain and the costs and work that go along with that. By connecting to a free web browser–based service, the small business can obtain near unlimited e-mail, contacts, and calendar solutions. But, there is no administrative control, and some security concerns, which we discuss in just a little bit.

Cloud computing services are generally broken down into several categories of services:

- **Software as a service (SaaS):** The most commonly used and recognized of the three categories, SaaS is when users access applications over the Internet that are provided by a third party. The applications need not be installed on the local computer. In many cases these applications are run within a web browser; in other cases the user connects with screen sharing programs or remote desktop programs. A common example of this is webmail.

> **NOTE**   Often compared to SaaS is the application service provider (ASP) model. SaaS typically offers a generalized service to many users. However, an ASP typically delivers a service (perhaps a single application) to a small number of users.

- **Infrastructure as a service (IaaS):** A service that offers computer networking, storage, load balancing, routing, and VM hosting. More and more organizations are seeing the benefits of offloading some of their networking infrastructure to the cloud.

- **Platform as a service (PaaS):** A service that provides various software solutions to organizations, especially the ability to develop applications in a virtual environment without the cost or administration of a physical platform. PaaS is used for easy-to-configure operating systems and on-demand computing. Often, this utilizes IaaS as well for an underlying infrastructure to the platform. Cloud-based virtual desktop environments (VDEs) and virtual desktop infrastructures (VDIs) are often considered to be part of this service, but can be part of IaaS as well.

- **Security as a service (SECaaS):** A service where a large service provider integrates its security services into the company/customer's existing infrastructure. The concept is that the service provider can provide the security more efficiently and more cost effectively than a company can, especially if it has a limited IT staff or budget. The Cloud Security Alliance (CSA) defines various categories to help businesses implement and understand SECaaS, including: encryption, data loss prevention (DLP), continuous monitoring, business continuity and disaster recovery (BCDR), vulnerability scanning, and much more.

> **NOTE**   Periodically, new services will arrive, such as monitoring as a service (MaaS)—a framework that facilitates the deployment of monitoring within the cloud in a continuous fashion. There are many types of cloud-based services. If they don't fall into the previous list, then they will often fall under the category "anything as a service" (XaaS).

A cloud service provider (CSP) might offer one or more of these services. Between 2005 and 2010, cloud services were slow to be adopted by organizations. One of the reasons for this is the inherent security issues that present themselves when an organization relegates its software, platforms, and especially infrastructure to a CSP. After 2010, however, implementation of cloud services has grown dramatically, with most companies either already running cloud services or in the planning stages. Similar to the CSP is the managed service provider (MSP), which can deliver network, application, system, and management services using a pay-as-you-go model.

There are different types of clouds used by organizations: public, private hybrid, and community. Let's discuss each briefly.

- **Public cloud:** When a service provider offers applications and storage space to the general public over the Internet. A couple of examples of this include free, web-based e-mail services, and pay-as-you-go business-class services. The main benefits of this include low (or zero) cost and scalability. Providers of public cloud space include Google, Rackspace, and Amazon.

- **Private cloud:** Designed for a particular organization in mind. The security administrator has more control over the data and infrastructure. A limited number of people have access to the cloud, and they are usually located behind a firewall of some sort in order to gain access to the private cloud. Resources might be provided by a third party, or could come from the security administrator's server room or data center.

- **Hybrid cloud:** A mixture of public and private clouds. Dedicated servers located within the organization and cloud servers from a third party are used together to form the collective network. In these hybrid scenarios, confidential data is usually kept in-house.

- **Community cloud:** Another mix of public and private, but one where multiple organizations can share the public portion. Community clouds appeal to organizations that usually have a common form of computing and storing of data.

The type of cloud an organization uses will be dictated by its budget, the level of security it requires, and the amount of manpower (or lack thereof) it has to administer its resources. While a private cloud can be very appealing, it is often beyond the ability of an organization, forcing that organization to seek the public or community-based cloud. However, it doesn't matter what type of cloud is used. Resources still have to be secured by someone, and you'll have a hand in that security one way or the other.

Cloud Security

Cloud security hinges on the level of control a security administrator retains and the types of security controls the admin implements. When an organization makes a decision to use cloud computing, probably the most important security control concern to administrators is the loss of physical control of the organization's data. A more in-depth list of cloud computing security concerns includes lack of privacy, lack of accountability, improper authentication, lack of administrative control, data sensitivity and integrity problems, data segregation issues, location of data and data recovery problems, malicious insider attack, bug exploitation, lack of investigative support when there is a problem, and finally, questionable long-term viability. In general, everything that you worry about for your local network and computers! Let's also mention that cloud service providers can be abused as well—attackers often attempt to use providers' infrastructure to launch powerful attacks.

Solutions to these security issues include the following:

- **Complex passwords:** Strong passwords are beyond important; they are critical, as I will mention many times in this text. As of the writing of this book, accepted password schemes include the following:

  — **For general security:** 10 characters minimum, including at least one capital letter, one number, and one special character

  — **For confidential data:** 15 characters minimum, including a minimum two each of capital letters, numbers, and special characters

  When it comes to the cloud, a security administrator might just opt to use the second option for every type of cloud. The reasoning is that public clouds can be insecure (you just don't know), and private clouds will most likely house the most confidential data. To enforce the type of passwords you want your users to choose, a strong server-based policy is recommended.

- **Powerful authentication methods:** Passwords are all well and good, but how the person is authenticated will prove to be just as important. Multifactor authentication can offer a certain amount of defense in depth. In this scenario, if one form of authentication is compromised, the other works as a backup.

For example, in addition to a password, a person might be asked for biometric confirmation such as a thumbprint or voice authorization, for an additional PIN, or to swipe a smart card. Multifactor authentication may or may not be physically possible, depending on the cloud environment being used, but if at all possible, it should be considered.

■ **Strong cloud data access policies:** We're talking the who, what, and when. When it comes to public clouds especially, you should specifically define which users have access, exactly which resources they have access to, and when they are allowed to access those resources. Configure strong passwords and consider two-factor authentication. Configure policies from servers that govern the users; for example, use Group Policy objects on a Windows Server domain controller. Audit any and all connected devices and apps. Consider storing different types of data with different services—some services do better with media files, for example. Remember that cloud storage is not backup. Approach the backing up of data as a separate procedure.

■ **Encryption:** Encryption of individual data files, whole disk encryption, digitally signed virtual machine files...the list goes on. Perhaps the most important is a robust public key infrastructure (PKI), which we discuss further in Chapter 15, "PKI and Encryption Protocols." That is because many users will access data through a web browser.

■ **Standardization of programming:** The way applications are planned, designed, programmed, and run on the cloud should all be standardized from one platform to the next, and from one programmer to the next. Most important is standardized testing in the form of input validation, fuzzing, and white-, gray-, or black-box testing.

■ **Protection of all the data!:** This includes storage area networks (SANs), general cloud storage, and the handling of big data (for example, astronomical data). When data is stored in multiple locations, it is easy for some to slip through the cracks. Detailed documentation of what is stored where (and how it is secured) should be kept and updated periodically. As a top-notch security admin, you don't want your data to be tampered with. So, implementing some cloud-based security controls can be very helpful. For example, consider the following: deterrent controls (prevent the tampering of data), preventive controls (increase the security strength of a system that houses data), corrective controls (reduce the effects of data tampering that has occurred), and detective controls (detect attacks in real time, and have a defense plan that can be immediately carried out).

NOTE We'll discuss security controls in more depth in Chapter 12, "Vulnerability and Risk Assessment."

What else are we trying to protect here? We're concerned with protecting the identity and privacy of our users (especially executives because they are high-profile targets). We need to secure the privacy of credit card numbers and other super-confidential information. We want to secure physical servers that are part of our server room or data center, because they might be part of our private cloud. We desire protection of our applications with testing and acceptance procedures. (Keep in mind that these things all need to be done within contractual obligations with any third-party cloud providers.) And finally, we're interested in promoting the availability of our data. After all of our security controls and methods have been implemented, we might find that we have locked out more people than first intended. So, our design plan should contain details that will allow for available data, but in a secure manner.

Customers considering using cloud computing services should ask for transparency—or detailed information about the provider's security. The provider must be in compliance with the organization's security policies; otherwise, the data and software in the cloud becomes far less secure than the data and software within the customer's own network. This concept, and most of the concepts in the first half of this chapter, should be considered when planning whether to have data, systems, and infrastructure contained on-premises, in a hosted environment, on the cloud, or a mix of those. If there is a mix of on-premises infrastructure and cloud-provider infrastructure, a company might consider a cloud access security broker (CASB)—a software tool or service that acts as the gatekeeper between the two, allowing the company to extend the reach of its security policies beyond its internal infrastructure.

Other "Cloud"-based Concerns

There are other technologies to watch out for that are loosely connected with what we call cloud technologies. One example is social media. Social media environments can include websites as well as special applications that are loaded directly on to the computer (mobile or desktop), among other ways to connect, both legitimate and illegitimate. People share the darndest things on social media websites, which can easily compromise the security of employees and data. The point? There are several ways to access social media platforms, and it can be difficult for a security administrator to find every website, application, service, and port that is used by social media. In cases such as these, an admin might consider more whitelisting of applications, so that users are better locked down.

Another thing to watch for is P2P networks. File sharing, gaming, media streaming, and all the world is apparently available to a user—if the user knows where to look. However, P2P often comes with a price: malware and potential system infiltration. By the latter I mean that computers can become unwilling participants in the sharing of data on a P2P network. This is one example in which the cloud invades client computers, often without the user's consent. Access to file sharing, P2P, and torrents also needs a permanent "padlock."

Then there's the darknet. Where Batman stores his data... No, a darknet is another type of P2P (often referred to as an F2F, meaning friends to friends) that creates connections between trusted peers (unlike most other P2Ps), but uses nonstandard ports and protocols. This makes it a bit more difficult to detect. Darknets are often the safe haven of illegal activities because they are designed specifically to resist surveillance. Computers that are part of an admin's network, and more often, virtual machines in the admin's cloud, can be part of these darknets, and can easily go undetected by the admin. In some cases, an employee of the organization (or an employee of the cloud provider) might have configured some cloud-based resources to join a darknet. This can have devastating legal consequences if illegal activities are traced to your organization. Thorough checks of cloud-based resources can help to prevent this. Also, screening of employees, careful inspection of service-level agreements with cloud providers, and the use of third-party IT auditors can avoid the possibility of darknet connectivity, P2P links, and improper use of social media.

Server Defense

Now we come down to it. Servers are the cornerstone of data. They store it, transfer it, archive it, and allow or disallow access to it. They need super-fast network connections that are monitored and baselined regularly. They require an admin to configure policies, check logs, and perform audits frequently. They exist in networks both large and small, within public and private clouds, and are often present in virtual fashion. What it all comes down to is that servers contain the data and the services that everyone relies on. So, they are effectively the most important things to secure on your network.

Let's break down five types of servers that are of great importance (in no particular order), and talk about some of the threats and vulnerabilities to those servers, and ways to protect them.

File Servers

File server computers store, transfer, migrate, synchronize, and archive files. Really any computer can act as a file server of sorts, but examples of actual server software include Microsoft Windows Server, macOS/OS X Server, and the various types of

Linux server versions (for example, Ubuntu Server or Red Hat Server), not to mention Unix. File servers are vulnerable to the same types of attacks and malware that typical desktop computers are. To secure file servers (and the rest of the servers on this list), employ hardening, updating, anti-malware applications, software-based firewalls, hardware-based intrusion detection systems (HIDSs), and encryption, and be sure to monitor the server regularly.

Network Controllers

A network controller is a server that acts as a central repository of user accounts and computer accounts on the network. All users log in to this server. An example of this would be a Windows Server system that has been promoted to a domain controller (runs Active Directory). In addition to the attacks mentioned for file servers, a domain controller can be the victim of LDAP injection. It also has Kerberos vulnerabilities, which can ultimately result in privilege escalation or spoofing. As mentioned in Chapter 5, LDAP injection can be prevented with proper input validation. But in the specific case of a Windows domain controller, really the only way to keep it protected (aside from the preventive measures mentioned for file servers) is to install specific security update hot patches for the OS, even if the latest service pack has been installed. This also applies to Kerberos vulnerabilities.

> **NOTE** An example of a Microsoft Security Bulletin addressing vulnerabilities in Kerberos can be found at the following link. You can see that even with the latest update, a server can still be vulnerable.
>
> https://technet.microsoft.com/library/security/ms11-013

E-mail Servers

E-mail servers are part of the message server family. When we make reference to a message server, we mean any server that deals with e-mail, faxing, texting, chatting, and so on. But for this section we'll concentrate strictly on the e-mail server. The most common of these is Microsoft Exchange. An Exchange Server might run POP3, SMTP, and IMAP, and allow for Outlook web-based connections. That's a lot of protocols and ports running. So, it's not surprising to hear some Exchange admins confess that running an e-mail server can be difficult at times, particularly because it is vulnerable to XSS attacks, overflows, DoS/DDoS attacks, SMTP memory exploits, directory traversal attacks, and of course spam. Bottom line, it has to be patched...a lot.

An admin needs to keep on top of the latest vulnerabilities and attacks, and possibly be prepared to shut down or quarantine an e-mail server at a moment's notice. New attacks and exploits are constantly surfacing because e-mail servers are a common and big target with a large attack surface. For spam, a hardware-based spam filter is most effective (such as one from Barracuda), but software-based filters can also help. To protect the integrity and confidentiality of e-mail-based data, an admin should consider DLP and encryption. Security could also come in the form of secure POP3 and secure SMTP, and we'll talk more about the specific secure e-mail protocols in Chapter 7. But also, security can come as encrypted SSL/TLS connections, security posture assessment (SPA), secure VPNs, and other encryption types, especially for web-based connections. Web-based connections can be particularly insecure—great care must be taken to secure these connections. For example, push notification services for mobile devices are quite common. While TLS is normally used as a secure channel for the e-mail connection, text and metadata can at times be sent as clear text. A solution to this is for the operating system to use a symmetrical key to encrypt the data payload. Vendors may or may not do this, so it is up to the e-mail admin to incorporate this added layer of security, or at least verify that push e-mail providers are implementing it.

Thinking a little outside of the box, an admin could consider moving away from Microsoft (which is the victim of the most attacks) and toward a Linux solution such as the Java-based SMTP server built into Apache, or with a third-party tool such as Zimbra (or one of many others). These solutions are not foolproof, and still need to be updated, but it is a well-known fact that historically Linux has not been attacked as often as Microsoft (in general), though the difference between the two in the number of attacks experienced has shrunk considerably since the turn of the millennium.

Web Servers

The web server could be the most commonly attacked server of them all. Examples of web servers include Microsoft's Internet Information Services (IIS), Apache HTTP Server (Linux), lighttpd (FreeBSD), Oracle iPlanet Web Server (Oracle), and iPlanet's predecessor Sun Java System Web Server (Sun Microsystems). Web servers in general can be the victim of DoS attacks, overflows, XSS and XSRF, remote code execution, and various attacks that make use of backdoors. For example, in IIS, if basic authentication is enabled, a backdoor could be created, and attackers could ultimately bypass access restrictions. An IIS admin must keep up to date with the latest vulnerabilities by reading Microsoft Security Bulletins, such as this one which addresses possible information disclosure: https://technet.microsoft.com/library/security/ms12-073.

In general, a security administrator should keep up to date with **Common Vulnerabilities and Exposures (CVE)** as maintained by MITRE (http://cve.mitre.org/). The latest CVE listings for applications and operating systems can be found there and at several other websites.

Aside from the usual programmatic solutions to vulnerabilities such as XSS (discussed in Chapter 5), and standard updating and hot patching, a security admin might consider adding and configuring a hardware-based firewall from Cisco, Juniper, Check Point, or other similar company. And, of course, HTTPS (be it SSL or, better yet, TLS) can be beneficial if the scenario calls for it. Once a server is secured, you can prove the relative security of the system to users by using an automated vulnerability scanning program (such as Netcraft) that leaves a little image on the web pages that states whether or not the site is secure and when it was scanned or audited.

Apache can be the casualty of many attacks as well, including privilege escalation, code injection, and exploits to the proxy portion of the software. PHP forms and the PHP engine could act as gateways to the Apache web server. Patches to known CVEs should be applied ASAP.

NOTE   A list of CVEs to Apache HTTP Server (and the corresponding updates) can be found at the following link: http://httpd.apache.org/security/.

When it comes to Apache web servers, security admins have to watch out for the web server attack called Darkleech. This takes the form of a malicious Apache module (specifically an injected HTML iframe tag within a PHP file). If loaded on a compromised Apache web server, it can initiate all kinds of attacks and deliver various payloads of malware and ransomware. Or, it could redirect a user to another site that contains an exploit kit such as the Blackhole exploit kit mentioned in Chapter 2. Though Darkleech is not limited to Apache, the bulk of Darkleech-infected sites have been Apache-based.

NOTE   So much for Microsoft being less targeted than Linux. As time moves forward, it seems that no platform is safe. A word to the wise—don't rely on any particular technology because of a reputation, and be sure to update and patch every technology you use.

As far as combating Darkleech, a webmaster can attempt to query the system for PHP files stored in folders with suspiciously long hexadecimal names. If convenient for the organization, all iframes can be filtered out. And, of course, the Apache server should be updated as soon as possible, and if necessary, taken offline while it is repaired. In many cases, this type of web server attack is very hard to detect, and sometimes the only recourse is to rebuild the server (or virtual server image) that hosts the Apache server.

> **NOTE**   Another tool that some attackers use is archive.org. This website takes snapshots of many websites over time and stores them. They are accessible to anyone, and can give attackers an idea of older (and possibly less secure) pages and scripts that used to run on a web server. It could be that these files and scripts are still located on the web server even though they are no longer used. This is a vulnerability that security admins should be aware of. Strongly consider removing older unused files and scripts from web servers.

FTP Server

An FTP server can be used to provide basic file access publicly or privately. Examples of FTP servers include the FTP server built into IIS, the Apache FtpServer, and other third-party offerings such as FileZilla Server and Pure-FTPd.

The standard, default FTP server is pretty insecure. It uses well-known ports (20 and 21), doesn't use encryption by default, and has basic username/password authentication. As a result, FTP servers are often the victims of many types of attacks. Examples include bounce attacks—when a person attempts to hijack the FTP service to scan other computers; buffer overflow attempts—when an attacker tries to send an extremely long username (or password or filename) to trigger the overflow; and attacks on the anonymous account (if utilized).

If the files to be stored on the FTP server are at all confidential, the security administrator should consider additional security. This can be done by incorporating FTP software that utilizes secure file transfer protocols such as FTPS or SFTP. Additional security can be provided by using FTP software that uses dynamic assignment of data ports, instead of using port 20 every time. We'll discuss more about ports and secure protocols in Chapter 7. Encryption can prevent most attackers from reading the data files, even if they are able to get access to them. Of course, if not a public FTP, the anonymous account should be disabled.

But there are other, more sinister attacks lurking, ones that work in conjunction with the web server, which is often on the same computer, or part of the same software suite—for instance, the web shell. There are plenty of variants of the web shell, but we'll detail its basic function. The web shell is a program that is installed on a web server by an attacker, and is used to remotely access and reconfigure the server without the owner's consent.

Web shells are remote access Trojans (RATs), but are also referred to as backdoors, since they offer an alternative way of accessing the website for the attacker. The reason I place the web shell attack here in the FTP section is because it is usually the FTP server that contains the real vulnerability—weak passwords. Once an attacker figures out an administrator password of the FTP server (often through brute-force attempts), the attacker can easily install the web shell, and effectively do anything desired to that web server (and/or the FTP server). It seems like a house of cards, and in a way, it is.

How can we prevent this from happening? First, increase the password security and change the passwords of all administrator accounts. Second, eliminate any unnecessary accounts, especially any superfluous admin accounts and the dreaded anonymous account. Next, strongly consider separating the FTP server and web server to two different computers or virtual machines. Finally, set up automated scans for web shell scripts (usually PHP files, lo and behold), or have the web server provider do so. If the provider doesn't offer that kind of scanning, use a different provider. If a web shell attack is accomplished successfully on a server, the security admin must at the very least search for and delete the original RAT files, and at worst re-image the system and restore from backup. This latter option is often necessary if the attacker has had some time to compromise the server. Some organizations have policies that state servers must be re-imaged if they are compromised in any way, shape, or form. It's a way of starting anew with a clean slate, but it means a lot of configuring for the admin. But again, the overall concern here is the complexity of, and the frequency of changing, the password.

That's the short list of servers. But there are plenty of others you need to be cognizant of, including: DNS servers (which we cover in Chapter 7), application servers, virtualization servers, firewall/proxy servers, database servers, print servers, remote connectivity servers such as RRAS and VPN (which we will discuss more in Chapter 10), and computer telephony integration (CTI) servers. If you are in charge of securing a server, be sure to examine the CVEs and bulletins for that software, and be ready to hot-patch the system at a moment's notice. This means having an RDP, VNC, or other remote connection to that specific server ready to go on your desktop, so that you can access it quickly.

Chapter Summary

Designing a secure network is more than just setting up a Microsoft Visio document and dragging a firewall onto the LAN. This might have been good security planning in 1998, but today we need a plan that includes many layers of protection, allowing for defense in depth. For instance, today's networks require specially secured devices such as switches, routers, and telephony equipment. And those networks might need demilitarized zones (DMZs), intrusion prevention systems (IPSs), content filters, network access control (NAC), subnetting, virtual local area networks (VLANs), and of course...firewalls.

Keep in mind that some of these technologies might exist on, or be moved to, the cloud. This opens up Pandora's box when it comes to security. The security administrator needs to be sure not only that resources are secured properly, but also that the cloud provider is reputable, and will take care of its end of the safety of the organization's data and infrastructures.

An organization has a lot of choices when it comes to the cloud. Software as a service (SaaS), infrastructure as a service (IaaS), platform as a service (PaaS), and security as a service (SECaaS) are some of the main types of cloud offerings. SaaS is probably the most common, and is used to run web-based applications remotely. IaaS offloads the network infrastructure of a company to the cloud and utilizes virtual machines to store entire operating systems. PaaS enables organizations to develop applications in a powerful virtual environment without using internal resources. SECaaS incorporates security services to a corporate structure on a subscription basis in an efficient way that many small/midsize companies cannot provide. Some organizations will opt to use more than one of these solutions.

Once the type of cloud solution is selected, an organization must select whether its resources will be kept publicly, privately, or a mixture of the two (hybrid or community-oriented). This will be based on the budget and manpower of the organization in question, but each option has its own set of security concerns.

Besides loss of administrative power, an organization going to the cloud might encounter data integrity issues, availability issues, and, worst of all, potential loss of confidentiality. That's the entire CIA triad right there, so making use of the cloud should be approached warily. To reduce the chance of data breaches on the cloud, organizations make use of complex passwords, password and cloud data access policies, strong authentication methods, encryption, and protection of data and applications on several levels.

It's the servers that are of greatest concern. They are attacked the most often, as it is they who contain the data. The common victims are the e-mail servers, web servers, and FTP servers, because they are so readily accessible, and because of the plethora of ways they can be compromised. Patching systems is an excellent method of protection—and keeping up to date with the latest Common Vulnerabilities and Exposures (CVE) is the best way to know exactly what needs to be patched.

As a final remark, a good security administrator has to remember that *any* platform is susceptible to attack, in one form or another. Every single server and networking device, either on the local network or on the cloud, should be secured accordingly.

Chapter Review Activities

Use the features in this section to study and review the topics in this chapter.

Review Key Topics

Review the most important topics in the chapter, noted with the Key Topic icon in the outer margin of the page. Table 6-5 lists a reference of these key topics and the page number on which each is found.

Table 6-5   Key Topics for Chapter 6

Key Topic Element	Description	Page Number
Bulleted list	Description of switch security implications	176
Figure 6-1	Example of public and private IPv4 addresses	181
Figure 6-2	3-leg perimeter DMZ	184
Table 6-4	Types of VLAN hopping	189

Define Key Terms

Define the following key terms from this chapter, and check your answers in the glossary:

MAC flooding, CAM table, fail-open mode, MAC spoofing, Spanning Tree Protocol (STP), network address translation, port address translation, static NAT, one-to-one mapping, demilitarized zone (DMZ), 3-leg perimeter, back-to-back perimeter, network access control (NAC), VLAN hopping, war-dialing, cloud computing, software as a service (SaaS), infrastructure as a service (IaaS), platform as a service (PaaS), security as a service (SECaaS), Common Vulnerabilities and Exposures (CVE)

Complete the Real-World Scenarios

Complete the Real-World Scenarios found on the companion website (www.pearsonitcertification.com/title/9780789758996). You will find a PDF containing the scenario and questions, and also supporting videos and simulations.

Review Questions

Answer the following review questions. Check your answers with the correct answers that follow.

1. Which of the following would you set up in a multifunction SOHO router?

   A. DMZ

   B. DOS

   C. OSI

   D. ARP

2. Which of the following is a private IPv4 address?

   A. 11.16.0.1

   B. 127.0.0.1

   C. 172.16.0.1

   D. 208.0.0.1

3. Which of these hides an entire network of IP addresses?

   A. SPI

   B. NAT

   C. SSH

   D. FTP

4. Which of the following statements best describes a static NAT?

   A. Static NAT uses a one-to-one mapping.

   B. Static NAT uses a many-to-many mapping.

   C. Static NAT uses a one-to-many mapping.

   D. Static NAT uses a many-to-one mapping.

5. Which of the following should be placed between the LAN and the Internet?

   A. DMZ

   B. HIDS

   C. Domain controller

   D. Extranet

6. You want to reduce network traffic on a particular network segment to limit the amount of user visibility. Which of the following is the best device to use in this scenario?

   A. Switch

   B. Hub

   C. Router

   D. Firewall

7. You receive complaints about network connectivity being disrupted. You suspect that a user connected both ends of a network cable to two different ports on a switch. What can be done to prevent this?

   A. Loop protection

   B. DMZ

   C. VLAN segregation

   D. Port forwarding

8. You see a network address in the command-line that is composed of a long string of letters and numbers. What protocol is being used?

   A. IPv4

   B. ICMP

   C. IPv3

   D. IPv6

9. Which of the following cloud computing services offers easy-to-configure operating systems?

   A. SaaS

   B. IaaS

   C. PaaS

   D. VM

10. Which of the following might be included in Microsoft Security Bulletins?

    A. PHP

    B. CGI

    C. CVE

    D. TLS

11. Which of the following devices would most likely have a DMZ interface?

   A. Switch

   B. VoIP phone

   C. Proxy server

   D. Firewall

12. Your network uses the subnet mask 255.255.255.224. Which of the following IPv4 addresses are able to communicate with each other? (Select the two best answers.)

   A. 10.36.36.126

   B. 10.36.36.158

   C. 10.36.36.166

   D. 10.36.36.184

   E. 10.36.36.224

13. You are implementing a testing environment for the development team. They use several virtual servers to test their applications. One of these applications requires that the servers communicate with each other. However, to keep this network safe and private, you do not want it to be routable to the firewall. What is the best method to accomplish this?

   A. Use a virtual switch.

   B. Remove the virtual network from the routing table.

   C. Use a standalone switch.

   D. Create a VLAN without any default gateway.

14. Your boss (the IT director) wants to move several internally developed software applications to an alternate environment, supported by a third party, in an effort to reduce the footprint of the server room. Which of the following is the IT director proposing?

   A. PaaS

   B. IaaS

   C. SaaS

   D. Community cloud

15. A security analyst wants to ensure that all external traffic is able to access an organization's front-end servers but also wants to protect access to internal resources. Which network design element is the best option for the security analyst?

    A. VLAN

    B. Virtualization

    C. DMZ

    D. Cloud computing

16. In your organization's network you have VoIP phones and PCs connected to the same switch. Which of the following is the best way to logically separate these device types while still allowing traffic between them via an ACL?

    A. Install a firewall and connect it to the switch.

    B. Create and define two subnets, configure each device to use a dedicated IP address, and then connect the whole network to a router.

    O. Install a firewall and connect it to a dedicated switch for each type of device.

    D. Create two VLANs on the switch connected to a router.

17. You ping a hostname on the network and receive a response including the address 2001:4560:0:2001::6A. What type of address is listed within the response?

    A. MAC address

    B. Loopback address

    C. IPv6 address

    D. IPv4 address

18. Analyze the following network traffic logs depicting communications between Computer1 and Computer2 on opposite sides of a router. The information was captured by the computer with the IPv4 address 10.254.254.10.

```
Computer1      Computer2
 [192.168.1.105]------[INSIDE 192.168.1.1 router OUTSIDE
    10.254.254.1] -----[10.254.254.10] LOGS
7:58:36 SRC 10.254.254.1:3030, DST 10.254.254.10:80, SYN
7:58:38 SRC 10.254.254.10:80, DST 10.254.254.1:3030, SYN/ACK
7:58:40 SRC 10.254.254.1:3030, DST 10.254.254.10:80, ACK
```

Given the information, which of the following can you infer about the network communications?

    A. The router implements NAT.

    B. The router filters port 80 traffic.

    C. 192.168.1.105 is a web server.

    D. The web server listens on a nonstandard port.

19. Your organization uses VoIP. Which of the following should be performed to increase the availability of IP telephony by prioritizing traffic?

    A. NAT

    B. QoS

    C. NAC

    D. Subnetting

20. You have been tasked with segmenting internal traffic between layer 2 devices on the LAN. Which of the following network design elements would most likely be used?

    A. VLAN

    B. DMZ

    C. NAT

    D. Routing

Answers and Explanations

1. **A.** A DMZ, or demilitarized zone, can be set up on a SOHO router (in the firewall portion) to create a sort of safe haven for servers. It is neither the LAN nor the Internet, but instead, a location in between the two.

2. **C.** 172.16.0.1 is the only address listed that is private. The private assigned ranges can be seen in Table 6-2 earlier in the chapter. 11.16.0.1 is a public IPv4 address, as is 208.0.0.1. 127.0.0.1 is the IPv4 loopback address.

3. **B.** NAT (network address translation) hides an entire network of IP addresses. SPI, or Stateful Packet Inspection, is the other type of firewall that today's SOHO routers incorporate. Secure Shell (SSH) is a protocol used to log in to remote systems securely over the network. The File Transfer Protocol (FTP) is used to copy files from one system to a remote system.

4. **A.** Static network address translation normally uses a one-to-one mapping when dealing with IP addresses.

5. **A.** A demilitarized zone, or DMZ, can be placed between the LAN and the Internet; this is known as a back-to-back perimeter configuration. This allows external users on the Internet to access services but segments access to the internal network. In some cases, it will be part of a 3-leg firewall scheme. Host-based intrusion detection systems are placed on an individual computer, usually within the LAN. Domain controllers should be protected and are normally on the LAN as well. An extranet can include parts of the Internet and parts of one or more LANs; normally it connects two companies utilizing the power of the Internet.

6. **A.** A switch can reduce network traffic on a particular network segment. It does this by keeping a table of information about computers on that segment. Instead of broadcasting information to all ports of the switch, the switch selectively chooses where the information goes.

7. **A.** Loop protection should be enabled on the switch to prevent the looping that can occur when a person connects both ends of a network cable to the same switch. A DMZ is a demilitarized zone that is used to keep servers in a midway zone between the Internet and the LAN. VLAN segregation (or VLAN separation) is a way of preventing ARP poisoning. Port forwarding refers to logical ports associated with protocols.

8. **D.** IPv6 uses a long string of numbers and letters in the IP address. These addresses are 128-bit in length. IPv4 addresses are shorter (32-bit) and are numeric only. ICMP is the Internet Control Message Protocol, which is used by ping and other commands. IPv3 was a test version prior to IPv4 and was similar in IP addressing structure.

9. **C.** Platform as a service (PaaS) is a cloud computing service that offers many software solutions, including easy-to-configure operating systems and on-demand computing. SaaS is software as a service, used to offer solutions such as webmail. IaaS is infrastructure as a service, used for networking and storage. VM stands for virtual machine, which is something that PaaS also offers.

10. **C.** Common Vulnerabilities and Exposures (CVE) can be included in Microsoft Security Bulletins and will be listed for other web server products such as Apache. PHP and CGI are pseudo-programming languages used within HTML for websites. Both can contain harmful scripts if used inappropriately. Transport Layer Security (TLS) is a protocol used by sites secured by HTTPS.

11. D. The firewall is the device most likely to have a separate DMZ interface. Switches connect computers on the LAN. VoIP phones are used by individuals to make and answer phone calls on a Voice over IP connection. A proxy server acts as a go-between for the clients on the LAN and the web servers that they connect to, and caches web content for faster access.

12. C and D. The hosts using the IP addresses 10.36.36.166 and 10.36.36.184 would be able to communicate with each other because they are on the same subnet (known as subnet ID 5). All of the other answer choices' IP addresses are on different subnets, so they would not be able to communicate with each other (or with the IP addresses of the correct answers) by default. Table 6-6 provides the complete list of subnets and their ranges for this particular subnetted network. It is noteworthy that the answer 10.36.36.224 is not even usable because it is the first IP of one of the subnets. Remember that the general rule is: you can't use the first and last IP within each subnet. That is because they are reserved for the subnet ID and the broadcast addresses, respectively.

Table 6-6 List of Subnets for 10.36.36.0/27 (255.255.255.224 Subnet Mask)

Subnet ID	Mathematical IP Range	Usable IP Range
ID 0	10.36.36.0–10.36.36.31	10.36.36.1–10.36.36.30
ID 1	10.36.36.32–10.36.36.63	10.36.36.33–10.36.36.62
ID 2	10.36.36.64–10.36.36.95	10.36.36.65–10.36.36.94
ID 3	10.36.36.96–10.36.36.127	10.36.36.97–10.36.36.126
ID 4	10.36.36.128–10.36.36.159	10.36.36.129–10.36.36.158
ID 5	10.36.36.160–10.36.36.191	10.36.36.161–10.36.36.190
ID 6	10.36.36.192–10.36.36.223	10.36.36.193–10.36.36.222
ID 7	10.36.36.224–10.36.36.255	10.36.36.225–10.36.36.254

13. A. The virtual switch is the best option. This virtual device will connect the virtual servers together without being routable to the firewall (by default). Removing the virtual network from the routing table is another possibility; but if you have not created a virtual switch yet, it should not be necessary. A physical standalone switch won't be able to connect the virtual servers together; a virtual switch (or individual virtual connections) is required. Creating a VLAN would also require a physical switch. In that scenario, you can have multiple virtual LANs each containing physical computers (not virtual computers), and each working off of the same physical switch. That answer would keep the VLAN from being routable to the firewall, but not virtual servers.

14. **B.** The IT director is most likely proposing that you use infrastructure as a service (IaaS). A cloud-based service, IaaS is often used to house servers (within virtual machines) that store developed applications. It differs from PaaS in that it is the servers, and already developed applications, that are being moved from the server room to the cloud. However, PaaS might also be required if the applications require further development. The most basic cloud-based service, software as a service (SaaS), is when users work with applications (often web-based) that are provided from the cloud. A community cloud is when multiple organizations share certain aspects of a public cloud.

15. **C.** The demilitarized zone (DMZ) is the best option in this scenario. By creating a DMZ, and placing the front-end servers within it (on a separate branch of the firewall), you create a type of compartmentalization between the LAN (important internal resources) and the front-end servers. A VLAN is used to separate a LAN into multiple virtual units. Virtualization is a general term that usually refers to the virtualizing of operating systems. Cloud computing is another possible option in this scenario, because you could take the front-end servers and move them to the cloud. However, a certain level of control is lost when this is done, whereas with a DMZ, the security analyst still retains complete control.

16. **D.** The best option is to create two VLANs on the switch (one for the VoIP phones, and one for the PCs) and make sure that the switch is connected to the router. Configure access control lists (ACLs) as necessary on the router to allow or disallow connectivity and traffic between the two VLANs. Installing a firewall and configuring ACLs on that firewall is a possibility, but you would also have to use two separate dedicated switches if VLANs are not employed. This is a valid option, but requires additional equipment, whereas creating the two VLANs requires no additional equipment (as long as the switch has VLAN functionality). While subnetting is a possible option, it is more elaborate than required. The VLAN (in this case port-based) works very well in this scenario and is the best option.

17. **C.** The address in the response is a truncated IPv6 address. You can tell it is an IPv6 address because of the hexadecimal numbering, the separation with colons, and the groups of four digits. You can tell it is truncated because of the single zero and the double colon. A MAC address is also hexadecimal and can use colons to separate the groups of numbers (though hyphens often are used), but the numbers are grouped in twos. An example is 00-1C-C0-A1-54-15. The loopback address is a testing address for the local computer. In IPv6 it is simply ::1, whereas in IPv4 it is 127.0.0.1. Finally, IPv4 addresses in general are 32-bit dotted-decimal numbers such as 192.168.1.100.

18. **A.** The only one of the listed answers that you can infer from the log is that the router implements network address translation (NAT). You can tell this from the first line of the log, which shows the inside of the router using the 192.168.1.1 IP address and the outside using 10.254.254.1. NAT is occurring between the two at the router. This allows the IP 192.168.1.105 to communicate with 10.254.254.10 ultimately. However, the rest of the logs only show the first step of that communication between 10.254.254.10 and the router at 10.254.254.1.

What's really happening here? The router is showing that port 3030 is being used on 10.254.254.1. That is the port used by an online game known as net-Panzer as well as a mass-e-mailing backdoor worm. The client (10.254.254.10) is using port 80 to make a web-based connection to the game. You can see the three-way TCP handshake occurring with the SYN, SYN/ACK, and ACK packets. Ultimately, 10.254.254.10 is communicating with 192.168.1.105, but we only see the first stage of that communication to the router. As a security analyst you would most likely want to shut down the use of port 3030, so that employees can be more productive and you have less overall chance of a network breach.

As far as the incorrect answers, the router definitely is not filtering out port 80, as traffic is successfully being sent on that port. 192.168.1.105 is not a web server; it is most likely used for other purposes. Finally, even though port 80 is used by the client computer, there is likely no web server in this scenario.

19. **B.** Quality of Service (QoS) should be configured on the router to prioritize traffic, promoting IP telephony traffic to be more available. You'll get some detractors of QoS, especially for the SOHO side of networks, but if used on the right device and configured properly, it can make a difference. This might sound like more of a networking question, but it ties in directly to the CIA triad of security. Data confidentiality and integrity are important, but just as important is availability—the ability for users to access data when required. NAT is network address translation, which interprets internal and external IP networks to each other. NAC is network access control—for example, 802.1X. Subnetting is when a network is divided into multiple logical areas through IP addressing/planning and subnet mask configuring.

20. **A.** You would most likely use a virtual LAN (VLAN). This allows you to segment internal traffic within layer 2 of the OSI model, by using either a protocol-based scheme or a port-based scheme. The DMZ is used to create a safe haven for servers that are accessed by outside traffic. NAT is network address translation, which is a layer 3 option used on routers. Because we are dealing with a layer 2 scenario, routing in general is not necessary.

This chapter covers the following subjects:

- **Ports and Protocols:** In this section, you learn the ports and their associated protocols you need to know for the exam and how to secure those ports. Sometimes the port needs to be closed; sometimes it needs to remain open. Once you understand if the port is necessary, you can decide whether to lock it down or to keep it ajar in a secure manner.

- **Malicious Attacks:** This section covers the basics about network attacks and how to defend against them. Study this section carefully; the CompTIA Security+ exam is bound to ask you several questions about these concepts.

Making client connections to servers means that the servers need to have open ports to facilitate their services. However, every open port is a vulnerability. It's important to know the common protocols used by servers and their respective ports and how to protect against threats that might try to exploit those server ports.

CHAPTER 7

Networking Protocols and Threats

The threats are many. Malicious attacks such as denial-of-service attacks, man-in-the-middle attacks, replay attacks, and session hijacking can all be devastating to individual computers and to entire networks. But once you have built a decent knowledge of ports and protocols, you can use that intelligence to better protect your servers and network against the plethora of attacks you will face.

One thing to remember is that there are always new network attacks being developed, and many that currently exist, but are unknown. Therefore, this chapter is incomplete in the sense that once it is written, it is out of date. Keep this in mind, and remember to always keep on top of your security bulletins, Common Vulnerabilities and Exposures (CVEs), and security updates.

Foundation Topics

Ports and Protocols

I can't stress enough how important it is to secure a host's ports and protocols. They are the doorways into an operating system. Think about it: An open doorway is a plain and simple invitation for disaster. And that disaster could be caused by one of many different types of malicious network attacks. The security administrator must be ever vigilant in monitoring, auditing, and implementing updated defense mechanisms to combat malicious attacks. Understanding ports and protocols is the first step in this endeavor.

Port Ranges, Inbound Versus Outbound, and Common Ports

Although some readers of this book will be familiar with ports used by the network adapter and operating system, a review of them is necessary because they play a big role in securing hosts and will most definitely appear on the exam in some way, shape, or form.

Ports act as logical communication endpoints for computers. Each protocol uses a specific port; for example, HTTP uses port 80 by default. These ports are ultimately controlled on the transport layer of the OSI model by protocols such as the Transmission Control Protocol (TCP) and User Datagram Protocol

(UDP). TCP is used for guaranteed, connection-oriented sessions such as the initial connection to a web page, and UDP is used for connectionless sessions such as the streaming of data. There are 65,536 ports altogether, numbering between 0 and 65,535. The ports are divided into categories, as shown in Table 7-1.

Table 7-1   Port Ranges

Port Range	Category Type	Description
0–1023	Well-Known Ports	This range defines commonly used protocols; for example, HTTP uses port 80. They are designated by the IANA (Internet Assigned Numbers Authority), which is operated by the ICANN (Internet Corporation for Assigned Names and Numbers).
1024–49,151	Registered Ports	Ports used by vendors for proprietary applications. These must be registered with the IANA. For example, Microsoft registered port 3389 for use with the Remote Desktop Protocol (RDP), also known as Remote Desktop Connection.
49,152–65,535	Dynamic and Private Ports	These ports can be used by applications but cannot be registered by vendors.

You need to understand the difference between inbound and outbound ports as described in the following two bullets and as illustrated in Figure 7-1.

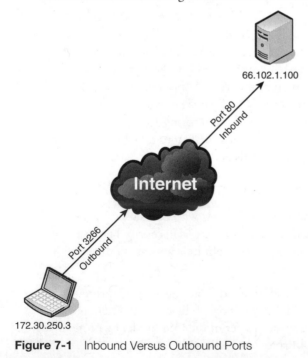

66.102.1.100

Port 80
Inbound

Internet

Port 3266
Outbound

172.30.250.3

Figure 7-1   Inbound Versus Outbound Ports

- **Inbound ports:** Used when another computer wants to connect to a service or application running on your computer. Servers primarily use inbound ports so that they can accept incoming connections and serve data. For example, in Figure 7-1, the server with the IP address 66.102.1.100 has inbound port 80 open to accept incoming web page requests.

- **Outbound ports:** Used when your computer wants to connect to a service or application running on another computer. Client computers primarily use outbound ports that are assigned dynamically by the operating system. For example, in Figure 7-1, the client computer with the IP address 172.30.250.3 has outbound port 3266 open to make a web page request to the server.

> **NOTE**   For a refresher about TCP, UDP, and ports, see the short 5-minute video at the following link: http://www.davidlprowse.com/articles/?p=911.

It's the inbound ports that a security administrator should be most concerned with. Web servers, FTP servers, database servers, and so on have specific inbound ports opened to the public. Any other unnecessary ports should be closed, and any open ports should be protected and monitored carefully. Although there are 1,024 well-known ports, for the exam you need to know only a handful of them, plus some that are beyond 1,024, as shown in Table 7-2. Remember that these inbound port numbers relate to the applications, services, and protocols that run on a computer, often a server. When it comes to the OSI model, the bulk of these protocols are application layer protocols. Examples of these protocols include HTTP, FTP, SMTP, SSH, DHCP, and POP3, and there are many more. Because these are known as application layer protocols, their associated ports are known as *application service ports*. The bulk of Table 7-2 is composed of application service ports. Some of the protocols listed make use of TCP transport layer connections only (for example, HTTP, port 80). Some make use of UDP only (for example, SNMP, port 161). Many can use TCP *or* UDP transport mechanisms. Note that some have secure versions listed as well. Study Table 7-2 carefully now, bookmark it, and refer to it often!

Key Topic

Table 7-2   Ports and Their Associated Protocols

Port Number	Associated Protocol (or Keyword)	TCP/UDP Usage	Secure Version and Port	Usage
21	FTP	TCP	FTPS, port 989/990	Transfers files from host to host.
22	SSH	TCP or UDP		Secure Shell: Remotely administers network devices and systems. Also used by Secure Copy (SCP) and Secure FTP (SFTP).

Port Number	Associated Protocol (or Keyword)	TCP/UDP Usage	Secure Version and Port	Usage
23	Telnet	TCP or UDP		Remotely administers network devices (deprecated).
25	SMTP	TCP	SMTP with SSL/TLS, port 465 or 587	Sends e-mail.
49	TACACS+	TCP		Remote authentication. Can also use UDP, but TCP is the default. Compare with RADIUS.
53	DNS	TCP or UDP	DNSSEC	Resolves hostnames to IP addresses and vice versa.
69	TFTP	UDP		Basic version of FTP.
80	HTTP	TCP	HTTPS (uses SSL/TLS), port 443	Transmits web page data.
88	Kerberos	TCP or UDP		Network authentication, uses tickets.
110	POP3	TCP	POP3 with SSL/TLS, port 995	Receives e-mail.
119	NNTP	TCP		Transports Usenet articles.
135	RPC/epmap/ dcom-scm	TCP or UDP		Used to locate DCOM ports. Also known as RPC (Remote Procedure Call).
137–139	NetBIOS	TCP or UDP		Name querying, sending data, NetBIOS connections.
143	IMAP	TCP	IMAP4 with SSL/TLS, port 993	Retrieval of e-mail, with advantages over POP3.
161	SNMP	UDP		Remotely monitor network devices.
162	SNMPTRAP	TCP or UDP		Traps and InformRequests are sent to the SNMP Manager on this port.

Port Number	Associated Protocol (or Keyword)	TCP/UDP Usage	Secure Version and Port	Usage
389	LDAP	TCP or UDP	LDAP over SSL/TLS, port 636	Maintains directories of users and other objects.
445	SMB	TCP		Provides shared access to files and other resources.
514	Syslog	UDP		Used for computer message logging, especially for router and firewall logs. A secure version (Syslog over TLS) uses TCP as the transport mechanism and port 6514.
860	iSCSI	TCP		IP-based protocol used for linking data storage facilities. Also uses port 3260 for the iSCSI target.
1433	Ms-sql-s	TCP		Opens queries to Microsoft SQL server.
1701	L2TP	UDP		VPN protocol with no inherent security. Often used with IPsec.
1723	PPTP	TCP or UDP		VPN protocol with built-in security.
1812/1813	RADIUS	UDP		An AAA protocol used for authentication (port 1812), authorization, and accounting (port 1813) of users. Also, ports 1645 and 1646.
3225	FCIP	TCP or UDP		Encapsulates Fibre Channel frames within TCP/IP packets. Contrast with Fibre Channel over Ethernet (FCoE), which relies on the data link layer and doesn't rely on TCP/IP directly.
3389	RDP	TCP or UDP		Remotely views and controls other Windows systems.
3868	Diameter	TCP (or SCTP)		An AAA protocol; can replace the RADIUS protocol.

> **NOTE**   You can find a complete list of ports and their corresponding protocols at the following link: http://www.iana.org/assignments/service-names-port-numbers/service-names-port-numbers.xhtml.

> **NOTE**   Not all protocols have set port numbers. For example, the Real-time Transport Protocol (RTP) and Secure RTP (SRTP) use a pair of port numbers determined by the application that is streaming the audio and video information via RTP. They are selected from a broad range of ports (between 16384 and 32767).

The IP address of a computer and the port number it is sending or receiving on are combined together to form a network socket address. An example of this would be 66.102.1.100:80. That is illustrated by the IP address of the server in Figure 7-1 and the inbound port number accepting a connection from the client computer. Notice that when they are written, the two are separated by a colon. The IP address precedes the colon and the port number follows it.

Figure 7-2 illustrates a few more examples of this within a Windows client computer. It shows some of the results of a `netstat -an` command after FTP, WWW, and mail connections were made by the client to two separate servers. Examine Figure 7-2 and then read on.

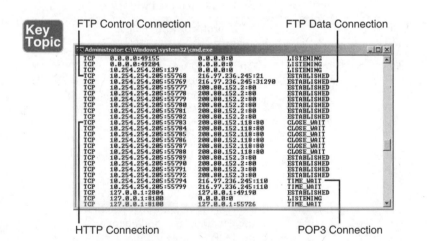

Figure 7-2   IP Addresses and Ports

The first callout in Figure 7-2 is the initial FTP connection. This happens when a user first connects to an FTP server with FTP client software. Notice that the local computer has the IP address 10.254.254.205 and uses the dynamically assigned outbound port 55768 to connect to the FTP server. The remote computer, on the other hand, has the IP address 216.97.236.245 and uses inbound port 21 (known as a command port) to accept the connection. Keep in mind that this is only the initial connection and login to the FTP server. Subsequent data connections are normally done on the server side via dynamically assigned ports. For example, the second call-out, FTP Data Connection, occurred when the client downloaded a file. It is a separate session in which the client used the dynamically assigned port number 55769. In reality, this isn't quite dynamic anymore; the client operating system is simply selecting the next port number available. Afterward, a subsequent and concurrent download would probably use port 55770. The server, on the other hand, used the dynamically assigned port number 31290.

Many FTP servers randomly select a different inbound port to use for each data connection to increase security. However, some active FTP connections still use the original port 20 for data connections, which is not as secure, not only because it is well known, but also because it is static. To secure FTP communications, consider using software that enables dynamically assigned ports during data transfers; for example, Pure-FTPd (https://www.pureftpd.org/project/pure-ftpd) on the server side and FileZilla (https://filezilla-project.org/) on the client side. If your FTP server enables it, you can also consider IPv6 connections, and as always, be sure to use strong, complex passwords. (I don't mean to sound like a broken record!)

The third callout in Figure 7-2 shows an HTTP connection. Note that this is being made to a different server (208.80.152.118) and uses port 80. And finally, the fourth callout shows a POP3 connection that was previously made to the same server IP as the FTP connection, but note that the port number reflects POP3—it shows port number 110. Always be mindful of securing connections; if you were making an encrypted POP3 connection using SSL/TLS, then the port number used would most likely be port 995.

These are just a few examples of many that occur between clients and servers all the time. Try making some connections to various servers from your client computer and view those sessions in the command-line.

Aside from servers, ports also become particularly important on router/firewall devices. These devices operate on the implicit deny concept, which means they deny all traffic unless a rule is made to open the port associated with the type of traffic desired to be let through. We talk more about firewalls in Chapter 8, "Network Perimeter Security."

You need to scan your servers, routers, and firewall devices to discern which ports are open. This can be done with the aforementioned `netstat` command, with an application such as Nmap (https://nmap.org/), or with an online scanner from a website. The most effective way is with an actual scanning application, which we show in depth in Chapter 12, "Vulnerability and Risk Assessment."

Afterward, unnecessary ports should be closed. This can be done in a few ways:

- **Within the operating system GUI:** For example, in Windows, open the Computer Management console. Then go to Services and Applications > Services. Right-click the appropriate service and select Properties. From here the service can be stopped and disabled.

- **Within the CLI:** For example, a service can be stopped in Windows by using the `net stop` *service* command, or with the `sudo stop` *service* command in Linux. (More about stopping services can be found in Chapter 4, "OS Hardening and Virtualization.")

- **Within a firewall:** Simply setting up a firewall normally closes and shields all ports by default. But you might have a service that was used previously on a server, and therefore a rule might have been created on the firewall to enable traffic on that port. Within the firewall software, the rule can be deleted, disabled, or modified as needed. In general, network firewalls protect all the computers on the network, so this is where you would normally go to close particular ports.

Unnecessary ports also include ports associated with nonessential protocols. For example, TFTP (port 69) is usually considered a nonessential protocol, as is Finger (port 79). Telnet (port 23) is insecure and as such is also considered nonessential. However, the list of nonessential protocols differs from one organization to the next. Always rescan the host to make sure that the ports are indeed closed. Then, make the necessary changes in documentation. Depending on company policy, you might need to follow change management procedures before making modifications to ports and services. For more information on this type of documentation and procedures, see Chapter 18, "Policies and Procedures."

> **NOTE** In some cases, you might find that a particular network interface is used either very infrequently or not at all. In these scenarios it is smart to consider disabling the entire interface altogether, either from the properties of the network adapter, in the Device Manager, or in the command-line of the OS in question. When the network adapter is disabled, all ports are effectively closed.

Port Zero Security

Let's talk about port zero for a moment. Although there is a total of 65,536 ports, only 65,535 of them can normally be exploited. The reason is that port zero usually redirects to another dynamically assigned port. Although the IANA listings say it is reserved, it is not considered to exist and is often defined as an invalid port number.

But programmers use port zero as a wildcard port, designing their applications to ask the operating system to assign a non-zero port. So, normally malware that exploits port zero will simply be redirected to another valid port. Again, this means that only 65,535 of the 65,536 ports can be exploited. In the future, port zero may become more of a security concern with the growth of legitimate raw socket programming. This is programming directly to network ports, bypassing the transport layer; an example would be the Internet Control Message Protocol (ICMP) involving ping operations. However, historically, raw sockets have been used by attackers to perform *TCP reset attacks*, which set the reset flag in a TCP header to 1, telling the respective computer to kill the TCP session immediately. Until recently, raw socket programming has been generally frowned upon.

Protocols That Can Cause Anxiety on the Exam

Unfortunately, a lot of the protocols look similar, behave similarly, and can be downright confusing. Let's discuss a few of the more difficult ones and try to dispel some of the confusion. We start with FTP and its derivatives.

You know about the FTP protocol and what it does. You probably also know that FTP can be inherently insecure. There are several ways to make FTP sessions more secure. We mentioned previously that you can use FTP software that randomizes which ports are selected to transfer each file. You can also select passive mode instead of active mode (most FTP clients default to passive). The difference is that in passive mode the server is required to open ports for incoming traffic, and in active mode both the server and the client open ports. Then, you could use an FTP protocol that is secured through encryption. Two examples are Secure FTP (SFTP) and FTP Secure (FTPS). SFTP uses SSH port 22 to make connections to other systems. Because of this it is also known as SSH FTP. However, FTPS works with SSL or TLS, and (in implicit mode) it uses ports 990 (control port) and 989 (data port) to make secure connections and send data, respectively. FTPS can work in two modes: explicit mode and the previously mentioned implicit mode. In explicit mode, the FTPS client must explicitly request security from an FTPS server and then mutually agree on the type of encryption to be used. In implicit mode, there is no negotiation, and the client is expected to already know the type of encryption used by the server. In general, implicit mode is considered to be more secure than explicit mode.

So, in summary, regular FTP uses port 21 as the control port by default, and possibly port 20 to do data transfers—or (and more likely), it uses random ports for data transfers, if the software allows it. SFTP uses port 22. FTPS uses port 990 to make connections, and port 989 to transfer data by default. TFTP (which is not really secure) uses port 69.

On a separate note, another file transfer program, Secure Copy (SCP), is an example of a protocol that uses an additional protocol (and its corresponding port) for security. It uses SSH, and ultimately uses port 22 to transfer data.

All those acronyms can be difficult to keep straight at times. Hopefully this section alleviates some of the confusion. For more help, be sure to memorize Table 7-2 to the best of your ability for the exam, and don't be afraid to ask me questions on my website!

Malicious Attacks

There are many types of malicious network attacks. We've mentioned some of these attacks in the preceding chapters as they relate to secure computing, but in this section we will better define them. Some attacks are similar to others, making it difficult to differentiate between them. Because of this, I've listed simple definitions and examples of each, plus mitigating techniques, and summarized them at the end of this section.

DoS

Denial-of-service (DoS) is a broad term given to many different types of network attacks that attempt to make computer resources unavailable. Generally, this is done to servers but could also be perpetuated against routers and other hosts. DoS attacks can be implemented in several ways, as listed here:

- **Flood attack:** An attacker sends many packets to a single server or other host in an attempt to disable it. There are a few ways to accomplish this, including:
  - **Ping flood:** Also known as an ICMP flood attack, this is when an attacker attempts to send many ICMP echo request packets (pings) to a host in an attempt to use up all available bandwidth. This works only if the attacker has more bandwidth available than the target. To deter this attack, configure the system not to respond to ICMP echoes. You might have noticed that several years ago, you could ping large companies' websites and get replies. But after ping floods became prevalent, a lot of these companies disabled ICMP echo replies. For example, try opening the command prompt and typing `ping microsoft.com` (Internet connection required). It should result in Request Timed Out, which tells you that Microsoft has disabled this.
  - **Smurf attack:** Also sends large amounts of ICMP echoes, but this particular attack goes a bit further. The attacking computer broadcasts the ICMP echo requests to every computer on its network or subnetwork. In addition, in the header of the ICMP echo requests will be a spoofed IP

address. That IP address is the target of the Smurf attack. Every computer that replies to the ICMP echo requests will do so to the spoofed IP. Don't forget that the original attack was broadcast, so, the more systems on the network (or subnetwork), the more echo replies that are sent to the target computer. There are several defenses for this attack, including configuring hosts not to respond to pings or ICMP echoes, configuring routers not to forward packets directed to broadcast addresses, implementing subnetting with smaller subnetworks, and employing network ingress filtering in an attempt to drop packets that contain forged or spoofed IP addresses (especially addresses on other networks). These defenses have enabled most network administrators to make their networks immune to Smurf and other ICMP-based attacks. The attack can be automated and modified using the exploit code known as Smurf.c.

— **Fraggle:** Similar to the Smurf attack, but the traffic sent is UDP echoes. The traffic is directed to port 7 (Echo) and port 19 (CHARGEN). To protect against this attack, again, configure routers not to forward packets directed to broadcast addresses, employ network filtering, and disable ports 7 and 19. These ports are not normally used in most networks. The attack can be automated and modified using the exploit code known as Fraggle.c.

NOTE A similar attack is known as a UDP flood attack, which also uses the connectionless User Datagram Protocol. It is enticing to attackers because it does not require a synchronization process.

SYN flood: Also known as a SYN attack, it occurs when an attacker sends a large amount of SYN request packets to a server in an attempt to deny service. Remember that in the TCP three-way handshake, a synchronization (SYN) packet is sent from the client to the server, then a SYN/ACK packet is sent from the server to the client, and finally, an acknowledgment (ACK) packet is sent from the client to the server. Attackers attempting a SYN flood either simply skip sending the ACK or spoof the source IP address in the original SYN. Either way, the server will never receive the final ACK packet. This ends up being a half-open connection. By doing this multiple times, an attacker seeks to use up all connection-oriented resources so that no real connections can be made. Some ways to defend against this include implementing **flood guards** (which can be implemented on some firewalls and other devices, otherwise known as attack guards), recycling half-open connections after a predetermined amount of time, and using intrusion detection systems

(IDSs) to detect the attack. You can find more information about IDSs in Chapter 8 and more information about SYN flood attacks and mitigation techniques at the following link: https://tools.ietf.org/html/rfc4987.

— **Xmas attack:** Also known as the Christmas Tree attack or TCP Xmas Scan attack, it can deny service to routers and other devices, or simply cause them to reboot. It is based on the Christmas Tree packet, which can be generated by a variety of programs; for example, Nmap can be used (with the `-sX` parameter) to produce this scanning packet. This type of packet has the FIN, PSH, and URG flags set, which gives a "Christmas Tree" appearance when viewing the flags in a network sniffer. If the packet is sent many times in a short period of time, it could possibly result in a DoS (which is why I placed this attack in the DoS flood section). But most routers and other devices today will block this type of packet, as it is a well-known attack. Otherwise, an IDS/IPS solution (if in place) can detect the packet and/or prevent the packet from denying service to a router or other device.

■ **Ping of Death:** POD is an attack that sends an oversized and malformed packet to another computer. It is an older attack; most computer operating systems today will not be affected by it, and most firewalls will block it before it enters a network. It entails sending a packet that is larger than 65,535 bytes in length, which according to RFC 791 is the largest size packet that can be used on a TCP/IP network without fragmentation. It should be noted that, normally, the maximum transmission unit (MTU) size of an Ethernet frame is 1500 bytes, and slightly less for the encapsulated TCP/IP packet. Going beyond this requires special means. Now, if a packet is sent that is larger than 65,535 bytes, it might overflow the target system's memory buffers, which can cause several types of problems, including system crashes. Windows computers do not allow ping sizes beyond 65,500 bytes. For example, `ping destination -l 65500` will work, but `ping destination -l 66000` will not work. However, on some systems, this maximum limitation can be hacked in the Registry, and there are also third-party applications that can send these "larger than life" packets. To protect against this type of attack, configure hosts not to respond to pings or ICMP echoes, make sure that operating systems run the latest service packs and updates, update the firmware on any hardware-based firewalls, and update any software-based firewalls as well. POD can be combined with a ping flood, but because most firewalls will block one or more PODs, it doesn't make much sense to attempt the attack, so most attackers opt for some other sort of packet flooding nowadays. This was one of the first DoS attacks. It and other attacks such as Nuke and WinNuke are considered by the security community to be deprecated.

- **Teardrop attack:** Sends mangled IP fragments with overlapping and over-sized payloads to the target machine. This can crash and reboot various operating systems due to a bug in their TCP/IP fragmentation reassembly code. For example, some older versions of Windows are particularly susceptible to teardrop attacks. Linux and Windows systems should be upgraded to protect from this attack. There are also software downloads available on the Internet for teardrop detection.

- **Permanent DoS attack:** Generally consists of an attacker exploiting security flaws in routers and other networking hardware by flashing the firmware of the device and replacing it with a modified image. This is also known as phlashing, or PDoS.

- **Fork bomb:** Works by quickly creating a large number of processes to saturate the available processing space in the computer's operating system. Running processes can be "forked" to create other running processes, and so on. They are not considered viruses or worms but are known as "rabbit malware," "wabbits," or "bacteria" because they might self-replicate but do not infect programs or use the network to spread. They are still considered DoS attacks though, due to their ability to stop a system from functioning.

There are other types of DoS attacks, but that should suffice for now. Keep in mind that new DoS attacks are always being dreamed up (and implemented), so as a security administrator, you need to be ready for new attacks and prepared to exercise new mitigation techniques.

DDoS

A **distributed denial-of-service (DDoS)** attack is when a group of compromised systems attacks a single target, causing a DoS to occur at that host. A DDoS attack often utilizes a botnet—which is a large group of computers known as robots or simply "bots." Often, these are systems owned by unsuspecting users. The computers in the botnet that act as attackers are known as zombies. An attacker starts the DDoS attack by exploiting a single vulnerability in a computer system and making that computer the zombie master, or DDoS master. The master system communicates with the other systems in the botnet. The attacker often loads malicious software on many computers (zombies). The attacker can launch a flood of attacks by all zombies in the botnet with a single command. DDoS attacks and botnets are often associated with exploit kits (such as the Blackhole kit) and ransomware.

DoS and DDoS attacks are difficult to defend against. Other than the methods mentioned previously in the DoS section, these attacks can be prevented to some extent by updated stateful firewalls, switches, and routers with access control lists, intrusion prevention systems (IPSs), and proactive testing. Several companies offer products that simulate DoS and DDoS attacks. By creating a test server and assessing its vulnerabilities with simulated DoS tests, you can find holes in the security of your server before you take it live. A quick web search for "DoS testing" shows a few of these simulation test companies. An organization could also opt for a "clean pipe," which attempts to weed out DDoS attacks, among other attacks. This solution is offered as a service by Verisign and other companies. Manual protection of servers can be a difficult task; to implement proper DDoS mitigation, your organization might want to consider anti-DDoS technology and emergency response from an outside source or from the organization's cloud-based provider. Finally, if you do realize that a DDoS attack is being carried out on your network, call your ISP and request that this traffic be redirected.

One specific type of DDoS is the **DNS amplification attack**. Amplification attacks generate a high volume of packets ultimately intended to flood a target website. In the case of a DNS amplification attack, the attacker initiates DNS requests with a spoofed source IP address. The attacker relies on *reflection*; responses are not sent back to the attacker, but are instead sent "back" to the victim server. Because the DNS response is larger than the DNS request (usually), it *amplifies* the amount of data being passed to the victim. An attacker can use a small number of systems with little bandwidth to create a sizable attack. However, a DNS amplification attack can also be accomplished with the aid of a botnet, which has proven to be devastating to sections of the Internet during the period when the attack was carried out.

The primary way of preventing this attack is to block spoofed source packets. It can also be prevented by blocking specific DNS servers, blocking open recursive relay servers, rate limiting, and updating one's own DNS server(s) often. Finally, make use of the Domain Name System Security Extensions (DNSSEC), which are specifications that provide for origin authentication and data integrity.

> **NOTE**   Smurf and Fraggle are also examples of amplification attacks.

Sinkholes and Blackholes

To combat DoS and DDoS attacks, security admins have the option to employ or make use of sinkholes, blackholes, and blackhole lists. A DNS sinkhole is a DNS server that can be configured to hand out false information to bots, and can detect and block malicious traffic by redirecting it to nonroutable addresses. However, the sinkhole can also be used maliciously to redirect unwary users to unwanted IP addresses and domains. A DNS blackhole is similar; it can be used to identify domains used by spammers, domains that contain malware, and so on, and block traffic to those domains. It can also be remotely triggered (known as a RTBH). A DNS blackhole list (DNSBL) is a published list of IP addresses within DNS that contains the addresses of computers and networks involved in spamming and other malicious activity such as DDoS attacks initiated by botnets. The list can be downloaded and used on an organization's DNS server to help block zombie computers and botnets.

Spoofing

A **spoofing** attack is when an attacker masquerades as another person by falsifying information. There are several types of spoofing attacks. The man-in-the-middle attack is not only a form of session hijacking (which we discuss in the next section), but it is also considered spoofing. Internet protocols and their associated applications can also be spoofed, especially if the protocols were poorly programmed in the first place. Web pages can also be spoofed in an attempt to fool users into thinking they are logging in to a trusted website; this is known as URL spoofing and is used when attackers are fraudulently **phishing** for information such as usernames, passwords, credit card information, and identities. Phishing can also be done through a false e-mail that looks like it comes from a valid source. Often, this is combined with e-mail address spoofing, which hides or disguises the sender information. Defending against these types of spoofing attacks is difficult, but by carefully selecting and updating applications that your organization uses, and through user awareness, spoofing can be held down to a minimum and when necessary ignored.

NOTE   A Uniform Resource Locator (URL) is a type of Uniform Resource Identifier (URI). URIs are strings of characters that are used to identify a resource—for example, a pointer to a file. The URL is the most well-known type of URI, so it is commonly spoofed, but any other type of URI can be spoofed as well.

Just about anything can be spoofed if enough work is put into it, and IP addresses are no exception. IP address spoofing is when IP packets are created with a forged source IP address in the header. This conceals where the packets originated from. Packet filtering and sessions that repeat authentication can defend against this type of spoofing. Also, updating operating systems and firmware and using newer operating systems and network devices helps to mitigate risks involved with IP spoofing. IP spoofing is commonly used in DoS attacks, as mentioned earlier, and is also common in TCP/IP hijacking, which we discuss more in the next section. MAC addresses can also be spoofed. MAC addresses are usually unique, which helps to identify a particular system. This is the best type of address to use to identify a malicious insider or other attacker, because it is more difficult to modify than an IP address. However, there are methods for attackers to change the MAC address of a network adapter (or mask it) so that the system cannot be identified properly.

A World Wide Name (WWN) can be spoofed too. World Wide Names (and their derivatives, pWWN and nWWN) are unique identifiers for SAS, ATA, and Fibre Channel equipment that are common to storage area networks (SANs). It's not really a name, but a hexadecimal address that includes a 3-byte vendor identifier and a 3-byte vendor-specified serial number. An attacker that is masquerading as an authorized WWN can be prevented by challenging the attacker to give unique information only known to an authorized user or device. For a user, this might be information that corresponds to a password. For devices, a secret is associated with the WWN of the port on the SAN switch. Proper authentication is also beneficial when combating these types of spoof attacks.

Session Hijacking

Session hijacking is the exploitation of a computer session in an attempt to gain unauthorized access to data, services, or other resources on a computer. A few types of session hijacks can occur:

- **Session theft:** Can be accomplished by making use of packet header manipulation (see Chapter 5, "Application Security") or by stealing a cookie from the client computer, which authenticates the client computer to a server. This is done at the application layer, and the cookies involved are often based off their corresponding web applications (such as WWW sessions). This can be combated by using encryption and long random numbers for the session key, and regeneration of the session after a successful login. The Challenge Handshake Authentication Protocol (CHAP) can also be employed to require clients to periodically re-authenticate. However, session hijacking can also occur at the network layer—for example, TCP/IP hijacking.

- **TCP/IP hijacking:** A common type of session hijacking, due to its popularity among attackers. It is when an attacker takes over a TCP session between two computers without the need of a cookie or any other type of host access. Because most communications' authentication occurs only at the beginning of a standard TCP session, an attacker can attempt to gain access to a client computer anytime after the session begins. One way would be to spoof the client computer's IP address, then find out what was the last packet sequence number sent to the server, and then inject data into the session before the client sends another packet of information to the server. Remember the three-way handshake that occurs at the beginning of a session; this is the only authentication that occurs during the session. A synchronization (SYN) packet is sent by the client to the server, then a SYN/ACK packet is sent by the server to the client, and finally, an acknowledgment (ACK) packet is sent by the client to the server. An attacker can jump in anytime after this process and attempt to steal the session by injecting data into the data stream. This is the more difficult part; the attacker might need to perform a DoS attack on the client to stop it from sending any more packets so that the packet sequence number doesn't increase. In contrast, UDP sessions are easier to hijack because no packet sequence numbers exist. Targets for this type of attack include online games and also DNS queries. To mitigate the risk of TCP/IP hijacking, employ encrypted transport protocols such as SSL, IPsec, and SSH. For more information about these encryption protocols, see Chapter 15, "PKI and Encryption Protocols."

- **Blind hijacking:** When an attacker blindly injects data into a data stream without being able to see whether the injection was successful. The attacker could be attempting to create a new administrator account or gain access to one.

- **Clickjacking:** When a user browsing the web is tricked into clicking something different than what the user thought he or she was clicking. It is usually implemented as a concealed link—embedded code or a script on a website that executes when the user clicks that element. For example, a Flash script—when clicked—could cause the user's webcam to turn on without the user's consent. The user is often redirected to the website from a malicious source. This can be prevented by updating the user's web browser and using third-party add-ons that watch for clickjacking code or scripts. On the server side, web page frames (such as iframes) must be managed carefully. There are JavaScript-based snippets that can be added and content security policies that can be configured to help manage frames.

- **Man-in-the-middle (MITM):** These attacks intercept all data between a client and a server. It is a type of active interception. If successful, all communications now go through the MITM attacking computer. The attacking computer can at this point modify the data, insert code, and send it to the receiving computer. This type of eavesdropping is only successful when the attacker can properly impersonate each endpoint. Cryptographic protocols such as Secure Sockets Layer (SSL) and Transport Layer Security (TLS) address MITM attacks by using a mutually trusted third-party certification authority (CA). These public key infrastructures (PKIs) should use strong mutual authentication such as secret keys and strong passwords. For more information about PKI, see Chapter 15.

- **Man-in-the-browser (MITB):** Similar to MITM, this attack makes use of a Trojan (from a proxy location) that infects a vulnerable web browser and modifies web pages and online transactions, in an attempt to ultimately steal money or data. For example, a user might make an online banking transaction, and the user would see confirmation of the exact transaction, but on the banking side, a different amount might have been actually transferred, with some of it going to a different location altogether. This can be prevented by updating the web browser, using transaction verification (often third-party), and updating the anti-malware on the computer in question.

■ **Watering hole attack:** This targeted attack is when an attacker profiles the websites that the intended victim accesses. The attacker then scans those websites for possible vulnerabilities. If the attacker locates a website that can be compromised, the website is then injected with a JavaScript or other similar code injection that is designed to redirect the user when the user returns to that site (also known as a pivot attack). The user is then redirected to a site with some sort of exploit code...and the rest is, well, history. The purpose is to infect computers in the organization's network, thereby allowing the attacker to gain a foothold in the network for espionage or other reasons. Watering hole attacks are often designed to profile users of specific organizations, and as such, an organization should develop policies to prevent these attacks. This can be done by updating anti-malware applications regularly, and by other security controls mentioned in Chapters 2 through 4, but also by using secure virtual browsers that have little connectivity to the rest of the system and the rest of the network. To avoid having a website compromised as part of this attack, the admin should use proper programming methods (discussed in Chapter 5) and scan the website for malware regularly.

On a semi-related note, *cross-site scripting (XSS)* is a type of vulnerability found in web applications that is used with session hijacking. The attacker manipulates a client computer into executing code that is considered trusted as if it came from the server the client was connected to. In this way, the attacker can acquire the client computer's session cookie (enabling the attacker to steal sensitive information) or exploit the computer in other ways. See Chapter 5 for ways on how to prevent XSS.

Replay

A **replay attack** is a network attack in which a valid data transmission is maliciously or fraudulently repeated or delayed. This differs from session hijacking in that the original session is simply intercepted and analyzed for later use. In a replay attack an attacker might use a packet sniffer to intercept data and retransmit it later. In this way, the attacker can impersonate the entity that originally sent the data. For example, if customers were to log in to a banking website with their credentials while an attacker was watching, the attacker could possibly sniff out the packets that include the usernames and passwords and then possibly connect with those credentials later on. Of course, if the bank uses SSL or TLS to secure login sessions, then the attacker would have to decrypt the data as well, which could prove more difficult. An organization can defend against this attack in several ways. The first is to use session tokens that are transmitted to people the first time they attempt to connect, and identify them subsequently. They are handed out randomly so that attackers cannot guess at token numbers. The second way is to implement timestamping and synchronization as in a Kerberos environment. A third way would be to use a time-stamped **nonce**, a random number issued by an authentication protocol that can be used only one time. We talk more about SSL, TLS, Kerberos, and other crypto-graphic solutions in Chapter 15. You can also implement CHAP-based authentica-tion protocols to provide protection against replay attacks.

NOTE   A replay attack should not be confused with SMTP relay, which is when one server forwards e-mail to other e-mail servers.

Null Sessions

A **null session** is a connection to the Windows interprocess communications share (IPC$). The null session attack is a type of exploit that makes unauthenticated Net-BIOS connections to a target computer. The attack uses ports 139 and 445, which are the NetBIOS session port and the Server Message Block (SMB) port, respec-tively. If successful, an attacker could find user IDs, share names, and various set-tings and could possibly gain access to files, folders, and other resources. An example of the initial code an attacker might use is

```
net use \\IP address\ipc$ "" /U: ""
```

Afterward, the attacker might use a program such as enum.exe or something simi-lar to extract information from the remote computer, such as usernames. Finally, an attacker might use a brute-force attack in an attempt at cracking passwords and gaining more access.

To protect against this attack, computers should be updated as soon as possible. However, the best way to defend against this attack is to filter out traffic on ports 139 and 445 with a firewall or a host-based intrusion prevention system. When a firewall is enabled, ports 139 and 445 will not appear to exist.

NOTE   Command-line scripting in general can be used for legitimate and illegiti-mate purposes: The former by security administrators, and the latter by malicious in-siders. Tools such as the Command Prompt, PowerShell, Windows Scripting Host, and the command-line in general, can all be used for malevolent purposes. To that effect, operating systems should be updated and patched often, and access to these programs should be secured by using permissions, UAC, and other similar tools.

Transitive Access and Client-Side Attacks

Transitive access is not really a specific attack, but a way or means of attacking a computer. It is based on the transitive property in mathematics, which states that whenever A is equal to B, and B is equal to C, then A is equal to C, summed up as

If A = B and B = C, then A = C

That's just a piece of the transitive property, but you get the gist of it. What we are really dealing with here is trust. Does one computer on the LAN trust another? Can that trust be manipulated? For example, let's say that computer C is a server that hosts a database. Now, let's say that computer B is a client on the LAN that frequently accesses the database and is authorized to do so. This is all well and good, and is normal. However, add in the attacker, at computer A. If the attacker can somehow create a trusted environment between computer A and computer B, then by way of transitivity, the attacker can obtain a trust with computer C, and then the database can become compromised. Normally, the attacker at computer A cannot access the database at computer C. But by compromising computer B, the attacker can then launch a client-side attack, one that is coming from a computer on the LAN that would otherwise be harmless.

Trusting relationships are created between computers (and sometimes networks) to save time and to bypass authentication methods. It would seem like a good idea at first, but when you think of all the vulnerable operating systems and applications on client computers, each one of which is a possible opening for transitive access, it makes sense that nowadays the general rule is to have every client computer authenticated whenever any session is started to another computer (perhaps even twice!). Implementing this practice along with the use of firewalls, intrusion detection/ prevention systems, and updates is the best way to prevent transitive access and client-side attacks. In many environments, the rule is that no one computer should trust any other by default, and if a computer needs to do so, it happens only temporarily, and in a secure fashion.

DNS Poisoning and Other DNS Attacks

DNS poisoning (or DNS cache poisoning) is the modification of name resolution information that should be in a DNS server's cache. It is done to redirect client computers to incorrect websites. This can happen through improper software design, misconfiguration of name servers, and maliciously designed scenarios exploiting the traditionally open architecture of the DNS system. Let's say a client wants to go to www.comptia.org. That client's DNS server will have a cache of information about domain names and their corresponding IP addresses. If CompTIA's site were visited in the recent past by any client accessing the DNS server, its domain name and IP should be in the DNS server's cache. If the cache is poisoned, it could be modified in such a way to redirect requests for www.comptia.org to a different IP address and website. This other site could be a phishing site or could be malicious in some other way. This attack can be countered by using Transport Layer Security (TLS) and digital signatures or by using Secure DNS (DNSSEC), which uses encrypted electronic signatures when passing DNS information, and finally, by patching the DNS server. You might use a Transaction Signature (TSIG) to provide authentication for DNS database updates. This protocol uses shared secret keys and one-way hashing to provide security. One item of note: the hashing procedure might not be secure enough for your organization, so you may want to consider alternatives when updating DNS databases.

Unauthorized zone transfers are another bane to DNS servers. Zone transfers replicate the database that contains DNS data; they operate on top of TCP. If a zone transfer is initiated, say through a reconnaissance attack, server name and IP address information can be stolen, resulting in the attacker accessing various hosts by IP address. To defend against this, zone transfers should be restricted and audited in an attempt to eliminate unauthorized zone transfers and to identify anyone who tries to exploit the DNS server in this manner. Vigilant logging of the DNS server and the regular checking of DNS records can help detect unauthorized zone transfers.

A Windows computer's hosts file can also be the victim of attack. The hosts file is used on a local computer to translate or resolve hostnames to IP addresses. This is the predecessor to DNS, and although the file is normally empty of entries, it is still read and parsed by Windows operating systems. Attackers may attempt to hijack the hosts file in an attempt to alter or poison it or to try to have the client bypass DNS altogether. The best defense for this is to modify the computer's hosts file permissions to read-only. It is located at the following path: \%systemroot%\System32\drivers\etc.

If the file has already been hijacked, and you don't use the file for any static entries, delete it, and Windows should re-create it automatically at the next system startup. If Windows does not, then a standard hosts file can be easily re-created by simply making a blank hosts.txt file and placing it in the path mentioned previously. The hosts file is used by some people as a security measure as well. This is done by adding entries that redirect known bad domains to other safe locations or the localhost. Generally, this is done in conjunction with disabling the DNS client service. However, in general, the DNS client service is required by the average Windows user.

Hosts files and vulnerable DNS software can also be victims of pharming attacks. **Pharming** is when an attacker redirects one website's traffic to another website that is bogus and possibly malicious. Pharming can be prevented by carefully monitoring DNS configurations and hosts files. Unfortunately, if an ISP's DNS server is compromised, that will be passed on to all the small office/home office routers that the ISP services. So, it becomes more important for end users to be conscious of pharming. They can prevent it by turning on phishing and pharming filters within the browser, and by being careful of which websites they access. Users can also check their local hosts files. By default, the file doesn't have any entries, so if they see entries and have never modified the file themselves, they should either delete the entries or delete the file entirely.

Although it is less of an actual attack, **domain name kiting** (or simply domain kiting) is the process of deleting a domain name during the five-day grace period (known as the add grace period, or AGP) and immediately reregistering it for another five-day period. This process is repeated any number of times with the end result of having the domain registered without ever actually paying for it. It is a malicious attack on the entire Domain Name System by misusing the domain-tasting grace period. The result is that a legitimate company or organization often cannot secure the domain name of its choice.

As you can see, the DNS server can be the victim of many attacks due to its visibility on the Internet. It should be closely monitored at all times. Other highly visible servers such as web servers and mail servers should be likewise monitored, audited, and patched as soon as updates are available.

ARP Poisoning

The Address Resolution Protocol (ARP) resolves IP addresses to MAC addresses. Any resolutions that occur over a set amount of time are stored in the ARP table. The ARP table can be poisoned or spoofed. **ARP poisoning** is an attack that exploits Ethernet networks, and it may enable an attacker to sniff frames of information, modify that information, or stop it from getting to its intended destination. The spoofed frames of data contain a false source MAC address, which deceives other devices on the network. The idea behind this is to associate the attacker's MAC address with an IP address of another device, such as a default gateway or router, so that any traffic that would normally go to the gateway would end up at the attacker's computer. The attacker could then perpetuate a man-in-the-middle attack, or a denial-of-service attack, in addition to MAC flooding. Some of the defenses for ARP poisoning include VLAN segregation/VLAN separation (creating multiple virtual LANs in an effort to thwart the attack), DHCP snooping, and an open source program called ArpON (http://arpon.sourceforge.net/).

Summary of Network Attacks

Table 7-3 summarizes important network attacks and mitigation techniques discussed in this chapter that you should know for the Security+ exam. Keep in mind that we covered some other device-oriented attacks in the previous chapter. Plus, there are always new attacks being invented. Keep abreast of the latest attacks and prevention methods.

Key Topic

Table 7-3 Summary of Important Network Attacks and Mitigation Techniques

Network Attack	Description	Mitigation Techniques
Ping flood	Type of DoS. When an attacker sends many ICMP echo request packets (pings) to a host in an attempt to use up all available bandwidth.	Configure the system not to respond to ICMP echoes.
Smurf attack	Type of DoS. Sends large amounts of ICMP echoes, broadcasting the ICMP echo requests to every computer on its network or subnetwork. The header of the ICMP echo requests will have a spoofed IP address. That IP address is the target of the Smurf attack. Every computer that replies to the ICMP echo requests will do so to the spoofed IP.	Configure hosts not to respond to pings or ICMP echoes. Configure routers not to forward packets directed to broadcast addresses. Implement subnetting with smaller subnetworks. Employ network ingress filtering.
Fraggle	Type of DoS. Similar to the Smurf attack, but the traffic sent is UDP echo traffic as opposed to ICMP echo traffic.	Configure routers not to forward packets directed to broadcast addresses. Employ network filtering, disabling ports 7 and 19.
SYN flood	Type of DoS. When an attacker sends a large amount of SYN request packets to a server in an attempt to deny service.	Recycle half-open connections after a predetermined amount of time. Use intrusion detection systems (IDSs) to detect the attack.
Ping of Death	Type of DoS. Sends an oversized and malformed packet to another computer.	Configure hosts not to respond to pings or ICMP echoes. Verify operating systems are running the latest service packs and updates. Update the firmware on any hardware-based firewalls, and update any software-based firewalls as well.
Teardrop attack	Type of DoS. Sends mangled IP fragments with overlapping and oversized payloads to the target machine.	Upgrade operating systems. Consider third-party downloads.

Network Attack	Description	Mitigation Techniques
DDoS	When a group of compromised systems attacks a single target, causing a DoS to occur at that host, possibly using a botnet.	Update firewalls. Use IPS. Utilize a "clean pipe."
DNS amplification attack	A DDoS consisting of a high volume of amplified DNS packets with a spoofed source IP address.	Block spoofed source packets. Update DNS servers. Block unnecessary DNS servers.
Spoofing	When an attacker masquerades as another person by falsifying information.	Carefully select applications. User awareness. In the case of IP spoofing, incorporate packet filtering, and repeat authentication schemes.
Session theft/ session hijacking	When an attacker attempts to steal a user's session using the owner's cookie and authentication information.	Use encryption. Use CHAP.
TCP/IP hijacking	When an attacker takes over a TCP session between two computers without the need of a cookie or any other type of host access.	Employ encrypted transport protocols such as SSL, IPsec, and SSH.
Man-in-the-middle (MITM)	Form of eavesdropping that intercepts all data between a client and a server, relaying that information back and forth.	Implement SSL/TLS using a mutually trusted third-party certification authority.
Man-in-the-browser (MITB)	Infects a vulnerable web browser in the hopes of modifying online transactions.	Update the web browser. Use a virtual browser. Use transaction verification. Update anti-malware.
Watering hole attack	When websites the victim visits are profiled, infected, and ultimately redirect the victim to illegitimate sites.	Update the browser or use a virtual browser or VM. Update anti-malware programs. Harden the system.

Network Attack	Description	Mitigation Techniques
Replay attack	Valid data transmission is maliciously or fraudulently repeated or delayed.	Use session tokens. Implement timestamping and synchronization. Use a nonce.
Null session	A connection to the Windows interprocess communications share (IPC$).	Update computers. Filter ports 139 and 445.
Transitive access	When one computer uses a second computer to attack a third, based on the trust of the second and third computers.	Authentication. Firewalls. IDS/IPS. Updates.
DNS poisoning	The modification of name resolution information that should be in a DNS server's cache.	Use TLS. Utilize Secure DNS.
Unauthorized zone transfers	Unauthorized transfer of DNS information from a DNS server.	Log the DNS server. Restrict and audit the DNS server.
Altered hosts file	When an attacker attempts to hijack the hosts file and have the client bypass the DNS server or access incorrect websites.	Change permission on the hosts file to read-only.
Domain name kiting	The process of deleting a domain name during the 5-day grace period (known as the add grace period, or AGP) and immediately reregistering it for another 5-day period.	Not many ways to defend against this other than creating rules that charge fees for people who kite domain names.
ARP poisoning	An attack that exploits Ethernet networks, and it may enable an attacker to sniff frames of information, modify that information, or stop it from getting to its intended destination.	VLAN segregation. DHCP snooping. Third-party tools like ArpON.

Chapter Summary

Just as cracks in a dam are vulnerabilities to anything standing in a nearby valley, open ports are vulnerabilities to computer networks. The teaming flood of network attacks is seemingly endless; and though new network attacks are constantly being devised, these threats have to be dealt with in a proactive manner.

All metaphors aside, this means you are required to have a thorough understanding of the many networking protocols in use today, and their corresponding port numbers. Knowledge of inbound ports is the most important because they correlate to the services that run on a server; these are the doorways that attackers use to access a system. Servers that run protocols such as HTTP, FTP, SMTP, and so on should be updated, hardened, and secured appropriately. Secure versions of these protocols should be implemented. Any nonessential protocols and services (such as the deprecated Telnet or, for instance, TFTP) should be stopped and disabled. This effectively closes the ports in question. Know it all! You should memorize the ports mentioned in this chapter because you will be scanning for open ports such as these in upcoming chapters. If there is ever confusion about a port or protocol, remember to access the IANA website for more information.

The whole point of reducing the attack surface of a system is so that malicious network attacks will have a more difficult time accessing that system. For example, let's say you have a server running Microsoft Internet Information Services (IIS) and have a website running on it that uses HTTP, but you unknowingly also have FTP running on that server, using port 21. The server could be easy prey for attacks designed to infiltrate via port 21. But it doesn't have to be this way! Using secure ports, closing ports, disabling services, and, of course, using firewalls are vital defenses. Chapter 8 covers additional equipment such as network intrusion detection systems, proxies, and the varying types of firewalls.

In this day and age there is a cornucopia of network attacks. When observing your network and servers, attacks such as denial-of-service (DoS), distributed DoS (DDoS), spoofing, hijacking, replays, amplification, and poisoning should be at the top of your list. But the security administrator must wear multiple hats. In addition to investigator, one of your roles is that of researcher. You must study the latest attacks and CVEs for a system, watch for updates and bulletins, and visit online forums and discussion groups often. However, the role of "watcher" is probably one of the best descriptive terms for a security administrator. You must constantly scrutinize your servers and network equipment. This everlasting vigil is part of the job. Those who are alert and observant shall prevail, and those who are not...well, they risk the danger of becoming enveloped by the flood of threats that lurks just outside (and sometimes inside) the computer network.

Chapter Review Activities

Use the features in this section to study and review the topics in this chapter.

Review Key Topics

Review the most important topics in the chapter, noted with the Key Topic icon in the outer margin of the page. Table 7-4 lists a reference of these key topics and the page number on which each is found.

Table 7-4   Key Topics for Chapter 7

Key Topic Element	Description	Page Number
Table 7-2	Ports and their associated protocols	219
Figure 7-2	IP addresses and ports	222
Table 7-3	Summary of network attacks and mitigation techniques	239

Define Key Terms

Define the following key terms from this chapter, and check your answers in the glossary:

denial-of-service (DoS), ping flood, Smurf attack, Fraggle, SYN flood, flood guard, Ping of Death, teardrop attack, permanent DoS attack, fork bomb, distributed denial-of-service (DDoS), DNS amplification attack, spoofing, phishing, TCP/IP hijacking, man-in-the-middle (MITM), man-in-the-browser (MITB), watering hole attack, replay attack, nonce, null session, DNS poisoning, pharming, domain name kiting, ARP poisoning

Complete the Real-World Scenarios

Complete the Real-World Scenarios found on the companion website (www.pearsonitcertification.com/title/9780789758996). You will find a PDF containing the scenario and questions, and also supporting videos and simulations.

Review Questions

Answer the following review questions. Check your answers with the correct answers that follow.

1. Which of the following is an example of a nonessential protocol?

   A. DNS

   B. ARP

   C. TCP

   D. TFTP

2. A person attempts to access a server during a zone transfer to get access to a zone file. What type of server is that person trying to manipulate?

   A. Proxy server

   B. DNS server

   C. File server

   D. Web server

3. Which one of the following can monitor and protect a DNS server?

   A. Ping the DNS server.

   B. Block port 53 on the firewall.

   C. Purge PTR records daily.

   D. Check DNS records regularly.

4. Which TCP port does LDAP use?

   A. 389

   B. 80

   C. 443

   D. 143

5. From the list of ports, select two that are used for e-mail. (Select the two best answers.)

   A. 110

   B. 3389

   C. 143

   D. 389

6. Which port number does the Domain Name System use?

   A. 53

   B. 80

   C. 110

   D. 88

7. John needs to install a web server that can offer SSL-based encryption. Which of the following ports is required for SSL transactions?

   A. Port 80 inbound

   B. Port 80 outbound

   C. Port 443 inbound

   D. Port 443 outbound

8. If a person takes control of a session between a server and a client, it is known as what type of attack?

   A. DDoS

   B. Smurf

   C. Session hijacking

   D. Malicious software

9. Making data appear as if it is coming from somewhere other than its original source is known as what?

   A. Hacking

   B. Phishing

   C. Cracking

   D. Spoofing

10. Which of the following enables an attacker to float a domain registration for a maximum of five days?

   A. Kiting

   B. DNS poisoning

   C. Domain hijacking

   D. Spoofing

11. What is the best definition for ARP?

    A. Resolves IP addresses to DNS names

    B. Resolves IP addresses to hostnames

    C. Resolves IP addresses to MAC addresses

    D. Resolves IP addresses to DNS addresses

12. You have three e-mail servers. What is it called when one server forwards e-mail to another?

    A. SMTP relay

    B. Buffer overflows

    C. POP3

    D. Cookies

13. A coworker goes to a website but notices that the browser brings her to a different website and that the URL has changed. What type of attack is this?

    A. DNS poisoning

    B. Denial of service

    C. Buffer overflow

    D. ARP poisoning

14. Which of the following misuses the Transmission Control Protocol handshake process?

    A. Man-in-the-middle attack

    B. SYN attack

    C. WPA attack

    D. Replay attack

15. For a remote tech to log in to a user's computer in another state, what inbound port must be open on the user's computer?

    A. 21

    B. 389

    C. 3389

    D. 8080

16. A DDoS attack can be best defined as what?

    A. Privilege escalation

    B. Multiple computers attacking a single server

    C. A computer placed between a sender and receiver to capture data

    D. Overhearing parts of a conversation

17. When users in your company attempt to access a particular website, the attempts are redirected to a spoofed website. What are two possible reasons for this?

    A. DoS

    B. DNS poisoning

    C. Modified hosts file

    D. Domain name kiting

18. What kind of attack is it when the packets sent do not require a synchronization process and are not connection-oriented?

    A. Man-in-the-middle

    B. TCP/IP hijacking

    C. UDP attack

    D. ICMP flood

19. Which of the following attacks is a type of DoS attack that sends large amounts of UDP echoes to ports 7 and 19?

    A. Teardrop

    B. IP spoofing

    C. Fraggle

    D. Replay

20. Don must configure his firewall to support TACACS+. Which port(s) should he open on the firewall?

    A. Port 53

    B. Port 49

    C. Port 161

    D. Port 22

21. Which of the following ports is used by Kerberos by default?

   A. 21

   B. 80

   C. 88

   D. 443

22. Which of the following is the best option if you are trying to monitor network devices?

   A. SNMP

   B. Telnet

   C. FTPS

   D. IPsec

23. What is a secure way to remotely administer Linux systems?

   A. SCP

   B. SSH

   C. SNMP

   D. SFTP

24. Your web server that conducts online transactions crashed, so you examine the HTTP logs and see that a search string was executed by a single user masquerading as a customer. The crash happened immediately afterward. What type of network attack occurred?

   A. DDoS

   B. DoS

   C. MAC spoofing

   D. MITM

   E. DNS amplification attack

25. Which port number is ultimately used by SCP?

   A. 22

   B. 23

   C. 25

   D. 443

26. A malicious insider is accused of stealing confidential data from your organization. What is the best way to identify the insider's computer?

    A. IP address

    B. MAC address

    C. Computer name

    D. NetBIOS name

27. What is the best way to utilize FTP sessions securely?

    A. FTPS

    B. FTP passive

    C. FTP active

    D. TFTP

28. Which of the following is the most secure protocol for transferring files?

    A. FTP

    B. SSH

    C. FTPS

    D. Telnet

29. Which of the following protocols allow for the secure transfer of files? (Select the two best answers.)

    A. SNMP

    B. SFTP

    C. TFTP

    D. SCP

    E. ICMP

30. Your organization wants to implement a secure e-mail system using the POP3 and SMTP mail protocols. All mail connections need to be secured with SSL. Which of the following ports should you be using? (Select the two best answers.)

    A. 25

    B. 110

    C. 143

    D. 465

    E. 993

    F. 995

Answers and Explanations

1. **D.** TFTP (Trivial File Transfer Protocol) is a simpler version of FTP that uses a small amount of memory. It is generally considered to be a nonessential protocol. The Domain Name System service (or DNS service) is required for Internet access and on Microsoft domains. The Address Resolution Protocol (ARP) is necessary in Ethernet networks that use TCP/IP. TCP stands for Transmission Control Protocol, an essential part of most network communications.

2. **B.** DNS servers are the only types of servers listed that do zone transfers. The purpose of accessing the zone file is to find out what hosts are on the network.

3. **D.** By checking a DNS server's records regularly, a security admin can monitor and protect it. Blocking port 53 on a firewall might protect it (it also might make it inaccessible depending on the network configuration) but won't enable you to monitor it. Pinging the server can simply tell you whether the server is alive. Purging pointer records (PTR) cannot help to secure or monitor the server.

4. **A.** The Lightweight Directory Access Protocol (LDAP) uses port TCP 389. Note: If you are working with secure LDAP, then you will be using port 636. Port 80 is used by HTTP. Port 443 is used by HTTPS. Port 143 is used by IMAP.

5. **A and C.** POP3 uses port 110; IMAP uses port 143; 3389 is used by the Remote Desktop Protocol; and 389 is used by LDAP.

6. **A.** The Domain Name System (DNS) uses port 53. Port 80 is used by HTTP; port 110 is used by POP3; and port 88 is used by Kerberos.

7. **C.** For clients to connect to the server via SSL, the server must have inbound port 443 open. The outbound ports on the server are of little consequence for this concept, and inbound port 80 is used by HTTP.

8. **C.** Session hijacking (or TCP/IP hijacking) is when an unwanted mediator takes control of the session between a client and a server (for example, an FTP or HTTP session).

9. **D.** Spoofing is when a malicious user makes data or e-mail appear to be coming from somewhere else.

10. **A.** Kiting is the practice of monopolizing domain names without paying for them. Newly registered domain names can be canceled with a full refund during an initial five-day window known as an AGP, or add grace period. Domain hijacking is another type of hijacking attack where the attacker changes the

registration of a domain name without the permission of the original owner/registrant.

11. **C.** The Address Resolution Protocol, or ARP, resolves IP addresses to MAC addresses. DNS resolves from IP addresses to hostnames, and vice versa. RARP is Reverse ARP; it resolves MAC addresses to IP addresses.

12. **A.** The SMTP relay is when one server forwards e-mail to other e-mail servers. Buffer overflows are attacks that can be perpetuated on web pages. POP3 is another type of e-mail protocol, and cookies are small text files stored on the client computer that remember information about that computer's session with a website.

13. **A.** DNS poisoning can occur at a DNS server and can affect all clients on the network. It can also occur at an individual computer. Another possibility is that spyware has compromised the browser. A denial-of-service is a single attack that attempts to stop a server from functioning. A buffer overflow is an attack that, for example, could be perpetuated on a web page. ARP poisoning is the poisoning of an ARP table, creating confusion when it comes to IP address-to-MAC address resolutions.

14. **B.** A synchronize (SYN) attack misuses the TCP three-way handshake process. The idea behind this is to overload servers and deny access to users. A man-in-the-middle (MITM) attack is when an attacker is situated between the legitimate sender and receiver and captures and (potentially) modifies packets in transit. Though not a common term, an example of a WPA attack would be the cracking of an access point's password. A replay attack is when data is maliciously repeated or delayed.

15. **C.** Port 3389 must be open on the inbound side of the user's computer to enable a remote tech to log in remotely and take control of that computer. Port 21 is the port used by FTP, and 389 is used by LDAP. 8080 is another port used by web browsers that takes the place of port 80.

16. **B.** When multiple computers attack a single server, it is known as a distributed denial-of-service attack, or DDoS. Privilege escalation is when a person who is not normally authorized to a server manages to get administrative permissions to resources. If a computer is placed between a sender and receiver, it is known as a man-in-the-middle attack. Overhearing parts of a conversation is known as eavesdropping.

17. **B and C.** DNS poisoning and a DNS server's modified hosts files are possible causes for why a person would be redirected to a spoofed website. DoS, or denial-of-service, is when a computer attempts to attack a server to stop it from functioning. Domain name kiting is when a person renews and cancels domains within five-day periods.

18. **C.** User Datagram Protocol (UDP) attacks, or UDP flood attacks, are DoS attacks that use a computer to send a large number of UDP packets to a remote host. The remote host will reply to each of these with an ICMP Destination Unreachable packet, which ultimately makes it inaccessible to clients. The man-in-the-middle (MITM) attack is when an attacker secretly relays and possibly alters information between two parties. TCP/IP hijacking is an attack that spoofs a server into thinking it is talking with a valid client when in reality it is not. An ICMP flood (or ping flood) is a basic DoS where many ICMP packets are sent out without waiting for replies.

19. **C.** A Fraggle attack is a type of DoS attack that sends large amounts of UDP echoes to ports 7 and 19. This is similar to the Smurf attack. Teardrop DoS attacks send many IP fragments with oversized payloads to a target. IP spoofing is when an attacker sends IP packets with a forged source IP address. The replay attack is when valid data transmissions are maliciously repeated or delayed.

20. **B.** Port 49 is used by TACACS+. Port 53 is used by DNS, port 161 is used by SNMP, and port 22 is used by SSH.

21. **C.** Port 88 is used by Kerberos by default. Port 21 is used by FTP, port 80 is used by HTTP, and port 443 is used by HTTPS (TLS/SSL).

22. **A.** SNMP (Simple Network Management Protocol) is the best protocol to use to monitor network devices. Telnet is a deprecated protocol that is used to remotely administer network devices. FTPS provides for the secure transmission of files from one computer to another. IPsec is used to secure VPN connections and other IP connections.

23. **B.** SSH (Secure Shell) is used to remotely administer Unix/Linux systems and network devices. SCP (Secure Copy) is a way of transferring files securely between two hosts—it utilizes SSH. SNMP is used to remotely monitor network equipment. SFTP is used to securely transfer files from host to host—it also uses SSH.

24. **B.** A denial-of-service (DoS) attack probably occurred. The attacker most likely used code to cause an infinite loop or repeating search, which caused the server to crash. It couldn't have been a DDoS (distributed denial-of-service) because only one attacker was involved. MAC spoofing is when an attacker disguises the MAC address of his network adapter with another number. MITM stands for the man-in-the-middle attack, which wasn't necessary since the attacker had direct access to the search fields on the web server. A DNS amplification attack is when an attacker spoofs DNS requests to flood a target website.

25. **A.** SCP (Secure Copy) uses SSH, which runs on port 22 by default. Port 23 is Telnet, port 25 is SMTP, and port 443 is HTTPS (SSL/TLS).

26. **B.** The MAC address is the best way because it is unique and is the hardest to modify or spoof. IP addresses are often dynamically assigned on networks and are easily modified. Computer names (which are effectively NetBIOS names) can easily be changed as well.

27. **A.** FTPS (FTP Secure) uses encryption in the form of SSL or TLS to secure file transfers. The other three options are basically variations on FTP; they do not use encryption, making them less secure.

28. **C.** FTPS (FTP Secure) is the most secure protocol (listed) for transferring files. It uses SSL or TLS to secure FTP transmissions utilizing ports 989 and 990. FTP by itself is inherently insecure and uses port 21 by default. The truly distracting answer here, SSH, allows a person to remotely access another computer securely, but it's the Secure FTP (SFTP) protocol that works on top of SSH that is considered a secure way of transferring files. Telnet is outdated and insecure. Because of this it is not found on most of today's operating systems, but if it is, it should be removed, or at least stopped and disabled.

29. **B and D.** The Secure FTP (SFTP) and Secure Copy (SCP) protocols provide for the secure transfer of files. The Simple Network Management Protocol (SNMP) is used to monitor various parts of the network. Trivial FTP (TFTP) is not secure by default. The Internet Control Message Protocol (ICMP) is the protocol initiated by ping to invoke responses from other computers.

30. **D and F.** To implement SSL encrypted e-mail communications you would use port 465 for SMTP (or perhaps 587) and port 995 for POP3. Other ports can be assigned by the admin, but they would have to be configured properly at the server side and the client side, and must not conflict with any other well-known ports or other ports currently in use within the organization's network. Port 25 is the default port for regular SMTP. Port 110 is the default for POP3. Port 143 is the default for IMAP. Port 993 is used by IMAP encrypted with SSL/TLS.

This chapter covers the following subjects:

- **Firewalls and Network Security:** In this section, you find out about one of the most important strategic pieces in your network security design—the firewall. Then we discuss other network security concepts such as packet filtering, access control lists, proxy servers, and honeypots.

- **NIDS Versus NIPS:** This section delves into the characteristics, advantages, disadvantages, and differences of network intrusion *detection* systems and network intrusion *prevention* systems.

This chapter is all about the network border, also known as the **network perimeter**. This should be a network security administrator's primary focus when it comes to securing the network because it contains the entrances that many attackers attempt to use.

CHAPTER 8

Network Perimeter Security

Allow me to analogize for a few moments. I've said it before; as you read this book, you are building yourself an impenetrable castle of knowledge, culminating in hands-on familiarity and the know-how to pass the exam. But we can use the castle analogy for your network as well. Imagine a big stone castle with tall walls, an expanse of clear land around the castle, or perhaps a moat surrounding it (with alligators, of course), and one or more drawbridges. The tall walls are meant to keep the average person out, sort of like a firewall in a computer network—not perfect, but necessary. The open area around the castle makes it difficult for people to sneak up on your castle; they would quickly be *detected*, just like malicious packets detected by a network intrusion detection system. Or better yet, if you had a moat, people trying to cross it would have a difficult time, would be easy targets for your bowmen, and would probably be gobbled up by your pet alligators. This would represent a network intrusion *prevention* system, which not only detects threats, but also eliminates those threats to the network.

The drawbridge, or drawbridges, could be seen as network ports open to the network. As drawbridges are part of the castle wall, so network ports are part of the firewall. You, as the network security administrator, have the ability and the right to close these ports at any time. At the risk of taking this analogy even further, you might decide to set traps for people; like a pool of quicksand that has an open netted bag of pyrite suspended above it, or maybe a false entry to the castle that, after a long corridor, is walled off on the inside, ultimately trapping the unwary. In a network environment, these would be known as honeypots. Of course, every once in a while, legitimate traffic needs to enter and exit your network, too! To do this in a more secure fashion, you can set up proxy servers to act as go-betweens for the computers inside your network and the servers they talk to on the Internet: kind of like a sentry in the tower of the castle that would relay an outsider's messages to someone inside the castle.

The network perimeter is less tangible in an actual network environment (thus the previous use of superfluous metaphor). Networking devices are commonly located in a single server room or data center, or perhaps are located in a hybrid of in-house and cloud-based locations. Either way, they can be difficult to visualize. To better envision your network, one of the best tips I can give you is to map out your network on paper, or create network documentation using programs such as Microsoft Visio and by utilizing network mapping tools (more on these tools in Chapter 12, "Vulnerability and Risk Assessment").

So, before we end up playing *Dungeons & Dragons*, let's talk about one of the most important parts of your strategic defense—the firewall.

Foundation Topics

Firewalls and Network Security

Nowadays, firewalls are everywhere. Businesses large and small use them, and many households have simpler versions of these protective devices as well. You need to be aware of several types of firewalls, and you definitely want to spend some time configuring hardware and software firewalls. There are many free software-based firewalls and firmware-based emulators that you can download. A quick search on the Internet will give you several options.

The firewall is there to protect the entire network, but other tools are often implemented as well; for example, proxy servers that help protect users and computers by keeping them anonymous; honeypots meant to attract hackers, crackers, and other types of attackers into a false computer or network; and data loss prevention (DLP) devices to keep confidential data from leaving the network. But by far, the most important element in your network will be the firewall, so let's begin with that.

Firewalls

In Chapter 3, "Computer Systems Security Part II," we discussed personal firewalls—you remember, the kind installed to an individual computer. Now let's broaden the scope of your knowledge with network-based firewalls. Network-based firewalls are primarily used to section off and protect one network from another. They are a primary line of defense and are *extremely* important in network security. There are several types of firewalls; some run as software on server computers, some as standalone dedicated appliances, and some work as just one function of many on a single device. They are commonly represented as a sort of "brick wall" between a LAN and the Internet, as shown in Figure 8-1.

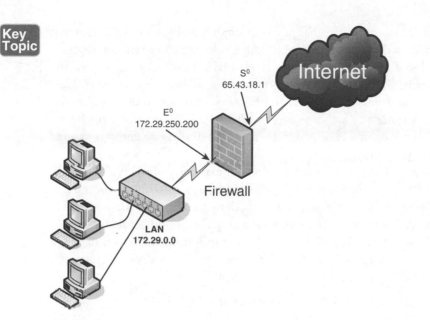

Figure 8-1   Diagram of a Basic Firewall Implementation

Just as a firewall in a physical building is there to slow the spread of a fire and contain it until the fire department arrives, a firewall in a computer network is there to keep fire at bay in the form of malicious attacks. Often, a firewall (or the device the firewall resides on) has NAT in operation as well. In Figure 8-1, note that the firewall has a local address of 172.29.250.200; this connects it to the LAN. It also has an Internet address of 65.43.18.1, enabling connectivity for the entire LAN to the Internet, while hiding the LAN IP addresses. By default, the IP address 65.43.18.1 is completely shielded. This means that all inbound ports are effectively closed and will not enable incoming traffic, unless a LAN computer initiates a session with another system on the Internet. However, a good security administrator always checks this to make sure; first, by accessing the firewall's firmware (or software application, as the case may be) and verifying that the firewall is on, and next by scanning the firewall with third-party applications such as Nmap (https://nmap.org) or with a web-based port scanning utility, as was shown in a Chapter 7 Real-world Scenario. If any ports are open, or unshielded, they should be dealt with immediately. Then the firewall should be rescanned for vulnerabilities. You can find more information on port scanning and vulnerability assessments in Chapter 12.

Important point: Firewalls should be used only as they were intended. The company firewall should not handle any other extraneous services—for example, acting as a web server or SMTP server. By using a firewall as it was intended, its vulnerability is reduced.

Generally, a firewall inspects traffic that passes through it and permits or denies that traffic based on rules set by an administrator. These rules are stored within **access control lists** (ACLs). In regards to firewalls, an ACL is a set of rules that applies to a list of network names, IP addresses, and port numbers. These rules can be configured to control inbound and outbound traffic. This is a bit different than ACLs with respect to operating systems, which we cover in Chapter 11, "Access Control Methods and Models," but the same basic principles apply: Basically, one entity is granted or denied permission to another entity. If you decide that a specific type of traffic should be granted access to your network, you would **explicitly allow** that traffic as a rule within an ACL. If on the other hand you decide that a specific type of traffic should *not* be granted access, you would **explicitly deny** that traffic within an ACL. And finally, if a type of network traffic is not defined in the firewall's rule set, it should be stopped by default. This is the concept of **implicit deny** and is usually a default rule found in a firewall's ACL. It is often added automatically to the end of a firewall's rule set (ACLs) and is also known as "block all."

Firewall rules should be specific. Here's an example of a firewall rule:

```
deny TCP any any port 53
```

This rule can be used to restrict DNS zone transfers (as they run on top of TCP and use port 53), but other DNS traffic will still function properly. The rule is specific; it gives the transport layer protocol to be filtered, and the exact port, and also states that it applies to *any* computer's IP address on the inbound and outbound side. Be careful with firewall rules and ACLs; they need to be written very cautiously so as not to filter required traffic.

> **NOTE**   Traffic can also be passed to other computers and servers, or to specific ports. For a quick tutorial on setting up virtual servers and port forwarding on a typical SOHO router/firewall, see the following link: http://www.davidlprowse.com/articles/?p=916.

A lot of today's firewalls have two types of firewall technologies built into them: SPI and NAT. However, you also should be aware of a couple other types of firewall methodologies:

Key Topic

- **Packet filtering:** Inspects each packet passing through the firewall and accepts or rejects it based on rules. However, there are two types: stateless packet inspection and **stateful packet inspection** (also known as SPI or a stateful firewall). A stateless packet filter, also known as pure packet filtering, does not retain memory of packets that have passed through the firewall; due to this, a stateless packet filter can be vulnerable to IP spoofing attacks. But a firewall running stateful packet inspection is normally not vulnerable to this because it keeps track of the state of network connections by examining the header in each packet. It can distinguish between legitimate and illegitimate packets. This function operates at the network layer of the OSI model.

- **NAT filtering:** Also known as NAT endpoint filtering, filters traffic according to ports (TCP or UDP). This can be done in three ways: by way of basic endpoint connections, by matching incoming traffic to the corresponding outbound IP address connection, or by matching incoming traffic to the corresponding IP address and port.

- **Application-level gateway (ALG):** Applies security mechanisms to specific applications, such as FTP or BitTorrent. It supports address and port translation and checks whether the type of application traffic is allowed. For example, your company might allow FTP traffic through the firewall, but might decide to disable Telnet traffic (probably a wise choice). The ALG checks each type of packet coming in and discards Telnet packets. Although this adds a powerful layer of security, the price is that it is resource-intensive, which could lead to performance degradation.

- **Circuit-level gateway:** Works at the session layer of the OSI model, and applies security mechanisms when a TCP or UDP connection is established; it acts as a go-between for the transport and application layers in TCP/IP. After the connection has been made, packets can flow between the hosts without further checking. Circuit-level gateways hide information about the private network, but they do not filter individual packets.

A firewall can be set up in several different physical configurations. For example, in Chapter 6, "Network Design Elements," we discussed implementing a DMZ. This could be done in a back-to-back configuration (two firewalls surrounding the DMZ), as shown in Figure 8-2, or as a 3-leg perimeter configuration.

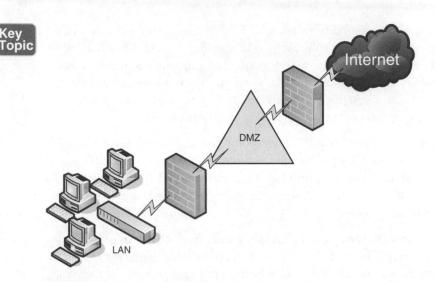

Figure 8-2   Back-to-Back Firewall/DMZ Configuration

Generally, there will be one firewall with the network and all devices and computers residing "behind" it. By the way, if a device is "behind" the firewall, it is also considered to be "after" the firewall, and if the device is "in front of" the firewall, it is also known as being "before" the firewall. Think of the firewall as the drawbridge of a castle. When you are trying to gain admittance to the castle, the drawbridge will probably be closed. You would be in front of the drawbridge, and the people inside the castle would be behind the drawbridge. This is a basic analogy but should help you to understand the whole "in front of" and "behind" business as it relates to data attempting to enter the network and devices that reside on your network.

Logging is also important when it comes to a firewall. Firewall logs should be the first thing you check when an intrusion has been detected. You should know how to access the logs and how to read them. For example, Figure 8-3 shows two screen captures: The first displays the Internet sessions on a basic SOHO router/firewall, and the second shows log events such as blocked packets. Look at the blocked Gnutella packet that is pointed out. I know it is a Gnutella packet because the inbound port on my firewall that the external computer is trying to connect to shows as port 6346; this associates with Gnutella. Gnutella is an older P2P file-sharing network. None of the computers on this particular network use or are in any way connected to the Gnutella service. These external computers are just random clients of the Gnutella P2P network trying to connect to anyone possible.

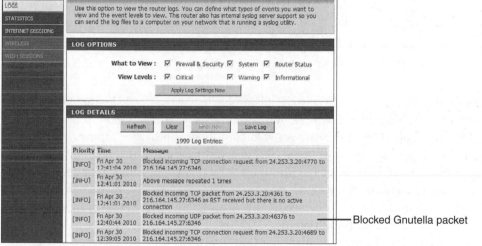

Figure 8-3 SOHO Router/Firewall Internet Sessions

It's good that these packets have been blocked, but maybe you don't want the IP
address shown (24.253.3.20) to have any capability to connect to your network at all.
To eliminate that IP, you could add it to an inbound filter or to an ACL.

So far, we have discussed host-based firewalls (in Chapter 3) and, just now, network-
based firewalls. However, both of these firewalls can also fall into the category of
application firewall. If either type runs protocols that operate on the application
layer of the OSI model, then it can be classified as an application firewall. That
means that it can control the traffic associated with specific applications. This is

something a stateful network firewall cannot do, as this function operates at the application layer of the OSI model. Many host-based firewalls fall into this category, but when it comes to network-based firewalls, it varies. A basic SOHO router with built-in firewalling capabilities would usually not fall into the application firewall category. However, more advanced network appliances from companies such as Barracuda, Citrix, Fortinet, and Smoothwall do fall into this category. This means that they allow for more in-depth monitoring of the network by controlling the input, output, and access to applications and services all the way up through the application layer of the OSI model. These appliances might also be referred to as *network-based application layer firewalls*. Now that's a mouthful—just be ready for multiple terms used by companies and technicians.

Going a step further, some of the aforementioned network appliances have tools that are designed to specifically protect HTTP sessions from XSS attacks and SQL injection. These types of tools are known as **web application firewalls**. WAFs can help to protect the servers in your environment.

NOTE   A firewall appliance needs more than one network adapter so that it can connect to more than one network; this is known as a *multihomed connection*. It might be dual-homed (two adapters), or perhaps it has more, maybe three network adapters, in case you want to implement a DMZ or another perimeter security technique.

Firewalls are often considered to be all-in-one devices, but actually they provide specific functionality as discussed in this section. Still, it is common to hear people refer to a firewall when they are really talking about another technology, or even another device. For example, many SOHO users have an all-in-one multifunction network device. This device has four ports for wired connections, plus a wireless antenna; it connects all the computers to the Internet, and finally has a firewall built-in. Because some users consider this to be simply a firewall, you should teach them about the benefits of disabling SSID broadcasting, and enabling MAC filtering. By disabling Service Set Identifier (SSID) broadcasting, the average user cannot connect wirelessly to the device. An attacker knows how to bypass this, but it is an important element of security that you should implement after all trusted computers have been connected wirelessly. MAC filtering denies access to any computer that does not have one of the MAC addresses you list, another powerful tool that we will cover more in Chapter 9, "Securing Network Media and Devices."

To make matters a bit more confusing, a firewall can also act as, or in combination with, a proxy server, which we discuss in the following section.

Proxy Servers

A **proxy server** acts as an intermediary for clients, usually located on a LAN, and the servers that they want to access, usually located on the Internet. By definition, *proxy* means go-between, or mediator, acting as such a mediator in between a private network and a public network. The proxy server evaluates requests from clients and, if they meet certain criteria, forwards them to the appropriate server. There are several types of proxies, including a couple you should know for the exam:

Key Topic

- **IP proxy:** Secures a network by keeping machines behind it anonymous; it does this through the use of NAT. For example, a basic four-port router can act as an IP proxy for the clients on the LAN it protects. An IP proxy can be the victim of many of the network attacks mentioned in Chapter 6, especially DoS attacks. Regardless of whether the IP proxy is an appliance or a computer, it should be updated regularly, and its log files should be monitored periodically and audited according to organization policies.

- **Caching proxy:** Attempts to serve client requests without actually contacting the remote server. Although there are FTP and SMTP proxies, among others, the most common caching proxy is the **HTTP proxy**, also known as a **web proxy,** which caches web pages from servers on the Internet for a set amount of time. Examples of caching proxies include WinGate (for Windows systems) and Squid (commonly used on Linux-based systems). An example of a caching proxy is illustrated in Figure 8-4. For example, let's say a co-worker of yours (Client A) accessed www.google.com, and that she was the first person to do so on the network. This client request will go through the HTTP proxy and be redirected to Google's web server. As the data for Google's home page comes in, the HTTP proxy will store or cache that information. When another person on your network (Client B) makes a subsequent request for www.google.com, the bulk of that information will come from the HTTP proxy instead of from Google's web server. This is done to save bandwidth on the company's Internet connection and to increase the speed at which client requests are carried out. Most HTTP proxies check websites to verify that nothing has changed since the last request. Because information changes quickly on the Internet, a time limit of 24 hours is common for storing cached information before it is deleted. Web browsers make use of a **proxy auto-configuration (PAC)** file, which defines how the browser can automatically choose a proxy server. The file itself and the embedded JavaScript function pose a security risk in that the file can be exploited and modified, ultimately redirecting the user to unwanted (and potentially malicious) websites. Consider disabling PAC files and auto-configuration in general within client web browsers.

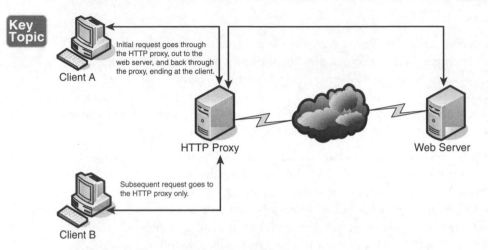

Figure 8-4   Illustration of an HTTP Proxy in Action

Other types of proxies are available to apply policies, block undesirable websites, audit employee usage, and scan for malware. One device or computer might do all these things or just one or two. It depends on the software used or appliance installed. Reverse proxies can also be implemented to protect a DMZ server's identity or to provide authentication and other secure tasks. This is done when users on the Internet are accessing server resources on your network. Generally, a proxy server has more than one network adapter so that it can connect to the various networks it is acting as a mediator for. Each of the network adapters in a proxy should be periodically monitored for improper traffic and for possible network attacks and other vulnerabilities. A proxy server might be the same device as a firewall, or it could be separate. Because of this, a multitude of network configurations are possible. Proxy servers, especially HTTP proxies, can be used maliciously to record traffic sent through them; because most of the traffic is sent in unencrypted form, this could be a security risk. A possible mitigation for this is to chain multiple proxies together in an attempt to confuse any onlookers and potential attackers.

Most often, a proxy server is implemented as a *forward proxy*. This means that clients looking for websites, or files via an FTP connection, pass their requests through to the proxy. However, there is also a *reverse proxy*, where *multiple* HTTP or FTP servers use a proxy server and send out content to one or more clients. These HTTP and FTP servers could be located in a server farm or similar grouping, and the reverse proxy might also undertake the role of load balancer in this situation. A reverse proxy can act as another layer of defense for an organization's FTP or HTTP servers. An *application proxy* might be used as a reverse proxy; for example, Microsoft's Web Application Proxy, which enables remote users to connect to the organization's internal network to access multiple servers. These are often multipurpose by design, allowing for HTTP, FTP, e-mail, and other types of data connections. However, it could be that you have a single application stored on several servers. Those servers can work together utilizing clustering technology. The clustering might be controlled by the servers themselves or, more commonly, a load balancer can be installed in front of the servers that distributes the network load among them. That load balancer in effect acts as a reverse proxy.

Regardless of the type of proxy used, it will often modify the requests of the "client computer," whatever that client is, providing for a level of anonymity. But in some cases, you might need a proxy that does not modify requests. This is known as a *transparent proxy*. While it allows for increased efficiency, there is less protection for the client system.

Another example of a proxy in action is Internet content filtering. An **Internet content filter**, or simply a content filter, is usually applied as software at the application layer and can filter out various types of Internet activities such as websites accessed, e-mail, instant messaging, and more. It often functions as a content inspection device, and disallows access to inappropriate web material (estimated to be a big percentage of the Internet!) or websites that take up far too much of an organization's Internet bandwidth. Internet content filters can be installed on individual clients, but by far the more efficient implementation is as an individual proxy that acts as a mediator between all the clients and the Internet. These proxy versions of content filters secure the network in two ways: one, by forbidding access to potentially malicious websites, and two, by blocking access to objectionable material that employees might feel is offensive. It can also act as a URL filter; even if employees inadvertently type an incorrect URL, they can rest assured that any objectionable material will not show up on their display.

Internet filtering appliances analyze just about all the data that comes through them, including Internet content, URLs, HTML tags, metadata, and security certificates such as the kind you would automatically receive when going to a secure site that starts with https. (However, revoked certificates and certificate revocation lists, or CRLs, will not be filtered because they are only published periodically. More on certificates and CRLs is provided in Chapter 15, "PKI and Encryption Protocols.") Some of these appliances are even capable of malware inspection. Another similar appliance is the web security gateway. **Web security gateways** (such as Forcepoint, previously known as Websense) act as go-between devices that scan for viruses, filter content, and act as data loss prevention (DLP) devices. This type of content inspection/content filtering is accomplished by actively monitoring the users' data streams in search of malicious code, bad behavior, or confidential data that should not be leaked outside the network.

As you can see, many, many options for security devices are available for your network, and many vendors offer them. Based on price, you can purchase all kinds of devices, from ones that do an individual task, to ones that are combinations of everything we spoke about so far, which are also known as *all-in-one security appliances* or unified threat management (UTM) devices (discussed in the upcoming "NIDS Versus NIPS" section).

> **NOTE**   Proxies, content filters, and web security gateways are examples of servers that probably face the Internet directly. These "Internet-facing servers" require security controls before they are installed. The two most important security controls are to keep the application up to date, and to review and apply vendor-provided hardening documentation. Remember to do these things before putting the proxy server (or other Internet-facing servers) in a live environment.

Honeypots and Honeynets

Honeypots and honeynets attract and trap potential attackers to counteract any attempts at unauthorized access of the network. This isolates the potential attacker in a monitored area and contains dummy resources that look to be of value to the perpetrator. While an attacker is trapped in one of these, their methods can be studied and analyzed, and the results of those analyses can be applied to the general security of the functional network.

A **honeypot** is generally a single computer but could also be a file, group of files, or an area of unused IP address space, whereas a **honeynet** is one or more computers, servers, or an area of a network; a honeynet is used when a single honeypot is not sufficient. Either way, the individual computer, or group of servers, will *usually* not house any important company information. Various analysis tools are implemented to study the attacker; these tools, along with a centralized group of honeypots (or a honeynet), are known collectively as a honeyfarm.

One example of a honeypot in action is the spam honeypot. Spam e-mail is one of the worst banes known to a network administrator; a spam honeypot can lure spammers in, enabling the network administrators to study the spammers' techniques and habits, thus allowing the network admins to better protect their actual e-mail servers, SMTP relays, SMTP proxies, and so on, over the long term. It might ultimately keep the spammers away from the real e-mail addresses, because the spammers are occupied elsewhere. Some of the information gained by studying spammers is often shared with other network admins or organizations' websites dedicated to reducing spam. A spam honeypot could be as simple as a single e-mail address or as complex as an entire e-mail domain with multiple SMTP servers.

Of course, as with any technology that studies attackers, honeypots also bear risks to the legitimate network. The honeypot or honeynet should be carefully firewalled off from the legitimate network to ensure that the attacker can't break through.

Often, honeypots and honeynets are used as part of a more complex solution known as a network intrusion detection system, discussed following a short review of data loss prevention.

Data Loss Prevention (DLP)

We mentioned DLP in Chapter 3. Let's discuss it briefly now as it relates to networks. **Data loss prevention (DLP)** systems are designed to protect data by way of content inspection. They are meant to stop the leakage of confidential data, often concentrating on communications. As such, they are also referred to as data leak prevention (DLP) devices, information leak prevention (ILP) devices, and extrusion prevention systems. Regardless, they are intended to be used to keep data from leaking past a computer system or network and into unwanted hands.

In network-based DLP, systems deal with data in motion and are usually located on the perimeter of the network. If data is classified in an organization's policy as confidential and not to be read by outsiders, the DLP system detects it and prevents it from leaving the network. Network-based DLP systems can be hardware-based or software-based. An example of a network-based DLP system would be one that detects and prevents the transfer of confidential e-mail information outside the network. Organizations such as Check Point offer DLP solutions, and there are some free open source applications as well. Going further, there are cloud based DLP solutions available. But it all depends on where you store your data. If you store some or all of your data on the cloud, or if you have a large bring your own device (BYOD) or choose your own device (CYOD) population, then cloud-based DLP becomes an important part of your security strategy. Because the data—and the security of that data—is now external from the company, planning becomes even more vital. Some key elements of the security mindset include: 1) planning for the mitigation of security risks; 2) adequate understanding of the cloud-based provider, where and how data is stored, and their service-level agreement (SLA); 3) in-depth analysis of code and the types of data that will be stored in the cloud; and 4) strong authentication, auditing, and logging. If all this is planned for and implemented properly, it can build the organization's confidence in the cloud, which can lead to a smoother transition, and ultimately reduce risk. However, all this becomes a bigger conversation: We'll talk more about general mindsets when dealing with cloud-based companies in Chapter 16, "Redundancy and Disaster Recovery," and Chapter 18, "Policies and Procedures."

As for DLP, the monitoring of possible leaked information could become a privacy concern. Before implementing a system of this nature, it is important to review your organization's privacy policies. Leaks can still occur due to poor implementation of DLP systems, so it is essential to plan what type of DLP solution your organization needs, exactly how it will be installed, and how it will be monitored.

NIDS Versus NIPS

It's not a battle royale, but you should be able to differentiate between a network intrusion *detection* system (NIDS) and a network intrusion *prevention* system (NIPS) for the exam. Previously, in Chapter 4, "OS Hardening and Virtualization," we discussed host-based intrusion detection systems (or HIDSs). Although a great many attacks can hamper an individual computer, just as many network attacks could possibly take down a server, switch, router, or even an entire network. Network-based IDSs were developed to detect these malicious network attacks, and network-based IPSs were developed in an attempt to prevent them.

NIDS

A **network intrusion detection system (NIDS)** by definition is a type of IDS that attempts to detect malicious network activities, for example, port scans and DoS attacks, by constantly monitoring network traffic. It can also be instrumental in rogue machine detection, including rogue desktops, laptops, and mobile devices, as well as rogue access points, DHCP servers, and network sniffers. Examples of NIDS solutions include open-source products such as Snort (https://www.snort.org/), Bro (https://www.bro.org/), and many other commercial hardware and software-based products. A NIDS should be situated at the entrance or gateway to your network. It is not a firewall but should be used with a firewall. Because the NIDS inspects every packet that traverses your network, it needs to be fast; basically, the slower the NIDS, the slower the network. So, the solution itself, the computer/device it is installed on, and the network connections of that computer/device all need to be planned out accordingly to ensure that the NIDS does not cause network performance degradation.

Figure 8-5 illustrates how a NIDS might be implemented on a network. Often it is placed in front of a firewall. The NIDS detects attacks and anomalies and alerts the administrator if they occur, whereas the firewall does its best to prevent those attacks from entering the network. However, a NIDS could be placed behind the firewall, or you might have multiple NIDS points strategically placed around the network. If the NIDS is placed in front of the firewall, it generates a lot more administrator alerts, but these can usually be whittled down within the firmware or software of the device running the NIDS. Regardless of where the NIDS is located, a network administrator should monitor traffic from time to time; to do so, the computer, server, or appliance that has the NIDS installed should have a network adapter configured to work in **promiscuous mode**. This passes all traffic to the CPU, not just the frames addressed to it.

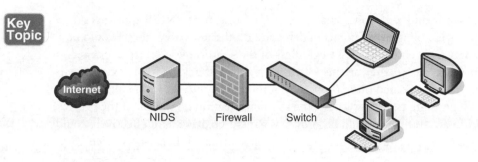

Figure 8-5 Illustration of NIDS Placement in a Network

The beauty of a NIDS is that you might get away with one or two NIDS points
on the network, and do away with some or all the HIDS installed on individual
computers, effectively lowering the bottom line while still doing a decent job of
mitigating risk. A couple of disadvantages of a NIDS, aside from possible network
performance issues, are that it might not be able to read encrypted packets of information and will not detect problems that occur on an individual computer. Therefore, to secure a network and its hosts, many organizations implement a mixture of
NIDS and HIDS. If a NIDS is placed in front of the firewall, it is subject to attack;
therefore, it should be monitored and updated regularly. Some NIDS solutions will
auto-update. Finally, the biggest disadvantage of a NIDS is that it is passive, meaning it only *detects* attacks; to protect against, or *prevent*, these attacks, you need something active, you need a NIPS.

NIPS

A **network intrusion prevention system (NIPS)** is designed to inspect traffic
and, based on its configuration or security policy, either remove, detain, or redirect malicious traffic that it becomes aware of. The NIPS (as well as the NIDS) is
considered to be an *application-aware device*, meaning it can divine different types of
packets, define what application they are based on, and ultimately permit or disallow
that traffic on the network. More and more companies are offering NIPS solutions
in addition to, or instead of, NIDS solutions. Examples of NIPS solutions include
Check Point security appliances (https://www.checkpoint.com), and the aforementioned Snort, which is actually a NIDS/NIPS software package that should be
installed on a dual-homed or multihomed server. Not only can a NIPS go above and
beyond a NIDS by removing or redirecting malicious traffic, it can also redirect a
recognized attacker to a single computer known as a padded cell, which contains no
information of value and has no way out.

Like a NIDS, a NIPS should sit inline on the network, often in front of the firewall, although it could be placed elsewhere, depending on the network segment
it protects and the network architecture. Whereas many NIPS solutions have two

connections only and are known as perimeter solutions, other NIPS appliances have up to 16 ports enabling many points of detection on the network—these would be known as network "core" devices. Regardless of the solution you select, as packets pass through the device, they are inspected for possible attacks. These devices need to be accurate and updated often (hopefully automatically) to avoid the misidentification of legitimate traffic, or worse, the misidentification of attacks. If the NIPS blocks legitimate traffic, it would be known as a **false positive**, and effectively could deny service to legitimate customers, creating a self-inflicted denial-of-service of sorts.

If the IPS does not have a particular attack's signature in its database, and lets that attack through thinking it is legitimate traffic, it is known as a **false negative**, also bad for obvious reasons! Many IPS systems can monitor for attack signatures and anomalies. More information on signatures can be found in Chapter 4 and Chapter 13, "Monitoring and Auditing." Another type of error that can occur with NIDS and NIPS is a subversion error; this is when the NIDS/NIPS has been altered by an attacker to allow for false negatives, ultimately leading to attacks creeping into the network. This can be deadly because the NIDS/NIPS often is the first point of resistance in the network. To protect against this, some devices have the capability to hide or mask their IP address. They might also come with an internal firewall. It is also important to select an IPS solution that has a secure channel for the management console interface.

One advantage of newer NIPS solutions is that some of them can act as protocol analyzers by reading encrypted traffic and stopping encrypted attacks. In general, the beauty of a NIPS compared to a host-based IPS (HIPS) is that it can protect non-computer-based network devices such as switches, routers, and firewalls. However, the NIPS is considered a single point of failure because it sits inline on the network. Due to this, some organizations opt to install a bypass switch, which also enables the NIPS to be taken offline when maintenance needs to be done.

A vital NIPS consideration is whether to implement a fail-close or fail-open policy—in essence, deciding what will happen if the NIPS fails. Fail-close means that all data transfer is stopped, while fail-open means that data transfer (including potential attacks) are passed through. Let's consider an example. Say that the NIPS was protecting an individual server (or router), and had a certain level of control over that system. Now let's say that the NIPS failed. In a fail-close scenario, it would disconnect the system that it is protecting, stopping all data transfer. This is unacceptable to some organizations that require near 100 percent uptime. These organizations are willing to accept additional risk, and therefore are more receptive to a fail-open scenario. However, in this case, if the NIPS fails, it continues to pass all traffic to the "protected" system, which could include possible attacks. Sometimes, fail-open scenarios are necessary. In these cases, defense in depth is the best strategy. For instance, you might opt to have a firewall filter the bulk of traffic coming into the network, but have the IPS filter only specific traffic, reducing the chances of IPS failure. This layered approach can offer greater security with less chance of attacks passing through, but often comes with increased cost and administration.

Summary of NIDS Versus NIPS

Table 8-1 summarizes NIDS versus NIPS.

Key Topic

Table 8-1   Summary of NIDS Versus NIPS

Type of System	Summary	Disadvantage/Advantage	Example
NIDS	Detects malicious network activities	Pro: Only a limited number of NIDSs are necessary on a network. Con: Only detects malicious activities.	Snort Bro IDS
NIPS	Detects, removes, detains, and redirects traffic	Pro: Detects and mitigates malicious activity. Pro: Can act as a protocol analyzer. Con: Uses more resources. Con: Possibility of false positives and false negatives.	Check Point Systems solutions

The Protocol Analyzer's Role in NIDS and NIPS

You might be familiar already with protocol analyzers such as Wireshark (previously Ethereal) or Network Monitor. These are loaded on a computer and are controlled by the user in a GUI environment; they capture packets, enabling the user to analyze them and view their contents. However, some NIDS/NIPS solutions are considered to be full protocol analyzers with no user intervention required. The protocol analyzer is built into the NIDS/NIPS appliance. It decodes application layer protocols, such as HTTP, FTP, or SMTP, and forwards the results to the IDS or IPS analysis engine. Then the analysis engine studies the information for anomalous or behavioral exploits. This type of analysis can block many exploits based on a single signature. This is superior to basic signature pattern recognition (without protocol analysis), because with signature-based IDS/IPS solutions, many signatures have to be constantly downloaded and stored in the device's database, and they don't enable dynamic understanding of new attacks. However, as with any powerful analysis, like protocol analysis, a premium is placed on processing power, and the price of these types of IDS/IPS solutions will undoubtedly be higher.

NOTE   There are also wireless versions of IDS: WIDS and WIPS. They monitor the radio spectrum for unauthorized access and rogue access points. However, these names might be incorporated into the concept of NIDS and NIPS by some organizations. Regardless, be sure to use an IDS (or IPS) for your wired and wireless connections!

Unified Threat Management

A relatively newer concept, **unified threat management (UTM)** is the culmination of everything we discussed in this chapter so far. As early as the year 2000, it was realized that the firewall was no longer enough to protect an organization's network. Other devices and technologies such as NIDS/NIPS systems, content filters, anti-malware gateways, data leak prevention, and virtual private networks were added to the network in order to better protect it. However, with all these extra devices and technologies come added cost and more administration. And so, UTM providers simplify the whole situation by offering all-in-one devices that combine the various levels of defense into one solution. The all-in-one device might also be referred to as a next-generation firewall (NGFW). Companies such as Cisco, Fortinet, and Sophos (to name a few) offer UTM and NGFW solutions; often this is a single device that sits last on the network before the Internet connection. They usually come with a straightforward web-based GUI, which is good news for the beleaguered security administrator who might be burning the midnight oil researching the latest attacks and prevention methods. There's a caveat to all this, and it is a common theme in network security: a single point of defense is a single point of failure. Get past the UTM, and your job as an attacker is done. Secondary and backup UTM devices, as well as server-based HIDSs, strike a balance and create a certain level of defense in depth, while still retaining a level of simplicity. Another consideration is that UTMs should be quick. If they are to take the place of several other devices, then their data processing and traffic flow requirements will be steep. The smart network administrator/security administrator will consider a device that exceeds their current needs and then some.

It was important to discuss each of the tools and technologies separately in this chapter so that you understand how to work with each. But keep in mind that many of these technologies are consolidated into a single solution, a trend that will likely continue as we move forward.

Chapter Summary

Well, it goes without saying that there are many potential attackers who would "storm the castle." The question presents itself: Have you performed your due diligence in securing your computer networking kingdom?

If you answered yes, then it most likely means you have implemented some kind of unified threat management solution; one that includes a firewall, content filter, anti-malware technology, IDS/IPS, and possibly other network security technologies. This collaborative effort makes for a strong network perimeter. The firewall is at the frontlines, whether it is part of a UTM or running as a separate device. Its importance can't be stressed enough, and you can't just implement a firewall; it has to be configured properly with your organization's policies in mind. ACLs, stateful packet inspection, and network address translation should be employed to solidify your firewall solution.

If you answered no, then prepare ye for more metaphorical expression. Remember that enemy forces are everywhere. They are lying in wait just outside your network, and they can even reside within your network—for example, the malicious insider, that dragon who has usurped the mountain and is perhaps in control of your precious treasure...your data. Analogies aside, this is all clear and present danger—it is *real*, and should be enough to convince you to take strong measures to protect your network.

Often, the act of securing the network can also provide increased efficiency and productivity. For example, a proxy server can act to filter content, and can provide anonymity, but also saves time and bandwidth for commonly accessed data. A honeypot can trap an attacker, thus securing the network, but the secondary result is that network bandwidth is not gobbled up by the powerful attacker. However, the same act can have the opposite effect. For example, a NIDS that is installed to detect anomalies in packets can slow down the network if it is not a powerful enough model. For increased efficiency (and lower all-around cost), consider an all-in-one device such as a UTM, which includes functionality such as firewalling, IDS/IPS, AV, VPN, and DLP. Just make sure it has the core processing and memory required to keep up with the amount of data that will flow through your network.

If you can find the right balance of security and performance while employing your network security solution, it will be analogous to your network donning the aegis, acting as a powerful shield against network attacks from within and without.

Chapter Review Activities

Use the features in this section to study and review the topics in this chapter.

Review Key Topics

Review the most important topics in the chapter, noted with the Key Topic icon in the outer margin of the page. Table 8-2 lists a reference of these key topics and the page number on which each is found.

Table 8-2   Key Topics for Chapter 8

Key Topic Element	Description	Page Number
Figure 8-1	Diagram of a basic firewall	257
Bulleted list	Types of firewalls	258
Figure 8-2	Back-to-back firewall/DMZ configuration	260
Bulleted list	Types of proxies	263
Figure 8-4	Illustration of an HTTP proxy in action	264
Figure 8-5	Illustration of NIDS placement in a network	269
Table 8-1	Summary of NIDS versus NIPS	271

Define Key Terms

Define the following key terms from this chapter, and check your answers in the glossary:

network perimeter, access control list, explicit allow, explicit deny, implicit deny, packet filtering, stateful packet inspection, application-level gateway, circuit-level gateway, application firewall, web application firewall, proxy server, IP proxy, HTTP proxy (web proxy), proxy auto-configuration (PAC), Internet content filter, web security gateway, honeypot, honeynet, data loss prevention (DLP), network intrusion detection system (NIDS), promiscuous mode, network intrusion prevention system (NIPS), false positive, false negative, unified threat management (UTM)

Complete the Real-World Scenarios

Complete the Real-World Scenarios found on the companion website (www.pearsonitcertification.com/title/9780789758996). You will find a PDF containing the scenario and questions, and also supporting videos and simulations.

Review Questions

Answer the following review questions. Check your answers with the correct answers that follow.

1. Which tool would you use if you want to view the contents of a packet?

   A. TDR

   B. Port scanner

   C. Protocol analyzer

   D. Loopback adapter

2. The honeypot concept is enticing to administrators because

   A. It enables them to observe attacks.

   B. It traps an attacker in a network.

   C. It bounces attacks back at the attacker.

   D. It traps a person physically between two locked doors.

3. James has detected an intrusion in his company network. What should he check first?

   A. DNS logs

   B. Firewall logs

   C. The Event Viewer

   D. Performance logs

4. Which of the following devices should you employ to protect your network? (Select the best answer.)

   A. Protocol analyzer

   B. Firewall

   C. DMZ

   D. Proxy server

5. Which device's log file will show access control lists and who was allowed access and who wasn't?

   A. Firewall

   B. Smartphone

   C. Performance Monitor

   D. IP proxy

6. Where are software firewalls usually located?

    A. On routers

    B. On servers

    C. On clients

    D. On every computer

7. Where is the optimal place to have a proxy server?

    A. In between two private networks

    B. In between a private network and a public network

    C. In between two public networks

    D. On all of the servers

8. A coworker has installed an SMTP server on the company firewall. What security principle does this violate?

    A. Chain of custody

    B. Use of a device as it was intended

    C. Man trap

    D. Use of multifunction network devices

9. You are working on a server and are busy implementing a network intrusion detection system on the network. You need to monitor the network traffic from the server. What mode should you configure the network adapter to work in?

    A. Half-duplex mode

    B. Full-duplex mode

    C. Auto-configuration mode

    D. Promiscuous mode

10. Which of the following displays a single public IP address to the Internet while hiding a group of internal private IP addresses?

    A. HTTP proxy

    B. Protocol analyzer

    C. IP proxy

    D. SMTP proxy

    E. PAC

11. If your ISP blocks objectionable material, what device would you guess has been implemented?

   A. Proxy server

   B. Firewall

   C. Internet content filter

   D. NIDS

12. Of the following, which is a collection of servers that was set up to attract attackers?

   A. DMZ

   B. Honeypot

   C. Honeynet

   D. VLAN

13. Which of the following will detect malicious packets and discard them?

   A. Proxy server

   B. NIDS

   C. NIPS

   D. PAT

14. Which of the following will an Internet filtering appliance analyze? (Select the three best answers.)

   A. Content

   B. Certificates

   C. Certificate revocation lists

   D. URLs

15. Which of the following devices would detect but not react to suspicious behavior on the network? (Select the most accurate answer.)

   A. NIPS

   B. Firewall

   C. NIDS

   D. HIDS

   E. UTM

16. One of the programmers in your organization complains that he can no longer transfer files to the FTP server. You check the network firewall and see that the proper FTP ports are open. What should you check next?

    A. ACLs

    B. NIDS

    C. AV definitions

    D. FTP permissions

17. Which of the following is likely to be the last rule contained within the ACLs of a firewall?

    A. Time of day restrictions

    B. Explicit allow

    C. IP allow any

    D. Implicit deny

18. Which of the following best describes an IPS?

    A. A system that identifies attacks

    B. A system that stops attacks in progress

    C. A system that is designed to attract and trap attackers

    D. A system that logs attacks for later analysis

19. What is a device doing when it actively monitors data streams for malicious code?

    A. Content inspection

    B. URL filtering

    C. Load balancing

    D. NAT

20. Allowing or denying traffic based on ports, protocols, addresses, or direction of data is an example of what?

    A. Port security

    B. Content inspection

    C. Firewall rules

    D. Honeynet

21. Which of the following should a security administrator implement to limit web-based traffic that is based on the country of origin? (Select the three best answers.)

   A. AV software

   B. Proxy server

   C. Spam filter

   D. Load balancer

   E. Firewall

   F. URL filter

   G. NIDS

22. You have implemented a technology that enables you to review logs from computers located on the Internet. The information gathered is used to find out about new malware attacks. What have you implemented?

   A. Honeynet

   B. Protocol analyzer

   C. Firewall

   D. Proxy

23. Which of the following is a layer 7 device used to prevent specific types of HTML tags from passing through to the client computer?

   A. Router

   B. Firewall

   C. Content filter

   D. NIDS

24. Your boss has asked you to implement a solution that will monitor users and limit their access to external websites. Which of the following is the best solution?

   A. NIDS

   B. Proxy server

   C. Block all traffic on port 80

   D. Honeypot

25. Which of the following firewall rules only denies DNS zone transfers?

    A. `deny IP any any`

    B. `deny TCP any any port 53`

    C. `deny UDP any any port 53`

    D. `deny all dns packets`

Answers and Explanations

1. **C.** A protocol analyzer has the capability to "drill" down through a packet and show the contents of that packet as they correspond to the OSI model. A TDR is a time-domain reflectometer, a tool used to locate faults in cabling. (I threw that one in for fun. It is a Network+ level concept, so you security people should know it!) A port scanner identifies open network ports on a computer or device; we'll discuss that more in Chapters 12 and 13. A loopback adapter is a device that can test a switch port or network adapter (depending on how it is used).

2. **A.** By creating a honeypot, the administrator can monitor attacks without sustaining damage to a server or other computer. Don't confuse this with a honeynet (answer B), which is meant to attract and trap malicious attackers in an entirely false network. Answer C is not something that an administrator would normally do, and answer D is defining a man trap.

3. **B.** If there was an intrusion, James should check the firewall logs first. DNS logs in the Event Viewer and the performance logs will most likely not show intrusions to the company network. The best place to look first is the firewall logs.

4. **B.** Install a firewall to protect the network. Protocol analyzers do not help to protect a network but are valuable as vulnerability assessment and monitoring tools. Although a DMZ and a proxy server could possibly help to protect a portion of the network to a certain extent, the best answer is firewall.

5. **A.** A firewall contains one or more access control lists (ACLs) defining who is enabled to access the network. The firewall can also show attempts at access and whether they succeeded or failed. A smartphone might list who called or e-mailed, but as of the writing of this book does not use ACLs. Performance Monitor analyzes the performance of a computer, and an IP proxy deals with network address translation, hiding many private IP addresses behind one public address. Although the function of an IP proxy is often built into a firewall, the best answer would be firewall.

6. **C.** Software-based firewalls, such as Windows Firewall, are normally running on the client computers. Although a software-based firewall could also be run on a server, it is not as common. Also, a SOHO router might have a built-in firewall, but not all routers have firewalls.

7. **B.** Proxy servers should normally be between the private network and the public network. This way they can act as a go-between for all the computers located on the private network. This applies especially to IP proxy servers but might also include HTTP proxy servers.

8. **B.** SMTP servers should not be installed on a company firewall. This is not the intention of a firewall device. The SMTP server should most likely be installed within a DMZ.

9. **D.** To monitor the implementation of NIDS on the network, you should configure the network adapter to work in promiscuous mode; this forces the network adapter to pass all the traffic it receives to the processor, not just the frames that were addressed to that particular network adapter. The other three answers have to do with duplexing—whether the network adapter can send and receive simultaneously.

10. **C.** An IP proxy displays a single public IP address to the Internet while hiding a group of internal private IP addresses. It sends data back and forth between the IP addresses by using network address translation (NAT). This functionality is usually built into SOHO routers and is one of the main functions of those routers. HTTP proxies store commonly accessed Internet information. Protocol analyzers enable the capture and viewing of network data. SMTP proxies act as a go-between for e-mail. PAC stands for proxy auto-config, a file built into web browsers that allows the browser to automatically connect to a proxy server.

11. **C.** An Internet content filter, usually implemented as content-control software, can block objectionable material before it ever gets to the user. This is common in schools, government agencies, and many companies.

12. **C.** A honeynet is a collection of servers set up to attract attackers. A honeypot is usually one computer or one server that has the same purpose. A DMZ is the demilitarized zone that is in between the LAN and the Internet. A VLAN is a virtual LAN.

13. **C.** A NIPS, or network intrusion prevention system, detects and discards malicious packets. A NIDS only detects them and alerts the administrator. A proxy server acts as a go-between for clients sending data to systems on the Internet. PAT is port-based address translation.

14. **A, B, and D.** Internet filtering appliances will analyze content, certificates, and URLs. However, certificate revocation lists will most likely not be analyzed. Remember that CRLs are published only periodically.

15. **C.** A NIDS, or network intrusion detection system, will detect suspicious behavior but most likely will not react to it. To prevent it and react to it, you would want a NIPS. Firewalls block certain types of traffic but by default do not check for suspicious behavior. HIDS is the host-based version of an IDS; it checks only the local computer, not the network. A UTM is an all-inclusive security product that will probably include an IDS or IPS—but you don't know which, so you can't assume that a UTM will function in the same manner as a NIDS.

16. **A.** Access control lists can stop specific network traffic (such as FTP transfers) even if the appropriate ports are open. A NIDS will detect traffic and report on it but not prevent it. Antivirus definitions have no bearing on this scenario. If the programmer was able to connect to the FTP server, the password should not be an issue. FTP permissions might be an issue, but since you are working in the firewall, you should check the ACL first; then later you can check on the FTP permissions, passwords, and so on.

17. **D.** Implicit deny (block all) is often the last rule in a firewall; it is added automatically by the firewall, not by the user. Any rules that allow traffic will be before the implicit deny/block all on the list. Time of day restrictions will probably be stored elsewhere but otherwise would be before the implicit deny as well.

18. **B.** An IPS (intrusion prevention system) is a system that prevents or stops attacks in progress. A system that only identifies attacks would be an IDS. A system designed to attract and trap attackers would be a honeypot. A system that logs attacks would also be an IDS or one of several other devices or servers.

19. **A.** A device that is actively monitoring data streams for malicious code is inspecting the content. URL filtering is the inspection of the URL only (for example, https://www.comptia.org). Load balancing is the act of dividing up workload between multiple computers; we'll discuss that more in Chapter 16, "Redundancy and Disaster Recovery." NAT is network address translation, which is often accomplished by a firewall or IP proxy.

20. **C.** Firewall rules (ACLs) are generated to allow or deny traffic. They can be based on ports, protocols, IP addresses, or which way the data is headed. Port security deals more with switches and the restriction of MAC addresses that

are allowed to access particular physical ports. Content inspection is the filtering of web content, checking for inappropriate or malicious material. A honeynet is a group of computers or other systems designed to attract and trap an attacker.

21. **B, E, and F.** The security administrator should implement a proxy server, a firewall, and/or a URL filter. These can all act as tools to reduce or limit the amount of traffic based on a specific country. AV software checks for, and quarantines, malware. Spam filters will reduce the amount of spam that an e-mail address or entire e-mail server receives. A load balancer spreads out the network load to various switches, routers, and servers. A NIDS is used to detect anomalies in network traffic.

22. **A.** A honeynet has been employed. This is a group of computers on the Internet, or on a DMZ (and sometimes on the LAN), that is used to trap attackers and analyze their attack methods, whether they are network attacks or malware attempts. A protocol analyzer captures packets on a specific computer in order to analyze them but doesn't capture logs per se. A firewall is used to block network attacks but not malware. A proxy is used to cache websites and act as a filter for clients.

23. **C.** A content filter is an application layer (layer 7) device that is used to prevent undesired HTML tags, URLs, certificates, and so on, from passing through to the client computers. A router is used to connect IP networks. A firewall blocks network attacks. A NIDS is used to detect anomalous traffic.

24. **B.** You should implement a proxy server. This can limit access to specific websites, and monitor who goes to which websites. Also, it can often filter various HTML and website content. A NIDS is used to report potentially unwanted data traffic that is found on the network. Blocking all traffic on port 80 is something you would accomplish at a firewall, but that would stop all users from accessing any websites that use inbound port 80 (the great majority of them!). A honeypot is a group of computers used to lure attackers in and trap them for later analysis.

25. **B.** The firewall rule listed that only denies DNS zone transfers is deny TCP any any port 53. As mentioned in Chapter 7, "Networking Protocols and Threats," DNS uses port 53, and DNS zone transfers specifically use TCP. This rule will apply to any computer's IP address initiating zone transfers on the inbound and outbound sides. If you configured the rule for UDP, other desired DNS functionality would be lost. Denying IP in general would have additional unwanted results. When creating a firewall rule (or ACL), you need to be very specific so that you do not filter out desired traffic.

This chapter covers the following subjects:

- **Securing Wired Networks and Devices:** In this section, you learn about how to reduce the risk of attack to your wired networks and the central connecting devices that control access to those networks. Concepts covered include security for common network devices such as SOHO routers and firewalls, and how to secure twisted-pair, fiber-optic, and coaxial cables.

- **Securing Wireless Networks:** Here, we delve into wireless networks, how you can secure your wireless access points and protect your wireless network from intruders, inside or outside the building. Wireless concepts covered include Wi-Fi security, Bluetooth security, and security of other over-the-air technologies such as RFID.

Imagine if you will that you are in charge of securing your organization's wired and wireless networks, and all the devices associated with them. There are several questions you should ask yourself: What kind of cables does your network use, what are the vulnerabilities of those cables, and how can they be secured? What are your future cabling plans? Do you have wireless networks, and if so, how can you protect data that is flinging through the air? How many devices can be accessed either from users on the network or remotely? And are there any older devices that need to be updated, or simply removed?

CHAPTER 9

Securing Network Media and Devices

Verifying that all network devices, cables, and other mediums are secure might sound like a daunting task at first, but let's take it step by step and discuss how this can be done. We begin with wired networks, cables, and the devices you might find on a wired network; then we move onto wireless transmissions. At the end of the chapter, we examine a final piece of network documentation that sums up many of the security precautions we implemented in Chapters 6 through 9.

Foundation Topics

Securing Wired Networks and Devices

Implementing a security plan for your wired network is critical. In Chapter 6, "Network Design Elements," we talked about the design elements of your network. In Chapter 7, "Networking Protocols and Threats," we discussed the possible threats to those design elements and to the computers and servers on the network. In Chapter 8, "Network Perimeter Security," we talked about some of the security tools, such as firewalls, that could be used to protect the network. But what connects it all together? Usually the wired network. Now let's get into the nitty-gritty of the wired network. Not only are the devices wired to the network targets for attack, but the wires could be targets as well. Some attacks could come from inside the network, whereas other attacks could be external. Let's start with some of the common vulnerabilities to network devices.

Network Device Vulnerabilities

Devices that reside on your network might include switches, routers, firewalls, NIDS/NIPS appliances, and more. Each of these devices can be vulnerable in its default state. Most devices are sold with simple default accounts and blank or weak passwords. In some cases, it's easy for users to escalate their privileges to gain access to resources that they normally would not have access to. Some devices and computers can be the victim of backdoors that programmers did not remove, or forgot to remove, which enable access for attackers. And of course, a good network administrator will protect against network attacks such as denial-of-service. Let's go through each of these one by one and show how to protect against these vulnerabilities to help mitigate risk.

Default Accounts

Many of the networking devices available to organizations are initially installed with a default set of user credentials; this is the **default account**. The default account might be called administrator, or admin, or something else similar. If possible, this default account should be changed to a new name, because attackers are aware of default account names. This also applies to computers and servers, as we mentioned in Chapter 4, "OS Hardening and Virtualization." By renaming the default account, or by removing it altogether, you add a layer of security that makes it more difficult for an attacker to figure out which account has administrative access to the device. One example of this is the SOHO router. Historically, these devices were set up by default with the username admin and a blank password. This is one of the first things you should change before you connect it to the Internet—that is, if the device doesn't prompt you to do it automatically. And a lot of these devices allow a separate user account as well, which might have varying levels of access depending on the device. This should either be set with a complex password or be disabled altogether.

If any guest accounts exist, it is recommended that you disable these accounts. And again, this applies to network devices and computers. The guest account will usually not be enabled, but you should always check this just in case. Of course, more important than the account name or the username is the password. If you have to use a guest account, set a complex password!

Weak Passwords

Passwords should be as complex as possible. A weak password can be cracked by an attacker in a short time. Many network devices come stock with no password at all; so, your first order of business should be to create a complex password. It is common knowledge that a strong password is important for protecting a user account, whether the account is with a bank, at work, or elsewhere. The same goes for network devices. But what is a strong password? Many organizations define a *strong* password as a password with at least eight (even ten) characters, including at least one uppercase letter, one number, and one special character. The *best* passwords have the same requirements but are 15 characters or more. Many password checker programs are available on the Internet; for example, the Password Meter or Kaspersky's password checker.

Let's look at Table 9-1, which gives some examples of weak passwords and strong passwords based on the criteria of a typical password checker.

Table 9-1   Weak, Strong, and Stronger Passwords

Password	Strength of Password
Prowse	Weak
DavidProwse	Medium (also known as "good")
|ocrIan7	Strong
This1sV#ryS3cure	Very strong (also known as "best")

> **NOTE**   Be aware that password checking programs can change their criteria over time. Also, never actually *use* a password that was entered into a checker! The purpose of the checker is to demonstrate the strength of a password so that you know what criteria to use for other passwords in the future.

The first password in Table 9-1 is weak; even though it has an uppercase P, it is only 6 characters in length. The second password is only medium strength; it has 11 characters but only 2 uppercase characters, and nothing else is special about it. However, notice the third password is using the pipe symbol instead of the letter L. This is a special character that shares the \ backslash key on the keyboard. Because the third password has a special character, an uppercase I, and a number, and is 8 characters in total, it is considered to be a strong password by the password checker. In the last password, we have 16 characters, including 3 uppercase letters, 2 numbers, and 1 special character. These methods make for an extremely strong password that would take a powerful desktop computer many years to crack.

Employ elastic thinking! Remember—a strong password this year might be a weak password next year. That's because computers increase in power and efficiency all the time (see Moore's Law). And let's not forget to mention that a botnet can use the collective power of many systems to brute-force a password much faster than one system could. That's something to keep in mind if you are the security admin for an organization that has high-profile employees.

Privilege Escalation

When an attacker exploits a bug or other flaw in an operating system or application in order to gain protected access to resources, it is known as **privilege escalation**. The original developer does not intend for the attacker to gain higher levels of access, but probably doesn't enforce a need-to-know policy properly and/or hasn't validated the code of the application appropriately. This technique is used by attackers to gain access to protected areas of operating systems, or to applications; for example, if a particular user can read another user's e-mail without authorization. Other programs, such as Cisco Unified Communications Manager (CallManager), have also been the victim of privilege escalations, although patches are regularly released if issues like these are discovered. Buffer overflows are used on Windows computers to elevate privileges as well. To bypass digital rights management (DRM) on games and music, attackers use a method known as jailbreaking, another type of privilege escalation, most commonly found on mobile devices. Malware also attempts to exploit privilege escalation vulnerabilities, if any exist on the system. Privilege escalation can also be attempted on network devices. Generally, the fix for this is simply to update the device and to check on a regular basis if any updates are available. For example, a typical SOHO router has a user account and an admin account. If a device like this isn't properly updated, an attacker can take advantage of a bug in the firmware to elevate the privileges of the user account. Couple this with the fact that a person forgot to put a password on the user account (or disable it) and your network could be in for some "fun." It is also possible on some devices to encrypt the firmware component. Following are a couple different types of privilege escalation:

Key Topic

- **Vertical privilege escalation:** When a lower privileged user accesses functions reserved for higher privileged users; for example, if a standard user can access functions of an administrator. This is also known as privilege elevation and is the most common description. To protect against this, update the network device firmware. In the case of an operating system, it should again be updated, and usage of some type of access control system is also advisable; for example, User Account Control (UAC).

- **Horizontal privilege escalation:** When a normal user accesses functions or content reserved for other normal users; for example, if one user reads another's e-mail. This can be done through hacking or by a person walking over to other people's computers and simply reading their e-mail! Always have your users lock their computer (or log off) when they are not physically at their desk!

There is also privilege de-escalation, when high privileged but segregated users can downgrade their access level to access normal users' functions. Sneaky admins can attempt this to glean confidential information from an organization. It's a two-way street when it comes to security; you should think three-dimensionally when securing your network!

Back Doors

A **backdoor** is a way of bypassing normal authentication in a system, securing illegal remote access to a computer, or gaining access to a cryptosystem through circumvention of the normal system of rules.

As mentioned in Chapter 2, "Computer Security Systems Part I," backdoors were originally used by developers as a legitimate way of accessing an application, but quickly became known to attackers and utilized as an illegitimate means of gaining access to the system. The beauty of the backdoor attack is that the attacker can easily remain undetected. Backdoors can take the form of programs such as remote access Trojans (RATs), or could be accessed via a rootkit.

Backdoors are less common nowadays, because their practice is usually discouraged by software manufacturers and by makers of network devices. So, as long as the *design* of the application or device was secure (and tested), attackers should not be able to gain access via the backdoor.

Network Attacks

Denial-of-service and many other network attacks can wreak havoc on your network devices. It is important to keep abreast of these latest attacks and to verify that all systems and network devices are updated accordingly. Use smart network intrusion prevention systems (NIPSs) to identify new attacks and prevent them from causing trouble on your networks. For more information on denial of service attacks and other types of network attacks, see the section "Malicious Attacks" in Chapter 7.

Other Network Device Considerations

Some network administrators use remote ports on their network devices to remotely administer those devices. These ports can be used maliciously as well. If the remote port is not to be used, it should be disabled. If it is to be used, a strong authentication system should be employed, and data encryption should be considered. This applies to routers, switches, servers, and PBX equipment. For more specific ways to protect your network devices, see the section "Network Design" in Chapter 6.

In some cases, a network administrator uses the Telnet program to access network equipment remotely from another site or from within the local area network. This practice should be shunned because Telnet by default is not secure; it does not encrypt data, including passwords, and default implementations of Telnet have no authentication scheme that ensures that communications will not be intercepted. In addition, most Telnet programs have other vulnerabilities and risk associated with them. Instead of using Telnet, administrators should opt for another protocol such as Secure Shell (SSH).

Cable Media Vulnerabilities

The most commonly overlooked item in a network is the cabling. The entire cabling infrastructure (or cabling plant) includes the cables themselves, network jacks, patch panels, punch blocks, and so on. You need to think about what types of cabling you are using, what vulnerabilities they have, and how to combat those vulnerabilities in an attempt to reduce risk. Following are three types of cabling that you might have implemented in your network:

- **Twisted-pair:** A copper-based cable with four pairs of wires (for a total of eight wires), each of which is twisted together along the length of the cable. It is the most common type of network cable; it sends electrical signals to transfer data and uses RJ45 plugs to connect to ports on hosts. The most common security problem with twisted-pair cable is crosstalk, which we discuss later.

- **Fiber-optic:** A glass/plastic-based cable that sends light (photons) instead of electricity. It is composed of one or more thin strands known as fibers that transfer the data. Generally, this is the most secure type of cable that can be used in a network. It is not susceptible to EMI, RFI, or data emanations (all of which are discussed shortly) and is the least susceptible cable to wiretapping. The two main categories of fiber-optic cables are single-mode (for the longest distances) and multimode (for shorter distances but longer than twisted-pair). Examples of places where fiber-optic cables are used include high-bandwidth networking technologies such as Fibre Channel (FCoE and FCIP) that use SC and LC connectors.

- **Coaxial:** A less used copper-based cable that has a single copper core. Although not used for connections to hosts anymore, you might see it used with special connections, perhaps for the Internet or for video. In smaller companies' networks, it is common to see an RG-6 cable used for the Internet connection. The most common security risk with coaxial cable is data emanation, which we discuss later.

Each of these cables has its own inherent vulnerabilities; let's talk about a few of these now.

Interference

Interference is anything that disrupts or modifies a signal traveling along a wire. There are many types of interference, but you should know about only a few for the exam, including the following:

- **Electromagnetic interference (EMI):** A disturbance that can affect electrical circuits, devices, and cables due to electromagnetic conduction or radiation. Just about any type of electrical device can cause EMI: TVs, microwaves, air-conditioning units, motors, unshielded electrical lines, and so on. Copper-based cables and network devices should be kept away from these electrical devices if at all possible. If not possible, shielded cables can be used, for example, shielded twisted-pair (STP). Or the device that is emanating EMI can be shielded. For example, an air-conditioning unit could be boxed in with aluminum shielding in an attempt to keep the EMI generated by the AC unit's motor to a minimum. In addition, electrical cables should be BX (encased in metal) and not Romex (not encased in metal); most municipalities require this to meet industrial and office space building code. EMI can also be used in a mischievous manner, known as radio jamming. But the methods listed here can help defend against this as well.

- **Radio frequency interference (RFI):** Interference that can come from AM/FM transmissions and cell towers. It is often considered to be part of the EMI family and is sometimes referred to as EMI. The closer a business is to one of these towers, the greater the chance of interference. The methods mentioned for EMI can be employed to help defend against RFI. In addition, filters can be installed on the network to eliminate the signal frequency broadcast by a radio tower, though this usually does not affect standard-wired Ethernet networks. Wireless signals from wireless networks and cell phones can interfere with speakers and other devices; try to keep speakers and monitors away from cell phones and wireless network adapters. Try to keep wireless access points away from computers, printers, monitors, and speakers; and switches, routers, and other network equipment.

Another common type of interference is crosstalk, discussed next.

Crosstalk

Crosstalk is when a signal transmitted on one copper wire creates an undesired effect on another wire; the signal "bleeds" over, so to speak. This first occurred when telephone lines were placed in close proximity to each other. Because the phone lines were so close, the signal could jump from one line to the next intermittently. If you have ever heard another conversation while talking on your home phone (not cell phones mind you) you have been the victim of crosstalk. This can happen with connections made by a modem as well, causing considerable havoc on the data transfer.

NOTE   With cell phones, crosstalk is also known as co-channel interference, or CCI.

To combat crosstalk, you can use twisted-pair cable. This helps when regular analog signals are sent across the wires and applies only to standard POTS connections and computer modems that use POTS connections. The beauty of the twists in twisted-pair cabling is that the signal has less chance of leaking to other wires, in comparison to straight wires next to each other and bundled together. If the signals are digital—for example, Ethernet data transfers or Voice over IP—you already have an environment less susceptible to crosstalk, in comparison to an analog environment.

Data can still bleed over to other wires, but it is less common because the twists of the wires have been precisely calculated by the manufacturer. Sometimes crosstalk occurs due to bunches of cables bundled too tightly, which could also cause crimping or other damage to the cable. If this is the case, a trusty continuity tester will let you know which cable has failed; normally this will have to be replaced. When it comes to twisted-pair cabling, crosstalk is broken down into two categories: near end crosstalk (NEXT) and far end crosstalk (FEXT). NEXT is when measured interference occurs between two pairs in a single cable, measured on the cable end nearest the transmitter. FEXT is when like interference occurs but is measured at the cable end farthest from the transmitter.

If crosstalk is still a problem, even though twisted-pair cable has been employed and digital data transmissions have been implemented, shielded twisted-pair (STP) could be used. Although twisting individual pairs can minimize crosstalk between wire pairs within a cable, shielding an entire cable minimizes crosstalk between cables. Normally, companies opt for regular twisted-pair cabling, which is unshielded (also known as UTP), but sometimes, too much interference exists in the environment to send data effectively, and STP must be utilized.

Data Emanation

Data emanation (or signal emanation) is the electromagnetic (EM) field generated by a network cable or network device, which can be manipulated to eavesdrop on conversations or to steal data. Data emanation is sometimes also referred to as eavesdropping, although this is not accurate.

Data emanation is the most commonly seen security risk when using coaxial cable, depending on the type of coaxial cable, but can also be a security risk for other copper-based cables. There are various ways to tap into these EM fields to get unauthorized access to confidential data. To alleviate the situation, there are several solutions. For example, you could use shielded cabling or run the cabling through metal conduits. You could also use electromagnetic shielding on devices that might be emanating an electromagnetic field. This could be done on a small scale by shielding the single device or on a larger scale by shielding an entire room, perhaps a server room; this would be an example of a **Faraday cage**. If an entire room is shielded, electromagnetic energy cannot pass through the walls in either direction. So, if a person attempts to use a cell phone inside the cage, it will not function properly, because the signal cannot go beyond the cage walls. More important, devices such as cell phones, motors, and wireless access points that create electromagnetic fields and are outside the cage cannot disrupt electromagnetic-sensitive devices that reside inside the cage. Server rooms and cabling should be protected in some way, especially if the data that travels through them is confidential. Studies are constantly done about signal emanations and how to contain them. A group of standards known as **TEMPEST** refers to the investigations of conducted emissions from electrical and mechanical devices, which could be compromising to an organization.

Tapping into Data and Conversations

This is a huge subject, and we could talk about it for days without scratching the surface. One item of note: ANY system can be tapped or hacked. It's just the lengths you must go to that can vary; it depends on the network, cabling, and security precautions already in place.

The term "tapping" originates from the days when an attacker would use a tool (such as a vampire tap) to physically bite into a wire or cable so that the attacker could monitor the network. Today, "tapping" takes on a whole new meaning. **Wiretapping** can mean any one of the following and more:

- **Connecting to a punch block, or RJ11 jack with a butt set:** A **butt set** (or lineman's handset) is a device that looks similar to a phone but has alligator clips that can connect to the various terminals used by phone equipment, enabling a person to test a new line or listen in to a conversation. The device is used primarily by telecommunications technicians but can obviously be used for malicious purposes as well. There are analog versions of this device (for POTS systems) and digital versions (for digital systems such as VoIP and so on) that act as packet capturing devices (sniffers). To protect against this, keep all punch blocks and other phone equipment in a physically secure server room or wiring closet. Although expensive, there are also lockable RJ11 jacks, but it would probably be less costly to install a network of cameras in the building, especially if your organization wants them for other purposes as well.

- **Plugging in to an open port of a twisted-pair network:** This could be either at an RJ45 wall plate or in the server room (not as easy) at an open port of a hub or switch. Unused ports, whether on a hub or switch or at a computer station's RJ45 jack, should be disabled. Also, central connecting devices such as hubs and switches should be locked in the server room, and only properly authenticated individuals should have access.

- **Splitting the wires of a twisted-pair connection:** This can be done anywhere along a cable but would disrupt communications for that individual computer or segment while it is being done. By cutting the twisted-pair cable and soldering a second twisted-pair cable to the appropriate wires (for example, Ethernet 568B networks use the orange and green pairs of wires by default), a person could eavesdrop on all communications on that segment. Cables should not be exposed if at all possible. Cable runs should be above the drop ceiling and inside the walls, perhaps run in conduit. It is understandable that computers need to connect to RJ45 jacks by way of patch cables; if a computer suddenly loses its connection to the network, an alert can be sent to junior administrators, prompting them to investigate why it occurred.

- **Using a spectral analyzer to access data emanations:** Spectral analyzers can measure the composition of electrical waveforms at specific frequencies (for example, 100 MHz, or 250 MHz on a twisted-pair network). These can also decode encrypted transmissions. These types of devices should not be allowed in the building (unless used by authorized personnel). A metal detector could be used at the entrance of the building, and again, video cameras can help detect this, and perhaps even prevent mischievous people from attempting to do so, just because they think they might be under surveillance.

- **Using a passive optical splitter for fiber-optic networks:** This is a more expensive device and would need access to a cable. Plus, the process of getting it to work is difficult. (And again, this would disrupt communications for a time.) The preceding listed methods apply to defending against this as well. Because it is difficult to implement an optical splitter properly, this could cause chromatic dispersion on the particular fiber segment. Chromatic dispersion (and subsequent loss of data) could also occur if the fiber-optic cable is too long. Administrators could monitor the network for dispersion and have alerts sent to them in the case that it occurs. The most common example of chromatic dispersion is the rainbow. For example, if light is sent through a prism, the light will be refracted (dispersed) into the rainbow of colors. Although not exactly how it would occur on a fiber-optic cable, if this were to happen, data transmissions would fail.

A quick word about wiring "closets." Generally, a commercial office building will have two types of wiring frameworks. First, there are intermediate distribution frame (IDF) rooms, usually one per floor. These rooms are where all the cabling for that floor is terminated—for example, twisted-pair cables are punched down here, either to patch panels or punch blocks, depending on the architecture. All IDF rooms then connect (in one way or another) to the second type, the main distribution frame (MDF) room, often on the first floor or in the basement. The MDF is where circuits merge and connect out to external ISPs, and other network providers. Both types of rooms are vulnerable attack points. Historically, MDF rooms have been better protected than IDF rooms, but today organizations are increasing security on both and treating them the same way they would treat data centers or high-end server rooms. Basic security such as a door lock is not enough. (Watch some DEF CON videos for quick proof of that.) Security admins should consider methods such as multifactor authentication, possibly including biometrics, and active surveillance systems. We'll discuss more about physical security in Chapter 10, "Physical Security and Authentication Models." However, an attacker might try to exploit IDF and MDF vulnerabilities from within and from *without*. By connecting to SNMP-monitored systems, such as power distribution units (PDUs), UPSs, and environmental devices, an attacker can circumnavigate other security safeguards that might be in place. Consider the security implications of SNMP carefully. We'll discuss that topic more in Chapter 13, "Monitoring and Auditing."

Some organizations and government agencies require the use of a **protected distribution system (PDS)** for wired connections. These *approved circuits* use all of the techniques mentioned previously in this section to secure the unencrypted transmission of classified information. It is all-encompassing: cables, terminals, and other equipment, including safeguards for electrical, electromagnetic, and acoustical concerns.

Keep in mind that the Security+ exam does not go too far in depth for this subject, but realize that you might get a question on wiretapping, and remember that any network can be hacked! It is more common to attempt hacking into wireless networks. So, let's delve into the basics of that immense subject next.

Securing Wireless Networks

Wireless networks pose a whole new set of problems for a network administrator. Wireless access points (WAPs) and wireless network adapters need to be secure from attackers that could be just about anywhere as long as they're within range of the wireless network. Several points we cover can help you secure your WAP, wireless network adapters, and any other wireless devices. In this section, you learn how to watch out for wireless transmission vulnerabilities that you should be aware of, including Wi-Fi, Bluetooth, and RFID.

Wireless Access Point Vulnerabilities

The wireless access point is the central connecting device for wireless network adapters that might exist in PCs, laptops, handheld computers, mobile devices, and other computers. You need to secure any broadcasts that the WAP might make and verify that transmissions are encrypted with a strong encryption technique. It's also important to watch out for rogue access points and round up any nomads on your network.

The Administration Interface

The first thing you should look at when it comes to WAPs is the administration interface, or console. The act of accessing the administration interface is sometimes referred to as "romming" into the access point. By default, most access points have a blank password or a simple and weak password (for example, "password" or "admin"). The first step you want to take is to access the administration interface and modify the password; change it to a complex password. Next, consider disabling remote administration if it is not necessary. Your organization might require it, but it depends on several factors. If you are dead set on leaving it enabled, be completely sure that the remote administration password is complex.

SSID Broadcast

The **service set identifier (SSID)** is one of several broadcasts that a WAP makes. It identifies the network and is the name of the WAP used by clients to connect to the wireless network. It is on by default. After all your clients have been connected to the wireless network, consider disabling the SSID broadcast. Though there will still be ways for attackers to get into your WAP, this at least provides a preliminary level of security. The average user cannot see the SSID and cannot connect to the wireless network. In the future if you need to add clients, simply enable the SSID temporarily, connect the client, and then disable the SSID. This might not be a factor if you are in a large building. But if you are in a smaller structure, the WAP's broadcast range may leak out beyond your organization's property. You can also try reducing the transmitter power of the WAP. Although not all WAPs have this function, some do and it can help to fine-tune the area that the WAP serves.

NOTE It wasn't mentioned yet, but clients can still connect to a wireless network that is not broadcasting the SSID. This can be done manually within the proprietary third-party wireless adapter settings or, in Windows, by first starting the WLAN AutoConfig service (wlansvc) and then accessing the Managing Wireless Networks link within the Network and Sharing Center. However, the person connecting must know the SSID, the type of encryption being used, and the encryption key. Some third-party wireless software applications won't allow for this to be manually entered. If that is the case, and the user needs to connect manually, the third-party software should be disabled and the client should connect using Windows.

Just remember, by default when the SSID broadcast is disabled, no new wireless clients can connect, unless they do so manually.

Rogue Access Points

Rogue APs can be described as unauthorized wireless access points/routers that allow access to secure networks. Sometimes companies lose track of the WAPs on their network. Keep track of all your devices with network documentation. Use network mapping programs and Microsoft Visio to detect and document any rogue APs. Older WAPs, especially ones with weak encryption, should be updated, disabled, or simply disconnected from the network. Some companies may have a dozen WAPs and additional wireless devices such as repeaters, and it may be difficult to keep track of these. In this case, a network mapping program can be one of your best friends. In addition, you can search for rogue APs with a laptop or handheld computer with Windows' wireless application, the wireless network adapter's built-in software, or third-party applications such as AirMagnet or NetStumbler. If traffic from a rogue AP does enter your network, a NIDS or NIPS solution can be instrumental in detecting and preventing that data and data that comes from other rogue devices. Organizations commonly perform site surveys to detect rogue APs, and other unwanted wireless devices. We'll discuss more details about site surveys later in this chapter.

Evil Twin

An **evil twin** is a rogue, counterfeit, and unauthorized wireless access point that uses the same SSID name as a nearby wireless network, often public hotspots. Like an evil twin antagonist found in many sci-fi books, the device is identical in almost all respects to the authorized WAP. While the antagonist in the sci-fi book usually has a beard or goatee, the WAP is controlled by a person with the same types of motives as the bearded evil twin. One of these motives is phishing. For example, an attacker might attempt to fool wireless users at an Internet café to connect to the counterfeit WAP to gain valuable information and passwords from the users. If the user is unlucky enough to connect to the evil twin, all the information within the session can easily be recorded and digested later on by the attacker. This attack can also be en-acted upon organizations. To protect against this, virtual private networks (VPNs) can be implemented that require external authentication outside the WAP. Administrators should scan the network often for rogue APs that might be evil twins. Users in general should be trained not to send passwords, credit card numbers, and other sensitive information over wireless networks.

Weak Encryption

Weak encryption or no encryption can be the worst thing that can happen to a wireless network. This can occur for several reasons—for example, if someone wanted to connect an older device or a device that hasn't been updated, and that device can run only a weaker, older type of encryption. It's important to have strong encryption in your network; as of this writing, Wi-Fi Protected Access 2 (WPA2) is the best wireless protocol you can use. It can be used with TKIP or, better yet, AES. Remember that the encryption level of the WAP and the encryption level of the network adapters that connect to it need to be the same. Table 9-2 defines some of the available wireless protocols and encryption types.

Key Topic

Table 9-2 Wireless Protocols

Wireless Protocol	Description	Encryption Level (Key Size)
WEP	Wired Equivalent Privacy (Deprecated)	64-bit Also 128-bit but uncommon
WPA	Wi-Fi Protected Access	128-bit
WPA2	Wi-Fi Protected Access Version 2	256-bit
TKIP	Temporal Key Integrity Protocol (Deprecated) Encryption protocol used with WEP and WPA	128-bit
CCMP	Counter Mode with Cipher Block Chaining Message Authentication Code (CBC-MAC) Protocol Encryption protocol used with WPA2 Addresses the vulnerabilities of TKIP Meets requirements of IEEE 802.11i	128-bit
AES	Advanced Encryption Standard Encryption protocol used with WPA/WPA2 Strongest encryption method in this table	128-bit, 192-bit, and 256-bit
WTLS	Wireless Transport Layer Security	Based on TLS

WEP is the weakest type of encryption; WPA is stronger, and WPA2 is the strongest of the three. However, it is better to have WEP as opposed to nothing. If this is the case, use encryption keys that are difficult to guess, and consider changing those keys often. Some devices can be updated to support WPA, whether it is through a firmware upgrade or through the use of a software add-on. Figure 9-1 shows a typical WAP with WPA2 and AES configured; AES is the cipher type. The **pre-shared key (PSK)** used to enable connectivity between wireless clients and the WAP is a complex passphrase. PSK is automatically used when you select WPA-Personal in the Security Mode section. The other option is WPA-Enterprise, which uses a RADIUS server in this WAP. So, if you ever see the term "WPA2-PSK," that means that the WAP is set up to use the WPA2 protocol with a pre-shared key, and not an external authentication method such as RADIUS.

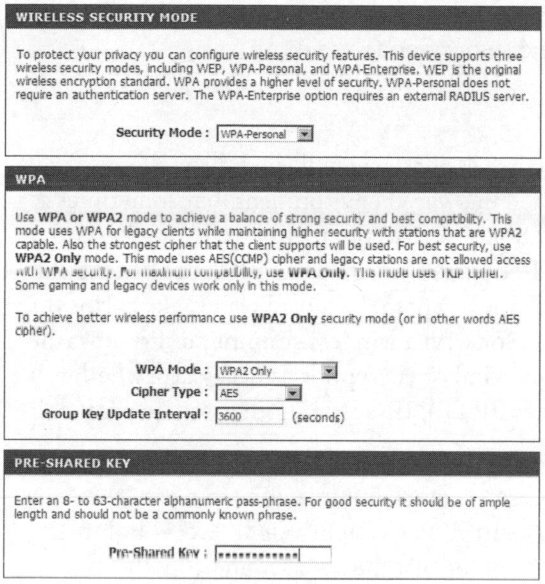

Key
Topic

WIRELESS SECURITY MODE

To protect your privacy you can configure wireless security features. This device supports three wireless security modes, including WEP, WPA-Personal, and WPA-Enterprise. WEP is the original wireless encryption standard. WPA provides a higher level of security. WPA-Personal does not require an authentication server. The WPA-Enterprise option requires an external RADIUS server.

Security Mode : [WPA-Personal ▼]

WPA

Use **WPA or WPA2** mode to achieve a balance of strong security and best compatibility. This mode uses WPA for legacy clients while maintaining higher security with stations that are WPA2 capable. Also the strongest cipher that the client supports will be used. For best security, use **WPA2 Only** mode. This mode uses AES(CCMP) cipher and legacy stations are not allowed access with WPA security. For maximum compatibility, use **WPA Only**. This mode uses TKIP cipher. Some gaming and legacy devices work only in this mode.

To achieve better wireless performance use **WPA2 Only** security mode (or in other words AES cipher).

WPA Mode : [WPA2 Only ▼]
Cipher Type : [AES ▼]
Group Key Update Interval : [3600] (seconds)

PRE-SHARED KEY

Enter an 8- to 63-character alphanumeric pass-phrase. For good security it should be of ample length and should not be a commonly known phrase.

Pre-Shared Key : [••••••••••••]

Figure 9-1 Wireless Security Configuration on a Typical Access Point

The **Wireless Transport Layer Security (WTLS)** protocol is part of the Wireless Application Protocol (WAP) stack used by mobile devices. It enables secure user sessions—for instance, banking transactions—using algorithms such as RSA, ECC, Triple DES, and MD5 or SHA, all of which are described in Chapter 14, "Encryption and Hashing Concepts."

Wi-Fi Protected Setup

Wi-Fi Protected Setup (WPS) is in of itself a security vulnerability. Created originally to enable users easy connectivity to a wireless access point, it was later suggested by all major manufacturers that it be disabled (if possible). In a nutshell, the problem with WPS was the eight-digit code. It effectively worked as two separate smaller codes that collectively could be broken by a brute-force attack within hours.

There isn't much that can be done to prevent the problem other than disabling WPS altogether in the WAP's firmware interface or, if WPS can't be disabled, upgrading to a newer device. In summary, WPS is a deprecated and insecure technology that should not be allowed on a wireless network.

Ad Hoc Networks

Ad hoc networks allow for wireless connections between clients without any centralized WAP or wireless LAN (WLAN) controller. This is inherently insecure. Most organizations have written policies that disallow ad hoc networks for Wi-Fi and other wireless technologies. In most scenarios, security admins should disable ad hoc functionality on Windows clients and other client operating systems, wireless devices, mobile computers, WAPs, and so on. Enough said.

VPN over Open Wireless

VPN connections are meant to be secure sessions accomplished through an encrypted tunnel. They are best secured in a wired environment, but sometimes a wireless VPN connection is required. Some devices offer this but in an inherently insecure manner—this is known as VPN over *open* wireless, with "open" being the operative word, meaning insecure and unencrypted. In most business scenarios this is unacceptable, and should be scanned for with a wireless scanning utility. Just the presence of a VPN is not enough; some kind of encryption is necessary, whether it be Point-to-Point Tunneling Protocol (PPTP), IPsec, or another secure protocol.

For example, in a standard Cisco wireless VPN configuration, the wireless client initiates a tunnel to a VPN server (a Cisco router), but it is done in a pass-through manner via a wireless LAN (WLAN) controller. (A Lightweight Access Point is often also part of the solution.) It's the router that must be set up properly, and in this scenario IPsec should be installed and configured. That will allow for the encryption of session data between the wireless client and the WLAN controller.

In other scenarios, especially in smaller offices or home offices, a single device will act as the all-in-one solution. Though wireless VPN connections are uncommon in SOHO environments, this solution presents only a single layer of defense and it can be easy to forget to initiate the proper encryption. There are many authentication mechanisms and possibilities, and several ways to encrypt the session. The key here is to remember to have clients authenticate in a secure manner, and handshake on an encryption protocol that will protect the data. We discuss authentication and concepts such as VPN in more depth in Chapter 10.

Wireless Access Point Security Strategies

Strategic placement of a WAP is vital. Usually, the best place for a WAP is in the center of the building. This way, equal access can be given to everyone on the perimeter of the organization's property, and there is the least chance of the signal bleeding over to other organizations. If needed, attempt to reduce the transmission power levels of the antenna, which can reduce the broadcast range of the WAP. Also, to avoid interference in the form of EMI or RFI, keep WAPs away from any electrical panels, cables, devices, motors, or other pieces of equipment that might give off an electromagnetic field. If necessary, shield the device creating the EM field, or shield the access point itself. Sheesh, I am starting to sound bossy! (Must be those two years I spent as a building contractor....)

Anyway, in order to really know how to best arrange and secure your wireless connections, you need to understand the different wireless systems and antenna types available. The most common wireless system is point-to-multipoint. This system is commonly used in WLANs where a single central device (such as a SOHO wireless router) will connect to multiple other wireless devices that could be located in any direction. Specifically, it makes use of omnidirectional antennas such as vertical omnis, ceiling domes, and so on. A typical wireless router might have two, three, four, or more vertical omnidirectional antennas. For example, a SOHO 802.11n wireless router might have three antennas that use multiple-input multiple-output (MIMO) technology to combine multiple data streams for significantly higher data throughput (up to eight streams for 802.11ac). These antennas can be rotated so that they are parallel to each other, or at an angle to each other; for example, 180 degrees is often a good configuration to, in essence, "sweep" the area for wireless transmissions. However, you might choose a different method. For example, you might have 100 computers on one floor and two WAPs to work with. The best method might be to position them at vertical angles from each other. One would be in the building's northeast corner and the other in the southwest corner. Then, each set of three antennas could be positioned in a 90-degree sweep as shown in Figure 9-2. As long as the building isn't larger than the range of the antennas, then this should allow for excellent wireless coverage.

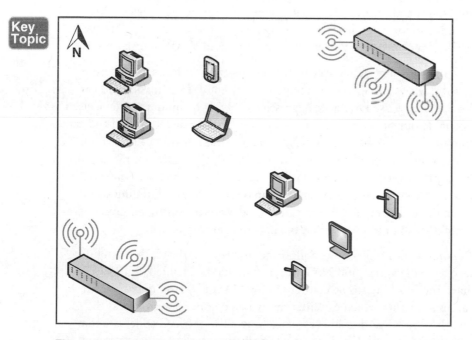

Figure 9-2   Wireless Point-to-Multipoint Layout

NOTE   Speaking of 802.11ac and 802.11n, channel selection and channel width selection can impact performance and security as well. 5-GHz frequency bands usually offer better performance than 2.4-GHz bands, but both can be monitored over-the-air by attackers. Some WAPs can be set to auto-configure, seeking the least used wireless frequencies/channels, which can be great for performance, but might be a security risk. Consider using less common channel numbers, and perhaps a narrower channel; for example, 40 MHz instead of 80 MHz for 802.11ac. And remember to reduce antenna power levels as much as possible. Once again, you must test carefully, and then balance performance and security for optimal organization efficiency.

There are also more simplistic point-to-point wireless systems where only two points need to be connected; these points are usually fixed in location. In this case you would use directional antennas; for example, a parabolic antenna (dish) or a Yagi antenna.

Whatever you implement, it's a good idea to perform a wireless site survey. There are three kinds of wireless surveys you might perform, each with its own purpose, and all of which are usually based on software that collects WLAN data and signal information (though hardware can also be used to measure radio frequencies). A passive site survey listens to WLAN traffic and measures signal strength. An active survey actually sends and receives data to measure data transfer rate, packet loss, and so on. A predictive survey is a simulated survey based on real data such as the WAP to be used, the distance between the average computer and WAP, and so on.

Surveys can be instrumental in uncovering nonaggressive interference such as neighboring radio waves and electrical equipment (RFI and EMI, mentioned earlier). Surveys can also be used to locate aggressive *jamming* techniques often caused by wireless signal jammers. A signal jammer can easily be purchased online and can be used to initiate a denial-of-service attack to the wireless network. This is done by creating random noise on the channel used by the WAP, or by attempting to short out the device with powerful radio signals. The right wireless software (such as Net-Stumbler) can be used to locate signal jammers in or around your building so that you can remove them. Wireless software can also be used to identify potential wireless replay attacks that might exist within the network infrastructure.

Many WAPs come with a built-in firewall. If the firewall is utilized, the stateful packet inspection (SPI) option and NAT filtering should be enabled. The WAP might also have the capability to be configured for **MAC filtering** (a basic form of network access control), which can filter out which computers can access the wireless network. The WAP does this by consulting a list of MAC addresses that have been previously entered. Only the network adapters with those corresponding MAC addresses can connect; everyone else cannot join the wireless network. In some cases, a device might broadcast this MAC table. If this is the case, look for an update for the firmware of the WAP, and again, attempt to fine-tune the broadcast range of the device so that it does not leak out to other organizations. Because MAC filtering and a disabled SSID can be easily circumvented using a network sniffer, it is very important to also use strong encryption, and possibly consider other types of network access control (such as 802.1X) and external authentication methods (such as RADIUS).

Some WAPs also support isolation. **AP isolation** (also known as isolation mode) means that each client connected to the WAP will not be able to communicate with any other clients connected to the WAP. Each client can still access the Internet (or other network that the WAP is connected to), but every wireless user will be segmented from the other wireless users.

It is also possible to include the IEEE 802.1X standard for port-based network access control that can provide for strong authentication. For a WAP to incorporate this kind of technology, it must also act as a router, which adds the duty of wireless gateway to the WAP.

Another option is to consider encryption technologies on the application layer, such as SSL, SSH, or PGP; these and others can help to secure data transmissions from attackers that have already gained access to the wireless network. For more information on encryption types, see the section "Security Protocols" in Chapter 15, "PKI and Encryption Protocols." When it comes down to it, authentication and a strong wireless protocol such as WPA2 with AES are the two security precautions that will best help to protect against network attacks.

We briefly mentioned wireless LAN controllers. If your organization has or needs multiple WAPs, a smart method is to wire them each to a WLAN controller. This device acts as a switch for all the WAPs, thus increasing data transfer speeds between them, and more importantly, centralizes the management of security options. Most of the WAP functionality is handed off to the controller. If this controller is physically stored in a server room or data center, the access to its functionality becomes inherently more secure (especially if a Faraday cage is implemented). In this scenario, the WAP devices are considered "thin access points" because of the reduced functionality. Contrast this to the typical "fat access point" that contains all functionality. Because the fat access point must be located close to users to be functional, it creates more potential for attackers to gain access to it. Most midsized companies and virtually all enterprise networks use WLAN controllers.

Finally, another option is to not run wireless at all. It's tough to hack into a wireless network that doesn't exist! Some companies opt for this, as strange and difficult as it may seem, because they have deduced that the costs of implementation, administration, maintenance, and security outweigh the benefits of having a wireless network.

(Personally, my home is cabled up 100 percent—bedrooms, bathrooms, attic, you name it...but I still use wireless devices!) However, if you decide to go down the anti-wireless road, make sure that any devices that enable wireless access have those wireless functions disabled. This includes wireless access points, laptops, and other mobile devices that have wireless adapters, and any Bluetooth, infrared, or other wireless transmitters.

Wireless Transmission Vulnerabilities

Because wireless networks can transmit information through air or space, data emanations are everywhere and can easily be identified by people using the right tools. One deed that can be considered an attack on wireless networks is known as **war-driving**; this is the act of searching for wireless networks by a person in a vehicle, through the use of a device with a wireless antenna, often a particularly strong antenna. A basic example of this would be a person in a car with a laptop, utilizing the freely downloadable NetStumbler software. When war-drivers find a network, they can attempt to crack the password or passphrase to gain access to the wireless network. This might be done by guessing; you'd be surprised how much this works. It is estimated that more than 40 percent of wireless networks are unprotected. It could also be done with dictionary or brute-force attacks. You can find more information on password cracking in the section "Assessing Vulnerability with Security Tools" in Chapter 12, "Vulnerability and Risk Assessment."

Ways to protect against war-driving include hiding the SSID of the WAP, proper positioning of the WAP, decreasing the power levels to the point where the signal doesn't leak past the organization's building, using strong encryption, and changing the passphrase (encryption key) at regular intervals.

An interesting item connected with public Wi-Fi is **war-chalking**. This is the act of physically drawing symbols in public places that denote open, closed, or protected wireless networks. This is done by attackers to let other attackers know about open wireless networks. However, some organizations use the symbols as well to let people know that they have an open wireless network available to the public. In this case, the symbols will be professionally presented. Various symbols are used including the open node (two half circles back to back), the closed node (a closed circle), and a circle with a W, which stands for a WEP- or WPA-encrypted network.

IV attacks are another vulnerability of wireless networks. The **IV attack** is a type of related-key attack, which is when an attacker observes the operation of a cipher using several different keys, and finds a mathematical relationship between those keys, allowing the attacker to ultimately decipher data. *IV* stands for initialization vector, a random fixed-sized input that occurs in the beginning of every WEP or WPA packet. For WEP, the IV size was small (24-bit) and led to many successful attacks on WEP. This is why WEP is considered to be deprecated and insecure. The best way to prevent IV attacks is to use stronger wireless protocols such as WPA2 and AES.

We've mentioned DoS attacks several times in this book already. These can be run against WAPs in a variety of ways. One way is through the use of spoofed MAC addresses. If an attacker emulates a large number of wireless clients, each with a different spoofed MAC address, and never allows authentication for these clients to finish, then legitimate clients will no longer be able to be serviced by the WAP, because all of the session spots will have been taken. This is a type of denial-of-service due to incomplete authentication. It can be prevented by configuring expiration timeouts for all sessions that have not had activity for a certain period of time. It can also be prevented by updating the WAP and implementing wireless frame protection. (Different providers will have different names for this; for example, Cisco Management Frame Protection.) Another type of wireless-based DoS is the **Wi-Fi disassociation attack**—also known as Wi-Fi deauthentication attack. The attacker targets a user that is connected to a Wi-Fi network by using a wireless scanner. Then the attacker forces that user's system to deauthenticate using special software, and then re-authenticate to the WAP. By capturing the packets during the authentication process, the attacker can find out the SSID or ESSID of the WAP and possibly WPA/WPA2 handshake information. After that, the attacker will attempt to find out the WPA passphrase using a dictionary attack. This sounds more difficult in theory than it actually is. Using automated software tools, this can all be accomplished by an attacker in under a minute. These types of "deauth" attacks can be prevented by using WPA2, by using complex passphrases, and by implementing technologies such as management frame protection by Cisco, which adds a hash value to management frames of information, such as the ones used by WPA/WPA2.

We previously pointed out that a WAP can fall victim to brute-force attacks if WPS is used. The key of the WAP can also be compromised by a brute-force attack known as an exhaustive key search. This can be prevented by limiting the number of times a password/passphrase can be tried, using time delays between attempts, and requiring complex answers during the authentication process. Also, as a corrective security control, attacking IP addresses can be blacklisted. We'll discuss brute-force/exhaustive key searches more in Chapter 14.

Bluetooth and Other Wireless Technology Vulnerabilities

Bluetooth, RFID, and NFC are not wireless networking technologies in the general sense the way Wi-Fi is. But anything that has two or more wireless devices that communicate with each other could technically be considered a wireless network. So, I decided to place these technologies here. "It seemed the proper way...."

Like any wireless technology, Bluetooth is vulnerable to attack as well. Bluejacking and bluesnarfing are two types of vulnerabilities to Bluetooth-enabled devices. Bluetooth is also vulnerable to conflicts with other wireless technologies. For example, some WLAN (or Wi-Fi) standards use the 2.4-GHz frequency range, as does Bluetooth, and even though Bluetooth uses frequency hopping, conflicts can occur between 802.11g or 802.11b networks and Bluetooth personal area networks (PANs). To avoid this, use Bluetooth version 1.2 devices or greater, which employ adaptive frequency hopping, improving resistance to radio interference. Also, consider placing Bluetooth access points (if they are used) and WLAN access points in different areas of the building. Some companies have policies governing Bluetooth usage; in some cases, it is not allowed if 802.11 standards are in place, and in some cases a company will enforce rules that say Bluetooth can be used only outside the building. In other cases, a company will put its 802.11 devices on specific channels or use WLAN standards that use the 5-GHz range.

Bluetooth-equipped devices can use *near field communication* (NFC), which allows two mobile devices (or a mobile device and a stationary computer) to be automatically paired and transmit data. NFC is not limited to Bluetooth, but Bluetooth is probably the most common technology used to transmit data wirelessly over short distances. Of course, even though the distance is short, it can still be eavesdropped on. In addition, NFC is a data transmission protocol, but not necessarily secure. Data can be destroyed by use of a jammer, and users are also at risk of replay attacks. At the writing of this book, NFC does not offer preventive security in this aspect, but a user can prevent these attacks by only using applications that offer SSL/TLS or other secure channels during an NFC session.

Bluejacking

Bluejacking is the sending of unsolicited messages to Bluetooth-enabled devices such as mobile phones and tablets. Bluejacking is usually harmless, but if it does occur, it may appear that the Bluetooth device is malfunctioning. Originally, bluejackers would send only text messages, but with newer Bluetooth-enabled mobile devices, it is possible to send images and sounds as well. Bluejacking is used in less-than-reputable marketing campaigns. Bluejacking can be stopped by setting the affected Bluetooth device to "undiscoverable" or by turning off Bluetooth altogether.

Bluesnarfing

I know what you are thinking: The names of these attacks are starting to get a bit ridiculous! I guarantee it will improve as we progress through the rest of this book! Anyway, **bluesnarfing** is the unauthorized access of information from a wireless device through a Bluetooth connection. Generally, bluesnarfing is the theft of data (calendar information, phonebook contacts, and so on). It is possible to steal other information as well, but to pilfer any of this data, a pairing must be made between the attacking Bluetooth device and the Bluetooth victim. Ways of discouraging bluesnarfing include using a pairing key that is not easy to guess; for example, stay away from 0000 or similar default Bluetooth pairing keys! Otherwise, Bluetooth devices should be set to "undiscoverable" (only after legitimate Bluetooth devices have been set up, of course), or Bluetooth can be turned off altogether, especially in areas that might be bluesnarfing playgrounds, such as Times Square in New York City. Bluesnarfing is considered by some to be a component of bluejacking, but for the exam, try to differentiate between the two.

More details about how to protect phones, laptops, and other devices that use Bluetooth can be found in Chapter 3, "Computer Systems Security Part II."

RFID and NFC

Radio-frequency identification (RFID) has many uses, but it all boils down to identifying and tracking tags that are attached to objects. In the security world that generally means authentication.

As with any wireless technology, RFID is susceptible to attack. For example, some RFID tags can be affected by skimming, man-in-the-middle (MITM) attacks, sniffing, eavesdropping/replaying, spoofing, and jamming (DoS). From an authentication standpoint, the attacker is using these attacks to try to find out the passcode. An RFID tag can also be reverse engineered if the attacker gets possession of it. Finally, power levels can be analyzed to find out passwords. On some RFID tags, correct passcodes emit a different level of power than incorrect passcodes. To prevent these attacks, a security admin (or team) should consider newer generation RFID devices, encryption, chip coatings, filtering of data, and multifactor authentication methods. Encryption is one of the best methods. Included in this prevention method are rolling codes, which are generated with a pseudorandom number generator (PRNG), and challenge-response authentication (CRA), where the user (or user's device) must present the valid response to the challenge.

RFID ranges vary depending on the EM band used—from 10 cm up to 200 meters. Many authentication readers can be as much as 1 meter, which is enough to facilitate skimming of information by attackers. One way to avoid this is to use newer RFID proximity readers and keys—ones that use lower frequencies—from respectable companies. Another way is to utilize the set of protocols called near field communication (NFC). NFC generally requires that communicating devices be within 4 cm of each other, which makes skimming of information difficult. If an employee uses a smartphone to enter a building instead of an RFID device, then NFC should be implemented. NFC has obvious benefits for contactless payment systems or any other non-contact-oriented communications between devices. However, for optimal security, use contact-oriented readers and cards.

More Wireless Technologies

Let's not forget about cellular connections. Many companies don't allow cellular access, meaning 2G, 3G, 4G, LTE, and so on. These are often denied within company premises, and instead the company will rely on Wi-Fi methods; for example Wi-Fi calling. This is common in choose your own device (CYOD) and corporate-owned, personally enabled (COPE) environments. But if cellular is necessary in a bring your own device (BYOD) environment, then security can be increased by using newer devices, updating the devices' OS, updating the preferred roaming list (PRL), updating identification technologies (such as IMEI and IMSI), and using a VPN for data connections over cellular. Use these methods for employees who must be on the road as well. And if there are foreseeable instances where cellular is not available for mobile employees, be sure that they understand the risks of open Wi-Fi networks and that they should avoid them as much as possible.

We talked about GPS in Chapter 3. Remember that the usage of GPS should be examined carefully. Weigh the benefits of GPS against the exploitable vulnerabilities inherent to the system. Disable it whenever possible. Also, consider disabling other GPS and geolocation-related technologies. For example, *geotagging* is when geographical identification information, such as latitude and longitude coordinates, is added to photographs, websites, SMS messages, and more. It is common in social media and can be a great tool, but it can also be an easy way for attackers to zero in on high-profile executives and other employees of an organization. Consider a *geofence*—a virtual fence defining the boundaries of an actual geographical area. Geofencing is an excellent way to be alerted to users entering and exiting an organization's physical premises and can provide security for wireless networks by defining the physical borders and allowing or disallowing access based on the physical location of the user, or more accurately, the user's computer or mobile device!

Some organizations rely on satellite communications (SATCOM): sometimes for long distance communications, and sometimes for communicating between buildings in a campus. Either way, it is important to understand that SATCOM devices can be at risk if their firmware is not updated. Exploits could include the installation of malicious firmware and the execution of arbitrary code. Updating may require physical access to the parabolic antenna using a laptop or terminal device. But remember, the easier it is to access these antennas, the more likely they can be hacked by a malicious individual. Of course, in some cases these antennas can be hacked remotely as well. Secure planning is necessary when it comes to physical access, firewalling (if possible), and especially updating.

Remember this: wireless technologies are always "evolving." But anything is hackable, given time and ingenuity. When it comes to over-the-air tech, be ever vigilant—know the latest exploits, and prepare a worthy defense.

Final Network Documentation

As promised in the beginning of this chapter, Figure 9-3 sums up a lot of the devices and security implementations that we discussed in Chapters 6 through 9. Note the different network elements, devices, cabling, and wireless connectivity included in the illustration. Also note that the firewall has four connections, one each to the LAN, DMZ, extranet, and Internet. Also worth noting is that the WAP is using WPA2 and AES. All network equipment and servers are stored in a secure server room, which also acts as the MDF room. Try to define each network element that you see, and remember the various ways to secure them. Then create your own set of documentation for your own dream network (with security implementations, of course) that includes all the elements discussed in Chapters 6–9.

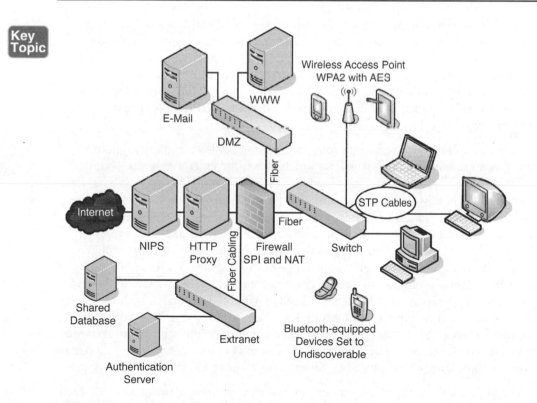

Figure 9-3 Final Network Documentation

Chapter Summary

If we all operated computers that never made any connections to other systems, we could say that those computers were pretty secure. What a wonderful world it would be, and for many end users, that was the world...in 1986. Today's computers usually *require* networking connections; otherwise they become useless. These past four chapters have shown that the majority of security concerns are network related... not all, but a huge chunk. Now here's a newsflash that even some technicians don't think of—disable the wired or wireless networking connection when the computer is not in use. Yes! In some cases, this method is feasible today. For example, configure a mobile device to go to airplane mode while you are sleeping. A good rule of thumb for end users is that, unless they have a server, their computers should sleep when the users sleep. As another example, configure an unused server to effectively shut down its network interface automatically between the hours of 2 a.m. and 7 a.m. (if there is little activity then). This kind of mentality can add up over time, and equate to a cleaner and more efficiently running network.

However, that is somewhat of a utopian mindset when it comes to the hardcore company that needs to do business 24/7. Therefore, we have to employ the measures discussed in this chapter. We focused on the wired and wireless connections of networks. Devices that control these wired and wireless networks often have weak security when it comes to account names and especially passwords. If you can change the administrator account name (or create a secondary admin account and disable the first) and set a complex password, you will have implemented the most important layer of security. And by complex, I mean COMPLEX! (That was me practically yelling the word.)

Today's complexity is multifaceted compared to last decade's complexity. There are various reasons for this—which we will discuss more in later chapters—but in essence, having a 10-character password for normal environments and a 15-character password for highly confidential environments is now the status quo (as of the writing of this book). Add on numerals, uppercase letters, and special characters, and you have the beginnings of a virtually uncrackable password. But remember, password cracking programs (and the computers that run them) are always getting stronger and faster. For example, an eight-character password that was considered uncrackable in 1999 might only take a week to crack today with the use of a typical desktop computer. This progression is directly related to Moore's Law, and as such will most likely continue. You might say: "But wait, Dave! Does this mean that, at some point, all passwords can be cracked?" Theoretically, yes, but that time probably won't come soon. It is better to be safe than sorry, and so you might also want to incorporate multifactor authentication, of which we will speak to in the following chapter.

Devices should have their firmware updated often to help close backdoors and weed out privilege escalation attempts. These updates will often have patches for the various network attacks that we have mentioned in the past few chapters.

Wired connections are still the lifeblood of a company. Wireless is great, but you don't run it in a server room or data center; and for stationary workstations, wired connections are king. The bulk of these connections are twisted-pair, which is inherently vulnerable to tapping. Use shielded cables to block EMI, resist wiretapping, and reduce data emanation and crosstalk. On a larger scale, consider shielding such as a Faraday cage or TEMPEST, especially in server rooms. Disable unused ports on switches and RJ45 wall terminals. Remove any network cabling that is not hidden from view, and, if you are really security conscious, consider using fiber-optic cabling. Your servers may already utilize this, but your clients probably do not. For computers that send the most confidential of information, a secure channel is great, but secure media (such as fiber-optic cabling) seals the deal.

Of course, when you have data that flies all over the air in your building, it can be more difficult to secure. It is more abstract, and not as easily measured. But it is still possible to secure a wireless network. It's really all about scanning the wireless network. Is your SSID easy to find? Is it possible that you could hide the SSID? Are there other SSIDs that show up on your scan? Rogue APs and evil twins need to be sniffed out and eliminated immediately. But that isn't as much a preventive security control as it is a detective security control. The real way to prevent issues on the wireless network is to employ encryption—strong encryption such as WPA2 and AES (with a PSK), or perhaps utilize a RADIUS server in combination with those. Get rid of WPS once and for all, and make sure that VPN connections made wirelessly are heavily encrypted. Consider setting wireless boundaries by implementing a geofence. Then it's just a matter of doing a site survey, and maximizing your data transfer rate in a secure way by using smart placement techniques of your WAPs and antennas. These methods will help to reduce the chance of a successful war-driving attack, or IV attack, or a brute-force attempt.

And wireless is not limited to WLAN. You might have Bluetooth, IR, GSM, 4G, RFID, SATCOM, and the list goes on. All wireless transmissions should be thoroughly scanned and tested before they are allowed in your organization. But that's another book (and certification) altogether. Where the Security+ certification expects a basic level of wireless security knowledge, other certifications such as the Certified Wireless Network Administrator (CWNA) take it to the next level and require in-depth knowledge of all wireless communications security techniques, especially WLAN. If your organization is highly dependent on its wireless communications, consider a wireless certification such as the CWNA to bolster your resume.

Every chapter in this book effectively deals with network security on some level. But these past four chapters are at the core of it. Remember the content in these chapters as you progress throughout the rest of the book—they build your foundation of networking and network security knowledge. Finally, when it comes to your network security, attempt to think outside the box. If necessary, take it to the next level and work out solutions that, even if they seem unorthodox, fit into your organization's business model. You might surprise yourself and come up with some great answers that work very well for you and your organization.

Chapter Review Activities

Use the features in this section to study and review the topics in this chapter.

Review Key Topics

Review the most important topics in the chapter, noted with the Key Topic icon in the outer margin of the page. Table 9-3 lists a reference of these key topics and the page number on which each is found.

Key Topic

Table 9-3   Key Topics for Chapter 9

Key Topic Element	Description	Page Number
Table 9-1	Weak, strong, and stronger passwords	287
Bulleted list	Privilege escalation types	288
Bulleted list	Cable types	290
Bulleted list	Interference types	290
Table 9-2	Wireless protocols	298
Figure 9-1	Wireless security configuration on a typical WAP	299
Figure 9-2	Wireless point-to-multipoint layout	301
Figure 9-3	Final network documentation	309

Define Key Terms

Define the following key terms from this chapter, and check your answers in the glossary:

default account, privilege escalation, backdoor, electromagnetic interference (EMI), radio frequency interference (RFI), crosstalk, data emanation, Faraday cage, TEMPEST, wiretapping, butt set, protected distribution system (PDS), service set identifier (SSID), rogue AP, evil twin, Wired Equivalent Privacy (WEP), Wi-Fi Protected Access (WPA), Advanced Encryption Standard (AES), Temporal Key Integrity Protocol (TKIP), pre-shared key (PSK), Wireless Transport Layer Security (WTLS), Wi-Fi Protected Setup (WPS), MAC filtering, AP isolation, war-driving, war-chalking, IV attack, Wi-Fi disassociation attack, bluejacking, bluesnarfing

Complete the Real-World Scenarios

Complete the Real-World Scenarios found on the companion website (www.pearsonitcertification.com/title/9780789758996). You will find a PDF containing the scenario and questions, and also supporting videos and simulations.

Review Questions

Answer the following review questions. Check your answers with the correct answers that follow.

1. Which of the following is the most secure protocol to use when accessing a wireless network?

   A. WEP

   B. WPA

   C. WPA2

   D. TKIP

2. What type of cabling is the most secure for networks?

   A. STP

   B. UTP

   C. Fiber-optic

   D. Coaxial

3. What should you configure to improve wireless security?

   A. Enable the SSID

   B. IP spoofing

   C. Remove repeaters

   D. MAC filtering

4. In a wireless network, why is an SSID used?

   A. To secure the wireless access point

   B. To identify the network

   C. To encrypt data

   D. To enforce MAC filtering

5. What is the most commonly seen security risk of using coaxial cable?

   A. Data that emanates from the core of the cable

   B. Crosstalk between the different wires

   C. Chromatic dispersion

   D. Jamming

6. Of the following, what is the most common problem associated with UTP cable?

    A. Crosstalk

    B. Data emanation

    C. Chromatic dispersion

    D. Vampire tapping

7. What two security precautions can best help to protect against wireless network attacks?

    A. Authentication and WEP

    B. Access control lists and WEP

    C. Identification and WPA2

    D. Authentication and WPA

8. Which of the following cables suffers from chromatic dispersion if the cable is too long?

    A. Twisted-pair cable

    B. Fiber-optic cable

    C. Coaxial cable

    D. USB cables

9. Which of the following cable media is the least susceptible to a tap?

    A. Coaxial cable

    B. Twisted-pair cable

    C. Fiber-optic cable

    D. CATV cable

10. Which of the following, when removed, can increase the security of a wireless access point?

    A. MAC filtering

    B. SSID

    C. WPA

    D. Firewall

11. A wireless network switch has connectivity issues but only when the air-conditioning system is running. What can be added to fix the problem?

    A. Shielding

    B. A wireless network

    C. A key deflector

    D. Redundant air-conditioning systems

12. Which of the following is the most secure type of cabling?

    A. Unshielded twisted-pair

    B. Shielded twisted-pair

    C. Coaxial

    D. Category 6

13. Which of the following is the least secure type of wireless encryption?

    A. WEP 64-bit

    B. WEP 128-bit

    C. WPA with TKIP

    D. WPA2 with AES

14. Which of the following is the unauthorized access of information from a Bluetooth device?

    A. Bluejacking

    B. Bluesnarfing

    C. Deep Blue

    D. The Blues Brothers

15. Which of the following can be described as the act of exploiting a bug or flaw in software to gain access to resources that normally would be protected?

    A. Privilege escalation

    B. Chain of custody

    C. Default account

    D. Backdoor

16. What does isolation mode on an AP provide?

    A. Hides the SSID

    B. Segments each wireless user from every other wireless user

    C. Stops users from communicating with the AP

    D. Stops users from connecting to the Internet

17. You scan your network and find a rogue AP with the same SSID used by your network. What type of attack is occurring?

    A. War-driving

    B. Bluesnarfing

    C. Evil twin

    D. IV attack

18. Which of the following is an unauthorized wireless router that allows access to a secure network?

    A. Rogue AP

    B. Evil twin

    C. War-driving

    D. AP isolation

19. Your boss asks you to limit the wireless signal of a WAP from going outside the building. What should you do?

    A. Put the antenna on the exterior of the building.

    B. Disable the SSID.

    C. Enable MAC filtering.

    D. Decrease the power levels of the WAP.

20. Which of the following should be considered to mitigate data theft when using Cat 6 wiring?

    A. Multimode fiber

    B. EMI shielding

    C. CCTV

    D. Passive scanning

21. Which of the following is a room or "closet" where wiring and circuits merge, creating a potential attack point?

    A. SATCOM

    B. NFC

    C. MDF

    D. TEMPEST

Answers and Explanations

1. **C.** Wi-Fi Protected Access 2 (WPA2) is the most secure protocol listed for connecting to wireless networks. It is more secure than WPA and WEP. Wired Equivalent Privacy (WEP) is actually a deprecated protocol that should be avoided. The WEP algorithm is considered deficient for encrypting wireless networks. TKIP is also deprecated and is replaceable with CCMP.

2. **C.** Fiber-optic is the most secure because it cannot be tapped like the other three copper-based cables; it does not emit EMI. Although shielded twisted-pair (STP) offers a level of security due to its shielding, it does not offer a level of security like that of fiber-optic and is not the best answer.

3. **D.** MAC filtering disallows connections from any wireless clients unless the wireless client's MAC address is on the MAC filtering list.

4. **B.** The SSID is used to identify the wireless network. It does not secure the WAP; one of the ways to secure a WAP is by disabling the SSID. The SSID does not encrypt data or enforce MAC filtering.

5. **A.** Some types of coaxial cables suffer from the emanation of data from the core of the cable, which can be accessed. Crosstalk occurs on twisted-pair cable. Chromatic dispersion occurs on fiber-optic cable. Jamming occurs when an attacker floods a specific EM spectrum in an attempt to block legitimate transmissions from passing through that medium.

6. **A.** Of the listed answers, crosstalk is the most common problem associated with UTP cable. Older versions of UTP cable (for example, Category 3 or 5) are more susceptible to crosstalk than newer versions such as Cat 5e or Cat 6. Although data emanation can be a problem with UTP cable, it is more common with coaxial cable, as is vampire tapping. Chromatic dispersion is a problem with fiber-optic cable.

7. **D.** The best two security precautions are authentication and WPA. Although WPA2 is more secure than WPA, the term "Identification" is not correct. WEP is a deprecated wireless encryption protocol and should be avoided.

8. **B.** Fiber-optic cable is the only one listed that might suffer from chromatic dispersion, because it is the only cable based on light. All the other answers are based on electricity.

9. **C.** Fiber-optic cable is the least susceptible to a tap because it operates on the principle of light as opposed to electricity. All the other answers suffer from data emanation because they are all copper-based. Wiretaps are easily obtainable for copper-based connections such the ones that use twisted-pair cables.

10. **B.** By removing the SSID (security set identifier), the WAP will be more secure, and it will be tougher for war-drivers to access that network. Of course, no new clients can connect to the WAP (unless they do so manually). MAC filtering, WPA, and firewalls are all components that increase the security of a WAP.

11. **A.** By shielding the network switch, we hope to deflect any interference from the air-conditioning system. Another option would be to move the network switch to another location.

12. **B.** Shielded twisted-pair is the most secure type of cabling listed. It adds an aluminum sheath around the wires that can help mitigate data emanation. By far, fiber-optic would be the most secure type of cabling because it does not suffer from data emanation because the medium is glass instead of copper.

13. **A.** WEP 64-bit is the least secure type of wireless encryption listed in the possible answers. The answers are listed in order from least secure to most secure.

14. **B.** Bluesnarfing is the unauthorized access of information from a Bluetooth device—for example, calendar information, phonebook contacts, and so on. Bluejacking is the sending of unsolicited messages to Bluetooth-enabled devices. Deep Blue is not a valid answer to this question as it was a chess-playing computer developed by IBM. And if you answered the Blues Brothers, you should re-read this entire chapter, and then watch the movie if you have some free time.

15. **A.** Privilege escalation is the act of exploiting a bug or flaw in software to gain access to resources that normally would be protected. Chain of custody is the chronological paper trail used as evidence. A default account is an account such as admin set up by the manufacturer on a device; it usually has a blank or simple password. A backdoor is used in computer programs to bypass normal authentication and other security mechanisms that might be in place.

16. **B.** AP isolation mode segments all wireless users so they can't communicate with each other. They can still communicate with the AP and access the Internet (or other network that the AP connects to). It does not hide the SSID.

17. C. An evil twin is a rogue access point that has the same SSID as another access point on the network. War-driving is when a person attempts to access a wireless network, usually while driving in a vehicle. Bluesnarfing is the unauthorized access of information through a Bluetooth connection. An IV attack is one that attempts to break the encryption of wireless protocols.

18. A. A rogue AP is an unauthorized wireless router (or WAP) that allows access to a secure network. An evil twin is a type of rogue AP, but it also uses the same SSID as the legitimate network. War driving is the act of trying to access a wireless network. AP isolation blocks each wireless user from communicating with each other.

19. D. To limit the wireless signal, decrease the power levels! This can easily be done in most WAP control panels. Putting the antenna on the exterior of the building would make it easier for war-drivers to access the network, and more difficult for actual users. Disabling the SSID has no effect on the signal level. Nor does MAC filtering, though both of those methods can increase the security of your wireless network.

20. B. You should implement EMI shielding. This will help to eliminate EMI and data emanation from the Cat 6 wiring (which by default is UTP and therefore not shielded). Multimode fiber would solve the problem, but only if you tore out all of the twisted-pair cabling and replaced it. Questions of this nature don't expect you to take those kinds of measures or accept those types of expenses. Instead, you should focus on securing the cabling that is already in place. CCTV is a detective control that allows you to monitor what transpires in your building via video. Passive scanning is a technique used to check the vulnerabilities of a computer.

21. C. A main distribution frame (MDF) room is where wiring and circuits merge and connect out to external ISPs, and other network providers. Both MDF and intermediate distribution frame (IDF) types of rooms are vulnerable attack points. An attacker can exploit MDF and IDF vulnerabilities from within or from without. Satellite communications (SATCOM) is sometimes used for long distance communications, and sometimes for communicating between buildings in a campus. SATCOM devices can be at risk if their firmware is not updated. Exploits could include the installation of malicious firmware and the execution of arbitrary code. Near field communication (NFC) is a data transmission protocol often used with Bluetooth devices, but it is not necessarily secure. Data can be blocked/destroyed by use of a jammer, and users are also at risk of replay attacks. A group of standards known as TEMPEST refers to the investigations of conducted emissions from electrical and mechanical devices, which could be compromising to an organization.

This chapter covers the following subjects:

- **Physical Security:** An organization's building is one of its greatest assets and as such it should be properly protected. This section details door access, biometric readers, access logs, and video surveillance to teach you some of the ways to protect the building, its contents, and its inhabitants and to ensure proper authentication when a person enters a building.

- **Authentication Models and Components:** You can use various methods and models to authenticate a person who wants to access computer networks and resources. This section delves into local authentication technologies such as Kerberos, LDAP, and 802.1X, and remote authentication types such as VPN and RADIUS.

I suppose that at times life on this planet is all about proving oneself. The world of security is no different. To gain access to an organization's building and ultimately to its resources, you must first prove yourself in a physical manner, providing indisputable evidence of your identity. Then, perhaps you can gain access by being authenticated, as long as the system authenticating you accepts your identification. Finally, if all this goes through properly, you should be authorized to specific resources such as data files, printers, and so on.

CHAPTER 10

Physical Security and Authentication Models

Some people use the terms *identification*, *authentication*, and *authorization* synonymously. Although this might be somewhat acceptable in everyday conversation, we need to delve a bit deeper and attempt to make some distinctions among the three.

- **Identification:** When a person is in a state of being identified. It can also be described as something that identifies a person such as an ID card.

- **Authentication:** When a person's identity is confirmed or verified through the use of a specific system. Authorization to specific resources cannot be accomplished without previous authentication of the user. This might also be referred to as access control, but generally authentication is considered to be a component of access control.

- **Authorization:** When a user is given permission to access certain resources. This can be accomplished only when authentication is complete.

The CompTIA Security+ exam concentrates most on the terms *authentication* and *access control*. This chapter focuses mostly on the authentication portion of access control. The rest of access control is covered in Chapter 11, "Access Control Methods and Models."

First, we cover the physical ways that a person can be authenticated. Then, we move on to ways that a person can be authenticated to a computer network, whether that person is attempting to connect locally (for example, on the LAN) or attempting to connect remotely (for example, via a VPN).

Authentication is required to gain access to a secure area of the building or to gain access to secure data. People might identify themselves in several ways depending on the authentication scheme used, by presenting one or more of the following:

- **Something the user knows:** Such as a password or personal identification number (PIN). These are also known as *knowledge* factors.

- **Something the user has:** Such as a smart card or ID card. These are also known as *possession* factors.

- **Something the user does:** Such as a signature or gesture.

- **Something the user is:** Such as a thumbprint or retina scan or other biometric. These are also known as *inherence* factors.

- **Somewhere the user is:** Such as "at work," "at the home office," or "on the road."

Another term you might hear in your travels is **identity proofing**, which is an initial validation of an identity. For example, when employees working for a government agency want to enter a restricted building, the first thing they must do is show their ID. A guard or similar person then does an initial check of that ID. Additional authentication systems would undoubtedly ensue. Identity proofing is also when an entity validates the identity of a person applying for a certain credential with that entity. It could be used for anonymous access as well.

As you go through this chapter and read about the following physical and logical authentication technologies, try to remember this introduction and apply these concepts to each of those authentication types.

Foundation Topics

Physical Security

To control access, physical security can be considered the first line of defense, sort of like a firewall is the first line of defense for a network. Implementing physical access security methods should be a top priority for an organization. Unfortunately, securing physical access to the organization's building sometimes slumps to the bottom of the list. Or a system is employed, but it fails to mitigate risk properly. In some cases, the system is not maintained well. Proper building entrance access and secure access to physical equipment are vital. And anyone coming and going should be logged and surveyed. Let's discuss a few of the ways that we can secure physical access to an organization's building.

General Building and Server Room Security

Protecting an organization's building is an important step in general security. The more security a building has, the less you have to depend on your authentication system. A building's perimeter should be surveyed for possible breaches; this includes all doors, windows, loading docks, and even the roof. The area around the building should be scanned for hiding places; if there are any they should be removed. The area surrounding the building should be well lit at night. Some companies may opt to use security guards and guard dogs. It is important that these are trained properly; usually an organization will enlist the services of a third-party security company. Video surveillance can also be employed to track an individual's movements. Video cameras should be placed on the exterior perimeter of the building in an area hard to access; for example, 12 feet or higher with no lateral or climbing access. The more well-hidden the cameras are the better. Video cameras can also be placed inside the building, especially in secure areas such as executive offices, wiring closets, server rooms, and research and development areas. Many organizations use **closed-circuit television (CCTV)**, but some opt for a wired/wireless IP-based solution. Either way, the video stream may be watched and recorded, but it should not be broadcast. Video cameras are an excellent way of tracking user identities. However, proper lighting is necessary inside and outside in order for the cameras to capture images well. Also, video cameras must be properly secured as they are prime targets for reverse-engineering techniques where the attacker attempts to gain access to the pan-tilt-zoom (PTZ) controls and redirect the video feed. Motion detectors and other sensors are also common as part of a total alarm system. They are often infrared-based (set off by heat) or ultrasonic-based (set off by certain higher frequencies). We could go on and on about general building security, but this chapter focuses on authentication. Besides, I think you get the idea. If your organization is extremely concerned about building security, and doubts that it has the knowledge to protect the building and its contents properly, consider hiring a professional.

The server room is the lifeblood in today's organizations. If anything happens to the server room, the company could be in for a disaster. We talk more about how an organization can recover from disasters in Chapter 16, "Redundancy and Disaster Recovery," but the best policy is to try to avoid disasters before they happen. So, there are some things you should think about when it comes to server room security. First, where is the server room to be placed? It's wise to avoid basements or any other areas that might be prone to water damage. Second, the room should be accessible only to authorized IT persons. This can be accomplished by using one of many door access systems. The room should also have video surveillance saved to a hard drive located in a different room of the building or stored offsite. All devices and servers in the server room should have complex passwords that only the authorized IT personnel have knowledge of. Devices and servers should be physically locked down with cable locks to prevent theft. If necessary, network cabling to each server should be approved circuits and meet the requirements for protected distribution systems. We discuss wired security in Chapter 9, "Securing Network Media and Devices," and talk more about server room security and building security in Chapter 16 and Chapter 18, "Policies and Procedures."

> **NOTE** Security doesn't just mean securing data; it also means user safety—keeping an organization's employees secure. To this end, properly planned fire drills, exit signs, escape plans, and escape routes are all vital. We'll discuss this more in Chapter 18.

For now, let's focus on how to impede unauthorized access. Secure door access is the number one way to stop intruders from getting into the building or server room. If the system is set up properly, then the intruder cannot be authenticated. Let's talk about door access in a little more depth.

Door Access

Lock the door! Sounds so simple, yet it is often overlooked. As a person in charge of security for a small business or even a midsized business, you must think about all types of security, including entrances to the building. Door locks are essential. When deciding on a locking system to use, you should take into account the type of area your building is in and the crime rate, and who will have authorized access to the building. If you purchase regular door locks that work with a key, it is recommended that you get two or three of them. The first one should be tested. Can you break in to it with a credit card, jeweler's screwdriver, or other tools? And a backup should always be on hand in case the current door lock gets jimmied in an attempt to force a break-in. Cipher locks are a decent solution when regular key locks are not enough but you don't want to implement an electronic system. The cipher lock uses a punch code to lock the door and unlock it. Though it will have a relatively low number of combinations, the fact that they have to be attempted manually makes it difficult to get past them.

Of course, many organizations (and especially government) get more technical with their door access systems. Electronic access control systems such as cardkey systems are common. These use scanning devices on each door used for access to the building. They read the cardkeys that you give out to employees and visitors. These cardkeys should be logged; it should be known exactly who has which key at all times. The whole system is guided by a cardkey controller. This controller should be placed in a wiring closet or in a server room, and that room should be locked as well (and protected by the cardkey system). Some companies implement separate cardkey systems for the server room and for the main entrances. Some systems use photo ID badges for identification and authentication to a building's entrance. They might have a magnetic stripe similar to a credit card, or they might have a barcode or use an RFID chip. A key card door access system is another good practice for tracking user identities.

NOTE Hardware-based **security tokens** are physical devices given to authorized users to help with authentication. These devices might be attached to a keychain or might be part of a card system. Hardware-based tokens might be used as part of the door access system or as something that gives access to an individual computer. As one example, RSA tokens carry and generate rolling one-time passwords (OTPs), each of which is valid for only one login session or transaction.

Another possibility is the smart card. The smart card falls into the category of "something a person has" and is known as a token. It's the size of a credit card and has an embedded chip that stores and transacts data for use in secure applications such as hotel guest room access, prepaid phone services, and more. Smart cards have multiple applications, one of which is to authenticate users by swiping the card against a scanner, thus securing a computer or a computer room. The smart card might have a photo ID as well. Examples of smart cards include the PIV card (Personal Identity Verification), which is required for all U.S. government employees and contractors, and the Common Access Card (CAC), which is used to identify Department of Defense (DoD) military personnel, other DoD civilian government employees, and so on. These cards not only identify the person and are responsible for authentication to buildings and systems, but can also encrypt and digitally sign e-mails. These cards might be used as part of a multifactor authentication scheme in which there is a combination of username/password (or PIN) and a smart card. Advanced smart cards have specialized cryptographic hardware that can use algorithms such as RSA and 3DES but generally use private keys to encrypt data. (More on encryption and these encryption types is provided in Chapter 14, "Encryption and Hashing Concepts.") A smart card might incorporate a microprocessor (as is the case with the PIV and CAC cards). A smart card security system usually is composed of the smart card itself, smart card readers, and a back-office database that stores all the smart card access control lists and history.

Older technologies use proximity sensors, but this is not considered very secure today. However, the more complex the technology, the more it costs. Often, in these situations, budgeting becomes more important to organizations than mitigating risk; and generally, the amount of acceptable risk increases as the budget decreases. So, you will probably see proximity-based door access systems. HID (also known as HID Global) is an example of a company that offers various levels of door access control systems.

To increase security of the entrances of the building, some organizations implement **mantraps**, which are areas between two doorways, meant to hold people until they are identified and authenticated. This might be coupled with security guards, video surveillance, multifactor authentication, and sign-in logs. The main purpose of a physical access log or sign-in log is to show who entered the facility and when.

Door access systems are considered by many to be the weakest link in an enterprise. This can be taken to the next level by also incorporating biometrics, thus creating a different type of multifactor authentication scheme.

Biometric Readers

Biometrics is the science of recognizing humans based on one or more physical characteristics. Biometrics is used as a form of authentication and access control. It is also used to identify persons who might be under surveillance.

Biometrics falls into the category of "something a person is." Examples of bodily characteristics that are measured include fingerprints, retinal patterns, iris patterns, voice patterns, and even facial/bone structure. Biometric readers (for example, fingerprint scanners) are becoming more common in door access systems and on laptops or as USB devices. Biometric information can also be incorporated into smart card technology. An example of a biometric door access system provider is Suprema, which has various levels of access systems, including some that incorporate smart cards and biometrics, together forming a multifactor authentication system. There are lots of providers of fingerprint scanners (also called fingerprint *readers*) for desktops and laptops also; these fingerprint recognition systems are usually USB-based.

Sometimes there are failures in which a biometric authentication system will improperly categorize people. These include the following:

- **False acceptance:** This is when a biometric system authenticates a user who should *not* be allowed access to the system.

- **False rejection:** This is when a biometric system denies a user who should actually be allowed access to the system.

A security admin should monitor the biometric system for errors. Generally, if either the false acceptance rate (FAR) or the false rejection rate (FRR) goes above 1%, it should be investigated further—perhaps .1% for some organizations. More importantly, the two should be collectively analyzed with the **crossover error rate (CER)**. This is also known as the equal error rate (EER) because the goal is to keep both the FAR and FRR errors at a common value, or as close as possible. The lower the CER, the better the biometric system in general. This is one of the main metrics to use when analyzing biometric system performance.

Biometrics can be seen in many movies and TV shows. However, many biometric systems historically have been easily compromised. It has only been of late that readily available biometric systems have started to live up to the hype. Thorough investigation and testing of a biometric system is necessary before purchase and installation. In addition, it should be used in a multifactor authentication scheme. The more factors the better, as long as your users can handle it. (You would be surprised what a little bit of training can do.) Voice recognition software has made great leaps and bounds since the turn of the millennium. A combination of biometrics, voice recognition, and PIN access would make for an excellent three-factor authentication system. But as always, only if you can get it through budgeting!

Authentication Models and Components

Now that we've covered some physical authentication methods, let's move into authentication models, components, and technologies used to grant or deny access to operating systems and computer networks.

The first thing a security administrator should do is plan what type of authentication model to use. Then, consider what type of authentication technology and how many factors of authentication will be implemented. Also for consideration is how the authentication system will be monitored and logged. Getting more into the specifics, will only local authentication be necessary? Or will remote authentication also be needed? And which type of technology should be utilized? Will it be Windows-based or a third-party solution? Let's discuss these concepts now and give some different examples of the possible solutions you can implement.

Authentication Models

Many small businesses and even some midsized businesses often have one type of authentication to gain access to a computer network—the username and password. In today's security-conscious world, this is not enough for the average organization. Some companies share passwords or fail to enforce password complexity. In addition, password-cracking programs are becoming more and more powerful and work much more quickly than they did just five years ago, making the username and password authentication scheme limiting. Not to say that it shouldn't be used, but perhaps it should be enforced, enhanced, and integrated with other technologies.

Because of the limitations of a single type of authentication such as username and password, organizations sometimes use multiple factors of authentication. **Multifactor authentication (MFA)** is when two or more types of authentication are used for user access control. An example of multifactor authentication would be when a user needs to sign in with a username and password and swipe some type of smart card or use some other type of physical token at the same time. Adding factors of authentication makes it more difficult for a malicious person to gain access to a computer network or an individual computer system. Sometimes an organization uses three factors of authentication—perhaps a smart card, biometrics, and a username/password. The disadvantages of a multifactor authentication scheme are that users need to remember more information and remember to bring more identification with them, and more IT costs and more administration will be involved. Another disadvantage of some MFA environments is that they are static—rules and whitelists/blacklists are usually configured manually. A more dynamic way of authenticating individuals is to utilize **context-aware authentication** (also known as context-sensitive access). It is an adaptive way of authenticating users based on their usage of resources, and the confidence that the system has in the user. It can automatically increase the level of identification required and/or increase or decrease the level of access to resources based on constant analysis of the user.

Some organizations have several computer systems that an individual user might need access to. By default, each of these systems will have a separate login. It can be difficult for users to remember the various logins. **Single sign-on (SSO)** is when a user can log in once but gain access to multiple systems without being asked to log in again. This is complemented by single sign-off, which is basically the reverse; logging off signs off a person from multiple systems. Single sign-on is meant to reduce password fatigue, or password chaos, which is when a person can become confused and possibly even disoriented when having to log in with several different usernames and passwords. It is also meant to reduce IT help desk calls and password resets. By implementing a more centralized authentication scheme such as single sign-on, many companies have reduced IT costs significantly. If implemented properly, single sign-on can also reduce phishing. In large networks and enterprise scenarios, it might not be possible for users to have a single sign-on, and in these cases, it might be referred to as *reduced* sign-on. Single sign-on can be Kerberos-based, integrated with Windows authentication, or token- or smart card-based.

SSO is a derivative of **federated identity management** (also called FIM or FIdM). This is when a user's identity, as well as the user's attributes, is shared across multiple identity management systems. These various systems can be owned by one organization; for example, Microsoft offers the Forefront Identity Manager software, which can control user accounts across local and cloud environments. Also, Google, Yahoo!, and Amazon are examples of companies that utilize this federation approach. But, some providers join forces so that information can be shared across multiple services and environments between the companies, yet still allow the user a single login. Shibboleth is an example of an SSO system that allows people to sign in with a single digital identity and connect to various systems run by federations of different organizations. SSO systems—and federated systems in general—will often incorporate the concept of transitive trust where two networks (or more) have a relationship such that users logging in to one network get access to data on the other.

While an SSO is easier for the user to remember, it acts as a single point of failure as well. In addition, sometimes a company might not be watching out for the user's best interests—either unwittingly or otherwise—and might fail to realize that multiple systems have been configured as a transitive trust. We mentioned the transitive trust concept in Chapter 7, "Networking Protocols and Threats." When it comes to authentication, it can be especially damaging. Let's say that a user has an account with Company A, and has a separate account with Company B. Imagine that Companies A and B have a two-way trust. Now, let's say there is a third organization, Company C, that has a two-way trust with Company B. At this point, the user's account information from Companies A and B could be shared with Company C, even though the user never signed up with that company. This kind of activity is frowned upon, but the user might not even know when it happens—two companies might merge, or a company might be bought out or otherwise absorbed by another. So, when it comes to authentication, it is sometimes wise to avoid trust relationships, and strongly consider whether single sign-on will ultimately be more beneficial or costly to your organization.

Another concern is web-based SSO. Web-based SSO can be problematic due to disparate proprietary technologies. To help alleviate this problem, the XML-based Security Assertion Markup Language (SAML) and the OpenID Connect protocol were developed. OpenID Connect is an interoperable authentication protocol based on the OAuth 2.0 family of specifications. It uses straightforward REST/JSON message flows with a design goal of "making simple things simple and complicated things possible." Both OpenID Connect and SAML specify separate roles for the user, the service provider, and the identity provider. Shibboleth is also based on SAML.

Whatever the type of authentication scheme used, it needs to be monitored periodically to make sure that it's working properly. The authentication system should block people who cannot furnish proper identification, and should allow access to people who do have proper identification. Let's talk about some of those authentication technologies now.

Localized Authentication Technologies

There are several types of technologies for authenticating a user to a local area network. Examples that are software-based include LDAP and Kerberos, whereas an example that includes physical characteristics would be 802.1X. Keep in mind that there is a gray area between localized and remote authentication technologies. I've placed each technology in the category in which it is used the most commonly.

During this section and the next one, we mention several encryption concepts that work with the various authentication technologies. These encryption concepts and protocols are covered in detail in Chapter 14 and Chapter 15, "PKI and Encryption Protocols."

802.1X and EAP

802.1X is an IEEE standard that defines port-based network access control (PNAC). Not to be confused with 802.11x WLAN standards, **802.1X** is a data link layer authentication technology used to connect hosts to a LAN or WLAN. 802.1X allows you to apply a security control that ties physical ports to end-device MAC addresses, and prevents additional devices from being connected to the network. It is a good way of implementing port security, much better than simply setting up MAC filtering.

It all starts with the central connecting device such as a switch or wireless access point. These devices must first enable 802.1X connections; they must have the 802.1X protocol (and supporting protocols) installed. Vendors that offer 802.1X-compliant devices (for example, switches and wireless access points) include Cisco, Symbol Technologies, and Intel. Next, the client computer needs to have an operating system, or additional software, that supports 802.1X. The client computer is known as the supplicant. All recent Windows versions support 802.1X. macOS/ OS X offers support as well, and Linux computers can use Open1X to enable client access to networks that require 802.1X authentication.

802.1X encapsulates the **Extensible Authentication Protocol (EAP)** over wired or wireless connections. EAP is not an authentication mechanism in itself, but instead defines message formats. 802.1X is the authentication mechanism and defines how EAP is encapsulated within messages. An example of an 802.1X-enabled network adapter is shown in Figure 10-1. In the figure, you can see that the box for enabling 802.1X has been checked, and that the type of network authentication method for 802.1X is EAP— specifically, Protected EAP (PEAP).

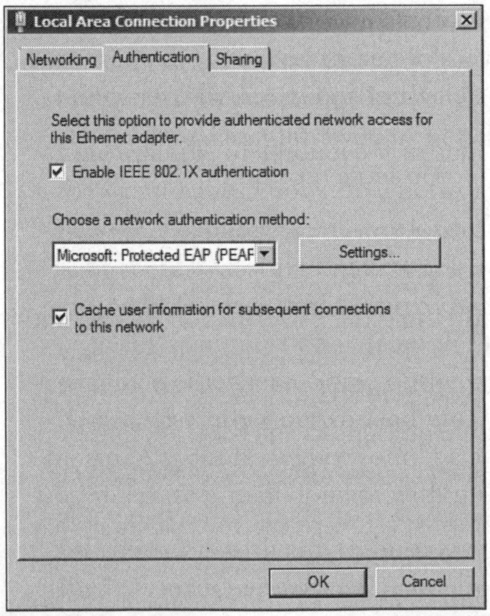

Figure 10-1 Example of an 802.1X-Enabled Network Adapter in Windows

NOTE 802.1X can be enabled in Windows by accessing the Local Area Connection Properties page.

Following are three components to an 802.1X connection:

- **Supplicant:** A software client running on a workstation. This is also known as an authentication agent.

- **Authenticator:** A wireless access point or switch.

- **Authentication server:** An authentication database, most likely a RADIUS server.

The typical 802.1X authentication procedure has four steps. The components used in these steps are illustrated in Figure 10-2.

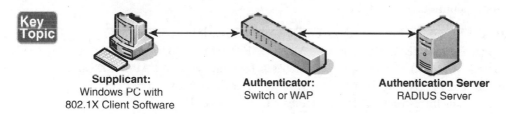

Figure 10-2 Components of a Typical 802.1X Authentication Procedure

Step 1.   **Initialization:** If a switch or wireless access point detects a new suppli-cant, the port connection enables port 802.1X traffic; other types of traf-fic are dropped.

Step 2.   **Initiation:** The authenticator (switch or wireless access point) periodi-cally sends EAP requests to a MAC address on the network. The suppli-cant listens for this address and sends an EAP response that might include a user ID or other similar information. The authenticator encapsulates this response and sends it to the authentication server.

Step 3.   **Negotiation:** The authentication server then sends a reply to the authen-ticator. The authentication server specifies which EAP method to use. (These are listed next.) Then the authenticator transmits that request to the supplicant.

Step 4.   **Authentication:** If the supplicant and the authentication server agree on an EAP method, the two transmit until there is either success or failure to authenticate the supplicant computer.

Following are several types of EAP authentication:

- **EAP-MD5:** This is a challenge-based authentication providing basic EAP support. It enables only one-way authentication and not mutual authentication.

- **EAP-TLS:** This version uses Transport Layer Security, which is a certificate-based system that does enable mutual authentication. This does not work well in enterprise scenarios because certificates must be configured or managed on the client side and server side.

- **EAP-TTLS:** This version is Tunneled Transport Layer Security and is basically the same as TLS except that it is done through an encrypted channel, and it requires only server-side certificates.

- **EAP-FAST:** This uses a protected access credential instead of a certificate to achieve mutual authentication. FAST stands for Flexible Authentication via Secure Tunneling.

- **PEAP:** This is the **Protected Extensible Authentication Protocol** (also known as Protected EAP). This uses MS-CHAPv2, which supports authentication via Microsoft Active Directory databases. It competes with EAP-TTLS and includes legacy password-based protocols. It creates a TLS tunnel by acquiring a public key infrastructure (PKI) certificate from a server known as a certificate authority (CA). The TLS tunnel protects user authentication much like EAP-TTLS. More information on PKI and CAs can be found in Chapter 15.

Cisco also created a proprietary protocol called LEAP (Lightweight EAP), and it is just that—proprietary. To use LEAP, you must have a Cisco device such as an Aironet WAP or Catalyst switch, or another vendor's device that complies with the Cisco Compatible Extensions program. Then you must download a third-party client on Windows computers to connect to the Cisco device. Most WLAN vendors offer an 802.1X LEAP download for their wireless network adapters.

Although 802.1X is often used for port-based network access control on the LAN, especially VLANs, it can also be used with VPNs as a way of remote authentication. Central connecting devices such as switches and wireless access points remain the same, but on the client side 802.1X would need to be configured on a VPN adapter, instead of a network adapter.

Many vendors, such as Intel and Cisco, refer to 802.1X with a lowercase x; however, the IEEE displays this on its website with an uppercase X, as does the IETF. The protocol was originally defined in 2001 (802.1X-2001) and has been redefined in 2004 and 2010 (802.1X-2004 and 802.1X-2010, respectively). There are several links to more information about 802.1X in the "View Recommended Resources" document on this book's companion website.

LDAP

The **Lightweight Directory Access Protocol (LDAP)** is an application layer protocol used for accessing and modifying directory services data. It is part of the TCP/IP suite. Originally used in WAN connections, it has developed over time into a protocol commonly used by services such as Microsoft Active Directory on Windows Server domain controllers. LDAP acts as the protocol that controls the directory service. This is the service that organizes the users, computers, and other objects within the Active Directory. An example of the Active Directory is shown in Figure 10-3. Take note of the list of users (known as objects of the Active Directory) from the Users folder that is highlighted. Also observe other folders such as Computers that house other objects (such as Windows client computers).

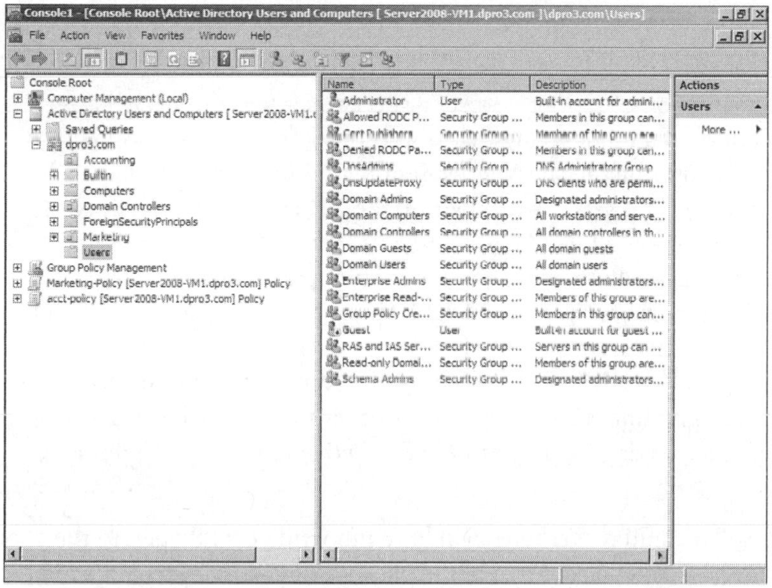

Figure 10-3 Example of Active Directory Showing User Objects

NOTE Windows servers running Active Directory use parameters and variables when querying the names of objects. For example, CN=dprowse, where *CN* stands for common name and *dprowse* is the username. Taking it to the next level: DC=ServerName. *DC* stands for domain component. *ServerName* is the variable and is the name of the server. Microsoft is famous for using the name "fabrikam" as its test name, but it would be whatever your server name is. In the case of fabrikam, an entire LDAP query might look something like this:

```
<LDAP://DC=Fabrikam, DC=COM>
```

A Microsoft server that has Active Directory and LDAP running will have inbound port 389 open by default. To protect Active Directory from being tampered with, Secure LDAP can be used—also known as LDAPS. This brings into play SSL (Secure Sockets Layer) on top of LDAP and uses inbound port 636 by default. Other implementations of LDAP use TLS (Transport Layer Security) over LDAP.

Kerberos and Mutual Authentication

Kerberos is an authentication protocol designed at MIT that enables computers to prove their identity to each other in a secure manner. It is used most often in a client-server environment; the client and the server both verify each other's identity. This is known as two-way authentication or **mutual authentication**. Often, Kerberos protects a network server from illegitimate login attempts, just as the mythological three-headed guard dog of the same name (also known as Cerberus) guards Hades.

A common implementation of Kerberos occurs when a user logs on to a Microsoft domain. (Of course, I am not saying that Microsoft domains are analogous to Hades!) The domain controller in the Microsoft domain is known as the key distribution center (KDC). This server works with **tickets** that prove the identity of users. The KDC is composed of two logical parts: the authentication server and the ticket-granting server. Basically, a client computer attempts to authenticate itself to the authentication server portion of the KDC. When it does so successfully, the client receives a ticket. This is actually a ticket to get other tickets—known as a ticket granting ticket (TGT). The client uses this preliminary ticket to demonstrate its identity to a ticket-granting server in the hopes of ultimately getting access to a service—for example, making a connection to the Active Directory of a domain controller.

The domain controller running Kerberos will have inbound port 88 open to the service logon requests from clients. Figure 10-4 shows a `netstat -an` command run on a Windows Server that has been promoted to a domain controller. It points out port 88 (used by Kerberos) and port 389 (used by LDAP) on the same domain controller.

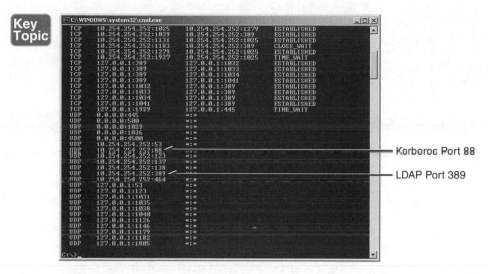

Figure 10-4 Results of the `netstat -an` Command on a Windows Server

Kerberos is designed to protect against replay attacks and eavesdropping. One of the drawbacks of Kerberos is that it relies on a centralized server such as a domain controller. This can be a single point of failure. To alleviate this problem, secondary and tertiary domain controllers can be installed that keep a copy of the Active Directory and are available with no downtime in case the first domain controller fails. Another possible issue is one of synchronicity. Time between the clients and the domain controller must be synchronized for Kerberos to work properly. If for some reason a client attempting to connect to a domain controller becomes desynchronized, it cannot complete the Kerberos authentication, and as an end result the user cannot log on to the domain. This can be fixed by logging on to the affected client locally and synchronizing the client's time to the domain controller by using the `net time` command. For example, to synchronize to the domain controller in Figure 10-4, the command would be

```
net time \\10.254.254.252 /set
```

Afterward, the client should be able to connect to the domain. We revisit Kerberos and how it makes use of encryption keys in Chapter 14.

Kerberos—like any authentication system—is vulnerable to attack. Older Windows operating systems that run, or connect to, Kerberos are vulnerable to privilege escalation attacks; and newer Windows operating systems are vulnerable to spoofing. Of course, Microsoft will quickly release updates for these kinds of vulnerabilities (as they are found), but for the security administrator who does not allow Windows Update to automatically update, it's important to review the CVEs for the Microsoft systems often.

NOTE In a Red Hat Enterprise environment that uses an SSO such as Kerberos, *pluggable authentication modules (PAMs)* can be instrumental in providing the systems admin/security admin flexibility and control over authentication, as well as fully documented libraries for the developer.

Remote Desktop Services

Remote Desktop Services enables the remote control of Windows computers (most importantly for this section, Windows servers) from a client computer. This client computer could be on the LAN or out on the Internet, so the term "remote" is used loosely. It can also be used to enable client access to specific applications.

In Windows Server 2008, it is configured within Remote Desktop Management Server, and in Windows Server 2012 R2 and higher it is configured via the Remote Desktop Services server role. This application is in charge of authenticating remote users and will do so if the user has been configured properly. For example, users in question must have Remote Access permissions enabled within the properties of their account. Remote Desktop Services authentication integrates directly with standard Windows Server authentication. The remote desktop will have inbound port 3389 open to accept connections from remote clients. Client sessions are stored at the Windows Server running Remote Desktop Services, which allows for disconnections and later reuse.

NOTE Remote Desktop Services is still often referred to as its original name, Terminal Services. In fact, the underlying service name is actually still called "TermService."

Some of the vulnerabilities to Remote Desktop Services—and the Remote Desktop Protocol in general, otherwise known as RDP—include an extremely well-known port, comparatively weak encryption, and a lack of multifactor authentication. Because of this, you might choose to utilize another remote control application. At this point, security is relative, and your decision on what tool to use will be based on the type of data you are protecting.

As mentioned, the port is 3389 by default, and is extremely well known. But it can be modified within the inbound computer's Registry at the following path:

```
HKEY_LOCAL_MACHINE\SYSTEM\CurrentControlSet\Control\Terminal Server\
   WinStations\RDP-Tcp
```

Third-party applications such as VNC, TeamViewer, and so on can be more secure in this respect because they can use web-based connections via HTTPS on port 443. Out-of-the-box, RDP is generally limited to SSL (TLS 1.0) with a 128-bit key based on the RC4 algorithm (which is considered crackable, though difficult to do so). However, RDP can also comply with Federal Information Processing Standard (FIPS) 140 encryption methods, but additional hardware and software modules are required, which might incur an unacceptable expense. On the other hand, third-party remote control applications such as the ones mentioned earlier will often use RSA encryption for the HTTPS connection, and the Advanced Encryption Standard (AES) with up to 256-bit keys for session security. Some third-party applications also offer multifactor authentication; for example, a passcode in combination with the standard username/password login. However, multifactor authentication could always be added to RDP as a separate module (at a price). Your final decision of what application to use will be based on cost, the number of remote connections required, the platforms you need to support, and, of course, the level of security you desire.

Captive Portals

Have you ever stayed at a hotel or gone to a coffee shop that had free Wi-Fi? What happens when you use that wireless network? Chances are you are redirected to a web page that asks for authentication prior to normal Internet use. Quite often you will have to create an account with a username (usually an e-mail address) and password, which is authenticated through e-mail. This is an example of a captive portal. So, the captive portal method forces the HTTP client (for instance, a web browser) of the wireless device to authenticate itself via a web page. The redirection could occur as HTTP or as DNS. Quite often, it is done through basic SSL-secured HTTPS web pages. This can often be circumvented with the use of a packet sniffer such as Wireshark. To avoid this potential hazard, an organization can opt for extended or multifactor authentication. There are many free, one-time charge, and subscription-based applications that an organization can use for Windows and Linux-based platforms. The whole point of the technology is to be able to track users who access the free wireless network. If the user performs any suspect actions, the user can be traced by way of e-mail address, IP address, and MAC address, in addition to other means if multifactor authentication is used.

Remote Authentication Technologies

Even more important than authenticating local users is authenticating *remote* users. The chances of illegitimate connections increase when you allow remote users to connect to your network. Examples of remote authentication technologies include RAS, VPN, RADIUS, TACACS+, and CHAP. Let's discuss these now.

Remote Access Service

Remote Access Service (RAS) began as a service that enabled dial-up connections from remote clients. Nowadays, more and more remote connections are made with high-speed Internet technologies such as cable Internet, DSL, and fiber-optic connections. But we can't discount the dial-up connection. It is used in certain areas where other Internet connections are not available, and is still used as a fail-safe in many network operation centers and server rooms to take control of networking equipment.

One of the best things you can do to secure a RAS server is to deny access to individuals who don't require it. Even if the user or user group is set to "not configured," it is wise to specifically deny them access. Allow access to only those users who need it, and monitor on a daily basis the logs that list who connected. If there are any unknowns, investigate immediately. Be sure to update the permissions list often in the case that a remote user is terminated or otherwise leaves the organization.

The next most important security precaution is to set up RAS authentication. One secure way is to use the **Challenge-Handshake Authentication Protocol (CHAP),** which is an authentication scheme used by the Point-to-Point Protocol (PPP), which in turn is the standard for dial-up connections. It uses a challenge-response mechanism with one-way encryption. Due to this, it is not capable of mutual authentication in the way that Kerberos is, for example. CHAP uses DES and MD5 encryption types, which we cover in Chapter 14. Microsoft developed its own version of CHAP known as MS-CHAP; an example of this is shown in Figure 10-5. The figure shows the Advanced Security Settings dialog box of a dial-up connection. Notice that this particular configuration shows that encryption is required, and that the only protocol allowed is MS-CHAPv2. It's important to use version 2 of MS-CHAP because it provides for mutual authentication between the client and the authenticator. Of course, the RAS server has to be configured to accept MS-CHAP connections as well. You also have the option to enable EAP for the dial-up connection. Other RAS authentication protocols include SPAP, which is of lesser security, and PAP, which sends usernames and passwords in clear text—obviously insecure and to be avoided.

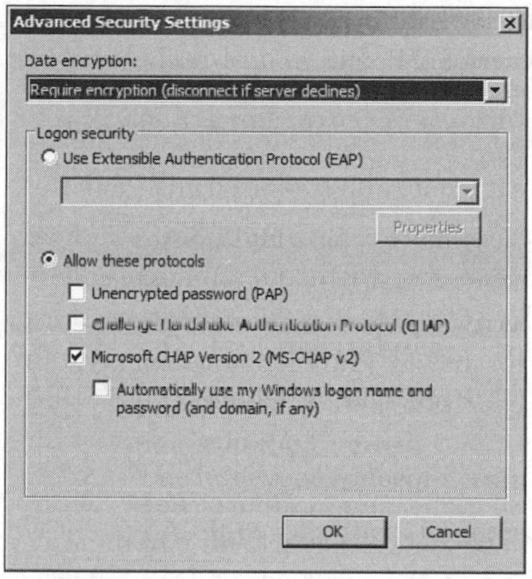

Figure 10-5 MS-CHAP Enabled on a Dial-Up Connection

NOTE Use CHAP, MS-CHAP, or EAP for dial-up connections. Verify that it is configured properly on the RAS server and dial-up client to ensure a proper handshake.

The CHAP authentication scheme consists of several steps. It authenticates a user or a network host to entities such as Internet access providers. CHAP periodically verifies the identity of the client by using a three-way handshake. The verification is based on a shared secret. After the link has been established, the authenticator sends a challenge message to the peer. The encrypted results are compared, and finally the client is either authorized or denied access.

The actual data transmitted in these RAS connections is encrypted as well. By default, Microsoft RAS connections are encrypted by the RSA RC4 algorithm. More information on this can also be found in Chapter 14.

Now you might say, "But Dave, who cares about dial-up connections?" Well, there are two reasons that they are important. First, the supporting protocols, authentication types, and encryption types are used in other technologies; this is the basis for those systems. Second, as I mentioned before, some organizations still use the dial-up connection—for remote users or for administrative purposes. And hey, don't downplay the dial-up connection. Old-school dial-up guys used to tweak the connection to the point where it was as fast as some DSL versions and as reliable. So, there are going to be die-hards out there as well. Plus, there are some areas of the United States, and the rest of the world, that have no other option than dial-up.

However, RAS now has morphed into something that goes beyond just dial-up. VPN connections that use dial-up, cable Internet, DSL, and so on are all considered remote access.

Virtual Private Networks

A **virtual private network (VPN)** is a connection between two or more computers or devices not on the same private network. Generally, VPNs use the Internet to connect one host to another. It is desirable that only proper users and data sessions make their way to a VPN device; because of this, data encapsulation and encryption are used. A "tunnel' is created through any LANs and WANs that might intervene; this tunnel connects the two VPN devices together. Every time a new session is initiated, a new tunnel is created, which makes the connection secure.

PPTP and L2TP are common VPN connections that can cause a lot of havoc if the security settings are not configured properly on the client side and the server side. This can cause errors; you can find a link to the list of these error codes in the "View Recommended Resources" document online. We cover PPTP and L2TP encryption methods in Chapter 15.

Figure 10-6 shows an illustration of a VPN. Note that the VPN server is on one side of the cloud, and the VPN client is on the other. It should be known that the VPN client will have a standard IP address to connect to its own LAN. However, it will receive a second IP address from the VPN server or a DHCP device. This second IP address works "inside" the original IP address. So, the client computer will have two IP addresses; in essence, the VPN address is encapsulated within the logical IP address. As previously mentioned, dial-up authentication protocols such as CHAP are also used in other technologies; this is one of those examples. VPN adapters, regardless of the Internet connection used, can use MS-CHAP, as shown in Figure 10-6. To further increase authentication security, a separate RADIUS server can be used with the VPN server—we talk more about RADIUS in the next section.

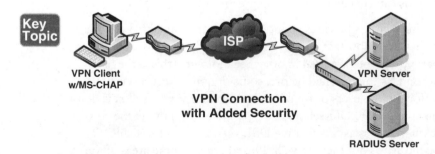

Figure 10-6 Illustration of a VPN

Figure 10-6 illustrates a single computer connecting to a VPN server at an office, which is typical and is known as VPN remote access. However, organizations sometimes need to connect multiple offices to each other. This is done with a *site-to-site* configuration, where each site has a VPN device (SOHO router, concentrator, or server) that takes care of VPN connections for each network of computers. Site-to-site VPNs are generally more secure because an admin can specify that only specific networks can connect—and can do it in a private intranet fashion. If a company is growing, site-to-site is the way to go, whether the company is flourishing geographically or is simply inhabiting a separate space of the same building. When separate networks are connected in the same building, it is often wise to use a VPN, because the physical wiring might pass through a public area.

A Microsoft VPN can be set up on a standard Windows Server by configuring Routing and Remote Access Service (RRAS). Remote access policies can be created from here that permit or deny access to groups of users for dial-in or VPN connections. In a typical Windows Server you would need to set up RRAS as part of the Network Policy and Access Services role. Then you would right-click the Remote Access Logging & Policies node and access the Network Policy Server (NPS) window to create a new RRAS policy. Figure 10-7 displays the initiation of a RRAS VPN policy.

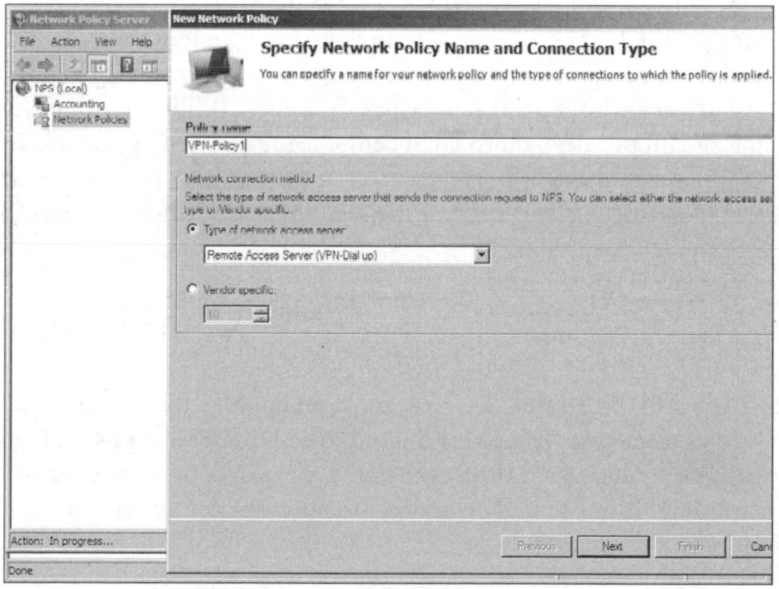

Figure 10-7 RRAS VPN Policy on a Windows Server

NOTE You could also configure DirectAccess if you have Windows Server 2008 R2 (or higher) and Windows 7 clients (or higher) to implement a Microsoft-based VPN.

You don't have to use a server for incoming VPN sessions. Hardware appliances are offered by several vendors. Larger organizations that need hundreds of simultaneous connections should opt for a **VPN concentrator** as their solution. Or, it might be part of your unified threat management (UTM) solution.

Older VPNs use either PPTP (port 1723) or L2TP (port 1701) with IPsec. They can also incorporate CHAP on the client side and RADIUS servers for authentication. Newer VPNs protect traffic by using SSL or TLS. For example, OpenVPN uses this type of encryption (https://openvpn.net/). SSL/TLS solutions for VPN improve on endpoint security and enable **always-on VPN** functionality—where a user can always have access via the VPN without the need to periodically disconnect and reconnect.

Watch out for *split tunneling*. This is when a client system (for example, a mobile device) can access a public network and a LAN at the same time using one or more network connections. For example, a remote user might connect to the Internet through a hotel's Wi-Fi network. If the user needs to access resources on the company LAN, the VPN software will take control. But if the user needs to connect to websites on the Internet, the hotel's gateway will provide those sessions. While this can provide for bandwidth conservation and increase efficiency, it can also bypass upper-layer security in place within the company infrastructure. While it is common, split tunneling should be tested thoroughly before being allowed by administrators. For example, simulate the split tunnel from a remote location, then perform vulnerability scans and capture packets. Analyze the session in depth and log your findings.

Cisco systems use the *Generic Routing Encapsulation (GRE)* protocol to encapsulate a lot of different data, namely, routing information that passes between VPN-enabled connected networks that use PPTP or IPsec. GRE might also make use of Multiprotocol Label Switching (MPLS), a packet-forwarding technology that uses labels to make data forwarding decisions. With MPLS, the Layer 3 header analysis is done just once (when the packet enters the MPLS domain). Label inspection drives subsequent packet forwarding. It is a natural evolution for networks that provide predictable IP services.

There is a minor amount of risk when using MPLS due to its open-ended nature, and when connecting from MPLS to non-MPLS networks. To mitigate this, the MPLS over GRE feature provides a mechanism for tunneling MPLS packets over a non-MPLS network. This feature utilizes MPLS over Generic Routing Encapsulation (MPLSoGRE) to encapsulate MPLS packets inside IP tunnels. The encapsulation of MPLS packets inside IP tunnels creates a virtual point-to-point link across non-MPLS networks.

RADIUS Versus TACACS

We mentioned RADIUS previously in this chapter and in Chapter 9, and said that it could be used in combination with a SOHO router in order to provide strong authentication. Let's define it further: The **Remote Authentication Dial-In User Service (RADIUS)** provides centralized administration of dial-up, VPN, and wireless authentication and can be used with EAP and 802.1X. To set this up on a Windows Server, the Internet Authentication Service must be loaded; it is usually set up on a separate physical server. RADIUS is a client-server protocol that runs on the application layer of the OSI model.

RADIUS works within the AAA concept: It is used to authenticate users, authorize them to services, and account for the usage of those services. RADIUS checks whether the correct authentication scheme such as CHAP or EAP is used when clients attempt to connect. It commonly uses port 1812 for authentication messages and port 1813 for accounting messages (both of which use UDP as the transport mechanism). In some proprietary cases, it uses ports 1645 and 1646 for these messages, respectively. Memorize these four ports for the exam!

Another concept you will encounter is that of *RADIUS federation*. This is when an organization has multiple RADIUS servers—possibly on different networks—that need to communicate with each other in a safe way. It is accomplished by creating trust relationships and developing a core to manage those relationships as well as the routing of authentication requests. It is often implemented in conjunction with 802.1X. This federated network authentication could also span between multiple organizations.

NOTE Another protocol similar to RADIUS—though not as commonly used—is the Diameter protocol. Once again, it's an AAA protocol. It evolves from RADIUS by supporting TCP or SCTP, but not UDP. It uses port 3868.

Moving on, the Terminal Access Controller Access-Control System (TACACS) is one of the most confusing-sounding acronyms ever. Now that we have reached the pinnacle of computer acronyms, let's really discuss what it is. TACACS is another remote authentication protocol that was used more often in Unix networks. In Unix, the TACACS service is known as the TACACS daemon. The newer and more commonly used implementation of TACACS is called **Terminal Access Controller Access-Control System Plus (TACACS+)**. It is not backward compatible with TACACS. TACACS+, and its predecessor XTACACS, were developed by Cisco.

TACACS+ uses inbound port 49 like its forerunners; however, it uses TCP as the transport mechanism instead of UDP. Let's clarify: the older TACACS and XTACACS technologies are not commonly seen anymore. The two common protocols for remote authentication used today are RADIUS and TACACS+.

There are a few differences between RADIUS and TACACS+. Whereas RADIUS uses UDP as its transport layer protocol, TACACS+ uses TCP as its transport layer protocol, which is usually seen as a more reliable transport protocol (though each will have its own unique set of advantages). Also, RADIUS combines the authentication and authorization functions when dealing with users; however, TACACS+ separates these two functions into two separate operations that introduce another layer of security. It also separates the accounting portion of AAA into its own operation.

RADIUS encrypts only the password in the access-request packet, from the client to the server. The remainder of the packet is unencrypted. Other information such as the username can be easily captured, without need of decryption, by a third party. However, TACACS+ encrypts the entire body of the access-request packet. So, effectively TACACS+ encrypts entire client-server dialogues, whereas RADIUS does not. Finally, TACACS+ provides for more types of authentication requests than RADIUS.

Table 10-1 summarizes the local and remote authentication technologies we have covered thus far.

Table 10-1 Summary of Authentication Technologies

Authentication Type	Description
802.1X	An IEEE standard that defines Port-based Network Access Control (PNAC). 802.1X is a data link layer authentication technology used to connect devices to a LAN or WLAN. Defines EAP.
LDAP	An application layer protocol used for accessing and modifying directory services data. It is part of the TCP/IP suite. Originally used in WAN connections, it has morphed into a protocol commonly used by services such as Microsoft Active Directory.
Kerberos	An authentication protocol designed at MIT that enables computers to prove their identity to each other in a secure manner. It is used most often in a client-server environment; the client and the server both verify each other's identity.
RAS	A service that enables dial-up and various types of VPN connections from remote clients.

Authentication Type	Description
CHAP	An authentication scheme used by the Point-to-Point Protocol (PPP) that is the standard for dial-up connections. It utilizes a challenge-response mechanism with one-way encryption. Derivatives include MS-CHAP and MS-CHAPv2.
RADIUS	Used to provide centralized administration of dial-up, VPN, and wireless authentication. It can be used with EAP and 802.1X. Uses ports 1812 and 1813, or 1645 and 1646, over a UDP transport.
TACACS+	Remote authentication developed by Cisco, similar to RADIUS but separates authentication and authorization into two separate processes. Uses port 49 over a TCP transport.

Chapter Summary

Users must constantly prove themselves to the world of technology. It's amazing how many times a person can be authenticated during a typical day. An authentication method could be as simple as typing an e-mail address and password; for example, when logging into a web-based e-mail system. Or, it could be as complex as a multifactor authentication system; where a user is required to enter a password, then a PIN, then swipe a smart card, and finally scan a thumb!

The complexity of the authentication system will be based on the confidentiality level of an organization's data and resources. If a person can supply the necessary identification and credentials, and the system is configured properly, that person should be authenticated to the system, and finally authorized to access data, or enter a server room, or whatever the case may be. The authentication system can include methods such as: something the user knows, something the user has, something the user does, something the user is, and some*where* the user is. These systems span from the physical (door access systems and biometrics) to the logical (localized and remote authentication software/hardware). In some cases, to make things easier for the end user, an SSO is utilized where the user need only remember one password. Sometimes it's not even the user who is authenticated, but the computer itself; for example, when a network adapter adheres to the 802.1X protocol.

Authentication systems can fail. For example, in biometric systems, the most common failures are *false acceptance*—when a system authenticates a user who should *not* be allowed access to the system, and *false rejection*—when a system denies a user who *should* be allowed access to the system. A system that has too many failures will cause user distress, and should be reconfigured and tested carefully. One of the best metrics to analyze this failure rate is the crossover error rate (CER), which compares the false acceptance rate (FAR) to the false rejection rate (FRR).

Examples of localized authentication systems include 802.1X, LDAP, Kerberos, and RDP. Examples of remote authentication systems include RAS, VPNs, and RADIUS. However, there is a gray area here. Some local systems can be used for remote access, and vice versa. Remember: This is not a cut-and-dried technology in general; for example, RDP could be used locally or over the Internet. It all hinges on what your organization needs for its end users. Nowadays, more and more people work from home or on the road, making remote authentication vital to the organization's efficiency and overall production.

One thing to keep in mind is that attackers (and con artists) are very smart. In fact, the sad truth is that they are sometimes smarter than IT people. A poorly designed authentication system is tantamount to leaving the physical key in the door. However, a well-planned authentication system can save an organization millions of dollars and untold man hours in the long run.

Chapter Review Activities

Use the features in this section to study and review the topics in this chapter.

Review Key Topics

Review the most important topics in the chapter, noted with the Key Topic icon in the outer margin of the page. Table 10-2 lists a reference of these key topics and the page number on which each is found.

Table 10-2 Key Topics for Chapter 10

Key Topic Element	Description	Page Number
Bulleted list	Authentication methods	322
Figure 10-1	Example of an 802.1X-enabled network adapter in Windows	330
Figure 10-2	Components of a typical 802.1X authentication procedure	331
Figure 10-3	Example of Active Directory showing user objects	333
Figure 10-4	Results of the `netstat -an` command on a Windows Server	335
Figure 10-5	MS-CHAP enabled on a dial-up connection	339
Figure 10-6	Illustration of a VPN	340
Table 10-1	Summary of authentication technologies	344

Define Key Terms

Define the following key terms from this chapter, and check your answers in the glossary:

identification, authentication, authorization, identity proofing, closed-circuit television (CCTV), security tokens, mantrap, biometrics, false acceptance, false rejection, crossover error rate (CER), multifactor authentication (MFA), context-aware authentication, single sign-on (SSO), federated identity management, 802.1X, Extensible Authentication Protocol (EAP), Protected Extensible Authentication Protocol (PEAP), Lightweight Directory Access Protocol (LDAP), Kerberos, mutual authentication, tickets, Remote Access Service (RAS), Challenge-Handshake Authentication Protocol (CHAP), virtual private network (VPN), VPN concentrator, always-on VPN, Remote Authentication Dial-In User Service (RADIUS), Terminal Access Controller Access-Control System Plus (TACACS+)

Complete the Real-World Scenarios

Complete the Real-World Scenarios found on the companion website (www.pearsonitcertification.com/title/9780789758996). You will find a PDF containing the scenario and questions, and also supporting videos and simulations.

Review Questions

Answer the following review questions. Check your answers with the correct answers that follow.

1. Which of the following is the verification of a person's identity?
    A. Authorization
    B. Accountability
    C. Authentication
    D. Password

2. Which of the following would fall into the category of "something a person is"?
    A. Passwords
    B. Passphrases
    C. Fingerprints
    D. Smart cards

3. Which of the following are good practices for tracking user identities? (Select the two best answers.)

    A. Video cameras

    B. Key card door access systems

    C. Sign-in sheets

    D. Security guards

4. What are two examples of common single sign-on authentication configurations? (Select the two best answers.)

    A. Biometrics-based

    B. Multifactor authentication

    C. Kerberos-based

    D. Smart card-based

5. Which of the following is an example of two-factor authentication?

    A. L2TP and IPsec

    B. Username and password

    C. Thumbprint and key card

    D. Client and server

6. What is the main purpose of a physical access log?

    A. To enable authorized employee access

    B. To show who exited the facility

    C. To show who entered the facility

    D. To prevent unauthorized employee access

7. Which of the following is not a common criteria when authenticating users?

    A. Something you do

    B. Something you are

    C. Something you know

    D. Something you like

8. Of the following, what two authentication mechanisms require something you physically possess? (Select the two best answers.)

   A. Smart card

   B. Certificate

   C. USB flash drive

   D. Username and password

9. Which of the following is the final step a user needs to take before that user can access domain resources?

   A. Verification

   B. Validation

   C. Authorization

   D. Authentication

10. To gain access to your network, users must provide a thumbprint and a username and password. What type of authentication model is this?

    A. Biometrics

    B. Domain logon

    C. Multifactor

    D. Single sign-on

11. The IT director has asked you to set up an authentication model in which users can enter their credentials one time, yet still access multiple server resources. What type of authentication model should you implement?

    A. Smart card and biometrics

    B. Three-factor authentication

    C. SSO

    D. VPN

12. Which of the following about authentication is false?

    A. RADIUS is a client-server system that provides authentication, authorization, and accounting services.

    B. PAP is insecure because usernames and passwords are sent as clear text.

    C. MS-CHAPv2 is not capable of mutual authentication of the client and server.

    D. CHAP is more secure than PAP because it encrypts usernames and passwords.

13. What types of technologies are used by external motion detectors? (Select the two best answers.)

   A. Infrared

   B. RFID

   C. Gamma rays

   D. Ultrasonic

14. In a secure environment, which authentication mechanism performs better?

   A. RADIUS because it is a remote access authentication service.

   B. RADIUS because it encrypts client-server passwords.

   C. TACACS+ because it is a remote access authentication service.

   D. TACACS+ because it encrypts client-server negotiation dialogues.

15. Which port number does the protocol LDAP use when it is secured?

   A. 389

   B. 443

   C. 636

   D. 3389

16. Which of the following results occurs when a biometric system identifies a legitimate user as unauthorized?

   A. False rejection

   B. FAR

   C. False acceptance

   D. CER

   E. False exception

17. Of the following, which is not a logical method of access control?

   A. Username/password

   B. Access control lists

   C. Biometrics

   D. Software-based policy

18. Which of the following permits or denies access to resources through the use of ports?

    A. Hub

    B. 802.11n

    C. 802.11x

    D. 802.1X

19. Your data center has highly critical information. Because of this you want to improve upon physical security. The data center already has a video surveillance system. What else can you add to increase physical security? (Select the two best answers.)

    A. A software-based token system

    B. Access control lists

    C. A mantrap

    D. Biometrics

20. Which authentication method completes the following in order: logon request, encrypts value response, server, challenge, compare encrypted results, and authorize or fail referred to?

    A. Security tokens

    B. Certificates

    C. Kerberos

    D. CHAP

21. What does a virtual private network use to connect one remote host to another? (Select the best answer.)

    A. Modem

    B. Network adapter

    C. Internet

    D. Cell phone

22. Two items are needed before a user can be given access to the network. What are these two items?

    A. Authentication and authorization

    B. Authorization and identification

    C. Identification and authentication

    D. Password and authentication

23. Kerberos uses which of the following? (Select the two best answers.)

    A. Ticket distribution service

    B. The Faraday cage

    C. Port 389

    D. Authentication service

24. Which of the following authentication systems makes use of a Key Distribution Center?

    A. Security tokens

    B. CHAP

    C. Kerberos

    D. Certificates

25. Of the following, which best describes the difference between RADIUS and TACACS+?

    A. RADIUS is a remote access authentication service.

    B. RADIUS separates authentication, authorization, and auditing capabilities.

    C. TACACS+ is a remote access authentication service.

    D. TACACS+ separates authentication, authorization, and auditing capabilities.

26. Which of the following best describes the proper method and reason to implement port security?

    A. Apply a security control that ties specific ports to end-device MAC addresses, and prevents additional devices from being connected to the network.

    B. Apply a security control that ties specific ports to end-device IP addresses, and prevents additional devices from being connected to the network.

    C. Apply a security control that ties specific ports to end-device MAC addresses, and prevents all devices from being connected to the network.

    D. Apply a security control that ties specific ports to end-device IP addresses, and prevents all devices from being connected to the network.

27. You are tasked with setting up a wireless network that uses 802.1X for authentication. You set up the wireless network using WPA2 and CCMP; however, you don't want to use a PSK for authentication. Which of the following options would support 802.1X authentication?

    A. Kerberos

    B. CAC card

    C. Pre-shared key

    D. RADIUS

28. Which two options can prevent unauthorized employees from entering a server room? (Select the two best answers.)

    A. Bollards

    B. CCTV

    C. Security guard

    D. 802.1X

    E. Proximity reader

29. What is the most secure method of authentication and authorization in its default form?

    A. TACACS

    B. Kerberos

    C. RADIUS

    D. LDAP

30. When attempting to grant access to remote users, which protocol uses separate, multiple-challenge responses for each of the authentication, authorization, and audit processes?

    A. RADIUS

    B. TACACS

    C. TACACS+

    D. LDAP

31. Before gaining access to the data center, you must swipe your finger on a device. What type of authentication is this?

    A. Biometrics

    B. Single sign-on

    C. Multifactor

    D. Tokens

32. Which of the following is an authentication system that uses UDP as the transport mechanism?

    A. LDAP

    B. Kerberos

    C. RADIUS

    D. TACACS+

33. Your organization provides employee badges that are encoded with a private encryption key and specific personal information. The encoding is used to provide access to the organization's network. What type of authentication method is being used?

    A. Token

    B. Biometrics

    C. Kerberos

    D. Smart card

34. You are in charge of training a group of technicians on the authentication method their organization uses. The organization currently runs an Active Directory infrastructure. Which of the following best correlates to the host authentication protocol used within that organization's IT environment?

    A. TACACS+

    B. Kerberos

    C. LDAP

    D. 802.1X

35. Which of the following is an authentication and accounting service that uses TCP as its transport mechanism when connecting to routers and switches?

    A. Kerberos

    B. RADIUS

    C. Captive portal

    D. TACACS+

Answers and Explanations

1. **C.** Authentication is the verification of a person's identity. Authorization to specific resources cannot be accomplished without previous authentication of the user.

2. **C.** Fingerprints are an example of something a person is. The process of measuring that characteristic is known as biometrics.

3. **A and B.** Video cameras enable a person to view and visually identify users as they enter and traverse a building. Key card access systems can be configured to identify a person as well, as long as the right person is carrying the key card!

4. **C and D.** Kerberos and smart card setups are common single sign-on configurations.

5. **C.** Two-factor authentication (or dual-factor) means that two pieces of identity are needed prior to authentication. A thumbprint and key card would fall into this category. L2TP and IPsec are protocols used to connect through a VPN, which by default require only a username and password. Username and password is considered one-factor authentication. There is no client and server authentication model.

6. **C.** A physical access log's main purpose is to show who entered the facility and when. Different access control and authentication models will be used to permit or prevent employee access.

7. **D.** Common criteria when authenticating users include something you do, something you are, something you know, something you have, and some*where* you are. A person's likes and dislikes are not common criteria; although, they may be asked as secondary questions when logging in to a system.

8. **A and C.** Two of the authentication mechanisms that require something you physically possess include smart cards and USB flash drives. Key fobs and cardkeys would also be part of this category. Certificates are granted from a server and are stored on a computer as software. The username/password mechanism is a common authentication scheme, but it is something that you type and not something that you physically possess.

9. **C.** Before a user can gain access to domain resources, the final step is to be authorized to those resources. Previously the user should have provided identification to be authenticated.

10. **C.** Multifactor authentication means that the user must provide two different types of identification. The thumbprint is an example of biometrics. Username and password are examples of a domain logon. Single sign-on would only be one type of authentication that enables the user access to multiple resources.

11. **C.** SSO (single sign-on) enables users to access multiple servers and multiple resources while entering their credentials only once. The type of authentication can vary but will generally be a username and password. Smart cards and biometrics is an example of two-factor authentication. VPN is short for virtual private network.

12. **C.** MS-CHAPv2 *is* capable of mutual authentication of the client and server. However, MS-CHAPv1 is not. That's why it is important to use MS-CHAPv2. Mutual authentication *is* accomplished with Kerberos. All the other statements are true.

13. **A and D.** Motion detectors often use infrared technology; heat would set them off. They also use ultrasonic technology; sounds in higher spectrums that humans cannot hear would set these detectors off.

14. **D.** Unlike RADIUS, TACACS+ (Terminal Access Controller Access-Control System Plus) encrypts client-server negotiation dialogues. Both protocols are remote authentication protocols.

15. **C.** Port 636 is the port used to secure LDAP (called LDAPS). Port 389 is the standard LDAP port number. Port 443 is used by HTTPS (SSL/TLS), and port 3389 is used by RDP.

16. **A.** If a biometric system identifies a legitimate user as unauthorized, and denies that user access, it is known as a false rejection. False acceptance on the other hand is when a biometric system authorizes an illegitimate user. FAR is the false acceptance rate—the lower the better. CER stands for crossover error rate, which is the comparison of the FAR and the FRR. False exceptions have to do with software that has failed and needs to be debugged.

17. **C.** The only answer that is not a logical method of access control is biometrics. Biometrics deals with the physical attributes of a person and is the most tangible of the answers. All the rest deal with software, so they are logical methods.

18. **D.** 802.1X permits or denies access to resources through the use of ports. It implements Port-based Network Access Control (PNAC). This is part of the 802.1 group of IEEE protocols. 802.1X should not be confused with 802.11x, which is an informal term used to denote any of the 802.11 standards including 802.11b, 802.11g, 802.11n, and 802.11ac. A hub connects computers by way of physical ports but does not permit or deny access to any particular resources; it is a simple physical connector of computers.

19. **C and D.** A mantrap is a device made to capture a person. It is usually an area with two doorways, the first of which leads to the outside and locks when the person enters, the second of which leads to the secure area and is locked until the person is granted access. Biometrics can help in the granting of this access

by authenticating the user in a secure way, such as thumbprint, retina scan, and so on. Software-based token systems and access control lists are both logical and do not play into physical security.

20. **D.** CHAP, the Challenge Handshake Authentication Protocol, authenticates a user or a network host to entities like Internet access providers. CHAP periodically verifies the identity of the client by using a three-way handshake; the verification is based on a shared secret. After a link has been established, the authenticator sends a challenge message to the peer; this does not happen in the other three authentication methods listed.

21. **C.** The Internet is used to connect hosts to each other in virtual private networks. A particular computer will probably also use a VPN adapter and/or a network adapter. Modems generally are used in dial-up connections and are not used in VPNs.

22. **C.** Before users can be given access to the network, the network needs to identify them and authenticate them. Later, users may be authorized to use particular resources on the network. Part of the authentication scheme may include a username and password. This would be known as an access control method.

23. **A and D.** Kerberos uses a ticket distribution service and an authentication service. This is provided by the Key Distribution Center. A Faraday cage is used to block data emanations. Port 389 is used by LDAP. One of the more common ports that Kerberos uses is port 88.

24. **C.** Kerberos uses a KDC (key distribution center) to centralize the distribution of certificate keys and keep a list of revoked keys.

25. **D.** Unlike RADIUS, TACACS+ separates authentication, authorization, and auditing capabilities. The other three answers are incorrect and are not differences between RADIUS and TACACS+.

26. **A.** You can achieve port security by applying a security control (such as 802.1X), which ties specific physical ports to end-device MAC addresses and prevents additional devices from being connected to the network. Note that port security solutions such as 802.1X are data link layer technologies (layer 2) so they deal with MAC addresses, not IP addresses. You wouldn't want to exclude all devices from being connected to the network as this would cause a severe problem with connectivity.

27. **D.** RADIUS is a common back-end authenticator for 802.1X. When setting up a wireless access point, the two security mode options are usually PSK (pre-shared key), which is stored on the WAP, and Enterprise, which usually refers authentication to an external RADIUS server. Kerberos deals with

authentication to Microsoft domains. CAC cards are smart cards that are used for ID and authentication to systems.

28. **C and E.** If a person doesn't have the proper proximity card, that person will be prevented from entering a server room or other protected room. Security guards can also prevent people from accessing unauthorized areas. However, bollards (short vertical posts) probably wouldn't stop a person, besides they aren't normally installed in front of a server room entrance. A barricade might stop a person, but again, would be out of place! CCTV video surveillance is a detective control, but not a preventive control. 802.1X deals with authentication, not with physical security.

29. **B.** Kerberos is the most secure method of authentication listed. It has a more complicated system of authentication than TACACS (which is outdated) and RADIUS (which is used in different scenarios than Kerberos). LDAP deals with directories (for example, the ones on a Microsoft domain controller), which Kerberos first needs to give access to.

30. **C.** TACACS+ is the only answer listed that uses separate processes for authentication, authorization, and auditing. That is one of the main differences between it and RADIUS. TACACS is deprecated and is not often seen in the field. LDAP deals with managing directories of information.

31. **A.** Fingerprint technology is part of the realm of biometrics. Single sign-on means that you can use one type of authentication to get access to more than one system. While that could be going on in this scenario, it is not explicit, so biometrics is the more accurate answer. Multifactor means that more than one type of authentication is needed; for example, a fingerprint and a PIN. Let's say that users were expected to type a PIN into a keypad to gain access to the data center. You might find over time that some persons who enter don't match the owner of the PIN. That uncertainty can be avoided by incorporating biometrics. Tokens are used to gain access to systems and networks, and might include rolling one-time passwords, but do not incorporate a person's physical characteristics such as a fingerprint.

32. **C.** RADIUS is the authentication system that uses UDP as the transport mechanism. The others all use TCP. Remember, RADIUS uses ports 1812 and 1813 (or 1645 and 1646), LDAP uses 389 (or 636 for secure LDAP), Kerberos uses port 88, and TACACS+ uses port 49.

33. **D.** A badge encoded with a private encryption key would be an example of a smart card. Tokens are software-based and could be used with a USB flash drive or could be stored on a mobile device. An example of biometrics is a thumbprint scan or retina scan. Kerberos is an authentication technology used by operating systems such as Windows (often in domain scenarios).

34. B. If the organization runs Active Directory, that means it has a Windows Server that is acting as a domain controller. These use the Kerberos authentication system by default. TACACS+ is an example of a remote authentication system, but is owned by Cisco, and is not a part of Active Directory. LDAP is the protocol in Windows that controls Active Directory objects, and works in conjunction with Kerberos, but is not the actual authentication method used. 802.1X is an authentication method used by network adapters on the data link layer.

35. D. TACACS+ is an authentication, accounting, and authorization service. It uses TCP as its transport mechanism. Kerberos authenticates only, and can use TCP and UDP. RADIUS performs authentication and accounting but uses UDP as the transport mechanism. A captive portal redirects people in an effort to authenticate them. It will often do this within a web browser, and might use TCP (HTTPS), but does not perform accounting services.

This chapter covers the following subjects:

- **Access Control Models Defined:** This section gets into access control models, such as MAC, DAC, RBAC, and ABAC, plus methodologies such as implicit deny and job rotation. Before creating and enforcing policies, a plan of action has to be developed, and the access control model to be used should be at the core of that plan.

- **Rights, Permissions, and Policies:** Here, we delve into users, groups, permissions, rights, and policies that can be created on a computer network. By configuring users, templates, and groups in a smart fashion, you can ease administration and increase security at the same time. Policies can control just about anything a user does on the network or on an individual computer. And security templates make it easier than ever to implement a secure set of policies.

Controlling user access is of paramount importance. You don't want just any Tom, Dick, or Harry to gain admittance to your computer network! The first step in controlling user access is to define who needs to have access and what they need to have access to. After this is done, an access control plan must be developed. This primarily consists of choosing an access control model. Which model you should choose depends on your organization's procedures and written policies, the level of security you need, and the amount of IT resources at your disposal. After a model has been selected, you should implement as many safe practices as possible to bolster the model's effectiveness. Then, you can actually implement security on the computers and network. This includes creating and organizing secure users, groups, and other network objects such as organizational units. More important, it incorporates the use of policies and Group Policy objects. By configuring computer-based policies for your users, groups, and computers, you are forcing them to abide by your organization's rules.

CHAPTER 11

Access Control Methods and Models

Access Control Models Defined

Access control models are methodologies in which admission to physical areas and, more important, computer systems is managed and organized. Access control, also known as an access policy, is extremely important when it comes to users accessing secure or confidential data. Some organizations also practice concepts such as separation of duties, job rotation, and least privilege. By combining these best practices along with an access control model, a robust plan can be developed concerning how users access confidential data and secure areas of a building.

There are several models for access control, each with its own special characteristics that you should know for the exam. Let's discuss these now.

Discretionary Access Control

Discretionary access control (DAC) is an access control policy generally determined by the owner. Objects such as files and printers can be created and accessed by the owner. Also, the owner decides which users are allowed to have access to the objects, and what level of access they may have. The levels of access, or permissions, are stored in access control lists (ACLs).

Originally, DAC was described in The Orange Book as the Discretionary Security Policy and was meant to enforce a consistent set of rules governing limited access to identified individuals. The Orange Book's proper name is the **Trusted Computer System Evaluation Criteria**, or TCSEC, and was developed by the U.S. Department of Defense (DoD); however, The Orange Book is old (they refer to it in the movie *Hackers* in the 1990s!), and the standard was superseded in 2005 by an international standard called the Common Criteria for Information Technology Security Evaluation (or simply Common Criteria). But the DAC methodology lives on in many of today's personal computers and client/server networks.

> **NOTE**   An entire set of security standards was published by the DoD in the 1980s and 1990s known as the "Rainbow Series." Although The Orange Book is the centerpiece of the series (maybe not in the color spectrum, but as far as security content), there are other ones you might come into contact with, such as The Red Book, which is the Trusted Network Interpretation standard. Some of the standards have been superseded, but they contain the basis for many of today's security procedures.

An example of DAC would be a typical Windows computer with two users. User A can log on to the computer, create a folder, stock it with data, and then finally configure permissions so that only she can access the folder. User B can log on to the computer, but cannot access User A's folder by default, unless User A says so, and configures it as so! However, User B can create his own folder and lock down permissions in the same way. Let's say that there was a third user, User C, who wanted both User A and User B to have limited access to a folder that he created. That is also possible by setting specific permission levels, as shown in Figure 11-1. The first Properties window shows that User C (the owner) has Full Control permissions. This is normal because User C created the folder. But in the second Properties window, you see that User A has limited permissions, which were set by User C.

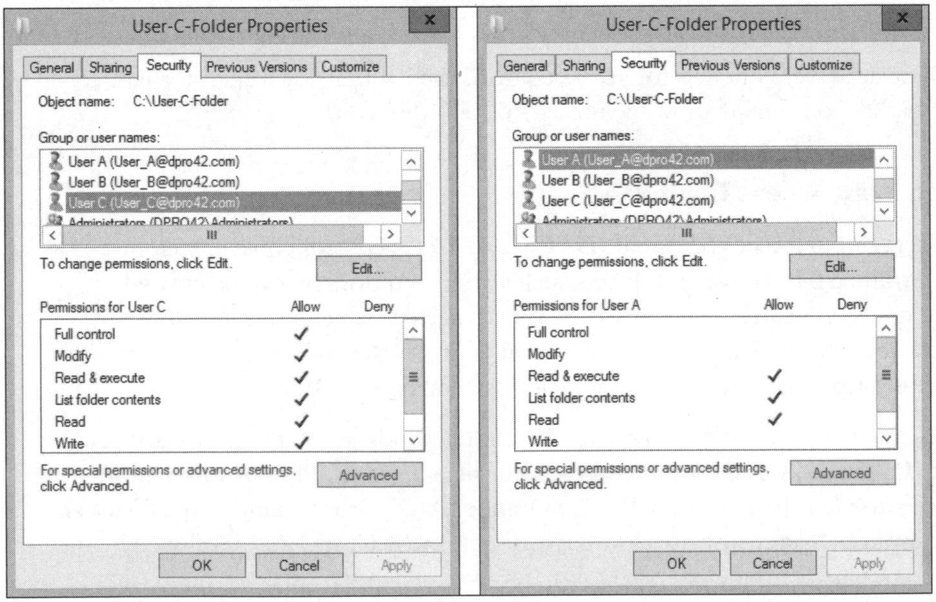

Figure 11-1   Example of Discretionary Access in Windows

NOTE   Take notice of standard naming conventions used in your organization. In Figure 11-1 the naming convention is *user@domainname*. For example, User_A@dpro42.com.

NOTE   The owner of a resource controls the permissions to that resource! This is the core of the DAC model.

Windows networks/domains work in the same fashion. Access to objects is based on which user created them and what permissions they assign to those objects. However, in Windows networks we can group users together and assign permissions by way of roles as well. More on that in the role-based access control (RBAC) section.

In a way, DAC, when implemented in client-server networks, is sort of a decentralized administration model. Even though an administrator still has control over most, or all, resources (depending on company policy), the owners retain a certain amount of power over their own resources. But, many companies take away the ability for users to configure permissions. They may create folders and save data to them, but the permissions list is often generated on a parent folder by someone else and is inherited by the subfolder.

There are two important points to remember when talking about the DAC model: First, every object in the system has an owner, and the owner has control over its access policy; and second, access rights, or permissions, can be assigned by the owner to users to specifically control object access.

Mandatory Access Control

Mandatory access control (MAC) is an access control policy determined by a computer system, not by a user or owner, as it is in DAC. Permissions are predefined in the MAC model. Historically, it has been used in highly classified government and military multilevel systems, but you will find lesser implementations of it in today's more common operating systems as well. The MAC model defines sensitivity labels that are assigned to *subjects* (users) and *objects* (files, folders, hardware devices, network connections, and so on). A subject's label dictates its security level, or level of trust. An object's label dictates what level of clearance is needed to access it, also known as a trust level (this is also known as *data labeling*). The access controls in a MAC system are based on the security classification of the data and "need-to-know" information—where a user can access only what the system considers absolutely necessary. Also, in the MAC model, data import and export are controlled. MAC is the strictest of the access control models.

An example of MAC can be seen in FreeBSD version 5.0 and higher. In this OS, access control modules can be installed that allow for security policies that label subjects and objects. The enforcement of the policies is done by administrators or by the OS; this is what makes it mandatory and sets it apart from DAC. Another example is Security-Enhanced Linux (SELinux), a set of kernel modifications to Linux that supports DoD-style mandatory access controls such as the requirement for trusted computing base (TCB). Though often interpreted differently, TCB can be described as the set of all hardware and software components critical to a system's security and all associated protection mechanisms. The mechanisms must meet a certain standard, and SELinux helps accomplish this by modifying the kernel of the Linux OS in a secure manner. Like DAC, MAC was also originally defined in The Orange Book, but as the Mandatory Security Policy—a policy that enforces access control based on a user's clearance and by the confidentiality levels of the data. Even though The Orange Book is deprecated, the concept of MAC lives on in today's systems and is implemented in two ways:

- **Rule-based access control:** Also known as label-based access control, this defines whether access should be granted or denied to objects by comparing the object label and the subject label.

- **Lattice-based access control:** Used for more complex determinations of object access by subjects. Somewhat advanced mathematics are used to create sets of objects and subjects and define how the two interact.

NOTE   Rule-based access control uses labels, is part of mandatory access control, and should not be confused with *role-based* access control.

NOTE   Other related access control models include Bell-LaPadula, Biba, and Clark-Wilson. Bell-LaPadula is a state machine model used for enforcing access control in government applications. It is a less common multilevel security derivative of mandatory access control. This model focuses on data confidentiality and controlled access to classified information. The Biba Integrity Model describes rules for the protection of data integrity. Clark-Wilson is another integrity model that provides a foundation for specifying and analyzing an integrity policy for a computing system.

Role-Based Access Control (RBAC)

Role-based access control (RBAC) is an access model that, like MAC, is controlled by the system, and, unlike DAC, not by the owner of a resource. However, RBAC is different from MAC in the way that permissions are configured. RBAC works with sets of permissions, instead of individual permissions that are label-based. A set of permissions constitutes a role. When users are assigned to roles, they can then gain access to resources. A role might be the ability to complete a specific operation in an organization as opposed to accessing a single data file. For example, a person in a bank who wants to check a prospective client's credit score would be attempting to perform a transaction that is allowed only if that person holds the proper role. So roles are created for various job functions in an organization. Roles might have overlapping privileges and responsibilities. Also, some general operations can be completed by all the employees of an organization. Because there is overlap, an administrator can develop role hierarchies; these define roles that can contain other roles, or have exclusive attributes.

Think about it. Did you ever notice that an administrator or root user is extremely powerful? Perhaps too powerful? And standard users are often not powerful enough to respond to their own needs or fix their own problems? Some operating systems counter this problem by creating mid-level accounts such as Power Users (Microsoft) or Operators (Solaris), but for large organizations, this is not flexible enough. Currently, more levels of roles and special groups of users are implemented in newer operating systems. RBAC is used in database access as well and is becoming more common in the healthcare industry and government.

Attribute-based Access Control (ABAC)

Attribute-based access control (ABAC) is an access model that is dynamic and context-aware. Access rights are granted to users through the use of multiple policies that can combine various user, group, and resource attributes together. It makes use of IF-THEN statements based on the user and requested resource. For example, *if* David is a systems administrator, *then* allow full control access to the \\dataserver\ adminfolder share. If implemented properly, it can be a more flexible solution. As of the writing of this book, many technologies—and organizations—are moving toward a more context-sensitive, context-aware mindset when it comes to authentication and access control.

Table 11-1 summarizes the four access control models just discussed: DAC, MAC, RBAC, and ABAC.

Key Topic

Table 11-1 Summary of Access Control Models

Access Control Model	Key Points
DAC	Every object in the system has an owner.
	Permissions are determined by the owner.

Access Control Model	Key Points
MAC	Permissions are determined by the system.
	Can be rule-based or lattice-based.
	Labels are used to identify security levels of subjects and objects.
RBAC	Based on roles, or sets of permissions involved in an operation.
	Controlled by the system.
ABAC	Context-aware, and dynamic authentication.
	Uses IF-THEN statements to allow access.

NOTE Another type of access control method is known as anonymous access control—for example, access to an FTP server. This method uses attributes before access is granted to an object. Authentication is usually not required.

NOTE In general, access control can be centralized or decentralized. *Centralized* access control means that one entity is responsible for administering access to resources. *Decentralized* access control means that more than one entity is responsible, and those entities are closer to the actual resources than the entity would be in a centralized access control scenario.

Access Control Wise Practices

After you decide on an access control model that fits your needs, you should consider employing some other concepts. Some of these are used in operating systems automatically to some extent:

- **Implicit deny:** This concept denies all traffic to a resource unless the users generating that traffic are specifically granted access to the resource. Even if permissions haven't been configured for the user in question, that person will still be denied access. This is a default setting for access control lists on a Cisco router. It is also used by default on Microsoft computers to a certain extent. Figure 11-2 shows an example of this. In the folder's permissions, you can see that the Users group has the Read & Execute, List Folder Contents, and Read permissions set to Allow. But other permissions such as Modify are not configured at all—not set to Allow or Deny. Therefore, the users in the Users group cannot modify data inside the folder because that permission is implicitly denied. Likewise, they can't take full control of the folder.

> **NOTE** Implicit deny will deny users access to a resource unless they are specifically allowed access.

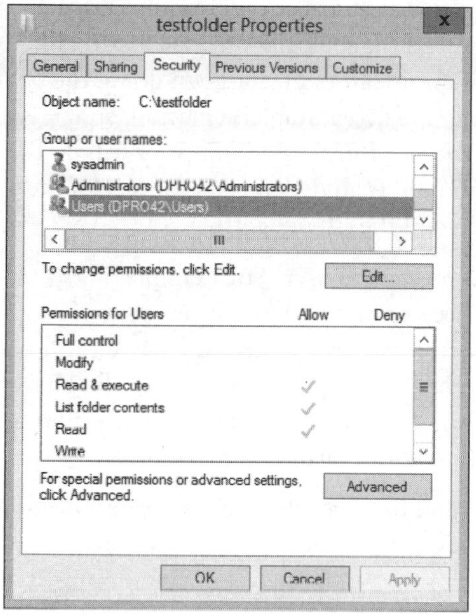

Figure 11-2 Example of Implicit Deny on a Windows Folder

- **Least privilege:** This is when users are given only the amount of privileges needed to do their job and not one iota more. A basic example of this would be the Guest account in a Windows computer. This account (when enabled) can surf the Web and use other basic applications but cannot make any modifications to the computer system. However, least privilege as a principle goes much further. One of the ideas behind the principle is to run the user session with only the processes necessary, thus reducing the amount of CPU power needed. This hopefully leads to better system stability and system security. Have you ever noticed that many crashed systems are due to users trying to do more than they really should be allowed? Or more than the computer can handle? The concept of *least* privilege tends to be absolute, whereas an absolute solution isn't quite possible in the real world. It is difficult to gauge exactly what the "least" amount of privileges and processes would be. Instead, a security administrator should practice the implementation of minimal privilege, reducing what a user has access to as much as possible. Programmers also practice this when developing applications and operating systems, making sure that the app has only the least privilege necessary to accomplish what it needs to do. This concept is also known as "the principle of least privilege."

■ **Separation of duties:** This is when more than one person is required to complete a particular task or operation. If one person has too much control and completes too many portions of a task, it can become a security risk. The more people involved, the less the chance that a job can be compromised. Checks and balances are employed to make sure that the proper equilibrium of users is maintained. One example of this would be the securing of a new network. There might be one or more security administrators in charge of doing the actual planning, and a couple more doing the actual implementation, and finally another group for testing; or perhaps, a third-party company will do the testing, keeping everything on the up and up. It all depends on the size of the organization and the internal trust level (and the IT budget!).

Separation of duties can also be applied to a single user. For example, if a user on a typical Windows computer (Vista or newer) has a specific set of privileges, but the user wants to do something on the system that requires administrative access, User Account Control (UAC) kicks in and asks for the proper credentials to perform the actions of that role. If the credentials cannot be supplied, UAC blocks the action, keeping the various duties separate.

■ **Job rotation:** This is one of the checks and balances that might be employed to enforce the proper separation of duties. Job rotation is when users are cycled through various assignments to

■ Increase user insight as to overall operations

■ Reduce employee boredom

■ Enhance employee skill level

■ Increase operation security

Job rotation creates a pool of people that can do an individual job and discourages hoarding of information. It also helps to protect the purity of an operation. By cross-training people in each department, you defend against fraud and increase awareness, making it easier to detect if it does happen.

By incorporating the implicit deny, least privilege, separation of duties, and job rotation concepts, your total access control plan can be improved greatly. These access control principles can be applied both to desktop computers and to mobile devices. However, the specific way they are applied will depend on the particular operating systems and the policies—both written and computerized—of the organization you work for.

Rights, Permissions, and Policies

Now that we have a plan for access control, we need to implement it in a tangible way. By strategically setting up organizational units, users, and groups, and by assigning permissions according to our chosen access control model, we can create a safe, guarded working area for all employees. In so doing, we can protect the data on the network.

Users, Groups, and Permissions

User accounts can be added to individual computers or to networks. For example, a Windows client, Linux computer, or Mac can have multiple users. And larger networks that have a controlling server, for example, a Windows domain controller, enable user accounts that can access one or more computers on the domain. In a Microsoft domain, users are added in Active Directory Users and Computers (ADUC), as shown in Figure 11-3.

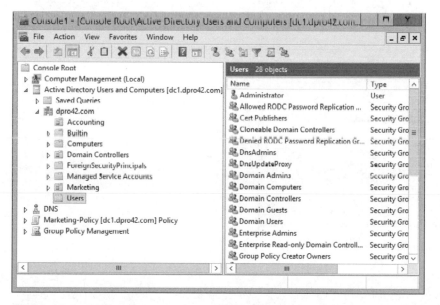

Figure 11-3 The Users Folder Within ADUC on a Windows Server

ADUC can be accessed from Administrative Tools or added as a snap-in to an MMC. Users can be added in one of two places:

- **In the Users folder:** This is located inside the domain name within ADUC.

- **In an OU:** Organizational units can be created within the domain. These are often made to mimic the departments of a company. In Figure 11-3, there are Accounting and Marketing OUs; users can be created within these OUs.

User rights can be modified within the particular user's Properties window. There are many more rights associated with a user account that is stored on a Windows Server domain controller than there are on an individual Windows client computer. For example, the Account tab can be configured so that the user account has an expiration date. You can see this in Figure 11-4, where at the bottom of the Properties window, we had configured Alice's account to expire on April 1, 2020—and that was no April Fools' prank! Immediately after that expiration date, the user couldn't log on to the domain unless her account was reconfigured or she logged on as someone else.

Key Topic

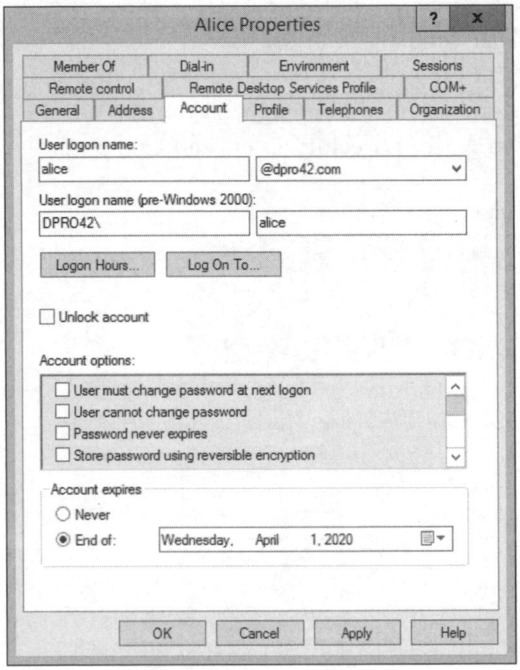

Figure 11-4 User Account Expiration Date

> **NOTE** Users cannot log on to a network after their account has expired. The Account Expiration date in Windows controls this.

By clicking the Logon Hours button, time-of-day restrictions can be configured so that a user can log on only at certain times throughout the week. An example of this is shown in Figure 11-5. In the figure, Alice's user account has been configured in such a way that she can log on to the domain only between 8 a.m. and 6 p.m. Monday through Friday. If she attempts to log on at any other time, the system will deny access. These kinds of access rights are available on domain controllers.

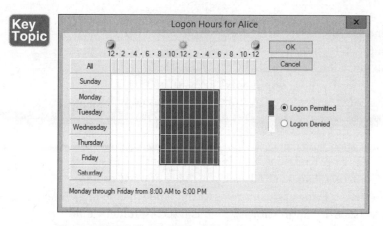

Figure 11-5 Time-of-Day Restrictions for a Standard User

NOTE Users can log on to the network only during their configured logon hours.

Sometimes users have more than one account. This might have been done to allow access to multiple systems or resources. There are plenty of different issues that can occur because of this. To mitigate problems that can develop from a user having two accounts, consider the consolidation of accounts, for example, utilizing a federated identity management (FIM) system, one that will incorporate single sign-on (SSO). User administration can also benefit from credential management, where passwords, certificates, and other logon credentials are stored in a special folder called a vault. A security administrator should also consider the use of roles (RBAC) and user groups.

Groups can be created to classify users and to ease administration when assigning permissions. If you refer to Figure 11-3, you see that a group is displayed with a two-headed icon (for example, the Domain Admins group). Single users are displayed with a single head, as is the case with the Administrator. By grouping users together, you can save a lot of time when assigning permissions to files and other resources; instead of assigning permissions to one user at a time, it can be done to the entire group in one shot.

Permissions such as file and printer access can be assigned to individual users or to groups. These permissions (also known as access modes) are examples of **access control lists (ACLs)**—specifically, file system access control lists (abbreviated as FACL or FSACL). An ACL is a list of permissions attached to an object. ACLs reside on firewalls, routers, and computers. Permissions in an ACL might allow access or deny access. It all depends on who is required to have access; then, the configuration is up to you.

> **NOTE** In a Windows environment, ACLs are broken down into individual access control entries (ACEs); for example, the user JohnT has read access to the marketing folder. Also, Microsoft uses the term *discretionary access control list (DACL)* to refer to an ACL that identifies trustees who are allowed or denied access to an object. It uses the term *system access control list (SACL)* to refer to an ACL that enables admins to log attempts to access a secured object.

In Windows, there are two types of permissions. Sharing permissions are basic permissions including Full Control, Change, and Read, which are applied to folders only. These are often ignored in favor of the more powerful (and superseding) NTFS permissions, also called security permissions, which can secure folders and individual files. In a standard Windows folder on a domain, the types of NTFS permissions include the following:

- Full Control
- Modify
- Read & Execute
- List Folder Contents
- Read
- Write

These are shown in Figure 11-6 on a Windows Server in the Properties window of a folder named "testfolder." Note that the Administrators group has full control of the folder. Also note that you can allow particular permissions, or specifically deny those permissions. If a permission is not set to Allow, it will be implicitly denied.

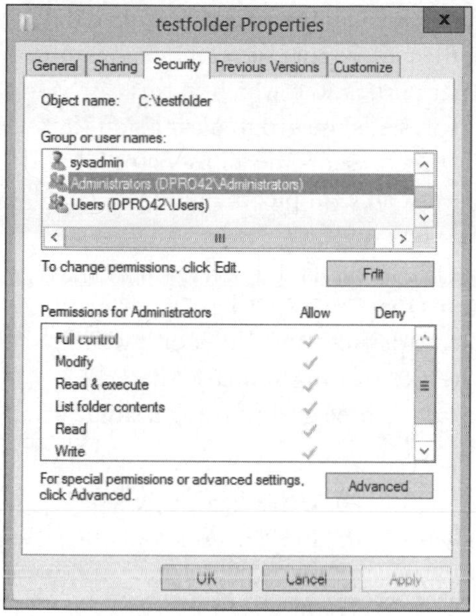

Figure 11-6 NTFS Permissions

In Linux, file permissions are broken down into three types: read, write, and execute (R, W, and X). They can be assigned to three different permission groups: owner, group, and all users (U, G, and O or A). These can be assigned and configured in the command-line with the chmod command (change mode), either by group letter or by using a designated numbering system. For example, in the latter case:

- R (Read) = 4

- W (Write) = 2

- X (Execute) = 1

These are added together to form each permission. For example, if a user was given read and write access, the number would be 6. If, however, the person was given read, write, and execute access, the number would be 7. Here's an example of the chmod command:

```
chmod 760 testfile
```

In the example we have the `chmod` command followed by the numbers 7, 6, and 0, and the name of the file, "testfile" (of course, the path to that file can be more complex). The first number, 7, represents the owner permission (which in this case is equal to full access). The second number, 6, represents the group permission (in this case read and write access). The final number, 0, represents the all users (or all *other* users) permission, which has no access. This is just an example; the numbers could be whatever you select for the three groups. You might see 777 when all groups have all permissions, though it is not normally recommended. It is common on a web server or file server to see 755, which means that the owner has all permissions, and the group and all users have read and execute permissions. You don't want a typical user to have write permissions on a web server! In summary, the `chmod` command is a great way to assign permissions to all three groups using a single command.

To avoid access violations when working with permissions, the "least privilege" or "minimal privilege" concept should be implemented. Give the users only the amount of access that they absolutely need. Note that permissions for long-term employees could suffer from *privilege creep* over time. To mitigate this, consider periodic user permission reviews and evaluation of ACLs. This permission auditing procedure will ensure that users have the access to the correct data. In general, this is known as *user access recertification*. Consider this procedure if a company has a particularly high attrition rate (hiring and terminating of employees). This will verify that users no longer with the company cannot log on to the network and cannot gain access to resources. It also ensures that new users can gain access to necessary resources.

Permission Inheritance and Propagation

If you create a folder, the default action it takes is to inherit permissions from the parent folder, which ultimately come from the root folder. So any permissions set in the parent are inherited by the subfolder. To view an example of this, locate any folder within an NTFS volume (besides the root folder), right-click it, and select Properties, access the Security tab, and click the Advanced button. That brings up a window as shown in Figure 11-7. If you look at the bottom of the figure, you can tell whether or not the folder is inheriting permissions from the parent. In this case, it is inheriting permissions.

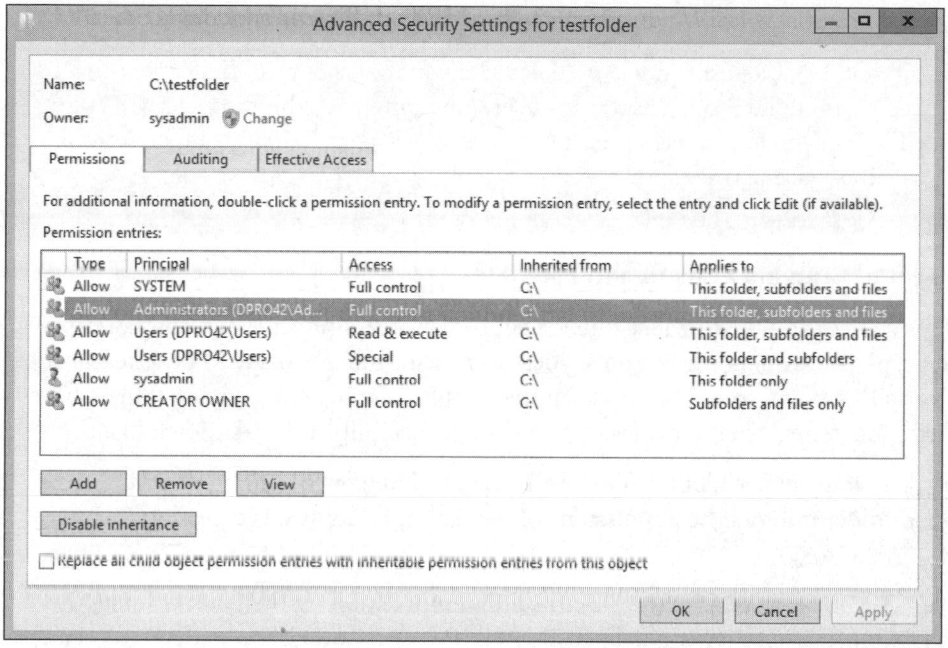

Figure 11-7 Inheritable Permissions

This means that any permissions added or removed in the parent folder will also be added or removed in the current folder. In addition, those permissions inherited cannot be modified in the current folder. To make modifications, you would have to disable inheritance, either by clicking the button shown in Figure 11-7 or by deselecting a checkbox on older versions of Windows Server. When you do so, you have the option to copy the permissions from the parent to the current folder or remove them entirely. To summarize, by default the parent is automatically propagating permissions to the subfolder, and the subfolder is inheriting its permissions from the parent.

You can also propagate permission changes to subfolders not inheriting from the current folder. To do so, select the Replace All Child Object Permission Entries... checkbox.

This might all seem a bit confusing, and you will probably not be asked many questions on the subject. Just remember that folders automatically inherit from the parent unless you turn off inheriting—and you can propagate permission entries to subfolders at any time by selecting the Replace option.

NOTE In a Windows environment there are two types of permissions: share permissions and NTFS permissions. By default, the more restrictive of the two sets of permissions is applied to the user. However, quite often an administrator will configure NTFS permissions to take precedence over share permissions—and effectively "ignore" the share permissions.

Moving and Copying Folders and Files

This subject and the previous one are actually more advanced Microsoft concepts, the type you would be asked on a Microsoft exam, and less likely to be asked on a CompTIA exam, so we'll try to keep this simple. Moving and copying folders have different results when it comes to permissions. Basically, it breaks down like this:

- If you *copy* a folder (or file) on the same volume or to a different volume, the folder inherits the permissions of the parent folder it was copied to (target directory).

- If you *move* a folder (or file) to a different location on the same volume, the folder retains its original permissions. (You cannot move a folder to a separate volume; if you attempt to do so it will automatically be copied to the other volume.)

NOTE Keep in mind that when you move data within a volume, the data isn't actually relocated; instead the pointer to the file or folder is modified. Accordingly, permissions are not really moved either, so they remain the same.

Usernames and Passwords

The most common type of authentication is the username/password combination. Usernames are usually based on a person's real name. Large organizations often use firstname.lastname as the standard naming convention (for example, david.prowse@company.com) or first initial and last name (dprowse@company.com). Smaller organizations might use the first name and last initial. The naming convention decided upon should be easy for you to implement without name confusion, and it should have the capability to be utilized for all systems on the network, including login, e-mail, database, file access, and so on.

The password is either set by the user or created automatically for the user by an administrator or system. Figure 11-8 shows an example of a password created by the administrator. However, in this case, the user is not blocked from changing the password (unless a policy was created for that purpose). Note that the second checkbox,

User Cannot Change Password, is not selected. As an administrator, you also have the option to select User Must Change Password at Next Logon. A user would have to pick a password when he first logs on to the domain, one that meets whatever complexity requirements your network calls for. This with the self-service password resetting (when users reset their own passwords at regular intervals) is necessary in larger networks to ease administration and increase security. The only caveat to this is account lockouts. Unlocking accounts that were locked by the system should be done only by an administrator or system operator.

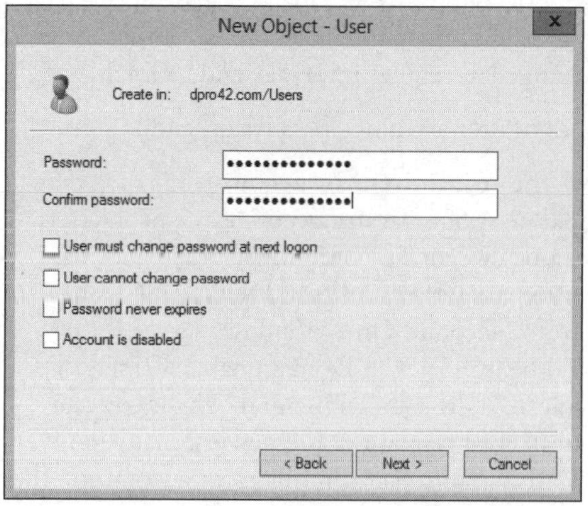

Figure 11-8 Password Phase of User Account Creation

At this point, it is common knowledge that a strong password is important for protecting a user account. Nowadays, many user accounts are compromised because of laziness; laziness on the part of the user for not configuring a strong password, or lethargic complacency on the part of the administrator for not enforcing the use of strong passwords.

But what is a strong password? That depends on the organization you deal with, but generally it is broken down into a few easy-to-remember points. Passwords should comply with the following:

- Contain uppercase letters
- Contain lowercase letters
- Contain numbers
- Contain special characters (symbols)
- Should be 8 to 10 characters or more. Some organizations that have extremely sensitive data will require 15 characters as a minimum.

The weak password and vendor-set default password can lead to data breaches. Attackers use weak or known passwords to access accounts and then perform unauthorized copying, transfer, and retrieval of data from servers—collectively known as *data exfiltration*. Data exfiltration is also known as data extrusion, data exportation, or simply stated—data theft. Whatever you call it, the complex password, and properly configured password policies, can help to prevent it.

Changing your password at regular intervals is important as well. The general rule of thumb is to change your password as often as you change your toothbrush. However, because this is a subjective concept (to put it nicely!), many organizations have policies concerning your password that we discuss in the next section. It might need to meet certain requirements, or be changed at regular intervals, and so forth.

Here are a few more tips when it comes to user accounts, passwords, and logons:

- **Rename and password protect the Administrator account:** It's nice that Windows has incorporated a separate Administrator account; the problem is that by default the account has no password. To configure this account, navigate to Computer Management > System Tools > Local Users and Groups > Users and locate the Administrator account. On a Windows server acting as a domain controller, this would be in ADUC > Domain name > Users. By right-clicking the account, you see a drop-down menu in which you can rename it and/or give it a password. (Just remember the new username and password!) Now it's great to have this additional Administrator account on the shelf just in case the primary account fails; however, your organization's policy might call for disabling it, which can be done by right-clicking the account and selecting Disable Account. (In older Windows systems, you would access the General tab of the account and select the Account Is Disabled checkbox.) Then, you would use that separate account previously created with administrative rights as your main administrative account. If you need access to the actual Administrator account later, it can be re-enabled using the methods previously described. Alternatively, open the command-line and type the following:

```
net user administrator /active:yes
```

  The way that the Administrator account behaves by default depends on the version of Windows. The Linux/Unix counterpart is the root account. The same types of measures should be employed when dealing with this account.

- **Verify that the Guest account (and other unnecessary accounts) is disabled:** This can be done by right-clicking the account in question, selecting Properties, and then selecting the checkbox named Account Is Disabled. It is also possible to delete accounts (aside from built-in accounts such as the Guest account); however, companies usually opt to have them disabled instead so that the company can retain information linking to the account. So, if an employee is terminated, the system administrator should generally implement the policy of account disablement. By disabling the account, the employee in question can no longer log in to the network, but the system administrator still has access to the history of that account.

- **Use Ctrl+Alt+Del:** Pressing Ctrl+Alt+Del before the logon adds a layer of security to the logon process by ensuring that users are communicating by means of a trusted path when entering passwords. This can be added in Windows 10 by going to Run and typing *netplwiz* (which opens the User Accounts dialog box), then going to the Advanced tab and selecting the checkbox for Require Users to Press Ctrl+Alt+Delete. Or, it can be added as a policy on individual Windows computers within the Local Group Policy Editor. It is implemented by default for computers that are members of a domain.

- **Use policies:** Policies governing user accounts, passwords, and so on can help you to enforce your rules, as discussed in the next section. Large organizations with a lot of users usually implement a self-service password management system. This means that users reset their own passwords after a given amount of time (set in a Group Policy); the administrator does not create passwords for users.

Policies

Policies are rules or guidelines used to guide decisions and achieve outcomes. They can be written or configured on a computer. The former are more difficult to enforce, whereas the latter would have to be hacked to be bypassed. Local computer policies and network policies are what really make an access control model effective.

Password policies can be implemented to enforce the usage of complex passwords and regulate how long passwords last. They can be configured on local computers, such as Windows operating systems, by navigating to Administrative Tools > Local Security Policy. When in the Local Security Settings window, continue to Security Settings > Account Policies > Password Policy.

More important, policies can be configured for an entire network; for example, on a Microsoft domain. This would be known as a group policy and there can be more than one. A group policy can affect the entire domain or an individual organizational unit. The main group policy is known as the Default Domain Policy. Figure 11-9 shows an example of the Default Domain Policy added to an MMC. To access the Password Policy section, you would navigate to Computer Configuration > Policies > Windows Settings > Security Settings > Account Policies > Password Policy.

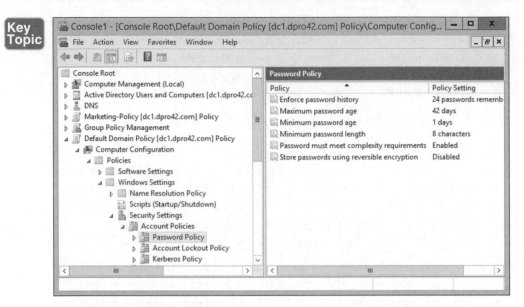

Figure 11-9   Password Policy on a Windows Server Domain Controller

> **NOTE**   The Default Domain Policy affects all users. This is okay for small networks, but for larger networks, separate organizational units should be created, each with its own security policy. From there, group-based privileges and individual user-based privileges can be expertly defined.

When Password Policy is selected, you see the following policies:

- **Enforce password history:** When this is defined, users cannot use any of the passwords remembered in the history. If you set the history to 3, the last three passwords cannot be reused when it is time to change the password.

- **Maximum and minimum password age:** This defines exactly how long a password can be used. The maximum is initially set to 42 days but does not affect the default Administrator account. To enforce effective password history, the minimum must be higher than zero. This is part of a category known as password expiration.

- **Minimum password length:** This requires that the password must be at least the specified number of characters. For a strong password policy, set this to 8 or more (as long as other complex requirements are also set; if not, the password should be longer).

- **Password must meet complexity requirements:** This means that passwords must meet three of these four criteria: uppercase characters, lowercase characters, digits between 0 and 9, and non-alphabetic characters (special characters).

To effectively stop users from reusing the same password, a security administrator should combine the Enforce Password History policy with the Minimum Password Age policy. The Minimum Password Age setting must be less than the Maximum Password Age setting and must be more than zero to enforce a password history policy. In addition, the security administrator might need to create a policy that states that passwords cannot be changed more than once a day: This would prevent users from changing their passwords X number of times in an attempt to bypass that password history policy.

Remember that all these policies, when enabled, affect all users to which the policy applies. If it is the Default Domain Policy (usually not recommended for configuration), it affects all users; if it is an OU policy, it affects all users in the OU.

Complexity and Length of a Password

You might see equations that represent the complexity and length of a password; for example, 26^n. In this case the 26 refers to the letters in the alphabet: "a" through "z" (lowercase), which comes to 26 characters in total. (This is sometimes referred to as a base-26 string.) If we also allowed uppercase letters, this number would be 52. If we added numbers, it would come to 62, and so on. But for now, let's stick with 26^n as the example. The superscript n is a variable that refers to the length of the password. When calculating a password, the number of characters should be raised to a particular power equal to the length of the password. So, if our policy dictates a password that is ten characters long, then it would be 26 to the power of 10, or 26^{10}. This would come to 141 trillion combinations. In this case $n = 10$, but it doesn't have to; n could be 12, 14, or whatever the security administrator sets the password length to within the password policy.

NOTE   For more information on password policies and password best practices, see the following link:

https://technet.microsoft.com/en-us/library/hh994572.aspx

There are plenty of other policies that you can configure. You can pretty much configure any policy on a domain. You can't configure how a person should shave in the morning, but anything computer-related can be modified and policed. One example is how many attempts a person will be allowed when typing in a password. This is known as the Account Lockout Threshold, as shown in Figure 11-10. Many companies adjust this to 3; this is known as the "3 strikes and you're out rule."

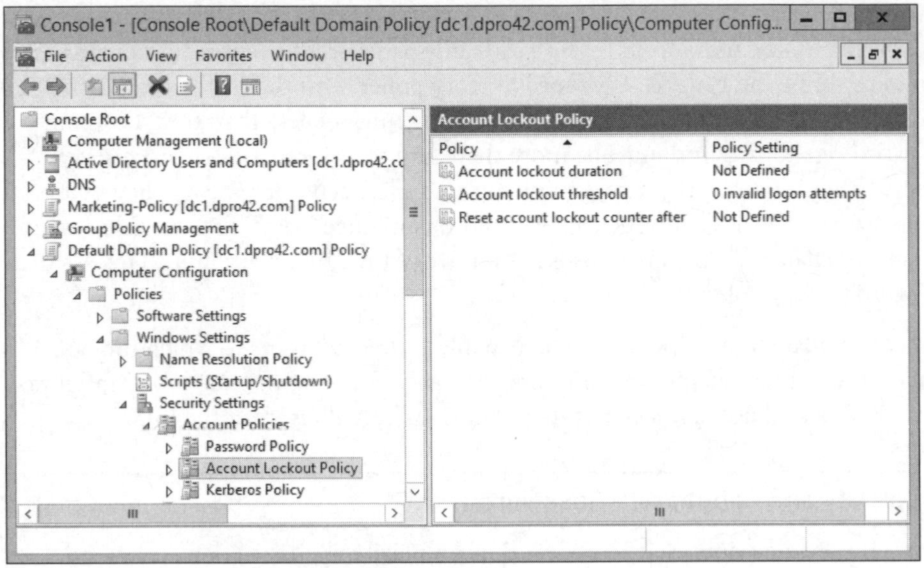

Figure 11-10   Account Lockout Threshold Policy

Another great tool is the previous logon notification. This can be configured in a policy and shows the user the last time the account logged in successfully—generally during the logon process. If users suspect that their account was compromised, they could check the previous logon notification and compare that with when they remember logging in.

It's important to note that when logging on to a Microsoft network, the logon process is secured by the Kerberos protocol, which is run by the domain controller. This adds a layer of protection for the username and password as they are authenticated across the network. When users take a break or go to lunch, they should lock the computer. This can be done by pressing Windows+L. When doing so, the operating system goes into a locked state, and the only way to unlock the computer is to enter the username and password of the person who locked the computer. The difference between this and logging out is that a locked computer keeps all the session's applications and files open, whereas logging out closes all applications and open files. A policy can also be configured to force locking after a certain amount of time has elapsed. Literally hundreds of policies are configurable. You could spend weeks doing it! Microsoft understands this and offers various levels of security templates that can be imported into your OU policy, making your job as an administrator a bit easier. A particular template might be just what you are looking for, or it might need a bit of tweaking. But in most cases it beats starting from scratch!

Policies can be developed on all kinds of software and systems, not just operating systems. For example, many organizations have websites, and a good portion of those organizations now set up bulletin board systems where authorized users can post messages. Bulletin boards are also known as forums or portals. Bulletin boards are often the playground for malicious activity; for example, users or bots posting spam messages. Various policies can be implemented on an interactive bulletin board system to prevent these types of problems. For example, when people first register, they would need to answer a question that requires something they know such as 2+4 = blank. The user would enter the answer (6) and continue on their merry way. Another viable option is to use **CAPTCHA** (Completely Automated Public Turing test to tell Computers and Humans Apart), which can display an image that has letters and numbers in it. The user must type the letters and numbers that they see before they can register, or perhaps to post any messages at all. This is a good deterrent for bots!

User Account Control (UAC)

User Account Control (UAC) is a security component of Windows that keeps every user (besides the actual Administrator account) in standard user mode instead of as an administrator with full administrative rights—even if the person is a member of the administrators group. It is meant to prevent unauthorized access, as well as avoid user error in the form of accidental changes. With UAC enabled, users perform common tasks as non-administrators, and, when necessary, as administrators, without having to switch users, log off, or use Run As.

Basically, UAC was created with two goals in mind:

- To eliminate unnecessary requests for excessive administrative-level access to Windows resources

- To reduce the risk of malicious software using the administrator's access control to infect operating system files

When a standard end user requires administrator privileges to perform certain tasks such as installing an application, a small pop-up UAC window appears, notifying the user that an administrator credential is necessary. If the user has administrative rights and clicks Continue, the task is carried out, but if the user does not have sufficient rights, the attempt fails. Note that these pop-up UAC windows do not appear if the person is logged on with the actual Administrator account.

NOTE   If necessary, UAC can be disabled in the Control Panel. However, it is not recommended.

There are other examples of generic account prohibition that work in the same manner as UAC. Third-party tools are available for Windows and Linux. An administrator might find that UAC does not have the configurability they desire. Regardless of the type of account prohibition used, it is important to conduct user access reviews—audits of what users have been able to access over time—and continuously monitor users' actions in this regard. We'll discuss this mindset in Chapter 13, "Monitoring and Auditing."

Chapter Summary

In order to have an efficient computer network, the security administrator needs to be *in control*. This is still feasible, even in today's complicated computer networks. An admin can choose from several basic access control models: discretionary access control (DAC), mandatory access control (MAC), role-based access control (RBAC), and attribute-based access control (ABAC). Probably the most common is DAC; many Windows-controlled and Linux-controlled networks utilize this model. Whatever the model, remember that they are based on subjects (users) and objects (data files and other resources).

For access control to work well, it is wise to implement certain concepts such as implicit deny, where all traffic is denied except for what a user specifically needs; least privilege, where a user is only given the permissions necessary to perform a task; separation of duties, where more than one person is required to complete a task; and job rotation, where a pool of people can work on the same individual job if necessary. Used together, an access control model can be very effective.

A lot of the concepts in the preceding two paragraphs are intangibles. To secure access to data in the technical sense, permissions and policies are your best friends. Both large and small networks can benefit from the use of permissions and groups of users: Using permissions enables a more secure system; using groups of users allows you to automate the distribution of permissions to multiple users at once. Permissions are also known as rights, access modes, and, depending on the scenario, access control lists (ACLs). The common Windows system uses a set of six NTFS permissions spanning from the ability to read files only, all the way to having full control of those files. In Unix/Linux-based systems, three types of permissions—read, write, and execute—are assigned to users, groups, and owners by way of a three-digit number and the chmod command.

Access control also hinges on authentication, the most common form of which is the username/password combination. The importance of complex passwords cannot be stressed enough. An organization will often require eight to ten characters minimum, including uppercase letters, numbers, and special characters. And all of this is usually enforced by a computerized policy. Password policies such as password history, maximum password age, minimum password length, and password complexity requirements, if configured properly, can offer your users a decent level of protection. The user accounts themselves can also be secured with the use of account lockouts, time-of-day restrictions, and User Account Control.

We mentioned in the beginning of the chapter that you don't want any Tom, Dick, or Harry to get access to your data. If you don't control access to your data, it is the equivalent of allowing the three stooges into your servers. You'd be surprised how many companies disregard best practices for access control. But when it comes to this layer of security, a little bit of planning and a modest piece of automated configuration can go a long way.

Chapter Review Activities

Use the features in this section to study and review the topics in this chapter.

Review Key Topics

Review the most important topics in the chapter, noted with the Key Topic icon in the outer margin of the page. Table 11-2 lists a reference of these key topics and the page number on which each is found.

Table 11-2 Key Topics for Chapter 11

Key Topic Element	Description	Page Number
Figure 11-1	Example of discretionary access in Windows	362
Table 11-1	Summary of access control models	365
Figure 11-2	Example of implicit deny on a Windows folder	367
Figure 11-4	User account expiration date	370
Figure 11-5	Time-of-day restrictions for a standard user	371
Figure 11-9	Password Policy on a Windows Server Domain Controller	380
Bulleted list	Password compliance	380

Define Key Terms

Define the following key terms from this chapter, and check your answers in the glossary:

access control model, discretionary access control (DAC), Trusted Computer System Evaluation Criteria (TCSEC), mandatory access control (MAC), role-based access control (RBAC), attribute-based access control (ABAC), implicit deny, least privilege, separation of duties, job rotation, permissions, access control list (ACL), CAPTCHA

Complete the Real-World Scenarios

Complete the Real-World Scenarios found on the companion website (www.pearsonitcertification.com/title/9780789758996). You will find a PDF containing the scenario and questions, and also supporting videos and simulations.

Review Questions

Answer the following review questions. Check your answers with the correct answers that follow.

1. Which of the following is the strongest password?

   A. |ocrian#

   B. Marqu1sD3S0d

   C. This1sV#ryS3cure

   D. Thisisverysecure

2. Which of these is a security component of Windows?

   A. UAC

   B. UPS

   C. Gadgets

   D. Control Panel

3. What key combination helps to secure the logon process?

   A. Windows+R

   B. Ctrl+Shift+Esc

   C. Ctrl+Alt+Del

   D. Alt+F4

4. Which of the following is the most common authentication model?

   A. Username and password

   B. Biometrics

   C. Key cards

   D. Tokens

5. Which of the following access control methods uses rules to govern whether object access will be allowed? (Select the best answer.)

   A. Rule-based access control

   B. Role-based access control

   C. Discretionary access control

   D. Mandatory access control

   E. Attribute-based access control

6. When using the mandatory access control model, what component is needed?

   A. Labels

   B. Certificates

   C. Tokens

   D. RBAC

7. Which of the following statements regarding the MAC model is true?

   A. Mandatory access control is a dynamic model.

   B. Mandatory access control enables an owner to establish access privileges to a resource.

   C. Mandatory access control is not restrictive.

   D. Mandatory access control users cannot share resources dynamically.

8. In the DAC model, how are permissions identified?

   A. Role membership.

   B. Access control lists.

   C. They are predefined.

   D. It is automatic.

9. Robert needs to access a resource. In the DAC model, what is used to identify him or other users?

    A. Roles

    B. ACLs

    C. MAC

    D. Rules

10. A company has a high attrition rate. What should you ask the network administrator to do first? (Select the best answer.)

    A. Review user permissions and access control lists.

    B. Review group policies.

    C. Review Performance logs.

    D. Review the Application log.

11. Your company has 1000 users. Which of the following password management systems will work best for your company?

    A. Multiple access methods

    B. Synchronize passwords

    C. Historical passwords

    D. Self-service password resetting

12. In a discretionary access control model, who is in charge of setting permissions to a resource?

    A. The owner of the resource

    B. The administrator

    C. Any user of the computer

    D. The administrator and the owner

13. Jason needs to add several users to a group. Which of the following will help him to get the job done faster?

    A. Propagation

    B. Inheritance

    C. Template

    D. Access control lists

14. How are permissions defined in the mandatory access control model?

    A. Access control lists

    B. User roles

    C. Defined by the user

    D. Predefined access privileges

15. Which of the following would lower the level of password security?

    A. After a set number of failed attempts, the server will lock the user out, forcing her to call the administrator to re-enable her account.

    B. Passwords must be greater than eight characters and contain at least one special character.

    C. All passwords are set to expire after 30 days.

    D. Complex passwords that users cannot change are randomly generated by the administrator.

16. Of the following access control models, which uses object labels? (Select the best answer.)

    A. Discretionary access control

    B. Role-based access control

    C. Rule-based access control

    D. Mandatory access control

    E. Attribute-based access control

17. Which of the following methods could identify when an unauthorized access has occurred?

    A. Two-factor authentication

    B. Session termination

    C. Previous logon notification

    D. Session lock

18. What would you use to control the traffic that is allowed in or out of a network? (Select the best answer.)

    A. Access control lists

    B. Firewall

    C. Address Resolution Protocol

    D. Discretionary access control

19. In an attempt to detect fraud and defend against it, your company cross-trains people in each department. What is this an example of?

   A. Separation of duties

   B. Chain of custody

   C. Job rotation

   D. Least privilege

20. What is a definition of implicit deny?

   A. Everything is denied by default.

   B. All traffic from one network to another is denied.

   C. ACLs are used to secure the firewall.

   D. Resources that are not given access are denied by default.

21. In an environment where administrators, the accounting department, and the marketing department all have different levels of access, which of the following access control models is being used?

   A. Role-based access control (RBAC)

   B. Mandatory access control (MAC)

   C. Discretionary access control (DAC)

   D. Rule-based access control (RBAC)

22. Which security measure should be included when implementing access control?

   A. Disabling SSID broadcast

   B. Time-of-day restrictions

   C. Changing default passwords

   D. Password complexity requirements

23. Which password management system best provides for a system with a large number of users?

   A. Locally saved passwords management system

   B. Synchronized passwords management system

   C. Multiple access methods management system

   D. Self-service password reset management system

24. You administer a bulletin board system for a rock and roll band. While reviewing logs for the board, you see one particular IP address posting spam multiple times per day. What is the best way to prevent this type of problem?

   A. Block the IP address of the user.

   B. Ban the user.

   C. Disable ActiveX.

   D. Implement CAPTCHA.

25. Your organization has enacted a policy where employees are required to create passwords with at least 15 characters. What type of policy does this define?

   A. Password length

   B. Password expiration

   C. Minimum password age

   D. Password complexity

26. Users are required to change their passwords every 30 days. Which policy should be configured?

   A. Password length

   B. Password recovery

   C. Password expiration

   D. Account lockout

27. You want to mitigate the possibility of privilege creep among your long-term users. What procedure should you employ?

   A. Mandatory vacations

   B. Job rotation

   C. User permission reviews

   D. Separation of duties

28. A security administrator implements access controls based on the security classification of the data and need-to-know information. Which of the following would best describe this level of access control?

   A. Least privilege

   B. Mandatory access control

   C. Role-based access control

   D. Implicit deny

29. Which of the following access control models would be found in a firewall?

   A. Mandatory access control

   B. Discretionary access control

   C. Role-based access control

   D. Rule-based access control

30. You are consulting for a small organization that relies on employees who work from home and on the road. An attacker has compromised the network by denying remote access to the company using a script. Which of the following security controls did the attacker exploit?

   A. Password complexity

   B. DoS

   C. Account lockout

   D. Password length

Answers and Explanations

1. **C.** The answer This1sV#ryS3cure incorporates case-sensitive letters, numbers, and special characters and is 16 characters long. The other answers do not have the complexity of This1sV#ryS3cure.

2. **A.** User Account Control (UAC) adds a layer of security to Windows that protects against malware and user error and conserves resources. It enforces a type of separation of duties.

3. **C.** Ctrl+Alt+Del is the key combination used to help secure the logon process. It can be added by configuring the Local Security policy.

4. **A.** By far the username and password combination is the most common authentication model. Although biometrics, key cards, and tokens are also used, the username/password is still the most common.

5. **A.** Rule-based access control uses rules to govern whether an object can be accessed. It is a type of mandatory access control (MAC).

6. **A.** Labels are required in the mandatory access control (MAC) model.

7. **D.** In the MAC (mandatory access control) model, users cannot share resources dynamically. MAC is not a dynamic model; it is a static model. Owners cannot establish access privileges to a resource; this would be done by the administrator. MAC is indeed very restrictive, as restrictive as the administrator wants it to be.

8. **B.** In the discretionary access control (DAC) model, permissions to files are identified by access control lists (ACLs). Role membership is used in RBAC.

The mandatory access control model predefines permissions. Either way, it is not identified automatically.

9. **B.** Access control lists (ACLs) are used in the discretionary access control model. This is different from role-based, rule-based, and MAC (mandatory access control) models.

10. **A.** The first thing administrators should do when they notice that the company has a high attrition rate (high turnover of employees) is to conduct a thorough review of user permissions, rights, and access control lists. A review of group policies might also be necessary but is not as imperative. Performance logs and the Application log will probably not pertain to the fact that the company has a lot of employees being hired and leaving the company.

11. **D.** It would be difficult for administrators to deal with thousands of users' passwords; therefore, the best management system for a company with 1000 users would be self-service password resetting.

12. **A.** In the discretionary access control (DAC) model, the owner of the resource is in charge of setting permissions. In a mandatory access control model, the administrator is in charge.

13. **C.** By using a template, you can add many users to a group at once simply by applying the template to the users. Propagation and inheritance deal with how permissions are exchanged between parent folders and subfolders. Access control lists show who was allowed access to a particular resource.

14. **D.** The mandatory access control model uses predefined access privileges to define which users have permission to resources.

15. **D.** To have a secure password scheme, passwords should be changed by the user. They should not be generated by the administrator. If an administrator were to generate the password for the user, it would have to be submitted in written (and unencrypted) form in some way to the user. This creates a security issue, especially if the user does not memorize the password and instead leaves a written version of it lying around. All the other answers would increase the level of password security.

16. **D.** The mandatory access control (MAC) model uses object and subject labels. DAC (discretionary access control), RBAC (role-based access control), and ABAC (attribute-based access control) do not. Rule-based access control is a portion of MAC, and although it might use labels, MAC is the best answer.

17. **C.** Previous logon notification can identify whether unauthorized access has occurred. Two-factor authentication means that person will supply two forms of identification before being authenticated to a network or system. Session termination is a mechanism that can be implemented to end an unauthorized access. Session lock mechanisms can be employed to lock a particular user or IP address out of the system.

18. **A.** Access control lists can be used to control the traffic that is allowed in or out of a network. They are usually included as part of a firewall, and they are the better answer because they specifically will control the traffic. Address Resolution Protocol (ARP) resolves IP addresses to MAC addresses. In the discretionary access control model, the owner controls permissions of resources.

19. **C.** When a company cross-trains people, it is known as job rotation. Separation of duties is in a way the opposite; this is when multiple people are needed to complete a single task. Chain of custody has to do with the legal paper trail of a particular occurrence. Least privilege is a mitigation technique to defend against privilege escalation attacks.

20. **D.** If a resource is not given specific access, it will be implicitly denied by default. Access control lists are used to permit or deny access from one network to another and are often implemented on a firewall.

21. **A.** Role-based access control is when different groups or roles are assigned different levels of permissions; rights and permissions are based on job function. (Note: Attribute-based access control [ABAC] is similar to RBAC, but uses Boolean logic such as IF-THEN statements.) In the mandatory access control model, an administrator centrally controls permissions. In the discretionary access control model, the owner of the user sets permissions. In the rule-based access control model, rules are defined by the administrator and are stored in an ACL.

22. **D.** By implementing password complexity requirements, users will be forced to select and enter complex passwords—for example, eight characters or more, uppercase characters, special characters, and more. Disabling the SSID deals with wireless networks, time-of-day restrictions are applied only after persons log in with their username and password, and changing default passwords should be part of a password policy.

23. **D.** If a network has a large number of users, the administrator should set up a system, and policies to enforce the system, that will allow for users to reset their own passwords. The passwords should be stored centrally, not locally. Also, it would be best if single sign-on were implemented and not a multiple access method.

24. **D.** By implementing CAPTCHA, another level of security is added that users have to complete before they can register to and/or post to a bulletin board. Although banning a user or the user's IP address can help to eliminate that particular person from spamming the site, the best way is to add another level of security, such as CAPTCHA. This applies to all persons who attempt to attack the bulletin board.

25. **A.** Password length is the policy that deals with how many characters are in a password. Password expiration and minimum (and maximum) password age define how long a password will be valid. Password complexity defines whether the password should have uppercase letters, numbers, and special characters.

26. **C.** The password expiration policy should be configured. For example, in Windows, the maximum password age policy should be set to 30 days. Password length deals with how many characters are in the password. Password recovery defines how (and if) a user can get back his password or create a new one. Account lockout policies dictate how many times the user has to type a password incorrectly to be locked out of the system, and for how long the user will remain locked out.

27. **C.** Conduct user permission reviews to ensure that long-term users are getting the proper permissions to data. Privilege creep is when, over time, additional permissions are given to a particular user because that user needs to access certain files on a temporary basis. Mandatory vacations are enforced on many personnel to ensure that there is no kind of fraud or other illegitimate activity going on. Job rotation is implemented so that multiple people can perform the same job, in the case that one person is not available. Separation of duties is when a group of users will each perform an individual task, which collectively forms the entire job.

28. **B.** When you are dealing with access controls based on the classification of data and need-to-know information, you are most likely working with a mandatory access control (MAC) system. Least privilege means the lowest amount of permissions possible. This differs from need-to-know in that a user configured as need-to-know might need to have access to a lot of data, and actually require a good deal of permissions. Role-based access control (RBAC), like MAC, is controlled by the system, but it works with sets of permissions based on user roles. Implicit deny means that unless otherwise configured, all access to data is denied.

29. **D.** Firewalls are most often considered to be based off of the rule-based access control model. This is because you indeed create rules (ACLs) that govern how data is transmitted through the firewall.

30. **C.** The attacker most likely exploited the account lockout policy, a security control originally implemented by the organization. The script modified the policy and caused all of the users to be locked out when they attempted to log in. Password complexity is the level of intricacy of a password; it usually entails using uppercase letters, numerals, and special characters, and is defined by a policy, just as the account lockout threshold is. DoS stands for denial-of-service, an attack that floods a network device (or server) with so much data that the device cannot perform its duties. Password length is the number of characters in a password, also definable by policy.

This chapter covers the following subjects:

- **Conducting Risk Assessments:** This section covers risk management and assessment. It discusses the differences between qualitative and quantitative risk and describes the methodologies of an important part of risk management—vulnerability management. Also covered are various ways to assess vulnerabilities and how to perform penetration tests.

- **Assessing Vulnerability with Security Tools:** In this section, you learn how to use common network security tools to measure the vulnerability of your computer systems and network devices. These tools include network mappers, vulnerability scanners, protocol analyzers, packet sniffers, and password crackers.

Let's take it to the next level and talk some serious security. As people, we're all vulnerable to something. They say that you need to "manage your own healthcare"—our computers are no different. The potential health of your computers and network is based on vulnerabilities. One of the most important tasks of a security administrator is to find vulnerabilities and either remove them or secure them as much as possible—within acceptable parameters. **Vulnerabilities** are weaknesses in your computer network design and individual host configuration. Vulnerabilities, such as open ports, unnecessary services, weak passwords, systems that aren't updated, lack of policy, and so on, are invitations to threats such as malicious attacks. Of course, your computer network can be vulnerable to other types of threats as well, such as environmental or natural threats, but these are covered in more depth in Chapter 16, "Redundancy and Disaster Recovery," and Chapter 18, "Policies and Procedures."

CHAPTER 12

Vulnerability and Risk Assessment

Vulnerability assessment is just part of overall risk management. Risk includes computer vulnerabilities, potential dangers, possible hardware and software failure, man hours wasted, and of course, monetary loss. Having a computer network is inherently a risky business, so we need to conduct risk assessments to define what an organization's risks are and how to reduce those risks.

Foundation Topics

Conducting Risk Assessments

When dealing with computer security, a **risk** is the possibility of a malicious attack or other threat causing damage or downtime to a computer system. Generally, this is done by exploiting vulnerabilities in a computer system or network. The more vulnerability—the more risk. Smart organizations are extremely interested in managing vulnerabilities, and thereby managing risk. **Risk management** can be defined as the identification, assessment, and prioritization of risks, and the mitigating and monitoring of those risks. Specifically, when talking about computer hardware and software, risk management is also known as **information assurance (IA)**. The two common models of IA include the well-known CIA triad (which we covered in Chapter 1, "Introduction to Security"), and the DoD "Five Pillars of IA," which comprise the concepts of the CIA triad (confidentiality, integrity, and availability) but also include authentication and non-repudiation.

Organizations usually employ one of the four following general strategies when managing a particular risk:

- Transfer the risk to another organization or third party.

- Avoid the risk.

- Reduce the risk.

- Accept some or all of the consequences of a risk.

It is possible to transfer *some* risk to a third party. An example of **risk transference** (also known as risk sharing) would be an organization that purchases insurance for a group of servers in a data center. The organization still takes on the risk of losing data in the case of server failure, theft, and disaster, but transfers the risk of losing the money those servers are worth in case they are lost.

Some organizations opt to avoid risk. **Risk avoidance** usually entails not carrying out a proposed plan because the risk factor is too great. An example of risk avoidance: If a high-profile organization decided not to implement a new and controversial website based on its belief that too many attackers would attempt to exploit it.

However, the most common goal of risk management is to *reduce* all risk to a level acceptable to the organization. It is impossible to eliminate all risk, but it should be mitigated as much as possible within reason. Usually, budgeting and IT resources dictate the level of **risk reduction**, and what kind of deterrents can be put in place. For example, installing antivirus/firewall software on every client computer is common; most companies do this. However, installing a high-end, hardware-based firewall at every computer is not common; although this method would probably make for a secure network, the amount of money and administration needed to implement that solution would make it unacceptable.

This leads to **risk acceptance**, also known as risk retention. Most organizations are willing to accept a certain amount of risk. Sometimes, vulnerabilities that would otherwise be mitigated by the implementation of expensive solutions are instead dealt with when and if they are exploited. IT budgeting and resource management are big factors when it comes to these risk management decisions.

After the risk transference, risk avoidance, and risk reduction techniques have been implemented, an organization is left with a certain amount of **residual risk**—the risk left over after a detailed security plan and disaster recovery plan have been implemented. There is always risk, as a company cannot possibly foresee every future event, nor can it secure against every single threat. Senior management as a collective whole is ultimately responsible for deciding how much residual risk there will be in a company's infrastructure, and how much risk there will be to the company's data. Often, no one person will be in charge of this, but it will be decided on as a group.

There are many different types of risks to computers and computer networks. Of course, before you can decide what to do about particular risks, you need to assess what those risks are.

Risk assessment is the attempt to determine the amount of threats or hazards that could possibly occur in a given amount of time to your computers and networks. When you assess risks, they are often recognized threats—but risk assessment can also take into account new types of threats that might occur. When risk has been assessed, it can be mitigated up until the point in which the organization will accept any additional risk. Generally, risk assessments follow a particular order, for example:

Step 1.   Identify the organization's assets.

Step 2.   Identify vulnerabilities.

Step 3.   Identify threats and threat likelihood.

Step 4.   Identify potential monetary impact.

The fourth step is also known as *impact assessment*. This is when you determine the potential monetary costs related to a threat. See the section "Vulnerability Management" later in this chapter for more on information on Steps 2 and 3, including how to mitigate potential threats.

An excellent tool to create during your risk assessment is a **risk register**, also known as a risk log, which helps to track issues and address problems as they occur. After the initial risk assessment, a security administrator will continue to use and refer to the risk register. This can be a great tool for just about any organization but can be of more value to certain types of organizations, such as manufacturers that utilize a supply chain. In this case, the organization would want to implement a specialized type of risk management called *supply chain risk management (SCRM)*. This is when the organization collaborates with suppliers and distributors to analyze and reduce risk.

The two most common risk assessment methods are qualitative and quantitative. Let's discuss these now.

Qualitative Risk Assessment

Qualitative risk assessment is an assessment that assigns numeric values to the probability of a risk and the impact it can have on the system or network. Unlike its counterpart, quantitative risk assessment, it does not assign monetary values to assets or possible losses. It is the easier, quicker, and cheaper way to assess risk but cannot assign asset value or give a total for possible monetary loss.

With this method, ranges can be assigned, for example, 1 to 10 or 1 to 100. The higher the number, the higher the probability of risk, or the greater the impact on the system. As a basic example, a computer without antivirus software that is connected to the Internet will most likely have a high probability of risk; it will also most likely have a great impact on the system. We could assign the number 99 as the probability of risk. We are not sure exactly when it will happen but are 99% sure that it will happen at some point. Next, we could assign the number 90 out of 100 as the impact of the risk. This number implies a heavy impact; probably either the system has crashed or has been rendered unusable at some point. There is a 10%

chance that the system will remain usable, but it is unlikely. Finally, we multiply the two numbers together to find out the qualitative risk: 99 × 90 = 8910. That's 8910 out of a possible 10,000, which is a high level of risk. **Risk mitigation** is when a risk is reduced or eliminated altogether. The way to mitigate risk in this example would be to install antivirus software and verify that it is configured to auto-update. By assigning these types of qualitative values to various risks, we can make comparisons from one risk to another and get a better idea of what needs to be mitigated and what doesn't.

The main issue with this type of risk assessment is that it is difficult to place an exact value on many types of risks. The type of qualitative system varies from organization to organization, even from person to person; it is a common source of debate as well. This makes qualitative risk assessments more descriptive than truly measurable. However, by relying on group surveys, company history, and personal experience, you can get a basic idea of the risk involved.

Quantitative Risk Assessment

Quantitative risk assessment measures risk by using exact monetary values. It attempts to give an expected yearly loss in dollars for any given risk. It also defines asset values to servers, routers, and other network equipment.

Three values are used when making quantitative risk calculations:

- **Single loss expectancy (SLE):** The loss of value in dollars based on a single incident.

- **Annualized rate of occurrence (ARO):** The number of times per year that the specific incident occurs.

- **Annualized loss expectancy (ALE):** The total loss in dollars per year due to a specific incident. The incident might happen once or more than once; either way, this number is the total loss in dollars for that particular type of incident. It is computed with the following calculation:

  SLE × ARO = ALE

So, for example, suppose we wanted to find out how much an e-commerce web server's downtime would cost the company per year. We would need some additional information such as the average web server downtime in minutes and the number of times this occurs per year. We also would need to know the average sale amount in dollars and how many sales are made per minute on this e-commerce web server. This information can be deduced by using accounting reports and by further security analysis of the web server, which we discuss later. For now, let's just say that over the past year our web server failed 7 times. The average downtime for each failure was 45 minutes. That equals a total of 315 minutes of downtime per year, close to 99.9% uptime. (The more years we can measure, the better our estimate will be.) Now let's say that this web server processes an average of 10 orders per minute with average revenue of $35. That means that $350 of revenue comes in per minute. As we mentioned, a single downtime averages 45 minutes, corresponding to a $15,750 loss per occurrence. So, the SLE is $15,750. Ouch! Some salespeople are going to be unhappy with your 99.9% uptime! But we're not done. We want to know the annualized loss expectancy (ALE). This can be calculated by multiplying the SLE ($15,750) by the annualized rate of occurrence (ARO). We said that the web server failed 7 times last year, so the SLE × ARO would be $15,750 × 7, which equals $110,250 (the ALE). This is shown in Table 12-1.

Key Topic

Table 12-1   Example of Quantitative Risk Assessment

SLE	ARO	ALE
$15,750	7	$110,250
Revenue lost due to each web server failure	Total web server failures over the past year	Total loss due to web server failure per year

Whoa! Apparently, we need to increase the uptime of our e-commerce web server! Many organizations demand 99.99% or even 99.999% uptime; 99.999% uptime means that the server will only have 5 minutes of downtime over the entire course of the year. Of course, to accomplish this we first need to scrutinize our server to see precisely why it fails so often. What exactly are the vulnerabilities of the web server? Which ones were exploited? Which threats exploited those vulnerabilities? By exploring the server's logs, configurations, and policies, and by using security tools, we can discern exactly why this happens so often. However, this analysis should be done carefully because the server does so much business for the company. We continue this example and show the specific tools you can use in the section "Assessing Vulnerability with Security Tools."

It isn't possible to assign a specific ALE to incidents that will happen in the future, so new technologies should be monitored carefully. Any failures should be documented thoroughly. For example, a spreadsheet could be maintained that contains the various technologies your organization uses, their failure history, their SLE, ARO, and ALE, and mitigation techniques that you have employed, and when they were implemented.

Although it's impossible to predict the future accurately, it can be quantified on an average basis using concepts such as **mean time between failures (MTBF)**. This term deals with reliability. It defines the average number of failures per million hours of operation for a product in question. This is based on historical baselines among various customers that use the product. It can be very helpful when making quantitative assessments.

NOTE Another way of describing MTBF is called failure in time (FIT), which is the number of failures per *billion* hours of operation.

There are two other terms you should know that are related to MTBF: mean time to repair (MTTR), which is the time needed to repair a failed device; and mean time to failure (MTTF), which is a basic measure of reliability for devices that cannot be repaired. All three of these concepts should also be considered when creating a disaster recovery (DR) plan, which we will discuss more in Chapter 16.

So, we can't specifically foretell the future, but by using qualitative and quantitative risk assessment methods we can get a feel for what is likely to happen (more so with the latter option), and prepare accordingly. Table 12-2 summarizes the risk assessment types discussed in this chapter.

Key Topic

Table 12-2 Summary of Risk Assessment Types

Risk Assessment Type	Description	Key Points
Qualitative risk assessment	Assigns numeric values to the probability of a risk, and the impact it can have on the system or network.	Numbers are arbitrary. Examples: 1–10 or 1–100.
Quantitative risk assessment	Measures risk by using exact monetary values. It attempts to give an expected yearly loss in dollars for any given risk.	Values are specific monetary amounts. SLE × ARO = ALE MTBF can be used for additional data.

NOTE Most organizations within the medical, pharmaceutical, and banking industries make use of quantitative risk assessments—they need to have specific monetary numbers to measure risk. Taking this one step further, many banking institutions adhere to the recommendations within the Basel I, II, and III accords. These recommended standards describe how much capital a bank should put aside to aid with financial and operational risks if they occur.

Security Analysis Methodologies

To assess risk properly, we must analyze the security of our computers, servers, and network devices. But before making an analysis, the computer, server, or other device should be backed up accordingly. This might require a backup of files, a complete image backup, or a backup of firmware. It all depends on the device in question. When this is done, an analysis can be made. Hosts should be analyzed to discern whether a firewall is in place, what type of configuration is used (or worse if the device is using a default configuration), what anti-malware software is installed, if any, and what updates have been made. A list of vulnerabilities should be developed, and a security person should watch for threats that could exploit these vulnerabilities; they might occur naturally, might be perpetuated by malicious persons using a variety of attack and threat vectors, or might be due to user error.

Security analysis can be done in one of two ways: actively or passively.

Active security analysis is when actual hands-on tests are run on the system in question. These tests might require a device to be taken off the network for a short time, or might cause a loss in productivity. Active scanning is used to find out if ports are open on a specific device, or to find out what IP addresses are in use on the network. A backup of the systems to be analyzed should be accomplished before the scan takes place. Active scanning (also known as intrusive scanning) can be detrimental to systems or the entire network, especially if you are dealing with a mission-critical network that requires close to 100% uptime. In some cases, you can pull systems off the network or run your test during off-hours. But in other cases, you must rely on passive security analysis.

Passive security analysis is when servers, devices, and networks are not affected by your analyses, scans, and other tests. It could be as simple as using documentation only to test the security of a system. For example, if an organization's network documentation shows computers, switches, servers, and routers, but no firewall, you have found a vulnerability to the network (a rather large one). Passive security analysis might be required in real-time, mission-critical networks or if you are conducting computer forensics analysis, but even if you are performing a passive security analysis, a backup of the system is normal procedure. Passive security analysis is also known as non-intrusive or non-invasive analysis.

One example of the difference between active and passive is fingerprinting, which is when a security person (or attacker) scans hosts to find out what ports are open, ultimately helping the person to distinguish the operating system used by the computer. It is also known as OS fingerprinting or TCP/IP fingerprinting. Active fingerprinting is when a direct connection is made to the computer starting with ICMP requests. This type of test could cause the system to respond slowly to other requests from legitimate computers. Passive fingerprinting is when the scanning host sniffs the network by chance, classifying hosts as the scanning host observes its traffic on the occasion that it occurs. This method is less common in port scanners but can help to reduce stress on the system being scanned.

Security analysis can also be categorized as either **passive reconnaissance** or **active reconnaissance**. If an attacker or white hat is performing passive reconnaissance, that person is attempting to gain information about a target system *without* engaging the system. For example, a basic port scan of a system, without any further action, can be considered passive reconnaissance. However, if the attacker or white hat then uses that information to exploit vulnerabilities associated with those ports, then it is known as active reconnaissance, and is a method used when performing penetration tests. (We'll further discuss penetration testing later in this chapter.)

Security Controls

Before we get into managing vulnerabilities, I'd like to revisit the concept of security controls. In Chapter 1 we discussed three basic security controls that are often used to develop a security plan: physical, technical, and administrative. However, there are additional categorical controls as described by the NIST. In short, the three can be described as the following:

- **Management controls:** These are techniques and concerns addressed by an organization's management (managers and executives). Generally, these controls focus on decisions and the management of risk. They also concentrate on procedures, policies, legal and regulatory, the software development life cycle (SDLC), the computer security life cycle, information assurance, and vulnerability management/scanning. In short, these controls focus on how the security of your data and systems is managed.

- **Operational controls:** These are the controls executed by people. They are designed to increase individual and group system security. They include user awareness and training, fault tolerance and disaster recovery plans, incident handling, computer support, baseline configuration development, and environmental security. The people who carry out the specific requirements of these controls must have technical expertise and understand how to implement what management desires of them.

- **Technical controls:** These are the logical controls executed by the computer system. Technical controls include authentication, access control, auditing, and cryptography. The configuration and workings of firewalls, session locks, RADIUS servers, or RAID 5 arrays would be within this category, as well as concepts such as least privilege implementation.

Once again, the previous controls are categorical. For the Security+ exam you should focus on these definitive security controls:

- **Preventive controls:** These controls are employed before the event and are designed to prevent an incident. Examples include biometric systems designed to keep unauthorized persons out, NIPSs to prevent malicious activity, and RAID 1 to prevent loss of data. These are also sometimes referred to as deterrent controls.

- **Detective controls:** These controls are used during an event and can find out whether malicious activity is occurring or has occurred. Examples include CCTV/video surveillance, alarms, NIDSs, and auditing.

- **Corrective controls:** These controls are used after an event. They limit the extent of damage and help the company recover from damage quickly. Tape backup, hot sites, and other fault tolerance and disaster recovery methods are also included here. These are sometimes referred to as compensating controls.

Compensating controls, also known as alternative controls, are mechanisms put in place to satisfy security requirements that are either impractical or too difficult to implement. For example, instead of using expensive hardware-based encryption modules, an organization might opt to use network access control (NAC), data loss prevention (DLP), and other security methods. Or, on the personnel side, instead of implementing *segregation of duties*, an organization might opt to do additional logging and auditing. (See Chapter 18 for more information on segregation of duties.) Approach compensating controls with great caution. They do not give the same level of security as their replaced counterparts.

And, of course, many security concepts can be placed in the category of physical as well as other categories listed previously. For example, a locking door would be an example of a physical control as well as a preventive control.

When you see technologies, policies, and procedures in the future, attempt to place them within their proper control category. Semantics will vary from one organization to the next, but as long as you can categorize security features in a general fashion such as the ones previously listed, you should be able to define and understand just about any organization's security controls.

Vulnerability Management

Vulnerability management is the practice of finding and mitigating software vulnerabilities in computers and networks. It consists of analyzing network documentation, testing computers and networks with a variety of security tools, mitigating vulnerabilities, and periodically monitoring for effects and changes. Vulnerability management can be broken down into five steps:

Step 1. **Define the desired state of security:** An organization might have written policies defining the desired state of security, or you as the security administrator might have to create those policies. These policies include access control rules, device configurations, network configurations, network documentation, and so on.

Step 2. **Create baselines:** After the desired state of security is defined, baselines should be taken to assess the current security state of computers, servers, network devices, and the network in general. These baselines are known as **vulnerability assessments**. The baselines should find as many vulnerabilities as possible utilizing vulnerability scans and other scanning and auditing methods. These baselines will be known as premitigation baselines and should be saved for later comparison.

Step 3. **Prioritize vulnerabilities:** Which vulnerabilities should take precedence? For example, the e-commerce web server we talked about earlier should definitely have a higher priority than a single client computer that does not have antivirus software installed. Prioritize all the vulnerabilities; this creates a list of items that need to be mitigated in order.

Step 4. **Mitigate vulnerabilities:** Go through the prioritized list and mitigate as many of the vulnerabilities as possible. This depends on the level of acceptable risk your organization allows. Mitigation techniques might include secure code review, and a review of system and application architecture and system design.

Step 5. **Monitor the environment:** When you finish mitigation, monitor the environment and compare the results to the original baseline. Use the new results as the post-mitigation baseline to be compared against future analyses. (Consider tools that can perform automated baseline reporting.) Because new vulnerabilities are always being discovered, and because company policies may change over time, you should periodically monitor the environment and compare your results to the post-mitigation baseline. Do this anytime policies change or the environment changes. Be careful to monitor for false positives—when a test reports a vulnerability as present when in fact there is none—they can be real time-wasters. If possible, use templates, scripts, and built-in system functionality to automate your monitoring efforts and employ continuous monitoring and configuration validation. All of these things will help to reduce risk.

This five-step process has helped me when managing vulnerabilities for customers. It should be noted again that some organizations already have a defined policy for their desired security level. You might come into a company as an employee or consultant who needs to work within the company's existing mindset. In other cases, an organization won't have a policy defined; it might not even know what type of security it needs. Just don't jump the gun and assume that you need to complete Step 1 from scratch.

The most important parts of vulnerability management are the finding and mitigating of vulnerabilities. Actual tools used to conduct vulnerability assessments include network mappers, port scanners, and other vulnerability scanners, ping scanners, protocol analyzers (also called network sniffers), and password crackers.

Vulnerability assessments might discover confidential data or sensitive data that is not properly protected, open ports, weak passwords, default configurations, prior attacks, system failures, and so on. Vulnerability assessments or vulnerability scanning can be taken to the next level by administering a penetration test.

Penetration Testing

Penetration testing is a method of evaluating the security of a system by simulating one or more attacks on that system. One of the differences between regular vulnerability scanning and penetration testing is that vulnerability scanning *may* be passive or active, whereas penetration testing *will* be active. Generally, vulnerability scans will not exploit found threats, but penetration testing will definitely exploit those threats. Another difference is that vulnerability scanning will seek out all vulnerabilities and weaknesses within an organization. But penetration tests are designed to determine the impact of a particular threat against an organization. For each individual threat, a different penetration test will be planned.

A penetration test—pen test for short—can be done blind, as in black-box testing, where the tester has little or no knowledge of the computer, infrastructure, or environment that is being tested. This simulates an attack from a person who is unfamiliar with the system. White-box testing is the converse, where the tester is provided with complete knowledge of the computer, user credentials, infrastructure, or environment to be tested. And gray-box testing is when the tester is given limited inside knowledge of the system or network. Generally, penetration testing is performed on servers or network devices that face the Internet publicly. This would be an example of external security testing—when a test is conducted from outside the organization's security perimeter.

One common pen test technique is the **pivot**. Once an attacker or tester has gained access to a system with an initial exploit, the pivot allows for movement to other systems in the network. Pivoting might occur through the same exploit used to compromise the first system; a second exploit; or information discovered when accessing a previous system—also known as pillaging. Pivoting can be prevented through the use of host-based IDS and IPS, secure coding, network-based solutions such as unified threat management (UTM), and, of course, good solid network and system planning.

Another technique is that of *persistence*. As the name implies, an attacker/tester will attempt to reconnect at a later date using a backdoor, privilege escalation, and cryptographic keys. Whatever the method, it would have to endure reboots of the target system. Consider developing systems that are non-persistent by using a master image, and then utilizing snapshots, reverting to known states, rolling back to known good configurations, and using live boot media.

Another exploit is the **race condition**. This is a difficult exploit to perform because it takes advantage of the small window of time between when a service is used and its corresponding security control is executed in an application or OS, or when temporary files are created. It can be defined as anomalous behavior due to a dependence on timing of events. Race conditions are also known as time-of-check (TOC) or time-of-use (TOU) attacks. Imagine that you are tasked with changing the permissions to a folder, or changing the rights in an ACL. If you remove all of the permissions and apply new permissions, then there will be a short period of time where the resource (and system) might be vulnerable. This depends on the system used, how it defaults, and how well you have planned your security architecture. That was a basic example, but the race condition is more common within the programming of an application. This exploit can be prevented by proper secure coding of applications, and planning of the system and network architecture.

Following are a couple methodologies for accomplishing penetration testing:

- **The Open Source Security Testing Methodology Manual (OSSTMM):** This manual and corresponding methodology define the proper way to conduct security testing. It adheres to the scientific method. The manual is freely obtained from ISECOM.

- **NIST penetration testing:** This is discussed in the document SP800-115. This document and methodology is less thorough than the OSSTMM; however, many organizations find it satisfactory because it comes from a department of the U.S. government. At times, it refers to the OSSTMM instead of going into more detail.

NOTE   Penetration testing can become even more intrusive (active) when it is associated with DLL injection testing. This is when dynamic link libraries are forced to run within currently used memory space, influencing the behavior of programs in a way the creator did not intend or anticipate.

OVAL

The **Open Vulnerability and Assessment Language (OVAL)** is a standard designed to regulate the transfer of secure public information across networks and the Internet utilizing any security tools and services available at the time. It is an international standard but is funded by the U.S. Department of Homeland Security. A worldwide OVAL community contributes to the standard, storing OVAL content in several locations, such as the MITRE Corporation (http://oval.mitre.org/). OVAL can be defined in two parts: the OVAL Language and the OVAL Interpreter.

- **OVAL Language:** Three different XML schemas have been developed that act as the framework of OVAL:

  1. System testing information
  2. System state analysis
  3. Assessment results reporting

  OVAL is not a language like C++ but is an XML schema that defines and describes the XML documents to be created for use with OVAL.

- **OVAL Interpreter:** A reference developed to ensure that the correct syntax is used by comparing it to OVAL schemas and definitions. Several downloads are associated with the OVAL Interpreter and help files and forums that enable security people to check their work for accuracy.

OVAL has several uses, one of which is as a tool to standardize security advisory distributions. Software vendors need to publish vulnerabilities in a standard, machine-readable format. By including an authoring tool, definitions repository, and definition evaluator, OVAL enables users to regulate their security advisories. Other uses for OVAL include vulnerability assessment, patch management, auditing, threat indicators, and so on.

Some of the entities that use OVAL include Hewlett-Packard, Red Hat Inc., CA Inc., and the U.S. Army CERDEC (Communications-Electronics Research, Development and Engineering Center).

Additional Vulnerabilities

Table 12-3 shows a list of general vulnerabilities that you should watch for and basic prevention methods. We'll discuss some of the security tools that you can use to assess vulnerabilities and prevent exploits in the following section.

Table 12-3 General Vulnerabilities and Basic Prevention Methods

Vulnerability	Prevention Methods
Improper input handling	Secure coding, SDLC (see Chapter 5)
Improper error handling	
Memory vulnerabilities	
Default configuration	Harden systems (see Chapter 4)
Design weaknesses	Proper network design (see Chapter 6)
Resource exhaustion	Properly configure and audit permissions (see Chapter 11)
Improperly configured accounts	

Vulnerability	Prevention Methods
System sprawl	Proper network auditing (see Chapter 6 and Chapter 13)
End-of-life systems	SDLC (see Chapter 5)
Vulnerable business processes	Implement secure policies (Chapter 18)
Weak ciphers	Upgrade encryption (see Chapter 14 and Chapter 9)
Improper certificates	Review certificates, use a CRL (see Chapter 15)
New threats	Keep abreast of latest CVEs and CWEs (see Chapter 6 and Chapter 5)
Zero-day attacks	Plan for unknowns (see Chapter 7)
Untrained users	Educate users about social engineering methods (see Chapter 17)
	Educate users about malware and attacks (see Chapter 2 and Chapter 7)

Assessing Vulnerability with Security Tools

Until now, we have talked about processes, methodologies, and concepts. But without actual security tools, testing, analyzing, and assessing cannot be accomplished. This section delves into the security assessment tools you might use in the field today, and shows how to interpret the results that you receive from those tools.

Computers and networks are naturally vulnerable. Whether it is an operating system or an appliance installed out-of-the-box, they are inherently insecure. Vulnerabilities could come in the form of backdoors or open ports. They could also be caused after installation due to poor design.

To understand what can be affected, security administrators should possess thorough computer and network documentation, and if they don't already, they should develop it themselves. Tools such as Microsoft Visio and network mapping tools can help to create proper network documentation. Then, tools such as vulnerability scanners, protocol analyzers, and password crackers should be used to assess the level of vulnerability on a computer network. When vulnerabilities are found, they should be eliminated or reduced as much as possible. Finally, scanning tools should be used again to prove that the vulnerabilities to the computer network have been removed.

You will find that most of the tools described in this section are used by security administrators and hackers alike. The former group uses the tools to find vulnerabilities and mitigate risk. The latter group uses the tools to exploit those vulnerabilities. However, remember that not all hackers are malevolent. Some are just curious, but they can cause just as much damage and downtime as a malicious hacker.

Network Mapping

Network documentation is an important part of defining the desired state of security. To develop adequate detailed network documentation, network mapping software should be used with network diagramming software. **Network mapping** is the study of physical and logical connectivity of networks. One example of automated network mapping software is the Network Topology Mapper by SolarWinds. This product can map elements on layers 1 through 3 of the OSI model, giving you a thorough representation of what is on the network. This type of network scan is not for the "weak of bandwidth." It should be attempted only during off-hours (if there is such a thing nowadays), if possible; otherwise, when the network is at its lowest point of usage. Most network mapping programs show routers, layer 3 switches, client computers, servers, and virtual machines. You can usually export the mapped contents directly to Microsoft Visio, a handy time-saver.

Plenty of other free and pay versions of network mapping software are available. A quick Internet search displays a list. Try out different programs, get to know them, and decide what works best for your infrastructure.

Wireless networks can be surveyed in a similar fashion. Applications such as Air-Magnet can map out the wireless clients on your network, and apps such as Net-Stumbler can locate the available WAPs. Both can output the information as you want to aid in your network documentation efforts.

When you are working on your network documentation, certain areas of the network probably need to be filled in manually. Some devices are tough to scan, and you have to rely on your eyes and other network administrators' knowledge to get a clear picture of the network. Network documentation can be written out or developed with a network diagramming program, such as Microsoft Visio. (A free trial is available at Microsoft's Office website.) Visio can make all kinds of diagrams and flowcharts that can be real time-savers and helpful planning tools for network administrators and security people. An example of a network diagram is shown in Figure 12-1. This network diagram was created by mapping a now-defunct network with network mapping software, exporting those results to Visio, and then making some tweaks to the diagram manually. Names and IP addresses (among other things) were changed to protect the innocent. This documentation helped to discover a few weaknesses such as the lack of firewalling and other DMZ issues such as the lack of CIDR notation on the DMZ IP network. Just the act of documenting revealed some other issues with some of the servers on the DMZ, making it much easier to mitigate risk. When the risks were mitigated, the resulting final network documentation acted as a foundation for later security analysis and comparison to future baselines.

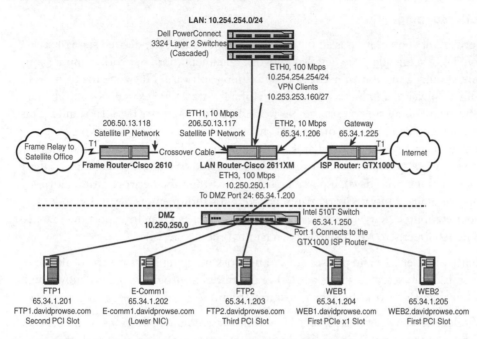

Figure 12-1 Network Diagram Created with Microsoft Visio

At times, you might be tempted to put passwords into a network diagram—don't do it! If there are too many passwords to memorize, and you need to keep passwords stored somewhere, the best way is to write them on a piece of paper and lock that paper in a fireproof, non-removable safe, perhaps offsite. The people (admins) who know the combination to the safe should be limited. Don't keep passwords on any computers!

You might also want to keep a list of IP addresses, computer names, and so on. This can be done on paper, within Excel or Access, or can be developed within your network mapping program and exported as you want. I find that Excel works great because I can sort different categories by the column header.

To summarize, network mapping can help in several of the vulnerability assessment phases. Be sure to use network mapping programs and document your network thoroughly. It can aid you when baselining and analyzing your networks and systems.

Vulnerability Scanning

Vulnerability scanning is a technique that identifies threats on your network, but does not exploit them. When you are ready to assess the level of vulnerability on the network, it is wise to use a general vulnerability scanner and a port scanner (or two). By scanning all the systems on the network, you determine the attack surface of those systems, and you can gain much insight as to the risks that you need to mitigate, and malicious activity that might already be going on underneath your nose. One such vulnerability scanner is called Nessus. This is one of many exploitation framework tools, but it is a very commonly deployed tool used to perform vulnerability, configuration, and compliance assessments. The tool can use a lot of resources, so it is wise to try to perform scans off-hours.

Sometimes, a full-blown vulnerability scanner isn't necessary (or within budget). There will be times when you simply want to scan ports or run other basic tests. As previously discussed in Chapter 7, an example of a good **port scanner** is Nmap. Although this tool has other functionality in addition to port scanning, it is probably best known for its port scanning capability. Figure 12-2 shows an example of a port scan with Nmap. This shows a scan (using the -sS parameter) to a computer that runs Kerberos (port 88), DNS (port 53), and web services (port 80), among other things. By using a port scanner like this one, you are taking a fingerprint of the operating system. The port scanner tells you what inbound ports are open on the remote computer and what services are running. From this, you can discern much more information, for example, what operating system the computer is running, what applications, and so on. In the example in Figure 12-2, you can gather that the scanned computer is a Microsoft domain controller running additional services. So, this is an example of OS fingerprinting.

Key Topic

```
C:\WINDOWS\system32\cmd.exe                                          _ 8 X

C:\>cd nmap

C:\nmap>nmap -sS 172.29.250.200

Starting nmap 3.75 ( http://www.insecure.org/nmap ) at 2009-02-04 12:06 Eastern Standard Time
Interesting ports on 2003DC (172.29.250.200):
(The 1645 ports scanned but not shown below are in state: closed)
PORT       STATE SERVICE
21/tcp     open  ftp
23/tcp     open  telnet
53/tcp     open  domain
80/tcp     open  http
88/tcp     open  kerberos-sec
135/tcp    open  msrpc
139/tcp    open  netbios-ssn
389/tcp    open  ldap
445/tcp    open  microsoft-ds
464/tcp    open  kpasswd5
593/tcp    open  http-rpc-epmap
636/tcp    open  ldapssl
1025/tcp   open  NFS-or-IIS
1027/tcp   open  IIS
1433/tcp   open  ms-sql-s
3268/tcp   open  globalcatLDAP
3269/tcp   open  globalcatLDAPssl
3389/tcp   open  ms-term-serv
MAC Address: 00:60:08:C0:09:8D (3com)

Nmap run completed -- 1 IP address (1 host up) scanned in 1.883 seconds

C:\nmap>_
```

Figure 12-2 Port Scan with Nmap

Open ports should be examined. You should be fully aware of the services or processes that use those ports. If services are unnecessary, they should be stopped and disabled. For example, if this computer was indeed a domain controller but wasn't supposed to be a DNS server, the DNS service (port 53) should be stopped. Otherwise, the DNS port could act as a vulnerability of the server. Afterward, the computer should be rescanned to ensure that the risk has been mitigated.

Nonessential services are often not configured, monitored, or secured by the network administrator. It is imperative that network administrators scan for nonessential services and close any corresponding ports. Even though services may be nonessential, that doesn't necessarily mean that they are not in use, maliciously or otherwise.

Another excellent tool is *netcat* (and Ncat), which is generally used in Linux/Unix platforms. It can be used for port scanning, port listening, transferring files, opening raw connections, and as a backdoor into systems. As discussed in Chapter 10, "Physical Security and Authentication Models, another tool that can be used to display the ports in use is the `netstat` command. Examples include the `netstat`, `netstat -a`, `netstat -n`, and `netstat -an` commands. However, this is only for the local computer, but it does show the ports used by the remote computer for the sessions that the local computer is running.

NOTE There are other basic port scanners you can use, such as Angry IP Scanner (and plenty of other free port scanners on the Internet). Some of these tools can be used as ping scanners, sending out ICMP echoes to find the IP addresses within a particular network segment.

Tools such as Nmap and Nessus are also known as network enumerators. *Enumeration* refers to a complete listing of items (such as port numbers); network enumerators extract information from servers including network shares, services running, groups of users, and so on. It is this additional extraction of information (enumerating) that sets them apart from a basic network mapping tool. This type of enumeration is also referred to as banner grabbing. **Banner grabbing** is a technique used to find out information about web servers, FTP servers, and mail servers. For example, it might be used by a network administrator to take inventory of systems and services running on servers. Or, it could be used by an attacker to grab information such as HTTP headers, which can tell the attacker what type of server is running, its version number, and so on. Examples of banner-grabbing applications include Netcat and Telnet. Aside from the security administrator (and perhaps auditors), no one should be running banner-grabbing tools, or network enumeration tools in general. A good security admin will attempt to sniff out any unpermitted usage of these tools.

Network Sniffing

For all intents and purposes, the terms *protocol analyzer*, *packet sniffer*, and *network sniffer* all mean the same thing. "Sniffing" the network is when you use a tool to find and investigate other computers on the network; the term is often used when capturing packets for later analysis. **Protocol analyzers** can tell you much more about the traffic that is coming and going to and from a host than a vulnerability scanner or port scanner might. In reality, the program captures Ethernet frames of information directly from the network adapter and displays the packets inside those frames within a capture window. Each packet is *encapsulated* inside a frame.

One common example of a protocol analyzer is Wireshark, which is a free download that can run on a variety of platforms. By default, it captures packets on the local computer that it was installed on. Figure 12-3 shows an example of a packet capture. This capture is centered on frame number 10, which encapsulates an ICMP packet. This particular packet is a ping request sent from the local computer (10.254.254.205) to the remote host (10.254.254.1). Although my local computer can definitely send out pings, it is unknown whether 10.254.254.1 should be replying to those pings. Perhaps there is a desired policy that states that this device (which is actually a router) should not reply to pings. As we learned in Chapter 7, "Networking Protocols and Threats," an ICMP reply can be a vulnerability. Now, if we look at frame 11 we see it shows an echo reply from 10.254.254.1—not what we want. So, to mitigate this risk and remove the vulnerability, we would turn off ICMP echo replies on the router.

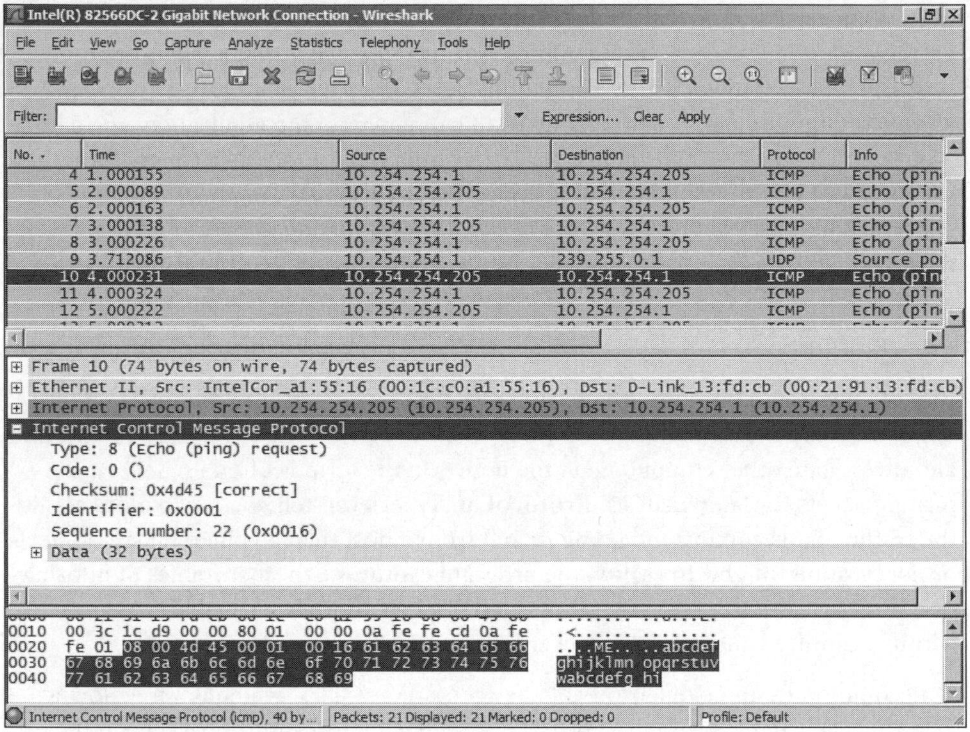

Figure 12-3 Packet Capture with Wireshark

This is just one example of many that we could show with this program. I've used this program to find, among other things, unauthorized FTP, gaming, and P2P traffic! You'd be surprised how often network admins and even regular old users set up these types of servers. It uses up valuable bandwidth and resources, so you can imagine that an organization would want these removed. Not only that, but they can be vulnerabilities as well. By running these services, a person opens up the computer system to a whole new set of threats. By removing these unauthorized servers, we are reducing risk. I know—I'm such a buzzkill. But really now, work is work, and play is play; that's how companies are going to look at it.

On the other side of things, malicious users will utilize a protocol analyzer to capture passwords and other confidential information. We discuss software-based protocol analyzers more in Chapter 13, "Monitoring and Auditing."

There are plenty of other software-based packet sniffers available on the Internet, but Wireshark is the industry standard. Also, hardware-based devices can analyze your networks and hosts; for example, Fluke Networks offers a variety of network testers. These handheld computers often have a built-in GUI-based system that can be used to monitor ports, troubleshoot authentication issues, identify network resources and IP addresses, and lots more. The name *Fluke* is used by some techs even if they use a handheld device by a different vendor; the brand is that well-known.

Password Analysis

Well, we've mapped the network, documented it, scanned for vulnerabilities, scanned ports, and analyzed packets. But wait, let's not forget about passwords. We've mentioned more than once in this book that weak passwords are the bane of today's operating systems and networks. This could be because no policy for passwords was defined, and people naturally gravitate toward weaker, easier-to-remember passwords. Or it could be that a policy was defined but is not complex enough, or is out of date. Whatever the reason, it would be wise to scan computers and other devices for weak passwords with a **password cracker**, which uses comparative analysis to break passwords and systematically guesses until it cracks the password. And of course, a variety of password-cracking programs can help with this. For Windows computers, there is the well-documented Cain & Abel password recovery tool. This program has a bit of a learning curve but is quite powerful. It can be used to crack all kinds of different passwords on the local system or on remote devices and computers. It sniffs out other hosts on the network the way a protocol analyzer would. This is an excellent tool to find out whether weak passwords are on the network, or to help if users forget their passwords (when password resets are not possible). Figure 12-4 shows an example of Cain & Abel. You can see hashed passwords (encrypted) that the program has discovered for various accounts on a test computer. From these hashes, the program can attempt to crack the password and deliver the original plaintext version of the password.

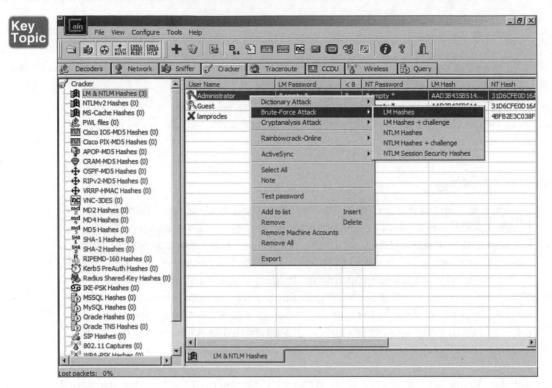

Figure 12-4 Password Cracking with Cain & Abel

We talk more about hashes and hashing algorithms in Chapter 14, "Encryption and Hashing Concepts."

Cain & Abel is a free download, and many other tools are available for various platforms; some free, some not, including ophcrack, John the Ripper, THC-Hydra, Aircrack-ng (used to crack WPA preshared keys), and RainbowCrack. Some of these tools have additional functionality but are known best as password/passphrase-cracking tools, although they can be used by security administrators in a legitimate sense as password recovery programs.

The following list shows the various password-cracking methods. Password recovery (or cracking) can be done in several different ways:

- **Guessing:** Weak passwords can be guessed by a smart person, especially if the person has knowledge of the user he is trying to exploit. Blank passwords are all too common. And then there are common passwords such as password, admin, secret, love, and many more. If a guessing attacker knew the person and some of the person's details, he might attempt the person's username as the password, or someone the person knows, date of birth, and so on. Reversing letters or adding a 1 to the end of a password are other common methods.

Although guessing is not as much of a technical method as the following three options, it reveals many passwords every day all over the world.

- **Dictionary attack:** Uses a prearranged list of likely words, trying each of them one at a time. It can be used for cracking passwords, passphrases, and keys. It works best with weak passwords and when targeting multiple systems. The power of the dictionary attack depends on the strength of the dictionary used by the password-cracking program.

- **Brute-force attack:** When every possible password instance is attempted. This is often a last resort due to the amount of CPU resources it might require. It works best on shorter passwords but can theoretically break any password given enough time and CPU power. For example, a four-character, lowercase password with no numbers or symbols could be cracked quickly. But a ten-character, complex password would take much longer; some computers will fail to complete the process. Also, you must consider whether the attack is online or offline. Online means that a connection has been made to the host, giving the password-cracking program only a short window to break the password. Offline means that there is no connection and that the password-cracking computer knows the target host's password hash and hashing algorithm, giving the cracking computer more (or unlimited) time to make the attempt. Some password-cracking programs are considered hybrids and make use of dictionary attacks (for passwords with actual words in them) and brute-force attacks (for complex passwords).

NOTE   Some attackers will utilize software that can perform hybrid attacks that consist of successive dictionary and brute-force attacks.

- **Cryptanalysis attack:** Uses a considerable set of precalculated encrypted passwords located in a lookup table. These tables are known as **rainbow tables**, and the type of password attack is also known as precomputation, where all words in the dictionary (or a specific set of possible passwords) are hashed and stored. This is done in an attempt to recover passwords quicker. It is used with the ophcrack and RainbowCrack applications. This attack can be defeated by implementing **salting**, which is the randomization of the hashing process.

Knowledgeable attackers understand where password information is stored. In Windows, it is stored in an encrypted binary format within the SAM hive. In Linux, the data used to verify passwords was historically stored in the /etc/passwd file, but in newer Linux systems the passwd file only shows an X, and the real password information is stored in another file, perhaps /etc/shadow, or elsewhere in an encrypted format.

Aside from using password-cracking programs, passwords can be obtained through viruses and Trojans, wiretapping, keystroke logging, network sniffing, phishing, shoulder surfing, and dumpster diving. Yikes! It should go without mentioning that protecting passwords is just as important as creating complex passwords and configuring complex password policies that are also periodically monitored and updated. Remember that password policies created on a Windows Server do not have jurisdiction where other vendors' devices are concerned, such as Cisco routers and firewalls or Check Point security devices. These need to be checked individually or by scanning particular network segments.

We could talk about password cracking for days because there are so many types of hashes, hashing algorithms, and password-cracking tools and ways to crack the passwords. But for the Security+ exam, a basic understanding of password cracking is enough.

Chapter Summary

It's a fact: As people, we are vulnerable to all kinds of medical conditions, injuries, maladies, and so on. However, the typical human being tends to find an equilibrium with himself or herself...and with nature. By this I mean that a person tends to automatically prevent medical problems from happening, and performs a certain level of self-healing when many problems do occur. We are intuitive. We drink water *before* we become dehydrated. We sleep before we become overtired. Most of the time, we automatically defend ourselves from germs and viruses, because we have consciously (and unconsciously) focused on preventative maintenance for our bodies and minds.

In a way, this philosophy can also be applied to technology. Your organization's technology environment—in all of its parts—can be treated as a sort of entity; similar to the bond a captain might have with a seagoing vessel. When this synergy happens, a person spends more productive time working on preventing problems, and as a result, spends less time fixing issues that occurred due to a compromise simply because compromises end up happening less frequently. Just as the captain will inspect the hull of a ship with a keen set of eyes, you must constantly inspect all parts of your technology for current and potential vulnerabilities. As Benjamin Franklin said, "An ounce of prevention is worth a pound of cure." It's a cliché, yet so necessary to revisit from time to time.

There are a great many terms, acronyms, and definitions when it comes to security analysis, but it all boils down to vulnerabilities, and how to prevent threats from exploiting them—that is, minimizing risk. You must plan ahead; not just for current attacks and CVEs, but also for what is on the horizon. Time must be spent considering what will happen to an installed device or computer in a year, or five years. That time will be here before you know it!

Define the risk, as it appears now, and as it will appear in the future. Reduce as much risk as possible, so that all but the most unlikely threats will be prevented. It's that prevention that is the key. Of all the security controls, prevention is the most important. One excellent way to be sure that you are doing your best to *prevent* problems is to use a vulnerability management process. This leaves nothing to chance. Another masterful way to manage vulnerabilities is to utilize automation. You can't clone yourself (yet), but you can clone your administrations. The size of your IT environment and the level of automation you employ should be proportionate.

Penetration testing, vulnerability scanning, port scanning, network sniffing, and password analysis are all just methods to be used within your risk and vulnerability assessments. You might use some methodologies, and not others, and you might perform assessments in an active or passive manner. That will depend on the particulars of your network and the level of criticality of your IT environment. And you may use different methods than the ones listed in this chapter, or develop new ones in the future. The list is in no way finite. The crucial point is to realize that you are taking the consolidated information you glean and using it to define the real risk to your organization in an intuitive way.

So, think of your IT infrastructure as a sort of living, breathing entity: One that relies on you as much as you rely on it.

Chapter Review Activities

Use the features in this section to study and review the topics in this chapter.

Review Key Topics

Review the most important topics in the chapter, noted with the Key Topic icon in the outer margin of the page. Table 12-4 lists a reference of these key topics and the page number on which each is found.

Table 12-4   Key Topics for Chapter 12

Key Topic Element	Description	Page Number
Table 12-1	Example of quantitative risk assessment	401
Table 12-2	Summary of risk assessment types	402

Key Topic Element	Description	Page Number
Bulleted list	Preventive, detective, and corrective security controls	404
Step list	Five steps of vulnerability management	405
Figure 12-2	Port scan with Nmap	413
Figure 12-3	Packet capture with Wireshark	416
Figure 12-4	Password cracking with Cain & Abel	418
Bulleted list	Password-cracking methods	418

Define Key Terms

Define the following key terms from this chapter, and check your answers in the glossary:

vulnerability, risk, risk management, information assurance (IA), risk transference, risk avoidance, risk reduction, risk acceptance, residual risk, risk assessment, risk register, qualitative risk assessment, risk mitigation, quantitative risk assessment, mean time between failures (MTBF), passive reconnaissance, active reconnaissance, vulnerability management, vulnerability assessment, penetration testing, pivot, race condition, Open Vulnerability and Assessment Language (OVAL), network mapping, vulnerability scanning, port scanner, banner grabbing, protocol analyzer, password cracker, dictionary attack, brute-force attack, cryptanalysis attack, rainbow tables, salting

Complete the Real-World Scenarios

Complete the Real-World Scenarios found on the companion website (www.pearsonitcertification.com/title/9780789758996). You will find a PDF containing the scenario and questions, and also supporting videos and simulations.

Review Questions

Answer the following review questions. Check your answers with the correct answers that follow.

1. Which type of vulnerability assessments software can check for weak passwords on the network?

   A. Wireshark

   B. Antivirus software

    C. Performance Monitor

    D. A password cracker

2. Which of the following has schemas written in XML?

    A. OVAL

    B. 3DES

    C. WPA

    D. PAP

3. Russ is using only documentation to test the security of a system. What type of testing methodology is this known as?

    A. Active security analysis

    B. Passive security analysis

    C. Hybrid security analysis

    D. Hands-on security analysis

4. Of the following, which is the best way for a person to find out what security holes exist on the network?

    A. Run a port scan.

    B. Use a network sniffer.

    C. Perform a vulnerability assessment.

    D. Use an IDS solution.

5. After using Nmap to do a port scan of your server, you find that several ports are open. Which of the following should you do next?

    A. Leave the ports open and monitor them for malicious attacks.

    B. Run the port scan again.

    C. Close all ports.

    D. Examine the services and/or processes that use those ports.

6. Which of the following is a vulnerability assessment tool?

    A. John the Ripper

    B. Aircrack-ng

    C. Nessus

    D. Cain & Abel

7. You are a consultant for an IT company. Your boss asks you to determine the topology of the network. What is the best device to use in this circumstance?

   A. Network mapper

   B. Protocol analyzer

   C. Port scanner

   D. Vulnerability scanner

8. Which of the following can enable you to find all the open ports on an entire network?

   A. Protocol analyzer

   B. Network scanner

   C. Firewall

   D. Performance monitor

9. What can attackers accomplish using malicious port scanning?

   A. "Fingerprint" of the operating system

   B. Topology of the network

   C. All the computer names on the network

   D. All the usernames and passwords

10. Many companies send passwords via clear text. Which of the following can view these passwords?

    A. Rainbow table

    B. Port scanner

    C. John the Ripper

    D. Protocol analyzer

11. Which of the following persons is ultimately in charge of deciding how much residual risk there will be?

    A. Chief security officer

    B. Security administrator

    C. Senior management

    D. Disaster recovery plan coordinator

12. To show risk from a monetary standpoint, which of the following should risk assessments be based upon?

   A. Survey of loss, potential threats, and asset value

   B. Quantitative measurement of risk, impact, and asset value

   C. Complete measurement of all threats

   D. Qualitative measurement of risk and impact

13. The main objective of risk management in an organization is to reduce risk to a level _____. (Fill in the blank.)

   A. the organization will mitigate

   B. where the ARO equals the SLE

   C. the organization will accept

   D. where the ALE is lower than the SLE

14. Why would a security administrator use a vulnerability scanner? (Select the best answer.)

   A. To identify remote access policies

   B. To analyze protocols

   C. To map the network

   D. To find open ports on a server

15. An example of a program that does comparative analysis is what?

   A. Protocol analyzer

   B. Password cracker

   C. Port scanner

   D. Event Viewer

16. Why do attackers often target nonessential services? (Select the two best answers.)

   A. Often they are not configured correctly.

   B. They are not monitored as often.

   C. They are not used.

   D. They are not monitored by an IDS.

17. Which of the following tools uses ICMP as its main underlying protocol?

   A. Ping scanner

   B. Port scanner

   C. Image scanner

   D. Barcode scanner

18. Which command would display the following output?

```
Active Connections
Proto  Local Address       Foreign Address      State
TCP    WorkstationA:1395   8.15.228.165:http    ESTABLISHED
```

   A. Ping

   B. Ipconfig

   C. Nbtstat

   D. Netstat

19. Which of the following is used when performing a quantitative risk analysis?

   A. Asset value

   B. Surveys

   C. Focus groups

   D. Best practices

20. You have been tasked with running a penetration test on a server. You have been given limited knowledge about the inner workings of the server. What kind of test will you be performing?

   A. White-box

   B. Gray-box

   C. Black-box

   D. Passive vulnerability scan

21. Which of the following is a technical control?

   A. Disaster recovery plan

   B. Baseline configuration development

   C. Least privilege implementation

   D. Categorization of system security

22. Which of the following is a detective security control?

   A. Bollards

   B. Firewall

   C. Tape backup

   D. CCTV

23. Which of the following would you make use of when performing a qualitative risk analysis?

   A. Judgment

   B. Asset value

   C. Threat frequency

   D. SLE

24. What is the best action to take when you conduct a corporate vulnerability assessment?

   A. Document your scan results for the change control board.

   B. Examine vulnerability data with a network sniffer.

   C. Update systems.

   D. Organize data based on severity and asset value.

25. You are implementing a new enterprise database server. After you evaluate the product with various vulnerability scans you determine that the product is not a threat in of itself but it has the potential to introduce new vulnerabilities to your network. Which assessment should you now take into consideration while you continue to evaluate the database server?

   A. Risk assessment

   B. Code assessment

   C. Vulnerability assessment

   D. Threat assessment

26. Why should penetration testing only be done during controlled conditions?

   A. Because vulnerability scanners can cause network flooding.

   B. Because penetration testing actively tests security controls and can cause system instability.

   C. Because white-box penetration testing cannot find zero-day attacks.

   D. Because penetration testing passively tests security controls and can cause system instability.

27. You are attempting to prevent unauthorized access to the desktop computers on your network. You decide to have the computers' operating systems lock after 5 minutes of inactivity. What type of security control is this?

    A. Detective

    B. Operational

    C. Management

    D. Technical

28. Which of the following methods can be used by a security administrator to recover a user's forgotten password from a password-protected file?

    A. Brute-force

    B. Packet sniffing

    C. Social engineering

    D. Cognitive password

29. A security admin is running a security analysis where information about a target system is gained without engaging or exploiting the system. Which of the following describes this type of analysis? (Select the best answer.)

    A. Banner grabbing

    B. ALE assessment

    C. Active reconnaissance

    D. Passive reconnaissance

Answers and Explanations

1. **D.** A password cracker can check for weak passwords on the network. Antivirus software can scan for viruses on a computer. Performance Monitor enables you to create baselines to check the performance of a computer. Wireshark is a protocol analyzer.

2. **A.** OVAL (Open Vulnerability and Assessment Language) uses XML as a framework for the language. It is a community standard dealing with the standardization of information transfer. 3DES is an encryption algorithm. WPA is a wireless encryption standard, and the deprecated PAP is the Password Authentication Protocol, used for identifying users to a server.

3. **B.** Passive security analysis or passive security testing would be one that possibly does not include a hands-on test. It is less tangible and often includes the

use of documentation only. To better protect a system or network, a person should also use active security analysis.

4. **C.** The best way to find all the security holes that exist on a network is to perform a vulnerability assessment. This may include utilizing a port scanner and using a network sniffer and perhaps using some sort of IDS.

5. **D.** If you find ports open that you don't expect, be sure to examine the services and/or processes that use those ports. You may have to close some or all those ports. When you finish with your examination, and after you have taken action, run the port scan again to verify that those ports are closed.

6. **C.** Nessus is a vulnerability assessment tool. Aircrack-ng is used to crack wireless encryption codes. John the Ripper and Cain & Abel are password-cracking programs.

7. **A.** A network mapper is the best tool to use to determine the topology of the network and to find out what devices and computers reside on that network. One example of this is the Network Topology Mapper.

8. **B.** A network scanner is a port scanner used to find open ports on multiple computers on the network. A protocol analyzer is used to delve into packets. A firewall protects a network, and a performance monitor is used to create baselines for and monitor a computer.

9. **A.** Port scanning can be used in a malicious way to find out all the openings to a computer's operating system; this is known as the "fingerprint" of the operating system. Port scanning cannot find out the topology of the network, computer names, usernames, or passwords.

10. **D.** A protocol analyzer can delve into the packets sent across the network and determine whether those packets contain clear-text passwords. Rainbow tables and John the Ripper deal with cracking passwords that were previously encrypted; they aren't necessary if the passwords were sent via clear text. Port scanners scan computers for any open ports.

11. **C.** Residual risk is the risk left over after a security plan and a disaster recovery plan have been implemented. There is always risk, because a company cannot possibly foresee every future event, nor can it secure against every single threat. Senior management as a collective whole is ultimately responsible for deciding how much residual risk there will be in a company's network. No one person should be in charge of this, but it should be decided on as a group. If the group decides that residual risk is too high, the group might decide to get insurance in addition to its security plan. The security administrator is in charge of finding and removing risks to the network and systems and should mitigate risks if possible. The disaster recovery plan (DRP) coordinator usually

assesses risks and documents them, along with creating strategies to defend against any disastrous problems that might occur from that risk, but that person does not decide on the amount of acceptable residual risk to a company.

12. **B.** When dealing with dollars, risk assessments should be based upon a quantitative measurement of risk, impact, and asset value.

13. **C.** The main objective of risk management is to reduce risk to a level that the organization or company will accept. Mitigation is the act of reducing threats in general.

14. **D.** The best answer for why a security administrator would use a vulnerability scanner is to find open ports on a particular computer. Although a vulnerability scanner can do more than scan for open ports, it is the best answer listed.

15. **B.** A password cracker is considered to be a program that does comparative analysis. It systematically guesses the password and compares all previous guesses before making new ones until it cracks the password.

16. **A and B.** Nonessential services are often not configured and secured by the network administrator; this goes hand-in-hand with the fact that they are not monitored as often as essential services. It is imperative that network administrators scan for nonessential services and close any corresponding ports. Even though services may be nonessential, that doesn't necessarily mean that they are not used. An IDS, if installed properly, should monitor everything on a given system.

17. **A.** A ping scanner uses the Internet Control Message Protocol (ICMP) to conduct its scans. Ping uses ICMP as its underlying protocol and IP and ARP. Image scanners are found in printers and as standalone items that scan images, photos, and text into a computer. Barcode scanners are used to scan barcodes, for example, at the supermarket.

18. **D.** Netstat shows sessions including the local computer and remote computer. It shows these connections by computer name (or IP) and port name (or number).

19. **A.** Asset value is assigned when performing quantitative risk analysis. Surveys, focus groups, and best practices might help with qualitative risk analysis but do not offer concrete data that a quantitative risk analysis requires. Money is the key ingredient here when it comes to quantitative risk analysis.

20. **B.** When you are given limited information of a system or network, it is known as gray-box testing. White-box testing is when you are given in-depth or complete information about the system. Black-box testing is when you know very little (or nothing) about the system to be tested. Penetration tests are active and are meant to test for a single threat and exploit it. Passive vulnerability

scans are different tests altogether and test for as many threats as they can find, without exploiting one of them.

21. **C.** The least privilege concept is executed as a technical control. A process that is severely limited in its functionality and a user who has very limited rights are some of the things that must be initiated technically. A disaster recovery plan and baseline configuration development would be operational controls. The categorization of system security would be a management control.

22. **D.** CCTV (closed-circuit television) is an example of a detective security control. It can detect who is entering a building and when it happened. Bollards (vertical posts often found in parking lots or in front of doorways) and firewalls are preventive controls, while tape backup is a corrective control.

23. **A.** When performing a qualitative risk analysis, a person often uses his own judgment. Asset value, threat frequency, and SLE (single loss expectancy) are all components of a quantitative risk analysis.

24. **D.** When conducting vulnerability assessments, you should organize the collected data by vulnerability and exploit severity as well as the asset value of the possibly affected equipment/systems. Documenting your scan results for a change control board may come later depending on some decision-making by the corporation. You should have already used a network sniffer to find vulnerabilities and possible exploits. Updating the systems will most likely happen at some point, but for the time being, it should be a recommendation within your vulnerability assessment. Management will decide how and if that will occur.

25. **A.** If a new solution poses the potential for new vulnerabilities to your network, you should run an in-depth risk assessment of the new product. In this case, you are not yet doing any coding, so a code assessment is not necessary, but should be implemented as part of a secure code review in the case that you make any programming changes to the database server. You have already run a vulnerability assessment when you did the vulnerability scans. You found that the solution is not a threat but could pose other threats. The risk assessment defines what kind of issues your organization could face due to the threats and vulnerabilities.

26. **B.** Penetration testing is an active test that seeks to exploit one vulnerability. It can indeed cause system instability, so it should be run only during controlled conditions and with express consent of the system owner. Vulnerability scanners are usually passive and should not cause network flooding. Zero-day attacks are based on vulnerabilities that are unknown to the system designer. In a white-box testing environment, zero-day vulnerabilities may become uncovered (at which point they are not quite zero-day anymore), but the fact remains that penetration testing can cause system instability.

27. **D.** An operating system lock (or screen saver lock) is an example of a technical control; it is also considered more technically to be a preventive control. An example of a detective control would be CCTV. An example of an operational control would be security awareness training. An example of a management security control would be the software development life cycle (SDLC).

28. **A.** The brute-force method can be used to recover a user's password from a protected file or otherwise protected area of an operating system. Tools such as these are used by security administrators to recover passwords, but are also used by attackers to crack password codes in order to obtain unauthorized access. Packet sniffing can be used to find passwords that have been sent over the network in clear text (which happens more often than you might suspect), but cannot crack the password stored in a protected file. Social engineering is when con artists attempt to find out information (such as a password) from unsuspecting users. But in the scenario of the question, the user has forgotten the password (thus the need for recovery), so social engineering would be pointless. The cognitive password is an authentication type where, in addition to the password, the user must answer a question of some sort; used collectively, the authentication system grants access if the answer and the password are correct. This is an excellent method to use in the case an attacker does crack a password, because that second level of authentication (based on the user's knowledge) is necessary. And that is when social engineering could perform wonders, attempting to elicit that information from the user. But again, for this question, brute-force is the answer, because the security administrator is simply trying to recover the password for the user.

29. **D.** If an attacker or white hat is performing passive reconnaissance, that person is attempting to gain information about a target system without engaging the system. For example, a basic port scan of a system, without any further action can be considered passive reconnaissance. However, if the attacker or white hat then uses that information to exploit vulnerabilities associated with those ports, then it is known as active reconnaissance. Banner grabbing is a technique used to find out information about web servers, FTP servers, and mail servers. For example, it might be used by a network administrator to take inventory of systems and services running on servers. Or, it could be used by an attacker to grab information such as HTTP headers, which can tell the attacker what type of server is running, its version number, and so on. Annualized loss expectancy (ALE) is the total loss in dollars per year due to a specific incident. It is computed with the following calculation: SLE × ARO = ALE.

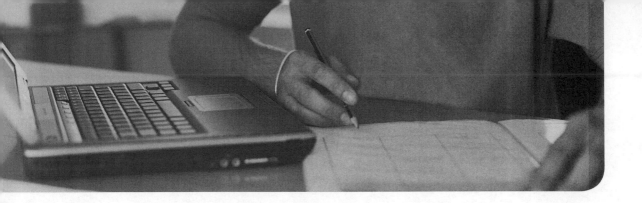

This chapter covers the following subjects:

- **Monitoring Methodologies:** Monitoring the network is extremely important, yet often overlooked by security administrators. In this section, you learn about the various monitoring methodologies that applications and IDS/IPS solutions use.

- **Using Tools to Monitor Systems and Networks:** Here, we delve into the hands-on again. Included in this section are performance analysis tools, such as Performance Monitor, and protocol analysis tools, such as Wireshark.

- **Conducting Audits:** Full-blown audits might be performed by third-party companies, but you as the security administrator should be constantly auditing and logging the network and its hosts. This section gives some good tips to follow when executing an audit and covers some of the tools you would use in a Windows server to perform audits and log them properly.

This chapter discusses monitoring and auditing. Key point: Monitoring alone does not constitute an audit, but audits usually include monitoring. So we cover some monitoring methodologies and monitoring tools before we get into computer security audits. This chapter assumes that you have read through Chapter 12, "Vulnerability and Risk Assessment," and that you will employ the concepts and tools you learned about in that chapter when performing an audit. Chapter 12 and this chapter are strongly intertwined; I broke them into two chapters because there was a bit too much information for just one, and I want to differentiate somewhat between risk and audits. But regardless, these two chapters are all about putting on your sleuthing hat. You might be surprised, but many networking and operating system security issues can be solved by using that old Sherlockian adage: "When you have eliminated the impossible, whatever remains, however improbable, must be the truth." This process of elimination is one of the cornerstones of a good IT troubleshooter and works well in the actual CompTIA Security+ exam.

CHAPTER 13

Monitoring and Auditing

Monitoring Methodologies

To operate a clean, secure network, you must keep an eye on your systems, applications, servers, network devices, power devices, and the entire network in general. One way to do this is to monitor the network. This surveillance of the network in of itself increases the security of your entire infrastructure. By periodically watching everything that occurs on the network, you become more familiar with day-to-day happenings and over time get quicker at analyzing whether an event is legitimate. It can help to think of yourself as Hercule Poirot, the Belgian detective—*seeing* everything that happens on your network, and ultimately *knowing* everything that happens. It might be a bit egotistical sounding, but whoever said that IT people don't have an ego?

This surveillance can be done in one of two ways: manual monitoring or automated monitoring. When manually monitoring the network, you are systematically viewing log files, policies, permissions, and so on. But this can also be automated. For example, there are several data mining programs available that can automatically sift through logs and other files for the exact information you want to know. In addition, applications such as antivirus, intrusion detection systems (IDSs), and intrusion prevention systems (IPSs) can automatically scan for errors, malicious attacks, and anomalies. The three main types of automated monitoring are signature-based, anomaly-based, and behavior-based.

Signature-Based Monitoring

In a **signature-based monitoring** scenario, frames and packets of network traffic are analyzed for predetermined attack patterns. These attack patterns are known as signatures. The signatures are stored in a database that must be updated regularly to have any effect on the security of your network. Many attacks today have their own distinct signatures. However, only the specific attack that matches the signature will be detected. Malicious activity with a slightly different signature might be missed. This makes signature-based monitoring vulnerable to false negatives—when an IDS, IPS, or antivirus system fails to detect an actual attack or error. To protect against this, the signature-based system should be updated to bring the system up to date with the latest signatures. When it comes to intrusion detection systems, the most basic form is the signature-based IDS. However, some signature-based monitoring systems are a bit more advanced and use heuristic signatures. These signatures incorporate an algorithm that determines whether an alarm should be sounded when a specific threshold is met. This type of signature is CPU-intensive and requires fine-tuning. For example, some signature-based IDS solutions use these signatures to conform to particular networking environments.

Anomaly-Based Monitoring

An **anomaly-based monitoring** system (also known as statistical anomaly-based) establishes a performance baseline based on a set of normal network traffic evaluations. These evaluations should be taken when the network and servers are under an average load during regular working hours. This monitoring method then compares current network traffic activity with the previously created baseline to detect whether it is within baseline parameters. If the sampled traffic is outside baseline parameters, an alarm will be triggered and sent to the administrator (as long as the system was configured properly). This type of monitoring is dependent on the accuracy of the baseline. An inaccurate baseline increases the likelihood of obtaining false indicators, such as false positives. Normally, false positives are when the system reads a legitimate event as an attack or other error. This can happen with an improperly configured IDS or IPS solution. If too many false indicator alerts are received by the security administrator, then the IDS/IPS should be reconfigured and baselines recollected, and/or those types of false alarms should be disabled.

Behavior-Based Monitoring

A **behavior-based monitoring** system looks at the previous behavior of applications, executables, and/or the operating system and compares that to current activity on the system. If an application later behaves improperly, the monitoring system will attempt to stop the behavior. This has advantages compared to signature-based and anomaly-based monitoring in that it can to a certain extent help with future events, without having to be updated. However, because there are so many types of applications, and so many types of relationships between applications, this type of monitoring could set off a high amount of false positives. Behavior monitoring should be configured carefully to avoid the system triggering alarms due to legitimate activity.

NOTE Heuristic analysis is often used in combination with behavior-based monitoring as it relates to antivirus software and IDS/IPS solutions. A heuristic in computer science is an algorithm that consistently performs quickly, and provides good results based on a set of rules. Heuristic analysis is designed to detect malicious behavior *without* uniquely identifying it (as is done in a signature-based system). It can find previously unknown malicious behavior by comparing it to known and similar malicious behavior. Then it "guesses" whether something is malicious or not. This can lead to low accuracy and a high percentage of false positives.

Table 13-1 summarizes the monitoring methods discussed. Keep in mind that some systems (IDS, IPS, and so on) might combine more than one of these monitoring methods.

Key Topic

Table 13-1 Summary of Monitoring Methodologies

Monitoring Methodology	Description
Signature-based monitoring	Network traffic is analyzed for predetermined attack patterns.
	These attack patterns are known as signatures.
Anomaly-based monitoring	Establishes a performance baseline based on a set of normal network traffic evaluations.
	Requires a baseline.
Behavior-based monitoring	Looks at the previous behavior of applications, executables, and/or the operating system and compares that to current activity on the system.
	If an application later behaves improperly, the monitoring system will attempt to stop the behavior.
	Requires a baseline.

Using Tools to Monitor Systems and Networks

All the methodologies in the world won't help you unless you know how to use some monitoring tools and how to create baselines. By using performance monitoring gizmos and software, incorporating protocol analyzers, and using other analytical utilities in the GUI and the command-line, you can really "watch" the network and quickly mitigate threats as they present themselves.

In this section, we use the Performance tool in Windows, the Wireshark protocol analyzer, and other analytical tools within the command-line and the GUI. These are just a couple examples of performance and network monitoring tools out there, but they are commonly used in the field and should give you a decent idea of how to work with any tools in those categories.

Performance Baselining

We mentioned in Chapter 4, "OS Hardening and Virtualization," that **baselining** is the process of measuring changes in networking, hardware, software, applications, and so on. Documenting and accounting for changes in a baseline is known as **baseline reporting**. Baseline reporting enables a security administrator to identify the **security posture** of an application, system, or network. The security posture can be defined as the risk level to which a system, or other technology element, is exposed. **Security posture assessments (SPAs)** use baseline reporting and other analyses to discover vulnerabilities and weaknesses in systems.

> **NOTE**   Ultimately, a security baseline will define the basic set of security objectives that must be met by any given service or system. Baseline deviation, meaning any changes or discrepancies as compared to the baseline, should be investigated right away, especially for mission-critical systems and RTOS-based computers.

Let's get into baselining a little more and show one of the software tools you can use to create a baseline.

Creating a baseline consists of selecting something to measure and measuring it consistently for a period of time. For example, we might want to know what the average hourly data transfer is to and from a server's network interface. There are a lot of ways to measure this, but we could possibly use a performance monitoring tool or a protocol analyzer to find out how many packets cross through the server's network adapter. This could be run for 1 hour (during business hours, of course) every day for 2 weeks. Selecting different hours for each day would add more randomness to the final results. By averaging the results together, we get a baseline. Then we can compare future measurements of the server to the baseline. This helps us define what the standard load of our server is and the requirements our server needs on a consistent basis. It also helps when installing other like computers on the network. The term *baselining* is most often used to refer to monitoring network performance, but it actually can be used to describe just about any type of performance monitoring and benchmarking. The term *standard load* is often used when referring to servers. A configuration baseline defines what the standard load of the server is for any measured objects. When it comes to performance-monitoring applications, objects are all of the components in the server (for example, CPU, RAM, hard disk, and so on). They are measured using counters. A typical counter would be the % Processor Time of the CPU. This is used by the Task Manager.

An example of one of these tools is the Performance Monitor tool in Windows. It can help to create baselines measuring network activity, CPU usage, memory, hard drive resources used, and so on. It should also be used when monitoring changes to the baseline. Figure 13-1 shows an example of Performance Monitor in Windows. The program works basically the same in all version of Windows, be it client or server, but the navigation to the program will vary. To simplify matters, go to the Run prompt and type `perfmon.exe` in Windows to open the program.

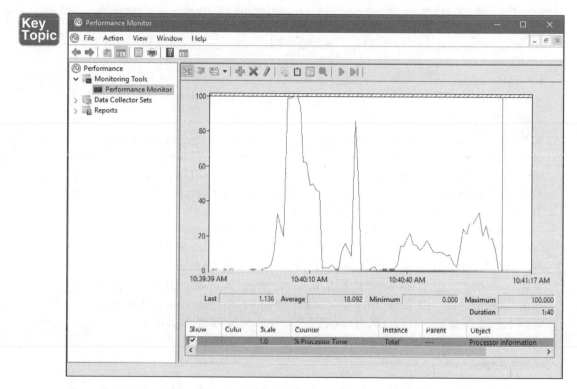

Figure 13-1 Performance Monitor in Windows

The CPU is probably the most important component of the computer. In Figure 13-1, the CPU counter hit 100% once, which is normal when opening applications or starting other processes. However, if the CPU maxes out often, then a percentage of clients will not be able to obtain access to resources on the computer. If the computer is a server, then that means trouble. CPU spiking could be due to normal usage, or it could be due to malicious activity or perhaps bad design. Further analysis would be necessary to determine the exact cause. If the system is a virtual machine, there is a higher probability of CPU spikes. Proper design of VMs is critical, and they must have a strong platform to run on if they are to serve clients properly. Known as a counter, the CPU % Processor Time is just one of many counters. A smart security auditor measures the activity of other objects such as the hard drive, paging file, memory (RAM), network adapter, and whatever else is specific to the organization's needs. Each object has several counters to select from. For example, if you are analyzing a web server, you would probably want to include the HTTP Service Request Queries object, and specifically the ArrivalRate and CurrentQueueSize counters, in your examination.

Now, Figure 13-1 shows the Performance Monitor screen, but this only gives us a brief look at our system. The window of time is only a minute or so before the information refreshes. However, we can record this information over x periods of time and create reports from the recorded information. By comparing the Performance Monitor reports and logs, we ultimately create the baseline. The key is to measure the same way at the same time each day or each week. This provides accurate comparisons. However, keep in mind that performance recording can be a strain on resources. Verify that the computer in question can handle the tests first before you initiate them.

Making reports is all fine and good (and necessary), but it is wise to also set up alerts. Alerts can be generated automatically by the system and sent to administrators and other important IT people. These alerts can be set off in a myriad of ways, all of your choosing; for example, if the CPU were to trip a certain threshold or run at 90% for more than a minute (although this is normal in some environments). Or maybe the physical disk was peaking at 100 MB/s for more than 5 minutes. If these types of things happen often, the system should be checked for malicious activity, illegitimate usage, or the need for an upgrade.

A tool similar to Performance Monitor used in Linux systems is called System Monitor. The different versions of Linux also have many third-party tools that can be used for performance monitoring. macOS/OS X uses Activity Monitor.

Protocol Analyzers

We've mentioned protocol analyzers a couple of times already in this book but haven't really delved into them too much. There are many protocol analyzers available, some free, some not, and some that are part of an operating system. In this section, we focus on Wireshark. Note that network adapters can work in one of two different modes:

- **Promiscuous mode:** The network adapter captures all packets that it has access to regardless of the destination of those packets.

- **Non-promiscuous mode:** The network adapter captures only the packets addressed to it specifically.

Packet capturing programs have different default settings for these modes. Some programs and network adapters can be configured to work in different modes.

Protocol analyzers can be useful in diagnosing where broadcast storms are coming from on your LAN. A **broadcast storm** (or extreme broadcast radiation) is when there is an accumulation of broadcast and multicast packet traffic on the LAN coming from one or more network interfaces. These storms could be intentional or could happen due to a network application or operating system error. The protocol analyzer can specify exactly which network adapter is causing the storm.

Protocol analyzers are also effective in finding header manipulation. Header manipulation can be accomplished by entering unvalidated data into the header of a packet and can ultimately enable XSS attacks, poisoning attacks, hijacking, and cookie manipulation. Header manipulation is common in HTTP response packets. The exploit can be prevented/corrected with proper input validation and detected with a protocol analyzer.

Protocol analyzers can look inside a packet that makes up a TCP/IP handshake. Information that can be viewed includes the SYN, which is the "synchronized sequence numbers," and the ACK, which is "acknowledgment field significant." By using the protocol analyzer to analyze a TCP/IP handshake, you can uncover attacks such as TCP hijacking. But that is just one way to use a protocol analyzer to secure your network. Let's talk about an industry standard protocol analyzer now.

Wireshark

Wireshark is a free download that works on several platforms. It is meant to capture packets on the local computer that it is installed on. But often, this is enough to find out vulnerabilities and monitor the local system and remote systems such as servers. Because Wireshark works in promiscuous mode, it can delve into packets even if they weren't addressed to the computer it runs on. To discern more information about the remote systems, simply start sessions from the client computer to those remote systems and monitor the packet stream. If that is not enough, the program can be installed on servers as well. However, you should check company policy (and get permission) before ever installing any software on a server.

NOTE   When installing Wireshark to a Windows system, you will also need the latest version of WinPcap. Pcap (sometimes shown as PCAP) stands for *packet capture*.

Imagine that you were contracted to find out whether an organization's web server was transacting secure data utilizing TLS version 1.0. But the organization doesn't want anyone logging in to the server—all too common! No problem; you could use Wireshark on a client computer, initiate a packet capture, make a connection to the web server's secure site, and verify that TLS 1.0 is being used by analyzing the packets, as shown in Figure 13-2. If you saw other protocols such as SSL 2.0 that should happen to raise a red flag, then you would want to investigate further, most likely culminating in a protocol upgrade or change.

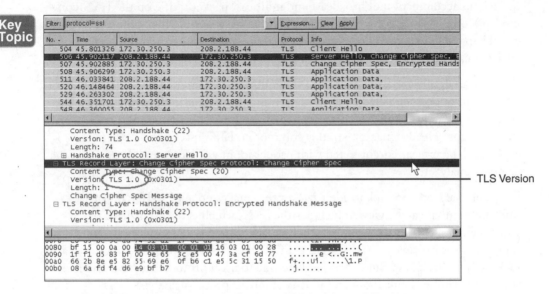

Figure 13-2 Wireshark Showing a Captured TLS Version 1.0 Packet

Always take screen captures and save your analysis as proof of the work that you did, and as proof of your conclusions and ensuing recommendations. You can also save the packet capture file (with the .pcap extension) for future analysis.

Remember that Wireshark can be used with a network adapter configured for promiscuous mode. It is set up by default to collect packets locally and from other sources. However, you can also capture and analyze packets using port mirroring or a network tap. **Port mirroring**, also known as SPAN, is when you configure one or more ports on a switch to forward all packets to another port. That destination port is where your packet capturing computer is plugged in. Know that this can place a considerable load on the CPU of the switch, which can lead to dropped packets. A network tap (as mentioned in Chapter 9) is a physical device that intercepts traffic between two points of the network. It commonly has three ports: two for the points to be monitored, and a third for the packet capturing computer. This is a costlier solution but can monitor all packets and frames of information with no risk of dropped packets.

How about another real-world example? Let's just say you were contracted to monitor an FTP server. The organization is not sure whether FTP passwords are truly being encrypted before being sent across the network. (By the way, some FTP programs with a default configuration do not encrypt the password.) You could use a packet sniffer to initiate a capture of packets on the monitoring server. Then, start up an FTP session on the monitoring server and log in to the FTP server. Afterward, stop the capture and view the FTP packets. Figure 13-3 shows an example of an FTP packet with a clear-text password. Notice that frame 1328 shows the password "locrian" in the details.

Key Topic

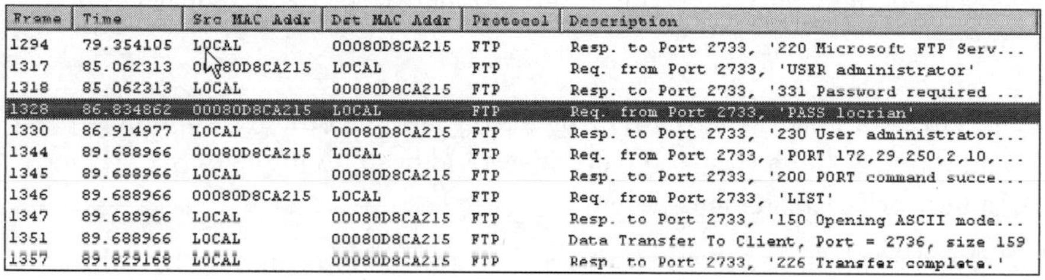

Frame	Time	Src MAC Addr	Dst MAC Addr	Protocol	Description
1294	79.354105	LOCAL	00080D8CA215	FTP	Resp. to Port 2733, '220 Microsoft FTP Serv...
1317	85.062313	00080D8CA215	LOCAL	FTP	Req. from Port 2733, 'USER administrator'
1318	85.062313	LOCAL	00080D8CA215	FTP	Resp. to Port 2733, '331 Password required ...
1328	86.834862	00080D8CA215	LOCAL	FTP	Req. from Port 2733, 'PASS locrian'
1330	86.914977	LOCAL	00080D8CA215	FTP	Resp. to Port 2733, '230 User administrator...
1344	89.688966	00080D8CA215	LOCAL	FTP	Req. from Port 2733, 'PORT 172,29,250,2,10,...
1345	89.688966	LOCAL	00080D8CA215	FTP	Resp. to Port 2733, '200 PORT command succe...
1346	89.688966	00080D8CA215	LOCAL	FTP	Req. from Port 2733, 'LIST'
1347	89.688966	LOCAL	00080D8CA215	FTP	Resp. to Port 2733, '150 Opening ASCII mode...
1351	89.688966	LOCAL	00080D8CA215	FTP	Data Transfer To Client, Port = 2736, size 159
1357	89.829168	LOCAL	00080D8CA215	FTP	Resp. to Port 2733, '226 Transfer complete.'

Figure 13-3 A Packet Sniffer Showing a Captured FTP Packet with Clear-Text Password

Clear-text passwords being passed across the network is a definite risk. The vulnerabilities could be mitigated by increasing the level of security on the FTP server and by using more secure programs. For example, if the FTP server were part of Windows IIS, domain-based or other authentication could be implemented. Or perhaps a different type of FTP server could be used, such as Pure-FTPd. And secure FTP client programs could be used as well. Instead of using the Command Prompt or a browser to make FTP connections, the FileZilla or WS_FTP programs could be used.

NOTE tcpdump is a Unix/Linux-based packet analyzer that runs in the command-line. It can be used for intercepting and displaying the communications of other systems, so it is often used by security techs and attackers alike. The Windows port for this is WinDump, another program that is reliant on WinPcap.

SNMP

The **Simple Network Management Protocol (SNMP)** is a TCP/IP protocol that aids in monitoring network-attached devices and computers. It's usually incorporated as part of a network management system, such as Windows SCCM/SCOM, or free SNMP-based monitoring software. A typical scenario that uses SNMP can be broken down into three components:

- **Managed devices:** Computers or other network-attached devices monitored through the use of agents by a network management system.

- **Agent:** Software deployed by the network management system that is loaded on managed devices. The software redirects the information that the NMS needs to monitor the remote managed devices.

- **Network management system (NMS):** The software run on one or more servers that controls the monitoring of network-attached devices and computers.

So, if the IT director asked you to install agents on several computers and network printers, and monitor them from a server, this would be an example of SNMP and the use of a network management system.

SNMP uses ports 161 and 162. SNMP agents receive requests on port 161; these requests come from the network management system or simply "manager." The manager receives notifications on port 162.

Because applications that use SNMP versions 1 and 2 are less secure, they should be replaced by software that supports SNMP version 3, as of the writing of this book, or whatever the latest version is. SNMPv3 provides confidentiality through the use of encrypted packets that prevent snooping and provide additional message integrity and authentication. However, there are vulnerabilities, such as power distribution units (PDUs) monitored by SNMP that use weak symmetric algorithms like CBC-DES. Packet analyzers and other third-party programs can be used to analyze SNMP devices, their packets, and any potential vulnerabilities.

Historically, SNMP-based monitoring and management tools have been *in-band*, meaning that the admin connects locally through the main company network itself. In-band management is very common. However, an admin might find the need to take an alternate path to manage network devices. In this case, the admin requires *out-of-band* management. This is common for devices that do not have a direct network connection, such as UPSs, PBX systems, and environmental controls. More importantly, in a mission-critical network, SNMP-based in-band management tools are not enough, because if the main LAN fails, then there is no path to manage the devices. That's when out-of-band management becomes crucial. Out-of-band tools that are based on RS-232 access, or even an entirely separate LAN, are required if the main network fails. The key here is that an access switch of some kind that is independent from the main (in-band) network is available to the managed devices. The decision of whether to use in-band or out-of-band management (or both) should be weighed carefully. Remember that every additional system or network increases the security risk, and needs to be protected appropriately—on a physical and a logical level. Then, this needs to be balanced against the level of criticality of your systems.

Analytical Tools

In this book, we try to distinguish between monitoring, auditing, vulnerability assessment, and forensics, but from a hands-on point of view, they are all quite similar. Many analytical tools can be used for multiple security purposes. This section discusses a few more tools that are more fine-tuned for monitoring, but that doesn't mean that they can't be used for other security purposes; and there are plenty of other tools not mentioned here that can also be used for monitoring.

You will probably want to monitor open sessions and files. In Windows, any files and shares that are being accessed by remote computers can be monitored within Computer Management (Run > compmgmt.msc). Inside Computer Management, navigate to System Tools > Shared Folders. From there you can see what shares and open files are being accessed, and what network sessions are open to that computer.

NOTE On some versions of Windows the Performance Monitor utility (discussed previously) can also be found within Computer Management.

One thing you can't see in this utility is the files that were opened locally. But for this you can use the `openfiles` command, which also allows you to see files opened by remote computers. The `openfiles` command must be run in elevated mode within the Command Prompt, and by default the Maintain Objects List global flag must be enabled, which can be done with the following syntax:

```
openfiles /local on
```

Then, simply run the `openfiles` command to see what files are opened locally, and by remote computers, as shown in Figure 13-4. Of course, there are switches that you can use to modify the command; view them with the `/?` option.

```
Administrator: Command Prompt                                                        _ |□| x|
528     WINWORD.EXE          C:\...\AppData\Local\Temp\~DF3A0BF75EBAA7A6E3.TMP
544     WINWORD.EXE          C:\...\Content.Word\~WRS0000.tmp
728     WINWORD.EXE          C:\..1e18e3b_8.0.50727.6195_none_cbf5e994470a1a8f
732     WINWORD.EXE          C:\..1e18e3b_8.0.50727.6195_none_d09154e044272b9a
736     WINWORD.EXE          C:\..1e18e3b_8.0.50727.6195_none_03ce2c7220594d3d3
740     WINWORD.EXE          C:\..\Nuance\NaturallySpeaking10\Program
744     WINWORD.EXE          C:\..1e18e3b_8.0.50727.6195_none_d09154e044272b9a
760     WINWORD.EXE          C:\..1e18e3b_8.0.50727.6195_none_d09154e044272b9a
820     WINWORD.EXE          C:\..\TechSmith\SnagIt 8\SnagIt Add-in.dot
832     WINWORD.EXE          C:\..\Microsoft Office\OFFICE11\MSWORD.OLB
840     WINWORD.EXE          C:\..\AppData\Local\Temp\~DFC4332B179C989A56.TMP
848     WINWORD.EXE          C:\..4ccf1df_6.0.7600.16385_none_421189da2b7fabfc
1016    WINWORD.EXE          D:\..\Chapters\CH12_Monitoring_and_Auditing.doc
1032    WINWORD.EXE          C:\..\AppData\Local\Temp\~DFBBF63EF4EB472091.TMP
1040    WINWORD.EXE
1044    WINWORD.EXE          C:\..\AppData\Local\Temp\~DF842CE9DB3B60B946.TMP
1116    WINWORD.EXE          C:\Windows\SysWOW64\en-US\KernelBase.dll.mui
1120    WINWORD.EXE          C:\..\microsoft shared\PROOF\MSHY2_EN.LEX
1132    WINWORD.EXE          C:\..\Content.Word\~WRF0001.tmp
1144    WINWORD.EXE          C:\PROGRA~2\COMMON~1\MICROS~1\VBA\VBA6\VBE6.DLL
1152    WINWORD.EXE          C:\PROGRA~2\COMMON~1\MICROS~1\VBA\VBA6\VBE6.DLL
1160    WINWORD.EXE          C:\..\microsoft shared\OFFICE11\MSO.DLL
1168    WINWORD.EXE          C:\Windows\SysWOW64\stdole2.tlb
1204    WINWORD.EXE          C:\PROGRA~2\COMMON~1\MICROS~1\SMARTT~1\FPERSON.DLL
1212    WINWORD.EXE          C:\PROGRA~2\COMMON~1\MICROS~1\SMARTT~1\FSTOCK.DLL
1224    WINWORD.EXE          C:\PROGRA~2\COMMON~1\MICROS~1\SMARTT~1\MOFL.DLL
1296    WINWORD.EXE          C:\..\MICROS~1\SMARTT~1\LISTS\1033\STOCKS.DAT
1316    WINWORD.EXE          C:\PROGRA~2\COMMON~1\MICROS~1\SMARTT~1\FDATE.DLL
1324    WINWORD.EXE          C:\PROGRA~2\COMMON~1\MICROS~1\SMARTT~1\FPLACE.DLL
1528    WINWORD.EXE          C:\..\microsoft shared\PROOF\MSSP3EN.LEX
1532    WINWORD.EXE          C:\PROGRA~2\COMMON~1\MICROS~1\SMARTT~1\FNAME.DLL
8       openfiles.exe        C:\Windows\System32
64      openfiles.exe        C:\Windows\System32\en-US\openfiles.exe.mui


Files opened remotely via local share points:
─────────────────────────────────────────────────

ID      Accessed By          Type        Open File <Path\executable>
======  ===================  ==========  =====================================
2       Lamprocles           Windows     D:\Data_Main\
35      Lamprocles           Windows     D:\Data_Main\Pearson
56      Lamprocles           Windows     D:\..\Pearson\Security+_CG_3rd-ed
66      Lamprocles           Windows     D:\..\Security+_CG_3rd-ed\Chapters
80      Lamprocles           Windows     D:\..dies - Videos - Simulations.doc
113     Lamprocles           Windows     D:\Data_Main\
139     Lamprocles           Windows     D:\..\Chapters\Thumbs.db
146     Lamprocles           Windows     D:\..ded Resources - PDF on disc.doc
409     Lamprocles           Windows     D:\..ded Resources - PDF on disc.doc

C:\Windows\system32>
```

Figure 13-4   openfiles Command Results in Windows

You might have to increase the screen buffer for the Command Prompt to see all of the results. As you can see in the figure, there is a long list of locally accessed files, but more importantly, the second list (starting with ID 2) shows any files that remote computers are connected to. You can also use openfiles to disconnect those remote computers. Example syntax for this is

```
openfiles /disconnect /id ##
```

where ## is the ID number associated with the file, shown at the left of the figure.

You might also find that files have been opened and possibly compromised. When you are not sure if the integrity of a file (or files) has been affected, you can use the FC command to compare the file that is suspected of compromise with an older version of the file.

Files can also be viewed and closed with the net file command (must be run in elevated mode). You'll probably also want to make use of the net config, net session, and net view commands. Better yet—just know the whole net command like the back of your hand. And of course there's the netstat command; for example, `netstat -an` is a good way to show open ports in numeric format, and `netstat -e` gives the amount of bytes and packets (and errors) sent and received.

We previously mentioned a few commands in Linux that can be used to view processes, services, and open files. Another command that can be used to show open files is `lsof` (list openfiles). The `netstat` command functions similarly in Linux as it does in Windows (with `netstat -l` being very informative).

Changing gears somewhat: What makes up a lot of the files stored on servers? Individual keystrokes—a bunch of them. And these, too, can be monitored, with keyloggers—both hardware based and software-based. The hardware variety is usually an inline (or pass-through) device that connects to the end of a keyboard's cable just before the port on the computer. These are tricky little devices that often look like a basic adapter. But in reality, they are fairly expensive devices that can store gigabytes of data and can transmit data wirelessly. You can identify a potential keylogger by the fact that it has the same port on each end, albeit one male and one female. Often, they are heavier than a basic adapter of similar size due to the additional processors and the antenna that are built in. The basic countermeasure for these is to deny physical access to areas of the building with important data, such as server rooms. If people have free access to your building, then there is a definite vulnerability. As a security administrator, you should lobby against such access, but if it is inescapable, then a thorough visual search of computers should be periodically undertaken. Sometimes, a computer's ports cannot be visualized very easily, but have no fear, there are software tools that can be used to locate these physical keyloggers as well. Speaking of software tools, keyloggers come in software format as well, and some are very difficult to detect (such as Actual Keylogger). These software tools can be prevented by using anti-keylogger software and security tokens. They can be detected using live USB/CD/DVD operating systems and network monitoring programs.

Use Static *and* Dynamic Tools

The list of analytical tools goes on and on, both integrated into the operating system and offered by third parties. Most of the analytical tools discussed in this section are static in nature. Because of this they are not best suited for monitoring environments where you are attempting to create a baseline. Other, more dynamic tools such as Performance Monitor and Wireshark will work better. However, there is something to be said about taking a snapshot of the moment with tools such as `openfiles` and getting a quick glimpse at what happened at just that moment. Taking it to the next level, it's the combination of static *and* dynamic tools that will allow you to properly conduct an audit.

Conducting Audits

Computer security audits are technical assessments conducted on applications, systems, or networks. They are an example of a detective security control. Audits can be done manually or with computer programs. Manual assessments usually include the following:

- Review of security logs
- Review of access control lists
- Review of user rights and permissions
- Review of group policies
- Performance of vulnerability scans
- Review of written organization policies
- Interviewing organization personnel

Programs used to audit a computer or network could be as simple as a program such as Belarc Advisor, or built-in auditing features within Windows and Linux, or more complex open source projects such as OpenXDAS.

When I have conducted IT security audits in the past, the following basic steps have helped me organize the entire process:

Step 1.   Define exactly what is to be audited.

Step 2.   Create backups.

Step 3.   Scan for, analyze, and create a list of vulnerabilities, threats, and issues that have already occurred.

Step 4.   Calculate risk.

Step 5.   Develop a plan to mitigate risk and present it to the appropriate personnel.

Although an independent security auditor might do all these things, a security administrator will be most concerned with the auditing of files, logs, and systems security settings.

Auditing Files

When dealing with auditing, we are interested in the who, what, and when. Basically, a security administrator wants to know *who* did *what* to a particular resource and *when* that person did it.

Auditing files can usually be broken down into a three-step process:

Step 1.   Turn on an auditing policy.

Step 2.   Enable auditing for particular objects such as files, folders, and printers.

Step 3.   Review the security logs to determine who did what to a resource and when.

As an example, let's use a Windows client computer. First, we would need to turn on a specific auditing policy such as "audit object access." This can be done within the Local Computer Policy, as shown in Figure 13-5. You can select from several different auditing policies such as logon events and privilege use, but object access is probably the most common, so we'll use that as the example.

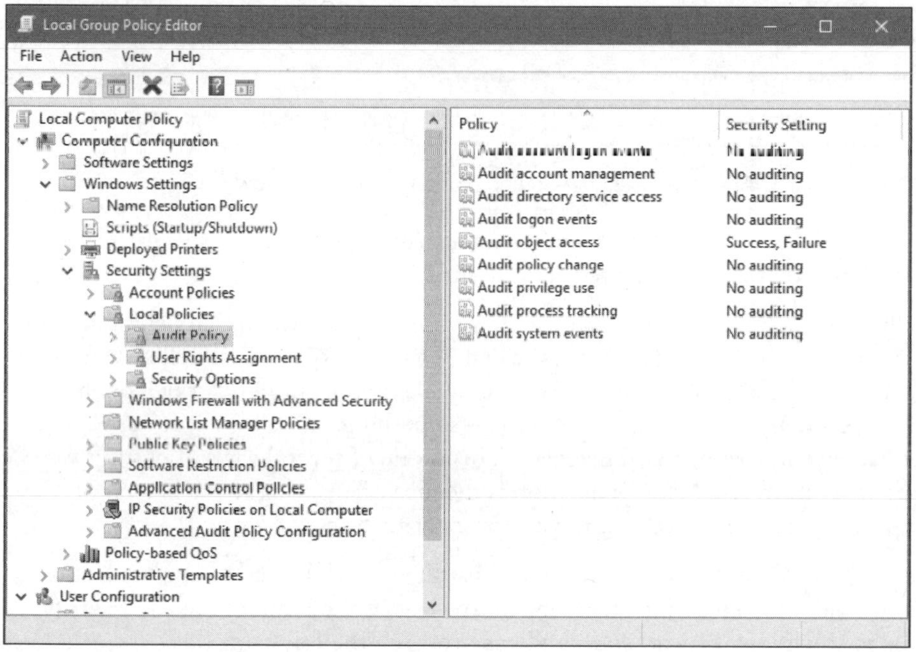

Figure 13-5   Audit Policy Within the Local Computer Policy of a Windows Computer

Next, we would need to enable auditing for particular objects. Let's say that we are auditing a folder of data. We would want to go to the Properties dialog box for that folder, then navigate to the Security tab, then click the Advanced button, and finally access the Auditing tab, as shown in Figure 13-6.

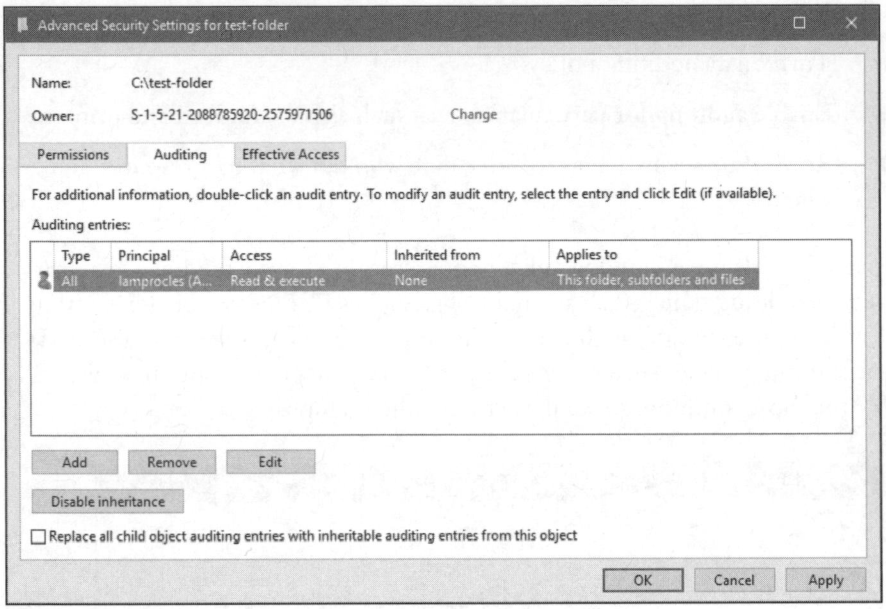

Figure 13-6 Auditing Advanced Security Settings for a Folder in Windows

From there, we can add users whom we want to audit, and we can specify one or more of many different attributes to be audited.

Finally, we need to review the security logs to see exactly what is happening on our system and who is accessing what and when. The security logs also tell us whether users have succeeded or failed in their attempts to access, modify, or delete objects. And if users deny that they attempted to do something, these logs act as proof that their user account was indeed involved. This is one of several ways of putting *non-repudiation* into force. Non-repudiation is the idea of ensuring that a person or group cannot refute the validity of your proof against them.

A common problem with security logs is that they fail to become populated, especially on older systems. If users complain to you that they cannot see any security events in the Event Viewer, you should ask yourself the following:

- Has auditing been turned on in a policy? And was it turned on in the correct policy?
- Was auditing enabled for the individual object?
- Does the person attempting to view the log have administrative capabilities?

In addition, you have to watch out for overriding policies. By default, a policy gets its settings from a parent policy; you might need to turn off the override option. On another note, perhaps the audit recording failed for some reason. Many auditing systems also have the capability to send an alert to the administrator in the case that a recording fails. Hopefully, the system attempts to recover from the failure and continue recording auditing information while the administrator fixes the issue. By answering all these questions and examining everything pertinent to the auditing scenario, you should be able to populate that security log! Now, security logs are just one component of logging that we cover in the next section.

Logging

When it comes to auditing an organized set of information, logging is the method of choice. Frequent monitoring of logs is an important part of being a security person. Possibly the most important log file in Windows is the Security log, as shown in Figure 13-7.

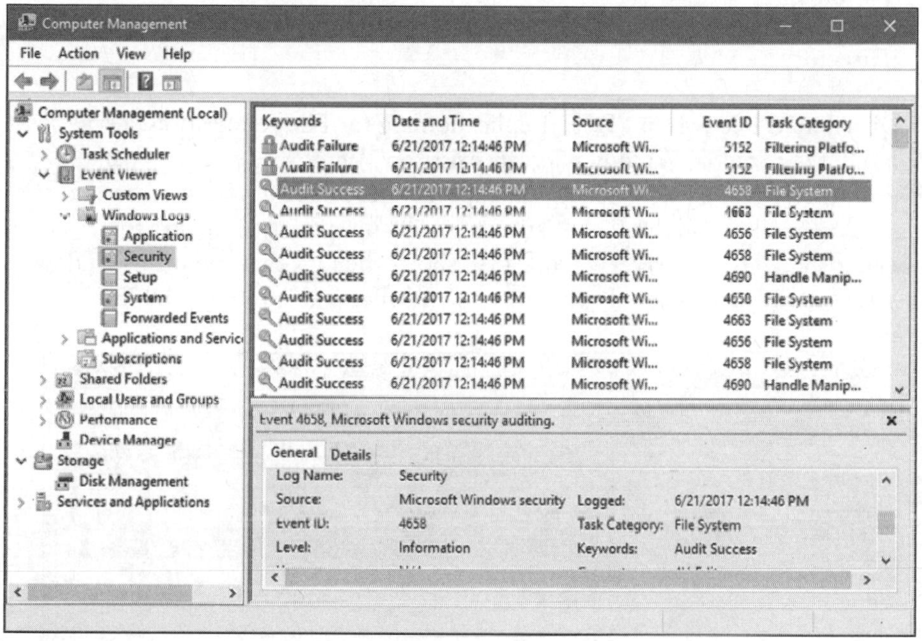

Figure 13-7   Security Log in Windows

The Security log can show whether a user was successful at doing a variety of things, including logging on to the local computer or domain; accessing, modifying, or deleting files; modifying policies; and so on. Of course, many of these things need to be configured first before they can be logged. Newer versions of Windows automatically log such events as logon or policy modification. All these Security log events can be referred to as **audit trails**. Audit trails are records or logs that show the tracked actions of users, whether the user was successful in the attempt or not.

A security administrator should monitor this log file often to keep on top of any breaches, or attempted breaches, of security. By periodically reviewing the logs of applications, operating systems, and network devices, we can find issues, errors, and threats quickly and increase our general awareness of the state of the network.

Several other types of Windows log files should be monitored periodically, including the following:

- **System:** Logs events such as system shutdown or driver failure
- **Application:** Logs events for operating system applications and third-party programs

The System and Application logs exist on client and server versions of Windows. A few log files that exist only on servers include the following:

- Distributed File System (DFS) Replication Service or File Replication Service
- DNS Server
- Directory Service

The Distributed File System (DFS) Replication log (or File Replication Service log on older versions of Windows Server) exists on Windows Servers by default. However, the Directory Service log will appear if the server has been promoted to a domain controller, and the DNS Server log will appear only if the DNS service has been installed to the server. Figure 13-8 shows the logs that run on a Windows Server that has been promoted to a domain controller and is running DNS.

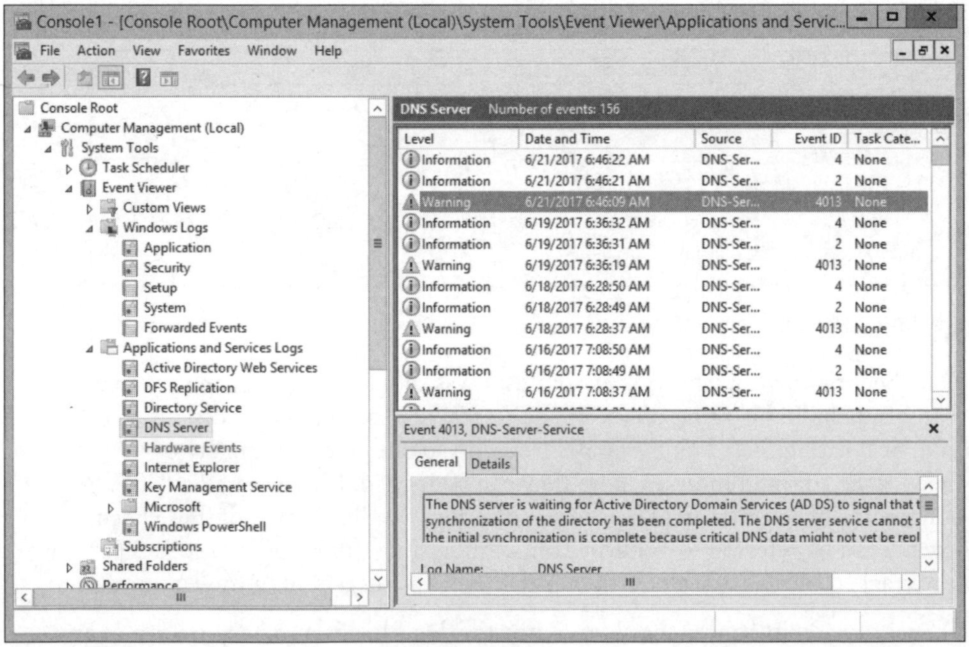

Figure 13-8   DNS Server Log in Windows Server

We've mentioned the importance of reviewing DNS logs previously in the book but it is worth reminding you that examining the DNS log can uncover unauthorized zone transfers and other malicious or inadvertent activity on the DNS server. In the case of Figure 13-8, we see a warning stating that Active Directory Domain Services (AD DS) has not signaled to DNS that synchronization of the directory has completed; we'll have to investigate that and probably fix that manually.

Let's not forget about web servers—by analyzing and monitoring a web server, you can determine whether the server has been compromised. Drops in CPU and hard disk speed are common indications of a web server that has been attacked. Of course, it could just be a whole lot of web traffic! It's up to you to use the log files to find out exactly what is going on.

Other types of operating systems, applications, and devices have their own set of log files—for example, applications such as Microsoft Exchange and SQL database servers, and firewalls. The firewall log especially is of importance, as shown in Figure 13-9. Note in the figure the dropped packets from addresses on the 169.254.0.0 network, which we know to be the APIPA network number. This is something that should be investigated further because most organizations have a policy against the use of APIPA addresses.

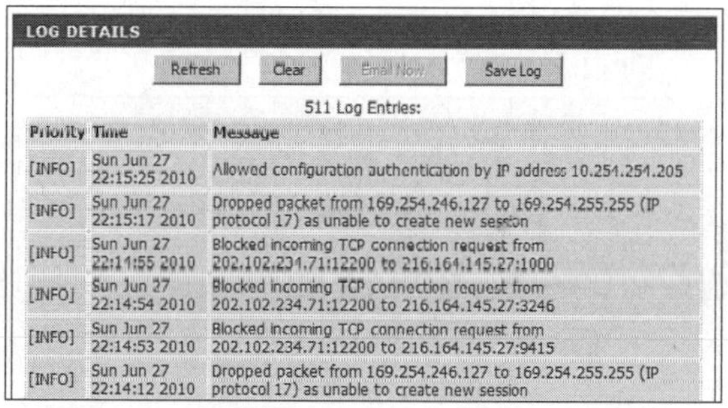

Figure 13-9   A Basic Firewall's Log

The firewall log can show all kinds of other things such as malicious port scans and other vulnerability scans. For example, when digging into a firewall log event, if you see the following syntax, you would know that a port scan attack has occurred:

S=207.50.135.54:53 – D=10.1.1.80:0

S=207.50.135.54:53 – D=10.1.1.80:1

S=207.50.135.54:53 – D=10.1.1.80:2

S=207.50.135.54:53 – D=10.1.1.80:3

S=207.50.135.54:53 – D=10.1.1.80:4

S=207.50.135.54:53 – D=10.1.1.80:5

Note the source IP address (which is public and therefore most likely external to your network) uses port 53 outbound to run a port scan of 10.1.1.80, starting with port 0 and moving on from there. The firewall is usually the first line of defense, but even if you have an IDS or IPS in front of it, you should review those firewall logs often.

A very useful tool for the security administrator is Syslog. Syslog is the standard for computer message logging. Most devices such as switches, routers, and firewalls use it, or can be updated to use it. For example, the log in Figure 13-9 was generated while adhering to the Syslog protocol. In addition, that log can be exported in real time to a computer running a Syslog server. The Syslog server is really just a repository for the logs that already exist on your routers and other devices. The key is that the Syslog server can run directly on your workstation, and pull the logs from those devices, so that you can easily monitor what is happening on those devices from the comfort of your seat. Yes, you could check the logs by logging in to the router or other device, but the logs won't be readily available; you will have to locate them, and different devices will store them in different places. With a Syslog server, you can view multiple devices' logs from one screen.

To illustrate this technology in action, take a look at Figure 13-10. This shows a Syslog program that is getting a log fed to it from a SOHO router. You can see that it is very easy to read the details of that log within the Syslog program; much easier than it would be to read them from within the SOHO router's interface.

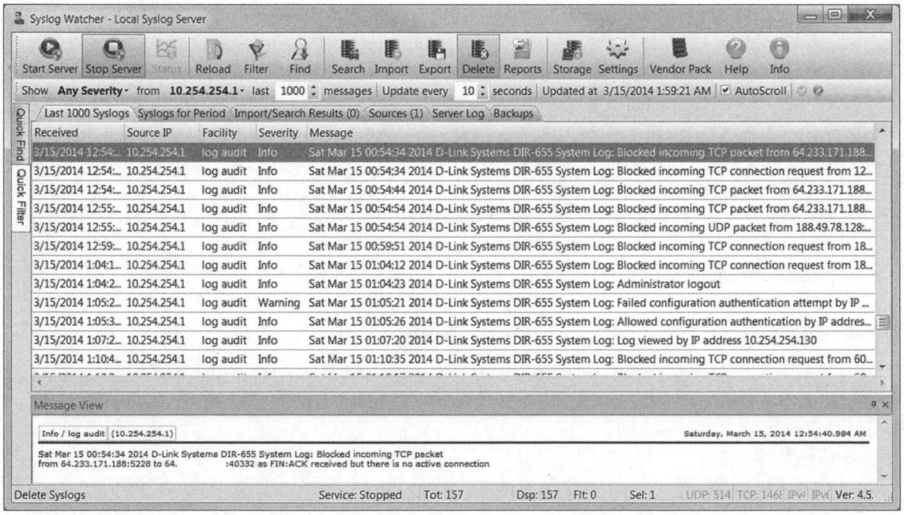

Figure 13-10   Syslog Program Running in Windows Detailing a SOHO Router Log

Figure 13-10 shows a list of logs. The one at the top is highlighted. It shows that the Source IP is 10.254.254.1. That is the internal IP address of the SOHO router—the device that is creating the log, and the one that is being monitored. The highlighted entry also has details at the bottom of the screen. You can see that the SOHO router blocked a TCP packet from the IP address 64.233.171.188 (in this case from port 5228). This is real, and it happens all the time as you can see from the log. It really reinforces the fact that you need to make sure your router (or other device) has its ports closed, and is patched and up to date!

By default, Syslog uses port 514 and works over a UDP transport mechanism. There are several companies that offer Syslog programs (SolarWinds Kiwi and Syslog Watcher, for example), and they all work in basically the same way, though some use a proprietary port number instead of the standard 514, and may offer TCP connectivity as well, to avoid packet loss. Port 6514 is used for secure connections known as Syslog over TLS.

> **NOTE**   Though Windows does not by default support exporting of logs to a Syslog server, there are utilities you can download that will convert event logs from the Event Viewer into Syslog messages.

Log File Maintenance and Security

The planning, maintenance, and security of the log files should be thoroughly considered. A few things to take into account include the configuration and saving of the log files, backing up of the files, and securing and encrypting of the files.

Before setting up any type of logging system, you should consider the amount of disk space (or other form of memory) that the log files will require. You should also contemplate all the different information necessary to reconstruct logged events later. Are the logs stored in multiple locations? Were they encrypted? Were they hashed for integrity? Also up for consideration is the level of detail you will allow in the log. Verbose logging is something that admins apply to get as much information as possible. Also, is the organization interested in exactly when an event occurred? If so, time stamping should be incorporated. Although many systems do this by default, some organizations opt to not use time stamping to reduce CPU usage.

Log files can be saved to a different partition of the logging system, or saved to a different system altogether; although, the latter requires a fast secondary system and a fast network. The size and overwriting configuration of the file should play into your considerations. Figure 13-11 shows an example of the properties of a Windows Server Security log file. Currently, the file is 74 MB but can grow to a maximum size of 131072 KB (128 MB). Although 128 MB might sound like a lot, larger organizations can eat that up quickly because they will probably audit and log a lot of user actions. When the file gets this big, log mining becomes important. There can be thousands and thousands of entries, making it difficult for an admin to sort through them all, but several third-party programs can make the mining of specific types of log entries much simpler. You can also note in the figure that the log is set to over-write events if the log reaches its maximum size. Security is a growing concern with organizations in general, so the chances are that they will not want events overwrit-ten. Instead, you would select Do Not Overwrite Events (Clear Log Manually). As an admin, you would save and back up the log monthly or weekly, and clear the log at the beginning of the new time period to start a new log. If the log becomes full for any reason, you should have an alert set up to notify you or another admin.

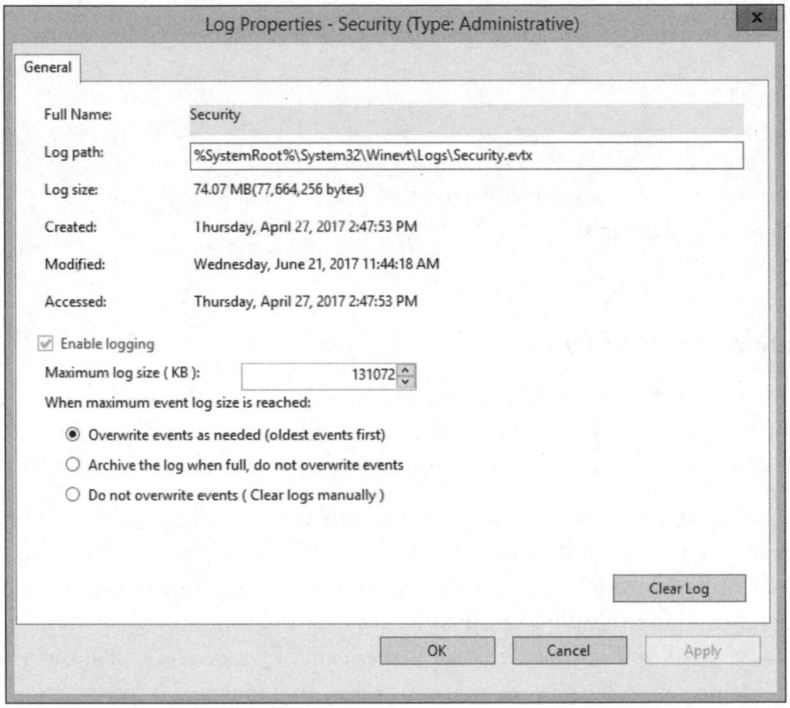

Figure 13-11   Windows Server Security Log Properties Dialog Box

As with any security configurations or files, the log files should be backed up. The best practice is to copy the files to a remote log server. The files could be backed up to a separate physical offsite location. Or, WORM (write once read many) media types could be utilized. WORM options such as DVD-R and other optical discs are good ways to back up log files, but not *re*-write optical discs, mind you. USB Flash drives and USB removable hard drives should not be allowed in any area where a computer stores log files. One way or another, a retention policy should be in place for your log files—meaning they should be retained for future reference.

Securing the log files can be done in several ways: First, by employing the afore-mentioned backup methods. Second, by setting permissions to the actual log file.

Figure 13-11 shows the filename for the Security log: Security.evtx, located in %SystemRoot%\System32\Winevt\Logs\. That is where you would go to configure NTFS permissions. Just remember that by default, this file inherits its permissions from the parent folder. File integrity is also important when securing log files. Encrypting the log files through the concept known as hashing is a good way to verify the integrity of the log files if they are moved and/or copied. And finally, you could flat-out encrypt the entire contents of the file so that other users cannot view it. We talk more about hashing and encryption in Chapter 14, "Encryption and Hashing Concepts," and Chapter 15, "PKI and Encryption Protocols."

Auditing System Security Settings

So far, we have conducted audits on object access and log files, but we still need to audit system security settings. For example, we should review user permissions and group policies.

For user access, we are most concerned with shared folders on the network and their permissions. Your file server (or distributed file system server) can easily show you all the shares it contains. This knowledge can be obtained on a Windows Server by navigating to Computer Management > System Tools > Shared Folders > Shares, as shown in Figure 13-12.

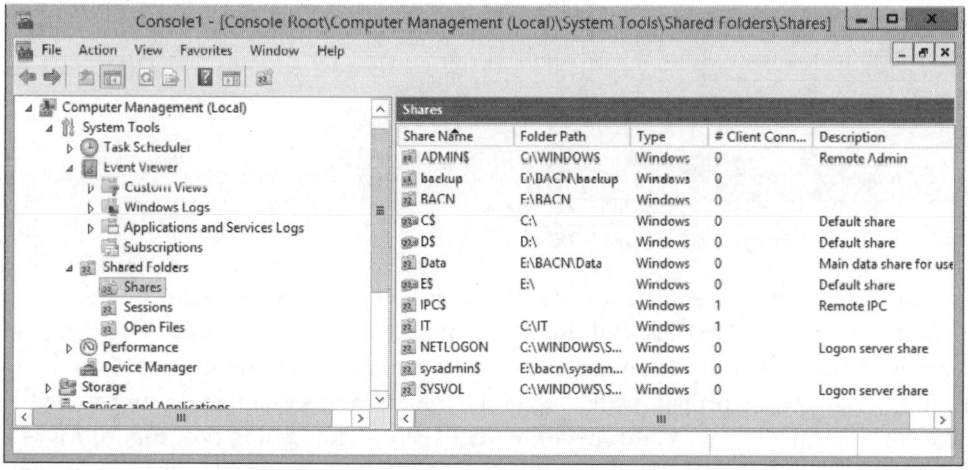

Figure 13-12 Network Shares on a Windows Server

Notice the IT share. There are a couple of things that pique my interest from the get-go. For starters, the shared folder is located in the C: drive of this server. Shared folders should actually be on a different partition, drive, or even a different computer. Second, it is in the root. That isn't a good practice either (blame the author).

Of course, this is just a test folder that we created previously, but we should definitely consider the location of our shared folders.

NOTE   Some companies opt to secure administrative shares, such as IPC$ and ADMIN$. Although this isn't actually an option on servers, it is a smart idea for client computers.

Either way, we now know where the IT share is located and can go to that folder's properties and review the permissions for it, as shown in Figure 13-13.

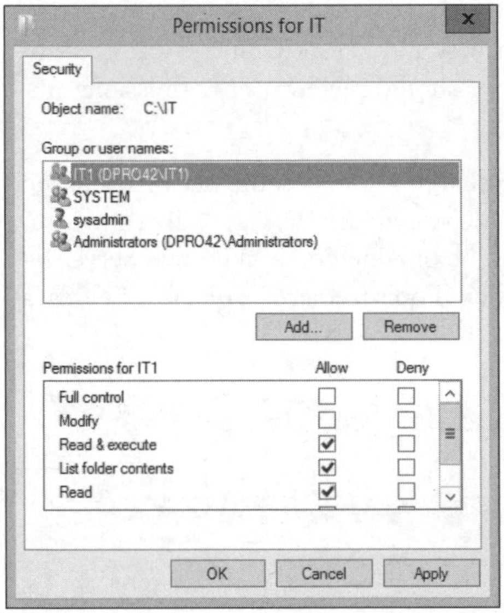

Figure 13-13   The IT Folder's Permissions

In the figure, you can see that the IT1 group has Read & Execute, List Folder Contents, and Read permissions. It is wise to make sure that individual users and groups of users do not have more permissions than necessary, or allowed. It is also important to verify proper ownership of the folder; in this example, it can be done by clicking the Advanced button within the IT Properties dialog box. Figure 13-14 shows that *sysadmin* is the owner of this resource. We want to make sure that no one else has inadvertently or maliciously taken control.

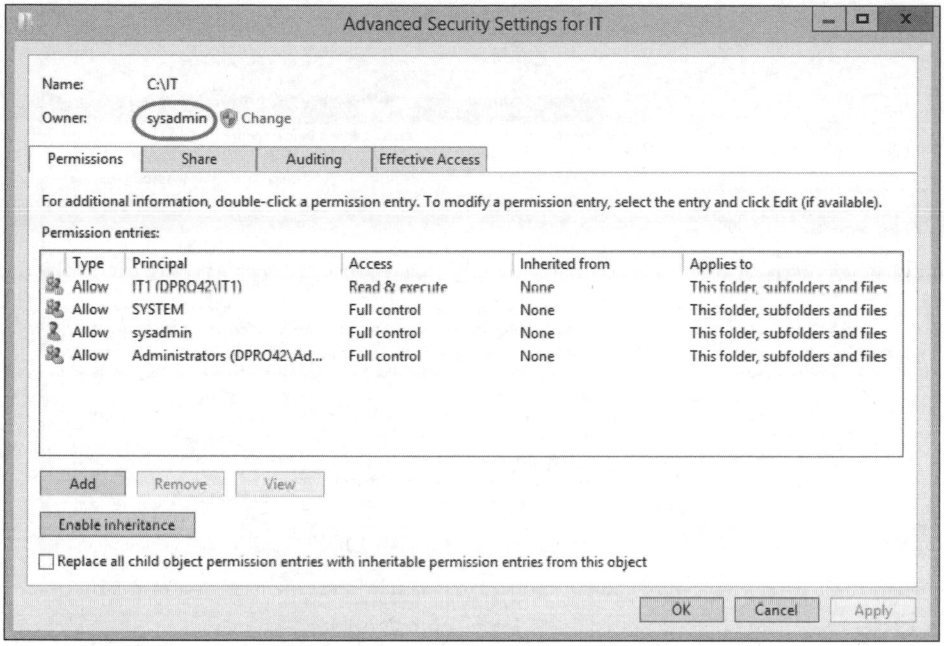

Figure 13-14 The IT Folder's Advanced Security Settings

While you are in the Advanced Security Settings dialog box, you can check what auditing settings have been implemented and whether they correspond to an organization's written policies.

Speaking of policies, computer policies should be reviewed as well. Remember that there might be different policies for each department in an organization. This would match up with the various organizational units on a Windows Server. Figure 13-15 shows the Security Settings section of the Marketing-Policy we created in Chapter 5, "Application Security." I haven't counted them, but there are probably thousands of settings. Due to this, an organization might opt to use a security template; if this is the case, verify that the proper one is being used, and that the settings included in that template take into account what the organization has defined as part of its security plan. Templates are accessed by right-clicking Security Settings and selecting Import Policy. If a template is not being used, you will need to go through as many policy objects as possible, especially things such as password policy, security options, and the audit policy itself.

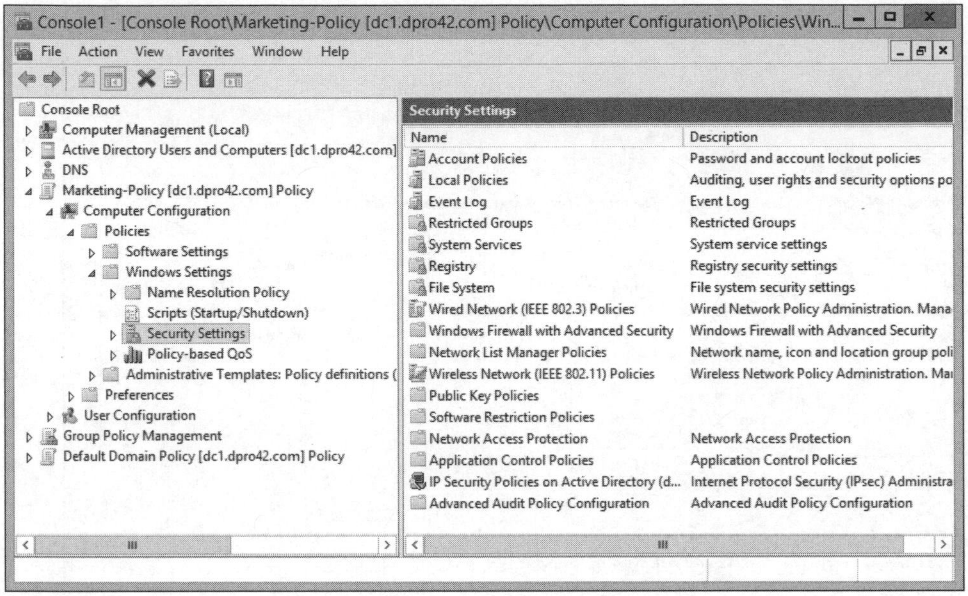

Figure 13-15 Security Settings Within the IT Policy on a Windows Server

Individual computers will probably use User Account Control and adhere to the policies created on the server. A spot check should be made of individual computers to verify that they are playing by the rules. In some cases, an organization will require that all client computers are checked. Auditing can be a lot of work, so plan your time accordingly, and be ready for a few hiccups along the way.

SIEM

Your security monitoring can be augmented by using a security information and event management (SIEM) solution. SIEM products combine security event management and security information management. Products such as HPE's ArcSight and IBM's QRadar offer real-time monitoring of systems and logs, and automation in the form of alerts and triggers. Some of the capabilities of a SIEM solution include: data aggregation, which can combine data from network devices, servers and applications; correlation engines, which automatically look for common attributes of events across the various monitored platforms; compliance with government regulatory auditing processes; and forensic analysis. SIEM also includes WORM functionality so that information once written, cannot be modified. When correlating data, it provides for automatic deduplication, or the elimination of redundant data. It may also include scanning for configuration compliance, also known as configuration compliance manager functionality.

Chapter Summary

In the previous chapter we discussed treating your IT infrastructure as more of an entity, and less of a collection of technologies. That philosophy of the synergy between man and computer is nothing novel—the idea dates back to John von Neumann. But the extension of this synergy between disparate IT systems—and the security administrators that protect them—is an outlook that is being applied by more and more IT professionals.

Protect is the key word here. To do so effectively means to apply hands-on, continuous monitoring that: enables an already secure organization to assess weaknesses in real-time; tracks the growth of the IT infrastructure; and provides a glimpse of what is to be. But then there is also the Monday morning quarterbacking, the investigation of negative occurrences, the reference to historical anomalies—in short, the auditing of the IT infrastructure. It's that interpretive digging into the past, coupled with protective monitoring, that can ensure the stability of an IT infrastructure.

Now we can wax poetic until we are blue in the face, but all the pontification in the world won't provide the hands-on execution required to meticulously, and methodically, defend the IT environment. For example, it's the IDS/IPS solutions that will provide you with actual statistics concerning the behavior of data, and any anomalies that may present themselves. It's the concrete baselining with tools such as Performance Monitor and Wireshark that supplies analytics about the health of your servers and the types of data passing through them.

There is a myriad of other analytical tools at your disposal. The command-line included with each type of operating system has a huge variety of utilities that can bestow the bulk of the answers you are looking for about your computers. Plus, there are seemingly countless third-party applications available—some free, and some for a fee—that can help to fill any knowledge gaps about your computer network.

The detective in you will require periodic audits. In some cases, an organization requires that this be done by an independent consultant. However, your honor will probably require that you conduct occasional audits as well. Review your ACLs, permissions, and policies. But especially, keep a watchful eye on your security logs. These are some of the most important analytics that you will possess. They explain who did what and when it occurred (and possibly why). Define strong auditing policies, implement them, enforce them, review them often, and back them up.

Finally, we made mention of the von Neumann mindset. As IT infrastructures become more complex, and data gets "bigger," and computers become "smarter," this ideal becomes all the more vital. I'm not saying to pat the server on the back and tell it everything is going to be okay, but rather provide your IT infrastructure with a sort of compassion that will nurture it and help it to grow. You may say: "Dave, it sounds like you treat your computer networks almost as if they are living beings!" Is that so strange? Is AI so far away? Time will tell. As of the writing of this book (2017) there are learning algorithms, self-healing servers and networks, super-computers such as Watson and Titan, and advances in robotics that were unimaginable just a decade ago. Besides, many of the geeks out there (and I use that term with high regard) do indeed already treat their servers—even entire IT environments—like pets or even friends. And so, that compassion manifests itself in the form of robust monitoring and scrupulous auditing. That is the *way* to the goal of providing the highest level of protection possible.

Chapter Review Activities

Use the features in this section to study and review the topics in this chapter.

Review Key Topics

Review the most important topics in the chapter, noted with the Key Topic icon in the outer margin of the page. Table 13-2 lists a reference of these key topics and the page number on which each is found.

Table 13-2   Key Topics for Chapter 13

Key Topic Element	Description	Page Number
Table 13-1	Summary of monitoring methodologies	437
Figure 13-1	Performance Monitor in Windows	439
Figure 13-2	Wireshark showing a captured TLS Version 1.0 packet	442
Figure 13-3	Captured FTP packet with clear-text password	443
Figure 13-5	Audit Policy within the Local Computer Policy of a Windows computer	449
Figure 13-7	Security log in Windows	451
Figure 13-10	Syslog program running in Windows	454
Figure 13-11	Windows Server Security Log Properties dialog box	456

Define Key Terms

Define the following key terms from this chapter, and check your answers in the glossary:

signature-based monitoring, anomaly-based monitoring, behavior-based monitoring, baselining, baseline reporting, security posture, security posture assessment (SPA), promiscuous mode, non-promiscuous mode, broadcast storm, port mirroring, Simple Network Management Protocol (SNMP), computer security audits, audit trail

Complete the Real-World Scenarios

Complete the Real-World Scenarios found on the companion website (www.pearsonitcertification.com/title/9780789758996). You will find a PDF containing the scenario and questions, and also supporting videos and simulations.

Review Questions

Answer the following review questions. Check your answers with the correct answers that follow.

1. Which of the following is a record of the tracked actions of users?
   - **A.** Performance Monitor
   - **B.** Audit trails
   - **C.** Permissions
   - **D.** System and event logs

2. What tool can alert you if a server's processor trips a certain threshold?
   - **A.** TDR
   - **B.** Password cracker
   - **C.** Event Viewer
   - **D.** Performance Monitor

3. The IT director has asked you to install agents on several client computers and monitor them from a program at a server. What is this known as?
   - **A.** SNMP
   - **B.** SMTP
   - **C.** SMP
   - **D.** Performance Monitor

4. One of your co-workers complains to you that he cannot see any security events in the Event Viewer. What are three possible reasons for this? (Select the three best answers.)

   A. Auditing has not been turned on.

   B. The log file is only 10 MB.

   C. The co-worker is not an administrator.

   D. Auditing for an individual object has not been turned on.

5. Which tool can be instrumental in capturing FTP GET requests?

   A. Vulnerability scanner

   B. Port scanner

   C. Performance Monitor

   D. Protocol analyzer

6. Your manager wants you to implement a type of intrusion detection system (IDS) that can be matched to certain types of traffic patterns. What kind of IDS is this?

   A. Anomaly-based IDS

   B. Signature-based IDS

   C. Behavior-based IDS

   D. Inline IDS

7. You are setting up auditing on a Windows computer. If set up properly, which log should have entries?

   A. Application log

   B. System log

   C. Security log

   D. Maintenance log

8. You have established a baseline for your server. Which of the following is the best tool to use to monitor any changes to that baseline?

   A. Performance Monitor

   B. Anti-spyware

   C. Antivirus software

   D. Vulnerability assessments software

9. In what way can you gather information from a remote printer?

   A. HTTP

   B. SNMP

   C. CA

   D. SMTP

10. Which of the following can determine which flags are set in a TCP/IP handshake?

    A. Protocol analyzer

    B. Port scanner

    C. SYN/ACK

    D. Performance Monitor

11. Which of following is the most basic form of IDS?

    A. Anomaly-based

    B. Behavioral-based

    C. Signature-based

    D. Statistical-based

12. Which of the following deals with the standard load for a server?

    A. Patch management

    B. Group Policy

    C. Port scanning

    D. Configuration baseline

13. Your boss wants you to properly log what happens on a database server. What are the most important concepts to think about while you do so? (Select the two best answers.)

    A. The amount of virtual memory that you will allocate for this task

    B. The amount of disk space you will require

    C. The information that will be needed to reconstruct events later

    D. Group Policy information

14. Which of the following is the best practice to implement when securing logs files?

    A. Log all failed and successful login attempts.

    B. Deny administrators access to log files.

    C. Copy the logs to a remote log server.

    D. Increase security settings for administrators.

15. What is the main reason to frequently view the logs of a DNS server?

    A. To create aliases

    B. To watch for unauthorized zone transfers

    C. To defend against denial-of-service attacks

    D. To prevent domain name kiting

16. As you review your firewall log, you see the following information. What type of attack is this?

```
S=207.50.135.54:53 - D=10.1.1.80:0
S=207.50.135.54:53 - D=10.1.1.80:1
S=207.50.135.54:53 - D=10.1.1.80:2
S=207.50.135.54:53 - D=10.1.1.80:3
S=207.50.135.54:53 - D=10.1.1.80:4
S=207.50.135.54:53 - D=10.1.1.80:5
```

    A. Denial-of-service

    B. Port scanning

    C. Ping scanning

    D. DNS spoofing

17. Of the following, which two security measures should be implemented when logging a server? (Select the two best answers.)

    A. Cyclic redundancy checks

    B. The application of retention policies on log files

    C. Hashing of log files

    D. Storing of temporary files

18. You suspect a broadcast storm on the LAN. Which tool is required to diagnose which network adapter is causing the storm?

    A. Protocol analyzer

    B. Firewall

    C. Port scanner

    D. Network intrusion detection system

    E. Port mirror

19. Which of the following should be done if an audit recording fails?

    A. Stop generating audit records.

    B. Overwrite the oldest audit records.

    C. Send an alert to the administrator.

    D. Shut down the server.

20. Which of the following log files should show attempts at unauthorized access?

    A. DNS

    B. System

    C. Application

    D. Security

21. To find out when a computer was shut down, which log file would an administrator use?

    A. Security

    B. System

    C. Application

    D. DNS

22. Which of the following requires a baseline? (Select the two best answers.)

    A. Behavior-based monitoring

    B. Performance Monitor

    C. Anomaly-based monitoring

    D. Signature-based monitoring

23. Jason is a security administrator for a company of 4000 users. He wants to store 6 months of security logs to a logging server for analysis. The reports are required by upper management due to legal obligations but are not time-critical. When planning for the requirements of the logging server, which of the following should not be implemented?

   A. Performance baseline and audit trails

   B. Time stamping and integrity of the logs

   C. Log details and level of verbose logging

   D. Log storage and backup requirements

24. One of the developers in your organization installs a new application in a test system to test its functionality before implementing into production. Which of the following is most likely affected?

   A. Application security

   B. Initial baseline configuration

   C. Application design

   D. Baseline comparison

25. Michael has just completed monitoring and analyzing a web server. Which of the following indicates that the server might have been compromised?

   A. The web server is sending hundreds of UDP packets.

   B. The web server has a dozen connections to inbound port 80.

   C. The web server has a dozen connections to inbound port 443.

   D. The web server is showing a drop in CPU speed and hard disk speed.

26. What kind of security control do computer security audits fall under?

   A. Detective

   B. Preventive

   C. Corrective

   D. Protective

27. You have been alerted to suspicious traffic without a specific signature. Under further investigation, you determine that the alert was a false indicator. Furthermore, the same alert has arrived at your workstation several times. Which security device needs to be configured to disable false alarms in the future? (Select the best answer.)

    A. Anomaly-based IDS

    B. Signature-based IPS

    C. Signature-based IDS

    D. UTM

    E. SIEM

28. You have been tasked with providing daily network usage reports of layer 3 devices without compromising any data during the information gathering process. Which of the following protocols should you select to provide for secure reporting in this scenario?

    A. ICMP

    B. SNMP

    C. SNMPv3

    D. SSH

29. Which of the following techniques enables an already secure organization to assess security vulnerabilities in real time?

    A. Baselining

    B. ACLs

    C. Continuous monitoring

    D. Video surveillance

30. Which of the following protocols are you observing in the packet capture below?

`16:42:01 - SRC 192.168.1.5:3389 - DST 10.254.254.57:8080 - SYN/ACK`

    A. HTTP

    B. HTTPS

    C. RDP

    D. SFTP

Answers and Explanations

1. **B.** Audit trails are records showing the tracked actions of users. Performance Monitor is a tool in Windows that enables you to track the performance of objects such as CPU, RAM, network adapter, physical disk, and so on. Permissions grant or deny access to resources. To see whether permissions were granted, auditing must be enabled. The System log and other logs record events that happened in other areas of the system—for example, events concerning the operating system, drivers, applications, and so on.

2. **D.** Performance Monitor can be configured in such a way that alerts can be set for any of the objects (processor, RAM, paging file) in a computer. For example, if the processor were to go beyond 90% usage for more than 1 minute, an alert would be created and could be sent automatically to an administrator. A TDR is a time-domain reflectometer, an electronic instrument used to test cables for faults. A password cracker is a software program used to recover or crack passwords; an example would be Cain & Abel. The Event Viewer is a built-in application in Windows that enables a user to view events on the computer such as warnings, errors, and other information events. It does not measure the objects in a server in the way that Performance Monitor does.

3. **A.** SNMP (Simple Network Management Protocol) is used when a person installs agents on client computers to monitor those systems from a single remote location. SMTP is used by e-mail clients and servers. SMP is symmetric multiprocessing, which is not covered in the Security+ exam objectives. Performance Monitor enables a person to monitor a computer and create performance baselines.

4. **A, C, and D.** To audit events on a computer, an administrator would need to enable auditing within the computer's policy, then turn on auditing for an individual object (folder, file, and so on), and then view the events within the Security log of the Event Viewer. The size of the log file won't matter in this case—aside from events being overwritten. However, the person should still be able to see some events if all the other criteria have been met because 10 MB is big enough for many events to be written to it.

5. **D.** A protocol analyzer captures data including things such as GET requests that were initiated from an FTP client. Vulnerability scanners and port scanners look for open ports and other vulnerabilities of a host. Performance Monitor is a Windows program that reports on the performance of the computer system and any of its parts.

6. **B.** When using an IDS, particular types of traffic patterns refer to signature-based IDS. Anomaly-based and behavior-based systems use different methodologies. Inline IDS means that the device exists on the network (often between a firewall and the Internet) and directly receives packets and forwards those packets to the intended destination.

7. **C.** After auditing is turned on and specific resources are configured for auditing, you need to check the Event Viewer's Security log for the entries. These could be successful logons or misfired attempts at deleting files; there are literally hundreds of options. The Application log contains errors, warnings, and informational entries about applications. The System log deals with drivers, system files, and so on. A System Maintenance log can be used to record routine maintenance procedures.

8. **A.** Performance monitoring software can be used to create a baseline and monitor for any changes to that baseline. An example of this would be the Performance console window within Windows Server. (It is commonly referred to as Performance Monitor.) Antivirus and anti-spyware applications usually go hand-in-hand and are not used to monitor server baselines. Vulnerability assessing software such as Nessus or Nmap is used to see whether open ports and other vulnerabilities are on a server.

9. **B.** SNMP (Simple Network Management Protocol) enables you to gather information from a remote printer. HTTP is the Hypertext Transfer Protocol that deals with the transfer of web pages. A CA is a certificate authority, and SMTP is the Simple Mail Transfer Protocol.

10. **A.** A protocol analyzer can look inside the packets that make up a TCP/IP handshake. Information that can be viewed includes SYN, which is synchronize sequence numbers, and ACK, which is acknowledgment field significant. Port scanners and Performance Monitor do not have the capability to view flags set in a TCP/IP handshake, nor can they look inside packets in general.

11. **C.** Signature-based IDS is the most basic form of intrusion detection system, or IDS. This monitors packets on the network and compares them against a database of signatures. Anomaly-based, behavioral-based, and statistical-based are all more complex forms of IDS. Anomaly-based and statistical-based are often considered to be the same type of monitoring methodology.

12. **D.** A configuration baseline deals with the standard load of a server. By measuring the traffic that passes through the server's network adapter, you can create a configuration baseline over time.

13. **B and C.** It is important to calculate how much disk space you will require for the logs of your database server and verify that you have that much disk space available on the hard drive. It is also important to plan what information will be needed in the case that you need to reconstruct events later. Group Policy information and virtual memory are not important for this particular task.

14. **C.** It is important to copy the logs to a secondary server in case something happens to the primary log server; this way you have another copy of any possible security breaches. Logging all failed and successful login attempts might not be wise, because it will create many entries. The rest of the answers are not necessarily good ideas when working with log files.

15. **B.** Security administrators should frequently view the logs of a DNS server to monitor any unauthorized zone transfers. Aliases are DNS names that redirect to a hostname or FQDN. Simply viewing the logs of a DNS server will not defend against denial-of-service attacks. Domain name kiting is the process of floating a domain name for up to five days without paying for the domain name.

16. **B.** The information listed is an example of a port scan. The source IP address perpetuating the port scan should be banned or blocked on the firewall. The fact that the source computer is using port 53 is of no consequence during the port scan and does not imply DNS spoofing. It is not a denial-of-service attack; note that the destination IP address ends in 80, but the number 80 is part of the IP address and is not the port.

17. **B and C.** The log files should be retained in some manner either on this computer or on another computer. By hashing the log files, the integrity of the files can be checked even after they are moved. Cyclic redundancy checks, or CRCs, have to deal with the transmission of Ethernet frames over the network. Temporary files are normally not necessary when dealing with log files.

18. **A.** A protocol analyzer should be used to diagnose which network adapter on the LAN is causing the broadcast storm. It is also useful for detecting flooding attacks and fragmented packets. A firewall cannot diagnose attacks perpetuated on a network. A port scanner is used to find open ports on one or more computers. A network intrusion detection system (NIDS) is implemented to locate and possibly quarantine some types of attacks but will not be effective when it comes to broadcast storms. A port mirror copies all packets from one or more ports to the monitoring port. It is preferred if you are doing a diagnosis of a broadcast storm, but it is not *required*, and may not even be possible in some cases.

19. **C.** If an audit recording fails, there should be sufficient safeguards employed that can automatically send an alert to the administrator, among other things. Audit records should not be overwritten and in general should not be stopped.

20. **D.** The Security log file should show attempts at unauthorized access to a Windows computer. The Application log file deals with events concerning applications within the operating system and some third-party applications. The System log file deals with drivers, system files, and so on. A DNS log will log information concerning the domain name system.

21. **B.** The System log will show when a computer was shut down (and turned on, for that matter, or restarted). The Security log shows any audited information on a computer system. The Application log deals with OS apps and third-party apps. The DNS log shows events that have transpired on a DNS server.

22. **A and C.** Behavior-based monitoring and anomaly-based monitoring require creating a baseline. Many host-based IDS systems will monitor parts of the dynamic behavior and the state of the computer system. An anomaly-based IDS will classify activities as either normal or anomalous; this will be based on rules instead of signatures. Both behavior-based and anomaly-based monitoring require a baseline to make a comparative analysis. Signature-based monitoring systems do not require this baseline because they are looking for specific patterns or signatures and are comparing them to a database of signatures. Performance Monitor can be used to create a baseline on Windows computers, but it does not necessarily require a baseline.

23. **A.** A performance baseline and audit trails are not necessarily needed. Security logs are usually not performance-oriented. For example, you might get this list from a Windows Server's Security log in the Event Viewer. Auditing this much information could be unfeasible for one person. However, it is important to implement time stamping of the logs and store log details. Before implementing the logging server, Jason should check whether he has enough storage and backup space to meet his requirements.

24. **B.** The initial baseline configuration is most likely affected. Because the application has just been installed, there is only an initial baseline, but no other baselines to yet compare with. Since it is a testing environment, and the developer has just installed the application, security is not a priority. The developer probably wants to see what makes the application tick, and possibly reverse engineer it, but is not yet at the stage of application design, and probably won't be until a new application or modification of the current application is designed.

25. **D.** If the web server is showing a drop in processor and hard disk speed, it might have been compromised. Further analysis and comparison to a preexisting baseline would be necessary. All the other answers are common for a web server.

26. **A.** A computer security audit is an example of a detective security control. If a security administrator found that a firewall was letting unauthorized ICMP echoes into the network, the administrator might close the port on the firewall—a corrective control, and for the future, a preventive control. The term *protective control* is not generally used in security circles as it is a somewhat ambiguous term.

27. **A.** Most likely, the anomaly-based IDS needs to be reconfigured. It is alerting you to legitimate traffic, which amounts to false positives. These are not actually anomalies. If the traffic being analyzed has no specific signature (or known signature), then a signature-based IDS or IPS will not be able to identify it as legitimate or illegitimate. A UTM is a unified threat management device. This device may or may not have an IDS or IPS, and even then, it may or may not be capable of anomaly-based analysis, so it is not as likely an answer as the anomaly-based IDS. SIEM stands for security information and event management, and comes in the form of a software product or service or an appliance; it deals with real-time monitoring.

28. **C.** SNMPv3 should be used because it provides a higher level of security (encryption of packets, message integrity, and authentication), allowing you to gather information without fear of the data being compromised. SNMPv1 and v2 do not have the elaborate security of SNMPv3. ICMP is the Internet Control Message Protocol used with the ping utility, among other things. It has little to do with monitoring. SSH is Secure Shell, which is a more secure way of remotely controlling systems; it acts as a secure alternative to Telnet.

29. **C.** Continuous monitoring will help an already secure organization to assess security vulnerabilities and weaknesses in real time. Baselining and ACLs are things that have happened, or were configured in the past. Video surveillance is surely in real time, but it is doubtful as to whether it can *assess* security vulnerabilities in real time, even if someone is watching the video stream as it happens.

30. **C.** You are observing a Remote Desktop Protocol (RDP) acknowledgement packet. You can tell because the source IP address (192.168.1.5) is using port 3389, the default port for RDP, and is sending the ACK to 10.254.254.57 (which was connecting on the secondary HTTP port 8080). So the client is using an HTTP port, but that is inconsequential because the packet is being generated by the source (SRC) IP. HTTPS (port 443) is not involved in this packet capture. Neither is SFTP, as it rides on SSH using port 22.

This chapter covers the following subjects:

- **Cryptography Concepts:** This section covers the basic terminology of cryptography, including encryption, ciphers, and keys. It also discusses private versus public keys, symmetric versus asymmetric encryption, and public key encryption.

- **Encryption Algorithms:** This section delves into the various symmetric algorithms, such as DES and AES, and some of the popular asymmetric algorithms such as RSA and elliptic curve.

- **Hashing Basics:** Here, we investigate the most common way to verify the integrity of files: hashing. We cover basic hashing concepts and cryptographic hash functions, such as MD5, SHA, and NTLM.

When data is encrypted, it is modified in such a way that it cannot be understood by anyone who does not have the correct key. If you have the correct key, you can decrypt the data, and it will once again become intelligible. Though almost everyone has dealt with encrypted data and/or encrypted Internet sessions of some sort, chances are that the majority of the readers of this book will have limited *hands-on* experience with encryption. Because of this, I have written this chapter, and the following one, in a very to-the-point manner with simple analogous examples. I cover only what you need to know about encryption concepts, methods, and types. Encryption by itself is an entire IT field, but the CompTIA Security+ exam requires that you know only the basics—the exam objectives only scrape the surface of encryption concepts. Keep all this in mind as you go through this chapter and the next. I have provided some links to more advanced encryption books and websites in the View Recommended Resources document online, although reading them is not necessary for the exam. That being said, the "basics" of cryptography is a pretty huge chunk of information—there is a lot to cover, and some of the topics can be difficult to understand.

CHAPTER 14

Encryption and Hashing Concepts

It can help to pose the following question: What is it that we need to encrypt? Without a doubt, it is the data that needs to be encrypted, but more specifically three types of data: data in use, data at rest, and data in transit. **Data in use** can be described as actively used data undergoing constant change; for example, it could be stored in databases or spreadsheets. **Data at rest** is inactive data that is archived—backed up to tape or otherwise. **Data in transit** (also known as data in motion) is data that crosses the network or data that currently resides in computer memory. Consider thinking in these terms as we progress through the chapter.

Foundation Topics

Cryptography Concepts

Cryptography is the practice of hiding the meaning of a message. The word is roughly derived from the Greek words *kryptos* (meaning "hidden") and *graphein* (meaning "to write"). However, in cryptography it is not the message that is hidden, but rather the significance of the message.

Let me give a basic example of cryptography. When I was younger, some of the kids I knew would keep a black book with names, phone numbers, and so on. You probably wouldn't use a black book today, but I digress... Anyway, a couple of those people did something that fascinated me—they would modify phone numbers according to a code they had developed. This was done to hide the true phone number of a special friend from their parents, or from teachers, and so on. It was a basic form of encryption, although at the time I didn't realize it. I just referred to it as a "code."

Essentially, it worked like this:

The person with the black book would take a real phone number such as 555-0386. They would then modify the number by stepping each number backward or forward *x* number of steps. Let's say the person decided to step each number between 0 and 9 backward by three steps; the resulting coded phone number would be 222-7053. I'm sure you see how that was done, but let's break it down so that we can make an analogy to today's data encryption. Table 14-1 shows the entire code used.

Key Topic

Table 14-1   Black Book Phone Number Encryption

Original Number	Modifier	Modified Number
0	Minus 3	7
1		8
2		9
3		0
4		1
5		2
6		3
7		4
8		5
9		6

In this example, each number between 0 and 9 corresponds to a number three digits behind it. By the way, the numbers cycle through: For example, the number 0 goes three steps back, starting at 0, to 9, 8, and then 7 in an "around-the-bend" fashion. This is an example of cryptographic substitution.

NOTE   This is based on the *Caesar Cipher* (more accurately the Caesar Shift Cipher), where messages sent in ancient Rome would have each letter shifted by one or more places. You may also have heard of the ROT13 substitution cipher—this replaces (or rotates) a letter with the letter 13 steps after it.

Let's analogize. Each of the components in the table can be likened to today's computer-based encryption concepts:

- The original number is like to original file data.
- The modifier is like to an encryption key.
- The modified number is like to encrypted file data.

I call this the "Black Book Example," but I would guess that others have used similar analogies. Of course, this is a basic example; however, it should serve to help you to associate actual computer-based encryption techniques with this more tangible idea.

Now, for other people to figure out the original phone numbers in the black book, they would have to do the following:

Step 1.   Gain access to the black book. This is just like gaining access to data. Depending on how well the black book is secured, this by itself could be difficult.

Step 2.   Break the code. This would be known as decrypting the data. Of course, if the owner of the black book was silly enough to put the phone number encryption table in the book, well, then game over; it would be easy to decode. But if the owner was smart enough to memorize the code (and tell it to no one), making it a secret code, it would be much more difficult for another person to crack. Plus, the person could make the code more advanced; for example, look at Table 14-2.

Table 14-2   Advanced Black Book Phone Number Encryption

Original Number	Modifier	Modified Number
0	Minus 9	1
1	Minus 8	3
2	Minus 7	5
3	Minus 6	7
4	Minus 5	9
5	Minus 4	1b
6	Minus 3	3b
7	Minus 2	5b
8	Minus 1	7b
9	Minus 0	9b

In this example, there is a different modifier (or key) for each original number. Because the modified numbers have duplicates, we place a letter next to each of the various duplicates to differentiate. This is tougher to decrypt due to the increased level of variations, but on the flipside, it is that much harder to memorize. Likewise, computers have a harder time processing more advanced encryption codes, and hackers (or crackers) have a difficult time processing their decryption.

At this point, only one person has legitimate access to the encryption codes. However, what if the person wanted to share phone numbers with another person, but still keep the numbers secret from everyone else? This would be known as a secret key.

We refer to this basic concept as we go through this chapter and the next.

Now that we have given a basic example, let's define some terminology in a more technical way. We start with cryptography, encryption, ciphers, and keys. You might want to read through this list twice because each definition builds on the last.

- **Cryptography:** By definition, **cryptography** is the practice and study of hiding information, or more accurately, hiding the meaning of the information. It is used in e-commerce and with passwords. Most commonly, encryption is used to hide a message's meaning and make it secret.

- **Encryption: Encryption** is the process of changing information using an algorithm (or cipher) into another form that is unreadable by others—unless they possess the key to that data. Encryption is used to secure communications and to protect data as it is transferred from one place to another. The reverse, decryption, can be accomplished in two ways: First, by using the proper key to unlock the data, and second, by cracking the original encryption key. Encryption enforces confidentiality of data.

- **Cipher:** A **cipher** is an algorithm that can perform encryption or decryption. A basic example would be to take the *plaintext* word "code" and encrypt it as a *ciphertext* using a specific algorithm. The end result could be anything, depending on the algorithm used, but, for example, let's say the end result was the ciphertext "zlab." I don't know about you, but "zlab" looks like gibberish to me. (Although if you Google it, I'm sure you'll find all kinds of endless fun.) You've probably already guessed at my cipher—each letter of the plaintext word "code" was stepped back three letters in the alphabet. Historical ciphers use substitution methods such as this, and transposition methods as well. However, actual algorithms today are much more complex. **Algorithms** are well-defined instructions that describe computations from their initial state to their final state. IF-THEN statements are examples of computer algorithms. The entire set of instructions is the cipher. We cover the various types of ciphers (again, also known as algorithms) in the section "Encryption Algorithms" later in this chapter.

- **Key:** The **key** is the essential piece of information that determines the output of a cipher. It is indispensable; without it there would be no result to the cipher computation. In the previous bullet, the key was the act of stepping back three letters. In the first black book example, the key was stepping back three numbers (a modifier of minus 3). Just like a person can't unlock a lock without the proper key, a computer can't decrypt information without the proper key (using normal methods). The only way to provide security is if the key is kept secret—or in the case that there are multiple keys, if one of them is kept secret. The terms *key* and *cipher* are sometimes used interchangeably, but you should remember that the key is the vital portion of the cipher that determines its output. The length of the key determines its strength. Shorter, weaker keys are desirable to attackers attempting to access encrypted data. When two users exchange encrypted messages, it starts with a key exchange. The method of this exchange will vary depending on the type of cryptographic algorithm.

Keys can be private or public. A **private key** is only known to a specific user or users who keep the key a secret. A **public key** is known to all parties involved in encrypted transactions within a given group. An example of a private key would be the usage of an encrypted smart card for authentication. Smart cards, ExpressCard/PC Card technology, and USB flash drives are examples of devices that can store keys. When private keys are stored on these types of devices and delivered outside of a network, it is known as out-of-band key exchange. An example of a public key would be when two people want to communicate securely with each other over the Internet; they would require a public key that each of them knows. When this key transfer happens over a network, it is known as in-band key exchange.

Encryption types, such as AES or RSA, are known as ciphers, key algorithms, or simply as algorithms; we refer to them as algorithms during the rest of this chapter and the next. There are basically two classifications of key algorithms: symmetric and asymmetric.

Symmetric Versus Asymmetric Key Algorithms

Some cryptographic systems use symmetric keys only, others use asymmetric keys only, and some use both symmetric and asymmetric. It is important to know the differences between the two, and how they can be used together.

Symmetric Key Algorithms

The **symmetric key algorithm** is a class of cipher that uses a single key, identical keys, or closely related keys for both encryption and decryption. The term *symmetric key* is also referred to as the following: secret key, private key, single key, and shared key. Examples of symmetric key algorithms include DES, 3DES, RC, and AES, all of which we discuss later in this chapter. Another example of a technology that uses symmetric keys is Kerberos. By default, Kerberos makes use of a third party known as a key distribution center (KDC) for the secure transmission of symmetric keys, also referred to as tickets.

NOTE   Kerberos can optionally use public key cryptography (covered later in this chapter) by making use of asymmetric keys. This is done during specific authentication stages. Kerberos is covered in more depth in Chapter 10, "Physical Security and Authentication Models."

The private key is common in the workplace. Let's say that a user encrypts a file with a private key. Generally, that same key (or a very similar private key) is needed to decrypt the data. Imagine that the user left the organization and that user's account (and therefore the user's key) was deleted. How would you get the data back? Well, if the system has a recovery agent, you could use that to decrypt the file; otherwise, the data will not be recoverable! It's important to understand that private keys, and by extension, symmetric key systems, must be approached carefully or data could become lost.

Following are two types of symmetric key algorithms:

- A **stream cipher** is a type of algorithm that encrypts each binary digit in the data stream, one bit at a time.

- A **block cipher** is a type of algorithm that encrypts a group of bits collectively as individual units known as blocks. For example, the Advanced Encryption Standard (AES) algorithm can use 128-bit or 256-bit block ciphers. Block ciphers can work in different modes including: Electronic Codebook (ECB), Cipher Block Chaining (CBC), Cipher Feedback (CFB), Output Feedback (OFB), Galois/Counter Mode (GCM), and Counter (CTR). The modes define how a message is divided into blocks and encrypted. For example, ECB divides a message into blocks of plaintext and each block is encrypted separately. CBC is a commonly used mode that builds on ECB by XORing each block of plaintext with the previous ciphertext block that was created. CBC is one of the modes that require a unique binary sequence (an initialization vector, or IV) for each encryption operation. The IV can be a vulnerability, as in the CBC IV attack, where a predictable IV can lead to the deciphering of all blocks, because each one is based on the block previous. Secure coding concepts should be employed when using CBC or a separate block mode should be selected altogether such as GCM, which is considered to be a more efficient mode. The mode chosen will depend on the purpose of the encryption and the application it is being developed for.

Symmetric key algorithms require a secure initial exchange of one or more secret keys to both the sender and the receiver. In our black book example, we mentioned that people might possibly want to share their cipher with someone else. To do so, they would need to make sure that they were alone and that no one was eavesdropping. It is also so with computers. The secure initial exchange of secret keys can be difficult depending on the circumstances. It is also possible to encrypt the initial exchange of the secret keys!

Symmetric encryption is the preferred option when encrypting and sending large amounts of data. This is in part because it usually takes far less time to encrypt and decrypt data than asymmetric encryption does.

Asymmetric Key Algorithms

Asymmetric key algorithms use a pair of different keys to encrypt and decrypt data. The keys might be related, but they are not identical or even close to it in the way symmetric keys are. The two asymmetric keys are related mathematically. Imagine that you are the night shift security guard for a warehouse that stores CPUs. When your shift is over you are required to lock up. But the warehouse uses a special lock. Your key can only lock the warehouse door; it cannot unlock it. Conversely, the morning watchman has a key that can only unlock the door but not lock it. There are physical and electronic locks of this manner. This is analogous to asymmetric keys used in encryption. One key is used to encrypt data; the other, dissimilar key is used to decrypt the data. Because of the difference in keys, asymmetric key management schemes (such as PKI) are considered to be the most complicated. Examples of asymmetric key algorithms include RSA, the Diffie-Hellman system, and elliptic curve cryptography. SSL and TLS protocols use asymmetric key algorithms but generally do so in a public key cryptographic environment.

Public Key Cryptography

Public key cryptography uses asymmetric keys alone or in addition to symmetric keys. It doesn't need the secure exchange of secret keys mentioned in the symmetric key section. Instead, the asymmetric key algorithm creates a secret private key and a published public key. The public key is well known, and anyone can use it to encrypt messages. However, only the owner(s) of the paired or corresponding private key can decrypt the message. The security of the system is based on the secrecy of the private key. If the private key is compromised, the entire system will lose its effectiveness. This is illustrated in Figure 14-1.

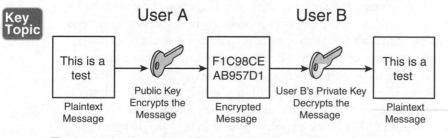

Figure 14-1   Illustration of Public Key Cryptography

Public key cryptography can become more intense. In some schemes, the private key is used to sign a message, and anyone can check the signature with the public key. This signing is done with a digital signature. A **digital signature** authenticates a document through math, letting the recipient know that the document was created and sent by the actual sender, and not someone else. So, it ensures integrity and non-repudiation, and it protects against forgery and tampering. The basic order of functions for the usage of asymmetric keys in this case would be encrypt, sign, decrypt, and verify.

> **NOTE**   Digital signatures can also be hashed (more on hashing later) for comparison once the document gets to its final destination.

In the Diffie-Hellman scheme, each user generates a public/private key pair and distributes a public key to everyone else. After two or more users obtain a copy of the others' public keys, they can be used to create a shared secret used as the key for a symmetric cipher. Due to the varying methods of public key cryptography, the whole subject can become somewhat confusing. Remember that there will always be a private key and a public key involved, and that public key cryptography can use asymmetric keys alone or in addition to symmetric keys.

Internet standards, such as SSL/TLS and PGP, use public key cryptography. Don't confuse the term *public key cryptography* with *public key infrastructure (PKI)*. Although they are related, they are not the same. PKI is an entire system of hardware, software, policies, and so on, that binds public keys with user identities by way of certificates and a certificate authority (server or other such device). A **certificate** is an electronic document that uses a digital signature to bind the key with the identity. We cover PKI more in Chapter 15, "PKI and Encryption Protocols."

Key Management

Key management deals with the relationship between users and keys; it's important to manage the generation, exchange, storage, and usage of those keys. It is crucial technically, and organizationally, because issues can present themselves due to poorly designed key systems and poor management. Keys must be chosen and stored securely. The generation of strong keys is probably the most important concept. Some algorithms have weak keys that make cryptanalysis easy. For example, DES uses a considerably weaker key than AES; the stronger the key, the stronger the key management. We detail several methods for the exchange of keys later in this chapter, including encapsulating one key within another, using key indicators, and exchanging symmetric session keys with an asymmetric key algorithm—in effect, ciphering our cipher. (We'll talk more about session keys in Chapter 15.)

Secure storage of keys often depends on users and passwords, or other authentication schemes. Proper storage of keys allows for availability, part of the CIA triad. Finally, keys should be replaced frequently. If a particular user uses a key for too long, it increases the chances of the key being cracked. Keys, like passwords, should be changed and/or recycled often.

Steganography

Although I have placed steganography within the cryptography section, it actually isn't cryptography, although it might be used with cryptography. **Steganography** is the science (and art) of writing hidden messages; it is a form of security through obscurity. The goal is that no one aside from the sender and receiver should even suspect that the hidden message exists. The advantage of steganography is that the clearly visible messages look to be just that, regular old messages that wouldn't usually attract attention to themselves. Most people know when they come into contact with an encrypted message, but far fewer people identify when a steganographic message has crossed their path. The classic example of steganography is from ancient Greece. A messenger would shave his head, and a leader would write a message on the person's scalp with indelible ink. After the messenger's hair grew long enough to hide the message, he would then deliver the message (time was not of the essence). When the messenger arrived at his destination, he would shave his head and the recipient could read the message. In Greek, *steganos* means "covered," and this is one example of hiding a message by covering it.

Steganography can hide messages within encrypted documents by inserting extra encrypted information. The hidden messages can also be found in sound files, image files, slowed-down video files, and regular Word documents or Excel spreadsheets. Messages can also be concealed within VoIP conversations (known as Lost Audio Packets Steganography, or LACK), and within any streaming service as well. They can also be obscured on a compromised wireless network with the HICCUPS system (Hidden Communication System for Corrupted Networks).

A common example of steganography is when using graphic files to send hidden messages. In this scenario, the least significant bit of each byte is replaced. For example, we could shade the color of a pixel (or triad) just slightly. This slight change would change the binary number associated with the color, enabling us to insert information. The color blue is represented as three bytes of data numbered 0, 0, and 255. We could change the color blue slightly to 1, 0, 255. This would not make the graphic look any different to the naked eye, but the change would be there nonetheless. This would be done in several or more pixels of the graphic to form the message. For this to work, the recipient would first need to have possession of the original file. Then the sender would transmit the modified steganographic file to be compared with the original by the recipient. There are several programs available on the Internet that facilitate and automate this process. Remember that one of the goals of steganography is to provide obfuscation, meaning making something obscure and unclear. This can be difficult to do manually, and more difficult to *undo* manually, so use reliable vendor-provided tools to aid in the process.

Encryption Algorithms

We mentioned previously that ciphers (or algorithms) can encrypt or decrypt data with the help of a key. We also pointed out that algorithms are well-defined instructions that describe computations from their initial state to their final state. In addition, we mentioned that there are symmetric and asymmetric algorithms. Now, let's talk about some of the actual algorithmic standards within both of those classifications. We start with symmetric types, including DES, 3DES, AES, and RC, and afterward move on to asymmetric types, including RSA, Diffie-Hellman, and the elliptic curve.

DES and 3DES

The **Data Encryption Standard (DES)** is an older type of block cipher selected by the U.S. federal government back in the 1970s as its encryption standard. But due to its weak key, it is now considered deprecated and has been replaced by other standards. Being a block cipher, it groups 64 bits together into encryption units. Today, a 64-bit cipher is not considered powerful enough; also, and more important, the key size is 56-bit, which can be cracked fairly easily with a brute-force attack or linear cryptanalysis attack. In addition to this, there are some theoretical weaknesses to the cipher itself. DES was replaced by Triple DES (3DES) in 1999. The actual algorithm is sometimes referred to as the Data Encryption Algorithm (DEA). The algorithm is based on the Feistel cipher, which has very similar, if not identical, encryption and decryption processes, reducing the amount of code required.

NOTE   The International Data Encryption Algorithm (IDEA) was designed as a replacement to DES and is an optional algorithm in the OpenPGP standard, though it suffers from a simple key schedule resulting in weak keys.

Triple DES, also known as 3DES or the Triple Data Encryption Algorithm (TDEA), is similar to DES but applies the cipher algorithm three times to each cipher block. The cipher block size is still 64-bit, but the key size can now be as much as 168-bit (three times the size of DES). This was a smart approach to defeating brute-force attacks without having to completely redesign the DES protocol. However, both DES and 3DES have been overshadowed by AES, which became the preferred standard in late 2001.

AES

In the late 1990s, the National Institute of Standards and Technology (NIST) started a competition to develop a more advanced type of encryption. There were 15 submissions, including Serpent, Twofish, RC6, and others, but the selected winner was Rijndael. This submission was then further developed into the **Advanced Encryption Standard (AES)** and became the U.S. federal government standard in 2002. AES is the successor to DES/3DES and is another symmetric key encryption standard composed of three different versions of block ciphers: AES-128, AES-192, and AES-256. Actually, each of these has the same 128-bit cipher block size, but the key sizes for each are 128-bit, 192-bit, and 256-bit, respectively.

AES is based on the substitution-permutation network, which takes plaintext and the key and applies x number of rounds to create the ciphertext. These rounds consist of substitution boxes and permutation boxes (usually in groups of 4×4 bytes) that convert the plaintext input bits to ciphertext output bits. AES specifies 10, 12, or 14 rounds for each of the respective versions.

AES is fast, uses minimal resources, and can be used on a variety of platforms. For example, it is the encryption algorithm of choice if you have a wireless network running the WPA2 protocol; the IEEE 802.11i standard specifies the usage of AES with WPA2, and in the process deprecates WEP. (See Chapter 9, "Securing Network Media and Devices," for more about WEP and WPA.) You will also find AES as the encrypting protocol for remote control applications. These are examples of data in motion (also called data in transit). Any network session that uses AES would fall into this category. But memory encryption would fall into that category as well. For example, there are programs that can encrypt passwords and other personally identifiable information (PII) as it is passing through RAM. They often use AES or Twofish.

In addition, AES is a good choice for transferring encrypted data quickly to a USB flash drive. It is also used as the Windows Encrypting File System (EFS) algorithm and in whole disk encryption techniques such as BitLocker.

AES is purportedly susceptible to the related-key attack, if the attacker has some information about the mathematical relationship between several different keys. Side-channel attacks can also circumvent the AES cipher using malware to obtain privilege escalation. These are ways of attacking the implementation of the protocol, but not the protocol itself.

Generally, AES is considered the strongest type of symmetric encryption for many scenarios. As of now, AES is used worldwide and has not been outright compromised, and some industry experts think it never will be.

You may have heard of the terms *DEK*, *KEK*, and *MEK*. These are different types of keys used during the encryption process. AES provides a good place to discuss these. Let's say you have data that you need encrypted and you decide to use AES to do so. When AES encrypts the data, it does so with a data encryption key (DEK). To make an encryption system more secure, you can store that DEK in an encrypted format. This is done with a key encryption key (KEK) and can be stored in a separate location for additional security if need be. A master encrypting key (MEK), or simply master key, is another type of key that describes either a DEK or KEK being used. For example, in a secure storage scenario, the master key will be a DEK that is used to encrypt data that is put in a user's protected storage area. It is encrypted by a KEK that is based on the user's password. That is a very basic explanation of DEK, KEK, and MEK. For the Security+ exam you should be able to define them, and understand that they can be instrumental in dealing with secure storage of data, potentially in multiple locations. However, unless you are a developer, you most likely won't be working with each type of key individually.

RC

RC stands for different things depending on who you talk to. Officially, it is known as Rivest Cipher but is playfully known as Ron's Code as well. There are multiple RC versions, most of which are not related aside from the fact that they are all encryption algorithms.

RC4 is a somewhat widely used stream cipher in protocols such as SSL, WEP, and RDP. It is known for its speed and simplicity. However, it is avoided when designing newer applications and technologies due to several vulnerabilities; when used with WEP on wireless networks, it can be cracked quickly with the use of aircrack-ptw. One way to avoid this to a certain extent is to use the Temporal Key Integrity Protocol (TKIP) with WEP. However, it still is recommended that AES and WPA2 be used in wireless networks. Some versions of Microsoft Remote Desktop Services use RC4 128-bit. However, Microsoft recommends disabling RC4 if at all possible, and using other encryption, such as Federal Information Processing Standard (FIPS)-compliant encryption (IPsec and EFS) and TLS for authentication.

> **NOTE** FIPS-compliant could be in the form of a hardware- or software-based crypto-module. For example, FIPS 140-1 and 140-2 specify Microsoft as a proper vendor; see this link for more: http://csrc.nist.gov/groups/STM/cmvp/documents/140-1/140val-all.htm. Microsoft includes a software library known as the Cryptographic Service Provider (CSP) that implements the Microsoft CryptoSPI (a system program interface).

RC5 is a block cipher noted for its simplicity and for its variable size (32-, 64-, or 128-bit). The strongest RC5 block cipher that has been cracked via brute-force as of the writing of this book is a 64-bit RC5 key, in 2001. This was done by distributed.net, a nonprofit organization which at the time had 30 TFLOPS of computational power. It is also working on cracking the 72-bit version of RC5, with substantially higher throughput at its disposal. This is cause for concern for some—because Moore's Law tells us of the effective doubling of CPU power every two years or so—but you must remember that stronger algorithms such as AES 256-bit are *exponentially* harder to crack.

RC6 is a block cipher entered into the AES competition and was one of the five finalists. Though it was not selected, it is a patented algorithm offered by RSA Security as an alternative to AES. It is similar to AES in block size and key size options but uses different mathematical methods than Rijndael.

Blowfish and Twofish

Blowfish and Twofish are two ciphers designed by Bruce Schneier. The original **Blowfish** is a block cipher designed as an alternative to DES (the name also pertains to a suite of products). It has a 64-bit block size and variable key size between 32 and 448 bits. Bruce Schneier recommends the newer **Twofish** cipher, which has a block size of 128 bits and a key size up to 256 bits and is also based on Feistel. There is also a newer Threefish block cipher with key sizes up to 1024-bit. These symmetrical ciphers have not been compromised, but they do have minor weaknesses that can be exploited by birthday attacks and key separation.

Summary of Symmetric Algorithms

Table 14-3 gives some comparisons of the algorithms up to this point and their key size. Key size is the number of bits in a cipher. It is also referred to as key length or key strength.

Key Topic

Table 14-3   Summary of Symmetric Algorithms

Algorithm Acronym	Full Name	Maximum/Typical Key Size
DES	Data Encryption Standard	56-bit
3DES	Triple DES	168-bit
AES	Advanced Encryption Standard	256-bit
RC4	Rivest Cipher version 4	128-bit typical
RC5	Rivest Cipher version 5	64-bit typical
RC6	Rivest Cipher version 6	256-bit typical
Twofish	Twofish	128-, 192-, 256-bit

RSA

Let's talk about some asymmetric key algorithms. The original and very common **RSA** (which stands for Rivest, Shamir, and Adleman, the creators) is a public key cryptography algorithm. As long as the proper size keys are used, it is considered to be a secure protocol and is used in many e-commerce scenarios. It is slower than symmetric key algorithms but has advantages of being suitable for signing and for encryption. It works well with credit card security and TLS/SSL. Key lengths for RSA are much longer than in symmetric cryptosystems. For example, 512-bit RSA keys have proven to be breakable over a decade ago; however, 1024-bit keys are currently considered unbreakable by most known technologies, but RSA still recommends using the longer 2048-bit key, which should deter even the most powerful super hackers. It is important to note that asymmetric algorithm keys need to be much larger than their symmetric key counterparts to be as effective. For example, a 128-bit symmetric key is essentially equal to a 2304-bit asymmetric key in strength.

The RSA algorithm uses what is known as integer factorization cryptography. It works by first multiplying two distinct prime numbers that cannot be factored. Then it moves on to some more advanced math in order to derive a set of two numbers. Finally, from these two numbers, it creates a private and public key pair.

The private key is used to decrypt data that has been encrypted with the public key. For example, if Alice (User A) sends Bob (User B) a message, Alice can find out Bob's public key from a central source and encrypt a message to Bob using Bob's public key. When Bob receives it, he decrypts it with his private key.

Bob can also authenticate himself to Alice, for example by using his private key to encrypt a digital certificate. When Alice receives it, she can use his public key to decrypt it. These concepts are summarized in Table 14-4.

Table 14-4   Summary of RSA Public and Private Key Usage

Task	Which Person's Key to Use	What Kind of Key
Send an encrypted message	Receiver's	Public key
Decrypt an encrypted message	Receiver's	Private key
Send an encrypted signature	Sender's	Private key
Decrypt an encrypted signature	Sender's	Public key

Other examples of RSA encryption include tokens in the form of SecurID USB dongles, and devices such as hardware security modules (HSMs) and trusted platform modules (TPMs). All these devices can store RSA asymmetric keys and can be used to assist in user authentication. RSA key distribution is vulnerable to man-in-the-middle attacks. However, these attacks are defensible through the use of digital certificates and other parts of a PKI system that we detail in the next chapter. It is also susceptible to timing attacks that can be defended against through the use of cryptographic blinding: This blind computation provides encryption without knowing actual input or output information. Due to other types of attacks, it is recommended that a secure padding scheme be used. Padding schemes work differently depending on the type of cryptography. In public key cryptography, padding is the addition of random material to a message to be sufficient, and incorporating a proof, making it more difficult to crack. A padding scheme is always involved, and algorithm makers such as RSA are always releasing improved versions.

In 2000, RSA Security released the RSA algorithm to the public. Therefore, no licensing fees are required if an organization decides to use or modify the algorithm. RSA published a group of standards known as PKCS (Public-Key Cryptography Standards) in an effort to promote its various public key techniques. For example, PKCS #1 defines the mathematical properties of RSA public and private keys. Another example is PKCS #11, which defines how HSMs utilize RSA. The entire list of standards can be found at the following link:

https://www.emc.com/emc-plus/rsa-labs/standards-initiatives/public-key-cryptography-standards.htm

Diffie-Hellman

The **Diffie-Hellman key exchange**, invented in the 1970s, was the first practical method for establishing a shared secret key over an unprotected communications channel. This asymmetric algorithm was developed shortly before the original RSA algorithm. It is also known as the Diffie-Hellman-Merkle key exchange due to Ralph Merkle's conceptual involvement.

Diffie-Hellman relies on secure key exchange before data can be transferred. This key exchange establishes a shared secret key that can be used for secret communications but over a public network. Originally, fictitious names were chosen for the "users": Alice and Bob. Basically, Alice and Bob agree to initial prime and base numbers. Then, each of them selects secret integers and sends an equation based on those to each other. Each of them computes the other's equation to complete the shared secret, which then allows for encrypted data to be transmitted. The secret integers are discarded at the end of the session. These were originally static keys, meaning that they were used for a long period of time.

Diffie-Hellman is considered secure against eavesdroppers due to the difficulty of mathematically solving the Diffie-Hellman problem. However, it is vulnerable to man-in-the-middle attacks. To prevent this, some method of authentication is used such as password authentication. This algorithm is used by the Transport Layer Security (TLS) protocol during encrypted web sessions. When used in this manner, it works in ephemeral mode, meaning that keys are generated during each portion of the key establishment process, and are used for shorter periods of time than with static keys. It is this ephemeral process that achieves *perfect forward secrecy (PFS)*, which ensures that the compromise of one message will not lead to the compromise of another message. This ephemeral version of Diffie-Hellman is called DHE, or sometimes Ephemeral Diffie-Hellman (EDH), because it uses an ephemeral key, meaning that the cryptographic key is generated for each execution of the key establishment process. One of the drawbacks to DHE is that it requires more computational power; however, there is an elliptic curve alternative, which we talk about in the next section.

NOTE   The Diffie-Hellman algorithm can also be used within a public key infrastructure (PKI), though the RSA algorithm is far more common.

Elliptic Curve

Elliptic curve cryptography (ECC) is a type of public key cryptography based on the structure of an elliptic curve. It uses logarithms calculated against a finite field and is based on the difficulty of certain mathematical problems. It uses smaller keys than most other encryption methods. Keys are created by graphing specific points on the curve, which were generated mathematically. All parties involved must agree on the elements that define the curve. This asymmetric algorithm has a compact design, leading to reduced computational power compared to other asymmetric algorithms, yet it creates keys that are difficult to crack.

Other algorithms have been adapted to work with elliptic curves, including Diffie-Hellman and the Digital Signature Algorithm (DSA). The Diffie-Hellman version (known as Elliptic Curve Diffie-Hellman, or ECDH) uses elliptic curve public/private key pairs to establish the secret key. Another variant, **Elliptic Curve Diffie-Hellman Ephemeral (ECDHE)**, runs in ephemeral mode, which as previously stated makes sure that a compromised message won't start a chain reaction, and that other messages maintain their integrity. By its very design, the elliptic curve solves the problem of the extra computational power required by DHE. DSA is a U.S. federal government standard public key encryption algorithm used in digital signatures. The elliptic version is known as ECDSA. In general, the size of the public key in an elliptic curve–based algorithm can be 1/6 the size of the non-elliptic curve version. For example, ECDSA has a public key that is 160 bits, but regular DSA uses a public key that is 1024 bits. This is part of the reasoning behind the reduced amount of CPU power needed.

ECC is used with smart cards, wireless security, and other communications such as VoIP and IPsec (with DSA). It can be susceptible to side-channel attacks (SCAs), which are attacks based on leaked information gained from the physical implementation (number and type of curves) of the cryptosystem, and fault attacks (a type of SCA), plus there are concerns about backdoors into the algorithm's random generator. Elliptic curve cryptography (as well as RSA and other algorithms) is also theoretically vulnerable to quantum cryptanalysis–based computing attacks.

Quantum Cryptography

The quantum computer (as of the writing of this book) is highly theoretical, but quantum encryption is more of a reality. More accurately known as quantum cryptography, it builds on quantum mechanics, and in particular, quantum communications.

In the standard digital encryption scenario, the "key" is established between two parties: One person encodes bits of information, and the other decodes them. Standard bits of information are used (1s and 0s). But in a quantum encryption scenario, the bits of the key can be encoded as quantum data (in which bits can exist in multiple states). This allows information to be encoded in such a way that would otherwise be impossible in classical digital encryption schemes.

Currently, quantum cryptography is a reality only in the form of quantum key distribution (QKD), which does have various protocols based on it. It commonly uses a fiber channel (fiber-optic matrix) to transmit quantum information, which can be very costly. In fact, the entire procedure is quite expensive and difficult to undertake, making it uncommon. But it is known to have flaws. Let's remember one general rule about security: There is no perfect, utopian, secure solution. Given time, every encryption technique is exploited and its vulnerabilities are exposed. It would follow that quantum encryption is no exception. And so continues the endless cycle of security control > hacking attempt > security control....

More Encryption Types

We have a couple more encryption types to speak of. They don't quite fit into the other sections, so I figured I would place them here. The first is the one-time pad, and the second is the Pretty Good Privacy (PGP) application and encryption method.

One-Time Pad

A **one-time pad** (also known as the Vernam cipher, named after the engineer Gilbert Vernam) is a stream cipher that encrypts plaintext with a secret random key that is the same length as the plaintext. It uses a string of bits that is generated at random (known as a keystream). Encryption is accomplished by combining the key-stream with the plaintext message using the bitwise XOR operator to produce the ciphertext. Because the keystream is randomized, even an attacker with a plethora of computational resources on hand can only guess the plaintext if the attacker sees the ciphertext.

Unlike other encryption types, it can be computed by hand with a pencil and paper (thus the word "pad" in the name), although today computers will be used to create a one-time pad algorithm for use with technology. It has been proven as impossible to crack if used correctly and is known as being "information-theoretically secure"; it is the only cryptosystem with theoretically perfect secrecy. This means that it provides no information about the original message to a person trying to decrypt it illegitimately. However, issues with this type of encryption have stopped it from being widely used. Because of this, the acronym *OTP* is more commonly associated with "one-time passwords," which we talk about later in this chapter.

One of the issues with a one-time pad is that it requires perfect randomness. The problem with computer-based random number generators is that they usually aren't truly random because high-quality random numbers are difficult to generate; instead, they are pseudorandom number generators (PRNGs), discussed a bit later. Another issue is that the exchange of the one-time pad data must be equal to the length of the message. It also requires proper disposal, which is difficult due to data remanence.

Regardless of these issues, the one-time pad can be useful in scenarios in which two users in a secure environment are required to also communicate with each other from two other separate secure environments. The one-time pad is also used in superencryption (or multiple encryption), which is encrypting an already encrypted message. In addition, it is commonly used in quantum cryptography, which uses quantum mechanics to guarantee secure communications. These last two concepts are far beyond the Security+ exam, but they show the actual purpose for this encryption type.

PGP

Pretty Good Privacy (PGP) is an encryption program used primarily for signing, encrypting, and decrypting e-mails in an attempt to increase the security of e-mail communications. You might remember that we previously discussed weaknesses of e-mail client programs when sending via POP3 and SMTP servers. PGP uses (actually wrote) the encryption specifications as shown in the OpenPGP standard; other similar programs use this as well. Today, PGP has an entire suite of tools that can encrypt e-mail, accomplish whole disk encryption, and encrypt zip files and instant messages. PGP uses a symmetric session key (also referred to as a preshared key, or PSK), and as such, you might hear PGP referred to as a program that uses symmetric encryption, but it also uses asymmetric RSA for digital signatures and for sending the session key. Because of this it is known as a hybrid cryptosystem, combining the best of conventional systems and public key cryptography.

When encrypting data, PGP uses key sizes of at least 128 bits. Newer versions allow for RSA or DSA key sizes ranging from 512 bits to 2048 bits. The larger the key, the more secure the encryption is, but the longer it takes to generate the keys; although, this is done only once when establishing a connection with another user. The program uses a combination of hashing, data compression, symmetric key cryptography, and public key cryptography. New versions of the program are not fully compatible with older versions because the older versions cannot decrypt the data that was generated by a newer version. This is one of the issues when using PGP; users must be sure to work with the same version. Newer versions of PGP support OpenPGP and S/MIME, which allows for secure communications with just about everyone.

Because it works with RSA, the security of PGP is based on the key size. It is considered secure and uncrackable as long as a sufficient key size is used. As an example, it has been suggested that a 2048-bit key should be safe against the strongest of well-funded adversaries with knowledgeable people and the latest in supercomputers until at least the year 2020; 1024-bit keys are considered strong enough for all but the most sensitive data environments.

Around the turn of the millennium, the creator of PGP, and many other security-minded people that used PGP, sensed that an open source alternative would be beneficial to the cryptographic community. This was presented to, and accepted by, the IETF, and a new standard called OpenPGP was developed. With this open source code, others could write software that could easily integrate with PGP (or replace it). One example of this is the **GNU Privacy Guard (GPG**, or GNuPG), which is compliant with the OpenPGP standard. Over time this has been developed for several platforms including various Linux GUIs, macOS/OS X, and Windows. GPG is a combination of symmetric key encryption and public key encryption.

PGP and its derivatives are used by many businesses and individuals worldwide so that files can be easily encrypted before transit. The original PGP (developed by Philip Zimmerman) has changed hands several times and, as of this writing, is owned by Symantec, which offers it as part of its products (for a fee). There are also several versions of PGP, as well as GNuPG, available for download for free. A good starting point is the following link: http://openpgp.org/.

Pseudorandom Number Generators

The **pseudorandom number generator (PRNG)** is used by cryptographic applications that require unpredictable output. They are primarily coded in C or Java and are developed within a cryptography application such as a key generator program.

Within that program there is a specific utility, for example SHA2PRNG, that is used to create the PRNG. (Remember to use SHA-256—as of the writing of this book—or higher.) For additional "randomness" a programmer will increase entropy, often by collecting system noise. One of the threats to PRNGs is the random number generator attack, which exploits weaknesses in the code. This can be prevented by implementing randomness, using AES, using newer versions of SHA, and maintaining physical control of the system where the PRNG is developed and stored.

AI and Genetic Algorithms

Algorithms are also used in the world of artificial intelligence, often by searching for particular information within a vast array of data. One example of this is the genetic algorithm, a type of evolutionary algorithm, which is inspired by natural, biological evolution. Algorithms such as this are programmed with languages like Python and C++.

A genetic algorithm can be used to identify a person from a very broad set of information. This could be based on a set of data gathered via data aggregation, or—and this is related to the book you are reading—it could involve stylometry. Stylometry is the study of linguistic style, music, and other forms of communication. It could be used to identify the author of this book without knowing any reference to the author, or to identify a songwriter. You know, name that tune in three notes!—except a computer does the naming. It's based on style and specific words (and their usage frequency) employed by the writer. A genetic algorithm used in stylometric analysis applies a set of rules (IF-THEN statements). It helps to know a key word that the writer uses somewhat frequently. For example, the word "known": In a chapter such as this, with 10,000 words, I might use that word 30 times. The rule could be "If the word *known* appears 3 or more times per every 1000 words, then the author is X." In this case, X would equal David L. Prowse, me, and possibly several other technical authors. Stylometry has its uses in identification, but can also be used to provide statistical analysis; for example, perhaps I should cut back on the word *known*! It might help to know overused words when a book such as this can commonly reach 2 million keystrokes. But more often than not it is used for identification of anonymous works. Stylometry is just one of many examples of applications that use genetic algorithms.

Hashing Basics

A **hash** is a summary of a file or message, often in numeric format. Hashes are used in digital signatures, in file and message authentication, and as a way to protect the integrity of sensitive data; for example, data entered into databases, or perhaps entire hard drives. A hash is generated through the use of a hash function to verify the integrity of the file or message, most commonly after transit over a network. A **hash**

function is a mathematical procedure that converts a variable-sized amount of data into a smaller block of data. The hash function is designed to take an arbitrary data block from the file or message, use that as an input, and from that block produce a fixed-length hash value. Basically, the hash is created at the source and is recalculated and compared with the original hash at the destination. Figure 14-2 illustrates this process. Note the hash that was created starting with ce114e and so on. This is the summary, or message digest, of the file to be sent. It is an actual representation of an MD5 hash (covered shortly) of a plaintext file with the words "This is a test," as shown in the message portion of Figure 14-2.

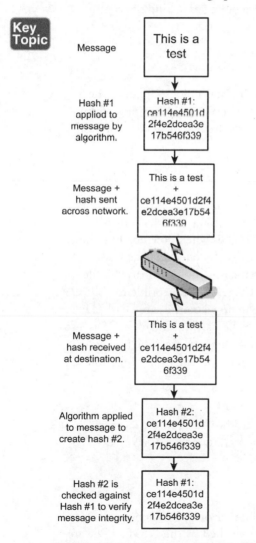

Figure 14-2   Illustration of the Hashing Process

Because the hash is a condensed version of the file/message, or a portion of it, it is also known as a message digest. It provides integrity to data so that a user knows that the message is intact, hasn't been modified during transit, and comes from the source the user expects. A hash can fall into the category of a **one-way function**. This means it is easy to compute when generated but difficult (or impossible) to compute in reverse. In the case of a hash, a condensed version of the message, initial computation is relatively easy (compared to other algorithms), but the original message should not be re-created from the hash. Contrast this concept to encryption methods that indeed can be reversed. A hash can be created without the use of an algorithm, but generally, the ones used in the field require some kind of cryptographic algorithm.

Cryptographic Hash Functions

Cryptographic hash functions are hash functions based on block ciphers. The methods used resemble that of cipher modes used in encryption. Examples of cryptographic hash functions include MD5 and SHA. Let's discuss a few types of hash functions now.

MD5

The **Message-Digest algorithm 5 (MD5)** is the newest of a series of algorithms designed by Ron Rivest. It uses a 128-bit key. This is a widely used hashing algorithm; at some point you have probably seen MD5 hashes when downloading files. This is an example of the attempt at providing integrity. By checking the hash produced by the downloaded file against the original hash, you can verify the file's integrity with a level of certainty. However, MD5 hashes are susceptible to collisions. A **collision** occurs when two different files end up using the same hash. Due to this low collision resistance, MD5 is considered to be harmful today. MD5 is also vulnerable to threats such as rainbow tables and pre-image attacks. The best solution to protect against these attacks is to use a stronger type of hashing function such as SHA-2 or higher.

NOTE A rainbow table is a precomputed table used to reverse engineer a cryptographic hash function. Rainbow tables are most often used to crack passwords.

SHA

The **Secure Hash Algorithm (SHA)** is one of a number of hash functions designed by the U.S. National Security Agency (NSA) and published by the NIST. They are used widely in the U.S. government. SHA-1 is no longer considered to be secure because there is the potential for successful collision-based attacks. It employs a

160-bit hash, and as of 2017 has been deprecated. Any websites or other applications using SHA-1 are required to be updated to a higher level of SHA or other hashing algorithm. SHA-2 is more secure; it has 256-bit and 512-bit block sizes, plus truncated derivatives of each. Keccak was selected from a group of algorithms in 2012 as the SHA-3 winner, but is not meant as a replacement for SHA-2, because no compromise of SHA-2 has yet been demonstrated (as of the writing of this book).

It is important that a hashing algorithm be collision-resistant. If it has the capability to avoid the same output from two guessed inputs (by an attacker attempting a collision attack), it is collision-resistant. When it comes to cryptography, "perfect hashing" is not possible because usually unknowns are involved, such as the data to be used to create the hash, and what hash values have been created in the past. Though perfect is not possible, it is possible to increase collision resistance by using a more powerful hashing algorithm.

Because MD5 and SHA-1 have vulnerabilities, some government agencies started using SHA-2 as early as 2011 (and most likely will use SHA-3 at some point). For added security, a software key (computed with either SHA or MD-5) might be compared to a hardware key. Some software activations require this in fact—if the hardware and software hash values don't match, then the software won't activate.

RIPEMD and HMAC

RIPEMD stands for the RACE Integrity Primitives Evaluation Message Digest. The original RIPEMD (128-bit) had a collision reported, and therefore it is recommended to use RIPEMD-160 (160-bit), RIPEMD-256, or RIPEMD-320. The commonly used RIPEMD-160 is a 160-bit message digest algorithm used in cryptographic hashing. It is used less commonly than SHA and was designed as an open source hashing algorithm.

HMAC stands for Hash-based Message Authentication Code. Let's step back for a moment: Message Authentication Code (MAC) is a short piece of information— a small algorithm—used to authenticate a message and to provide integrity and authenticity assurances on the message. It checks the integrity of the cipher used and notifies the receiver if there were any modifications to the encrypted data. This way, the data cannot be denied (repudiated) when received.

Building on this concept, HMAC is a calculation of a MAC through the use of a cryptographic hash function such as MD5 or SHA-1. If for example SHA-1 is used, the corresponding MAC would be known as HMAC-SHA1, or better yet, if using SHA-2 (due to SHA-1 deprecation) then you would probably use HMAC-SHA256 (or higher). Warning: Be very careful selecting the type and version of hash function that you use!

LANMAN, NTLM, and NTLMv2

Passwords can also be hashed using algorithms. Some password hashes are more secure than others, whereas older ones have been cracked and are therefore compromised. This section details the Windows-based LANMAN, NTLM, and NTLMv2 hashes starting from the oldest. These three types of authentication are what attempts to make your login to the Windows computer secure, unless you log in to a domain where Kerberos is used by default.

LANMAN

The **LANMAN hash**, also known as the LAN Manager hash or simply LM hash, was the original hash used to store Windows passwords. It was used in Windows operating systems before Windows NT but is supported by some versions of Windows in an attempt to be backward compatible. This backward compatibility can be a security risk because the LM hash has several weaknesses and can be cracked easily.

Its function is based on the deprecated DES algorithm and can only be a maximum of 14 characters. These weaknesses are compounded by the fact that the ASCII password is broken into two pieces, one of which is converted to uppercase, essentially removing a large portion of the character set. Plus, it can store a maximum of only seven uppercase characters. Due to this, brute-force attacks can crack alphanumeric LM hashes in a matter of hours.

Due to all these weaknesses, it is highly recommended that the LANMAN hash be disabled on operating systems that run it by default. It should also be checked on operating systems such as Windows Vista/Server 2008 *and higher* that are supposed to have it disabled by default, just in case the setting was modified.

The following step-by-step procedure shows how to disable the storage of LM hashes in Windows:

Step 1.   Open the Run prompt and type `secpol.msc` to display the Local Security Policy window.

Step 2.   Navigate to Local Policies > Security Options.

Step 3.   In the right pane, double-click the policy named Network Security: Do Not Store LAN Manager Hash Value on Next Password Change.

Step 4.   Click Enabled (if it isn't already), as shown in Figure 14-3, and click OK. (Remember that in a situation such as this you are enabling a negative.)

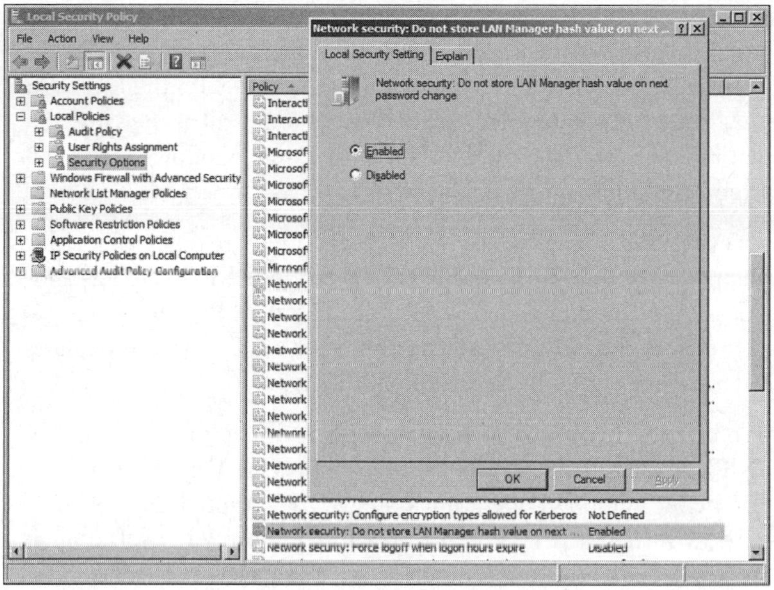

Figure 14-3 LM Hash in the Local Group Policy

NOTE For Windows Server domain controllers, you need to access the Group Policy Editor, not Local Group Policy. Generally, this would be done at the default domain policy, but it could also be accomplished at a single OU's policy, if necessary.

You can also disable the storage of LM hash passwords by modifying the Registry. This process is necessary for older versions of Windows. For more information, see the link to Microsoft's website in the "View Recommended Resources" document on the accompanying website.

If, for whatever reason, the storing of LM hashes for passwords cannot be turned off, Microsoft recommends using a 15-character-minimum password. When this is done, an LM hash and an NTLM hash value are stored. In this situation, the LM hash cannot be used solely to authenticate the user; therefore, it cannot be solely cracked. The NTLM hash would have to be cracked as well. Because 15 characters might be beyond some organizations' policies—or some users' ability, for that matter—it is highly recommended that the LM hash policy be disabled.

NTLM and NTLMv2

Well, we talked a lot about why the LM hash is insufficient. Let's get into the replacements. The first is the **NTLM hash**, also known as the NT LAN Manager hash. The NTLM algorithm was first supplied with Windows NT 3.1; it provides Unicode support and, more important to this conversation, the RC4 cipher. Although the RC4 cipher enables a more powerful hash known as NTLM for storing passwords, the systems it ran on were still configured to be backward compatible with the LM hash. So, as long as the LM hash was not disabled, those systems were still at the same risk as older systems that ran the LM hash only. Windows Vista and Windows Server 2008 operating systems (and higher) disable the older LM hash by default.

While NTLM uses cyclic redundancy checks (CRCs) and message digest algorithms for integrity, the main issue with NTLM is that it is based on the RC4 cipher, and not any recent cryptographic methods such as AES or SHA-256. RC4 has been compromised, and therefore the NTLM hash is compromised. Due to the weakness of NTLM, we need a stronger hashing algorithm: NTLMv2.

The **NTLMv2** hash uses an HMAC-MD5 hash, making it difficult to crack; it is a 128-bit system. NTLMv2 has been available since Windows NT 4.0 SP4 and is used by default on newer Windows operating systems. Even though NTLMv2 responds to the security issues of the LM hash and NTLM, most Microsoft domains use Kerberos as the logon authentication scheme because of its level of security when dealing with one computer logging in to another or in to an entire network/domain. NTLMv2 is used either when Kerberos isn't available, users log in with local accounts, or a connecting OS doesn't support Kerberos.

Hashing Attacks

A cryptographic hash is difficult to reverse engineer, but not impossible. A powerful computer can decrypt some hashes…it just takes time. But time is of the essence, and so attackers will attempt other methods, such as creating collisions, using side-channel attacks, or utilizing privilege escalation. Let's discuss a couple of ways that hashes can be exploited.

Pass the Hash

A **pass the hash** attack is when an attacker obtains the password hash of one or more user accounts and reapplies the hash to a server or other system in order to fool the system into thinking that the attacker is authentic. The goal is for the attacker to gain access to the system, often a Windows Server, and gain another user's credentials with the potential to escalate privileges.

The attack starts with the attacker obtaining the hashes from a target system. That's the hard part. Access to the system is required in one way or another, then the attacker can use a hash dumping utility to collect the hashes for user passwords. Next, the attacker utilizes a "pass the hash" program to place the hashes within the server. For example, within the Local Security Authority Subsystem Service (LSASS) in Windows Server. This can be done using a side-channel attack so that the attacker can impersonate one of the users. If done properly, the attacker does not need to know the password of an account, does need to brute-force the password, and does not need to reverse engineer the hash. While the attack can be carried out on an individual client system also, it is more often something that is focused on Windows Servers (namely domain controllers) because they house many user account credentials.

Prevention includes the following: Only allowing clients that are trusted operating systems to connect to a server; configuring Windows domain trusts securely, using multifactor authentication; using tokens; and implementing the principle of least privilege for user accounts. When employing least privilege, be sure to include domain accounts *and* local admin accounts. Finally, standard network security discussed in Chapter 6 through 9 should also be implemented, including IDS/IPS solutions, firewall restrictions, and so on.

Happy Birthday!

Not when a birthday attack is involved. A **birthday attack** is an attack on a hashing system that attempts to send two different messages with the same hash function, causing a collision. It is based on the birthday problem in probability theory (also known as the birthday paradox). This can be summed up simply as the following: A randomly chosen group of people will have a pair of persons with the same calendar date birthday. Given a standard calendar year of 365 days, the probability of this occurring with 366 people is 100% (367 people on a leap year). So far, this makes sense and sounds logical.

The paradox (thoughtfully and mathematically) comes into play when fewer people are involved. With only 57 people, there is a 99% probability of a match (a much higher percentage than one would think), and with only 23 people, there is a 50% probability. Imagine that and blow out your candles! And by this, I mean use hashing functions with strong collision resistance. Because if attackers can find any two messages that digest the same way (use the same hash value), they can deceive a user into receiving the wrong message. To protect against a birthday attack, use a secure transmission medium, such as SSH, or encrypt the entire message that has been hashed.

Additional Password Hashing Concepts

Remember that hashed passwords are one-way functions. The process of hashing takes the password and converts it into a fixed-length binary value that cannot be reversed. The converted number is usually represented in hexadecimal. Due to the nature of the conversion, even slightly different passwords will have completely different hashes.

Know that password hashes can be cracked. I know, I said the number cannot be reversed, and it can't, because it is a one-way function. But the hash can be cracked in a variety of ways. A person could try to guess the password, or use the dictionary attack method, or try the brute-force attack method. Attackers will also make use of lookup tables, reverse lookup tables, and rainbow tables. These vulnerabilities make your password policies—and the type of hash you use—very important. Of course, in some scenarios, you might be limited as to the length of password you can have your users select. For example, let's say you are using a web server technology with a somewhat weak password methodology, and you are concerned about hash collisions. There are other ways to increase the security of the password.

One way is to use key stretching. A **key stretching** technique will take a weak key, process it, and output an enhanced and more powerful key. Often, this process will increase the size of the key to 128 bits, making attacks such as brute-force attacks much more difficult, if not impossible. Examples of key stretching software include PBKDF2 and bcrypt.

These utilities also incorporate salting to protect against dictionary attacks, brute-forcing, and rainbow table attacks. Salting is additional random data that is added to a one-way cryptographic hash. It is one character or more, but defined in bits. The person with the weaker web server password key, or perhaps the admin with the NTLM hash, would do well to consider key stretching or salting. Another technique used is the *nonce* (number used once). It can be added to password-based authentication schemes where a secure hash function (such as SHA) is used. It is a unique number (that is difficult for attackers to find) that can only be used once. As such, it helps to protect users from replay attacks.

Of course, an admin needs to remember that the primary line of defense when it comes to passwords is to use complexity *and* length; not just one or the other. There are a couple of myths connected with passwords in general. The first is that complexity is better than length. This isn't always true; it will depend on the type of attack (dictionary or brute-force), the level of complexity, and the length of the password. So again, if at all possible, define policies that specify complexity plus length. And if length cannot be incorporated into your password scheme, use key stretching, or salting, or strongly consider using a different hash altogether. Another myth is that password checkers ensure strong passwords. Password checkers can help you get an idea of whether a password is secure, but may interpret some weak passwords as strong.

Remember also to limit the number of times that a password can be tried via policy; for example, limiting password attempts to five or even as little as three (remember the three strikes and you're out rule?). Also, define delays between consecutive password attempts. This is especially important on websites. It can help to defend against exhaustive key searches. Better yet, use one-time passwords (OTPs), such as the HMAC-based OTP (HOTP). Extend that concept by supporting a time-based moving factor that must be changed each time a new password is generated, and you have the time-based OTP (TOTP).

It may seem like we've covered a dizzying array of password technologies and acronyms, but we can quickly get our bearings by creating a checklist and going through it every time we design a password scheme: Use a strong hash, and if not possible, utilize key stretching. Incorporate salting. Consider OTPs, and create meticulously defined policies governing passwords. Finally, if working on a website that accepts passwords (especially public passwords), implement secure programming techniques, particularly input validation.

Chapter Summary

If there's one thing you should take away from this chapter it's that my phone number was probably never in any black books, either as plaintext or as ciphertext! (Just making sure you are reading the chapter summaries…be thankful I am not anthropomorphizing computers this time.) Seriously, though, it's amazing how many children can easily understand and design code with which to hide information. It's not surprising that there are so many cryptographers and cryptanalysts in this day and age, and a huge assortment of ciphers to work with.

The art of secret communication can basically be broken down into two categories: steganography and cryptography. Both have been used for millennia. But one is inherently insecure, and the other is inherently crackable. Steganography hides the entire message, but if the message is found, the message is instantly compromised. Remember the discussion of the Greek messenger who shaved his head, had a message written on his scalp, and re-grew his hair? If he had been asked by a guard at a border to shave his head (and had complied), the message would have been seen right away. That's why insecurity is built right into the scheme. Cryptography, on the other hand, is used to hide the *meaning* of the message. The message could be there for everyone to see, but they won't understand it unless they have the *key* to the message. Of course, all ciphers can be cracked; it's built into their DNA, so to speak. But, with the proper key size and appropriately designed ciphers, it can be very difficult, if not impossible, to crack the code. So, encryption is the weapon of choice for most data transfers.

However, you will also see some scenarios where a message is encrypted and then hidden as well, effectively combining the two concepts of cryptography and steganography. For example, User A might e-mail User B with an attachment containing a photo of the Grand Canyon—a slightly altered Grand Canyon, where some of the pixels' colors have been changed, but the changes are not visible to the naked eye. User B already has an unaltered version of the original photo stored on the computer. User B compares the two, and locates all of the modified pixels (or has a program do it). The modified colors could translate to letters in the alphabet: for example, a certain shade of red's three-byte color would be written numerically as FF 00 66 (255 0 102 in decimal). It could have been decided earlier that the third number of the three bytes would be the modified color. Furthermore, 102 is equal to the letter *f* in ASCII, which might be the first letter of the first sentence of a message. The process would continue until the complete message emerges from a group of modified colors. That's pretty hidden, wouldn't you say? But now, encryption could be employed based on a predetermined code. It could be as simple as a Caesar Cipher where the letters are shifted over three places, so instead of the ciphertext *f*, we get the plaintext *c*. So now, the message is hidden *and* the meaning of the message is hidden. And we can get as complex as we want with the cipher, either by utilizing a published algorithm or by designing our own.

Dating back to ancient times, cryptographers would create a code, and cryptanalysts would attempt to crack it. Every time a code was cracked, it was then considered compromised, and a new code would be created. This concept has been even more pronounced during the computer age. That's why there are so many algorithms in this chapter—the cyclic mousetrap effect has been in play for decades.

Symmetric algorithms use a single key, or more than one identical key (or very similar keys). One of the most powerful symmetric algorithms is the Advanced Encryption Standard (AES), which can have a maximum key length of 256 bits. That is considered uncrackable, so instead of trying to crack the code, attackers will usually attempt to maneuver around it and assault the implementation of the algorithm. Asymmetric algorithms, on the other hand, use a pair of different keys for encryption and decryption. For instance, take public key cryptography, where there will be a well-known public key that is used to encrypt messages, and a secret private key that is used to decrypt them. A common example of an asymmetric algorithm is RSA.

It is often desirable to create a summary of a message, known as a hash. Hashes are used in digital downloads to allow users to verify the integrity of a message or file. They are also used to protect passwords. A common hash used on the Internet is SHA-2—remember, SHA-1 is deprecated and should be replaced if it's currently in use. A common hash used to protect passwords in Windows is NTLMv2.

By combining all of these techniques and technologies, you can provide a decent amount of security for your files and passwords—essentially protecting your data *and* the access to that data.

Chapter Review Activities

Use the features in this section to study and review the topics in this chapter.

Review Key Topics

Review the most important topics in the chapter, noted with the Key Topic icon in the outer margin of the page. Table 14-5 lists a reference of these key topics and the page number on which each is found.

Table 14-5   Key Topics for Chapter 14

Key Topic Element	Description	Page Number
Table 14-1	Black book phone number encryption	478
Figure 14-1	Illustration of public key cryptography	483
Table 14-3	Summary of symmetric algorithms	489
Table 14-4	Summary of RSA public and private key usage	490
Figure 14-2	Illustration of the hashing process	497
Figure 14-3	LM hash in the Local Group Policy	501

Define Key Terms

Define the following key terms from this chapter, and check your answers in the glossary:

data in use, data at rest, data in transit, cryptography, encryption, cipher, algorithms, key, private key, public key, symmetric key algorithm, stream cipher, block cipher, asymmetric key algorithm, public key cryptography, digital signature, certificate, steganography, Data Encryption Standard (DES), Triple DES (3DES), Advanced Encryption Standard (AES), Blowfish, Twofish, RSA, Diffie-Hellman key exchange, elliptic curve cryptography (ECC), Elliptic Curve Diffie-Hellman Ephemeral (ECDHE), one-time pad, Pretty Good Privacy (PGP), GNU Privacy Guard (GPG), pseudorandom number generator (PRNG), hash, hash function, one-way function, cryptographic hash functions, Message-Digest algorithm 5 (MD5), collision, Secure Hash Algorithm (SHA), LANMAN hash, NTLM hash, NTLMv2 hash, pass the hash, birthday attack, key stretching

Complete the Real-World Scenarios

Complete the Real-World Scenarios found on the companion website (www.pearsonitcertification.com/title/9780789758996). You will find a PDF containing the scenario and questions, and also supporting videos and simulations.

Review Questions

Answer the following review questions. Check your answers with the correct answers that follow.

1. Which type of encryption technology is used with the BitLocker application?

    A. Symmetric

    B. Asymmetric

    C. Hashing

    D. WPA2

2. Which of the following will provide an integrity check?

    A. Public key

    B. Private key

    C. WEP

    D. Hash

3. Why would an attacker use steganography?

    A. To hide information

    B. For data integrity

    C. To encrypt information

    D. For wireless access

4. You need to encrypt and send a large amount of data. Which of the following would be the best option?

    A. Symmetric encryption

    B. Hashing algorithm

    C. Asymmetric encryption

    D. PKI

5. Imagine that you are an attacker. Which would be most desirable when attempting to compromise encrypted data?

   A. A weak key

   B. The algorithm used by the encryption protocol

   C. Captured traffic

   D. A block cipher

6. What is another term for secret key encryption?

   A. PKI

   B. Asymmetrical

   C. Symmetrical

   D. Public key

7. Your boss wants you to set up an authentication scheme in which employees will use smart cards to log in to the company network. What kind of key should be used to accomplish this?

   A. Private key

   B. Public key

   C. Cipher key

   D. Shared key

8. The IT director wants you to use a cryptographic algorithm that cannot be decoded by being reversed. Which of the following would be the best option?

   A. Asymmetric

   B. Symmetric

   C. PKI

   D. One-way function

9. Which of the following concepts does the Diffie-Hellman algorithm rely on?

   A. Usernames and passwords

   B. VPN tunneling

   C. Biometrics

   D. Key exchange

10. What does steganography replace in graphic files?

    A. The least significant bit of each byte

    B. The most significant bit of each byte

    C. The least significant byte of each bit

    D. The most significant byte of each bit

11. What does it mean if a hashing algorithm creates the same hash for two different downloads?

    A. A hash is not encrypted.

    B. A hashing chain has occurred.

    C. A one-way hash has occurred.

    D. A collision has occurred.

12. Which of the following methods will best verify that a download from the Internet has not been modified since the manufacturer released it?

    A. Compare the final LANMAN hash with the original.

    B. Download the patch file over an AES encrypted VPN connection.

    C. Download the patch file through an SSL connection.

    D. Compare the final MD5 hash with the original.

13. Which of the following encryption methods deals with two distinct, large prime numbers and the inability to factor those prime numbers?

    A. SHA-1

    B. RSA

    C. WPA

    D. Symmetric

14. Which of the following is not a symmetric key algorithm?

    A. RC4

    B. ECC

    C. 3DES

    D. Rijndael

15. You are attempting to move data to a USB flash drive. Which of the following enables a rapid and secure connection?

   A. SHA-2

   B. 3DES

   C. AES-256

   D. MD5

16. Which of the following is used by PGP to encrypt the session key before it is sent?

   A. Asymmetric key distribution system

   B. Asymmetric scheme

   C. Symmetric key distribution system

   D. Symmetric scheme

17. Which of the following encryption algorithms is used to encrypt and decrypt data?

   A. SHA-256

   B. RC5

   C. MD5

   D. NTLM

18. Of the following, which statement correctly describes the difference between a secure cipher and a secure hash?

   A. A hash produces a variable output for any input size; a cipher does not.

   B. A cipher produces the same size output for any input size; a hash does not.

   C. A hash can be reversed; a cipher cannot.

   D. A cipher can be reversed; a hash cannot.

19. When encrypting credit card data, which would be the most secure algorithm with the least CPU utilization?

   A. AES

   B. 3DES

   C. SHA-512

   D. MD5

20. A hash algorithm has the capability to avoid the same output from two guessed inputs. What is this known as?

   A. Collision resistance

   B. Collision strength

   C. Collision cipher

   D. Collision metric

21. Which of the following is the weakest encryption type?

   A. DES

   B. RSA

   C. AES

   D. SHA

22. Give two examples of hardware devices that can store keys. (Select the two best answers.)

   A. Smart card

   B. Network adapter

   C. PCI Express card

   D. USB flash drive

23. What type of attack sends two different messages using the same hash function, which end up causing a collision?

   A. Birthday attack

   B. Bluesnarfing

   C. Man-in-the-middle attack

   D. Logic bomb

24. Which of the following might a public key be used to accomplish?

   A. To decrypt the hash of a digital signature

   B. To encrypt web browser traffic

   C. To digitally sign a message

   D. To decrypt wireless messages

25. Which of the following combines the keystream with the plaintext message using the bitwise XOR operator to produce the ciphertext?

    A. One-time pad

    B. Obfuscation

    C. PBKDF2

    D. ECDH

26. WEP improperly uses an encryption protocol and therefore is considered to be insecure. What encryption protocol does it use?

    A. AES

    B. RSA

    C. RC6

    D. RC4

27. The fundamental difference between symmetric key systems and asymmetric key systems is that symmetric key systems do which of the following?

    A. Use the same key on each end

    B. Use different keys on each end

    C. Use multiple keys for non-repudiation purposes

    D. Use public key cryptography

28. Last week, one of the users in your organization encrypted a file with a private key. This week the user left the organization, and unfortunately the systems administrator deleted the user's account. What are the most probable outcomes of this situation? (Select the two best answers.)

    A. The data is not recoverable.

    B. The former user's account can be re-created to access the file.

    C. The file can be decrypted with a PKI.

    D. The data can be decrypted using the recovery agent.

    E. The data can be decrypted using the root user account.

29. You are tasked with ensuring that messages being sent and received between two systems are both encrypted and authenticated. Which of the following protocols accomplishes this?

    A. Diffie-Hellman

    B. BitLocker

    C. RSA

    D. SHA-384

30. Which of the following is not a valid cryptographic hash function?

    A. RC4

    B. SHA-512

    C. MD5

    D. RIPEMD

31. A network stream of data needs to be encrypted. Jason, a security administrator, selects a cipher that will encrypt 128 bits at a time before sending the data across the network. Which of the following has Jason chosen?

    A. Stream cipher

    B. Block cipher

    C. Hashing algorithm

    D. RC4

32. You are tasked with selecting an asymmetric encryption method that allows for the same level of encryption strength, but with a lesser key length than is typically necessary. Which encryption method fulfills your requirement?

    A. RSA

    B. ECC

    C. DHE

    D. Twofish

Answers and Explanations

1. **A.** BitLocker uses symmetric encryption technology based on AES. Hashing is the process of summarizing a file for integrity purposes. WPA2 is a wireless encryption protocol.

2. **D.** A hash provides integrity checks; for example, MD5 hash algorithms. Public and private keys are the element of a cipher that allows for output of encrypted information. WEP (Wired Equivalent Privacy) is a deprecated wireless encryption protocol.

3. **A.** Steganography is the act of writing hidden messages so that only the intended recipients know of the existence of the message. This is a form of security through obscurity. Steganographers are not as concerned with data integrity or encryption because the average person shouldn't even know that a message exists. Although steganography can be accomplished by using compromised wireless networks, it is not used to gain wireless access.

4. **A.** Symmetric encryption is the best option for sending large amounts of data. It is superior to asymmetric encryption. PKI is considered an asymmetric encryption type, and hashing algorithms don't play into sending large amounts of data.

5. **A.** The easiest way for an attacker to get at encrypted data is if that encrypted data has a weak encryption key. The algorithm isn't of much use to an attacker unless it has been broken, which is a far more difficult process than trying to crack an individual key. Captured traffic, if encrypted, still needs to be decrypted, and a weak key will aid in this process. The block cipher is a type of algorithm.

6. **C.** Symmetric key encryption uses a secret key. The term *symmetric key* is also referred to as the following: private key, single key, and shared key (and sometimes as session key). PKI and public keys at their core are asymmetrical.

7. **A.** A private key should be used by users when logging in to the network with their smart card. The key should certainly not be public. A key actually determines the function of a cipher. Shared key is another term for symmetric key encryption but does not imply privacy.

8. **D.** In cryptography, the one-way function is one option of an algorithm that cannot be reversed, or is difficult to reverse, in an attempt to decode data. An example of this would be a hash such as SHA-2, which creates only a small hashing number from a portion of the file or message. There are ways to crack asymmetric and symmetric encryptions, which enable complete decryption (decoding) of the file.

9. **D.** The Diffie-Hellman algorithm relies on key exchange before data can be sent. Usernames and passwords are considered a type of authentication. VPN tunneling is done to connect a remote client to a network. Biometrics is the science of identifying people by one of their physical attributes.

10. **A.** Steganography replaces the least significant bit of each byte. It would be impossible to replace a byte of each bit, because a byte is larger than a bit; a byte is eight bits.

11. **D.** If a hashing algorithm generates the same hash for two different messages within two different downloads, a collision has occurred and the implementation of the hashing algorithm should be investigated.

12. **D.** The purpose of the MD5 hash is to verify the integrity of a download. SHA is another example of a hash that will verify the integrity of downloads. LAN-MAN hashes are older, deprecated hashes used by Microsoft LAN Manager for passwords. Encrypted AES and SSL connections are great for encrypting the data transfer but do not verify integrity.

13. **B.** The RSA encryption algorithm uses two prime numbers. If used properly they will be large prime numbers that are difficult or impossible to factor. SHA-1 is an example of a Secure Hash Algorithm—albeit a deprecated one. WPA is the Wi-Fi Protected Access protocol, and RSA is an example of an asymmetric method of encryption.

14. **B.** ECC (elliptic curve cryptography) is an example of public key cryptography that uses an asymmetric key algorithm. All the other answers are symmetric key algorithms.

15. **C.** AES-256 enables a quick and secure encrypted connection for use with a USB flash drive. It might even be used with a whole disk encryption technology, such as BitLocker. SHA-2 and MD5 are examples of hashes. 3DES is an example of an encryption algorithm but would not be effective for sending encrypted information in a highly secure manner and quickly to a USB flash drive.

16. **D.** Pretty Good Privacy (PGP) encryption uses a symmetric key scheme for the session key data, and asymmetric RSA for the *sending* of the session key, plus a combination of hashing and data compression. Key distribution systems are part of an entire encryption scheme, which typically includes a technology such as Kerberos (key distribution center) or quantum cryptography.

17. **B.** RC5 (Rivest Cipher version 5) can encrypt and decrypt data. SHA-256 is a type of SHA-2. It and MD5 are used as hashing algorithms, and NTLM (NT LAN Manager) is used by Microsoft as an authentication protocol and a password hash.

18. **D.** Ciphers can be reverse engineered but hashes cannot when attempting to re-create a data file. Hashing is not the same as encryption; hashing is the digital fingerprint, so to speak, of a group of data. Hashes are not reversible.

19. **A.** AES (Advanced Encryption Standard) is fast and secure, more so than 3DES. SHA-512 (a type of SHA-2) and MD5 are hashing algorithms. Not listed is RSA, which is commonly implemented to secure credit card transactions.

20. **A.** A hash is collision resistant if it is difficult to guess two inputs that hash to the same output.

21. **A.** DES (Data Encryption Standard) was developed in the 1970s; its 56-bit key has been superseded by 3DES (max 168-bit key) and AES (max 256-bit key). DES is now considered to be insecure for many applications. RSA is definitely stronger than DES even when you compare its asymmetric strength to a relative symmetric strength. SHA is a hashing algorithm.

22. **A and D.** Smart cards and USB flash drives can be used as devices that carry a token and store keys; this means that they can be used for authentication to systems, often in a multifactor authentication scenario. Network adapters and PCI Express cards are internal to a PC and would not make for good key storage devices.

23. **A.** A birthday attack exploits the mathematics behind the birthday problem in probability theory. It deals with two different messages using the same hash function, generating the same message digest. Bluesnarfing deals with Bluetooth devices. The man-in-the-middle attack is when a person or computer intercepts information between a sender and the receiver. A logic bomb is a malicious attack set to go off at a particular time; often it is stored on a zombie computer.

24. **A.** Public keys can be used to decrypt the hash of a digital signature. Session keys are used to encrypt web browser traffic. Private keys are used to digitally sign a message and decrypt wireless messages.

25. **A.** A one-time pad is a stream cipher that encrypts plaintext with a secret random key that is the same length as the plaintext. Encryption is accomplished by combining the keystream with the plaintext message using the bitwise XOR operator to produce the ciphertext. Obfuscation means to make something obscure and unclear. PBKDF2 is an example of key-stretching software. Elliptic Curve Diffie-Hellman, or ECDH, uses elliptic curve public/private key pairs to establish the secret key.

26. **D.** RC4 has several vulnerabilities when used incorrectly by protocols such as WEP. WEP does not use AES, RSA, or RC6, all of which are secure protocols if used correctly.

27. **A.** Symmetric key systems use the same key on each end during transport of data. Asymmetric key systems (such as public key cryptography systems) use different keys.

28. **A and D.** Many systems have a recovery agent that is designed just for this purpose. If the account that encrypted the file is deleted, it cannot be recreated (without different IDs and therefore no access to the file), and the recovery agent will have to be used. If there is no recovery agent (which in some cases needs to be configured manually), then the file will be unrecoverable. This file was encrypted with a private key and needs to be decrypted with a private key—PKI is a system that uses asymmetric key pairs (private and public). The root user account does not have the ability to recover files that were encrypted by other users.

29. **C.** RSA can both encrypt and authenticate messages. Diffie-Hellman encrypts only. BitLocker is a type of whole disk encryption (WDE), which deals with encrypting entire hard drives but is not used to send and receive messages. SHA-384 is a cryptographic hash function used to preserve the integrity of files.

30. **A.** RC4 is a symmetric encryption algorithm that uses a stream cipher. It is the only listed answer that is not a valid cryptographic hash function.

31. **B.** Jason chose a block cipher; for example, the 128-bit version of AES. Don't let the phrase "network stream" fool you; stream ciphers will encrypt each bit in the stream. Hashing algorithms are not used to encrypt network streams of data. RC4 is a stream cipher.

32. **B.** The ECC (elliptic curve cryptography) method allows for lesser key lengths but at the same level of strength as other asymmetric methods. This reduces the computational power needed. RSA and Diffie-Hellman require more computational power due to the increased key length. DHE especially uses more CPU power because of the ephemeral aspect. (ECDHE would be the solution in that respect.) Twofish is a symmetric algorithm.

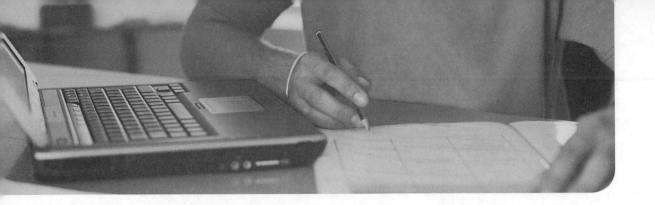

This chapter covers the following subjects:

- **Public Key Infrastructure:** In this section, we discuss PKI and its components, including private and public keys, certificates, certificate authorities, and the web of trust model.

- **Security Protocols:** Here, we define more security protocols such as S/MIME, SSL, TLS, SSH, and VPN-related protocols such as PPTP, L2TP, and IPsec. And three cheers if you want—these are the last of the TCP/IP security protocols in the book!

This short chapter wraps up the rest of the encryption concepts you need to know for the Security+ exam. You are required to understand public key infrastructures and should have the ability to explain what is entailed when a secure connection is made, for example, to a secure e-commerce web server. There is an entire system involved with public key infrastructures, from the users to servers, encryption methods, and much more. It's a big topic that can be confusing due to how many and what variety of keys are used. Take it slow, and reread the section if necessary. Several protocols use public key infrastructures as well, many of which you have probably heard of, such as S/MIME, SSL, TLS, SSH, and so on. Keep in mind that the security protocols discussed in this section are intertwined with the concepts of a public key infrastructure.

CHAPTER 15

PKI and Encryption Protocols

Public Key Infrastructure

A **public key infrastructure (PKI)** is an entire system of hardware and software, policies and procedures, and people. It is used to create, distribute, manage, store, and revoke digital certificates. If you have connected to a secure website in the past, you have been a part of a PKI! But a PKI can be used for other things as well, such as secure e-mail transmissions and secure connections to remote computers and remote networks. The PKI is all encompassing: It includes users, client computers, servers, services, and most of all, encryption. Don't confuse PKI with public key encryption. Though they are related, PKI is a way of accomplishing public key encryption, but not all public key encryption schemes are PKI. PKI creates asymmetric key pairs, a public key and a private key: The private key is kept secret, whereas the public key can be distributed. If the key pair is generated at a server, it is considered to be centralized, and the public key is distributed as needed. If the key pair is generated at a local computer, it is considered to be decentralized, and the keys are not distributed; instead, they are used by that local system. An example of public key usage would be a certificate obtained by a web browser during an encrypted session with an e-commerce website. An example of private key usage would be when a user needs to encrypt the digital signature of a private e-mail. The difference is the level of confidentiality. The public key certificate obtained by the web browser is public and might be obtained by thousands of individuals. The private key used to encrypt the e-mail is not to be shared with anyone.

In a nutshell, public key infrastructures are set up in such a way so as to bind public keys with user identities. This is usually done with certificates distributed by a certificate authority. Less commonly it is done by means of a web of trust.

Let's go ahead and describe these concepts in a little more detail.

Certificates

Certificates are digitally signed electronic documents that bind a public key with a user identity. The identity information might include a person's name and organization, or other details relevant to the user to whom the certificate is to be issued. Most certificates are based on the **X.509** standard, which is a common PKI standard developed by the ITU-T that often incorporates the single sign-on (SSO) authentication method. This way, a recipient of a single X.509 certificate has access to multiple resources, possibly in multiple locations. Although difficult, X.509 certificates that use MD5 and SHA1 hashes can be compromised. A more powerful hashing algorithm such as SHA2 should be implemented with the certificate. X.509 is the core of the PKIX, which is the IETF's Public Key Infrastructure (X.509) working group. Components of an X.509 certificate include the following:

- Owner (user) information, including their public key

- Certificate authority information, including their name, digital signature, serial number, issue and expiration dates, and version

Certificates can be used for connections to websites, for e-mail, and for many other things in the Internet world, as well as encryption done locally. For example, a user working in a Windows environment might want to use the Encrypting File System (EFS) to encrypt data locally. The Windows domain can be configured to allow for user certificates governing and enhancing this encryption process. So, certificates can be used internally or externally, but most people are more familiar with the certificate used to make secure HTTP connections, usually with SSL/TLS-based certificates. We'll focus mostly on that type of certificate as we move forward.

SSL Certificate Types

It's a good idea to classify certificates the way the companies that sell them do. This includes domain, organizational, and extended validation certificates. Domain validation (DV) certificates are where the certificate authority checks the rights of the applicant to use a specific domain name. We'll discuss the term *certificate authority (CA)* later in the chapter, but for now, simply put, it is the entity that issues the certificate. Organizational validation (OV) certificates go beyond this by also conducting some vetting of the organization involved, the result of which is displayed to customers. Extended validation (EV) certificates go further by conducting a thorough vetting of the organization. Issuance of these certificates is strictly defined.

Many companies have subdomains for their websites. For example, I own davidlprowse.com. I might also opt to create subdomains such as tools.davidlprowse.com and software.davidlprowse.com. Generally, if you connect to a secure website that uses subdomains, a single certificate will allow for connections to the main website and the subdomains. This is known as a **wildcard certificate**; for example, *.davidlprowse.com, meaning all subdomains of davidlprowse.com. Your organization might allow this, or for additional security might use a different certificate for each subdomain (possibly from different providers), but this can prove to be expensive. For small businesses and organizations, the single certificate is usually enough. In fact, if the provider allows it, a small organization can use a multidomain certificate. By modifying the **subject alternative name (SAN)** field, an organization can specify additional hostnames, domain names, IP addresses, and so on.

Single-Sided and Dual-Sided Certificates

Most communication sessions, such as secure web sessions, use single-sided certificates. This is when the server validates itself to recipients of the certificate, such as users who are accessing the website. In these types of scenarios, users do not need to validate their own identity. This would be resource-intensive, especially for a secure web server that might have thousands of concurrent connections.

Sometimes, an organization might choose to have the server *and* the user validate their identities. This would be using a dual-sided certificate; it works well when a limited number of computers and sessions are involved. When more computers are added to the mix, the amount of resources necessary might be a strain on the issuing CA.

Certificate Chain of Trust

A certificate chain is a list of certificates that utilizes the chain of trust concept. This is where each component of the system is validated from the bottom up. In a certificate chain, also known as a certification path, the anchor for this trust is the root certificate authority. At the bottom of the chain we have the end-entity certificate for a machine/computer. That's the certificate that you would see if you looked at the details of a secure HTTPS session in your web browser. That then handshakes with an intermediate certificate belonging to a subordinate certificate authority. This certificate signs the end-entity certificate. That then handshakes with the root certificate, which represents the root certificate authority. It signs the intermediate certificate and in and of itself is self-signing, which means that it not only creates the certificate, but signs it as well. It signs it with its own private key. The root CA will employ code signing: digitally signing and time stamping the certificate to provide integrity and authenticity. However, even this can be defeated, so the security admin has to always be on the lookout for CVEs detailing revoked certificates, and even entire issuing certificate companies that may have been compromised.

Certificate Formats

There are several certificate formats you should know for the exam. They can be identified in part by their file extension or encoding type used. First, let's briefly discuss the ITU-T X.690 encoding formats:

- **Basic Encoding Rules (BER):** This is the original ruleset governing the encoding of ASN.1 data structures. Any data created is encoded with a type identifier, a length description, and the content's value. BER can use one of several encoding methods.

- **Canonical Encoding Rules (CER):** This is a restricted version of BER in that it only allows the use of one encoding type; all others are restricted.

- **Distinguished Encoding Rules (DER):** Another restricted variant of BER, this only allows for one type of encoding, and has restrictive rules for length, character strings, and how elements are sorted. It is widely used for X.509 certificates. For example, certificate enrollment in Windows Servers uses DER exclusively.

Now, let's briefly define the certificate formats and extensions you might encounter. PEM is a very common format that uses base64-encoded ASCII files. It stands for Privacy-enhanced Electronic Mail and can be identified with the .pem file extension, though the format might also use .crt (for example, Microsoft), .cer, or .key extensions. It uses the DER encoding method. If the certificate uses a file extension different from .pem, you can tell if it is a PEM by opening the file with a text editor and looking for the "Begin Certificate" and "End Certificate" statements. However, if the certificate uses the .der extension, then the certificate file is in binary form instead of ASCII. Because it is in binary, you will not see the Begin and End Certificate statements that are displayed in a .pem.

P12/PFX is a binary format based on PKCS#12 used to store a server certificate, intermediate certificates, and the private key in one encryptable file. It is typically used to import and export certificates and private keys. You may see the .pfx and .p12 extensions associated with PKCS#12-based files. .pfx stands for Personal Information Exchange and is used by Microsoft for release signing. The certificate and its private and public keys are stored in the .pfx file. A .pfx file can also be developed by combining a private key with a PKCS #7 .p7b file, as might be done in Windows Internet Information Services (IIS). Or, .p7b format certificates can be used by themselves in IIS as the basis for S/MIME and single sign-on.

NOTE   Some of these extensions will also be used for different types of data such as private keys, and not only for certificates. It is also possible to convert from one format to another using tools such as OpenSSL.

Certificate Authorities

A **certificate authority (CA)** is the entity (usually a server) that issues certificates to users. In a PKI system that uses a CA, the CA is known as a trusted third party. Most PKI systems use a CA. The CA is also responsible for verifying the identity of the recipient of the certificate. An example of a technology that uses certificates would be secure websites. If you opened your browser and connected to a secure site, the browser would first check the certificate that comes from VeriSign or another similar company; it would *validate* the certificate. You (the user) and the website are the two parties attempting to communicate. The CA is a third party that negotiates the security of the connection between you and the website. For a user to obtain a digital identity certificate from a CA, the user's computer must initiate a *certificate signing request (CSR)* and present two items of information: The first is proof of the user's identity; the second is a public key. This public key is then matched to the CA's private key, and if successful the certificate is granted to the user.

A basic example of this would be if you connect to www.paypal.com. When connecting to this website, it automatically redirects you to https://www.paypal.com, which is secured by way of a VeriSign-issued certificate. You know you have been redirected to a secure site because the browser has various indicators. For instance, the web browser will probably show a padlock in the locked position and it and the name of the company will be displayed in green, as shown in Figure 15-1.

Figure 15-1   Example of a Secure Connection, Shown in Firefox

If you were to click on the green area of the address field in Firefox, you could ultimately get to the certificate details. Figure 15-2 shows the default General tab for the certificate associated with this domain name.

Key Topic

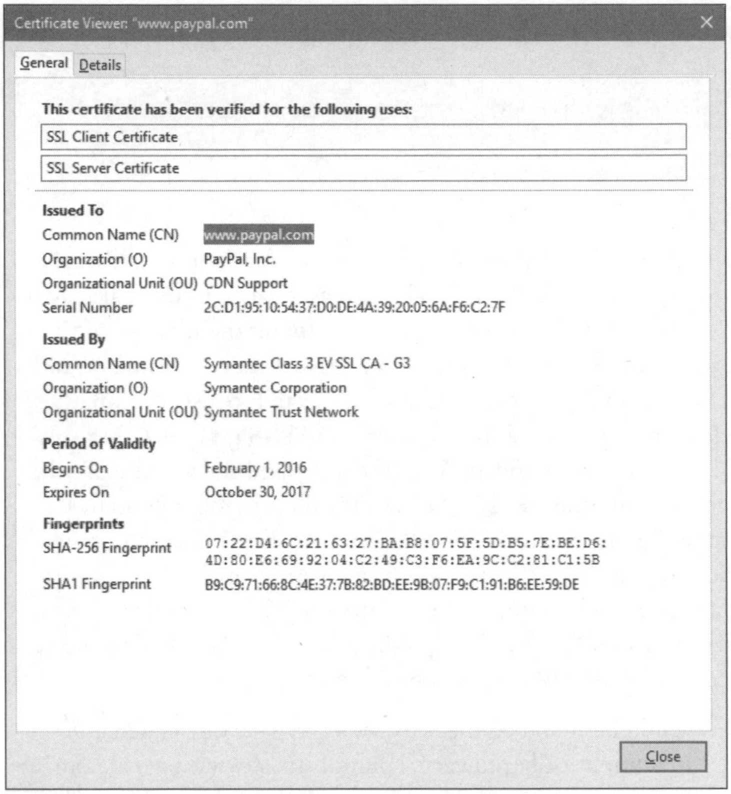

Certificate Viewer: "www.paypal.com"   ×

General _Details_

This certificate has been verified for the following uses:

SSL Client Certificate

SSL Server Certificate

Issued To
Common Name (CN)   www.paypal.com
Organization (O)   PayPal, Inc.
Organizational Unit (OU) CDN Support
Serial Number   2C:D1:95:10:54:37:D0:DE:4A:39:20:05:6A:F6:C2:7F

Issued By
Common Name (CN)   Symantec Class 3 EV SSL CA - G3
Organization (O)   Symantec Corporation
Organizational Unit (OU) Symantec Trust Network

Period of Validity
Begins On   February 1, 2016
Expires On   October 30, 2017

Fingerprints
SHA-256 Fingerprint   07:22:D4:6C:21:63:27:BA:B8:07:5F:5D:B5:7E:BE:D6:
                                      4D:80:E6:69:92:04:C2:49:C3:F6:EA:9C:C2:81:C1:5B

SHA1 Fingerprint   B9:C9:71:66:8C:4E:37:7B:82:BD:EE:9B:07:F9:C1:91:B6:EE:59:DE

                                                                                              Close

Figure 15-2 Details of a Typical VeriSign Certificate

The General tab shows that the certificate gets a super-long hexadecimal serial number, and shows when the certificate was originally issued and when it expires, among other information. You can also note that the certificate has been finger-printed with SHA-256 (a variant of SHA-2) and SHA1, enabling you or the website (or issuer) to verify the integrity of the certificate. If for some reason the certificate cannot be verified by any of the parties, and the issuer confirms this, then the issuer would need to revoke it and place it in the certificate revocation list (CRL). The Details tab gives us advanced and more complete information about the certificate used. I suggest you take a look at a few more websites that use SSL/TLS certificates and peruse the General and Details tabs. Compare the certificates with each other to learn more about the different levels of encryption, different levels of fingerprinting, and the different issuing companies.

One way to add security to the certificate validation process is to use certificate pin-ning, also known as SSL pinning or public key pinning. This can help to detect and block many types of MITM attacks by adding an extra step beyond normal X.509 certificate validation. Essentially, a client obtains a certificate from a CA in the normal way, but also checks the public key in the server's certificate against a hashed public key used for the server *name*. This functionality must be incorporated into the client side, so it is important to use a secure and up-to-date web browser on each client in order to take advantage of certificate pinning.

Recipients can use one or more certificates. Certificate mapping defines how many certificates are associated with a particular recipient. If an individual certificate is mapped to a recipient, it is known as a **one-to-one mapping**. If multiple certificates are mapped to a recipient, it is known as **many-to-one mapping**. Multiple certificates might be used if the recipient requires multiple secure (and separate) communications channels.

In some cases, a **registration authority (RA)** is used to verify requests for certificates. If the request is deemed valid, the RA informs the CA to issue the certificate. An RA might also be used if the organization deals with several CAs. In this case, the RA is at the top of a hierarchical structure and verifies the identity of the user. An RA isn't necessary in a PKI, but if you are centrally storing certificates, a CA is necessary.

Certificate authorities aren't just for the rich and famous (for example, PayPal using VeriSign as the issuer). You can have a CA, too! If you are running a Windows Server, you can install your own CA—for example, one that utilizes L2TP or possibly SSL/TLS; more on those protocols later in this chapter. Of course, a server's built-in certificates are not necessarily secure. If you were to implement this technology in a secure environment in your organization, you would probably want to obtain proper certificates from a trusted source to use with the Windows Server. When implementing certificates in Windows Server, you would use the Active Directory Certificate Services (AD CS) utility. From there you can define object identifiers (OIDs), which are built into AD CS for either low, medium, or high assurance. Or, you can have Windows randomly assign them. For security purposes, obtain the OID before completing the configuration of the CA.

Certificate authorities can be subverted through the use of social engineering. If a person posing as a legitimate company managed to obtain certificates from a trusted source, those certificates would appear to be valid certificates and could cause widespread damage due to connections made by unsuspecting users. That is, until the certificates were revoked. This happens sometimes, but the CA issuer usually finds out quickly and takes steps to mitigate the problem, including revoking the certificate(s) and notifying any involved parties of the incident.

The **certificate revocation list (CRL)** is a list of certificates that are no longer valid or that have been revoked by the issuer. There are two possible states of revocation: revoked, which is when a certificate has been irreversibly revoked and cannot be used again, and hold, which is used to temporarily invalidate a certificate. Reasons for revoking a certificate include the compromising or theft of a certificate or entire

CA, unspecified certificates, superseded certificates, held certificates, and key or encryption compromise. The CRL is published periodically, usually every 24 hours. This enables users of an issuer's certificates to find out whether a certificate is valid. CRLs, like the certificates themselves, carry digital signatures to prevent DoS and spoofing attacks; the CRL is digitally signed by the CA.

An alternative to the CRL is the **Online Certificate Status Protocol (OCSP)**. It contains less information than a CRL does, and the client side of the communication is less complex. However, OCSP does not require encryption, making it less secure than CRL. An alternative to OCSP is OCSP stapling (previously known as TLS Certificate Status Request), which allows the presenter of the certificate to bear the cost involved when providing OCSP responses.

Certificate keys can also be held in escrow. **Key escrow** is when a secure copy of a user's private key is held in case the key is lost. This may be necessary so that third parties such as government or other organizations can ultimately gain access to communications and data encrypted with that key. If data loss is unacceptable, you should implement key escrow in your PKI.

When installing a certificate authority to a Windows Server, you can set up a recovery agent for lost or corrupted keys. To do this, you need Windows Server and need to set up an Enterprise-level CA. In this configuration, the certificates (or private keys) are archived at the CA. If a **key recovery agent** has been configured, lost, or corrupted, keys can be restored. It's important to use some type of software that can archive and restore keys in case of an incident or disaster.

Another way to avoid single points of failure, such as a single CA, is to organize certificate authorities in a hierarchical manner. At the top of the tree is a root CA; underneath are subordinate, or intermediate, CAs that offer redundancy and can sign certificates on behalf of the root CA. Though CA exclusivity is common, it is not the only type of architecture used to bind public keys to users. In some cases, a centralized model for certificates is not required or desired.

Remember that if a root CA is compromised, all of its certificates are then also compromised, which could affect an entire organization and beyond. The entire certificate *chain of trust* can be affected. One way to add a layer of security to avoid root CA compromise is to set up an offline root CA. Because it is offline, it will not be able to communicate over the network with the subordinate CAs, or any other computers for that matter. Certificates are transported to the subordinate CAs *physically* using USB flash drives or other removable media. We discussed the mindset of offline computing in Chapter 9, "Securing Network Media and Devices"; this is yet another example. Of course, you would need to have secure policies regarding the use and transport of media, and would need to incorporate data loss prevention (DLP), among other things. But the offline root CA has some obvious security advantages compared to an online root CA. Consider this *offline* mindset when dealing with critical data and encryption methods.

> **NOTE**   One thing you can take away from this discussion of certificates is that there have been many certificate exploits in the past and lots of vulnerabilities still exist. Be very careful during the planning stage of certificates.

Web of Trust

A **web of trust** is a *decentralized* trust model that addresses issues associated with the public authentication of public keys common to CA-based PKIs. It is considered peer-to-peer in that there is no root CA; instead, self-signed certificates are created and used that have been attested to by the creator. Users can decide what certificates they want to trust and can share those trusted certificates with others, making the web of trust grow larger. Of course, one of the most common reasons that a certificate issuer is not recognized by a web browser is due to unknown self-signed certificates. This model can also interoperate with standard CA architectures inherent to PKI. The more people that show trust of a certificate, the higher the chance that it is legitimate. This model is used by PGP, which enables users to start their own web of trust, self-publishing their own public key information.

Security Protocols

You can use a variety of security protocols to allow for more secure connections to other systems and networks. But the question is: What should be secured when connecting to other computers? I like to break it down into four categories:

- **E-mail and other communications:** This can be accomplished with the use of S/MIME or PGP.

- **E-commerce and web logins:** This can be brought about with the aid of protocols such as SSL and TLS.

- **Direct connections to other computers:** This can be done with a protocol such as SSH.

- **Virtual connections to remote networks:** This can be achieved with virtual private networks and protocols such as PPTP and L2TP.

Each of these scenarios builds on the concepts you learned in the previous PKI section. Let's define each of these scenarios and the security protocols used in more depth.

S/MIME

Originally developed by RSA Security, **Secure/Multipurpose Internet Mail Extensions (S/MIME)** is an IETF standard that provides cryptographic security for electronic messaging such as e-mail. It is used for authentication, message integrity, and non-repudiation of origin. Most e-mail clients have S/MIME functionality built-in. S/MIME uses a separate session key for each e-mail message.

S/MIME relies on PKI and the obtaining and validating of certificates from a CA, namely X.509v3 certificates. It also relies on digital signatures when attempting to establish non-repudiation. S/MIME enables users to send both encrypted and digitally signed e-mail messages.

S/MIME can be implemented in Outlook by first obtaining a certificate known as a Digital ID, publishing the certificate within Outlook, and then modifying the settings for Outlook, as shown in Figure 15-3.

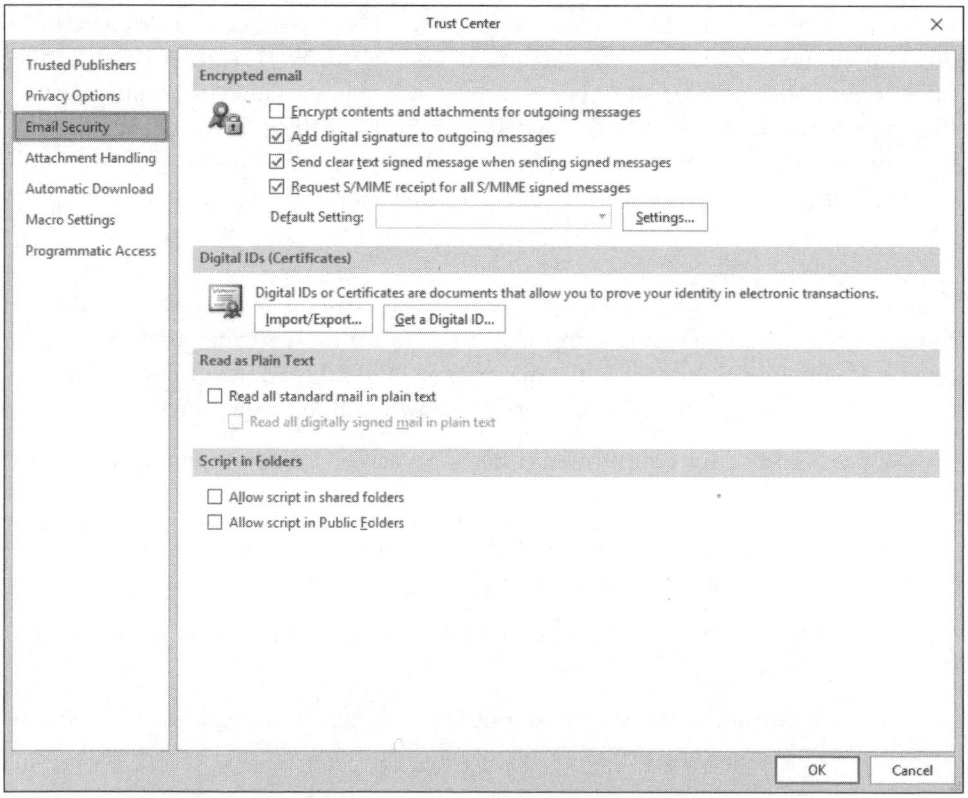

Figure 15-3 S/MIME Settings in Outlook

One of the issues with S/MIME is that it encrypts not only messages but also any malware that found its way into the message. This could compromise systems between the sender and receiver. To defeat this, scan messages at a network gateway that has a copy of the private keys used with S/MIME. Do this after decryption. If an e-mail program stores an S/MIME-encrypted message and the private key used for encryption/decryption is lost, deleted, or corrupted, the message cannot be decrypted.

SSL/TLS

Secure Sockets Layer (SSL) and its successor **Transport Layer Security (TLS)** are cryptographic protocols that provide secure Internet communications such as web browsing, instant messaging, e-mail, and VoIP. These protocols rely on a PKI for the obtaining and validating of certificates.

Many people refer to the secure connections they make to websites as SSL, but actually some of these will be TLS. The last version of SSL, version 3, was released in 1996. TLS is a more secure solution; version 1 of TLS supersedes SSLv3. As of the writing of this book, the latest version of TLS is 1.2 (defined in 2008), with 1.3 as a working draft and an eventuality. However, what you should be most interested in is the strength of the cipher—something to keep in mind when inquiring as to SSL or TLS certificates. TLS and SSL work in much the same manner. Two types of keys are required when any two computers attempt to communicate with the SSL or TLS protocols: a public key and a session key. Asymmetric encryption is used to encrypt and share session keys, and symmetric encryption is used to encrypt the session data. Session keys used by protocol such as TLS are used only once—a separate session key is utilized for every connection. A recovery key will be necessary if any data is lost in an SSL/TLS session. SSL and TLS encrypt segments of network connections that start at the transport layer of the OSI model. The actual encryption occurs at the session layer. In general, SSL and TLS are known as application layer protocols.

If a server running SSL/TLS requires additional processing, consider a SSL/TLS accelerator. This can be another computer, or more commonly, an add-on card that solely works on the CPU-intensive public-key encryption, namely the SSL/TLS handshake process. Your organization might have a policy that states that SSL/TLS-encrypted data needs to be decrypted when it reaches the internal network, and then analyzed for malware and potential attacks. It is often then re-encrypted and sent to its final destination. This is also very CPU intensive, and an SSL/TLS accelerator can provide the additional power required. Know that SSL/TLS decryption and re-encryption can be a security risk and a privacy issue (especially for BYOD users).

Careful consideration is required regarding where the decryption/re-encryption will take place, how it is implemented, and how people are notified about this policy.

HTTPS, which stands for Hypertext Transfer Protocol Secure, is a combination of HTTP and either SSL or TLS. Web servers that enable HTTPS inbound connections must have inbound port 443 open. This is common for e-commerce. If you connect to an online shopping portal such as Amazon, your credit card transactions should be protected by HTTPS, and you should see the protocol within the address bar of your browser when you enter a secure area of the website. HTTPS should not be confused with Secure HTTP (SHTTP). SHTTP is an alternative to HTTPS that works in much the same way. Because SHTTP was neglected by Microsoft, Netscape, and others in the 1990s, and because SHTTP encrypts only application layer messages, HTTPS became the widely used standard. HTTPS can encrypt all data passed between the client and the server, including data passing through layer 3.

E-mail protocols can use SSL/TLS as well. For example, there is SSL/TLS-encrypted POP (which uses port 995), SSL/TLS SMTP (uses port 465), and SSL/TLS IMAP (uses port 993).

One attack to watch for is the **downgrade attack**—when a protocol is downgraded from a high-quality mode or higher version to a low-quality mode or lower version. Many types of encryption protocols can be downgraded, but perhaps the most commonly targeted protocols are SSL and TLS. This is accomplished when backward compatibility is enabled on a system, and is often implemented as part of an MITM attack. Obviously, the removal of backward compatibility can help prevent the attack on the server side and on the client side, but also preventive measures against MITM and similar enveloping attacks can be beneficial. For example, using an IDS/IPS solution within the company network, and utilizing encrypted VPN tunnels for data sessions, are preventive measures that can be used against downgrade attacks.

SSL can be used by attackers as well. SSL-encrypted malware such as the Zeus or Gameover banking Trojans utilize the secure nature of SSL to exist undetected. Victims are often spammed a false update program that (if opened) downloads the Trojan payload through an SSL-encrypted connection from an infected website. The only way an individual user can protect from this is to have updated anti-malware running, and not open any unknown attachments. However, organizations can use *next-generation firewalls (NGFWs)* to filter out SSL-encrypted traffic. They might use these in addition to their regular firewalls, used for unencrypted traffic.

SSH

Secure Shell (SSH) is a protocol that can create a secure channel between two computers or network devices, enabling one computer or device to remotely control the other. Designed as a replacement for Telnet, it is commonly used on Linux and Unix systems, and nowadays also has widespread use on Windows clients. It depends on public key cryptography to authenticate remote computers. One computer (the one to be controlled) runs the SSH daemon, while the other computer runs the SSH client and makes secure connections to the first computer (which is known as a server), as long as a certificate can be obtained and validated.

Computers that run the SSH daemon have inbound port 22 open. If a proper SSH connection is made, files can also be transferred securely using SFTP (Secure File Transfer Protocol) or SCP (Secure Copy Protocol). Tunneling is also supported.

Vulnerabilities to SSH 1 and 1.5, such as the unauthorized insertion of content, the forwarding of client authentications to other servers (daemons), and integer overflow, precipitated the development of SSH 2.0, which is incompatible with SSH version 1. Improvements to SSH 2.0 include usage of the Diffie-Hellman key exchange and integrity checking with message authentication codes (MACs).

PPTP, L2TP, and IPsec

Virtual private networks (VPNs) were developed to enable quick, secure, remote connections using the inherent capacity of the Internet. They were also developed to take advantage of faster Internet connections such as cable, DSL, and so on but still work with dial-up connections. The issue with VPNs is how to secure those connections. Basically, there are two common protocols used to do so: PPTP and L2TP (with the aid of IPsec).

PPTP

The **Point-to-Point Tunneling Protocol (PPTP)** is a protocol used in VPNs. It encapsulates PPP packets, ultimately sending encrypted traffic. PPP by itself is useful for dial-up connections but is not suitable for a VPN by itself without a protocol such as PPTP. Servers and other devices running the PPTP protocol and accepting incoming VPN connections need to have inbound port 1723 open.

PPTP can be used with CHAP-based authentication protocols. Because the protocol MSCHAPv1 is considered inherently insecure, and MSCHAPv2 is vulnerable to dictionary attacks, PPTP is often deemed to be vulnerable. These authentication vulnerabilities can be dismissed if PPTP is used with an authentication method such as EAP-TLS. This relies on the existence of a PKI for the client and server computers. If this infrastructure is not readily available, PEAP can be used instead, as long as the computers are running the Windows Vista operating system or newer. Otherwise, L2TP with IPsec or other tunneling protocols is recommended for environments in which session and data security is of paramount importance.

L2TP

The **Layer 2 Tunneling Protocol (L2TP)** is a tunneling protocol used to connect VPNs. In essence, it creates an unencrypted tunnel if used by itself (which would be unwise). It does not include confidentiality or encryption on its own, but when paired with a security protocol such as IPsec it is considered a formidable tunneling protocol.

Its starting point is based on the Layer 2 Forwarding Protocol (L2F) and PPTP. The latest version is L2TPv3, which has improved encapsulation and increased security features. Servers and other devices accepting incoming VPN connections need to have inbound port 1701 open.

When installed on a Windows Server, it uses a PKI. Valid certificates need to be downloaded to clients before they can make a VPN connection to the server. Security must be configured on the server side and the client side. Generally, the IPsec protocol is used to accomplish the secure connection within the L2TP tunnel.

IPsec

Internet Protocol Security (IPsec) authenticates and encrypts IP packets, effectively securing communications between the computers and devices that use this protocol. IPsec operates at the network layer of the OSI model. It differs from SSH, SSL, and TLS in that it is the only protocol that does not operate within the upper layers of the OSI model. It can negotiate cryptographic keys and establish mutual authentication. IPsec is made up of three other protocols that perform its functions, including:

Key Topic

- **Security association (SA):** This is the establishment of secure connections and shared security information, using either certificates or cryptographic keys. It is set up most often through the Internet Key Exchange (IKE) or via Kerberized Internet Negotiation of Keys. The IKE can select varying levels of security protocols for the computers in a connection, which can differ in a VPN due to the dissimilar computers (with disparate protocols) that might attempt to connect to it.

- **Authentication header (AH):** This offers integrity and authentication. The authentication information is a keyed hash based on all the bytes in the packet. It can be used with the Encapsulating Security Payload (ESP) protocol. It can protect against replay attacks by employing sliding window protocols, which put limits on the total amount of packets that can be transceived in a given timeframe but ultimately enables an unlimited number of packets to be communicated using fixed-size sequence numbers.

- **Encapsulating Security Payload (ESP):** This provides integrity, confidentiality, and authenticity of packets. Protected data is encapsulated and encrypted.

IPsec can be implemented in two ways:

- **Transport mode:** In host-to-host transport mode, the payload of the IP packet is encrypted, but the header information is not. The AH is still hashed though. This mode allows for the secure transfer of data among computers in a LAN or other private, internal type of network. It can be used for transmission over networks, using NAT traversal (NAT-T), but tunnel mode is more often used for that purpose.

- **Tunnel mode:** Network tunneling mode is when the entire IP packet is encrypted. It takes the regular IP packet and encapsulates that inside of a new IP packet with a separate header. This mode is the more commonly used mode for transmission between networks, and is the one that facilitates VPNs. Keep in mind that an organization might favor *on-demand VPNs* (which make use of SSL/TLS certificates) over IPsec-based VPNs.

IPsec uses algorithms such as SHA2 (and possibly HMAC-SHA1) for integrity and authenticity, which hashes the packets of data; afterward the hash is encrypted. It can also use Triple DES and AES for confidentiality.

Chapter Summary

Because public keys are common knowledge, they must be protected from compromise. One way to do this is to implement a public key infrastructure (PKI). This is a complete environment for the public key, including hardware, software, and procedures.

Users who want to access a website securely are required to request a certificate; this will bind the user identity with the public key. The certificate is issued from a certificate authority (CA) such as VeriSign. To be validated, a user's computer initiates a certificate signing request (CSR) with proof of the user's identity. If a certificate used by a website is no longer valid, or is suspected to be compromised, it needs to be revoked right away and placed on a public certificate revocation list (CRL).

PKI is used during secure web sessions (HTTPS, for example) that use SSL or TLS protocols, e-mail sessions that use S/MIME, and secure sessions between computers with SSH. Virtual private networks can also use a PKI; for example, a VPN that relies on L2TP and therefore certificates as well. To further secure an L2TP tunneled connection, IPsec is implemented. Keep in mind that always-on VPN technology is also available, which makes use of SSL/TLS instead of PPTP or L2TP.

However, PKI is most commonly used for secure web transactions. Within that system, a certificate will employ asymmetric encryption (such as RSA or ECC) and a cryptographic hash (such as SHA) for the key exchange. Afterward, the rest of the session's data will be encrypted in a symmetric format (such as AES or RC4), which uses less computational power than asymmetric encryption.

As you travel the Internet, check on the validity (and level of security) of the certificates used by websites. Any site that you can log into, or conduct any type of transaction regarding anything of value, should have an HTTPS connection, as well as SSL or TLS, RSA or ECC, SHA-2 or MD5, and AES or RC4 cryptographic protocols.

Chapter Review Activities

Use the features in this section to study and review the topics in this chapter.

Review Key Topics

Review the most important topics in the chapter, noted with the Key Topic icon in the outer margin of the page. Table 15-1 lists a reference of these key topics and the page number on which each is found.

Key Topic

Table 15-1   Key Topics for Chapter 15

Key Topic Element	Description	Page Number
Figure 15-1	Example of a secure connection, shown in Firefox	525
Figure 15-2	Details of a typical VeriSign certificate	526
Bulleted list	IPsec protocols	534

Define Key Terms

Define the following key terms from this chapter, and check your answers in the glossary:

public key infrastructure (PKI), certificates, X.509, wildcard certificate, subject alternative name (SAN), certificate authority (CA), one-to-one mapping, many-to-one mapping, registration authority (RA), certificate revocation list (CRL), Online Certificate Status Protocol (OCSP), key escrow, key recovery agent, web of trust, Secure/Multipurpose Internet Mail Extensions (S/MIME), Secure Sockets Layer (SSL), Transport Layer Security (TLS), downgrade attack, Secure Shell (SSH), Point-to-Point Tunneling Protocol (PPTP), Layer 2 Tunneling Protocol (L2TP), Internet Protocol Security (IPsec)

Complete the Real-World Scenarios

Complete the Real-World Scenarios found on the companion website (www.pearsonitcertification.com/title/9780789758996). You will find a PDF containing the scenario and questions, and also supporting videos and simulations.

Review Questions

Answer the following review questions. Check your answers with the correct answers that follow.

1. Which of the following does not apply to an X.509 certificate?

   A. Certificate version

   B. The issuer of the certificate

   C. Public key information

   D. Owner's symmetric key

2. What two items are included in a digital certificate? (Select the two best answers.)

   A. User's private key

   B. Certificate authority's digital signature

   C. The user's public key

   D. Certificate authority's IP address

3. Rick has a local computer that uses software to generate and store key pairs. What type of PKI implementation is this?

   A. Distributed key

   B. Centralized

   C. Hub and spoke

   D. Decentralized

4. Which of the following is usually used with L2TP?

   A. IPsec

   B. SSH

   C. PHP

   D. SHA

5. What ensures that a CRL is authentic and has not been modified?

    A. The CRL can be accessed by anyone.

    B. The CRL is digitally signed by the CA.

    C. The CRL is always authentic.

    D. The CRL is encrypted by the CA.

6. Which of the following encryption concepts is PKI based on?

    A. Asymmetric

    B. Symmetric

    C. Elliptical curve

    D. Quantum

7. You are in charge of PKI certificates. What should you implement so that stolen certificates cannot be used?

    A. CRL

    B. CAD

    C. CA

    D. CRT

8. Which of the following are certificate-based authentication mapping schemes? (Select the two best answers.)

    A. One to-many mapping

    B. One-to-one mapping

    C. Many-to-many mapping

    D. Many-to-one mapping

9. Which of the following network protocols sends data between two computers while using a secure channel?

    A. SSH

    B. SMTP

    C. SNMP

    D. P2P

10. Which of the following protocols uses port 443?

    A. SFTP

    B. HTTPS

    C. SSHTP

    D. SSLP

11. Which of the following protocols creates an unencrypted tunnel?

    A. L2TP

    B. PPTP

    C. IPsec

    D. VPN

12. In a public key infrastructure setup, which of the following should be used to encrypt the signature of an e-mail?

    A. Private key

    B. Public key

    C. Shared key

    D. Hash

13. Two computers are attempting to communicate with the SSL protocol. Which two types of keys will be used? (Select the two best answers.)

    A. Recovery key

    B. Session key

    C. Public key

    D. Key card

14. Which layer of the OSI model does IPsec operate at?

    A. Data link

    B. Network

    C. Transport

    D. Application

15. Which layer of the OSI model is where SSL provides encryption?

    A. Network

    B. Transport

    C. Session

    D. Application

16. Which of the following details one of the primary benefits of using S/MIME?

    A. S/MIME expedites the delivery of e-mail messages.

    B. S/MIME enables users to send e-mail messages with a return receipt.

    C. S/MIME enables users to send both encrypted and digitally signed e-mail messages.

    D. S/MIME enables users to send anonymous e-mail messages.

17. What should you do to make sure that a compromised PKI key cannot be used again?

    A. Renew the key.

    B. Reconfigure the key.

    C. Revoke the key.

    D. Create a new key.

18. Which of the following statements is correct about IPsec authentication headers?

    A. The authentication information is a keyed hash based on half of the bytes in the packet.

    B. The authentication information is a keyed hash based on all the bytes in the packet.

    C. The authentication information hash will remain the same even if the bytes change on transfer.

    D. The authentication header cannot be used in combination with the IP Encapsulating Security Payload.

19. Which of the following protocols is not used to create a VPN tunnel and not used to encrypt VPN tunnels?

    A. PPTP

    B. L2TP

    C. PPP

    D. IPsec

20. Which of the following answers are not part of IPsec? (Select the two best answers.)

   A. TKIP

   B. Key exchange

   C. AES

   D. Authentication header

21. What should you publish a compromised certificate to?

   A. CRL

   B. CA

   C. PKI

   D. AES

22. You have been asked to set up authentication through PKI, and encryption of a database using a different cryptographic process to decrease latency. What encryption types should you use?

   A. Public key encryption to authenticate users and public keys to encrypt the database

   B. Public key encryption to authenticate users and private keys to encrypt the database

   C. Private key encryption to authenticate users and private keys to encrypt the database

   D. Private key encryption to authenticate users and public keys to encrypt the database

23. Which of the following uses an asymmetric key to open a session, and then establishes a symmetric key for the remainder of the session?

   A. TLS

   B. SFTP

   C. HTTPS

   D. SSL

   E. TFTP

24. Which of the following describes key escrow?

    A. Maintains a secured copy of the user's private key for the purpose of recovering the CRL

    B. Maintains a secured copy of the user's private key for the purpose of recovering the key if it is lost

    C. Maintains a secured copy of the user's public key for the purpose of recovering messages if the key is lost

    D. Maintains a secured copy of the user's public key for the purpose of increasing network performance

25. When a user's web browser communicates with a CA, what PKI element does the CA require from the browser?

    A. Public key

    B. Private key

    C. Symmetric key

    D. Secret key

Answers and Explanations

1. **D.** In X.509, the owner does not use a symmetric key. All the other answers apply to X.509.

2. **B and C.** A digital certificate includes the certificate authority's (CA) digital signature and the user's public key. A user's private key should be kept private and should not be within the digital certificate. The IP address of the CA should have been known to the user's computer before obtaining the certificate.

3. **D.** When creating key pairs, PKI has two methods: centralized and decentralized. Centralized is when keys are generated at a central server and are transmitted to hosts. Decentralized is when keys are generated and stored on a local computer system for use by that system.

4. **A.** IPsec is usually used with L2TP. SSH is a more secure way of connecting to remote computers. PHP is a type of language commonly used on the web. SHA is a type of hashing algorithm.

5. **B.** Certificate revocation lists (CRLs) are digitally signed by the certificate authority for security purposes. If a certificate is compromised, it will be revoked and placed on the CRL. CRLs are later generated and published periodically.

6. **A.** The public key infrastructure, or PKI, is based on the asymmetric encryption concept. Symmetric, elliptical curve, and quantum cryptography are all different encryption schemes that PKI is not associated with.

7. **A.** You should implement a CRL (certificate revocation list) so that stolen certificates, or otherwise revoked or held certificates, cannot be used.

8. **B and D.** When dealing with certificate authentication, asymmetric systems use one-to-one mappings and many-to-one mappings.

9. **A.** SSH, or Secure Shell, enables two computers to send data via a secure channel. SMTP is the Simple Mail Transfer Protocol, which deals with e-mail. SNMP is the Simple Network Management Protocol, which enables the monitoring of remote systems. P2P is an abbreviation of peer-to-peer network.

10. **B.** Port 443 is used by HTTPS, which implements TLS/SSL for security. SFTP is the Secure File Transfer Protocol. There are no protocols named SSHTP and SSLP.

11. **A.** In VPNs (virtual private networks), Layer Two Tunneling Protocol (L2TP) creates an unencrypted tunnel between two IP addresses. It is usually used with IPsec to encrypt the data transfer. PPTP is the Point-to-Point Tunneling Protocol, which includes encryption.

12. **A.** A private key should be used to encrypt the signature of an e-mail in an asymmetric system such as PKI. Public keys and shared keys should never be used to encrypt this type of information. A hash is not used to encrypt in this fashion; it is used to verify the integrity of the message.

13. **B and C.** In an SSL session, a session key and a public key are used. A recovery key is not necessary unless data has been lost. A key card would be used as a physical device to gain access to a building or server room.

14. **B.** IPsec is a dual-mode, end-to-end security scheme that operates at layer 3, the network layer of the OSI model, also known as the Internet layer within the Internet Protocol suite. It is often used with L2TP for VPN tunneling, among other protocols.

15. **C.** The session layer provides encryption. SSL, or Secure Sockets Layer, and its successor, Transport Layer Security (TLS), encrypt segments of network connections that start at the transport layer. The actual encryption is done at the session layer, and the protocol is known as an application layer protocol.

16. **C.** S/MIME (Secure/Multipurpose Internet Mail Extensions) enables users to send both encrypted and digitally signed e-mail messages, enabling a higher level of e-mail security. It does not make the delivery of e-mail any faster, nor does it have anything to do with return receipts. Return receipts are usually

controlled by the SMTP server. Anonymous e-mail messages would be considered spam, completely insecure, and something that a security administrator wants to reduce, and certainly does not want users to implement.

17. **C.** Key revocation is the proper way to approach the problem of a compromised PKI key. The revoked key will then be listed in the CRL (certificate revocation list).

18. **B.** The only statement that is true is that the authentication information is a keyed hash that is based on all the bytes in the packet. A hash will not remain the same if the bytes change on transfer; a new hash will be created for the authentication header (AH). The authentication header can be used in combination with the Encapsulating Security Payload (ESP).

19. **C.** PPP, or Point-to-Point Protocol, does not provide security and is not used to create VPN connections. You will see PPP used in dial-up connections, and it is an underlying protocol used by L2TP, PPTP, and IPsec, which are all used in VPN connections.

20. **A and C.** IPsec contains (or uses) a key exchange (either Internet Key Exchange or Kerberized Internet Negotiation of Keys) and an authentication header (in addition to many other components). TKIP and AES are other encryption protocols.

21. **A.** A compromised certificate should be published to the CRL (certificate revocation list). The CA is the certificate authority that houses the CRL. PKI stands for public key infrastructure—the entire system that CRLs and CAs are just components of. AES is an encryption protocol.

22. **B.** PKI uses public keys to authenticate users. If you are looking for a cryptographic process that allows for decreased latency, then symmetrical keys (private) would be the way to go. So, the PKI system uses public keys to authenticate the users, and the database uses private keys to encrypt the data.

23. **C.** HTTPS will govern the entire session when a person attempts to connect to a website securely (for example, HTTPS://www.*yourbanknamehere*.com). It initiates a key exchange using SSL or TLS, riding on asymmetric encryption such as RSA or ECC. Then, it performs the rest of the session data transfer using symmetric encryption such as AES. SFTP is Secure FTP, based on SSH. TFTP is Trivial FTP, which has little security.

24. **B.** Key escrow is implemented to secure a copy of the user's private key (not the public key) in case it is lost. It has nothing to do with the CRL.

25. **A.** The browser must present the public key, which is matched against the CA's private key. Symmetric and secret keys are other names for private keys.

This chapter covers the following subjects:

- **Redundancy Planning:** This section is all about ensuring your network and servers are fault tolerant. By setting up redundant power, data, servers, and even ISPs, you can avoid many disasters that could threaten the security of your organization.

- **Disaster Recovery Planning and Procedures:** A disaster is when something happens to your network that your fault-tolerant methods cannot prevent. To help recover after a disaster, data should be backed up, and a proper disaster recovery plan should be designed, practiced, and implemented if necessary.

The typical definition of "redundant" means superfluous or uncalled for. However, it is not so in the IT field. Being redundant is a way of life. It is a way of enhancing your servers, network devices, and other equipment. It is a way of developing fault tolerance—the capability to continue functioning even if there is an error.

CHAPTER 16

Redundancy and Disaster Recovery

This chapter discusses how to prevent problems that might occur that could threaten the security of your servers, network equipment, and server room in general. A good network security administrator should have plenty of redundancy and fault-tolerant methods in place that can help combat threats and help avoid disaster.

However, no matter how much redundancy you implement, there is always a chance that a disaster could arise. A disaster could be the loss of data on a server, a fire in a server room, or the catastrophic loss of access to an organization's building. To prepare for these events, a disaster recovery plan should be designed, but with the thought in mind that redundancy and fault tolerance can defend against most "disasters." The best admin is the one who avoids disaster and, in the rare case that it does happen, has a plan in place to recover quickly from it. This chapter also covers how to plan for disasters and discusses a plan of action for recovering swiftly.

Foundation Topics

Redundancy Planning

Most networks could do with a little more redundancy. I know…a lot of you are probably wondering why I keep repeating myself! It's because so many customers of mine in the past, and network admins who have worked for and with me, insist on avoiding the issue. Redundancy works—use it!

This section discusses redundant power in the form of power supplies, UPSs, and backup generators. It also talks about redundant data, servers, ISPs, and sites. All these things, when planned properly, create an environment that can withstand most failures barring total disaster.

The whole concept revolves around single points of failure. A **single point of failure** is an element, object, or part of a system that, if it fails, causes the whole system to fail. By implementing redundancy, you can bypass just about any single point of failure.

There are two methods to combating single points of failure. The first is to use redundancy. If employed properly, redundancy keeps a system running with no downtime. However, this can be pricey, and we all know there is only so much IT budget to go around. So, the alternative is to make sure you have plenty of spare parts lying around. This is a good method if your network and systems are not time-critical. Installing spare parts often requires you to shut down the server or a portion of a network. If this risk is not acceptable to an organization, you'll have to find the cheapest redundant solutions available. Research is key, and don't be fooled by the hype—sometimes the simplest sounding solutions are the best.

Here's the scenario (and we apply this to the rest of this "Redundancy Planning" section). Your server room has the following powered equipment:

- Nine servers
- Two Microsoft domain controllers
- One DNS server
- Two file servers
- One database server
- Two web servers (which second as FTP servers)
- One mail server
- Five 48-port switches
- One master switch
- Three routers
- Two CSU/DSUs
- One PBX
- Two client workstations (for remote server access without having to work directly at the server); these are within the server room as well.

It appears that there is already some redundancy in place in your server room. For example, there are two domain controllers. One of them has a copy of the Active Directory and acts as a secondary DC in the case that the first one fails. There are also two web servers, one ready to take over for the other if the primary one fails. This type of redundancy is known as failover redundancy. The secondary system is inactive until the first one fails. Also, there are two client workstations used to remotely control the servers; if one fails, another one is available.

Otherwise, the rest of the servers and other pieces of equipment are one-offs—single instances in need of something to prevent failure. There are a lot of them, so we truly need to *redundacize*. Hey, it's a word if IT people use it! It's the detailed approach to preparing for problems that can arise in a system that will make for a good IT contingency plan. Try to envision the various upcoming redundancy methods used with each of the items listed previously in our fictitious server room.

But before we get into some hard-core redundancy, let's quickly discuss the terms fail-open and fail-closed. *Fail-open* means that if a portion of a system fails, the rest of the system will still be available or "open." *Fail-closed* means that if a portion of a system fails, the entire system will become inaccessible or simply shut down. Depending on the level of security your organization requires, you might have a mixture of fail-open and fail-closed systems. In the previous server room example, we have a DNS server and a database server. Let's say that the DNS server forwards information to several different zones, and that one of those zones fails for one reason or another. We might decide that it is more beneficial to the network to have the rest of the DNS server continue to operate and service the rest of the zones instead of shutting down completely, so we would want the DNS server to fail-open. However, our database server might have confidential information that we cannot afford to lose, so if one service or component of the database server fails, we might opt to have the database server stop servicing requests altogether, or in other words, to fail-closed. Another example would be a firewall/router. If the firewall portion of the device failed, we would probably want the device to fail-closed. Even though the network connectivity could still function, we probably wouldn't want it to since there is no firewall protection. It all depends on the level of security you require, and the risk that can be associated with devices that fail-open. It also depends on whether the server or device has a redundancy associated with it. If the DNS server mentioned previously has a secondary redundant DNS server that is always up and running and ready to take requests at a moment's notice, we might opt to instead configure the first DNS server to fail-closed and let the secondary DNS server take over entirely. This leads to clustering, which we discuss later in this chapter.

Redundant Power

Let's begin with power because that is what all our devices and computers gain "sustenance" from. Power is so important—when planning for redundancy it should be at the top of your list. When considering power implications, think like an engineer; you might even need to enlist the help of a coworker who has an engineering background, or a third party, to help plan your electrical requirements and make them a reality.

We are most interested in the server room. Smart companies store most of their important data, settings, apps, and so on in that room. So power is critical here, whereas it is not as important for client computers and other client resources. If power fails in a server room or in any one component within the server room, it could cause the network to go down, or loss of access to resources. It could also cause damage to a server or other device.

When considering power, think about it from the inside out. For example, start with individual computers, servers, and networking components. How much power does each of these things require? Make a list and tally your results. Later, this plays into the total power needed by the server room. Remember that networking devices such as IP phones, cameras, and some wireless access points are powered over Ethernet cabling, which can require additional power requirements at the Ethernet switch (or switches) in the server room. Think about installing redundant power supplies in some of your servers and switches. Next, ponder using UPS devices as a way of defeating short-term power loss failures. Then, move on to how many circuits you need, total power, electrical panel requirements, and also the cleanliness of power coming in from your municipality. Finally, consider backup generators for longer-term power failures.

Using proper power devices is part of a good preventative maintenance/security plan and helps to protect a computer. You need to protect against several things:

- **Surges:** A **surge** in electrical power means that there is an unexpected increase in the amount of voltage provided. This can be a small increase, or a larger increase known as a spike.

- **Spikes:** A **spike** is a short transient in voltage that can be due to a short circuit, tripped circuit breaker, power outage, or lightning strike.

- **Sags:** A **sag** is an unexpected decrease in the amount of voltage provided. Typically, sags are limited in time and in the decrease in voltage. However, when voltage reduces further, a brownout could ensue.

- **Brownouts:** A **brownout** is when the voltage drops to such an extent that it typically causes the lights to dim and causes computers to shut off.

- **Blackouts:** A **blackout** is when total loss of power for a prolonged period occurs. Another problem associated with blackouts is the spike that can occur when power is restored. In the New York area, it is common to have an increased amount of tech support calls during July; this is attributed to lightning storms! Often, damage to systems is due to improper protection.

- **Power supply failure:** Power supplies are like hard drives in two ways: One, they will fail. It's not a matter of if; it's a matter of when. Two, they can cause intermittent issues when they begin to fail, issues that are hard to troubleshoot. If you suspect a power supply failure, then you should replace the supply. Also consider using a redundant power supply.

Some devices have specific purposes, and others can protect against more than one of these electrical issues. Let's talk about three of them now: redundant power supplies, uninterruptible power supplies, and backup generators.

Redundant Power Supplies

A proper **redundant power supply** is an enclosure that contains two (or more) complete power supplies. You make one main power connection from the AC outlet to the power supply, and there is one set of wires that connects to the motherboard and devices. However, if one of the power supplies in the enclosure fails, the other takes over immediately without computer failure. These are common on servers, especially RAID boxes. They are not practical for client computers, but you might see them installed in some powerful workstations. In our scenario, we should install redundant power supplies to as many servers as possible, starting with the file servers and domain controllers. If possible, we should implement redundant power supplies for any of our switches or routers that will accept them, or consider new routers and switches that are scalable for redundant power supplies.

In some cases (pun intended), it is possible to install two completely separate power supplies so that each has a connection to an AC outlet. This depends on your server configuration but is less common due to the amount of redundancy it requires of the devices inside the server. Either look at the specifications for your server's case or open it up during off-hours to see if redundant power supplies are an option.

Vendors such as HP and manufacturers such as Thermaltake and Enlight offer redundant power supply systems for servers, and vendors such as Cisco offer redundant AC power systems for their networking devices.

This technology is great in the case that a power supply failure occurs, but it does not protect from scenarios in which power to the computer is disrupted.

Uninterruptible Power Supplies

It should go without saying, but surge protectors are not good enough to protect power issues that might occur in your server room. A UPS is the proper device to use. An **uninterruptible power supply (UPS)** takes the functionality of a surge suppressor and combines that with a battery backup. So now, our server is protected not only from surges and spikes, but also from sags, brownouts, and blackouts. Most UPS devices also act as line conditioners that serve to clean up dirty power. Noise and increases/decreases in power make up dirty power. Dirty power can also be caused by too many devices using the same circuit, or because power coming from the electrical panel or from the municipal grid fluctuates, maybe because the panel or the entire grid is under- or overloaded. If a line-conditioning device such as a

UPS doesn't fix the problem, a quick call to your company's electrician should result in an answer and possibly a long-term fix.

If you happen to be using a separate line-conditioning device *in addition to* a UPS, it should be tested regularly. Line-conditioning devices are always supplying power to your devices. A UPS backup battery will kick in only if a power loss occurs.

Battery backup is great, but the battery can't last indefinitely! It is considered emergency power and typically keeps your computer system running for 5 to 30 minutes depending on the model you purchase. UPS devices today have a USB connection so that your computer can communicate with the UPS. When there is a power outage, the UPS sends a signal to the computer telling it to shut down, suspend, or stand-by before the battery discharges completely. Most UPSs come with software that you can install that enables you to configure the computer with these options.

The more devices that connect to the UPS, the less time the battery can last if a power outage occurs; if too many devices are connected, there may be inconsistencies when the battery needs to take over. Thus many UPS manufacturers limit the amount of battery backup–protected receptacles. Connecting a laser printer to the UPS is *not* recommended due to the high current draw of the laser printer; and *never* connect a surge protector or power strip to one of the receptacles in the UPS, to protect the UPS from being overloaded.

The UPS normally has a lead-acid battery that, when discharged, requires 10 hours to 20 hours to recharge. This battery is usually shipped in a disconnected state. Before charging the device for use, you must first make sure that the leads connect. If the battery ever needs to be replaced, a red light usually appears accompanied by a beeping sound. Beeping can also occur if power is no longer supplied to the UPS by the AC outlet.

There are varying levels of UPS devices, which incorporate different technologies. For example, the cheaper standby UPS (known as an SPS) might have a slight delay when switching from AC to battery power, possibly causing errors in the computer operating system. If a UPS is rack mounted, it will usually be a full-blown UPS (perhaps not the best choice of words!); this would be known as an "online" or "continuous" UPS—these cost hundreds or even thousands of dollars. If it is a smaller device that plugs into the AC outlet and lies freely about, it is probably an SPS—these cost between $25 and $100. You should realize that some care should be taken when planning the type of UPS to be used. When data is crucial, you had better plan for a quality UPS!

Just about everything in the server room should be connected to a UPS (you will most likely need several) to protect from power outages. This includes servers, monitors, switches, routers, CSU/DSUs, PBX equipment, security cameras, workstations, and monitors—really, everything in the server room!

Backup Generators

What if power to the building does fail completely? Most would consider this a disaster, and over the long term it could possibly be. However, most power outages are 5 minutes or less on the average, and most of the time a UPS can pick up the slack for these short outages but not for the less common, longer outages that might last a few hours or days. And, a UPS powers only the devices you plug into it. If your organization is to keep functioning, it will need a backup generator to power lights, computers, phones, and security systems over short term outages, or longer ones.

A **backup generator** is a part of an emergency power system used when there is an outage of regular electric grid power. Some emergency power systems might include special lighting and fuel cells, whereas larger, more commercial backup generators can power portions of a building, or an entire building, as long as fuel is available. For our scenario we should make sure that the backup generator powers the server room at the very least.

Backup generator fuel types include gasoline, diesel, natural gas, propane, and solar. Smaller backup generators often use gasoline, but these are not adequate for most companies. Instead, many organizations use larger natural gas generators. Some of these generators need to be started manually, but the majority of them are known as **standby generators**. These are systems that turn on automatically within seconds of a power outage. Transfer switches sense any power loss and instruct the generator to start. Standby generators may be required by code for certain types of buildings with standby lighting, or buildings with elevators, fire-suppression systems, and life-support equipment. You should always check company policy and your municipal guidelines before planning and implementing a backup generator system.

Backup generators can be broken into three types:

- **Portable gas-engine generator:** The least expensive and run on gasoline or possibly solar power. They are noisy, high maintenance, must be started manually, and usually require extension cords. They are a carbon monoxide risk and are only adequate for small operations and in mobile scenarios. Gas-powered inverters are quieter but often come with a higher price tag per watt generated.

- **Permanently installed generator:** Much more expensive, with a complex installation. These almost always run on either natural gas or propane. They are quieter and can be connected directly to the organization's electrical panel. Usually, these are standby generators and, as such, require little user interaction.

- **Battery-inverter generator:** These are based on lead-acid batteries, are quiet, and require little user interaction aside from an uncommon restart and change of batteries. They are well matched to environments that require a low amount of wattage or are the victims of short power outages only. Battery-inverter systems can be stored indoors, but because the batteries can release fumes, the area they are stored in should be well ventilated, such as an air-conditioned server room with external exhaust. Uninterruptible power supplies fall into the battery-inverter generator category.

Some of the considerations you should take into account when selecting a backup generator include the following:

- **Price:** As with any organizational purchase, this will have to be budgeted.

- **How unit is started:** Does it start automatically? Most organizations require this.

- **Uptime:** How many hours will the generator stay on before needing to be refueled? This goes hand-in-hand with the next bullet.

- **Power output:** How many watts does the system offer? Before purchasing a backup generator, you should measure the total maximum load your organization might use by running all computers, servers, lights, and other devices simultaneously, and measure this at the main electrical panel. Alternatively, you could measure the total on paper by adding the estimated power requirements of all devices together.

- **Fuel source:** Does it run on natural gas, gasoline, and so on? If it is an automatically starting system, the options will probably be limited to natural gas and propane.

Some vendors that offer backup generators include Generac, Gillette, and Kohler. These devices should be monitored periodically; most companies attempt to obtain a service contract from you, which might be wise depending on the size of your organization. We discuss service contracts and service-level agreements in Chapter 18, "Policies and Procedures."

Remember that your mission-critical devices, such as servers, should constantly be drawing power from a line-conditioning device. Then, if there is a power outage to the server, a UPS should kick in. (In some cases, the UPS also acts as the line-conditioning device.) Finally, if necessary, a backup generator will come online and feed all your critical devices with power.

Redundant Data

Now that we have power taken care of, we can move on to the heart of the matter—data. Data can fail due to file corruption and malicious intent, among other things. Power failures, hard drive failures, and user error can all lead to data failure. As always, it's the data that we are most interested in securing, so it stands to reason that the data should be redundant as well. But which data? There is so much of it! Well, generally file servers should have redundant data sets of some sort. If an organization has the budgeting, next on the list would be databases and then web and file servers. However, in some instances these additional servers might be better off with failover systems as opposed to redundant data arrays. And certainly, the majority of client computers' data does not constitute a reason for RAID. So we concentrate on the file servers in our original scenario in the beginning of the chapter.

The best way to protect file servers' data is to use some type of redundant array of disks. This is referred to as RAID (an acronym for redundant array of independent disks, or inexpensive disks). RAID technologies are designed to either increase the speed of reading and writing data or to create one of several types of fault-tolerant volumes, or to do both. From a security viewpoint, we are most interested in the availability of data, the fault tolerance (the capability to withstand failure) of our disks. A RAID array can be internal or external to a computer. Historically, RAID arrays were configured as SCSI chains, but nowadays you also find SATA, eSATA, and Fibre Channel. Either way, the idea is that data is being stored on multiple disks that work with each other. The number of disks and the way they work together is dependent on the level of RAID. For the exam, you need to know several levels of RAID including RAID 0, RAID 1, RAID 5, RAID 6, and RAID 10 (also known as RAID 1+0). Table 16-1 describes each of these. Note that RAID 0 is the only one listed that is *not* fault tolerant, so from a security perspective it is not a viable option. Nevertheless, you should know it for the exam.

Key Topic

Table 16-1 RAID Descriptions

RAID Level	Description	Fault Tolerant?	Minimum Number of Disks
RAID 0	Striping Data is striped across multiple disks to increase performance.	No	Two

RAID Level	Description	Fault Tolerant?	Minimum Number of Disks
RAID 1	Mirroring Data is copied to two identical disks. If one disk fails, the other continues to operate. See Figure 16-1 for an illustration. This RAID version allows for the least amount of downtime because there is a complete copy of the data ready at a moment's notice. When each disk is connected to a separate controller, this is known as **disk duplexing**.	Yes	Two (and two only)
RAID 5	Striping with Parity Data is striped across multiple disks; fault-tolerant parity data is also written to each disk. If one disk fails, the array can reconstruct the data from the parity information. See Figure 16-2 for an illustration.	Yes	Three
RAID 6	Striping with Double Parity Data is striped across multiple disks as it is in RAID 5, but there are two stripes of parity information. This usually requires another disk in the array. This system can operate even with two failed drives and is more adequate for time-critical systems.	Yes	Four
RAID 0+1	Combines the advantages of RAID 0 and RAID 1. Requires a minimum of four disks. This system contains two RAID 0 striped sets. Those two sets are mirrored.	Yes	Four
RAID 10 (also known as 1+0)	Combines the advantages of RAID 1 and RAID 0. Normally requires a minimum of four disks. This system contains at least two RAID 1 mirrors that are then striped.	Yes	Four

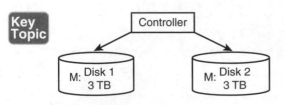

Figure 16-1   RAID 1 Illustration

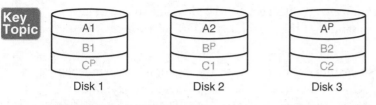

Figure 16-2 RAID 5 Illustration

Figure 16-1 shows an illustration of RAID 1; you can see that data is written to both disks and that both disks collectively are known as the M: drive or M: *volume*. Figure 16-2 displays an illustration of RAID 5. In a RAID 5 array, blocks of data are distributed to the disks (A1 and A2 are a block, B1 and B2 are a block, and so on), and parity information is written for each block of data. This is written to each disk in an alternating fashion (A^p, B^p, and such) so that the parity is also distributed. If one disk fails, the parity information from the other disks will reconstruct the data. It is important to make the distinction between fault tolerance and backup. *Fault tolerance* means that the hard drives can continue to function (with little or no downtime) even if there is a problem with one of the drives. *Backup* means that we are taking the data and copying it (and possibly compressing it) to another location for archival in the event of a disaster. An example of a disaster would be if *two* drives in a RAID 5 array were to fail. If an organization is worried that this disaster could happen, it should consider RAID 6, or RAID 10.

Windows servers support RAID 0, 1, and 5 (and possibly 6 depending on the version) within the operating system. But most client operating systems cannot support RAID 1, 5, and 6. However, they *can* support hardware controllers that can create these arrays. Some motherboards have built-in RAID functionality as well.

Hardware is always the better way to go when it comes to RAID. Having a separate interface that controls the RAID configuration and handling is far superior to trying to control it with software within an operating system. The hardware could be an adapter card installed inside the computer, or an external box that connects to the computer or even to the network. When it comes to RAID in a network storage scenario, you are now dealing with network attached storage (NAS). These NAS points can be combined to form a storage area network (SAN), but any type of network attached storage will cost more money to an organization.

You can classify RAID in three different ways; these classifications can help when you plan which type of RAID system to implement.

- **Failure-resistant disk systems:** Protect against data loss due to disk failure. An example of this would be RAID 1 mirroring.

- **Failure-tolerant disk systems:** Protect against data loss due to any single component failure. An example of this would be RAID 1 mirroring with duplexing.

- **Disaster-tolerant disk systems:** Protect data by the creation of two independent zones, each of which provides access to stored data. An example of this would be RAID 0+1.

As mentioned, whatever you implement, the data must be accessible, and in many cases highly available. The properly planned RAID system will have high availability (HA) and will be scalable; for example, a RAID 6 system that allows you to dynamically add hot-swappable disks—and the space to add them! You want the system to be elastic as well. Some RAID systems have better elasticity than others, meaning the ability to adapt to workload changes. You might even consider moving certain data away from internal RAID and on to the cloud for additional elasticity.

Of course, no matter how well you protect the data from failure, users still need to access the data, and to do so might require some redundant networking.

Redundant Networking

Network connections can fail as well. And we all know how users need to have the network up and running—or there will be heck to pay. The security of an organization can be compromised if networking connections fail. Some types of connections you should consider include the following:

- Server network adapter connections

- Main connections to switches and routers

- The Internet connection

So basically, when I speak of redundant networking, I'm referring to any network connection of great importance that could fail. Generally, these connections will be located in the server room.

Redundant network adapters are commonly used to decrease or eliminate server downtime in the case that one network adapter fails. However, you must consider how they will be set up. Optimally, the second network adapter will take over immediately when the first one fails, but how will this be determined? There are applications that can control multiple network adapters, or the switch that they connect to can control where data is directed in the case of a failure. Also, multiple network adapters can be part of an individual collective interface. What you decide will be dictated by company policy, budgeting, and previously installed equipment. As a rule of thumb, you should use like network adapters when implementing redundancy; check the model and the version of the particular model to be exact. When installing multiple network adapters to a server, that computer then becomes known as a multihomed machine. It is important to consider how multiple adapters (and their operating systems) will behave normally and during a failure. Microsoft has some notes about this; I left a link in the "View Recommended Resources" online document that accompanies this book. In some cases, you will install multiple physical network adapters, and in others you might opt for a single card that has multiple ports, such as a multi-Ethernet port Intel network adapter. This is often a cheaper solution than installing multiple cards but provides a single point of failure in the form of one adapter card and one adapter card slot. In our original scenario we had domain controllers, database servers, web servers, and file servers; these would all do well with the addition of redundant network adapters.

Companies should always have at least one backup switch sitting on the shelf. If the company has only one switch, it is a desperate single point of failure. If a company has multiple switches stacked in a star-bus fashion, the whole stack can be a single point of failure unless special backup ports are used (only available on certain switches). These special ports are often fiber-optic-based and are designed either for high-speed connections between switches or for redundancy. This concept should be employed at the master switch in a hierarchical star as well to avoid a complete network collapse. However, the hierarchical star is more secure than a star-bus configuration when it comes to network failure. In a hierarchical star, certain areas of the network still function even if one switch fails. This is a form of redundant topology.

Finally, your ISP is susceptible to failure as well—as I'm sure you are well aware. Most organizations rely on just one Internet connection for their entire network. This is another example of a single point of failure. Consider secondary connections to your ISP, such as redundant fiber-optics, forming what is known as a **redundant ISP**. Or, if you have a T-1 line, perhaps a BRI connection will do. Or if you have a T-3, perhaps a PRI connection would be best. At the very least, a set of dial-up connections can be used for redundancy. Some companies install completely fault-tolerant, dual Internet connections, the second of which comes online immediately following a failure. If you use a web host for your website and/or e-mail, consider a mirror site or more than one. Basically, in a nutshell, it's all about not being caught with your pants down. If an organization is without its Internet connection for more than a day (or hours in some cases), you know it will be the network admin and the security admin who will be the first on the chopping block, most likely followed by the ISP.

NOTE   Network devices will fail. It's just a matter of time. Chapter 12, "Vulnerability and Risk Assessment," mentioned the concept of mean time between failures (MTBF)—a reliability term used to provide an average number of failures for a device per million hours of use. MTBF, along with mean time to repair (MTTR) and mean time to failure (MTTF), should be incorporated into your thought process when considering redundant networking.

Redundant Servers

Let's take it to the next level and discuss redundant servers. When redundant network adapters and disks are not enough, you might decide to cluster multiple servers together that act as a single entity. This will be more costly and require more administration but can provide a company with low downtime and a secure feeling. Two or more servers that work with each other are a **cluster**.

The clustering of servers can be broken down into two types:

Key Topic

- **Failover clusters:** Otherwise known as high-availability clusters, these are designed so that a secondary server can take over in the case that the primary one fails, with limited or no downtime. A failover cluster can reduce the chance of a single point of failure on a server, regardless of what failed on that server—hard disk, CPU, memory, and so on. An example of a failover cluster would be the usage of two Microsoft domain controllers. When the first domain controller fails, the secondary domain controller should be ready to go at a moment's notice. There can be tertiary and quaternary servers and beyond as well. It all depends on how many servers you think might fail concurrently. Another example would be the DNS server we talked about in the beginning of the chapter. If we wanted the DNS server to fail-closed, then we should set up a secondary DNS server as a failover, one that will be ready to go at a moment's notice.

- **Load-balancing clusters:** Load-balancing clusters are multiple computers connected together for the purpose of sharing resources such as CPU, RAM, and hard disks. In this way, the cluster can share CPU power, along with other resources, and balance the CPU load among all the servers. Microsoft's Cluster Server is an example of this (although it can also act in failover mode), enabling for parallel, high-performance computing. Several third-party vendors offer clustering software for operating systems and virtual operating systems as well. It is a common technique in web and FTP server farms, as well as in IRC servers, DNS servers, and NNTP servers.

Data can also be replicated back and forth between servers as it often is with database servers and web servers. This is actually a mixture of redundant data (data replication) and server clustering.

However, it doesn't matter how many servers you install in a cluster. If they are all local, they could all be affected by certain attacks or, worse yet, disasters. Enter the redundant site concept.

Redundant Sites

Well, we have implemented redundant arrays of disks, redundant network adapters, redundant power, and even redundant servers. What is left? Devising a mirror of the entire network! That's right, a redundant site. Within the CIA triad, redundant sites fall into the category of *availability*. In the case of a disaster, a redundant site can act as a safe haven for your data and users. Redundant sites are sort of a gray area between redundancy and a disaster recovery method. If you have one and need to use it, a "disaster" has probably occurred. But, the better the redundant site, the less time the organization loses, and the less it seems like a disaster and more like a failure that you have prepared for. Of course, this all depends on the type of redundant site your organization decides on.

When it comes to the types of redundant sites, I like to refer to the story of Goldilocks and the three bears' three bowls of porridge. One was too hot, one too cold—and one just right. Most organizations opt for the warm redundant site as opposed to the hot or cold. Let's discuss these three now.

Key Topic

- **Hot site:** A near duplicate of the original site of the organization that can be up and running within minutes (maybe longer). Computers and phones are installed and ready to go, a simulated version of the server room stands ready, and the vast majority of the data is replicated to the site on a regular basis in the event that the original site is not accessible to users for whatever reason. Hot sites are used by companies that would face financial ruin in the case that a disaster makes their main site inaccessible for a few days or even a few hours. This is the only type of redundant site that can facilitate a full recovery.

- **Warm site:** Has computers, phones, and servers, but they might require some configuration before users can start working on them. The warm site will have backups of data that might need to be restored; they will probably be several days old. This is chosen the most often by organizations because it has a good amount of configuration yet remains less expensive than a hot site.

- **Cold site:** Has tables, chairs, bathrooms, and possibly some technical setup—for example, basic phone, data, and electric lines. Otherwise, a lot of configuration of computers and data restoration is necessary before the site can be properly utilized. This type of site is used only if a company can handle the stress of being nonproductive for a week or more.

Although they are redundant, these types of sites are generally known as backup sites because if they are required, a disaster has probably occurred. A good network security administrator tries to plan for, and rely on, redundancy and fault tolerance as much as possible before having to resort to disaster recovery methods.

Redundant People

Well—not really redundant people (which I suppose would be clones), but rather the redundancy of a person's role in the organization. A person doesn't work for a company forever; in fact, the average length of employment for IT management persons is less than five years. This level of attrition is in part made up of persons who move to other departments, leave for another job, take leaves of absence, or retire. This leads to the important concept of *succession planning*: identifying *internal* people who understand the IT infrastructure and can take over in the event an important decision-maker departs; for example, IT directors, CIOs, CTOs, and other IT management persons. The concept trickles down to any IT person who works for the organization. That is where the concepts of job rotation and separation of duties become very important. A high attrition rate requires cross-training of employees. In smaller companies, the loss of one smart IT person could be tantamount to a disaster if no one else understands (or has access to) the critical systems. That could truly be a disaster from a personnel standpoint, but much more lethal is a disaster concerning actual data.

Disaster Recovery Planning and Procedures

Regardless of how much you planned out redundancy and fault tolerance, when disaster strikes, it can be devastating. There are three things that you should be concerned with as a network security administrator when it comes to disasters—your data, your server room, and the site in general. You need to have a powerful backup plan for your data and a comprehensive disaster recovery plan as well.

Data Backup

Disaster recovery (or DR for short) is pretty simple in the case of data. If disaster strikes, you better have a good data backup plan; one that fits your organization's needs and budget. Your company might have a written policy as to what should be backed up, or you might need to decide what is best. Data can be backed up to various media, other computers, SANs, NAS devices, and to the cloud, but generally, one of the best local mediums is tape backup.

There are several tape backup types you should be aware of for the exam. Most operating systems and third-party backup utilities support these types. Keep in mind that this list is not the end-all of backup types, but it gives a basic idea of the main types of data backups used in the field. When performing any of these types of backups, the person must select what to back up. It could be a folder or an entire volume. For the sake of simplicity, we call these folders.

- **Full backup:** Backs up all the contents of a folder. The full backup can be stored on one or more tapes. If more than one is used, the restore process would require starting with the oldest tape and moving through the tapes chronologically one by one. Full backups can use a lot of space, causing a backup operator to use a lot of backup tapes, which can be expensive. Full backups can also be time-consuming if there is a lot of data. So, often, incremental and differential backups are used with full backups as part of a backup plan.

- **Incremental backup:** Backs up only the contents of a folder that has changed since the last full backup or the last incremental backup. An incremental backup must be preceded by a full backup. Restoring the contents of a folder or volume would require a person to start with the full backup tape and then move on to each of the incremental backup tapes chronologically, ending with the latest incremental backup tape. Incremental backups started in the time of floppy disks when storage space and backup speed were limited. Some operating systems and backup systems associate an archive bit (or archive flag) to any file that has been modified; this indicates to the backup program that it should be backed up during the next backup phase. If this is the case, the incremental backup resets the bit after backup is complete.

- **Differential backup:** Backs up only the contents of a folder that has changed since the last full backup. A differential backup must be preceded by a full backup. To restore data, a person would start with the full backup tape and then move on to the differential tape. Differential backups do not reset the archive bit when backing up. This means that incremental backups will not see or know that a differential backup has occurred.

Table 16-2 shows an example of a basic one-week backup schedule using the full and incremental backup types. A full backup is done on Monday, and incremental backups are done Tuesday through Friday.

Table 16-2   Example Incremental Backup Schedule

Day	Backup Type	Time
Monday	Full backup	6 p.m.
Tuesday	Incremental backup	6 p.m.

Day	Backup Type	Time
Wednesday	Incremental backup	6 p.m.
Thursday	Incremental backup	6 p.m.
Friday	Incremental backup	6 p.m.

In this schedule, five backup tapes are required, one for each day. Let's say that the backups are done at 6 p.m. daily. Often an organization might employ a sixth tape, which is a dummy tape. This tape is put in the tape drive every morning by the backup operator and is replaced with the proper daily tape at 5:30 p.m. when everyone has left the building. This prevents data theft during the day. The real tapes are kept locked up until needed. Tapes might be reused when the cycle is complete, or an organization might opt to archive certain tapes each week, for example, the full backup tapes, and use new tapes every Monday. Another option is to run a complete full backup (which might be time-consuming) over the weekend and archive that tape every Monday. As long as no data loss is reported, this is a feasible option.

Let's say that this backup procedure was used to back up a server. Now, let's say that the server crashed on Wednesday at 9 p.m., and the hard drive data was lost. A backup operator arriving on the scene Thursday morning would need to review any logs available to find out when the server crashed. Then, after an admin fixes the server, the backup operator would need to restore the data. This would require starting with the Monday full backup tape and continuing on to the Tuesday and Wednesday incremental backup tapes. So three tapes in total would be needed to complete the restore.

Table 16-3 shows another possible backup schedule where a full backup is done on Monday and differential backups are done on Wednesday and Friday.

Table 16-3   Example Differential Backup Schedule

Day	Backup Type	Time
Monday	Full backup	6 p.m.
Tuesday	None	
Wednesday	Differential backup	6 p.m.
Thursday	None	
Friday	Differential backup	6 p.m.

Let's say the backup operator needed to restore data on Monday morning due to a failure over the weekend. The backup operator would need two backup tapes, the previous Monday full backup and the Friday differential backup, because the differential backup would have backed up everything since the last full backup. The Wednesday differential backup would not be necessary for recovery; contrast this with the incremental backup schedule from Table 16-2 where each tape would be needed for restoration. In a differential backup scenario the "clear archive bit" is not selected, so a differential backup will back up things that may have already been backed up by a previous differential backup. In an incremental backup scenario, the "clear archive bit" option *is* selected, and so items that are backed up by an incremental are not backed up by a subsequent incremental.

Some operating systems such as Windows Server manage full and incremental backups for the administrator. Windows Server 2008 R2 and higher create incremental backups that behave as full backups. Any item can be recovered if need be, but the backup only occupies the space needed for an incremental backup.

Now, the schedules we just showed in Tables 16-2 and 16-3 are basic backup methods, also known as backup rotation schemes. Organizations might also do something similar over a two-week period. However, you should also be aware of a couple of other backup schemes used in the field. These might use one or more of the backup types mentioned previously.

- **10 tape rotation:** This method is simple and provides easy access to data that has been backed up. It can be accomplished during a two-week backup period; each tape is used once per day for two weeks. Then the entire set is recycled. Generally, this is similar to the one-week schedule shown previously; however, the second Monday might be a differential backup instead of a full backup. And the second Friday might be a full backup, which is archived. There are several options; you would need to run some backups and see which is best for you given the amount of tapes required and time spent running the backups.

- **Grandfather-father-son:** This backup rotation scheme is probably the most common backup method used. When attempting to use this scheme, three sets of backup tapes must be defined—usually they are daily, weekly, and monthly, which correspond to son, father, and grandfather. Backups are rotated on a daily basis; normally the last one of the week will be graduated to father status. Weekly (father) backups are rotated on a weekly basis, with the last one of the month being graduated to grandfather status. Often, monthly (grandfather) backups, or a copy of them, are archived offsite.

- **Towers of Hanoi:** This backup rotation scheme is based on the mathematics of the Towers of Hanoi puzzle. This also uses three backup sets, but they are rotated differently. Without getting into the mathematics behind it, the basic idea is that the first tape is used every second day, the second tape is used every fourth day, and the third tape is used every eighth day. Table 16-4 shows an example of this. Keep in mind that this can go further; a fourth tape can be used every 16th day, and a fifth tape every 32nd day, and so on, although it gets much more complex to remember what tapes to use to back up and which order to go by when restoring. The table shows an example with three tape sets represented as sets A, B, and C.

Table 16-4 Example of Towers of Hanoi Three-Tape Schedule

Day of the Cycle							
1	2	3	4	5	6	7	8
Tape A		A		A		A	
	B				B		
			C				C

To avoid the rewriting of data, start on the fourth day of the cycle with tape C. This rotation scheme should be written out and perhaps calculated during the planning stage before it is implemented. Also, due to the complexity of the scheme, a restore sequence should be tested as well.

Tapes should be stored in a cool, dry area, away from sunlight, power lines, and other power sources. Most tape backup vendors have specific guidelines as to the temperature and humidity ranges for storage, along with other storage guidelines. Tape backup methods and tape integrity should always be tested by restoring all or part of a backup.

It's also possible to archive data to a third party. This could be for backup purposes or for complete file replication. Several companies offer this type of service, and you can usually select to archive data over the Internet or by courier.

So far, we have been discussing how to back up groups of files. However, you can also back up entire systems or architectural instances. For instance, a **snapshot backup** backs up an entire application, drive, or system. It is also known as an image backup, especially when referring to backing up an entire operating system. Most of the time, this is done when a new system is installed and configured, but it can also be done when major changes are made to a system. Some organizations even back up images of all systems every month, even every week. This requires a lot of resources and a decent IT budget and so it must be planned accordingly.

Many organizations back up to tape. But some organizations are far too large for tape backup, and/or don't have the personnel or equipment necessary to archive properly. In these "big data" scenarios, data might be stored on the cloud, or archived with a third-party such as Iron Mountain. Whatever your data backup method, make sure that there is some kind of archival offsite in the case of a true disaster. Optimally, this will be in a sister site in another city but regardless should be geographically distant from the main site. It is an integral part of disaster recovery planning.

DR Planning

Before we can plan for disasters, we need to define exactly what disasters are possible and list them in order starting with the most probable. Sounds a bit morbid, but it's necessary to ensure the long-term welfare of your organization.

What could go wrong? Let's focus in on the server room in the beginning of the chapter as our scenario. As you remember, we have nine servers, networking equipment, a PBX, and a few workstations—a pretty typical server room for a midsized company. Keep in mind that larger organizations will have more equipment, bigger server rooms, and more to consider when it comes to DR planning.

Disasters can be divided into two categories: natural and manmade. Some of the disasters that could render your server room inoperable include the following:

- **Fire:** Fire is probably the number one planned-for disaster. This is partially because most municipalities require some sort of fire suppression system, as well as the fact that most organizations' policies define the usage of a proper fire suppression system. We discuss fire protection in more depth in Chapter 17, "Social Engineering, User Education, and Facilities Security," but for now, the three main types of fire extinguishers include A (for ash fires), B (for gas and other flammable liquid fires), and C (for electrical fires). Unfortunately, these and the standard sprinkler system in the rest of the building are not adequate for a server room. If there were a fire, the material from the fire extinguisher or the water from the sprinkler system would damage the equipment, making the disaster even worse! Instead, a server room should be equipped with a proper system of its own such as DuPont FM-200. This uses a large tank that stores a clean agent fire extinguishant that is sprayed from one or more nozzles in the ceiling of the server room. It can put out fires of all types in seconds. A product such as this can be used safely when people are present; however, most systems also employ a *very* loud alarm that tells all personnel to leave the server room. It is wise to run through several fire suppression alarm tests and fire drills, ensuring that the alarm will sound when necessary and that personnel know what do to when the alarm sounds. For example, escape plans should be posted, and battery-backup exit signs should be installed in various locations throughout the building so that employees know the quickest escape route in the case of a fire. Fire drills (and other safety drills) should be performed periodically so that the organization can analyze the security posture of their safety plan.

- **Flood:** The best way to avoid server room damage in the case of a flood is to locate the server room on the first floor or higher, not in a basement. There's not much you can do about the location of a building, but if it is in a flood zone, it makes the use of a warm or hot site that much more imperative. And a server room could also be flooded by other things such as boilers. The room should not be adjacent to, or on the same floor as, a boiler room. It should also be located away from other water sources such as bathrooms and any sprinkler systems. The server room should be thought of three-dimensionally; the floors, walls, and ceiling should be analyzed and protected. Some server rooms are designed to be a room within a room and might have drainage installed as well.

- **Long-term power loss:** Short-term power loss should be countered by the UPS, but long-term power loss requires a backup generator and possibly a redundant site.

- **Theft and malicious attack:** Theft and malicious attack can also cause a disaster, if the right data is stolen. Physical security such as door locks/access systems and video cameras should be implemented to avoid this. Servers should be cable-locked to their server racks, and removable hard drives (if any are used) should have key access. Not only does a security administrator have the task of writing policies and procedures that govern the security of server rooms and data centers, but that person will often have the task of *enforcing* those policies—meaning muscle in the form of security guards, and dual-class technician/guards—or by otherwise having the right to terminate employees as needed, contact and work with the authorities, and so on. Physical security is covered in more depth in Chapter 10, "Physical Security and Authentication Models." Malicious network attacks also need to be warded off; these are covered in depth in Chapter 7, "Networking Protocols and Threats."

- **Loss of building:** Temporary loss of the building due to gas leak, malicious attack, inaccessibility due to crime scene investigation, or natural event will require personnel to access a redundant site. Your server room should have as much data archived as possible, and the redundant site should be warm enough to keep business running. A plan should be in place as to how data will be restored at the redundant site and how the network will be made functional.

Disaster recovery plans (DRPs) should include information regarding redundancy, such as sites and backup, but should not include information that deals with the day-to-day operations of an organization, such as updating computers, patch management, monitoring and audits, and so on. It is important to include only what is necessary in a disaster recovery plan. Too much information can make it difficult to use when a disaster does strike.

Although not an exhaustive set, the following written disaster recovery policies, procedures, and information should be part of your disaster recovery plan:

- **Contact information:** Who you should contact if a disaster occurs and how employees will contact the organization.

- **Impact determination:** A procedure to determine a disaster's full impact on the organization. This includes an evaluation of assets lost and the cost to replace those assets.

- **Recovery plan:** This will be based on the determination of disaster impact. This will have many permutations depending on the type of disaster. Although it is impossible to foresee every possible event, the previous list gives a good starting point. The recovery plan includes an estimated time to complete recovery and a set of steps defining the order of what will be recovered and when. It might also include an after action report (AAR), which is a formal document designed to determine the effectiveness of a recovery plan in the case that it was implemented.

- **Business continuity plan:** A BCP defines how the business will continue to operate if a disaster occurs; this plan is often carried out by a team of individuals. A BCP is also referred to as a continuity of operations plan (COOP). Over the years, BCPs have become much more important, and depending on the organization, the BCP might actually encompass the entire DRP. It also comprises **business impact analysis**—the examination of critical versus non-critical functions. These functions are assigned two different values or metrics: **recovery time objective (RTO)**, the acceptable amount of time to restore a function (for example, the time required for a service to be restored after a disaster), and **recovery point objective (RPO)**, the acceptable latency of data, or the maximum tolerable time that data can remain inaccessible after a disaster. It's impossible to foresee exactly how long it will take to restore service after a disaster, but with the use of proper archival, hot/warm/cold sites, and redundant systems, a general timeframe can be laid out, and an organization will be able to decide on a maximum timeframe to get data back online. This in effect is IT contingency planning (ITCP).

Some organizations will have a continuity of operation planning group or crisis management group that meets every so often to discuss the BCP. Instead of running full-scale drills, they might run through tabletop exercises, where a talk-through of simulated disasters (in real time) is performed—a sort of role-playing, if you will. This can save time and be less disruptive to employees, but it is more than just a read-through of the BCP. It can help to identify critical systems and mission-essential functions of the organization's network as well as failover functionality, and alternate processing sites. It can also aid in assessing the impact of a potential disaster on privacy, property, finance, the reputation of the company, and most importantly, life itself.

- **Copies of agreements:** Copies of any agreements with vendors of redundant sites, ISPs, building management, and so on should be stored with the DR plan. We discuss agreements in Chapter 18, "Policies and Procedures."

- **Disaster recovery drills and exercises:** Employees should be drilled on what to do if a disaster occurs. These exercises should be written out step-by-step and should conform to safety standards.

- **Hierarchical list of critical systems and critical data:** This is a list of all the mission-essential data and systems necessary for business operations: domain controllers, firewalls, switches, DNS servers, file servers, web servers, and so on. They should be listed by priority. Systems such as client computers, test computers, and training systems would be last on the list or not listed at all. You should also include (somewhere in the DRP) some geographic considerations. For example: Are there offsite backups or virtualization in place? What is the physical distance to those backups and virtual machines? And, are there legal implications? For instance, are there data sovereignty implications—meaning, will it be difficult to gain access to data and VMs stored in a different country based on the laws of that country?

Generally, the chief security officer (CSO) or other high-level executive will be in charge of DR planning, often with the help of the information systems security officer (ISSO). However, it all depends on the size of the organization and the types of management involved. That said, any size organization can benefit from proper DR planning. This information should be accessible at the company site, and a copy should be stored offsite as well. It might be that your organization conforms to special compliance rules; these should be consulted when designing a DR plan. Depending on the type of organization, there might be other items that go into your DR plan. We cover some of these in more depth in Chapter 18.

Chapter Summary

This chapter defined in the strictest sense how to protect against potential failures, and how to recover from would-be disasters. Redundancy of data, services, and power is your best bet when it comes to the failure of equipment and servers. Data archiving and procedural planning are vitally important considerations when you are preparing for the unlikely scenario of disaster.

Any single point of failure is a bad thing. In a system of parts, that single point will cause the entire system to fail. It's common knowledge that hard drives will fail, power supplies will fail, power will fail, networking connections will fail, and so on. If you run your systems long enough, a failure will occur—over enough time the probability becomes 100%.

It's the redundancy that can save you: RAID systems and clustered servers for data; multiple power supplies, UPS devices, and generators for power; multihomed servers and multiple Internet connections for the networking of data; even entire secondary worksites and people waiting in the wings to take over when necessary. All these things can provide for a redundant IT infrastructure. But be wary, too much redundancy might blow your IT budget, leaving you little for maintenance, future planning, and disaster planning.

Although the chances of a disaster are slim, they do happen. The list of possible disasters in this chapter is not a complete one either, but it shows the more common tragedies you might encounter. The prepared organization will have a well-defined archival plan that should include a minimum of tape backup that is stored offsite. That protects the bulk of the data, but a DR plan is necessary to protect the employees, servers, and other equipment as well. And in the case of a loss of building, a backup worksite becomes imperative.

Many companies will have one person who spearheads the development of a DR plan, but it should be reviewed and mocked up by a group of people, with one person always ready to succeed the DR plan developer in the case that person leaves the organization.

Chapter Review Activities

Use the features in this section to study and review the topics in this chapter.

Review Key Topics

Review the most important topics in the chapter, noted with the Key Topic icon in the outer margin of the page. Table 16-5 lists a reference of these key topics and the page number on which each is found.

Table 16-5   Key Topics for Chapter 16

Key Topic Element	Description	Page Number
Bulleted list	Power failures	550
Table 16-1	RAID descriptions	555
Figure 16-1	RAID 1 illustration	556
Figure 16-2	RAID 5 illustration	557
Bulleted list	Server cluster types	560
Bulleted list	Types of redundant sites	561
Bulleted list	Backup types	563
Table 16-2	Example incremental backup schedule	563
Table 16-3	Example differential backup schedule	564
Bulleted list	Backup rotation schemes	565

Define Key Terms

Define the following key terms from this chapter, and check your answers in the glossary:

single point of failure, surge, spike, sag, brownout, blackout, redundant power supply, uninterruptible power supply (UPS), backup generator, standby generator, RAID 1, disk duplexing, RAID 5, RAID 6, RAID 10, redundant ISP, cluster, failover clusters, load-balancing clusters, hot site, warm site, cold site, full backup, incremental backup, differential backup, 10 tape rotation, grandfather-father-son, Towers of Hanoi, snapshot backup, disaster recovery plan (DRP), business impact analysis (BIA), recovery time objective (RTO), recovery point objective (RPO)

Complete the Real-World Scenarios

Complete the Real-World Scenarios found on the companion website (www.pearsonitcertification.com/title/9780789758996). You will find a PDF containing the scenario and questions, and also supporting videos and simulations.

Review Questions

Answer the following review questions. Check your answers with the correct answers that follow.

1. Which of the following RAID versions offers the least amount of performance degradation when a disk in the array fails?

    A. RAID 0

    B. RAID 1

    C. RAID 4

    D. RAID 5

2. Which of the following can facilitate a full recovery within minutes?

    A. Warm site

    B. Cold site

    C. Reestablishing a mirror

    D. Hot site

3. What device should be used to ensure that a server does not shut down when there is a power outage?

    A. RAID 1 box

    B. UPS

    C. Redundant NIC

    D. Hot site

4. Which of the following tape backup methods enables daily backups, weekly full backups, and monthly full backups?

    A. Towers of Hanoi

    B. Incremental

    C. Grandfather-father-son

    D. Differential

    E. Snapshot

5. To prevent electrical damage to a computer and its peripherals, the computer should be connected to what?

   A. Power strip

   B. Power inverter

   C. AC to DC converter

   D. UPS

6. Which of the following would not be considered part of a disaster recovery plan?

   A. Hot site

   B. Patch management software

   C. Backing up computers

   D. Tape backup

7. Which of the following factors should you consider when evaluating assets to a company? (Select the two best answers.)

   A. Their value to the company

   B. Their replacement cost

   C. Where they were purchased from

   D. Their salvage value

8. You are using the following backup scheme: A full backup is made every Friday night at 6 p.m., and differential backups are made every other night at 6 p.m. Your database server fails on a Thursday afternoon at 4 p.m. How many tapes will you need to restore the database server?

   A. One

   B. Two

   C. Three

   D. Four

9. Of the following, what is the worst place to store a backup tape?

   A. Near a bundle of fiber-optic cables

   B. Near a power line

   C. Near a server

   D. Near an LCD screen

10. Critical equipment should always be able to get power. What is the correct order of devices that your critical equipment should draw power from?

    A. Generator, line conditioner, UPS battery

    B. Line conditioner, UPS battery, generator

    C. Generator, UPS battery, line conditioner

    D. Line conditioner, generator, UPS battery

11. What is the best way to test the integrity of a company's backed up data?

    A. Conduct another backup

    B. Use software to recover deleted files

    C. Review written procedures

    D. Restore part of the backup

12. Your company has six web servers. You are implementing load balancing. What is this an example of?

    A. UPS

    B. Redundant servers

    C. RAID

    D. Warm site

13. Your company has a fiber-optic connection to the Internet. Which of the following can enable your network to remain operational even if the fiber-optic line fails?

    A. Redundant network adapters

    B. RAID 5

    C. Redundant ISP

    D. UPS

14. Which action should be taken to protect against a complete disaster in the case that a primary company's site is permanently lost?

    A. Back up all data to tape, and store those tapes at a sister site in another city.

    B. Back up all data to tape, and store those tapes at a sister site across the street.

    C. Back up all data to disk, and store the disk in a safe deposit box at the administrator's home.

    D. Back up all data to disk, and store the disk in a safe in the building's basement.

15. Of the following backup types, which describes the backup of files that have changed since the last full or incremental backup?

   A. Incremental

   B. Differential

   C. Full

   D. Copy

16. Michael's company has a single web server that is connected to three other distribution servers. What is the greatest risk involved in this scenario?

   A. Fraggle attack

   B. Single point of failure

   C. Denial-of-service attack

   D. Man-in-the-middle attack

17. Which of the following defines a business goal for system restoration and *acceptable* data loss?

   A. RPO

   B. Warm site

   C. MTBF

   D. MTTR

18. Which of the following uses multiple computers to share work?

   A. RAID

   B. VPN concentrator

   C. Load balancing

   D. Switching

19. You have been tasked with increasing the level of server fault tolerance, but you have been given no budget to perform the task. Which of the following should you implement to ensure that servers' data can withstand hardware failure?

   A. RAID

   B. Hardware load balancing

   C. A cold site

   D. Towers of Hanoi

20. Which of the following provides for the best application availability and can be easily expanded as an organization's demand grows?

    A. RAID 6

    B. Server virtualization

    C. Multi-CPU motherboards

    D. Load balancing

Answers and Explanations

1. **B.** RAID 1 is known as mirroring. If one drive fails, the other will still function and there will be no downtime and no degraded performance. All the rest of the answers are striping-based and therefore have either downtime or degraded performance associated with them. RAID 5 is the second best option because in many scenarios it will have zero downtime and little degraded performance. RAID 0 will not recover from a failure; it is not fault tolerant.

2. **D.** A hot site can facilitate a full recovery of communications software and equipment within minutes. Warm and cold sites cannot facilitate a full recovery but may have some of the options necessary to continue business. Reestablishing a mirror will not necessarily implement a full recovery of data communications or equipment.

3. **B.** A UPS (uninterruptible power supply) ensures that a computer will keep running even if a power outage occurs. The number of minutes the computer can continue in this fashion depends on the type of UPS and battery it contains. A backup generator can also be used, but it does not guarantee 100% uptime, because there might be a delay between when the power outage occurs and when the generator comes online. RAID 1 has to do with the fault tolerance of data. Redundant NICs (network interface cards, also known as network adapters) are used on servers in the case that one of them fails. Hot sites are completely different places that a company can inhabit. Although the hot site can be ready in minutes, and although it may have a mirror of the server in question, it does not ensure that the original server will not shut down during a power outage.

4. **C.** The grandfather-father-son (GFS) backup scheme generally uses daily backups (the son), weekly backups (the father), and monthly backups (the grandfather). The Towers of Hanoi is a more complex strategy based on a puzzle. Incremental backups are simply one-time backups that back up all data that has changed since the last incremental backup. These might be used as the son in a GFS scheme. Differential backups back up everything since the last full backup. A snapshot is a backup type, not a method; it is primarily designed to image systems.

5. **D.** A UPS (uninterruptible power supply) protects computer equipment against surges, spikes, sags, brownouts, and blackouts. Power strips, unlike surge protectors, do not protect against surges.

6. **B.** Patching a system is part of the normal maintenance of a computer. In the case of a disaster to a particular computer, the computer's OS and latest service pack would have to be reinstalled. The same would be true in the case of a disaster to a larger area, like the building. Hot sites, backing up computers, and tape backup are all components of a disaster recovery plan.

7. **A and B.** When evaluating assets to a company, it is important to know the replacement cost of those assets and the value of the assets to the company. If the assets were lost or stolen, the salvage value is not important, and although you may want to know where the assets were purchased from, it is not one of the best answers.

8. **B.** You need two tapes to restore the database server—the full backup tape made on Friday and the differential backup tape made on the following Wednesday. Only the last differential tape is needed. When restoring the database server, the technician must remember to start with the full backup tape.

9. **B.** Backup tapes should be kept away from power sources, including power lines, CRT monitors, speakers, and so on. And the admin should keep backup tapes away from sources that might emit EMI. LCD screens, servers, and fiber-optic cables have low EMI emissions.

10. **B.** The line conditioner is constantly serving critical equipment with clean power. It should be first and should always be on. The UPS battery should kick in only if there is a power outage. Finally, the generator should kick in only when the UPS battery is about to run out of power. Often, the line conditioner and UPS battery will be the same device. However, the line conditioner function will always be used, but the battery comes into play only when there is a power outage, or brownout.

11. **D.** The best way to test the integrity of backed up data is to restore part of that backup. Conducting another backup will tell you if the backup procedure is working properly, and if isn't, after testing the integrity of the backup and after the restore, a person might need to use software to recover deleted files. It's always important to review written procedures and amend them if need be.

12. **B.** Load balancing is a method used when you have redundant servers. In this case, the six web servers will serve data equally to users. The UPS is an uninterruptible power supply, and RAID is the redundant array of inexpensive disks. A warm site is a secondary site that a company can use if a disaster occurs; a warm site can be up and running within a few hours or a day.

13. **C.** A secondary ISP enables the network to remain operational and still gain Internet access even if the fiber-optic connection (or whatever connection) fails. This generally means that there will be a second ISP and a secondary physical connection to the Internet. Redundant network adapters are used on servers so that the server can have a higher percentage of uptime. RAID 5 is used for redundancy of data and spreads the data over three or more disks. A UPS is used in the case of a power outage.

14. **A.** In the case that a building's primary site is lost, data should be backed up to tape stored at a sister site in another city. Storing information across the street might not be good enough, especially if the area has to be evacuated. Company information should never be stored at an employee's home. And of course if the data were stored in the primary building's basement and there were a complete disaster at the primary site, that data would also be lost.

15. **A.** An incremental backup backs up only the files that have changed since the last incremental or full backup. Generally it is used as a daily backup. Differential backups are meant to be used to back up files that have changed since the last full backup. A full backup backs up all files in a particular folder or drive, depending on what has been selected; this is regardless of any previous differential or incremental backups. Copies of data can be made, but they will not affect backup rotations that include incremental, differential, and full backups. Technically, this question could be answered "Incremental" or "Differential," but "Incremental" is the accepted (and therefore best) answer. The CompTIA objectives expect a person to understand that an incremental backup will back up anything that was created/changed since the last incremental backup, or the last full backup if that was the last one completed.

16. **B.** The greatest risk involved in this scenario is that the single web server is a single point of failure regardless that it is connected to three other distribution servers. If the web server goes down or is compromised, no one can access the company's website. A Fraggle is a type of denial-of-service attack. Although denial-of-service attacks are a risk to web servers, they are not the greatest risk in this particular scenario. A company should implement as much redundancy as possible.

17. **A.** An RPO (recovery point objective) defines acceptable data loss. A warm site is a secondary site that will have computers and phones ready for users, but data and services need to be configured and loaded before work can commence. MTBF is the mean time between failure, which defines the average number of failures per million hours, and is usually a number derived from multiple customers of a product. MTTR is the mean time to repair. Both of these are more similar to RTO as opposed to RPO.

18. **C.** Load balancing uses multiple computers to share work, for example, in a load-balancing cluster configuration. RAID uses multiple hard drives to increase speed or create fault tolerance. VPN concentrators allow for remote access of multiple employees over the Internet. Switching (in its simplest form) is the moving of data across the LAN.

19. **A.** RAID should be employed; specifically a fault-tolerant version of RAID (1, 5, 6, and so on). This will ensure that data will still be accessible if one drive fails. Load balancing uses multiple computers to share the load of processing data—often in the form of CPU and RAM collectives—but it does not ensure that data will be accessible in the case of a failure. A cold site is not fault tolerant because it takes at least a day or two to get it up and running. Towers of Hanoi is a tape backup schedule, and as such is not fault tolerant either.

20. **D.** Load balancing is the best option for application availability and expansion. You can cluster multiple servers together to make a more powerful super-computer of sorts—one that can handle more and more simultaneous access requests. RAID 6 is meant more for data files, not applications. It may or may not be expandable depending on the system used. Multi-CPU motherboards are used in servers and power workstations, but are internal to one system. The CPUs are indeed used together, but will not help with expandability, unless used in a load-balancing scenario.

This chapter covers the following subjects:

- **Social Engineering:** This section delves into the methods and techniques that social engineers can employ to gain access to buildings and systems and obtain company data and personal information. It also covers the various ways that these social engineers can be defeated.

- **User Education:** Here we briefly discuss how to train up your users on the basics of security. Don't forget, it's not all about tech; the user is a vulnerability and can be exploited too. The key is understanding—the more the users know, the better equipped they will be to properly secure *themselves*.

- **Facilities Security:** An organization's facilities, such as its building, vehicles, and other property and equipment, can all be targets. Proper management and securing of facilities can help to protect company assets as well as the employees. It is important for a security person to consider fire suppression methods, heating, cooling, ventilation, shielding, and how to protect the server room. This section covers fire suppression methods, such as fire extinguishers, sprinkler systems, and special hazard protection, as well as HVAC, shielding, and some basic vehicle security.

The idea behind this chapter is to examine people and their behavior, and your organization's facilities.

CHAPTER 17

Social Engineering, User Education, and Facilities Security

When I say "people," I mean both kinds of people: social engineers who might try to exploit your organization, and the employees of an organization. In this chapter and the next we'll discuss how to protect employees' privacy, while still protecting your infrastructure from *them*! Policies and procedures can help to protect legitimate individuals and help protect the infrastructure from malicious individuals and social engineers.

An organization's facilities include the building and its environmental controls, vehicles, and anything else owned by the organization. Everything is connected these days, so everything needs to be protected. Server rooms and data centers can be protected through the use of fire suppression systems, shielding, and more. But even those systems, and other systems such as electrical systems, should be implemented with an eye on security at all times.

The concepts covered in this chapter are a bit of a hodge-podge; content is less about computers, and more on the periphery of technology security, but I have tried to line everything up in a way that will make for easy reading and recall. We start with social engineering. No matter how much technology you implement, people still have to deal with people, and that opens the door for con artists. Then we'll move on to user education. The best way to prevent social engineering attacks is to increase your users' knowledge. Finally, we'll get into the organization's building and facilities. It's all connected—attackers who use social engineering methods will target users and the facilities of an organization.

Foundation Topics

Social Engineering

Let's discuss a low note in our society. Because that is what information security–based social engineering is—a low form of behavior, but an effective one. It is estimated that 1 out of 10 people is conned every year through social engineering methods, and as many as half of them don't even know it has occurred. It's glorified in the movies, but in real life it can have devastating consequences to an organization and to innocent individuals.

We mentioned in Chapter 1, "Introduction to Security," that *social engineering* is the act of manipulating users into revealing confidential information or performing other actions detrimental to the user. Examples of social engineering are common in everyday life. A basic example would be a person asking for your username and password over the phone; often the person uses flattery to gain information. Malicious people use various forms of social engineering in an attempt to steal whatever you have of value: your money, information, identity, confidential company data, or IT equipment. Social engineering experts use techniques and principles such as the following:

- Authority

- Intimidation

- Bold impersonation

- Urgency, scarcity, and even emergency

- The grooming of trust/familiarity/liking

- Persistence and patience

- Relating to the user: using company jargon, consensus/popular decision, and social facts and proof

- Embedding of questions within conversations

Social engineers will rely on information. For example, open source intelligence (OSINT) is a way that attackers can gain knowledge about a target. OSINT includes media, public government data, commercial data, and academic publications. That's one of the reasons I don't accurately detail specific exploits in this book, because it could be a source of data for a potential attacker! Social engineers also use tools such as social networking sites and P2P software to obtain information disclosure either directly or through data aggregation. The main reason that social engineering succeeds is due to a lack of user awareness. But social engineering can also be effective in environments in which the IT personnel have little training, and in public areas; for example, public buildings with shared office space. Let's discuss some of the more common types of social engineering.

Pretexting

Pretexting is when a person invents a scenario, or pretext, in the hope of persuading a victim to divulge information. Preparation and some prior information are often needed before attempting a pretext; impersonation is often a key element. By impersonating the appropriate personnel or third-party entities, a person performing a pretext hopes to obtain records about an organization, its data, and its personnel. IT people and employees should always be on the lookout for impersonators and always ask for identification. If there is any doubt, the issue should be escalated to your supervisor and/or a call should be made to the authorities.

Malicious Insider

The malicious insider is one of the most insidious threats. Instead of impersonating personnel as is done in pretexting, the person actually *becomes* personnel! This attack is often used as part of a corporate espionage plan. Think that all IT techs are 100% honorable? In high-tech, you will find an assortment of atrocities, including the malicious insider threat. The insider might have been sent by a competing organization to obtain a job/consulting position with a certain company, or perhaps is approached by the competing organization while already working for the company that is the target. It is often initiated by organizations from another country. Once the insider is situated, that person can easily get access to secure data, PII, financials, engineering plans, and so on, and pass them on to the infiltrating organization. Of course, the penalties for this are high, but the potential rewards can be quite enticing to the properly "motivated" individual. Companies will therefore often run thorough background checks and credit checks and have human resources go through an entire set of psychological questions. Then, when a person is hired, there is a sort of trial period where the person is allowed very little access to secure data and secure environments.

Now, a malicious insider doesn't necessarily have to be a person. It could be a device or bug that was inserted into the organization by a person using social engineering skills; for example, rogue PIN pad devices, audio and video sensors (bugs), keyloggers, and so on. This requires physical access to the building in one way or another, so identification and authentication become of paramount importance.

Warning! As of the writing of this book, malicious insider threats are severely underappreciated by many organizations. They shouldn't be, because the malicious insider has the best chance of obtaining a desired result; a far better chance than the outsider. Think about it: if you wanted to steal 100,000 credit card numbers so that you could charge $1 to each—making a fortune, but causing no great stress to the credit card holders—how would you do it? Would you attempt a whole lot of MITM attacks? Would you try to hack through the bank's firewall and IDS/IPS, tip-toe around the honeypot, and so on? Or would you attempt to get *inside*. The risk is greater, of course, for the person. It is much easier to get caught. But the potential for success outweighs the risk in comparison to trying to hack the system from the outside. The number of compromises to banks and chains of stores done in this manner is staggering.

Diversion Theft

Diversion theft is when a thief attempts to take responsibility for a shipment by diverting the delivery to a nearby location. This happens more often than you would think, and millions of dollars' worth of IT equipment is stolen in this manner every day. It is important that couriers and other shippers know exactly where they are supposed to be delivering items, and that they are given an organization contact name, number, and possibly security code in case there is any confusion.

Phishing

Phishing is the attempt at fraudulently obtaining private information. A phisher usually masquerades as someone else, perhaps another entity. There are two main differences between phishing and pretexting. First, phishing is usually done by electronic communication, not in person. Second, little information about the target is necessary. A phisher may target thousands of individuals without much concern as to their background. An example of phishing would be an e-mail that requests verification of private information. The e-mail probably leads to a malicious website designed to lure people into a false sense of security to fraudulently obtain information. The website often looks like a legitimate website. A common phishing technique is to pose as a vendor (such as an online retailer or domain registrar) and send the target e-mail confirmations of orders that they supposedly placed.

This is a triple-whammy. First, the orders are obviously fake; a person might say "Hey, wait! I didn't place these orders!" and perhaps click the link(s) in the e-mail, leading the person to the false web page. Second, if a person thinks it's a legitimate order (perhaps the person does many orders, and the fraudulent one looks like another legitimate one), the person might click a link to track the order, again leading to the bogus web page. Third, once at the web page, the person is asked to enter her credentials for her account (which then leads to credit card fraud and ID theft), and in addition to that the page might have Trojans and other malicious scripts that are delivered to the unsuspecting person on exit. Sheesh, talk about cyber-bullying!

Generally, no information about the target is necessary for a phishing attack. However, some "phishermen" actually target specific groups of people or even specific individuals. This is known as **spear phishing**. And when an attacker targets senior executives (CEOs, CFOs, and so on) it is known as **whaling**. Whaling attacks are much more detailed and require that the attacker know a good deal of information about the target (much of which is freely available on the Internet).

The concept of phishing is also accomplished by telephone. Phone phishing, known as **vishing**, works in the same manner as phishing but is initiated by a phone call (often using VoIP systems). The phone call often sounds like a prerecorded message from a legitimate institution (bank, online retailer, donation collector, and so on). The message asks the unsuspecting person for confidential information such as name, bank account numbers, codes, and so on; all under the guise of needing to verify information for the person's protection. It's really the opposite, of course, and many people are caught unawares by these types of scams every day. By using automated systems (such as the ones telemarketers use), vishing can be perpetuated on large groups of people with little effort.

NOTE   A similar technique using automated systems is known as *war-dialing*. This is when a device (modem or other system) is used to scan a list of telephone numbers and dial them in search of computer systems and fax machines. The technique sifts out the phone numbers associated with voice lines, and the numbers associated with computers. It results in a list that can later be used by other attackers for various purposes.

Many different types of social engineering are often lumped into what is referred to as phishing, but actual phishing for private information is normally limited to e-mail and websites. To defend against this, a phishing filter or add-on should be installed and enabled on the web browser. Also, a person should be trained to realize that institutions will *not* call or e-mail requesting private information. If people are not sure, they should hang up the phone or simply delete the e-mail. A quick way to find out whether an e-mail is phishing for information is to hover over a link. You will see a URL domain name that is far different from that of the institution that the phisher is claiming to be, probably a URL located in a distant country. Many of these phishers are also probably engaging in spy-phishing: a combination of spyware and phishing that effectively makes use of spyware applications. A spyware application of this sort is downloaded to the target, which then enables additional phishing attempts that go beyond the initial phishing website.

Hoaxes

A **hoax** is the attempt at deceiving people into believing something that is false. The differences between hoaxes and phishing can be quite gray. However, hoaxes can come in person, or through other means of communication, whereas phishing is generally relegated to e-communication and phone. Although phishing can occur at any time, and with the specific goal of obtaining private information, a hoax can often be perpetuated on holidays or other special days and could be carried out simply for fun. Regardless, hoaxes can use up valuable organization resources: e-mail replies, Internet bandwidth used, time spent, and so on. An example of a "harmless" hoax was Google's supposed name change to "Topeka" on April Fools'

Day 2010. An example of a financially harmful hoax was the supposed assassination of Bill Gates on April Fools' Day 2003. This hoax led to stock market fluctuations and loss of profit in Asia. Some companies place a time limit on jokes and hoaxes indicating that the affected person has become nonproductive; for example, 3% of the workday.

Pretexting, malicious insider attempts, diversion theft, phishing, and hoaxes are all known as *confidence tricks*, thus the term *con*, and are committed by "bunko" artists. However, there are even lower ways to get access to people's information; these often are used with the previous methods. These include shoulder surfing, eavesdropping, dumpster diving, baiting, and piggybacking.

Shoulder Surfing

Shoulder surfing is when a person uses direct observation to find out a target's password, PIN, or other such authentication information. The simple resolution for this is for the user to shield the screen, keypad, or other authentication-requesting devices. A more aggressive approach is to courteously ask the suspected shoulder surfer to move along. Also, private information should never be left on a desk or out in the open. Computers should be locked or logged off when the user is not in the immediate area. From a more technical perspective, password masking can be implemented (if not already), where typed passwords only show as asterisks or dots on the screen. Always check if your systems, applications, and devices use password masking. Some lesser devices (such as SOHO routers) may not implement password masking by default, and that might go against company policy due to the inherent lack of security. Shoulder surfing, along with eavesdropping, and dumpster diving are examples of no-tech hacking.

Eavesdropping

Eavesdropping is when a person uses direct observation to "listen" in to a conversation. This could be a person hiding around the corner or a person tapping into a phone conversation. Soundproof rooms are often employed to stop eavesdropping, and encrypted phone sessions can also be implemented.

Dumpster Diving

Dumpster diving is when a person literally scavenges for private information in garbage and recycling containers. Any sensitive documents should be stored in a safe place as long as possible. When they are no longer necessary, they should be shredded. (Some organizations incinerate their documents.) Information might be found not only on paper, but also on hard drives or removable media. Proper recycling and/or destruction of hard drives is covered later in this chapter.

Baiting

Baiting is when a malicious individual leaves malware-infected removable media such as a USB drive or optical disc lying around in plain view. It might have an interesting logo or distinctive look about it. When a person takes it and connects it to his computer, the malware infects the computer and attempts to take control of it and/or the network the computer is a member of.

Piggybacking/Tailgating

Piggybacking is when an unauthorized person tags along with an authorized person to gain entry to a restricted area—usually with the person's consent. **Tailgating** is essentially the same with one difference: it is usually without the authorized person's consent. Both of these can be defeated through the use of mantraps. A **mantrap** is a small space that can usually only fit one person. It has two sets of interlocking doors; the first set must be closed before the other will open, creating a sort of waiting room where people are identified (and cannot escape!). This technique is often used in server rooms and data centers. Multifactor authentication is often used in conjunction with a mantrap; for example, using a proximity card and PIN at the first door, and biometric scan at the second. A mantrap is an example of a preventive security control. Turnstiles, double entry doors, and employing security guards are other less expensive (and less effective) solutions to the problem of piggybacking and tailgating and help address confidentiality in general.

Watering Hole Attack

The **watering hole attack** is a strategy that targets users based on the common websites that they frequent. The attacker loads malware beforehand on one or more websites in the hopes that the user(s) will access those sites and activate the malware, ultimately infecting the user's system and possibly spreading through the network. To figure out the browsing habits of users, the attacker might guess or use direct observation. So, this attack may also build upon other social engineering methods such as eavesdropping, pretexting, and phishing.

Popular websites such as Google, Microsoft, and so on will be difficult to infect with malware. It's the smaller websites that the attacker will go after. For example, let's take a company that manufactures widgets. Chances are that the company will need to purchase plastic and other resources to build the widgets. It follows that users will connect to suppliers' websites often via the Internet or possibly an intranet. Typically, suppliers' websites are known for a lack of security and make excellent targets. If many users in the company go to these same websites, and often, it's just a matter of time before one clicks on the wrong website element, or gets tricked in another manner. Then, malware gets installed to the client computer and possibly spreads throughout the company. An attacker might also redirect users to other websites where other scams or more hardcore malware (such as ransomware) are located.

The problem is that you as a security administrator can't actively prevent the malware on the targeted websites. You can suggest prevention methods to those companies—such as software patches and secure coding—but can't force them into action. So, you should focus on localized prevention methods including user training, reducing web browser functionality, blacklisting of websites, and monitoring in the form of anti-malware software, IDS/IPS, and more—essentially, all of the methods we have discussed earlier in this book.

Summary of Social Engineering Types

Table 17-1 summarizes the various types of social engineering we have discussed in this section.

Key Topic

Table 17-1 Summary of Social Engineering Types

Type	Description
Pretexting	When a person invents a scenario, or pretext, in the hope of persuading a victim to divulge information.
Malicious insider threat	When a person works at an organization with the secret purpose of obtaining secret information, financial information, design work, and PII.
Diversion theft	When a thief attempts to take responsibility for a shipment by diverting the delivery to a nearby location.
Phishing	The attempt at fraudulently obtaining private information, usually done electronically. Vishing is done by phone. Spear phishing targets specific individuals. Whaling targets senior executives.
Hoax	The attempt at deceiving people into believing something that is false.
Shoulder surfing	When a person uses direct observation to find out a target's password, PIN, or other such authentication information.
Eavesdropping	When a person uses direct observation to "listen" in to a conversation. This could be a person hiding around the corner or a person tapping into a phone conversation.
Dumpster diving	When a person literally scavenges for private information in garbage and recycling containers.

Type	Description
Baiting	When a malicious individual leaves malware-infected removable media such as a USB drive or optical disc lying around in plain view in the hopes that unknowing people will bring it back to their computer and access it.
Piggybacking/tailgating	When an unauthorized person tags along with an authorized person to gain entry to a restricted area.
Watering hole attack	When an attacker targets users' specific browsing habits in the hopes that they will access particular websites and activate the malware hidden within them.

In some cases, social engineering is easier than other, more technical ways of hacking information. For example, if a malicious individual wanted a person's password, it might be a lot easier to trick the person into giving her password than to try to crack it.

User Education

The user could be the single most exploitable resource of a company. I think that the previous section about social engineering provides a good argument to support that opinion. People aren't computers. Some might be compared to robots (perhaps unfairly), but no matter how logical and disciplined a person might be, there is always the potential for human error. So, until firewalls are developed for people's brains, education becomes the best method to prevent social engineering attacks and malware infection, not to mention user error.

As an IT manager, I've always made it a point to incorporate technology and security training for as many employees as possible. This would include classroom/ conference room training, written materials, digital courses, even funny posters in the cafeteria. I'd use whatever platform I could to get the point across. The key is to make it accessible to the user, and to make it interesting and fun.

There are several roadblocks when it comes to user training. The first is organizational acceptance. Are the executives of a company on board with the idea? As time moves on, we see that more and more executives include user education as a matter of course. However, if you come across an individual who is against the idea because of a "lack" of budgeting or time, then your counter is to simply show that person a news article about one of the many successful attacks that have occurred recently. Then show a case study of the amount of time and money that the affected company lost due to the attack, and—in most cases—how easily it could have been prevented. Then, there are the employees to be trained themselves. Some will put up a fight when it comes to education. Again, the secret ingredient here is to pique the interest of the users. Get them involved, make it fun, create a reward system, and use your imagination. Some organizations employ IT trainers on a full-time basis or as consultants. Good IT trainers know how to get through to the typical employee. Other organizations will offer incentives for attending training, or penalties for not attending—though statistics show that incentives usually work better than penalties.

You can also attempt role-playing. I'm not talking about a role-playing game such as *Dungeons & Dragons*! Rather, having the employees act out different organizational roles, such as system administrators, privileged users, executive users, data owners, system owners, and of course, typical end users. Throw in the hacker and/or con artist as the "bad guy" roles and you can really teach in a fun way. Create scenarios where people can learn in a tangible way how attacks are carried out and how they can be prevented. Quiz the employees, but keep it light. The idea is for employees to expand their knowledge into other areas of the company, a sort of table-top job rotation so to speak. Develop the situations and solutions properly, and the whole organization becomes a stronger and more secure unit, thanks to you. Come on, you know you always aspired to be a Dungeon Master!

Finally, there is the time factor. People have projects and tasks to complete, and usually aren't even given enough time for that! Where does the time for training come from? This is when the mindset of loyalty to the company comes in—and human resources can usually be helpful in cultivating that mindset. The whole outlook should be based on the idea of overall efficiency and benefits to the company and individual. By sitting in on security training, the user will save time over the long term and will ultimately become a more knowledgeable person.

Anyway, for the Security+ certification, *how* the training gets accomplished isn't as important as *what* is covered in training. The following is a basic list of rules you can convey when training employees:

- Never, under any circumstances, give out any authentication details such as passwords, PINs, company ID, tokens, smart cards, and so on.

- Always shield keypads and screens when entering authentication information.

- Adhere to the organization's *clean desk policy*, which states that all documents, electronics, personally owned devices, and other items be put away (or locked away) when the user is not at his or her desk, or other work area.

- Always screen your e-mail and phone calls carefully and keep a log of events. This is also known as communications *vetting*.

- Use encryption when possible to protect e-mails, phone calls, and data.

- If there is any doubt as to the legitimacy of a person, e-mail, or phone call, document the situation and escalate it to your supervisor, security, or the authorities.

- Never pick up, and make use of, any unknown removable media.

- Always shred any sensitive information destined for the garbage or recycling.

- Always comply with company policy when it comes to data handling and disposal. For example, if a hard drive, USB flash drive, memory stick, or optical disc is no longer being used, make sure it is disposed of properly. If the user is not sure, contact the IT department or facilities department of the organization to find out if it should be recycled, or destroyed.

- Always track and expedite shipments.

- *** Be extremely careful when using a web browser. Double-check everything that is typed before pressing Enter or clicking Go. Don't click on anything unless you know exactly what it is. I triple-starred this one because web-based attacks account for a huge percentage of damage to organizations.

When training employees, try to keep them interested; infuse some fun and be silly if you want to. For instance, the first bullet said to *never* give out authentication details. Pundits tell us to never say never. Well, if it's okay for them, then it's okay for us. And in this case, it's vital to the health of your organization—not to mention you. You see what I mean? Or, if you don't want to be silly, then consider imparting some real examples. Use examples of social engineering so that your trainees can make the connection between actual social engineering methods and their defenses. Make them understand that social engineers don't care how powerful an organization's firewall is or how many armed guards the company has. They get past technology and other types of security by exploiting the weaknesses inherent in human nature.

The previous lists of social engineering methods and defenses are in no way finite. There are so many ways to con a person and so many ways to defend against the con. However, some of the best weapons against social engineering, aside from user education and awareness, are policies and procedures, and their constant analysis. We'll be discussing those in the following chapter.

Facilities Security

Although it is usually the duty of the IT director and building management to take care of the installation, maintenance, and repair of facilities related to technology, you also should have a basic knowledge of how these systems function. Significant concepts include environmental controls such as fire suppression and HVAC, shielding of equipment, and company vehicles. By far, the concept a person would spend the most time dealing with when planning a server room or data center is fire suppression.

Fire Suppression

We talked about fire suppression somewhat in Chapter 16, "Redundancy and Disaster Recovery," but we need to dig a bit deeper into the types you can employ, and some of the policies and procedures involved with fire suppression. **Fire suppression** is the process of controlling and/or extinguishing fires to protect an organization's employees, its data, and its equipment. There are basically three types of fire suppression you should know: handheld fire extinguisher solutions, sprinkler systems, and special hazard protection systems such as those used in server rooms.

Fire Extinguishers

Be careful when selecting a handheld fire extinguisher. There are several types to choose from; they vary depending on what type of environment you work in. Keep in mind that any one of these will probably cause damage to computers, phones, and other electronics. With only a couple exceptions, these solutions should not be used in a server room or other critical areas of your organization. Here are some of the classifications of fires and their indicators on corresponding fire extinguishers:

Key Topic

- **Fire Class A:** Denoted by a green triangle, this class defines use for ordinary fires consuming solid combustibles such as wood. Think A for "ash" to help remember this type. Water-based extinguishers are suitable for Class A fires only and should not be used in a server room.

- **Fire Class B:** Represented by a red square, this type defines use for flammable liquid and gas fires. I like to remember this by associating B with "butane" because butane is a highly flammable gas.

- **Fire Class C:** Indicated with a blue circle, this type defines use for electrical fires—for example, when an outlet is overloaded. Think C for "copper" as in copper electrical wiring to aid in memorizing this type. If a fire occurs in a server room, and you don't have a special hazard system (not wise), the multipurpose BC extinguisher (CO_2) is the best handheld extinguisher to use. Electrical fires are the most likely type of fire in a server room.

- **Fire Class D:** Designated with a yellow decagon, this type defines use for combustible metal fires such as magnesium, titanium, and lithium. A Class D extinguisher is effective in case a laptop's batteries spontaneously ignite. Chemical laboratories and PC repair labs should definitely have one of these available. Metal fires can easily and quickly spread to become ordinary fires. These fire extinguishers are usually yellow; it is one of only a couple that deviate from the standard red color. Also, this is the only other exception when it comes to the use of extinguishers in a critical area of your organization. Because of those two reasons, I like to remember it by associating D with "deviate."

- **Fire Class K:** Symbolized as a black hexagon, this type is for cooking oil fires. This is one type of extinguisher that should be in any kitchen. This is important if your organization has a cafeteria with cooking equipment. Think K for "kitchen" when remembering this type.

The previous bulleted list is not an official standard but is used by most manufacturers of fire extinguishers in the United States. Other countries might have a slightly different system.

In general, the most common type of fire extinguisher used in a building is the multipurpose dry-chemical ABC extinguisher. However, this is extremely messy—it gets into everything! Plus, it can cause corrosion to computer components over time. For server rooms, BC extinguishers are sometimes employed; the most common is the carbon dioxide (CO_2) extinguisher. The CO_2 extinguisher displaces oxygen, which is needed for a fire to burn, in addition to heat and fuel, which collectively make up the fire triangle. CO_2 extinguishers are relatively safe for computer components, especially compared to ABC extinguishers. However, the CO_2 extinguisher can possibly cause damage to computer components from electrostatic discharge (ESD), although this is rare. Also, if carbon dioxide is released in an enclosed space where people are present, there is a risk of suffocation. If the organization has the money, it is far more preferable to use an ABC-rated Halotron extinguisher in the server room—or better yet, a special hazard protection system.

Older extinguishants, such as halon, are not used anymore because they are harmful to the environment. Less-developed countries might still use them, but most governments have banned the use of halon. If you see one of these, it should be replaced with a newer extinguisher that uses environment-safe halocarbon agents such as Halotron or FE-36. These are known as gaseous clean agents that are not only safe on humans and safe for IT equipment, but are better for the environment as well. Gaseous fire suppression systems are the best for server rooms.

Sprinkler Systems

The most common type of fire sprinkler system consists of a pressurized water supply system that can deliver a high quantity of water to an entire building via a piping distribution system. This is known as a **wet pipe sprinkler system**. Typical to these systems are sprinkler heads with glass bulbs (often red) or two-part metal links. When a certain amount of predetermined heat reaches the bulb or link, it causes it to shatter or break, applying pressure to the sprinkler cap and initiating the flow of water from that sprinkler and perhaps others in the same zone. The entire system is usually controlled by a valve assembly, often located in the building's basement. Some organizations might have a need for a dry pipe system, which is necessary in spaces where the temperature of that area of the building can be cold enough to freeze the water in a wet pipe system. In this type of system, the pipes are pressurized with air, and water is sent through the system only if necessary; for example, during a fire.

Regardless of the system, an organization should conduct periodic fire drills to simulate a real fire and sprinkler system activation. Afterward, the security administrator should simulate disaster recovery procedures, as detailed in Chapter 16.

Most local municipalities require that organizations possess a sprinkler system that covers all the building's floor space. However, the standard wet pipe or dry pipe systems are not acceptable in server rooms because if set off, they will most likely damage the equipment within. If a person were working in the server room and somehow damaged a pipe, it could discharge; possibly sending a few servers to the scrap heap. Instead, another option for a server room would be a pre-action sprinkler system (and possibly a special hazard protection system in addition to that). A **pre-action sprinkler system** is similar to a dry pipe system, but there are requirements for it to be set off such as heat or smoke. So, even if a person were to damage one of the pipes in the sprinkler system, the pre-action system would not be set off.

Special Hazard Protection Systems

I've mentioned several times that your server room contains the livelihood of your organization—its data. If you don't protect the data, you'll be out of a job. One way to protect the server room is by installing a clean agent fire suppression system. Special clean agent fire extinguishers, such as Halotron and FE-36, are recommended for server rooms because they leave no residue after the fire is extinguished, reducing the likelihood of damage to computer systems and networking equipment. Also, they are rated as ABC, so they can put out not only electrical fires, but also the ash fire that will most likely ensue. All the other systems mentioned up to this point can easily cause computer failure if they are discharged.

The ultimate solution would be to equip the server room with a **special hazard protection system**, a clean agent system, such as FM-200. This gaseous system would be installed in addition to the pre-action system (or other dry pipe system) if the organization can afford it. This system uses a large tank that stores a clean agent fire extinguishant in the form of a liquid. It is sprayed from one or more nozzles in the ceiling of the server room in gas form. A system such as this can put out most classes of fires in seconds. This type of product does not do damage to equipment and can be used safely when people are present. However, most of these systems also employ a *very* loud alarm that tells all personnel to leave the server room; it's usually so loud and abrasive that you are compelled to leave! It is wise to run through fire suppression alarm tests and fire drills, ensuring that the alarm will sound when necessary and that IT personnel know what to do when the alarm sounds, namely, leave. In some cases, these systems will shut the door automatically after a certain timeout. In these cases, procedures should be written out specifying what to do if a fire occurs. Drilling is of utmost importance in these environments to make certain that everyone knows to leave the server room quickly if a fire occurs. Again, after drills have been completed, the appropriate IT personnel should simulate disaster recovery procedures, if necessary. If the system was installed properly and does its job, this simulation should be minimal.

HVAC

HVAC, or heating, ventilating, and air conditioning, is important for server rooms, data centers, and other technology-oriented areas of your building. Servers run hot—their CPUs can make the temperature inside the case skyrocket. This heat needs to be dissipated and exhausted outside the case. All the heat from servers and other networking equipment is enough to make your server room fry!

To alleviate the situation, organizations install a heavy-duty air-conditioning system used solely for the server room. This can provide an appropriate ambient temperature for the servers. Often, the system also includes a humidity control. As we know, static electricity is our enemy. By increasing humidity, we decrease the buildup of static electricity and the chance of ESD. Also, this can enable us to keep our equipment from getting too humid, which can also cause failure. It is important to have this system on its own dedicated circuit that is rated properly.

Because most AC systems use refrigerant, it is important to locate the device and any pipes away from where servers and other equipment will be situated, or use a pipeless system. The controls for this system should be within the server room, perhaps protected by a key code. This way, only authorized IT personnel (who have access to the server room) can change the temperature or humidity. This control can also be hooked up to the door access system or other monitoring systems to log who made changes and when.

Another way to improve the heat situation is to circulate the air, and one smart way to do this is to install **hot and cold aisles**. To illustrate this concept, imagine that you had several rows of servers inside cabinets, all of which are resting on a raised floor. You would set up the fronts of the cabinets of each row to face each other, forming a cold aisle (the row you would normally walk down to access the servers). The cold air is pumped into this aisle from the raised floor. Since most servers and other IT equipment use front-to-back heat dissipation, the heat should be exhausted out behind the row. That's where the hot aisle is, along with network cables, power cables, and so on. The hot air is exhausted through the raised floor or through exhaust ducts in the ceiling.

A heating system is rarely needed in a server room, unless the organization's building is in the coldest of environments. This is due to the amount of heat that all the servers give off, and the fact that they usually run 24/7.

If there is a power failure that cannot be alleviated by use of a UPS and/or backup generator, you might opt to shut down all but the most necessary of systems temporarily. Some organizations enforce this by way of a written policy. To help monitor HVAC systems and their power consumption, industrial control systems (ICSs) such as the **supervisory control and data acquisition (SCADA)** computer-controlled system will be used. A system such as SCADA combines hardware monitoring devices (pressure gauges, electrodes, remote terminal units that connect to sensors) with software that is run on an admin's (or building management employee's) workstation, allowing the admin to monitor the HVAC system in real time. There could also be a human-machine interface (HMI) that displays SCADA animations on a separate screen in a strategic place in the building. SCADA systems are vulnerable to viruses (such as Stuxnet) that can be used to access design files. To protect against this, the workstation that runs the software portion of SCADA should have its AV software updated, and any separate physical interfaces, displays, and sensors should be secured and perhaps be placed within view of a CCTV system.

Aside from monitoring HVAC, heating and ventilation systems are usually beyond the knowledge of the IT people, and any maintenance or repair of such systems should be directed to qualified professionals. Sometimes, the building management is responsible for such systems, but more than likely the organization is responsible for the installation, repair, and maintenance. What's important to know for the exam is that HVAC systems address the need for *availability* of data.

NOTE ANT, a proprietary wireless sensor technology originally incorporated into sports and fitness sensors, is also finding its way into industrial applications, as well as health-based devices, home automation, and more. Watch out for proprietary technologies that can communicate wirelessly and devise means to detect them and prohibit them from accessing your organization's network.

Shielding

We have already established that EMI and RFI can corrupt legitimate signals and can possibly create unwelcome emanations. Shielding can help to prevent these problems. Although these have been briefly discussed previously, let's get into a little more detail with a few examples:

- **Shielded twisted-pair (STP) cable:** By using STP cable, you employ a shield around the wires inside the cable, reducing the levels of interference on the cable segment. This can help with computers suffering from intermittent data loss.

- **HVAC shielding:** By installing a shield around air conditioners and other similar equipment, you end up shielding them, and thereby keep EMI generated by that equipment inside the shield.

- **Faraday cage:** There are several types of Faraday cages. Screened cables such as coaxial cables for TV are basic examples. Booster bags lined with aluminum foil would be another example. But the term *Faraday cage* is usually applied to an entire room. If an entire room is shielded, electromagnetic energy cannot pass through the walls in either direction. So, if a person attempts to use a cell phone inside the cage, it will not function properly, because the signal cannot go beyond the cage walls; the cell phone cannot acquire a signal from a cell phone tower. More important, devices such as cell phones, motors, and wireless access points that create electromagnetic fields and are outside the cage cannot disrupt electromagnetic-sensitive devices that reside inside the cage.

By using shielding effectively, you can limit just about any type of interference. Some server rooms are shielded entirely to stop any type of wireless transmissions from entering or exiting the room. This can be an expensive proposition and is more common in data centers and advanced technology computer rooms. The pinnacle of shielding technology and research is **TEMPEST**, which, according to some organizations, stands for Transient ElectroMagnetic Pulse Emanations Standard, though the U.S. government has denied that the word is an acronym at all. The TEMPEST standards (as defined by the U.S. government) deal with the studies into compromising emissions, which are broken down into different levels according to particular environments and strictness of shielding necessary to those environments. Because computers and monitors give off electromagnetic radiation, there is a chance, if an attacker uses the proper antenna, that information could be recorded. The TEMPEST standards govern the limiting of EM radiation, reducing the chance of the leakage of data. A TEMPEST-certified building can prevent wireless devices from being hacked by war-driving attacks and other similar wireless attacks. TEMPEST shielding (and other types of shielding) can also help to prevent damage caused by a *high-energy* electromagnetic pulse (EMP). Also known as a spike or a pinch, a high-energy EMP can be generated in a nuclear or non-nuclear fashion. The chances of a high-energy EMP occurring near your facility is very rare, but some organizations and many government facilities require protection from it.

Vehicles

An organization's vehicles might include cars, trucks, tractor trailers, boats, planes, drones, and more. Nowadays, they all have integrated computers, and so, of course, they are all hackable. Plus, the operator of the vehicle will probably carry some kind of mobile device, which may or may not interface with the vehicle. We just opened up a can of worms—of the mobile variety.

Have no fear though, by applying the principles in this book, we can prevent most of the attacks and issues that can occur, because most of them are similar.

To start, many vehicles are equipped with Apple CarPlay, Android Auto, or a similar mobile device projection standard, allowing for seamless integration with the operator's smartphone or tablet. Depending on the policies of an organization embracing BYOD, CYOD, or COPE, the organization might consider disabling this technology as it can pose a separate security risk. In some cases, malware stored on a mobile device can be transferred to the automotive computer(s), when connected via USB. With any group of connected systems, it is possible to subvert one technology to gain access to another. For example, an automobile will use the **Controller Area Network (CAN)** bus to allow communications between the dozens of control units, including the engine control unit and possibly the onscreen display. There are potential vulnerabilities all over the place if the system isn't designed well. And with so many auto manufacturers and models, the risk level only increases.

Because of this, many organizations will opt for fleet vehicles that do not include an in-dash computer/mobile device projection system to reduce risk and to save money. Vehicles might also have an SD card slot, used to update GPS/maps or other automotive software. Infected SD cards could possibly be used (by a person with physical access) to corrupt the GPS system of the vehicle with the potential for location information being sent via the operator's mobile device or from the vehicle itself. SD card slots can be disabled on some vehicles and the settings for the on-board computer can be blocked with a passcode or password.

Manufacturers and organizations will also implement a network security measure known as an air gap. An **air gap** is a method of isolating an entity, effectively separating it from everything else—the entity could be a CPU, a system, or an entire network. The concept could be applied to just about anything. As we know, one of the best ways to secure a thing is to isolate it. In the case of the CAN bus, the engine control unit is usually air gapped. Industrial control systems such as SCADA are often air gapped. So are mission-critical and life-critical controls used in nuclear power plants or aviation vehicles. It could also be an entire network that needs to be separated—this is common in military and government scenarios, and might also require the implementation of a Faraday cage or TEMPEST solution. If two entities are involved in an air gap, for example, two networks, they are often categorized as classified (secure or high side) and unclassified (insecure or low side), but it's the classified entity that is considered to be the real air-gapped system. Data can easily be transferred from the low side to the high side, but for high side to low side data transfer, the procedures are much more strict, and quite possibly require physical moving of the data. For example, in Chapter 15, "PKI and Encryption Protocols," we discussed the concept of the offline certificate authority (CA), where certificates and keys are physically moved from that system to subsidiary CAs, and in fact are also done vice versa, making the air gap more secure.

It should go without saying that all vehicles should have appropriate locking systems and possibly additional authentication methods such as passcodes, proximity keys, and biometrics. By preventing access to unwanted individuals, you can protect many of the internal systems of a vehicle.

But what about wireless systems? Many vehicles now use Wi-Fi and Bluetooth, as well as proprietary technologies. We have detailed many vulnerabilities to these already. Use the prevention methods described previously in the book. Also, consider if Wi-Fi and/or Bluetooth are really necessary, and if not, disable them within the vehicle's on-board computer settings. Or, utilize passcodes for Bluetooth. And consider the geofencing mindset: reduce the Wi-Fi power levels in order to decrease the Wi-Fi area.

Another vehicle that has become much more common is the *unmanned aerial vehicle (UAV)*, commonly known as a drone. The applications of a UAV are seemingly endless, including security and defense applications. From a larger perspective, the risk associated with UAV technology is a double-edged sword—because you have organization-operated UAVs and attacker-operated UAVs. First, if an organization owns and uses UAV technology, it can be exploited like any other technology. For example, a UAV can be a target for command and control (C2) attacks, data link jamming, sensor jamming, and spoofing. An attacker might be trying to capture information, or compromise the UAV to take over navigation. The organization that owns the UAV can prevent this by using best coding practices (SDLC), encryption, mutual authentication, and UAV-specific security standards. Secondly, a well-funded attacker might *own* UAV technology and use it for reconnaissance, potentially spying on an organization, or gaining access to a wireless network—if properly equipped. On the prevention side, an organization should once again consider their geofencing policy, and have strong Wi-Fi encryption protocols in place. Plus, physical security methods (as discussed in Chapter 10, "Physical Security and Authentication Models") should be in place as well as no-fly-zone policies.

The bottom line is this: Incorporate your security policies and procedures into any vehicles that your organization uses. It's all part of that attitude we've used throughout the book—essentially, anything with a CPU and memory is a computer, and any computer can be compromised given time and effort. As a last note, by this definition of "computer," we can safely say that computers are just about everywhere. Govern them accordingly.

Chapter Summary

So that wraps up this chapter about people and facilities. It was a bit helter-skelter as far as the listing of content, but in a way, all the concepts are intertwined. For example, you don't want attackers to gain access to your building. But if they do, then you don't want them to gain access to your server room (among other things). So, you implement things such as multifactor authentication, and just in case, you implement shielding to help prevent any wireless intrusion. These are physical security controls and are easily understood.

If only it were so easy to shield people from the con: from what we call social engineering. Any technology can be ultimately exploited by a smart person and some social engineering skills—and this is less tangible, and not as easily understood or as easily prevented. People who employ social engineering rely on authority, intimidation, impersonation, trust, persistence, and a lot of patience. This enables them to perform cons such as pretexting and hoaxes, and steal information through phishing, baiting, shoulder surfing, eavesdropping, and other methods. While this whole book is full of ways to prevent the con artist from obtaining data, secrets, and PII, it is the user education and awareness that might be the best defense. Knowledge is power, but users need to be trained in an interesting manner in order to effectively stop the threat of social engineering.

Environmental controls are security controls that are put in place to protect employees, servers, and the organization's data. They include fire extinguishers, sprinkler systems, special hazard systems (such as FM-200), hot and cold aisles, SCADA-based systems, and shielding. The security of these depends on physical keys, proximity and smart card systems, video surveillance, security guards, alarms, and so forth. When it comes to building facilities, environmental controls might be a large piece of what you will be called on to secure, in addition to vehicles, equipment, electrical systems, and anything else that falls under that category. We've only scratched the surface when it comes to what is within the realm of "facilities." You will not be expected to know everything on the subject. However, be ready to work with your organization's facilities department and human resources department to accomplish what we have discussed in this chapter.

Chapter Review Activities

Use the features in this section to study and review the topics in this chapter.

Review Key Topics

Review the most important topics in the chapter, noted with the Key Topic icon in the outer margin of the page. Table 17-2 lists a reference of these key topics and the page number on which each is found.

Table 17-2   Key Topics for Chapter 17

Key Topic Element	Description	Page Number
Table 17-1	Summary of social engineering types	590
Bulleted list	Fire extinguisher types	594
Bulleted list	Shielding types	599

Define Key Terms

Define the following key terms from this chapter, and check your answers in the glossary:

pretexting, diversion theft, phishing, spear phishing, whaling, vishing, hoax, shoulder surfing, eavesdropping, dumpster diving, baiting, piggybacking, tailgating, mantrap, watering hole attack, fire suppression, wet pipe sprinkler system, pre-action sprinkler system, special hazard protection system, hot and cold aisles, supervisory control and data acquisition (SCADA), Faraday cage, TEMPEST, Controller Area Network (CAN), air gap

Complete the Real-World Scenarios

Complete the Real-World Scenarios found on the companion website (www.pearsonitcertification.com/title/9780789758996). You will find a PDF containing the scenario and questions, and also supporting videos and simulations.

Review Questions

Answer the following review questions. Check your answers with the correct answers that follow.

1. Jeff wants to employ a Faraday cage. What will this accomplish?

    A. It will increase the level of wireless encryption.

    B. It will reduce data emanations.

    C. It will increase EMI.

    D. It will decrease the level of wireless emanations.

2. If a fire occurs in the server room, which device is the best method to put it out?

    A. Class A extinguisher

    B. Class B extinguisher

    C. Class C extinguisher

    D. Class D extinguisher

3. What devices will not be able to communicate in a Faraday cage? (Select the two best answers.)

    A. Smartphones

    B. Servers

    C. Tablets

    D. Switches

4. You go out the back door of your building and notice someone looking through your company's trash. If this person were trying to acquire sensitive information, what would this attack be known as?

    A. Browsing

    B. Dumpster diving

    C. Phishing

    D. Hacking

5. User education can help to defend against which of the following? (Select the three best answers.)

    A. Social engineering

    B. Phishing

    C. Rainbow tables

    D. Dumpster diving

6. Which of these is an example of social engineering?

    A. Asking for a username and password over the phone

    B. Using someone else's unsecured wireless network

    C. Hacking into a router

    D. Virus

7. What is the most common reason that social engineering succeeds?

    A. Lack of vulnerability testing

    B. People sharing passwords

    C. Lack of auditing

    D. Lack of user awareness

8. In which two environments would social engineering attacks be most effective? (Select the two best answers.)

    A. Public building with shared office space

    B. Company with a dedicated IT staff

    C. Locked building

    D. Military facility

    E. An organization whose IT personnel have little training

9. Of the following definitions, which would be an example of eavesdropping?

    A. Overhearing parts of a conversation

    B. Monitoring network traffic

    C. Another person looking through your files

    D. A computer capturing information from a sender

10. Of the following, which type of fire suppression can prevent damage to computers and servers?

    A. Class A

    B. Water

    C. CO_2

    D. ABC extinguishers

11. A man pretending to be a data communications repair technician enters your building and states that there is networking trouble and he needs access to the server room. What is this an example of?

   A. Man-in-the-middle attack

   B. Virus

   C. Social engineering

   D. Chain of custody

12. Turnstiles, double entry doors, and security guards are all preventative measures for what kind of social engineering?

   A. Dumpster diving

   B. Impersonation

   C. Piggybacking

   D. Eavesdropping

13. In addition to bribery and forgery, which of the following are the most common techniques that attackers use to socially engineer people? (Select the two best answers.)

   A. Flattery

   B. Assuming a position of authority

   C. Dumpster diving

   D. WHOIS search

14. You need to protect your data center from unauthorized entry at all times. Which is the best type of physical security to implement?

   A. Mantrap

   B. Video surveillance

   C. Nightly security guards

   D. 802.1X

15. Which of the following targets specific people?

   A. Pharming

   B. Phishing

   C. Vishing

   D. Spear phishing

16. Why would you implement password masking?

    A. To deter tailgating

    B. To deter shoulder surfing

    C. To deter impersonation

    D. To deter hoaxes

17. A targeted e-mail attack is received by your organization's CFO. What is this an example of?

    A. Vishing

    B. Phishing

    C. Whaling

    D. Spear phishing

18. Which of the following environmental variables reduces the possibility of static discharges (ESD)?

    A. Humidity

    B. Temperature

    C. EMI

    D. RFI

19. Which of the following is a strategy that targets users based on the common websites that they frequent?

    A. Pre-action

    B. Hot/cold aisle

    C. SCADA

    D. Watering hole

20. You have been ordered to implement a secure shredding system as well as privacy screens. What two attacks is your organization attempting to mitigate?

    A. Shoulder surfing

    B. Impersonation

    C. Phishing

    D. Dumpster diving

    E. Tailgating

Answers and Explanations

1. **B.** The Faraday cage will reduce data emanations. The cage is essentially an enclosure (of which there are various types) of conducting material that can block external electric fields and stop internal electric fields from leaving the cage, thus reducing or eliminating data emanations from such devices as cell phones.

2. **C.** When you think Class C, think copper. Extinguishers rated as Class C can suppress electrical fires, which are the most likely kind in a server room.

3. **A and C.** Signals cannot emanate outside a Faraday cage. Therefore, smart-phones and tablets (by default) will not work inside the Faraday cage. Generally, a Faraday cage is "constructed" for a server room, data center, or other similar location. Servers and switches are common in these places and are normally wired to the network, so they should be able to communicate with the outside world.

4. **B.** Dumpster diving is when a person goes through a company's trash to find sensitive information about an individual or a company. Browsing is not an attack but something you do when connected to the Internet. Phishing is known as acquiring sensitive information through the use of electronic communication. Nowadays, hacking is a general term used to describe many different types of attacks.

5. **A, B, and D.** User education and awareness can help defend against social engineering attacks, phishing, and dumpster diving. Rainbow tables are lookup tables used when recovering passwords.

6. **A.** Social engineering is the practice of obtaining confidential information by manipulating people. Using someone else's network is just theft. Hacking into a router is just that, hacking. And a virus is a self-spreading program that may or may not cause damage to files and applications.

7. **D.** User awareness is extremely important when attempting to defend against social engineering attacks. Vulnerability testing and auditing are definitely important as part of a complete security plan but will not necessarily help defend against social engineering and definitely will not help as much as user awareness training. People should not share passwords.

8. **A and E.** Public buildings with shared office space and organizations with IT employees who have little training are environments in which social engineering attacks are common and would be most successful. Social engineering will be less successful in secret buildings, buildings with a decent level of security such as military facilities, and organizations with dedicated and well-trained IT staff.

9. **A.** Eavesdropping is when people listen to a conversation that they are not part of. A security administrator should keep in mind that someone could always be listening, and thus should always try to protect against this.

10. **C.** CO_2 is the best answer that will prevent damage to computers because CO_2 is air-based, not water-based. CO_2 displaces oxygen. Fire needs oxygen; without it the fire will go out. All the other options have substances that can damage computers. However, because CO_2 can possibly cause ESD damage, the best solution in a server room would be Halotron or FE-36.

11. **C.** Any person pretending to be a data communications repair person would be attempting a social engineering attack.

12. **C.** Turnstiles, double entry doors, and security guards are all examples of preventative measures that attempt to defeat piggybacking. Dumpster diving is when a person looks through a coworker's trash or a building's trash to retrieve information. Impersonation is when a person attempts to represent another person, possibly with the other person's identification. Eavesdropping is when a person overhears another person's conversation.

13. **A and C.** The most common techniques that attackers use to socially engineer people include flattery, dumpster diving, bribery, and forgery. Although assuming a position of authority is an example of social engineering, it is not one of the most common. A WHOIS search is not necessarily malicious; it can be accomplished by anyone and can be done for legitimate reasons. This type of search can tell a person who runs a particular website or who owns a domain name.

14. **A.** Mantraps are the best solution listed—they are the closest to foolproof of the listed answers. Mantraps (if installed properly) are strong enough to keep a human inside until he completes the authentication process or is escorted off the premises. This is a type of preventive security control meant to stop tailgating and piggybacking. Video surveillance will not prevent an unauthorized person from entering your data center; rather, it is a detective security control. Security guards are a good idea, but if they work only at night, then they can't prevent unauthorized access at all times. 802.1X is an excellent authentication method, but it is logically implemented as software and devices; it is not a physical security control.

15. **D.** Spear phishing is a targeted attack, unlike regular phishing, which usually works by contacting large groups of people. Pharming is when a website's traffic is redirected to another, illegitimate, website. Vishing is the phone/VoIP version of phishing.

16. **B.** Password masking is when the characters a user types into a password field are replaced, usually by asterisks. This is done to prevent shoulder surfing. Tailgating is when an unauthorized person follows an authorized person into a secure area, without the second person's consent. Impersonation is when a person masquerades as another, authorized user. A hoax is an attempt at deceiving people into believing something that is false.

17. **C.** Whaling is a type of spear phishing that targets senior executives such as CFOs. Regular old phishing does not target anyone, but instead tries to contact as many people as possible until an unsuspecting victim can be found. Vishing is the telephone-based version of phishing. Spear phishing does target individuals but not senior executives.

18. **A.** Humidity (if increased) can reduce the chance of static discharges. Temperature does not have an effect on computer systems (within reason). EMI and RFI are types of interference that in some cases could possibly increase the chance of static discharge.

19. **D.** The watering hole attack is a strategy that targets users based on the common websites that they frequent. A pre-action sprinkler system is similar to a dry pipe system, but there are requirements for it to be set off such as heat or smoke. Implementing hot and cold aisles in server rooms is a way to improve air circulation. Supervisory control and data acquisition (SCADA) systems combine hardware monitoring devices (pressure gauges, electrodes, remote terminal units that connect to sensors) with software that is run on an admin's (or building management employee's) workstation, allowing the admin to monitor the HVAC system in real time.

20. **A and D.** The privacy screens are being implemented to prevent shoulder surfing. The secure shredding system is being implemented to mitigate dumpster diving. Impersonation is when an unauthorized person masquerades as a legitimate, authorized person. Phishing is when an attacker attempts to fraudulently obtain information through e-mail scams. Tailgating is when a person (without proper credentials) attempts to gain access to an unauthorized area by following someone else in.

This chapter covers the following subjects:

- **Legislative and Organizational Policies:** In this section, you learn about ways to classify data, laws that protect individual privacy, personnel security policies and how to implement them, service-level agreements, and the safe disposal of computers.

- **Incident Response Procedures:** Here we discuss the processes and procedures involved in computer security incident management. Proper planning for incident response is key, as is the ability to document the lessons learned.

- **IT Security Frameworks:** This short section gets into the basics of security frameworks and how they can help to organize your IT processes and procedures.

This is the last chapter of actual objective content for the Security+ exam, but you will no doubt see several questions on the exam about these topics. This chapter is all about procedures and policies. Conceptually, this chapter is a bit more "high level." It deals with larger concepts concerning the organization and its employees. Like the last chapter, it is less tech-oriented, and more people-oriented. When going through this chapter, try to keep an open mind as to the different roles a security person might be placed in. Imagine branching out beyond computers, servers, and networks and developing security for the entire organization and its personnel.

CHAPTER 18

Policies and Procedures

Some smaller companies don't have much in the way of policies. Arguably, that is why a percentage of them fail. You will see many companies of all sizes create their own policies or embrace ones that other organizations are using, or perhaps apply for a company-wide standards certification from an organization such as the International Organization for Standardization (ISO). Some organizations are bound by legislative policy and organized protocols. In general, policies are designed to protect employees and make the organization more productive and efficient.

It's important to distinguish between policies and procedures. A *policy* is something that an individual employee, or entire organization, should adhere to, but is usually expressed in broad terms. A *procedure* is usually much more specific. Although it is often stated in detail, it can potentially be interpreted more loosely. Standard operating procedures used by corporations, government, and the military are usually pretty tight. But other procedures might be a bit more relaxed, and as long as the employee gets to the final goal efficiently, procedures can often be overlooked to a certain degree. However, incident response procedures—once developed by an organization—are usually followed to the letter. Otherwise there can be legal repercussions. Keep in mind that a procedure could be a part of an overall policy.

To help organize the many procedures and policies, we need a plan. An IT security framework is just that—it's like the blueprint for your organization's security goals. It defines, organizes, and interconnects the various policies and procedures that can make people giddy.

The concepts in this chapter are meant to oversee everything else in the book from a more managed perspective. By using a well-planned IT security framework (or frameworks), our procedures and policies, and technology in general, all start to flow together.

Foundation Topics

Legislative and Organizational Policies

There are myriad legislative laws and policies. For the Security+ exam, we are concerned only with a few that affect, and protect, the privacy of individuals. In this section, we cover those and some associated security standards.

More important for the Security+ exam are organizational policies. Organizations usually define policies that concern how data is classified, expected employee behavior, and how to dispose of IT equipment that is no longer needed. These policies begin with a statement or goal that is usually short, to the point, and open-ended. They are normally written in clear language that can be understood by most everyone. They are followed by procedures (or guidelines) that detail how the policy will be implemented.

Table 18-1 shows an example of a basic policy and corresponding procedure.

Table 18-1   Example of a Company Policy

Policy	Procedure

Employees will identify themselves in a minimum of two ways when entering the complex.	1. When employees enter the complex, they will first enter a guard room. This will begin the authentication process.
	
	2. In the guard room, they must prove their identification in two ways:
	
	   ■ By showing their ID badge to the on-duty guard.
	
	   ■ By being visible to the guard so that the guard can compare their likeness to the ID badge's photo. The head of the employee should not be obstructed by hats, sunglasses, and so on. In essence, the employee should look similar to the ID photo. If the employee's appearance changes for any reason, that person should contact human resources for a new ID badge.
	
	   * If guards cannot identify the "employee," they will contact the employee's supervisor, human resources, or security in an attempt to confirm the person's identity. If the employee is not confirmed, they will be escorted out of the building by security.
	
	3. After the guard has acknowledged the identification, employees will swipe their ID badge against the door scanner to complete the authentication process and gain access to the complex.

Keep in mind that this is just a basic example; technical documentation specialists will tailor the wording to fit the feel of the organization. Plus, the procedure will be different depending on the size and resources of the organization and the type of authentication scheme used, which could be more or less complex. However, the *policy* (which is fairly common) is written in such a way as to be open-ended, allowing for the *procedure* to change over time. We talk about many different policies as they relate to the Security+ exam in this section.

Data Sensitivity and Classification of Information

Sensitive data is information that can result in a loss of security, or loss of advantage to a company, if accessed by unauthorized persons. Often, information is broken down into two groups: classified (which requires some level of security clearance) and nonclassified.

ISO/IEC 27002:2013 (which revises the older ISO/IEC 27002:2005) is a security standard that among other things can aid companies in classifying their data. Although you don't need to know the contents of that document for the Security+ exam, you should have a basic idea of how to classify information. For example, classification of data can be broken down, as shown in Table 18-2.

Table 18-2 Example of Data Sensitivity Classifications

Class	Description
Public information	Information available to anyone. Also referred to as unclassified or nonclassified.
Internal information	Used internally by a company, but if it becomes public, no critical consequences result. This, and the next three levels, is known as *private* information. It might also be classified as *proprietary* information.
Confidential information	Information that can cause financial and operational loss to the company.
Secret information	Data that should never become public and is critical to the company.
Top secret information	The highest sensitivity of data; few people should have access, and security clearance may be necessary. Information is broken into sections on a need-to-know basis.

In this example, loss of public and internal information probably won't affect the company very much. However, unauthorized access, misuse, modification, or loss of confidential, secret, or top secret data can affect users' privacy, trade secrets, financials, and the general security of the company. By setting data roles such as owner, custodian, and privacy officer, and by classifying data and enforcing policies that govern who has access to what information, a company can limit its exposure to security threats. Different organizations will classify data in various ways, but they will usually be similar to Table 18-2. For example, you might also see the high, medium, and low classifications. Or, for instance, Red Hat Linux uses the Top Secret, Secret, and Confidential classifications (just as in Table 18-2), but considers everything else simply unclassified. All of these types of interpretations of data classifications are implementations of mandatory access control (MAC) discussed in Chapter 11, "Access Control Methods and Models." It's the incorporation of these types of classifications that is a key element in the multilevel security of Trusted Operating Systems (TOSs). Trusted Operating Systems such as Red Hat, OS X 10.6 and higher, and HP-UX utilize multilevel security concepts such as these to meet government requirements.

NOTE   Regardless of the format used, if data exists that is considered to be secret or confidential, then the security admin should strongly consider using data-handling electronics (DHE) devices. Data handling is the process of ensuring that research data is stored, archived, or disposed of in a safe and secure manner during and after the conclusion of a research project.

Moving beyond government classification requirements, many companies need to be in compliance with specific *laws* when it comes to the disclosure of information. In the United States there are a few acts you should know about, as shown in Table 18-3. In addition, there are several bills in process that could be passed in the near future regarding data breach notification.

Key Topic

Table 18-3   Acts Passed Concerning the Disclosure of Data, Personally Identifiable Information (PII), and Protected Health Information (PHI)

Act	Acronym	Description
Privacy Act of 1974	n/a	Establishes a code of fair information practice.
		Governs the collection, use, and dissemination of personally identifiable information about persons' records maintained by federal agencies.
Sarbanes-Oxley	SOX	Governs the disclosure of financial and accounting information. Enacted in 2002.
Health Insurance Portability and Accountability Act	HIPAA	Governs the disclosure and protection of health information. Enacted in 1996.

Act	Acronym	Description
Gramm-Leach-Bliley Act	GLB	Enables commercial banks, investment banks, securities firms, and insurance companies to consolidate. Enacted in 1999.
		Protects against pretexting. Individuals need proper authority to gain access to nonpublic information such as Social Security numbers.
Help America Vote Act of 2002	HAVA	Main goal was to replace punchcard and lever-based voting systems.
		Governs the security, confidentiality, and integrity of personal information collected, stored, or otherwise used by various electronic and computer-based voting systems.
California SB 1386	SB 1386	Requires California businesses that store computerized personal information to immediately disclose breaches of security.
		Enacted in 2003.

Many computer technicians have to deal with SOX and HIPAA at some point in their careers, and although these types of acts create a lot of paperwork and protocol, the expected result is that, in the long run, they will help companies protect their data and keep sensitive information private.

NOTE SOX sparked another concept known as governance, risk, and compliance (GRC), which deals with the continuous security monitoring of: overall management of information systems and control structures; risk management processes; and compliance with stated requirements, be they government related or otherwise.

Personnel Security Policies

Most organizations have policies governing employees. The breadth and scope of these policies vary from organization to organization. For example, a small company might have a few pages defining how employees should behave (a code of ethics) and what to do in an emergency. Larger organizations might go so far as to certify to a particular standard such as ISO 9001:2015 and ISO 9001:2008. This means that the organization will comply with a set of quality standards that is all-encompassing, covering all facets of the business. An organization would have to be examined and finally accredited by an accrediting certification body to state that it is ISO certified. This is a rigorous process and is not for the average organization. For many companies, this would create too much documentation and would bog the company down in details and minutia.

We as IT people are more interested in policies that deal with the security of the infrastructure and its employees. As a security administrator, you might deal with procedural documentation specialists, technical documentation specialists, and even outside consultants. You should become familiar with policies and as many procedures as possible, focusing on policies that take security into account, but remember that actual work must take precedence!

Let's define a few types of policies that are common to organizations. We focus on the security aspect of these policies.

Privacy Policies

The Privacy Act of 1974 sets many standards when it comes to the security of personally identifiable information (PII). However, most organizations will go further and define their own privacy policy, which explains how users' identities and other similar information will be secured. For example, if an organization has an Internet-based application that internal and external users access, the application will probably retain some of their information—possibly details of their identity. Not only should this information be secured, but the privacy policy should state in clear terms what data is allowed to be accessed, and by whom, as well as how the data will be retained and distributed (if at all). An organization might also enact a policy that governs the labeling of data to ensure that all employees understand what data they are handling, and to prevent the mishandling of confidential information. Before any systems administrators or other personnel gather information about these users, they should consult the privacy policy.

Acceptable Use

Acceptable use policies (AUPs) define the rules that restrict how a computer, network, or other system may be used. They state what users are, and are not, allowed to do when it comes to the technology infrastructure of an organization. Often, an AUP must be signed by the employees before they begin working on any systems. This protects the organization, but it also defines to employees exactly what they should, and should not, be working on. If a director asks a particular employee to repair a particular system that was outside the AUP parameters, the employee would know to refuse. If employees are found working on a system that is outside the scope of their work, and they signed an AUP, it is grounds for termination. As part of an AUP, employees enter into an agreement acknowledging they understand that the unauthorized sharing of data is prohibited. Also, employees should understand that they are not to take any information or equipment home without express permission from the various parties listed in the policy. This can sometimes be in conflict with a BYOD policy where users are permitted to bring their own devices into work and use them for work purposes. At that point, strong policies for data ownership need to be developed, identifying what portion of the data on a mobile device is owned by the organization, and what portion is owned by the employee. Any organizational data on a mobile device should be backed up.

Change Management

Change management is a structured way of changing the state of a computer system, network, or IT procedure. The idea behind this is that change is necessary, but that an organization should adapt with change, and be knowledgeable of it. Any change that a person wants to make must be introduced to each of the heads of various departments that it might affect. They must approve the change before it goes into effect. Before this happens, department managers will most likely make recommendations and/or give stipulations. When the necessary people have signed off on the change, it should be tested and then implemented. During implementation, it should be monitored and documented carefully.

Because there are so many interrelated parts and people in an IT infrastructure, it is sometimes difficult for the left hand to know what the right hand is doing, or has done in the past. For example, after a network analysis, a network engineer might think that an unused interface on a firewall doesn't necessarily need to exist anymore. But does he know this for sure? Who installed and configured the interface? When was it enabled? Was it ever used? Perhaps it is used only rarely by special customers making a connection to a DMZ; perhaps it is used with a honeynet; or maybe it is for future use or for testing purposes. It would be negligent for the network engineer to simply modify the firewall without at least asking around to find out whether the interface is necessary. More likely, there will be forms involved that require the network engineer to state the reason for change and have it signed by several other people before making the change. In general, this will slow down progress, but in the long run it will help to cover the network engineer. People were warned, and as long as the correct people involved have signed off on the procedure or technical change, the network engineer shouldn't have to worry. In a larger organization that complies with various certifications such as ISO 9001:2015, it can be a complex task. IT people should have charts of personnel and department heads. There should also be current procedures in place that show who needs to be contacted in the case of a proposed change.

Separation of Duties/Job Rotation

Separation of duties is when more than one person is required to complete a particular task or operation. This distributes control over a system, infrastructure, or particular task. Job rotation is one of the checks and balances that might be employed to enforce the proper separation of duties. It is when two or more employees switch roles at regular intervals. It is used to increase user insight and skill level, and to decrease the risk of fraud and other illegal activities. Both of these policies are enforced to increase the security of an organization by limiting the amount of control a person has over a situation and by increasing employees' knowledge of what other employees are doing. For more information on these and similar concepts, see Chapter 11.

Mandatory Vacations

Some organizations require employees to take X number of consecutive days of vacation over the course of a year as part of their annual leave. For example, a company might require an IT director to take five consecutive days' vacation at least once per year to force another person into his role for that time period. Although a company might state that this helps the person to rest and focus on his job, and incorporate job rotation, the underlying security concept is that **mandatory vacations** can help to stop any possible malicious activity that might occur such as fraud, sabotage, embezzlement, and so on. Because IT people are smart, and often access the network remotely in a somewhat unobserved fashion, auditing becomes very important.

Onboarding and Offboarding

Onboarding is when a new employee is added to an organization, and to its identity and access management system. It incorporates training, formal meetings, lectures, and human resources employee handbooks and videos. It can also be implemented when a person changes roles within an organization. It is known as a socialization technique used to ultimately provide better job performance and higher job satisfaction. Onboarding is associated with federated identity management discussed in Chapter 11. It is also sometimes connected to an employee's *role* in the company, and therefore role-based access control (RBAC).

Offboarding is the converse, and correlates to procedurally removing an employee from a federated identity management system, restricting rights and permissions, and possibly debriefing the person or conducting an exit interview. This happens when a person changes roles within an organization, or departs the organization altogether.

An organization will commonly work with business partners, but no business relationship lasts forever, and new ones are often developed. So, onboarding and offboarding can apply to business partners as well. The main concerns are access to data. In Chapter 6, "Network Design Elements," we discussed extranets and the community cloud, which are both commonly used technologies with business partners. These technologies allow an organization to carefully select which data the business partner has access to. As relationships with business partners are severed, a systematic audit of all shared data should be made, including the various types of connectivity, permissions, policies, and even physical access to data.

Due Diligence

When it comes to information security, **due diligence** is ensuring that IT infrastructure risks are known and managed. An organization needs to spend time assessing risk and vulnerabilities and might state in a policy how it will give due diligence to certain areas of its infrastructure. It can help to study the history of the company, particularly the failures, errors, and user issues that have been documented—essentially, *lessons learned*.

Due Care

Due care is the mitigation action that an organization takes to defend against the risks that have been uncovered during due diligence.

Due Process

Due process is the principle that an organization must respect and safeguard personnel's rights. This is to protect the employee from the state and from frivolous lawsuits.

User Education and Awareness Training

With so many possible organizational policies, employees need to be trained to at least get a basic understanding of them. Certain departments of an organization require more training than others. For example, Human Resources personnel need to understand many facets of the business and their corresponding policies, especially policies that affect personnel. HR people should be thoroughly trained in guidelines and enforcement. Sometimes the HR people train management and other employees on the various policies that those trainees are expected to enforce. In other cases, the trainer would be an executive assistant or outside consultant.

Security awareness training is an ongoing process. Different organizations have varying types of security awareness training, and employees with different roles in the organization receive different types of training. This type of training is often coupled with the signing of a user agreement. The user, when signing this, accepts and acknowledges specific rules of conduct, rules of behavior, and possibly the non-disclosure of any training (known as a nondisclosure agreement, or NDA).

NOTE   Historically, the CompTIA exams themselves require that you sign an NDA. This means that you agree not to share any of the contents of the exam with anyone else.

All employees should be trained on **personally identifiable information (PII)**. This is information used to uniquely identify, contact, or locate a person. This type of information could be a name, birthday, Social Security number, biometric information, and so on. Employees should know what identifies them to the organization and how to keep that information secret and safe from outsiders. Another key element of user education is the dissemination of the password policy. They should understand that passwords should be complex, and know the complexity requirements. They should also understand never to give out their password or ask for another person's password to any resource.

IT personnel should be trained on what to do in the case of account changes—for example, temporarily disabling the account of employees when they take a leave of absence or disabling the account (or deleting it, less common) of an employee who has been terminated. All IT personnel should be fluent in the organization's password policy, lockout policy, and other user-related policies so that they can explain them to any other employees.

Some users might need to take additional privacy training, HIPAA training, or other types of security awareness training depending on the type of organization they work for. This user training might take the form of role-based training, where the instructors and trainees act out the roles they might play, such as network administrator, security analyst, and so on. Instructors will often devise their training to take advantage of learning management systems and training metrics so that they can gauge the effectiveness of the training, validate compliance with policies, and analyze the security posture of the trainees in general.

Summary of Personnel Security Policies

Table 18-4 breaks down and summarizes the various policy types mentioned in this section.

Table 18-4   Summary of Policy Types

Type	Description
Acceptable use	Policy that defines the rules that restrict how a computer, network, or other system may be used.
Change management	A structured way of changing the state of a computer system, network, or IT procedure.
Separation of duties	When more than one person is required to complete a task.
Job rotation	When a particular task is rotated among a group of employees.
Mandatory vacations	When an organization requires employees to take X number of consecutive days' vacation over the course of a year as part of their annual leave.

Type	Description
Onboarding	When a new employee is added to an organization, and to its identity and access management system. It is associated with user training, federated identity management, and RBAC. *Offboarding* correlates to removing an employee from a federated identity management system.
Due diligence	Ensuring that IT infrastructure risks are known and managed.
Due care	The mitigation action that an organization takes to defend against the risks that have been uncovered during due diligence.
Due process	The principle that an organization must respect and safeguard personnel's rights.

How to Deal with Vendors

Before we begin, I should mention that the following information is *not* intended as legal advice. Before signing any contracts, an organization should strongly consider consulting with an attorney.

An organization often has in-depth policies concerning vendors. I can't tell you how many times I've seen issues occur because the level of agreement between the organization and the vendor was not clearly defined. A proper **service-level agreement (SLA)** that is analyzed by the organization carefully before signing can be helpful. A basic service contract is usually not enough; a service contract with an SLA will have a section within it that formally and clearly defines exactly what a vendor is responsible for and what the organization is responsible for—a demarcation point so to speak. It might also define performance expectations and what the vendor will do if a failure of service occurs, timeframes for repair, backup plans, and so on. To benefit the organization, these will usually be legally binding and not informal. Due to this, it would benefit the organization to scrutinize the SLA before signing, and an organization's attorney should be involved in that process.

For instance, a company might use an ISP for its T3 connection. The customer will want to know what kind of fault-tolerant methods are on hand at the ISP and what kind of uptime they should expect, which should be monitored by a network admin. The SLA might have some sort of guarantee of measurable service that can be clearly defined; perhaps a minimum level of service and a target level of service. Before signing an SLA such as this, it is recommended that an attorney, the IT director, and other organizational management review the document carefully and make sure that it covers all the points required by the organization.

On a separate note: A business partners agreement (BPA) is a type of contract that can establish the profits each partner will get, what responsibilities each partner will have, and exit strategies for partners.

> **NOTE**   You will also see *BPA* stand for something else. An SLA that requires products and services over and over again is known as a blanket purchase agreement (BPA)—similar to a blanket order. These are common in government contracts, but some organizations use them also. One thing to make sure is that there is some type of ending for the contract length. Some less than reputable cloud providers will design open-ended BPAs—try to avoid these.

Sometimes, multiple government agencies will enter into a **memorandum of understanding (MoU)**, or a letter of intent, in regard to a BPA; it could be that two agencies have a sort of convergence when it comes to ordering services.

Another type of agreement is the **interconnection security agreement (ISA)**. It is an agreement that is established between two (or more) organizations that own and operate connected IT systems and data sets. Its purpose is to specifically document the technical and security requirements of the interconnection between the organizations. This is the type of agreement you need in this scenario because the data is sensitive and the CIO requires that there is a clear understanding of security controls to be implemented and agreed upon. As far as governing the security of data and systems, it is a more precise agreement than an SLA.

The ISA differs from the SLA, BPA, and MoU in the following ways:

- An SLA is a contract between a service provider and a customer that specifies the nature of the service to be provided and the level of service that the provider will offer to the customer. It can be a very basic agreement, or it could also state the technical and performance parameters, but it will probably not include any specific security controls.

- A BPA does not have any inherent security planning in the way an ISA does.

- An MoU is not an agreement at all, but an understanding between two organizations or government agencies. It does not specify any security controls either. However, a memorandum of *agreement* (MoA) will constitute a legal agreement between two parties wishing to work together on a project, but still will not detail any security controls.

Now, I don't expect you to go out and get a postgraduate degree in business law, but it's a good idea to know these terms in case you need to interface with the business people at your organization, and to better understand the special contractual relationships between your organization and other organizations. That said, let's get back to some tech talk!

How to Dispose of Computers and Other IT Equipment Securely

Organizations might opt to recycle computers and other equipment or donate them. Rarely do organizations throw away equipment. It might be illegal to do so depending on your location and depending on what IT equipment is to be thrown away. The first thing an IT person should do is consult the organization's policy regarding computer disposal, and if necessary, consult local municipal guidelines.

A basic example of a policy and procedure that an organization enforces might look like the following:

Policy: Recycle or donate IT equipment that has been determined to be outdated and nonproductive to the company.

Step 1 Define the equipment to be disposed of.

Step 2. Obtain temporary storage for the equipment.

Step 3. Have the appropriate personnel analyze the equipment.

- Verify whether the equipment is outdated and whether it can be used somewhere else in the organization.

- If a device can be used in another area of the organization, it should be formatted, flashed, or otherwise reset to the original default, and then transported to its new location.

- If a device cannot be reused in the organization, move to Step 4.

Step 4. Sanitize the devices or computers.

- Check for any removable media inside, or connected to, the computer. These should be analyzed and recycled within the organization if possible.

- Remove any RAM, label it, and store it.

- Remove the hard drive, sanitize it, and store it. If necessary based on organizational policies, pulverize or otherwise destroy the device.

- Reset any UEFI/BIOS or other passwords to the default setting.

Step 5. Recycle or donate items as necessary.

Again, this is just an example of a basic recycle policy and procedure, but it gives you an idea of the type of method an organization might employ to best make use of its IT equipment and to organize the entire recycling/donating process.

In Step 4, the policy specifies to sanitize the hard drive; sanitizing the hard drive is a common way of removing data, but not the only one. The way data is removed might vary depending on its proposed final destination. Data removal is the most important element of computer recycling. Proper data removal goes far beyond file deletion or the formatting of digital media. The problem with file deletion/formatting is data remanence, or the residue, that is left behind, from which re-creation of files can be accomplished with the use of software such as SpinRite or other data recovery applications. Companies typically employ one of three options when met with the prospect of data removal:

- **Clearing:** This is the removal of data with a certain amount of assurance that it cannot be reconstructed. The data is actually recoverable with special techniques. In this case, the media is recycled and used within the company again. The data-wiping technique is used to clear data from media by overwriting new data to that media or by performing low-level formats. A regular format within the operating system is not enough because it can leave data behind, known as *data remanence*. Data remanence can exist within cluster tips. A cluster tip is the last bit of a cluster that is not used by a file, and typically is not automatically erased with the rest of the cluster when doing standard formatting or deleting. Remnants of data can exist in these cluster tips, which can be removed by using specific third-party data-wiping software, purging, or low-level formats. The low-level format is initiated through third-party software (or, in some cases, in the BIOS), which formats the drive in a way that is similar to when the drive first came from the manufacturer. In some cases, patterns of ones and zeros are written to the entire drive. Several software programs are available to accomplish this. Low-level formats are often frowned upon because they can reduce the lifespan of a drive, and so might not be acceptable if the drive is to be recycled within the company.

- **Purging:** Also known as sanitizing, this is once again the removal of data, but this time, it's done in such a way so that it cannot be reconstructed by any known technique; in this case the media is released outside the company. Special bit-level erasure software (or other means) is employed to completely destroy all data on the media. This type of software will comply with the U.S. Department of Defense (DoD) 5220.22-M standard, which requires seven full passes of rewrites. It is also possible to degauss the disk, which renders the data unreadable but might also cause physical damage to the drive. Tools such as electromagnetic degaussers and permanent magnet degaussers can be used to permanently purge information from a disk.

- **Destruction:** This is when the storage media is physically destroyed through pulverizing, shredding, pulping, incineration, and so on. At this point, the media can be disposed of in accordance with municipal guidelines. Some organizations require a certificate of destruction to show that a drive has indeed been destroyed. This is obtained from the third-party vendor that performs the drive destruction.

The type of data removal used will be dictated by the data stored on the drive. If there is no personally identifiable information, or other sensitive information, it might simply be cleared and released outside the company. But in many cases, organizations will specify purging of data if the drive is to leave the building. In cases where a drive previously contained confidential or top secret data, the drive will usually be destroyed.

Incident Response Procedures

Incident response is a set of procedures that an investigator follows when examining a computer security incident. Incident response procedures are a part of computer security **incident management**, which can be defined as the monitoring and detection of security events on a computer network and the execution of proper responses to those security events.

However, often, IT employees of the organization discover the incident. Sometimes they act as the investigators also. It depends on the resources and budget of the organization. So, it is important for the IT personnel to be well briefed on policies regarding the reporting and disclosure of incidents.

Don't confuse an incident with an event. An example of a single event might be a single stop error on a Windows computer. In many cases, the blue screen of death (BSOD) won't occur again, and regardless, it has been logged in case that it does. The event should be monitored, but that is about all. An example of an incident would be when several DDoS attacks are launched at an organization's web servers over the course of a work day. This will require an incident response team that might include the security administrator, IT or senior management, and possibly a liaison to the public and local municipality.

You will find that organizations might use varying incident response processes. The National Institute of Standards and Technology (NIST) breaks the process down into four main phases. The CompTIA Security+ objectives include six phases. In the past, I have worked with organizations that break the process down into as many as ten phases. The key is to know the policies/procedures of whatever organization *you* work for. As far as the CompTIA Security+ objectives' incident response plan (IR), the process can be summed up as follows:

Key Topic

Phase 1.   **Preparation:** It all comes down to preparation. Consider a data breach, for example. An organization with no planning will take much longer to repair the problem and will have a hard time controlling the damage and loss. But an organization with a well-planned incident response procedure (in advance), a strong security posture, and a knowledgeable chief information security officer (CISO) will be able to limit the damage (to data and to the company reputation) by: quickly discovering the breach; having an internal response team ready to take action; obtaining forensics data quickly; and beginning a seamless notification process and inquiry response plan.

Phase 2.   **Identification:** The recognition of whether an event that occurs should be classified as an incident. Once identified, you might be required to make contact with other groups or escalate the problem if necessary.

Phase 3.   **Containment:** Isolating the problem. For example, if it is a network attack, the attacker should be extradited to a padded cell where the attacker can be analyzed and monitored. Or if only one server has been affected so far by a worm or virus, it should be physically disconnected from the network. The same goes for devices—they should be removed from the network or from a connected computer if the incident concerns them. This phase might also include evidence gathering (in a way that preserves the evidence's integrity) and further investigation so that you can ascertain exactly what happened and why.

Phase 4.   **Eradication:** Removal of the attack or threat, quarantine of the computer(s), device removal if necessary, and other mitigation techniques covered previously in this book.

Phase 5.   **Recovery:** Retrieve data, repair systems, re-enable servers and networks, reconstitute server rooms and/or the IT environment, and so on. Damage and loss control comes into play here; it can be a very slow process to make sure that as much data is recovered as possible.

Phase 6.   **Lessons learned:** The scenario should be reviewed to define what went wrong and why, ultimately defining the lessons to be learned—how the organization can improve. Document the process and make any changes to procedures and processes that are necessary for the future. Damage and loss should be calculated and that information should be shared with the accounting department of the organization. The affected systems should be monitored for any repercussions.

NOTE   At any time during these steps, you might be required to notify your superior and/or escalate the problem to someone with more experience than you. That will depend on your organization's rules and whether you encounter something that you don't understand. It happens, and you need to be able to swallow your pride and escalate if necessary.

Of course, an incident response policy can be much more in depth, specify exact procedures, and vary in content from organization to organization. To find out more about common practices and standards for incident response, see the ISO/IEC 27002:2013 (or 27002:2005) standard, or NIST Special Publication 800-61 Revision 2. Due to the length and breadth of the information, there is far too much to cover in this book. (I supplied some links to these resources in the "View Recommended Resources" document online, or you can search the Internet for one of several documents that whittles down the content to a more manageable size—but still pretty hefty reading material!) The Security+ exam expects you to know only the basics of incident response.

The six-phase process listed previously is a typical example; however, an organization might have more or fewer phases, and its procedures might vary. An organization's typical incident response policy and procedures generally detail the following:

- **Initial incident management process:** This includes who first found the problem, tracking tickets, and various levels of change controls. It also defines **first responders** who perform preliminary analysis of the incident data and determine whether the incident is actually an incident or just an event, and the criticality of the incident.

- **Emergency response detail:** If the incident is deemed to be an emergency, this details how the event is escalated to an emergency incident. It also specifies a coordinator of the incident, how and when the cyber incident response team will meet, lock-down procedures, containment of the incident, repair and test of systems, and further investigation procedures to find the culprit (if there is one).

- **Collection and preservation of evidence:** Sherlock Holmes based his investigations on traditional clues such as footprints, fingerprints, and cigar ash. Analogous to this, a security investigator needs to collect log files, alerts, captured packets, and so on, and preserve the integrity of this information by retaining forensic images of data. Modification of any information or image files during the investigative process will most likely void its validity in a court of law. One way to preserve evidence properly is to establish a **chain of custody**—the chronological documentation or paper trail of evidence. This is something that should be set up immediately at the start of an investigation; it documents who had custody of evidence all the way up to litigation or a court trial (if necessary) and verifies that the evidence has not been modified. Your work might also be affected by a *legal hold*, which is a notification that the normal disposition of data, media, and documents is suspended. An incident response policy lists proper procedures when it comes to the procurement of evidence.

- **Damage and loss control:** The incident response policy also covers how to stop the spread of damage to other IT systems and how to minimize or completely curtail loss of data.

But a lot of this is really just posturing. The toughest part of the job is figuring out what happened during an incident, and how it happened. That means hardcore forensics. This might be taken care of internally, but more often than not it will be a job for third-party vendors—forensics consultants and specialists.

The incident response policy might define how computer forensics (or digital forensics) should be carried out. It might detail how information is to be deciphered from a hard disk or other device. Often, it dictates the use of hard drive hashing so that computer forensics experts can identify tampering by outside entities. It might also specify a list of rules to follow when investigating what an attacker did. For example, forensics investigators verify the integrity of data to ensure that it has not been tampered with. It is important that computer forensics investigations are carried out properly in case legal action is taken. Policies detailing the proper collection and preservation of evidence can be of assistance when this is the case.

There are some basic forensic procedures concerning data acquisition that can be utilized within the incident response process. Most commonly, these are applied during the containment phase, but could be performed during other phases as well. Some of these include:

- **Capture and hash system images:** If a computer's data is to be used as evidence, the entire drive should be imaged (copied) before it is investigated. The imaging process should be secured and logged, and the image itself should be hashed; the hashing process should take place before and after the image is created. This will protect the image from tampering and prove the integrity of the image. Generally, imaging is done to the hard drive of the computer, but if the computer is on, memory and other components/media can also be imaged. It is important to consider order of volatility (OOV) when imaging any media, as discussed further down in this list. LiveCDs, LiveDVDs, and flash drives are commonly used to take an image of a computer. These are operating systems that run directly off of removable media. Because they are outside of the computer's regular OS environment, they are excellent options if you don't want to disturb the system. Examples of these include Knoppix and BackTrack.

- **Analyze data with software tools:** The data files may have to be analyzed carefully. Forensic toolkits (FTKs) can be invaluable for this. Examples include Guidance Software's EnCase, AccessData's Forensic Toolkit, The Sleuth Kit (open source), Disk Investigator (freeware), and Defiant Technologies' DiskDigger, to name a few.

- **Capture screenshots:** A computer that is being investigated might be compromised. Therefore, it is usually not wise to use screen-capturing software that is installed on the affected computer. Instead, take actual photos of the various screens you wish to capture using a camera.

- **Review network traffic captures and logs:** As part of an investigation, an analyst will review network captures made with a network sniffing program such as Wireshark (covered in Chapters 12, "Vulnerability and Risk Assessment," and 13, "Monitoring and Auditing"). Logs should also be preserved, hashed, and stored, including firewall logs, server logs, and router/switch logs. Various network device logs are discussed in Chapters 6 through 9.

- **Capture video:** Any video surveillance equipment that recorded an incident will need to be analyzed. Before doing so, recorded video should be captured to a computer or to an external media device. Once again, the process should be secured and logged so that a person cannot claim that the evidence has been tampered with. Different municipalities, governments, and organizations will have varying policies on how this is to be accomplished. A forensic analyst should be well versed on these policies before responding to an incident. Keep in mind that the time stamp for video might be incorrect. When this happens, the investigator should establish what "real" time is, using a legitimate time server. The "real" time should be compared to the time stamp of the video. The difference between the two is known as the *record time offset*.

- **Consider the order of volatility (OOV):** OOV can be summarized as the life expectancy of various types of captured data during forensic analysis. For example, optical discs can be preserved for tens of years, and USB flash drives and tape backup can usually be preserved for years. Hard drives can be expected to last from 1 to 5 years. However, information stored in memory, cache, or CPU registers, and any running processes, only last for seconds (or even milliseconds or nanoseconds). The OOV of media and captured data should be considered when gathering evidence that will be used in a court of law.

- **Take statements from witnesses:** Witnesses are people who were present during an event and were cognizant of what happened during the event. They are used during court cases and investigations to describe what they saw, heard, smelled, felt, and so on. A witness can corroborate evidence that was gathered from video, computer logs, captures, and other technical evidence.

- **Review licensing:** Depending on the situation, you might need to locate licenses (or lack thereof) for software, client connections, and hardware; for example, the client access licenses (CALs) being used to access a Windows Server. *License compliance violation* can have legal ramifications, not to mention availability and integrity repercussions.

- **Track man hours and expenses:** Every action that is taken by the investigators of an incident response team should be logged and documented so as to act as a proper audit trail. Investigators normally need to sign in before being allowed access to an affected area or computer. The total man hours, sign in and sign out times, as well as any expenses incurred should be thoroughly documented. Man hours might be tracked through a computer system. For more information on the login of users, and policies governing how and when they can log in, see Chapter 11.

When an examiner collects digital evidence, he or she should abide by *best practices*. One best practice is to document everything (a fairly simple concept that we have mentioned so many times that you should now have documentation on the brain). But best practices can be more encompassing. For example, the following example procedure defines a best practice for preserving evidence (including live, volatile data in memory):

1. Photograph the computer and scene.

2. If the computer is off, *do not* turn it on. (Skip to #7.)

3. If the computer is on, photograph the screen.

4. Collect live data from the RAM image.

5. Collect other live data such as logged-on users, the network connection state, and so on.

6. Only if the drive is encrypted, collect a logical image of the drive. Special software will be required.

7. Unplug the power cord from the computer. If the computer is a laptop or mobile device and it does not shut down properly, then remove the battery.

8. Diagram and label all cords.

9. Document all device model numbers and serial numbers that are visible.

10. Disconnect all cords and devices.

11. Collect an image of the hard drive using a hardware imager. Or, if a hardware imager is not available, use one of the software tools mentioned previously in this section. However, if that is the case, this step should be moved to earlier in the sequence (before all cables were disconnected). Next, hash the image.

12. Package all components using antistatic evidence bags.

13. Collect additional storage media and store it using antistatic evidence bags.

14. Keep all media away from magnets, radio transmitters, and so on.

15. Collect instruction manuals, documentation, and notes.

16. Document all steps performed during the seizure.

That is a general procedure. But it will vary depending on the scene, the tools you have at your disposal, and whether or not the computer was on (or sleeping) when you arrived.

Now, in general, I know what you are thinking: With all these policies and procedures in place, how does anything ever get done?! And how do incidents get analyzed quickly enough so as not to become a disaster? Well, training is important. Personnel need to be trained quickly and efficiently without getting too much into the minutia of things. They also need to be trained to *take action* quickly. By narrowing down an organization's policies to just what an employee needs to know, you can create a short but sweet list of key points for the employee to remember. *Need-to-know* is in itself an important security concept in companies. It is designed as much to hide information from people as it is to prevent information overload. For example, if a person were choking, the information you want to know is how to perform the Heimlich Maneuver; you don't care why a person chokes, what the person ate for breakfast, or how specifically the maneuver works. This concept helps when there is an event or incident; the employees don't need to sift through wads of policies to find the right action to take, because they are on a need-to-know basis and will quickly execute what they have been trained to do. Need-to-know also comes into play when confidential or top secret information is involved. In classified environments, top secret information is divided into pieces, only some of which particular people have access to. This compartmentalizing of information not only helps to secure data, it also increases productivity and efficiency in the workforce.

IT Security Frameworks

We have discussed a lot in this book so far. It can leave some people's heads spinning. One way to reduce the chaos is to implement an IT security framework. This could be something that your organization devises or it could be a widely accepted set of standards. The goal of an IT security framework is to provide an implementable set of security controls for the IT environment and document the processes, procedures, and policies used to perform the implementation.

While an organization might opt to create its own framework, it makes sense for organizations—especially larger ones—to use standards that have already been thoroughly planned out, or at least base their framework on those standards; for example, the ISO/IEC 27000 family of information security standards. We mentioned ISO/IEC 27002:2013 already but you will find that there are several others. You can find more information at this link: https://www.iso.org/isoiec-27001-information-security.html. Then there is the NIST, which defines all kinds of guidelines and recommendations within the SP 800 and SP 1800 publication groups. See this link for more information: http://csrc.nist.gov/publications/PubsSPs.html. Next, there is ISACA's Control Objectives for Information and Related Technologies (COBIT) framework, which divides IT into four sections: 1) plan and organize; 2) acquire and implement; 3) deliver and support; and 4) monitor and evaluate. That pretty much sums up everything we've talked about in this book! Also, you might be interested in the Information Technology Infrastructure Library (ITIL), Business Information Services Library (BiSL), and Project Management Body of Knowledge (PMBOK). A good NIST document that combines the usage of several of these can be found at this link: https://www.nist.gov/sites/default/files/documents/cyberframework/cybersecurity-framework-021214.pdf. You will also find that the U.S. government and military have their own resources on the subject, or depending on the scenario, will use one of the aforementioned standards.

So, some of these are regulatory, and you as an employee *must* abide by any of them that are applicable to your organization or profession. Some are nonregulatory, but usually the organization strongly urges its employees to accept them. Most of what I detailed so far are used in the United States, but there are other specific standards and guidelines used by other countries. In some cases, for example in the European Union, guidelines are international.

Reference frameworks can also be industry-specific, or could define how precise tasks and problems within an organization are to be approached. For example, the company you work for might repair mobile devices for corporations. This company would require a specific secure configuration guide detailing how the mobile devices are repaired, stored, handled, and so on. Or, you might be interested in benchmarking your servers. A detailed list of procedures is vital so that you obtain reliable results in a controlled environment. Then there is software development: When building software, you might embrace the concept of *use case analysis*, which is a requirement analysis technique practiced in software engineering. The use case analysis can benefit from well-written procedures within an IT security framework. Let's not forget about software-defined networking (SDN), which is an approach to computer networking that allows admins to programmatically control and manage network behavior via open interfaces such as OpenFlow and Cisco's Open Network Environment. SDN can benefit greatly from a well-thought-out framework.

Your IT security framework might include risk analysis and vulnerability assessment tools and how to use them. For example, using the Security Content Automation Protocol (SCAP) to automate vulnerability management. The framework might also incorporate how to properly utilize enterprise resource planning (ERP) software, which is used to manage and automate many back-office functions of technology in a larger organization. The examples are endless—really, just about anything we talked about in this book can be incorporated into your IT security framework.

So you see, the IT security framework could be large or small. It might deal with a specific task, or many tasks within an organization. But often, the content in the framework can be applied to many different solutions and implementations. The goal is to organize a group of processes, procedures, and policies of your organization into a single cohesive agenda that all employees can easily understand and work within.

From a security perspective, what this means is that the IT security framework—if designed properly—can help an organization to provide for defense in depth of systems and networks, and increase the confidentiality, integrity, and availability of data.

Chapter Summary

For an organization to realize a high level of security, the implementation of policies and procedures is highly recommended, and in some cases may be mandatory. Data sensitivity can be classified to better define which users are allowed to access specific data. Personnel policies such as privacy policies, acceptable use, change management, separation of duties, job rotation, succession planning, and onboarding are all very useful to an organization in that they help to identify exactly what a user is supposed to be doing—and not doing—and how the user will be trained and brought into the mold, so to speak.

Policies are also used to describe what happens to data when it is no longer needed, and what should be done with the media that holds the data; whether it is the clearing of data, the purging of data and other methods of sanitizing data, or even the destruction of the media. This might be necessary at the end of a particular device's lifespan.

The terms *policy* and *procedure* are sometimes used interchangeably—it will depend on the organization. However, for many companies, the policy is often a broader concept, whereas the procedure is a very specific step-by-step instruction. Perhaps the most important procedure is the one that defines what an organization will do during an *incident*. One thing that we can easily forget to do is to try to learn from incidents—because they will happen at some point. Proper documentation can really drive home the idea of the *lesson learned*. It can help us to recall what the specific problem was and why it occurred, ultimately allowing us to define ways to prevent it from happening again. It's all of these policies and procedures, and the people who implement them, that contribute to the overall security plan of an organization. All of the technical know-how and the assessments and analysis that we discussed throughout the book can be leveraged by the power of well-defined organizational policies and procedures. And those can collectively be planned and organized through the use of an IT security framework.

Chapter Review Activities

Use the features in this section to study and review the topics in this chapter.

Review Key Topics

Review the most important topics in the chapter, noted with the Key Topic icon in the outer margin of the page. Table 18-5 lists a reference of these key topics and the page number on which each is found.

Key Topic

Table 18-5   Key Topics for Chapter 18

Key Topic Element	Description	Page Number
Table 18-3	Acts passed concerning the disclosure of data and PII	616
Table 18-4	Summary of policy types	622
Numbered list	Six phases of incident response process	628
Bulleted list	Forensic procedures	630

Define Key Terms

Define the following key terms from this chapter, and check your answers in the glossary:

change management, separation of duties, acceptable use policy (AUP), mandatory vacations, onboarding, due diligence, due care, due process, personally identifiable information (PII), service-level agreement (SLA), memorandum of understanding (MoU), interconnection security agreement (ISA), incident response, incident management, first responders, chain of custody

Complete the Real-World Scenarios

Complete the Real-World Scenarios found on the companion website (www.pearsonitcertification.com/title/9780789758996). You will find a PDF containing the scenario and questions, and also supporting videos and simulations.

Review Questions

Answer the following review questions. Check your answers with the correct answers that follow.

1. Which method would you use if you were disposing hard drives as part of a company computer sale?

    A. Destruction

    B. Purging

    C. Clearing

    D. Formatting

2. Which of these governs the disclosure of financial data?

    A. SOX

    B. HIPAA

    C. GLB

    D. Top secret

3. You are told by your manager to keep evidence for later use at a court proceeding. Which of the following should you document?

    A. Disaster recovery plan

    B. Chain of custody

    C. Key distribution center

    D. Auditing

4. Which law protects your Social Security number and other pertinent information?

    A. HIPAA

    B. SOX

    C. The National Security Agency

    D. The Gramm-Leach-Bliley Act

5. Which of the following is not one of the steps of the incident response process?

   A. Eradication

   B. Recovery

   C. Containment

   D. Non-repudiation

6. Your company expects its employees to behave in a certain way. How could a description of this behavior be documented?

   A. Chain of custody

   B. Separation of duties

   C. Code of ethics

   D. Acceptable use policy

7. You are a forensics investigator. What is the most important reason for you to verify the integrity of acquired data?

   A. To ensure that the data has not been tampered with

   B. To ensure that a virus cannot be copied to the target media

   C. To ensure that the acquired data is up to date

   D. To ensure that the source data will fit on the target media

8. You are the security administrator for your organization. You have just identified a malware incident. Of the following, what should be your first response?

   A. Containment

   B. Removal

   C. Recovery

   D. Monitoring

9. Employees are asked to sign a document that describes the methods of accessing a company's servers. Which of the following best describes this document?

   A. Acceptable use policy

   B. Chain of custody

   C. Incident response

   D. Privacy Act of 1974

10. One of the developers for your company asks you what he should do before making a change to the code of a program's authentication. Which of the following processes should you instruct him to follow?

    A. Chain of custody

    B. Incident response

    C. Disclosure reporting

    D. Change management

11. As a network administrator, one of your jobs is to deal with Internet service providers. You want to ensure that a provider guarantees end-to-end traffic performance. What is this known as?

    A. SLA

    B. VPN

    C. DRP

    D. WPA

12. When it comes to security policies, what should HR personnel be trained in?

    A. Maintenance

    B. Monitoring

    C. Guidelines and enforcement

    D. Vulnerability assessment

13. In a classified environment, clearance to top secret information that enables access to only certain pieces of information is known as what?

    A. Separation of duties

    B. Chain of custody

    C. Non-repudiation

    D. Need to know

14. What is documentation that describes minimum expected behavior known as?

    A. Need to know

    B. Acceptable usage

    C. Separation of duties

    D. Code of ethics

15. You are the security administrator for your company. You have been informed by human resources that one of the employees in accounting has been terminated. What should you do?

    A. Delete the user account.

    B. Speak to the employee's supervisor about the person's data.

    C. Disable the user account.

    D. Change the user's password.

16. Your organization already has a policy in place that bans flash drives. What other policy could you enact to reduce the possibility of data leakage?

    A. Disallow the saving of data to a network share

    B. Enforce that all work files have to be password protected

    C. Disallow personal music devices

    D. Allow unencrypted HSMs

17. Which of the following requires special handling and policies for data retention and distribution? (Select the two best answers.)

    A. Phishing

    B. Personal electronic devices

    C. SOX

    D. PII

18. One of the accounting people is forced to change roles with another accounting person every three months. What is this an example of?

    A. Least privilege

    B. Job rotation

    C. Mandatory vacation

    D. Separation of duties

19. Your organization uses a third-party service provider for some of its systems and IT infrastructure. Your IT director wants to implement a governance, risk, and compliance (GRC) system that will oversee the third party and promises to provide overall security posture coverage. Which of the following is the most important activity that should be considered?

    A. Baseline configuration

    B. SLA monitoring

    C. Security alerting and trending

    D. Continuous security monitoring

20. Which of the following is the least volatile when performing incident response procedures?

    A. RAM

    B. Registers

    C. Hard drive

    D. RAID cache

21. Which of the following is a *best practice* when a mistake is made during a forensic examination?

    A. The examiner should document the mistake and work around the problem.

    B. The examiner should attempt to hide the mistake during the examination.

    C. The examiner should disclose the mistake and assess another area of the disc.

    D. The examiner should verify the tools before, during, and after an examination.

Answers and Explanations

1. **B.** Purging (or sanitizing) removes all the data from a hard drive so that it cannot be reconstructed by any known technique. If a hard drive were destroyed, it wouldn't be of much value at a company computer sale. Clearing is the removal of data with a certain amount of assurance that it cannot be reconstructed; this method is usually used when recycling the drive within the organization. Formatting is not nearly enough to actually remove data because it leaves data residue, which can be used to reconstruct data.

2. **A.** SOX, or Sarbanes-Oxley, governs the disclosure of financial and accounting data. HIPAA governs the disclosure and protection of health information. GLB, or the Gramm-Leach-Bliley Act of 1999, enables commercial banks, investment banks, securities firms, and insurance companies to consolidate. Top secret is a classification given to confidential data.

3. **B.** A chain of custody is the chronological documentation or paper trail of evidence. A disaster recovery plan details how a company will recover from a disaster with such methods as backup data and sites. A key distribution center is used with the Kerberos protocol. Auditing is the verification of logs and other information to find out who did what action and when and where.

4. **D.** The Gramm-Leach-Bliley Act protects private information such as Social Security numbers. HIPAA deals with health information privacy. SOX, or the Sarbanes-Oxley Act of 2002, applies to publicly held companies and accounting firms and protects shareholders in the case of fraudulent practices.

5. **D.** Non-repudiation, although an important part of security, is not part of the incident response process. Eradication, containment, and recovery are all parts of the incident response process.

6. **C.** The code of ethics describes how a company wants its employees to behave. A chain of custody is a legal and chronological paper trail. Separation of duties means that more than one person is required to complete a job. Acceptable use policy is a set of rules that restricts how a network or a computer system may be used.

7. **A.** Before analyzing any acquired data, you need to make sure that the data has not been tampered with, so you should verify the integrity of the acquired data before analysis.

8. **A.** Most organizations' incident response procedures will specify that containment of the malware incident should be first. Next would be the removal, then recovery of any damaged systems, and finally monitoring that should actually be going on at all times.

9. **A.** Acceptable use (or usage) policies set forth the principles for using IT equipment such as computers, servers, and network devices. Employees are commonly asked to sign such a document that is a binding agreement that they will try their best to adhere to the policy.

10. **D.** He should follow the change management process as dictated by your company's policies and procedures. This might include filing forms in paper format and electronically, and notifying certain departments of the proposed changes before they are made.

11. **A.** An SLA, or service-level agreement, is the agreement between the Internet service provider and you, defining how much traffic you are allowed and what type of performance you can expect. A VPN is a virtual private network. A DRP is a disaster recovery plan. And WPA is Wi-Fi Protected Access.

12. **C.** Human resources personnel should be trained in guidelines and enforcement. A company's standard operating procedures will usually have more information about this. However, a security administrator might need to train these employees in some areas of guidelines and enforcement.

13. **D.** In classified environments, especially when accessing top secret information, a person can get access to only what he needs to know.

14. **D.** A code of ethics is documentation that describes the minimum expected behavior of employees of a company or organization. Need to know deals with the categorizing of data and how much an individual can access. Acceptable usage defines how a user or group of users may use a server or other IT equipment. Separation of duties refers to a task that requires multiple people to complete.

15. **C.** When an employee has been terminated, the employee's account should be disabled, and the employee's data should be stored for a certain amount of time, which should be dictated by the company's policies and procedures. There is no need to speak to the employee's supervisor. It is important not to delete the user account because the company may need information relating to that account later on. Changing the user's password is not enough; the account should be disabled.

16. **C.** By creating a policy that disallows personal music devices, you reduce the possibility of data leakage. This is because many personal music devices can store data files, not just music files. This could be a difficult policy to enforce since smartphones can play music and store data. That's when you need to configure your systems so that those devices cannot connect to the organization's network. DLP devices would also help to prevent data leakage. Network shares are part of the soul of a network; without them, there would be chaos as far as stored data. If network shares are configured properly, there shouldn't be much of a risk of data leakage. Password protecting files is something that would be hard to enforce, and the encryption used could very easily be subpar and easily cracked. Hardware security modules (HSMs) are inherently encrypted; that is their purpose. To allow an HSM would be a good thing, but there are no unencrypted HSMs.

17. **B and D.** PII (personally identifiable information) must be handled and distributed carefully to prevent ID theft and fraud. In a BYOD environment, personal electronic devices should also be protected and secured and require special policies as well because the devices are being used for personal *and* business purposes. Phishing is the attempt at obtaining information fraudulently. SOX (Sarbanes-Oxley) is an act that details the disclosure of banking information.

18. **B.** Job rotation is when people switch jobs, usually within the same department. This is done to decrease the risk of fraud. It is closely linked with separation of duties, which is when multiple people work together to complete a task; each person is given only a piece of the task to accomplish. Least privilege is when a process (or a person) is given only the bare minimum needed to complete its function. Mandatory vacations are when an employee is forced to take X number of consecutive days of vacation away from the office.

19. **D.** The most important activity when implementing a GRC system in this scenario is continuous security monitoring. It will provide for a secure posture while overseeing the work of the third-party vendor. Baselining is important as well as part of vulnerability management, but the answer "baseline configuration" refers more to the building of a baseline, and not the constant monitoring of that baseline. An SLA is a service-level agreement, which, once agreed to, isn't something you normally *monitor* so to speak. It is a contract of sorts. Security alerting and trending is a part of continuous security monitoring.

20. **C.** Of the listed answers, a hard drive would be considered the least volatile when performing incident response procedures. The order of volatility defines any type of registers as the most volatile, and cache and RAM as slightly less volatile. On the other hand, backup tapes are less volatile than hard drives, and optical discs are less volatile as well. Those last two options make for good options if forensics data needs to be stored over the long term.

21. **A.** The best practice in this scenario is to document. In fact, you should always document. Document everything to be on the safe side. Work around the problem as best you can. Never try to hide anything. It could be costly to the investigation, and your livelihood. You shouldn't have to assess another area of the disc, because you have made a copy (or more than one) and should be able to still access that portion of the disc where the mistake occurred. You should always verify the tools and software used, but this is more of a standard procedure and less of a *best practice*; besides, it doesn't necessarily have to do with the mistake.

This chapter covers the following subjects:

- **Getting Ready and the Exam Preparation Checklist:** This section gives you a step-by-step list on how to go about taking the exam. It also shows one of my favorite study methods—the cheat sheet.

- **Tips for Taking the Real Exam:** In this section, you learn all my certification test taking techniques that I have developed over the past 20 years.

- **Beyond the CompTIA Security+ Certification:** This section briefly discusses your future and the possibilities that are out there.

Now you've done it! You've accessed the final chapter. We are at the final countdown! This chapter shows you how to go about taking the exam. Then it goes over some tips and tricks I have used over the years that have helped me to pass multiple certification exams. Finally, we discuss some of the possible future avenues that can lead you to a career in IT security.

CHAPTER 19

Taking the Real Exam

Getting Ready and the Exam Preparation Checklist

The CompTIA Security+ certification exam can be taken by anyone. There are no prerequisites, although CompTIA recommends prior networking experience and the Network+ certification. For more information on CompTIA and the Security+ exam, go to the following link: https://certification.comptia.org/.

To acquire your Security+ certification, you need to pass the SY0-501 exam. This exam consists of multiple-choice and performance-based questions. The exam is administered by Pearson VUE. You need to register with that test agency in order to take the exam. To do so, go to the following link: http://www.pearsonvue.com/comptia/.

NOTE If you have never taken a CompTIA exam before, and depending on your location, you might have to create an account with CompTIA first before registering for an exam with a testing agency. Receiving your CompTIA ID could take up to 48 hours to complete. I recommend you check this ahead of time so that there are no surprises once you are ready to register for the exam.

CompTIA uses a somewhat unorthodox grading scale, so it can be difficult to estimate what percentage of questions you need to get correct to pass the exam. To be safe, the best bet is to attempt to know as much as possible and shoot for 90% correct or higher when taking the practice exams provided with this book.

It is important to be fully prepared for the exam, so I created a checklist that you can use to make sure you have covered all the bases. The checklist is shown in Table 19-1. It assumes that you have read this entire book up to this point.

Place a check in the status column as each item is completed. Historically, my readers and students have benefited greatly from this type of checklist.

Table 19-1   Exam Preparation Checklist

Step	Item	Details	SY0-501 Status
1.	Review the end-of-chapter questions.	The first step in your exam preparation checklist is to review all the end-of-chapter questions. There are over 400 of them in total, offering you a lot of prep before you move on to the practice exams. You can review them in the text or, if you have the accompanying disc, electronically. Make sure you understand the concepts thoroughly before moving on to the following steps. Note: During this stage you might also want to check your local testing center and see whether there are any delays for the Security+ exam. If you are under a deadline and you see that there are delays of up to a week or two, consider other testing center locations, or consider scheduling your exam now to save your seat. If you do, be sure to commit to your study schedule. Otherwise, if there are no delays, continue through the steps as normal.	
2.	Complete simulations and watch videos.	You can find more than 30 videos and 30 simulations on the accompanying website (www.pearsonitcertification.com/title/9780789758996). Go through them and be sure to practice any corresponding hands-on skills on your own computers and networks. This hands-on practice will help you with the performance-based questions on the real exam, and more importantly will strengthen you for the IT field.	

Step	Item	Details	SY0-501 Status
3.	Complete the Practice Exam in the book.	Directly after this chapter is an 80-question practice exam. Your goal should be to get at least 90% correct on this exam the *first time through*. Do not continue to any other exams until you can score at least 90% correct on this exam (100% would be even better!). Additional practice exams can be found on the accompanying website. When using the practice exams, be sure to understand why the correct answer is correct and also why incorrect answers are incorrect. The explanations should help you in this regard. However, if any names, acronyms, or concepts seem new to you, go back to the chapter and section where the concept is covered and review them. Also, review the names and acronyms in the glossary, which is located after the practice exam.	
4.	Visit my website.	Make use of the Security+ section of my website: www.davidlprowse.com. Feel free to ask questions about any of the practice exam questions and explanations, or other items within this book. That's why I am here! On the site you will also find the book's errata page and additional helpful videos.	
5.	Create a cheat sheet.	A cheat sheet can be very helpful for late-stage studying. See Table 19-2 for an example. The act of writing down important details helps to commit them to memory. This sheet should have facts that are tough to memorize. Due to this, each person's cheat sheet will vary. Keep in mind that you will not be allowed to take this into the actual testing room. (It's not actually for "cheating!") One great way to help build your "cheat" sheet is to go back through all of the key topics in the book.	

Step	Item	Details	SY0-501 Status
6.	Register for the exam.	Do not register until you have completed the previous steps; you shouldn't register until you are fully prepared (unless you saw that the testing center was delayed during step 1). When you are ready, schedule the exam to commence within a day or two so that you won't forget what you learned!	
		Registration can be done over the phone or online; although, online is much easier for many people. Register at Pearson VUE at the following website: http://www.pearsonvue.com/comptia/.	
		You need to input your personal information into a secure website. Afterward, you will be assigned an ID#, which you can refer to for all your exams. They accept payment by major credit card for the exam fee.	
		Note: Watch for discounts, discount codes, and reimbursement programs.	
7.	Final study.	Study from the cheat sheet (and perhaps the practice exams) during the day or two between when you registered and the day of the exam.	
		If you need to delay your exam for any reason, reschedule, then go back to steps 1 and 2 (and optionally 3), and retake the practice exams until the test day is a day or two away. Remember that you must give the testing center at least 48 hours' notice if you wish to reschedule. Note: This timeframe can change at any time.	
8.	Take the exam!	Good luck! Check mark the column to the right when you pass. Let me know on my website when you have passed the exam!	

Table 19-2 gives a partial example of a cheat sheet that you can create to aid in your studies. For example, the first row shows common ports. Add information that you think is important or difficult to memorize. Keep the descriptions short and to the point. A few examples are listed in the table.

Table 19-2 Example Cheat Sheet

Concept	Fill in the Appropriate Information Here
Common port numbers	FTP: Port 21
	SSH: Port 22
	SMTP: Port 25 (465 for SSL/TLS encrypted SMTP)
	(Complete for all ports.)
Access control models	MAC: Mandatory access control—Uses labels, has predefined privileges.
	DAC: Discretionary access control—Uses ACLs, or access control lists. Owner of list establishes access permissions.
	RBAC: Role-based access control—Permissions are assigned to roles instead of individual users. Users are assigned roles.
	ABAC: Attribute-based access control—Dynamic and context-aware model that grants rights to users using IF-THEN statements.
NIDS and NIPS	(Spell out the acronym and give a brief description.)
The CIA of computer security	(Spell out the acronym and give a brief description.)
Etc.*	

* Continue Table 19-2 in this fashion on paper. The idea is to write down various technologies, processes, step-by-step tasks, and so on to commit them to memory.

Tips for Taking the Real Exam

Some of you will be new to certification exams. This section is for you. For others who have taken CompTIA exams before, feel free to skip this section or use it as a review.

The exam is conducted on a computer and has two types of questions. The bulk of the exam consists of multiple-choice questions, where you select one or more correct answers from a list of possibilities. However, there are also some performance-based questions. These might ask you to drag and drop correct answers into their respective slots, or they might ask you to complete a simulation, either within the operating system, in the command-line, or otherwise. This is where your hands-on knowledge is tested. But it shouldn't matter what type of question you receive; if you have studied this book in its entirety, you should be ready for just about anything.

Note that you have the option to skip questions. If you do so, be sure to "flag" or "mark" them before moving on. Feel free to mark any other questions that you have answered but are not completely sure about, or any questions that you think are taking you too long to answer. When you get to the end of the exam, there will be an item review section, which shows you any questions that you did not answer and any that you marked. Though you should try to avoid marking many items and skipping around, sometimes it is unavoidable and can save time in the long run if a question is overly difficult. A good rule of thumb is to keep the marked questions between 10% and 20%. Just be sure to allow some time at the end of the exam to finish up those marked questions!

The following list includes tips and tricks that I have learned over the years when it comes to taking exams. By utilizing these points, you can easily increase your score.

First, let's talk about some good general practices for taking exams:

- **Pick a good time for the exam:** It would appear that the least amount of people are at test centers on Monday and Friday mornings. Consider scheduling during these times. Otherwise, schedule a time that works well for you, when you don't have to worry about anything else. Keep in mind that Saturdays can be busy.

- **Don't over study the day before the exam:** Some people like to study hard the day before; some don't. My recommendation is to study off the cheat sheet you created, but in general, don't overdo it. It's not a good idea to go into overload the day before the exam.

- **Get a good night's rest:** A good night's sleep (7 hours to 9 hours) before the day of the exam is probably the best way to get your mind ready for an exam.

- **Eat a decent breakfast:** Eating is good! Breakfast is number two when it comes to getting your mind ready for an exam, especially if it is a morning exam. Just watch out for the coffee and tea. Too much caffeine for a person who is not used to it can be detrimental to the thinking process.

- **Show up early:** Both testing agencies recommend that you show up 30 minutes prior to your scheduled exam time. This is important; give yourself plenty of time, and make sure you know where you are going. You don't want to have to worry about getting lost or being late. (If it is the first time going to the testing center, consider a test drive a couple days before.) Stress and fear are mind killers. Work on reducing any types of stress the day of and the day before the exam. By the way, you really do need extra time, because when you get to the testing center, you need to show ID, sign forms, get your personal belongings situated, and be escorted to your seat. Have two forms of ID (one, a photo ID, both signed) ready for the administrator of the test center. Turn your phone off when you get to the test center; they'll check that, too.

- **Bring ear plugs:** You never know when you will get a loud testing center—or worse yet, a loud test taker next to you. Ear plugs help to block out any unwanted noise that might show up. Just be ready to show your ear plugs to the test administrator.

- **Brainstorm before starting the exam:** Write down as much as you can remember from the cheat sheet before starting the exam. The testing center is obligated to give you something to write on; make use of it! By getting all the memorization out of your head and on "paper" first, it clears the brain somewhat so that it can tackle the questions. I put "paper" in quotation marks because it might not be paper; it could be a mini dry-erase board or something similar.

- **Take small breaks while taking the exam:** Exams can be brutal. You have to answer up to 100 questions while staring at a screen for an hour or more. Sometimes these screens are old and have seen better days; these older flickering monitors can cause a strain on your eyes. I recommend small breaks and breathing techniques. For example, after going through every 25 questions or so, close your eyes, and slowly take a few deep breaths, holding each one for 5 seconds or so, and releasing each one slowly. Think about nothing while doing so. Remove the test from your mind during these breaks. It takes only half a minute but can really help to get your brain refocused.

- **Be confident:** You have studied hard, gone through the practice exams, created your cheat sheet—done everything you can to prep. These things alone should build confidence. But really, you just have to be confident. You are great...I am great...there is no disputing this!

Now let's talk about some methods to use when faced with difficult questions:

- **Use the process of elimination:** If you are not sure about an answer, first eliminate any answers that are definitely incorrect. You might be surprised how often this works. This is one of the reasons why it is recommended that you not only know the correct answers to the practice exams' questions, but also know why the wrong answers are wrong. The testing center should give you something to write on; use it by writing down the letters of the answers that are incorrect to keep track.

NOTE   Check out this chapter's video. It shows me going through a couple of questions as if I were taking an exam and shows some of my tips and tricks to taking the exam.

- **Be logical in the face of adversity:** The most difficult questions are when two answers appear to be correct, even though the test question requires you to select only one answer. Real exams do not rely on "trick" questions. Sometimes you need to slow down, think logically, and really compare the two possible correct answers.

- **Use your gut instinct:** Sometimes a person taking a test just doesn't know the answer; it happens to everyone. If you have read through the question and all the answers and used the process of elimination, sometimes the gut instinct is all you have left. In some scenarios you might read a question and instinctively know the answer, even if you can't explain why. Tap into this ability. Some test takers write down their gut instinct answer before delving into the question and then compare their thoughtful answer with their gut instinct answer.

- **Don't let one question beat you!:** Don't let yourself get stuck on any one question (especially the performance-based variety). Mark it, move on to the next question, and return to it later. When you spend too much time on one question, the brain gets sluggish. The thing is, with these exams you either know it or you don't. And don't worry too much about it; chances are you are not going to get a perfect score. Remember that the goal is only to pass the exam; how many answers you get right after that is irrelevant. If you have gone through this book thoroughly, you should be well prepared, and you should have plenty of time to go through all the exam questions with time to spare to return to the ones you skipped and marked.

- **If all else fails, guess:** Remember that the exams might not be perfect. A question might seem confusing or appear not to make sense. Leave questions like this until the end, and when you have gone through all the other techniques mentioned, make an educated, logical guess. Try to imagine what the test is after, and why they would be bringing up this topic, vague or strange as it might appear.

And when you finish:

- **Review all your answers:** Use the time allotted to you to review the answers. Chances are you will have time left over at the end, so use it wisely! Make sure that everything you have marked has a proper answer that makes sense to you. But try not to overthink! Give it your best shot and be confident in your answers.

Beyond the CompTIA Security+ Certification

After you pass the exam, consider thinking about your technical future. Technical growth is important. Keeping up with new technology and keeping your technical skills sharp are what can keep you in demand. This technical growth equals job security.

Information Technology (IT) people need to keep learning to foster good growth in the field. Consider additional college courses (or even degrees). Contemplate taking other certification exams after you complete the Security+. The CompTIA Security+ certification acts as a springboard to other certifications. For example, you might choose to go for other more difficult non-vendor certifications such as the CISSP or the CEH. And, of course, there are vendor-specific certifications from Microsoft, Cisco, Check Point, and many others. Now that you know exactly how to go about passing a security-based certification exam, consider more certifications to bolster your resume, and maybe even a computer security degree. Most importantly, keep learning and practicing in a hands-on manner. Experience is the most important element of a resume.

The best advice I can give is to do what you love. From an IT perspective, I usually break that down by technology or concept, as opposed to by the vendor. Products and vendors come and go. Knowledge of a particular device or a distinct program can be fleeting. But skill sets that are based on conceptual technology will have more value in the long-term. Whatever segment (or segments) of security you decide to pursue, learn as much as you can about that field(s) *and* all its vendors. Read up on the latest technologies, visit security websites, read security periodicals, and keep in touch with fellow security people. Consider security conferences and seminars and ongoing training. Taking it to the next level, you might decide that there is a specific security threat that you would like to address. Who knows, in the future you might be interested in developing a security application or a secure hardware device. My advice is this: Good engineering can usually defy malicious individuals; the better you plan your security product, the less chance of its being compromised.

Whatever you decide, I wish you the best of luck in your IT career endeavors. And remember that I am available to answer any of your questions about this book via my website: www.davidlprowse.com.

David L. Prowse

Practice Exam 1: SY0-501

The 80 multiple-choice questions provided here help you determine how prepared you are for the actual exam and which topics you need to review further. Write down your answers on a separate sheet of paper so that you can take this exam again if necessary. Compare your answers against the answer key that follows this exam. Following the answer key are detailed explanations for each question. Additional practice exams can be found on the accompanying Pearson website, www.pearsonitcertification.com/title/9780789758996.

1. As a security administrator, you must be constantly vigilant and always be aware of the security posture of your systems. Which of the following supports this goal?

    A. Establishing baseline reporting

    B. Disabling unnecessary services

    C. Training staff on security policies

    D. Installing anti-malware applications

2. Your network has a DHCP server, AAA server, LDAP server, and e-mail server. Instead of authenticating wireless connections locally at the WAP, you want to utilize RADIUS for the authentication process. When you configure the WAP's authentication screen, what server should you point to, and which port should you use?

    A. The DHCP server and port 67

    B. The AAA server and port 1812

    C. The LDAP server and port 389

    D. The e-mail server and port 143

3. What is it known as when traffic to a website is redirected to another, illegitimate site?

    A. Phishing

    B. Whaling

    C. Pharming

    D. Spim

4. Which of the following protocols operates at the highest layer of the OSI model?

    A. IPsec

    B. TCP

    C. ICMP

    D. SCP

5. What can happen if access mechanisms to data on an encrypted USB hard drive are not implemented correctly?

    A. Data on the USB drive can be corrupted.

    B. Data on the hard drive can be vulnerable to log analysis.

    C. The security controls on the USB drive can be bypassed.

    D. User accounts can be locked out.

6. The helpdesk department for your organization reports that there are increased calls from clients reporting malware-infected computers. Which of the following steps of incident response is the most appropriate as a *first* response?

    A. Recovery

    B. Lessons learned

    C. Identification

    E. Containment

    F. Eradication

7. You want to secure data passing between two points on an IP network. What is the best method to protect from all but the most sophisticated APTs?

    A. Transport encryption

    B. Key escrow

    C. Block ciphers

    D. Stream ciphers

8. You are analyzing why the incident response team of your organization could not identify a recent incident that occurred. Review the following e-mail and then answer the question that follows.

E-mail from the incident response team:

```
A copyright infringement alert was triggered by IP address 11.128.50.1 at
02: 30: 01 GMT.

After reviewing the following logs for IP address 11.128.50.1 we cannot correlate
and identify the incident.
- 02: 25: 23 11.128.50.1 http://externalsite.com/login.asp?user=steve
- 02: 30: 15 11.128.50.1 http://externalsite.com/login.asp?user=amy
- 03: 30: 01 11.128.50.1 http://externalsite.com/access.asp?file=movie.mov
- 03: 31: 08 11.128.50.1 http://externalsite.com/download.asp?movie.mov=ok
```

Why couldn't the incident response team identify and correlate the incident?

A. The logs are corrupt.

B. The chain of custody was not properly maintained.

C. Incident time offsets were not accounted for.

D. Traffic logs for the incident are not available.

9. A security administrator for your organization utilized a heuristic system to detect an anomaly in a desktop computer's baseline. The admin was able to detect an attack even though the signature-based IDS and antivirus software did not detect it. Upon further review, it appears that the attacker had downloaded an executable file on the desktop computer from a USB port and executed it, triggering a privilege escalation. What type of attack has occurred?

A. Directory traversal

B. XML injection

C. Zero day

D. Baiting

10. The security administrator has added the following information to a SOHO router:

```
PERMIT      00:1C:C0:A2:56:18
DENY        01:23:6D:A9:55:EC
```

Now, a mobile device user reports a problem connecting to the network. What is preventing the user from connecting?

A. Port filtering has been implemented.

B. IP address filtering has been implemented.

C. Hardware address filtering has been implemented.

D. WPA2-PSK requires a supplicant on the mobile device.

11. Which of the following can be implemented in hardware or software to protect a web server from XSS attacks?

   A. Flood guard

   B. IDS

   C. URL content filter

   D. WAF

12. Your organization has suffered from several data leaks as a result of social engineering attacks that were conducted over the phone. Your boss wants to reduce the risk of another leak by incorporating user training. Which of the following is the *best* method for reducing data leaks?

   A. Social media and BYOD

   B. Acceptable use

   C. Information security awareness

   D. Data handling and disposal

13. A security administrator is required to submit a new CSR to a CA. What is the first step?

   A. Generate a new private key based on AES

   B. Generate a new public key based on RSA

   C. Generate a new public key based on AES

   D. Generate a new private key based on RSA

14. Bob wants to send an encrypted e-mail to Alice. Which of the following will Alice need to use to verify the validity of Bob's certificate? (Select the two best answers.)

   A. Bob's private key

   B. Alice's private key

   C. The CA's private key

   D. Bob's public key

   E. Alice's public key

   F. The CA's public key

15. What are LDAP and Kerberos commonly used for?

   A. To sign SSL wildcard certificates

   B. To utilize single sign-on capabilities

   C. To perform queries on a directory service

   D. To store usernames and passwords in a FIM system

16. Your server room has most items bolted down to the floor, but some items—such as network testing tools—can be easily removed from the room. Which security control can you implement to allow for automated notification of the removal of an item from the server room?

    A. Environmental monitoring

    B. RFID

    C. EMI shielding

    D. CCTV

17. Your organization uses a SOHO wireless router all-in-one device. The network has five wireless BYOD users and two web servers that are wired to the network. What should you configure to protect the servers from the BYOD users' devices? (Select the two best answers.)

    A. Implement EAP-TLS

    B. Change the default HTTP port

    C. Create a VLAN for the servers

    D. Deny incoming connections to the outside router interface

    E. Disable physical ports

    F. Create an ACL to access the servers

18. You have been tasked with blocking DNS requests and zone transfers coming from outside IP addresses. You analyze your organization's firewall and note that it implements an implicit allow and currently has the following ACL configured for the external interface:

    ```
    permit TCP any any 80
    permit TCP any any 443
    ```

    Which of the following rules would accomplish your goal? (Select the two best answers.)

    A. Change the implicit rule to an implicit deny

    B. Remove the current ACL

    C. Add the following ACL at the top of the current ACL:
       ```
       deny TCP any any 53
       ```

    D. Add the following ACL at the bottom of the current ACL:
       ```
       deny ICMP any any 53
       ```

    E. Apply the current ACL to all interfaces of the firewall

    F. Add the following ACL at the bottom of the current ACL:
       ```
       deny IP any any 53
       ```

19. An employee of your organization was escorted off of the premises for suspicion of fraudulent activity, but the employee had been working for two hours before leaving. You have been asked to find out what files have changed since last night's integrity scan. Which protocols could you use to perform your task? (Select the two best answers.)

   A. MD5

   B. ECC

   C. AES

   D. PGP

   E. HMAC

   F. Blowfish

20. Alice has read and write access to a database. Bob, her subordinate, only has read access. Alice needs to leave to go to a conference. Which access control type should you implement to trigger write access for Bob when Alice is not onsite?

   A. Discretionary access control

   B. Mandatory access control

   C. Rule-based access control

   D. Role-based access control

   E. Attribute-based access control

21. An attacker gained access to your server room by physically removing the proximity reader from the wall near the entrance. This caused the electronic locks on the door to release. Why did the locks release?

   A. The proximity reader was improperly installed.

   B. The system used magnetic locks and the locks became demagnetized.

   C. The system was designed to fail-open for life safety.

   D. The system was installed in a fail-close configuration.

22. Which of the following offer the best protection against brute-forcing passwords? (Select the two best answers.)

   A. MD5

   B. SHA2

   C. Bcrypt

D. AES

E. PBKDF2

F. CHAP

23. On Monday, all employees of your organization report that they cannot connect to the corporate wireless network, which uses 802.1X with PEAP. A technician verifies that no configuration changes were made to the wireless network and its supporting infrastructure, and that there are no outages. Which of the following is the most likely cause of the problem?

   A. The Remote Authentication Dial-In User Service certificate has expired.

   B. The DNS server is overwhelmed with connections and is unable to respond to queries.

   C. There have been too many incorrect authentication attempts and this caused users to be temporarily disabled.

   D. The company IDS detected a wireless attack and disabled the wireless network.

24. The organization you work for, a video streaming company, hired a security consultant to find out how customer credit card information was stolen. He determined that it was stolen while in transit from gaming consoles. What should you implement to secure this data in the future?

   A. Firmware updates

   B. WAF

   C. TCP Wrapper

   D. IDS

25. In a scenario where data integrity is crucial to the organization, which of the following is true about input validation regarding client/server applications?

   A. It must rely on the user's knowledge of the application.

   B. It should be performed on the server side.

   C. It should be performed on the client side only.

   D. It must be protected by SSL.

26. In an environment where the transmission and storage of PII data needs to be encrypted, what methods should you select? (Select the two best answers.)

   A. TFTP

   B. TKIP

   C. SSH

   D. PGP

   E. SNMP

   F. NTLM

27. Your organization is attempting to reduce risk concerning the use of unapproved USB devices to copy files. What could you implement as a security control to help reduce risk?

   A. IDS

   B. DLP

   C. Content filtering

   D. Auditing

28. Alice wishes to send a file to Bob using a PKI. Which of the following types of keys should Alice use to *sign* the file?

   A. Alice's private key

   B. Alice's public key

   C. Bob's public key

   D. Bob's private key

29. Which of the following techniques supports availability when considering a vendor-specific vulnerability in critical industrial control systems?

   A. Verifying that antivirus definitions are up to date

   B. Deploying multiple firewalls at the network perimeter

   C. Incorporating diversity into redundant design

   D. Enforcing application whitelists

30. To achieve multifactor security, what should you implement to accompany password usage and smart cards?

   A. Badge readers

   B. Passphrases

    C. Hard tokens

    D. Fingerprint readers

31. Which port and transport mechanism protocol must be opened on a firewall to allow incoming SFTP connections?

    A. 21 and UDP

    B. 22 and UDP

    C. 21 and TCP

    D. 22 and TCP

32. Users in your organization receive an e-mail encouraging them to click a link to obtain exclusive access to the newest version of a popular smartphone. What is this an example of?

    A. Trust

    B. Intimidation

    C. Scarcity

    D. Familiarity

33. You have been tasked by your boss with calculating the annualized loss expectancy (ALE) for a $5000 server that crashes often. In the past year, the server crashed 10 times, requiring a reboot each time, which resulted in a 10% loss of functionality. What is the ALE of the server?

    A. $500

    B. $5000

    C. $10,000

    D. $50,000

34. A security administrator analyzed the following logs:

```
Host: 10.248.248.67
[02: 15: 11]Successful Login: 045 10.248.248.67:local
[02: 15: 16]Unsuccessful Login: 067 208.159.67.23: RDP
  10.248.248.67
[02: 15: 16]Unsuccessful Login: 072 208.159.67.23: RDP
  10.248.248.67
[02: 15: 16]Unsuccessful Login: 058 208.159.67.23: RDP
  10.248.248.67
[02: 15: 16]Unsuccessful Login: 094 208.159.67.23: RDP
  10.248.248.67
```

What should the security administrator implement as a mitigation method against further attempts?

A. System log monitoring

B. IDS

C. Hardening

D. Reporting

35. What are the best ways for a web programmer to prevent website application code from being vulnerable to XSRF attacks? (Select the two best answers.)

A. Validate input on the client and the server side

B. Ensure HTML tags are enclosed within angle brackets

C. Permit URL redirection

D. Restrict the use of special characters in form fields

E. Use a web proxy to pass website requests between the user and the application

36. Which of the following is a step in deploying a WPA2-Enterprise wireless network?

A. Install a DHCP server on the authentication server

B. Install a digital certificate on the authentication server

C. Install an encryption key on the authentication server

D. Install a token on the authentication server

37. Which of the following is used to validate whether trust is in place and accurate by retuning responses of "good," "unknown," or "revoked"?

A. OCSP

B. PKI

C. CRL

D. RA

38. You have found vulnerabilities in your SCADA system. Unfortunately, changes to the SCADA system cannot be made without vendor approval, which can take months to obtain. Which of the following is the best way to protect the SCADA system in the interim?

A. Install a firewall in the SCADA network

B. Update AV definitions on the SCADA system

    C. Deploy a NIPS at the edge of the SCADA network

    D. Enable auditing of accounts on the SCADA system

39. Your organization's server uses a public, unencrypted communication channel. You are required to implement protocols that allow clients to securely negotiate encryption keys with the server. What protocols should you select? (Select the two best answers.)

    A. ECDHE

    B. PBKDF2

    C. Steganography

    D. Diffie-Hellman

    E. Symmetric encryption

40. Your Internet café operates a public wireless hotspot. Which of the following should you implement?

    A. Disable the SSID

    B. Open system authentication

    C. MAC filter

    D. Reduce the power level

41. There is an important upcoming patch to be released. You are required to test the installation of the patch a dozen times before the patch is distributed to the public. What should you perform to test the patching process quickly and often?

    A. Create a virtualized sandbox and utilize snapshots

    B. Create an image of a patched PC and replicate it to the servers

    C. Create an incremental backup of an unpatched PC

    D. Create a full disk image to restore after each installation

42. Which of the following is the greatest security risk of two or more companies working together under a memorandum of understanding?

    A. An MoU between two parties cannot be held to the same legal standards as a SLA.

    B. MoUs are generally loose agreements that do not have strict guidelines governing the transmission of sensitive data.

    C. Budgetary considerations may not have been written into the MoU.

    D. MoUs have strict policies concerning services performed between entities.

43. An administrator configures Unix accounts to authenticate to a non-Unix server on the internal network. The configuration file incorporates the following information: DC=ServerName and DC=COM. Which service is being used?

   A. SAML

   B. RADIUS

   C. LDAP

   D. TACACS+

44. Your organization (ABC-Services Corp.) has three separate wireless networks used for varying purposes. You conducted a site survey and found the following information from your scans:

```
SSID - State - Channel - Level
ABC-WAP1 - Connected - 1 - 80 dbm
ABC-WAP2 - Connected - 6 - 90 dbm
ABC-WAP3 - Connected - 11 - 75 dbm
ABC-WAP4 - Connected - 4 - 65 dbm
```

   What is occurring here?

   A. Jamming

   B. Packet sniffing

   C. Near field communication

   D. Rogue access point

45. Which of the following is vulnerable to spoofing?

   A. WPA-LEAP

   B. WPA-PEAP

   C. Enabled SSID

   D. MAC filtering

46. Your organization has decided to move large sets of sensitive data to a SaaS cloud provider in order to limit storage and infrastructure costs. Your CIO requires that both the cloud provider and your organization have a clear understanding of the security controls that will be implemented to protect the sensitive data. What kind of agreement is this?

   A. SLA

   B. ISA

   C. MoU

   D. BPA

47. Which of the following is a type of malware that is difficult to reverse engineer?

   A. Logic bomb

   B. Worm

   C. Backdoor

   D. Armored virus

48. Why would you deploy a wildcard certificate?

   A. To extend the renewal date of the certificate

   B. To reduce the burden of certificate management

   C. To increase the certificate's encryption key length

   D. To secure the certificate's private key

49. In the event of a short term power loss to the server room, what should be powered on first in order to establish DNS services?

   A. Apache server

   B. Exchange server

   C. RADIUS

   D. BIND server

50. Which of the following are the best options when it comes to increasing the security of passwords? (Select the two best answers.)

   A. Password age

   B. Password expiration

   C. Password complexity

   D. Password history

   E. Password length

51. You are in the middle of the information gathering stage of the planning and deployment of a role-based access control model. Which of the following is most likely required?

   A. Clearance levels of personnel

   B. Rules under which certain systems can be accessed

   C. Group-based privileges already in place

   D. Matrix of job titles with required privileges

52. Your organization has several conference rooms with wired RJ45 jacks that are used by employees and guests. The employees need to access internal organizational resources, but the guests only need to access the Internet. Which of the following should you implement?

     A. VPN and IPsec

     B. 802.1X and VLANs

     C. Switches and a firewall

     D. NAT and DMZ

53. Which of the following is a secure wireless authentication method that uses a RADIUS server for the authenticating?

     A. CCMP

     B. WEP-PSK

     C. LEAP

     D. WPA2-PSK

54. While running a new network line, you find an active network switch above the ceiling tiles of the CEO's office with cables going in various directions. What attack is occurring?

     A. Impersonation

     B. MAC flooding

     C. Packet sniffing

     D. Spear phishing

55. A security auditing consultant has completed a security assessment and gives the following recommendations:

     1. Implement fencing and additional lighting around the perimeter of the building.

     2. Digitally sign new releases of software.

        Categorically, what is the security consultant recommending? (Select the two best answers.)

     A. Encryption

     B. Availability

     C. Confidentiality

     D. Safety

     E. Fault tolerance

     F. Integrity

56. In the event that a mobile device is stolen, what two security controls can prevent data loss? (Select the two best answers.)

    A. GPS

    B. Asset tracking

    C. Screen locks

    D. Inventory control

    E. Full device encryption

57. What is the technique of adding text to a password when it is hashed?

    A. Rainbow tables

    B. Symmetric cryptography

    C. NTLMv2

    D. Salting

58. What port and transport mechanism does TFTP use by default?

    A. 68 and TCP

    B. 69 and TCP

    C. 68 and UDP

    D. 69 and UDP

59. Your boss has tasked you with ensuring that reclaimed space on a hard drive has been sanitized while the computer is in use. What job should you perform?

    A. Individual file encryption

    B. Full disk encryption

    C. Cluster tip wiping

    D. Storage retention

60. The IT director asks you to verify that the organization's virtualization technology is implemented securely. What should you do?

    A. Verify that virtual machines are multihomed

    B. Perform penetration testing on virtual machines

    C. Subnet the network so that each virtual machine is on a different network segment

    D. Verify that virtual machines have the latest updates and patches installed

61. You have been commissioned by a customer to implement a network access control model that limits remote users' network usage to normal business hours only. You create one policy that applies to all the remote users. What access control model are you implementing?

   A. Role-based access control

   B. Mandatory access control

   C. Discretionary access control

   D. Rule-based access control

62. You review the system logs for your organization's firewall and see that an implicit deny is within the ACL. Which is an example of an implicit deny?

   A. When an access control list is used as a secure way of moving traffic from one network to another.

   B. Implicit deny will deny all traffic from one network to another.

   C. Items not specifically given access are denied by default.

   D. Everything will be denied because of the implicit deny.

63. You suspect that files are being illegitimately copied to an external location. The file server that the files are stored on does not have logging enabled. Which log should you access to find out more about the files that are being copied illegitimately?

   A. DNS log

   B. Firewall log

   C. Antivirus log

   D. System log

64. You look through some graphic files and discover that confidential information has been encoded into the files. These files are being sent to a sister company outside your organization. What is this an example of?

   A. Confidentiality

   B. Cryptography

   C. Digital signature

   D. Steganography

65. You are designing the environmental controls for a server room that contains several servers and other network devices. What roles will an HVAC system play in this environment? (Select the two best answers.)

    A. Shield equipment from EMI

    B. Provide isolation in case of a fire

    C. Provide an appropriate ambient temperature

    D. Maintain appropriate humidity levels

    E. Vent fumes from the server room

66. The IT director recommends that you require your service provider to give you an end-to-end traffic performance guarantee. What document will include this guarantee?

    A. Chain of custody

    B. SLA

    C. DRP

    D. Incident response procedures

67. The IT director asks you to create a solution to protect your network from Internet-based attacks. The solution should include pre-admission security checks and automated remediation and should also integrate with existing network infrastructure devices. Which of the following solutions should you implement?

    A. NAC

    B. NAT

    C. VLAN

    D. Subnetting

68. Your network is an Active Directory domain controlled by a Windows Server domain controller. The Finance group has read permission to the Reports and History shared folders and other shared folders. The Accounting group has read and write permissions to the Reports, AccountRecs, and Statements shared folders. Several users are members of both the Finance and Accounting groups. All the folders are located on a file server. The Everyone group is granted the Full Control NTFS permission for each folder through inheritance, but non-administrative users do not have the right to log on locally at the server. Access to the shared folders is managed through share permissions. It is determined that the Finance group should no longer have read access to the Reports folder.

This change should not affect access permissions granted through membership in other groups. What is the best solution to the problem?

- **A.** Deny the read permission to the Finance group for the Reports folder
- **B.** Deny the read permission individually for each member of the Finance group for the Reports folder
- **C.** Remove the read permission from the Finance group for the Reports folder
- **D.** Delete the Finance group

69. Your network is a Windows domain controlled by a Windows Server domain controller. Your goal is to configure user access to file folders shared to the network. In your organization, directory access is dependent upon a user's role in the organization. You need to keep to a minimum the administrative overhead needed to manage access security. You need to be able to quickly modify a user's permissions if that user is assigned to a different role. A user can be assigned to more than one role within the organization. What solutions should you implement? (Select the two best answers.)

- **A.** Create security groups and assign access permissions based on organizational roles
- **B.** Place users in OUs based on organizational roles
- **C.** Create an OU for each organizational role and link GPOs to each OU
- **D.** Place users' computers in OUs based on user organizational roles
- **E.** Assign access permission explicitly by user account

70. You are in charge of your organization's backup plan. You need to make sure that the data backups are available in case of a disaster. However, you need to keep the plan as inexpensive as possible. Which of the following solutions should you implement?

- **A.** Implement a hot site
- **B.** Implement a cold site
- **C.** Back up data to removable media and store a copy offsite
- **D.** Implement a remote backup solution

71. You are in charge of recycling computers. Some of the computers have hard drives that contain personally identifiable information (PII). What should be done to the hard drive before it is recycled?

    A. The hard drive should be sanitized.

    B. The hard drive should be reformatted.

    C. The hard drive should be destroyed.

    D. The hard drive should be stored in a safe area.

72. Your LAN is isolated from the Internet by a perimeter network. You suspect that someone is trying to gather information about your LAN. The IT director asks you to gather as much information about the attacker as possible while preventing the attacker from knowing that the attempt has been detected. What is the best method to accomplish this?

    A. Deploy a DMZ

    B. Deploy a proxy server in the perimeter network

    C. Deploy a NIPS outside the perimeter network

    D. Deploy a honeypot in the perimeter network

73. You are reviewing your organization's continuity plan, which specifies an RTO of six hours and an RPO of two days. Which of the following is the plan describing?

    A. Systems should be restored within six hours and no later than two days after the incident.

    B. Systems should be restored within two days and should remain operational for at least six hours.

    C. Systems should be restored within six hours with a maximum of two days' worth of data latency.

    D. Systems should be restored within two days with a minimum of six hours' worth of data.

74. One of your servers (10.254.254.201) is only allowing slow and intermittent connections to clients on the network. You check the logs of the server and see a large number of connections from the following IP addresses:

```
10.254.254.38
10.254.254.79
10.254.254.102
11.57.86.86
198.155.201.214
212.119.64.32
```

The connections from these six hosts are overloading the server and causing it to stop responding to requests from clients. What type of attack is happening?

   A. Xmas tree

   B. XSS

   C. DoS

   D. DDoS

75. You have been tasked with sending a decommissioned SSL certificate server's hard drives to be destroyed by a third-party company. What should you implement before sending the drives out? (Select the two best answers.)

   A. Disk wiping

   B. Data retention policies

   C. Removable media encryption

   D. Full disk encryption

   E. Disk hashing

76. During a software development review, the cryptographic engineer advises the project manager that security can be improved by significantly slowing down the runtime of the hashing algorithm and increasing entropy by passing the input and salt back during each iteration. Which of the following best describes what the engineer is trying to achieve?

   A. Key stretching

   B. Confusion

   C. Diffusion

   D. Root of Trust

   E. Monoalphabetic cipher

   F. PRNG

   G. Pass the hash

77. Your organization must achieve compliance for PCI and SOX. Which of the following would best allow the organization to achieve compliance and ensure security? (Select the three best answers.)

   A. Establish a company framework

   B. Compartmentalize the network

   C. Centralize management of all devices on the network

   D. Apply technical controls to meet compliance regulations

   E. Establish a list of users who must work with each regulation

   F. Establish a list of devices that must meet regulations

78. You are a security administrator for a midsized company that uses several applications on its client computers. After the installation of a specialized program on one computer, a software application executed an online activation process. Then, a few months later, the computer experienced a hardware failure. A backup image of the operating system was restored on a newer revision of the same brand and model computer. After that restoration, the specialized program no longer works. Which of the following is the most likely cause of the problem?

   A. The restored image backup was encrypted with the wrong key.

   B. The hash key summary of the hardware and the specialized program no longer match.

   C. The specialized program is no longer able to perform remote attestation due to blocked ports.

   D. The binary files used by the specialized program have been modified by malware.

79. You are a security tester for a penetration testing security company. You are currently testing a website and you perform the following manual query:

`http://www.davidlprowse.com/cookies.jsp?products=5%20and%201=1`

The following response is received in the payload:

`"ORA-000001: SQL command not properly ended"`

Based on the query and the response, what technique are you employing?

   A. Cross-site scripting

   B. SQL injection

   C. Privilege escalation

   D. Fingerprinting

   E. Remote code execution

   F. Zero day

80. You are the security administrator working for a large corporation with many remote workers. You are tasked with deploying a remote access solution for both staff *and* contractors. Company management favors Remote Desktop Services because of its ease of use. Your current risk assessment suggests that you protect Windows as much as possible from direct ingress traffic exposure. Which of the following solutions should you choose?

   A. Change remote desktop to a non-standard port, and implement password complexity for the entire Active Directory domain.

   B. Distribute new IPsec VPN client software to applicable parties, and then virtualize the remote desktop services functionality.

   C. Place the remote desktop server(s) on a screened subnet, and implement two-factor authentication.

   D. Deploy a remote desktop server on your internal LAN, and require an Active Directory integrated SSL connection for access.

Answers to Practice Exam 1

1. A	25. B	49. D	73. C
2. B	26. C and D	50. C and E	74. D
3. C	27. B	51. D	75. A and D
4. D	28. A	52. B	76. A
5. C	29. C	53. C	77. B, D, and F
6. C	30. D	54. C	78. B
7. A	31. D	55. D and F	79. D
8. C	32. C	56. C and E	80. C
9. C	33. B	57. D	
10. C	34. C	58. D	
11. D	35. A and D	59. C	
12. C	36. B	60. D	
13. D	37. A	61. A	
14. D and F	38. C	62. C	
15. B	39. A and D	63. B	
16. B	40. B	64. D	
17. C and F	41. A	65. C and D	
18. A and F	42. B	66. B	
19. A and E	43. C	67. A	
20. C	44. D	68. C	
21. C	45. D	69. A and C	
22. C and E	46. B	70. C	
23. A	47. D	71. A	
24. C	48. B	72. D	

Answers with Explanations

1. Answer: A. Establishing baseline reporting

   Explanation: The key words of the question are "security posture." One of the best methods of monitoring the security posture of your systems is establishing baseline reporting. Baselining is the process of measuring changes in networking, hardware, software, and so on. Creating a baseline consists of selecting something to measure and measuring it consistently for a period of time. It is this baselining (and automated reporting with baselining tools such as Performance Monitor or Wireshark) that allows you to be vigilant and watch over your network carefully in real time.

   See the section "Monitoring Methodologies" in Chapter 13, "Monitoring and Auditing," for more information.

   Incorrect answers: Disabling unnecessary services is an important security concept, but this refers to *hardening* the system, and reducing the attack surface. Training staff on security policies is *educating the user* and is extremely important when attempting to reduce the consequences of successful social engineering attacks. Installing anti-malware applications also hardens the system, and secures it in general against viruses, worms, Trojans, and other forms of malware.

2. Answer: B. The AAA server and port 1812

   Explanation: AAA in computer security is an acronym that refers to authentication, authorization, and accounting. RADIUS (Remote Authentication Dial-In User Service) is an example of an AAA server, and would be the server that takes care of authentication for the wireless access point (WAP) in this scenario. By default, the RADIUS server uses port 1812 for authentication. Also by default, it does this over a UDP transport mechanism (though it can use TCP as well).

   See the section "Authentication Models and Components" in Chapter 10, "Physical Security and Authentication Models," for more information.

   Incorrect answers: The DHCP server (which uses ports 67 and 68) takes care of assigning IP addresses to computers on the network that require dynamic assignment. The Lightweight Directory Access Protocol (LDAP) server is used to maintain directory information, for example, in a Microsoft domain controller or an e-mail server. It uses port 389. It is based on the X.500 specification, and allows either unencrypted authentication or encrypted authentication via Transport Layer Security (TLS). An e-mail server that uses port 143 has the Internet Message Access Protocol (IMAP) e-mail protocol running.

Though this server may be involved in the authentication of e-mail logins, it does not authenticate for connections made to a WAP.

3. Answer: C. Pharming

Explanation: Pharming (a portmanteau of farming and phishing) is an attack that redirects traffic from a legitimate site to a different illegitimate and possibly malicious site. It can occur because of an exploited DNS server (which would affect many users), or can occur by modifying the hosts file of one or more computers (which would affect those computers only). If a hosts file is modified, it can be easily fixed by deleting the file, and either re-creating the file or letting the operating system re-create it. Individual computers can also be protected by configuring anti-phishing in the web browser or adding on third-party anti-phishing software, and using updated antivirus software. DNS servers can be protected through careful monitoring of DNS configurations and log files.

See the section "Malicious Attacks" in Chapter 7, "Networking Protocols and Threats," for more information.

Incorrect answers: Phishing is an attempt at obtaining private information from someone. It is usually done by e-mail. Whereas pharming attacks are often designed to "phish" for information, phishing can be accomplished in a variety of ways in addition to pharming. Whaling is a subset of phishing and refers to when an attacker targets senior executives, which is an example of spear phishing. Spim is the abuse of messaging systems other than e-mail.

4. Answer: D. SCP

Explanation: SCP (Secure Copy) is a protocol/application used to transfer files securely between computers. It relies on Secure Shell (SSH) and uses port 22, and it is an application, and therefore resides on the application layer (layer 7), the highest layer of the OSI model, as does SSH. Because the OSI model is normally represented with a top-down approach, the application layer is at the top, and is considered "highest."

See the section "Ports and Protocols" in Chapter 7, "Networking Protocols and Threats," for more information.

Incorrect answers: IPsec is a protocol used to secure IP communications, for example, within Layer 2 Tunneling Protocol (L2TP) VPN connections. It is a network layer (layer 3) protocol. TCP resides on the transport layer (layer 4). ICMP (Internet Control Message Protocol) resides on the network layer (layer 3), and is instrumental in testing networking connections; for example, with the `ping` command.

5. Answer: C. The security controls on the USB drive can be bypassed.

Explanation: If access mechanisms such as permissions and policies are not implemented correctly on a USB hard drive (or any hard drive for that matter), then those security controls for that drive can be bypassed by an attacker.

See the section "Securing Computer Hardware and Peripherals" in Chapter 3, "Computer Systems Security Part II," for more information.

Incorrect answers: The possibility of data corruption usually happens because a hard drive physically fails or becomes too fragmented, not because of security controls being bypassed. Data on the USB drive should not be vulnerable to log analysis because the logs are normally stored in the system partition of the operating system. That drive is internal to the computer, whereas a USB hard drive will be external to the computer. The same holds true for user accounts. Those accounts are stored within the OS, and again on the main drive, not on a USB hard drive.

6. Answer: C. Identification

Explanation: The *first* response within the incident response that should be taken in this scenario is identification. The malware needs to be identified, the computers affected need to be identified, and so on. Identification is usually the first step of an organization's incident response process.

See the section "Incident Response Procedures" in Chapter 18, "Policies and Procedures," for more information.

Incorrect answers: An example of the main phases of incident response (as listed in CompTIA Security+ exam objective 5.4) is as follows: 1. Preparation; 2. Identification; 3. Containment; 4. Eradication; 5. Recovery, and finally; 6. Lessons learned. (This list can vary from one organization to the next and from one standardization body to the next.) A pre-step to this list is preparation—being ready with tools, knowledge, and training before an incident occurs. Validation can occur during steps 5 through 7, depending on the type of validation. Follow-up can be considered part of the documenting and monitoring step.

7. Answer: A. Transport encryption

Explanation: When securing data that passes between two points on an IP network, you need some kind of transport layer communications encryption protocol. Examples include Transport Layer Security (TLS) and Secure Sockets Layer (SSL). Protocols such as these operate on layer 4 of the OSI model; they encrypt the transmissions between IP-based computers, protecting the session data from eavesdroppers, and are thus known as transport layer encryption protocols. They make use of X.509 certificates and a public key infrastructure

(PKI). These protocols can utilize block ciphers (for instance, Advanced Encryption Standard [AES]) or stream ciphers (for example, RC4), but more commonly use the former. By the way, *APT* stands for advanced persistent threat, a group of continuous hacking processes often performed by multiple attackers. APTs are carried out by knowledgeable groups of people using very sophisticated attacks; often they reside in another country.

See the section "Security Protocols" in Chapter 15, "PKI and Encryption Protocols," for more information.

Incorrect answers: Key escrow is when decryption keys are held in escrow (placed in the custody of a third party), in the case that they are needed to gain access to data. They are common in PKI systems. This is a concept of where keys are stored, but not a method of encrypting data transmissions between two hosts. The answers "block ciphers" and "stream ciphers" are not specific enough. You can use either as part of an overall solution to secure data passing between two points on an IP network, but more often than not you will encounter SSL certificates that make use of RSA (for the key exchange) and AES (the actual cipher used for the transfer of session data).

8. Answer: C. Incident time offsets were not accounted for.

Explanation: In this scenario, the copyright infringement alert was triggered at 02: 30: 01 GMT. This means that it happened at 2:30 AM (during the first second) and that the incident, and the logs, are based on GMT (Greenwich Mean Time), the global time standard. Note the third log shows that a movie file was accessed at 03: 30: 01. There is exactly a one-hour difference between the copyright infringement alert and the log file that shows the file access that occurred (which is the infringement). This could be due to the fact that the server hosting the file has its time based on a different time zone. There are several other possibilities why the incident time offset occurred, but it did occur. When scanning for incident time offsets (because your log files will probably be large), look for incidents that happened during the same minute and second, but on a different hour. Ultimately, what you (and the incident response team) need to find out is who downloaded the movie and triggered the copyright infringement. It could be that Amy was the downloader, based on the time offset, but you would need to analyze the situation further to be sure.

See the section "Incident Response Procedures" in Chapter 18, "Policies and Procedures," for more information.

Incorrect answers: The logs are certainly not corrupt, and they are definitely available, because the incident response team was able to access them and send them (or a copy of them) to you to review. You don't know if the chain of custody was properly maintained. It is beyond your understanding because the incident response team has the log files. You only received a copy of some of the log file information.

9. Answer: C. Zero day

    Explanation: A zero day attack (such as a zero day virus) is one that up until the point of time when the attack occurs was previously unknown to antivirus software companies and IDS companies. So, for the attack in question there was no AV or IDS signature available to detect it—it is an unknown and undocumented exploit. The admin found it by utilizing a heuristic system, which is a more advanced type of IDS. In a similar scenario, if a malicious exploit is found in an application and you inquire with the software vendor about remediation steps, and then find that no patches are available, you have most likely found a zero day attack. In these situations, you will have to *improvise*.

    See the section "Secure Programming" in Chapter 5, "Application Security," for more information.

    Incorrect answers: The rest of the answers are known attacks. Directory traversal is a method of accessing unauthorized parent directories on web servers. XML injection is a type of code injection used on website forms. Baiting is a type of social engineering attack where a USB flash drive or other type of removable media (often containing malware) is left out in the open for an unsuspecting person to pick up and (hopefully) insert into a computer.

10. Answer: C. Hardware address filtering has been implemented.

    Explanation: The security administrator denied one MAC address at the SOHO router: 01:23:6D:A9:55:EC. This is most likely the MAC address of the mobile device that cannot connect to the network. Individual octets of a MAC address are often separated by colons when working in a router. However, in an operating system such as Windows they are often separated by hyphens. Be able to identify both. Note that the admin also permitted (or allowed) a particular MAC address to connect to the network. Access control lists (ACLs), or rules, such as these are created on the router to allow or disallow access.

    See the section "Firewalls and Network Security" in Chapter 8, "Network Perimeter Security," for more information.

    Incorrect answers: Port filtering could mean physical ports or logical TCP/IP ports such as port 80 HTTP. IP address filtering means that entire IP addresses (such as 10.254.254.101) have been filtered out. Both of these answers are incorrect because this scenario clearly deals with MAC addresses.

WPA2-PSK is a method of connecting, but the "PSK" portion implies that it does not require a supplicant the way a technology such as 802.1X does. PSK means pre-shared key, a key that the admin selects and inputs into the router, which the user must know in order to connect to a wireless network.

11. Answer: D. WAF

Explanation: A WAF (web application firewall) can be implemented as hardware or software. Among other things it can protect from XSS (cross-site scripting) and SQL injection attacks. The WAF can be an appliance, server software, or plug-in, and applies a set of rules to HTTP sessions to protect from various attacks. WebKnight and ModSecurity are examples of open source WAFs. Unlike other devices such as network intrusion detection systems (NIDSs), routers, and some firewalls, the WAF operates at layer 7 of the OSI model (application layer).

See the section "Firewalls and Network Security" in Chapter 8, "Network Perimeter Security," for more information.

Incorrect answers: A flood guard is a separate feature of firewalls that can protect against SYN flood attacks. *IDS* stands for intrusion detection system—a device or software that monitors network activities and *alerts* an administrator to various types of malicious activities. A URL content filter is a software filter that monitors for specific URLs (domain names and website names) that are undesirable and disallows access to them.

12. Answer: C. Information security awareness

Explanation: Information security awareness means training users on how to screen calls and e-mails; not to give out personally identifiable information (PII); not to share confidential organizational data; and in general, to protect data and PII. This will be the best method for reducing the chances of another data leak due to social engineering attacks. By the way, if the social engineering attacks were conducted by phone, the attack type is known as *vishing*, a form of phishing.

See the section "User Education" in Chapter 17, "Social Engineering, User Education, and Facilities Security," for more information.

Incorrect answers: The use of social media and the option to bring your own device (BYOD) often lead to increased social engineering (in the form of spim, phishing, and possibly pharming), and additional security is required to meet that threat. When it comes to BYOD, the main security concern is that there is a lack of controls in place to ensure that the devices have the latest system patches and signature files. Mobile device management (MDM) systems can alleviate that situation. Acceptable use is usually stated in policy form, and basically describes what people are allowed to do with company-owned computers and data. Though adherence to this policy can potentially help to reduce data leaks, it is not the best or most effective solution.

> **NOTE**   This is an example of a question for which two answers could arguably be correct. When taking the CompTIA Security+ exam, be sure to analyze the question carefully and select the best answer for most situations.

Data handling and disposal is also important, but training in them won't reduce the type of social engineering attack in the question that was perpetrated on the organization; that attack was vishing. However, data handling policies can help with shoulder surfing, dumpster diving, and a variety of other attacks.

13. Answer: D. Generate a new private key based on RSA

Explanation: When a person is required to submit a CSR (certificate signing request) to a CA (certificate authority), the first step—before generating the CSR—is to create a private key. This will be an asymmetric key such as RSA, commonly a 2048-bit key. (In fact, since the end of 2013 it is mandated that the key be 2048-bit or larger.) The next steps are to generate the CSR, submit the CSR for signing (the crucial part of the process), and finally install the signed certificate. It is important to keep the original RSA private key safe and secure. No one, including the CA, should know the RSA key. The CA should only know the CSR generated, which is based on the private RSA key.

See the section "Public Key Infrastructure" in Chapter 15, "PKI and Encryption Protocols," for more information.

Incorrect answers: Symmetric keys such as AES are not used for this process; asymmetric keys such as RSA are the standard. The security administrator must use and keep safe a private key that only he or she knows. Later, when people connect to the organization's website or network, they will make use of the public key portion.

14. Answers: D and F. Bob's public key or the CA's public key

Explanation: The key word here is *verify*. If Alice is to verify the validity of Bob's certificate, she will need either Bob's public key or the CA's public key. Table 1 sums up the keys required for encrypting/decrypting data, signatures, and certificates. This table is based on RSA, but usually these rules of thumb hold true for any scenario where a public/private key pair are used.

Table 1 Summary of RSA Public and Private Key Usage

Task	Which Person's Key to Use	Type of Key
Send an encrypted message	Receiver's	Public key
Decrypt an encrypted message	Receiver's	Private key
Send an encrypted signature	Sender's	Private key
Decrypt an encrypted signature or verify a certificate	Sender's	Public key

As you can see from the last row of the table, to decrypt an encrypted signature or verify a certificate, you would need the sender's public key; in this case, Bob's public key (or the CA's public key).

See the section "Cryptography Concepts" in Chapter 14, "Encryption and Hashing Concepts," for more information.

Incorrect answers: Alice cannot use her own key to verify the certificate, and cannot use anyone else's private keys. She would have to use the public key of the sender, be it Bob's or the CA's. Table 1 shows that there are a variety of possibilities depending on the scenario, and depending on who is sending what. For example, if Bob sent an encrypted *message* to Alice, he would need to use her public key to encrypt the message, and Alice would need to use her private key to decrypt the message.

15. Answer: B. To utilize single sign-on capabilities

   Explanation: Both LDAP and Kerberos can be used for single sign-on (SSO). This eases the burden on users of having to remember different usernames and passwords and allows a single login to multiple systems.

   See the section "Authentication Models and Components" in Chapter 10, "Physical Security and Authentication Models," for more information.

   Incorrect answers: A CA is used to sign certificates, including wildcard certificates. Queries on a directory service can be made with LDAP, but not with Kerberos. SSO is a derivative of federated identity management (FIM), but FIM will be its own system altogether separate of LDAP and Kerberos.

16. Answer: B. RFID

   Explanation: RFID (radio-frequency identification) tags could be attached to mobile items such as network testers, laptops, and so on. These tags can be extremely small and hard for an intruder to notice. Any proximity point that the item is not supposed to go past can be configured to automatically set off an alert or alarm when the RFID tag passes it.

See the section "Physical Security" in Chapter 10, "Physical Security and Authentication Models," for more information.

Incorrect answers: None of the other answers allow for automatic notification of item removal. Environmental monitoring is the real-time analysis of controls and programs that concern heating, ventilation, and air conditioning (HVAC) and supervisory control and data acquisition (SCADA). Electromagnetic interference (EMI) shielding is used to reduce or eliminate crosstalk and data emanation. CCTV (closed-circuit television) is used to monitor and record things that transpire within the work area, but again cannot (without the help of other software/technology) alert an administrator automatically.

17. Answers: C and F. Create a VLAN for the servers, and create an ACL to access the server.

Explanation: If the servers and the BYOD users are on the same network, then the BYOD users could easily access the servers, regardless of whether a computer is connected in a wired fashion or wireless fashion by default. So to protect the servers from the users' mobile devices, you could first create a virtual LAN (VLAN) for the servers. This VLAN would separate the servers and you could then control who is allowed access to the servers via access control lists (ACLs) within the firewall portion of the SOHO all-in-one wireless router. If the SOHO router supported it, you could also place the web servers in a DMZ.

See the section "Network Design" in Chapter 6, "Network Design Elements," and "Rights, Permissions, and Policies" in Chapter 11, "Access Control Methods and Models," for more information.

Incorrect answers: The EAP-TLS authentication scheme should not be necessary for this scenario; it is used, for example, to authenticate wireless clients to a wireless network, which was not specified in the question. Changing the default HTTP port (which is normally 80) would cause your Internet guests some difficulty in finding the web servers, and is not necessary in this scenario either. Denying incoming connections to the outside router interface would also make it difficult for Internet users to access the web servers, and is therefore not recommended. If a physical port is disabled, anything connected to that port will be effectively offline. This also compounds the issue instead of solving it.

18. Answers: A and F. Change the implicit rule to an implicit deny and add the following ACL at the bottom of the current ACL: deny IP any any 53

Explanation: First of all, a firewall should not be set with an implicit allow by default. That would allow just about any kind of traffic through the firewall.

Plus, it would make the already configured ACL unnecessary. So, the firewall should be changed to an implicit *deny* for all connections. That is the default settings for firewalls and it disallows all traffic coming from the Internet through the inbound interface (unless otherwise stated with an ACL). Second, you would add the ACL deny IP any any 53 at the bottom of the current ACL. This will deny any DNS traffic (because DNS uses port 53) including DNS requests and zone transfers. It does this for any type of IP connection (including TCP and UDP) and for all IP addresses on the local and remote ends.

See the section "Firewalls and Network Security" in Chapter 8, "Network Perimeter Security," for more information.

Incorrect answers: Removing the current ACL would do nothing because the firewall is currently configured with an implicit allow. However, if you changed that default rule to an implicit deny and removed the ACL, Internet users would no longer be able to connect to the web server (which uses ports 80 and 443). That doesn't solve your problem; in fact, it creates another one. It doesn't really matter where you place the new ACL to block DNS requests—top, bottom, doesn't make a difference because when you are finished, the firewall will have an implicit deny, and then two separate ACLs that pretty much work independently of each other. However, you would normally place the ACLs in order, and this would mean placing the new ACL below the first. The key with the other two possible ACLs in the answers is that they are not blocking enough traffic. One shows TCP, which is not enough; you need to block TCP and UDP—this is done by simply stating IP. ICMP is not correct, because that deals with layer 3 testing, such as the ping utility.

19. Answers: A and E. MD5 and HMAC.

Explanation: The key word in this question is *integrity*. When we are dealing with the integrity of files, we often employ hashing. The only two hashing options in the supplied answers are MD5 and HMAC. Those cryptographic hash values could be compared to last night's integrity scan to find out which files have been changed in the two hours that the employee was working today.

See the section "Hashing Basics" in Chapter 14, "Encryption and Hashing Concepts," for more information.

Incorrect answers: Elliptic curve cryptography (ECC), Advanced Encryption Standard (AES), Pretty Good Privacy (PGP), and Blowfish are all encryption protocols used to encrypt files. None of them are cryptographic hashing functions.

20. Answer: C. Rule-based access control

Explanation: You would want to write a rule that automatically gives Bob write access to the database when Alice is gone. This is an example of rule-based access control. In this type of access control model, the security administrator writes the rule and allows the computer to automate the action of the rule when necessary.

See the section "Access Control Models Defined" in Chapter 11, "Access Control Methods and Models," for more information.

Incorrect answers: Discretionary access control (DAC) is when the user has ownership of the resource in question and can create permissions as necessary. Mandatory access control (MAC) is similar to rule-based access control; in fact, rule-based access control is a subset of MAC. However, MAC is controlled by the system and does not work at this type of depth concerning rules. Role-based access control (RBAC) concerns users and their roles in the organization, including which groups they are members of, and applies rights and permissions accordingly. Attribute-based access control (ABAC) is a context-aware model that utilizes dynamic authentication and bases its decisions on the results of IF-THEN statements.

21. Answer: C. The system was designed to fail-open for life safety.

Explanation: In this scenario, the system did what it was supposed to do. In the case of a failure, the security administrator designed the system to *fail-open*, meaning that the door would unlock, allowing people to leave the server room in the event of an emergency (thus the meaning of life safety). The attacker probably had knowledge of this design, and so planned the attack accordingly. To protect against the attacker's gaining access in this scenario, multifactor authentication could be implemented: for example, adding biometrics, a passcode, or other form of authentication.

See the section "NIDS Versus NIPS" in Chapter 8, "Network Perimeter Security," for more information.

Incorrect answers: The proximity reader was definitely installed properly. It's just that the system has vulnerabilities, one of which the attacker has exploited. These vulnerabilities are built into the design of the system for safety. We don't know whether or not the system uses magnetic locks; there is not enough information in the question to make that assumption. The system was not designed in a fail-close configuration. If it were, the door would have remained locked when the proximity reader was broken.

22. Answers: C and E. Bcrypt and PBKDF2

Explanation: Bcrypt and PBKDF2 are examples of key stretching software. This software takes a weaker password key and *stretches* the key length, in the end outputting an enhanced and more powerful key, usually to 128 bits in length. This makes brute-force attacks difficult if not impossible. Bcrypt also adds salting (additional data added to the password hash), which helps protect against dictionary attacks and rainbow table attacks.

See the section "Hashing Basics" in Chapter 14, "Encryption and Hashing Concepts," for more information.

Incorrect answers: MD5 and SHA2 are cryptographic hashing protocols, used to verify the integrity of files. AES is a common symmetric encryption protocol used to encrypt files and session data. CHAP is an authentication scheme, one that could be used by a RADIUS server or other authentication system.

23. Answer: A. The Remote Authentication Dial-In User Service certificate has expired.

Explanation: 802.1X secure network access can be used to connect to wireless networks. It can use EAP, CHAP, or PEAP authentication. It can also utilize centralized authentication such as RADIUS. Though the scenario does not say so specifically, you can assume an 802.1X/PEAP/RADIUS configuration. If the RADIUS certificate expires, none of the wireless users would be able to connect.

See the section "Authentication Models and Components" in Chapter 10, "Physical Security and Authentication Models," for more information.

Incorrect answers: The DNS server is a separate service altogether. If it was overwhelmed (perhaps by a DDoS attack), then DNS queries would fail, but those queries would be to items on the domain, or websites, and so on. It should not affect the wireless network. Too many incorrect authentication attempts could cause some users to be disabled, but most likely this will be a temporary loss of service. In the scenario, *all* employees report no service to the wireless network. The scenario also states the technician verified that there were *no outages*, so the IDS should not have disabled the wireless network.

24. Answer: C. TCP Wrapper

Explanation: TCP Wrapper is a host-based ACL program that provides protection against host name and host address spoofing in Linux and Unix environments. Most gaming consoles are Linux-based, and the video streaming servers they connect to are most likely Linux- or Unix-based as well. By using this program, rules can be configured to restrict access to TCP services. For example, attackers can easily determine when an unprotected Linux-based system is idle, and then attempt to access that system when it is unattended. The TCP Wrapper program acts as a pseudo-firewall in that it monitors incoming packets for authorization, thereby blocking the potential attacker. Programs used for streaming can be compiled with TCP Wrapper, and these can also be encrypted to further foil the would-be attacker. (Often this program is also referred to as TCP Wrappers.) By the way, credit card numbers should usually be stored in a transactional database that encrypts down to the database field level, not only the file level.

See the section "Firewalls and Network Security" in Chapter 8, "Network Perimeter Security," for more information.

Incorrect answers: Firmware updates are important for any system, but will not stop the problem being described. Some kind of software such as TCP Wrapper (an application layer program) is needed. A web application firewall (WAF) isn't the correct type of firewalling required by video streaming servers and the gaming consoles that connect to them. Plus, WAF along with IDS are solutions that are installed at the server side. This scenario calls for secure coding of the program that transmits data between the gaming consoles and the video streaming servers.

25. Answer: B. It should be performed on the server side.

Explanation: The best answer is that it should be performed on the server side. Given the choice between server-side and client-side input validation, server-side wins out. However, both should be incorporated as secure coding methods.

See the section "Secure Programming" in Chapter 5, "Application Security," for more information.

Incorrect answers: Using the client side only can actually create additional vulnerabilities at the server. As a programmer, you don't really care about the user's knowledge level; you have to assume that smart users or attackers will come along at some point and try to hack your forms, web pages, or other applications, and design the client and server sides of the application appropriately. Even SSL-protected pages can be hacked into if they weren't properly validated. In fact, SSL doesn't really have too much effect on the matter, especially when it comes to web forms built in PHP or other similar web programming languages.

26. Answers: C and D. SSH and PGP

Explanation: SSH (Secure Shell) can secure connections to remote machines and is instrumental in encrypting data in motion over the network. PGP (Pretty Good Privacy) encrypts data that is meant for transit via e-mail or for data that is meant to be *at rest*, or simply stored somewhere for an indeterminate amount of time. These are the only answers listed that will encrypt data and/or data sessions (and are not outdated).

See the section "Ports and Protocols" in Chapter 7, "Networking Protocols and Threats," and "Encryption Algorithms" in Chapter 14, "Encryption and Hashing Concepts," for more information.

Incorrect answers: TFTP is used to send small and basic files in an unsecure manner between two hosts on a LAN. It does not encrypt data. The Temporal Key Integrity Protocol (TKIP) is used as a security protocol in wireless networks but is outdated and should be replaced by either Counter Mode CBC-MAC Protocol (CCMP) or Advanced Encryption Standard (AES). TKIP is insecure because it makes use of RC4, which is considered outdated. The Simple Network Management Protocol (SNMP) concerns the monitoring of networks and network devices and hosts. NTLM (NT LAN Manager hash) is a cryptographic hashing protocol used with Windows passwords. This is also outdated and should be replaced with NTLMv2.

27. Answer: B. DLP

Explanation: DLP (data loss prevention) methods are often implemented in scenarios where USB mass storage devices are utilized (such as USB flash drives and external hard drives). A storage-based DLP system monitors data at rest, and performs content inspection in order to prevent unauthorized use of the data.

See the section "Implementing Security Applications" in Chapter 3, "Computer Systems Security Part II," for more information.

Incorrect answers: An IDS (intrusion detection system) is used to detect attacks and anomalies on the network. Content filtering is performed by proxy servers and Internet content filters—usually relating to Internet content. Auditing is when files and other resources are investigated in real time to see who accessed what and when.

28. Answer: A. Alice's private key

Explanation: Alice should use her own private key to sign the file. Refer to Table 14-4 in the book. It shows that to send an encrypted signature, Alice (the sender) would need her own private key. To decrypt the signature, Bob (the recipient) would need Alice's (the sender's) public key.

See the section "Cryptography Concepts" in Chapter 14, "Encryption and Hashing Concepts," for more information.

Incorrect answers: In this scenario, Bob's keys don't even come into play because he is the receiver. However, in a scenario where Alice had sent Bob an encrypted *message*, Bob's public and private keys would be utilized for the encrypting and decrypting of the message, respectively.

29. Answer: C. Incorporating diversity into redundant design

Explanation: The key word in the question is *availability*. One of the best ways to encourage availability is to have redundancy. The more diverse the redundancy, the more fault tolerant the system.

See the section "Redundancy Planning" in Chapter 16, "Redundancy and Disaster Recovery," and "Facilities Security" in Chapter 17, "Social Engineering, User Education, and Facilities Security," for more information.

Incorrect answers: Some industrial control systems do not have the option to run AV software, but even if they did, AV software does not promote availability directly. It helps to secure from viruses and other malware, but it is not a method of fault tolerance. Multiple firewalls, for example, a back-to-back perimeter configuration, will help to block network-based attacks, but also do not increase availability. Application whitelists, if not configured properly, could actually reduce availability. They are meant to restrict users to specific allowed applications.

30. Answer: D. Fingerprint readers

Explanation: The best answer is to use a biometric solution such as fingerprint readers. This is a different factor of authentication, and works well with smart cards and passwords. Biometric authentication falls into the factor category of something you *are*.

See the section "Physical Security" in Chapter 10, "Physical Security and Authentication Models," for more information.

Incorrect answers: The rest of the answers are within the categories of factors already mentioned in the question. Badge readers would be used with smart cards (or proximity cards) as would hard tokens; they are within the category of something you *have*. Passphrases are essentially the same as passwords; they are within the category of something you *know*.

31. Answer: D. 22 and TCP

Explanation: SFTP (Secure FTP) uses port 22 and rides on SSH to make connections. It uses TCP as the transport mechanism. Most secure connections of this sort require guaranteed, connection-oriented transmission of data—thus TCP.

See the section "Ports and Protocols" in Chapter 7, "Networking Protocols and Threats," for more information.

Incorrect answers: Port 21 is used by plain FTP, with no security. FTP also uses TCP as the transport mechanism. The answers listed might have appeared tricky at first, but if you know your protocols and associated port numbers and transport mechanisms used, you will prevail. Be sure to memorize Table 7-2 in the book!

32. Answer: C. Scarcity

Explanation: Scarcity refers to a limited supply, something in short supply, thus "exclusive access" in the question. Some users, especially the ones at the top of the marketing pyramid—the innovators—don't want to be left out of the latest, newest, exclusive smartphone offers. It is these people who are targeted by social engineers with the method of scarcity. Most likely, the link is bogus, and leads to another website altogether unexpected by the user.

See the section "Social Engineering" in Chapter 17, "Social Engineering, User Education, and Facilities Security," for more information.

Incorrect answers: It is possible that the e-mail could use the other methods mentioned in the incorrect answers, but they are not described in the scenario. An example of trust would be a money-back guarantee, or using some kind of knowledge of the user. An example of intimidation could be the use of hoax ransomware, or perhaps the e-mail says you are required to appear in court, and so on. An example of familiarity would be if a social engineer shows sympathy or empathy for a user, usually with previously learned information about the user.

33. Answer: B. $5000

Explanation: If the server had a 10% loss of functionality, then that would be $500, or 1/10 of the server value. If this happened 10 times per year, then you would multiply that individual loss of $500 × 10, resulting in a $5000 loss for the year. Remember that the ALE is the total loss in dollars per year for a specific incident. The entire quantitative risk assessment equation is

SLE × ARO = ALE

In this case, the single loss expectancy (SLE) is 10%, which equals $500. The annualized rate of occurrence (ARO) is the number of times per year that the incident occurred—in this case, 10. So:

$500 × 10 = $5000. The ALE = $5000, which just happens to be the value of the server. Hmmm, time for a replacement? At the very least, some investigative work needs to be done to find out why the server is going down so often.

See the section "Conducting Risk Assessments" in Chapter 12, "Vulnerability and Risk Assessment," for more information.

Incorrect answers: The other answers of $500, $10,000, and $50,000 are not correct because they do not fit the equation of SLE × ARO = ALE. Math doesn't lie.

34. Answer: C. Hardening

Explanation: It appears that an external IP address (208.159.67.23) is attempting to connect remotely to the local computer (10.248.248.67), possibly using the Remote Desktop Connection program. The connections were unsuccessful, but hardening is required at the local system and at the firewall to ensure that this IP address cannot connect through to the local computer. Services should be analyzed and, if necessary, shut down at the local computer. Ports should be scanned and, if necessary, closed at the firewall.

See the section "Hardening Operating Systems" in Chapter 4, "OS Hardening and Virtualization," for more information.

Incorrect answers: System log monitoring is incorrect because the logs are present, and they have been monitored and analyzed, resulting in the answer that additional hardening is necessary. An IDS (intrusion detection system) looks for attacks and will notify an administrator (and possibly shut down a firewall if necessary), but it is not working correctly at this point. To truly mitigate the problem, the IDS should be reconfigured and hardened, or an IPS (intrusion prevention system) should be implemented. Reporting, along with the logs, seems to be working properly.

35. Answers: A and D. Validate input on the client and the server side, and restrict the use of special characters in form fields

Explanation: Input validation is extremely important when it comes to website attacks such as XSRF (cross-site request forgery) and cross-site scripting (XSS) attacks. Forms and other documents should be validated on the client side and the server side (if at all possible). Special characters should be restricted and sanitized within form fields and URLs. This is all part of secure coding.

See the section "Secure Programming" in Chapter 5, "Application Security," for more information.

Incorrect answers: Using angle brackets for HTML code (for example < and >) is just good programming. Without angle brackets, the HTML statement won't work, but it has nothing to do with *input* validation. The more redirection that occurs, the more the chance of vulnerabilities being exploited. URL redirection should be limited if not eliminated. Web proxies make for more efficient web connections in a variety of ways but do nothing for input validation.

36. Answer: B. Install a digital certificate on the authentication server

Explanation: If you are running a WPA2-Enterprise wireless network, then the wireless access point (WAP) will need to access a RADIUS server for the authentication portion of the wireless connection. This scenario calls for a digital certificate to be loaded on the RADIUS server.

See the section "Authentication Models and Components" in Chapter 10, "Physical Security and Authentication Models," for more information.

Incorrect answers: A DHCP server might be utilized at the WAP (or other all-in-one network device), or there could be a separate DHCP server, but this is a different task altogether that the RADIUS server is not normally responsible for. The RADIUS server needs a digital certificate; the encryption key for WPA2 would be stored on the WAP. A token is not necessary, but is often used with swipeable smart cards for physical authentication.

37. Answer: A. OCSP

Explanation: OCSP (Online Certificate Status Protocol) is used as a lightweight (albeit less secure) alternative to the CRL. It validates certificates by returning responses such as "good," "unknown," and "revoked."

See the section "Public Key Infrastructure" in Chapter 15, "PKI and Encryption Protocols," for more information.

Incorrect answers: *PKI* stands for public key infrastructure, which OCSP is a part of. The PKI is the entire set of software, hardware, users, computers, certificates, and so on—it is an entire infrastructure. CRL stands for certificate revocation list, which is a list of certificates that are no longer valid. The RA is the registration authority, which is used to verify requests for certificates; it forwards the response to the CA.

38. Answer: C. Deploy a NIPS at the edge of the SCADA network

Explanation: The only answer that does not require modifications to the actual SCADA (supervisory control and data acquisition) system and network is to deploy a NIPS (network intrusion prevention system) at the *edge* of the SCADA network. This will monitor for (and protect against) attacks on the SCADA system, but does not require that the SCADA system be modified.

See the section "Facilities Security" in Chapter 17, "Social Engineering, User Education, and Facilities Security," for more information.

Incorrect answers: Installing a firewall, updating AV definitions, and enabling auditing all require modifications to the SCADA system and network. While you wait for testing to be completed and obtain vendor approval, these avenues should be explored, but not implemented.

39. Answers: A and D. ECDHE and Diffie-Hellman

Explanation: Standard Diffie-Hellman and ECDHE (Elliptic Curve Diffie-Hellman in ephemeral mode) were designed to securely negotiate encryption keys over an unencrypted channel.

See the section "Encryption Algorithms" in Chapter 14, "Encryption and Hashing Concepts," for more information.

Incorrect answers: PBKDF2 is a program used for key lengthening; it is often used to make weak keys stronger. Steganography is the art of hiding messages, for example, within pictures or photographs. Symmetric encryption is not used in this scenario. Both answers (and other solutions) will be asymmetric methods.

40. Answer: B. Open system authentication

Explanation: The best answer listed is to use open system authentication. In a public hotspot wireless network, this means that anyone can connect as long as she knows the password or passphrase. You could also utilize a captive portal, which forces the wireless client to authenticate via a special web page and possibly supply an e-mail address as part of the authentication process.

See the section "Securing Wireless Networks" in Chapter 9, "Securing Network Media and Devices," for more information.

Incorrect answers: Disabling the SSID would make it difficult for a computer to find the wireless network, and therefore difficult (if not impossible) for patrons to use the Internet. A MAC filter would be very inefficient as the proprietor of the establishment would need to find out the MAC address of each person coming through the door. Reducing the WAP power level is a good way to reduce the chances of war-driving, but isn't necessary in this scenario, though it is a good practice.

41. Answer: A. Create a virtualized sandbox and utilize snapshots

Explanation: You should create a virtualized sandbox—a place where you can work with many virtualized images and test them frequently. By utilizing snapshots, you are taking limited images of the systems at a specific point, most likely before and after the patch installation. The snapshot is a set of information at a particular point in time, and not necessarily an entire image.

See the section "Secure Programming" in Chapter 5, "Application Security," for more information.

Incorrect answers: Creating a single image of a patched PC is not enough. Good patch management requires that the security administrator do thorough testing; in the scenario you are required to test the patch a dozen times. Incremental backups are used as a part of an efficient backup plan that usually includes incremental and full backups. But this—and the fact that the PC is unpatched—does not help a security administrator to test the patching process quickly and often. A full disk image after each patch installation could be very time consuming. Instead, snapshots are the better option.

42. Answer: B. MoUs are generally loose agreements that do not have strict guidelines governing the transmission of sensitive data.

Explanation: An MoU is generally a loose agreement. It differs from a service level agreement (SLA) and an interconnection security agreement (ISA) in that those are very specific regarding legal issues and security concerns.

See the section "Legislative and Organizational Policies" in Chapter 18, "Policies and Procedures," for more information.

Incorrect answers: It could be said that an MoU between two parties cannot be held to the same legal standards as an SLA. However, that is a legal risk and not a security risk. Because the MoU may not have budgetary considerations written carefully, an entity may be left to absorb unexpected cost, but this is a financial risk, not a security risk. MoUs do not generally have strict policies concerning services performed between entities. The name implies a lot: memorandum of understanding. It is an understanding that has been met, not an *agreement*.

43. Answer: C. LDAP

Explanation: DC=ServerName and DC=COM imply the use of a Microsoft Windows domain controller (thus the DC parameter). Lightweight Directory Access Protocol (LDAP) is a directory access and authentication service used by Windows domain controllers, among other technologies.

See the section "Authentication Models and Components" in Chapter 10, "Physical Security and Authentication Models," for more information.

Incorrect answers: SAML (Security Assertion Markup Language) is used to address single sign-on (SSO) solutions between two providers; it is based on XML. RADIUS and TACACS+ are other types of authentication servers and are not necessarily Microsoft domain–based. (In fact, TACACS+ is Cisco-based.) Also, they are more often used for remote authentication, whereas the scenario implies a local authentication technology.

44. Answer: D. Rogue access point

Explanation: It appears from the information given that there is a rogue access point (ABC-WAP4). This could be a WAP that was forgotten about, or one that was purposely and maliciously placed inside the network. Note that the question stated there are *three* wireless networks, and that the first three WAPs utilize nonoverlapping channels (1, 6, and 11). However, the fourth WAP uses channel 4 (which would overlap with the ABC-WAP1), and has a lower power level reading, meaning that it is probably somewhere near the physical perimeter of your building. To mitigate the issue, this WAP should be physically located and taken offline.

See the section "Securing Wireless Networks" in Chapter 9, "Securing Network Media and Devices," for more information.

Incorrect answers: Wireless jamming would cause one or more of the WAPs to fail, and would ultimately cause connectivity issues for wireless users; this is not mentioned in the scenario. Packet sniffing is the capturing of data that crosses the network. This could possibly be happening if an attacker is monitoring the fourth WAP, but you do not know this. Near field communication (NFC) is a standard used by smartphones to establish radio communications easily over short distances (often by touching the two devices together or bringing them very close to each other).

45. Answer: D. MAC filtering

Explanation: When MAC filtering is enabled on a WAP, it actually broadcasts information wirelessly. This makes it vulnerable to spoofing. Because MAC filtering and a disabled SSID can be easily circumvented using a network sniffer, it is very important to also use strong encryption, and possibly consider other types of network access control (such as 802.1X) and external authentication methods (such as RADIUS).

See the section "Malicious Attacks" in Chapter 7, "Networking Protocols and Threats," for more information.

Incorrect answers: WPA-LEAP and WPA-PEAP are authentication protocols designed specifically to counter spoofing and other attacks. If the SSID is enabled, there is no need to do any spoofing because the SSID can be easily scanned for by war-drivers and other attackers.

46. Answer: B. ISA

Explanation: An ISA is an interconnection security agreement. It is an agreement that is established between two (or more) organizations that own and operate connected IT systems and data sets. Its purpose is to specifically document the technical and security requirements of the interconnection between the organizations. This is the type of agreement you need in this scenario because the data is sensitive and the CIO requires that there is a clear understanding of security controls to be implemented and agreed upon.

See the section "Legislative and Organizational Policies" in Chapter 18, "Policies and Procedures," for more information.

Incorrect answers: An SLA (service level agreement) is a contract between a service provider and a customer that specifies the nature of the service to be provided and the level of service that the provider will offer to the customer. It can be a very basic agreement, or it could also state the technical and performance parameters, but it will probably not include any specific security controls. An MoU is not an agreement at all, but a memorandum of understanding between two organizations or government agencies. It does not specify any security controls either. A BPA (business partners agreement) is a type of contract that can establish the profits each partner will get, what responsibilities each partner will have, and exit strategies for partners. Note that you might see the acronym *BPA* used for other things as well in the business and IT worlds.

47. Answer: D. Armored virus

Explanation: The armored virus protects itself from AV programs by tricking the program into thinking that it is located in a different place than where it actually resides. It thwarts attempts at analysis of its code. This makes it difficult to reverse engineer, and therefore makes building a defense against it difficult.

See the section "Malicious Software Types" in Chapter 2, "Computer Systems Security Part I," for more information.

Incorrect answers: A logic bomb is code that is inserted into software that "detonates" one of many types of malware when specific criteria are met. So, the logic bomb is more of a method of delivery for malware than the malware itself. The same holds true for backdoors; they are coded entrances to a system that either were designed for testing and forgotten about or are openings that were never found during a secure code review. A worm is similar to a virus except that it self-replicates. However, worms are fairly easy to detect and locate, making reverse engineering at least feasible.

48. Answer: B. To reduce the burden of certificate management

Explanation: A wildcard certificate (usually associated with SSL certificates) secures a website URL and an unlimited number of its subdomains. For example, it could secure www.davidlprowse.com, as well as the fictitious subdomains sy0-501.davidlprowse.com, blog.davidlprowse.com, and so on. Instead of having multiple SSL certificates, you could use a single wildcard SSL certificate. This can make the management of certificates easier, and can possibly save time and money.

See the section "Public Key Infrastructure" in Chapter 15, "PKI and Encryption Protocols," for more information.

Incorrect answers: Extending the renewal date of a certificate is incorrect because, generally, a renewal of a certificate simply means that a new certificate is purchased; a CSR is generated (with a new RSA private key) and submitted for approval. The same goes for increasing a certificate's encryption key length. Normally, this is not done, and a new certificate is purchased. Due to a mandate with a deadline of December 31, 2013, companies began renewing any certificates that were based on RSA encryption lower than 2048-bit. So, any older 1024-bit certificates were also added to the organization's certificate revocation list (CRL). Securing the certificate's private key is incorrect because the wildcard functionality has nothing to do with this. The certificate is based on the RSA private key, but this key should not be known by anyone accept the person who generated it. Again, this key should be 2048-bit.

49. Answer: D. BIND server

Explanation: *BIND* stands for Berkeley Internet Name Domain. It is the most widely used DNS server on the Internet and was originally designed at the University of California at Berkeley. It normally runs on Unix systems. This would have to be booted first in order to establish DNS services; in fact, it is the only server listed that will establish DNS services in this scenario.

See the section "Cloud Security and Server Defense" in Chapter 6, "Network Design Elements," for more information.

Incorrect answers: Apache is a type of web server. Exchange is a type of e-mail server. RADIUS is an authentication server. None of these establish DNS services, unless DNS has also been loaded on those computers separately.

50. Answer: C and E. Password complexity and password length

Explanation: The two best ways to increase security of passwords are to have longer passwords (for example, 10 to 15 characters in length) and to make the passwords more complex (for example, adding uppercase letters, numerals, and special characters). It is these two methods that will make a password difficult to crack. Finally, the best way to enforce the creation of complex passwords is to configure a policy within the computer system.

See the section "Rights, Permissions, and Policies" in Chapter 11, "Access Control Methods and Models," for more information.

Incorrect answers: It is also important to have a maximum password age before expiration, and disallow the use of passwords that were previously used in history. However, these are minor methods compared to password complexity and password length.

51. Answer: D. Matrix of job titles with required privileges

Explanation: The information gathering stage of a task such as this requires a matrix of job titles and required privileges, preferably something in spreadsheet format that can easily be entered into the system quickly. Each employee in the matrix would fall into a specific role in the RBAC model.

See the section "Access Control Models Defined" in Chapter 11, "Access Control Methods and Models," for more information.

Incorrect answers: The important information here for the RBAC model is the names of employees, job titles, and their required privileges. The clearance levels are also important, but they should be translated into required privileges before they are sent to the security administrator planning the RBAC model. Rules under which certain systems can be accessed aren't required here; besides, that would be an example of *rule*-based access control, not *role*-based access control. Any group-based privileges already in place will most likely be wiped clean once the new RBAC system is up and running, so they probably aren't necessary either.

52. Answer: B. 802.1X and VLANs

Explanation: In this question the RJ45 wired jacks are the key. You don't want just anyone connecting to the wired jacks and having access to internal resources. So, implementing 802.1X and VLANs is an excellent solution. This will authenticate computers; only systems with the proper 802.1X adapter will be authenticated to internal resources. Other computers that connect will only be able to connect to the Internet. The virtual LAN can be port-based, with a VLAN per conference room, or perhaps protocol-based, defining which computers are allowed to internal resources and which are allowed to the Internet only.

See the section "Authentication Models and Components" in Chapter 10, "Physical Security and Authentication Models," for more information.

Incorrect answers: A virtual private network (VPN) is used so that remote users can gain access to the network. The scenario speaks only to localized conference rooms and resources, so a VPN (and the supporting IPsec used in L2TP connections) is not necessary. The organization will most likely have at least one switch and firewall already. However, the switch can be used as the *authenticator* of the 802.1X system. NAT (network address translation) is used in IPv4 networks to mask internal IP addresses when they access the Internet. This will most likely already be implemented by default, so any guests accessing the Internet will enjoy the security benefits of NAT. However, a demilitarized zone (DMZ) has little to do with the scenario; this is when servers (such as WWW and FTP) are placed in an area outside the LAN but still within the organization's network, making it easier for people on the Internet to access them.

53. Answer: C. LEAP

Explanation: LEAP (Lightweight Extensible Authentication Protocol) is Cisco's version of EAP. It allows for dynamic Wired Equivalent Privacy (WEP) keys and mutual authentication with a RADIUS server.

See the section "Authentication Models and Components" in Chapter 10, "Physical Security and Authentication Models," for more information.

Incorrect answers: The other answers do not use a RADIUS server; they all rely on the pre-shared key (PSK). Counter Mode CBC-MAC Protocol (CCMP) is a secure alternative to Temporal Key Integrity Protocol (TKIP), both of which are used with a protocol such as WPA or WPA2. Both WEP-PSK and WPA2-PSK use pre-shared keys (PSK) that the administrator enters locally at the WAP. However, WEP should not be used in this manner, as it is deprecated. It can, however, be used in conjunction with a RADIUS server. In that scenario, it is possible to use WEP in a secure fashion.

54. Answer: C. Packet sniffing

Explanation: The network switch is probably intercepting cables to and from the CEO's office, and is probably replaying information to an attacker somewhere (perhaps a malicious insider), where packets are being analyzed by a packet sniffer such as Wireshark.

See the section "Assessing Vulnerability with Security Tools" in Chapter 12, "Vulnerability and Risk Assessment," for more information.

Incorrect answers: Impersonation is when a person attempts to gain access to a building by posing as someone else; it is a form of social engineering. Spear phishing, another type of social engineering, is when one or more individuals are targeted specifically. It is a derivative of phishing. The highly specific version of that—whaling—could possibly be happening here; you don't know without further analysis. MAC flooding is when a switch's content addressable memory (CAM) table is flooded with numerous packets, causing the switch to switch to fail-open mode and broadcast information instead of functioning as a proper switch.

55. Answers: D and F. Safety and integrity

Explanation: The fencing and additional lighting are for employee safety, especially at night. Digitally signing software, or anything else, speaks to keeping the integrity of the software intact. Hashing is another concept that could be implemented.

See the section "Conducting Audits" in Chapter 13, "Monitoring and Auditing," and "Physical Security" in Chapter 10, "Physical Security and Authentication Models," for more information.

Incorrect answers: Encryption would infer confidentiality. If the security consultant were to say that data is not secure in transit or at rest, then encryption would be a viable option. Fault tolerance infers availability. If the security consultant were to say that there are too many single points of failure, then fault-tolerant methods such as a redundant array of inexpensive [or independent] disks (RAID) array would be worth considering.

56. Answers: C and E. Screen locks and full device encryption

Explanation: Screen locks (especially the password and passcode variety) can make it difficult for an attacker to get to the data stored on the device. Better yet, full device encryption will make it virtually impossible to read the data. These are the best options, but not the only options. For example, a security administrator might opt to install a remote wipe program. Once it is known the mobile device has been stolen, the admin can trigger the wipe from a central location. However, there is a time delay concerning this method, so it should be used with the previous techniques.

See the section "Securing Mobile Devices" in Chapter 3, "Computer Systems Security Part II," for more information.

Incorrect answers: From a security standpoint, a global positioning system (GPS) is usually more of a hindrance than a security control. It might help in recovering the device, but by that point the damage has probably already been done. Inventory control and the tracking of assets are important (and are sometimes done with the aid of GPS), but remember that an unprotected mobile device can have its data downloaded by an attacker in a matter of minutes. So these things are great from a management standpoint, but not from a security standpoint.

57. Answer: D. Salting

Explanation: Salting is additional random data that is added to a one-way cryptographic hash. It can be used by itself or with key stretching if the hash has a weak key.

See the section "Hashing Basics" in Chapter 14, "Encryption and Hashing Concepts," for more information.

Incorrect answers: Rainbow tables are used to reverse cryptographic password hashes. Salting can help to deter this attack. Symmetric cryptography deals with the encryption of data using symmetric protocols such as the Advanced Encryption Standard (AES) and the Data Encryption Standard (DES). NTLMv2 is a newer Microsoft password hash used by Windows.

58. Answer: D. 69 and UDP

Explanation: TFTP, the Trivial File Transfer Protocol, uses port 69 by default, and utilizes the UDP (User Datagram Protocol) connectionless transport mechanism. This makes for a simple, lightweight protocol used to automate the transfer of basic files such as boot files in a localized environment. For example, if a PXE-compliant client computer boots off of the network, it might make use of an embedded TFTP program within the network card to transfer the appropriate boot files from a server located somewhere on the local area network. TFTP is inherently insecure, so it is not recommended for use on the Internet.

See the section "Ports and Protocols" in Chapter 7, "Network Perimeter Security," for more information.

Incorrect answers: Port 68 is used by the Dynamic Host Configuration Protocol (DHCP) (client side) and the client side of the Bootstrap Protocol (BOOTP). TCP is the Transmission Control Protocol, which offers a guaranteed, connection-oriented transport mechanism, in contrast to UDP. TCP is not used by TFTP via port 69 or DHCP via port 68 (or port 67 for that matter).

59. Answer: C. Cluster tip wiping

Explanation: A cluster tip is the last portion of a hard drive's cluster that is not used by a file. Often, files take up more than a single cluster. The cluster remainders don't get erased by default, but could possibly contain data remanence. So, some disk cleanup programs contain an option to wipe the cluster tips, thus better sanitizing the drive. This can even be performed while the computer is in use.

See the section "Legislative and Organizational Policies" in Chapter 18, "Policies and Procedures," for more information.

Incorrect answers: Encryption of any type does not sanitize the drive. Storage retention and data retention usually manifest themselves as policies. For example, an organization might have a storage retention policy that states a hard drive must be kept in storage for a minimum of three years before being fully sanitized and/or destroyed. This is common in high-security environments where data is extremely confidential, or where auditing and other logging information must be kept for a specific amount of time.

60. Answer: D. Verify that virtual machines have the updates and patches installed

    Explanation: One of the most important security precautions you can take is to install the updates and patches. This concept applies to regular operating systems, applications, and virtual machines.

    See the section "Virtualization Technology" in Chapter 4, "OS Hardening and Virtualization," for more information.

    Incorrect answers: It is unnecessary for virtual machines to be multihomed because this will not increase their security. In fact, the more network connections a VM has, the less security it has. Penetration testing should be completed before the virtual machines have been implemented. Subnetting is not necessary for virtual machines, although it can increase security. Subnetting should be taken into account during the planning and implementation stage.

61. Answer: A. Role-based access control

    Explanation: Role-based access control (RBAC) works with sets of permissions; each set of permissions constitutes a role. Users are assigned to roles to gain access to resources. Examples of user groups that are assigned to roles include remote users, extranet users, guests, and so on. In this question, the remote users are the group that has been assigned a role that enables them to access the network only during normal business hours.

    See the section "Access Control Models Defined" in Chapter 11, "Access Control Methods and Models," for more information.

    Role-based access control should not be confused with rule-based access control, which is a type of mandatory access control (MAC). MAC is an access control policy determined by a computer system and not by a user or owner. Discretionary access control (DAC) is generally determined by the owner of a resource.

62. Answer: C. Items not specifically given access are denied by default.

    Explanation: If a user or group of users does not have permissions to gain access to a resource, many systems will deny access by default; this is known as implicit deny and is common in firewalls and Windows operating systems. Default access control lists, or ACLs, will be set up for implicit deny and remain that way unless they are changed.

    See the section "Access Control Models Defined" in Chapter 11, "Access Control Methods and Models," for more information.

Incorrect answers: ACLs are not a secure way of moving traffic, but rather they are a secure way of permitting or denying traffic to pass through a firewall or permitting or denying a user or group of users access to resources. Implicit deny does not deny all traffic, only traffic that has not been previously allowed.

63. Answer: B. Firewall log

Explanation: The firewall log can help you find out whether files are being illegitimately copied to an external location. This is the only log listed that can give you any information about files being copied to an external or remote location.

See the section "Conducting Audits" in Chapter 13, "Monitoring and Auditing," for more information.

Incorrect answers: The DNS log can help you find out whether unauthorized zone transfers or DNS poisoning has occurred. The antivirus log shows what viruses have been detected and quarantined on a system. The System log is a log file within the Event Viewer that provides information about the operating system and device drivers.

64. Answer: D. Steganography

Explanation: Steganography is the science and art of writing hidden messages. It is a form of security through obscurity. The goal is that no one aside from the sender and receiver should even suspect that a hidden message exists. Although steganography can come in different forms, it is most commonly found in image files.

See the section "Cryptography Concepts" in Chapter 14, "Encryption and Hashing Concepts," for more information.

Confidentiality means preventing the disclosure of information to unauthorized persons. By definition, cryptography is the practice and study of hiding information. In computer science, cryptography uses encryption to hide information and make it secret, whereas steganography, if accomplished correctly, does not imply that a hidden message even exists. If a person were to see an encrypted cryptographic message, they would know it for what it is and may try to crack it. A digital signature authenticates a document or e-mail, letting the recipient know that the document was created and sent by the actual sender and not someone else.

65. Answers: C and D. Provide an appropriate ambient temperature, and maintain appropriate humidity levels

Explanation: The HVAC system's primary responsibilities are to provide an appropriate ambient temperature for the equipment and to maintain appropriate humidity levels. This keeps the equipment from overheating and prevents electrostatic discharge (ESD).

See the section "Facilities Security" in Chapter 17, "Social Engineering, User Education, and Facilities Security," for more information.

Incorrect answers: HVAC equipment cannot shield other equipment from EMI. However, some HVAC equipment needs to be shielded to reduce EMI after it is installed. Isolation can be provided by other methods such as the material used in the perimeter of the room (for example, physical firewalls). A separate ventilation system can be installed to vent fumes away from the server room; however, there shouldn't be any fumes. Products that contain fumes should be stored in a separate and specially secured area. And if a fire were to occur, the sprinkler system or special hazards system should end that threat, eliminating any fumes that were a result of the fire.

66. Answer: B. SLA.

Explanation: An SLA, service-level agreement, is the part of a service contract in which the level of service is formally defined. This might include traffic performance guarantees, restoration guarantees, and minimum downtime guarantees.

See the section "Legislative and Organizational Policies" in Chapter 18, "Policies and Procedures," for more information.

Incorrect answers: A chain of custody is the chronological documentation of evidence. *DRP* stands for disaster recovery plan, which includes contact information, determination of impact, a recovery plan, and so on. Incident response procedures are sets of procedures that an investigator will use when examining a computer security incident. They might include preparation, identification, containment, eradication, recovery, and lessons learned.

67. Answer: A. NAC

Explanation: NAC, or network access control, makes security checks of the users or the actual connections that are made before sessions are initiated. It can also remediate issues automatically if configured properly. 802.1X is an example of network access control.

See the section "Network Design" in Chapter 6, "Network Design Elements," for more information.

Incorrect answers: NAT (network address translation) converts one set of IP addresses to another. VLAN is a virtual local area network. Subnetting compartmentalizes IP networks by way of IP addresses and mathematics.

68. Answer: C. Remove the read permission from the Finance group for the Reports folder

Explanation: Removing the read permission from the Finance group for the Reports folder will ensure that members of the Finance group solely cannot access the folder. However, members with dual membership, such as users who are part of the Accounting group and the Finance group, will still be able to access the folder.

See the section "Rights, Permissions, and Policies" in Chapter 11, "Access Control Methods and Models," for more information.

Incorrect answers: Denying the read permission to the Finance group for the Reports folder is incorrect because if the Finance group is denied access, that will override any other permissions, including anyone who is a member of the Finance department and a member of another department (such as Accounting) that is normally allowed access. Bottom line: deny access overrides any other permissions. Denying the read permission individually for each member of the Finance group for the Reports folder is incorrect for the same reason, but this time each individual user of the Finance group is being denied, which again would include users with dual membership. It is never wise to delete a group because that would have serious implications for all the users involved.

69. Answers: A and C. Create security groups and assign access permissions based on organizational roles, and create an OU for each organizational role and link GPOs to each OU

Explanation: The first thing you should do as a network administrator is create organizational units (OUs) for each of the departments in your organization; this helps to categorize and classify where users will ultimately end up. Each OU will be considered a different role. Next on the list is creating Group Policy objects (GPOs), modifying the security policies, and applying those to each individual OU. Then, you should create the users and place them in their correct OUs according to the department that they will be working in and the role that they will play. Finally, you should create security groups, add users to the appropriate security group or groups, and apply access permissions to the groups, instead of the users, to save time and keep administrative overhead to a minimum.

See the section "Rights, Permissions, and Policies" in Chapter 11, "Access Control Methods and Models," for more information.

Incorrect answers: Placing the user's computer in an OU could cause issues when it comes time to move a user account to another OU; the computer account would need to be moved with it. Access permissions should not be assigned solely by the individual user account; this would increase administrative overhead by a great deal.

70. Answer: C. Back up data to removable media and store a copy offsite

Explanation: Backing up data to removable media and storing it offsite is the least expensive solution.

See the section "Disaster Recovery Planning and Procedures" in Chapter 16, "Redundancy and Disaster Recovery," for more information.

Incorrect answers: Hot sites and cold sites can cost the organization a lot of money, especially hot sites. Implementing a remote backup solution usually requires some sort of service with a monthly fee. You, as the network administrator, can back up data to removable media and store it offsite without incurring any other fees except for the cost of the removable media.

71. Answer: A. The hard drive should be sanitized.

Explanation: Before a hard drive is recycled, it should be sanitized. Also known as purging, sanitizing is the removal of data in such a way that it cannot be reconstructed by any known technique. At this point the drive can be recycled within the organization or recycled with the rest of the computer.

See the section "Legislative and Organizational Policies" in Chapter 18, "Policies and Procedures," for more information.

Incorrect answers: Reformatting the drive is not enough because reformatting leaves data remanence, or data residue. Destroying the drive can render it useless and therefore cannot be recycled. Storing the drive in a safe area is not recycling the drive.

72. Answer: D. Deploy a honeypot in the perimeter network

Explanation: A honeypot can be used to lure attackers in and trap them while you analyze their methods. The honeypot is usually placed within the perimeter network, which is the DMZ.

See the section "Firewalls and Network Security" in Chapter 8, "Network Perimeter Security," for more information.

Incorrect answers: Proxy servers are usually not placed in the perimeter network; they act as go-betweens, or mediators, for users on the LAN and servers on the Internet. A NIPS (network intrusion prevention system) can be placed in or out of a perimeter network, but it does not lure in attackers; instead, a NIPS attempts to prevent attacks from happening.

73. Answer: C. Systems should be restored within six hours with a minimum of two days' worth of data.

Explanation: *RTO* stands for recovery time objective, the acceptable amount of time to restore a function, service, or entire system. In the question the RTO is six hours, and so systems should be restored within six hours. *RPO* stands for recovery point objective, the acceptable latency of data, or the maximum tolerable time that data can remain inaccessible after a disaster. In the question the RPO is two days, and so there should be a maximum of two days' worth of data latency.

See the section "Disaster Recovery Planning and Procedures" in Chapter 16, "Redundancy and Disaster Recovery," for more information.

Incorrect answers: All of the other answers give incorrect descriptions of RTO and RPO. Know your acronyms!

74. Answer: D. DDoS

Explanation: A DDoS (distributed denial of service) attack is occurring. Most likely there is a botnet with computers on the Internet (such as 212.119.64.32) and computers on the LAN (such as 10.254.254.102) that are all zombies—and part of the botnet—concentrating an attack on the server at 10.254.254.201. It is known as a distributed attack because the entire attack is broken up among multiple computers. These attacks often happen on a large scale, where thousands of computers simultaneously attack a well-known server.

See the section "Malicious Attacks" in Chapter 7, "Networking Protocols and Threats," for more information.

Incorrect answers: The Xmas tree attack is one where special packets are sent that have specific flags set. It can ultimately act as a denial of service (DoS) attack if launched correctly. But it is not used for distributed DoS attacks. *XSS* stands for cross-site scripting, a type of code injection attack that exploits a computer programming flaw, often in web server forms. As mentioned, *DoS* stands for denial of service, an attack often performed by a single computer, not six or thousands in the way that a DDoS attack would occur.

75. Answers: A and D. Disk wiping and full disk encryption

Explanation: You don't want anyone else to get a hold of your SSL certificates, even if they are expired. The best solution in the scenario is to either destroy the drives yourself or store them in a secure location for a period of time. However, if you are sending them to a third party for destruction, the best option would be to fully wipe the drives; sanitize them with powerful software, and strong methods such as the Gutmann method. Barring that, you would want to consider full disk encryption (FDE) that utilizes AES or another powerful cipher. This way, the third party, and anyone else between you and the third party, will not be able to learn the RSA keys that the certificates are based on.

See the section "Legislative and Organizational Policies" in Chapter 18, "Policies and Procedures," for more information.

Incorrect answers: A data retention policy states how long data must be stored by an organization. If the drives are going to another company, then this policy is moot in this case. The server's hard drives that are referred to in the question are most likely internal drives, so removable media encryption (for things such as USB flash drives) has no bearing here. Disk hashing is not necessary. You are not interested in the data anymore, so there is no reason to hash it.

76. Answer: A. Key stretching

Explanation: Key stretching techniques will take a weak key, process it, and output an enhanced and more powerful key. This is often based on a password, and will include salting, making dictionary attacks and brute-forcing difficult to accomplish. The phrase "...slowing down the runtime of the hashing algorithm and increasing entropy by passing the input and salt back during each iteration" is the key. Salting usually happens in conjunction with key stretching, so that was the first hint. Next, "each iteration" is another hint meaning the original hash is re-hashed over and over. Warning: too many iterations can slow down the server where passwords are being checked.

See the section "Hashing Basics" in Chapter 14, "Encryption and Hashing Concepts," for more information.

Incorrect answers: When dealing with ciphers, *confusion* refers to making the relationship between a key and the ciphertext as complex as possible, and *diffusion* refers to the structure of the plaintext being dissipated into the ciphertext. In encryption, *substitution* is commonly used for confusion and *transposition* is commonly used for diffusion. The Root of Trust (RoT) is the set of functions in trusted computing that are always trusted by the operating system. A monoalphabetic cipher is one that uses fixed substitution, such as in the Caesar cipher or ROT13. *PRNG* stands for pseudorandom number generator, which is most likely being used in this scenario as part of the hashing process, but it is not what the engineer is referring to directly. *Pass the hash* is a hacking technique where an attacker obtains the password hash of one or more user accounts, and reapplies them to a server or other system in order to fool the system into thinking that the attacker is authentic—we use key stretching and hashing to make passwords more secure so that we can avoid attacks such as pass the hash.

77. Answers: B, D, F. Compartmentalize the network, apply technical controls to meet compliance regulation, and establish a list of devices that must meet regulations

Explanation: Of the listed options, the best ones for achieving compliance with PCI (Payment Card Industry) and SOX (Sarbanes-Oxley) regulations include the following:

1) Compartmentalize the network—divvy up the network with methods such as VLANs, subnetting, DMZs, whatever security boundary necessary to protect servers and clients that deal with sensitive data.

2) Apply technical controls to meet compliance regulations—for example, vulnerability management, monitoring, protecting data, and so on.

3) Establish a list of devices that must meet regulations: Any devices and computers that will have payment info, health info, or PII of any kind flowing through them should be analyzed, secured, and continually monitored.

PCI compliance requirements can be summed up as the following:

- Protect cardholder data
- Build and maintain a secure network
- Maintain an information security policy
- Maintain a vulnerability management program
- Implement strong access control measures
- Regularly monitor and test systems and networks

See the section "Legislative and Organizational Policies" in Chapter 18, "Policies and Procedures," for more information.

Incorrect answers: Establish a company framework is somewhat vague but could refer to creating an IT security framework. This is a very good idea, but it is more of a high-level plan on how to execute actual procedures and policies, and not the procedures and policies themselves. Centralizing management of all devices might be a good idea from a management perspective, but for security, certain devices will no doubt need to be compartmentalized. Establishing a list of users who work with each regulation is a good idea, but not as important as the technical controls previously mentioned. Note: Remember to familiarize yourself with whatever policies and procedures your organization employs, whether they are related to PCI, SOX, ISO, or other compliance and regulatory methods.

78. Answer: B. The hash key summary of the hardware and the specialized program no longer match.

Explanation: Some software activations are based on a hardware key, or a hardware key and a software key that are compared. The key is normally a hash value (computed with either MD5 or SHA-256, for instance), and if the hash values don't match, then the specialized program won't be able to execute the online activation process, which is required because the image was restored to the new computer (with a new and different key). This, of course, is the most likely cause, but not the only possible reason for why the specialized program stopped functioning.

See the section "Hashing Basics" in Chapter 14, "Encryption and Hashing Concepts," for more information.

Incorrect answers: If the image file to be restored was encrypted with the wrong key, then you wouldn't be able to complete the restoration, and the computer would not function. In trusted computing, remote attestation is when a client computer authenticates its hardware and software configuration to a remote server with the goal being to determine the level of trust—often using a PKI. Remote attestation might indeed be failing, but it is less likely being caused by blocked ports. The software configuration of the affected computer should not have changed, even after the restoration. Plus, the scenario doesn't mention any network changes, so the configuration of ports, ACLs, and so on should be the same. The least likely answer is that the binary files of the specialized program have been modified by malware. Malware can target binary files, but it is less common compared to other types of files such as executables. Many application developers will protect their binary files with transport layer security encryption, making them difficult (if not impossible) to modify.

79. Answer: D. Fingerprinting

Explanation: The technique being used here is fingerprinting, which is used to find out information about a system. It can be done passively by sniffing packets between hosts, or actively by sending special packets to a target and analyzing the responses. It can be done by scanning ports, or by using commands in a browser's URL bar as is the case in this scenario. By adding syntax to the end of a domain, you can "test" the web server and ascertain information about it based on the results. In this case, we see "ORA-000001: SQL command not properly ended" is the result. This tells us that the website is running an Oracle database (a relational SQL-oriented database). From there an attacker could limit attack techniques to that particular type of server, saving time. Now, if you were to run that actual syntax against my website, you would not see anything about Oracle, but you might get a 404 Not Found error. Underneath it would tell you that the server is running Apache web server software, OpenSSL, and more. Unless, that is, we improved upon our input validation and secure coding concepts, which is exactly why these tests are performed—to uncover these vulnerabilities.

See the section "Secure Programming" in Chapter 5, "Application Security," and "Conducting Risk Assessments" in Chapter 12, "Vulnerability and Risk Assessment," for more information.

Incorrect answers: Cross-site scripting (XSS) exploits the trust a user's browser has in a website through code injection, often in web forms, but not in the URL bar. SQL injection is a type of code injection when user input in database web forms is not filtered correctly and is executed improperly. Privilege escalation is the act of exploiting a bug or design flaw in a software or firmware application to gain access to resources that normally would've been protected from an application or user. Remote code execution (RCE) is when an attacker obtains control of a target computer through some sort of vulnerability. Finally, a zero day attack is one that is executed on a vulnerability in software before that vulnerability is known to the creator. Unfortunately, as a security administrator, you are expected to be able to predict the future to a certain extent, and protect against the unknown. Don't worry, though; the more experienced you get, the easier this becomes!

80. Answer: C. Place the remote desktop server(s) on a screened subnet, and implement two-factor authentication.

Explanation: The key phrase here is that the risk assessment suggests that Windows should be protected from ingress traffic. That mainly implies the Windows clients, but could include the Windows server as well. Either way, to that end, one of the best ways to secure the server is to compartmentalize the remote desktop server on a screened subnet. Remember that contractors will be using this server too, so you don't want it to be anywhere near other important servers in your network, and possibly it should be isolated from any and all servers. The two-factor authentication is the icing on the cake, and is an excellent solution for remote workers where theft/loss of laptops can occur. All in all, it's the best of the listed answers.

See the sections "Network Design" in Chapter 6, "Network Design Elements," and "Authentication Models and Components" in Chapter 10, "Physical Security and Authentication Models," for more information.

Incorrect answers:

"Change remote desktop to a non-standard port, and implement password complexity for the entire active directory domain."—Changing the remote desktop port is commonly implemented. For example, Microsoft remote desktop services uses 3389 inbound by default. Any attacker with a little experience knows this. So, changing the port is a good idea, but from the answer you can assume that the server is not in a screened subnet, DMZ, or similar protected area. Implementing password complexity for the Active Directory domain implies that the remote desktop server is located in the domain. You probably don't want that, or at least need to compartmentalize it in some way. Also, password complexity should already have been enabled, especially if this is an enterprise-level corporate network.

"Distribute new IPsec VPN client software to applicable parties, and then virtualize the remote desktop services functionality."—It's kind of a given: you would have to distribute *some kind* of VPN client software in order for remote users to connect. However, IPsec implies an L2TP connection. There are better, more secure options such as a Cisco GRE tunnel, or an always-on SSL/TLS-based VPN. But that doesn't tackle the problem of server location. Also, "virtualize the remote desktop services functionality" is vague. Are we talking about the clients? Server? Both? Most likely clients, and virtualizing apps can have security benefits, but remote desktop client apps aren't commonly virtualized. And if this is a large enterprise network (implying lots of remote users), then a virtualized remote access server is probably not a good idea from a performance standpoint.

"Deploy a remote desktop server on your internal LAN, and require an active directory integrated SSL connection for access."—We definitely don't want the remote access server on the LAN. No, it should be located somewhere more secure such as a DMZ, subnet, on the cloud, etc. Active Directory with SSL (meaning LDAP over SSL, port 636) is a good idea, but it again implies that the remote desktop server is on the LAN. Using a subnet or DMZ and using multifactor authentication dismisses most of the security issues associated with this incorrect answer's solution.

Remember to carefully secure your remote desktop servers using a layered defense strategy, especially if that server requires communication with a domain controller or other server on the LAN.

That is the end of the practice exam answers and explanations. Next, be sure to visit the companion website (www.pearsonitcertification.com/title/9780789758996) for additional practice exams, real-world scenarios, videos, and simulations. And visit my personal website as well (www.davidlprowse.com) for articles and videos relating to computer security.

Glossary

This glossary contains the key terms from the book. All the terms from each chapter's "Define Key Terms" tasks are defined here.

3-leg perimeter   A type of DMZ where a firewall has three legs that connect to the LAN, the Internet, and the DMZ.

10 tape rotation   A backup rotation scheme in which ten backup tapes are used over the course of two weeks.

802.1X   An authentication technology used to connect devices to a LAN or WLAN. It is an example of port-based network access control (NAC).

acceptable use policy (AUP)   Policy that defines the rules that restrict how a computer, network, or other system may be used.

access control list (ACL)   A list of permissions attached to an object specifying what level of access a user, users, or groups have to that object. When dealing with firewalls, an ACL is a set of rules that applies to a list of network names, IP addresses, and port numbers.

access control model   Specifies methodologies by which admission to physical areas and, more importantly, computer systems is managed and organized.

account expiration   The date when a user's account he uses to log on to the network expires.

accounting   The tracking of data, computer usage, and network resources. Often it means logging, auditing, and monitoring of the data and resources.

active interception   Normally refers to placing a computer between the sender and the receiver in an effort to capture and possibly modify information.

active reconnaissance   Gaining information about a target system using active, engaging techniques.

ad filtering   Ways of blocking and filtering out unwanted advertisements; pop-up blockers and content filters are considered to be ad filtering methods.

address space layout randomization (ASLR)   A technique used to prevent the exploitation of memory vulnerabilities.

Advanced Encryption Standard (AES)   A symmetric key encryption standard, used with WPA and WPA2, that is the successor to DES/3DES and is composed of three different block ciphers: AES-128, AES-192, and AES-256.

advanced persistent threat (APT)   A set of computer-attacking processes that targets private organizations or nation states. Also refers to a group (often a government) that persistently targets a specific entity.

adware   Type of spyware that pops up advertisements based on what it has learned about the user.

agile model   A type of SDLC based on being adaptive to change, and cooperation between business people, customers, and developers. *See* software development life cycle (SDLC). *Compare with* waterfall model.

air gap   A method of securing a control unit, system, or network through isolation and possibly shielding.

algorithms   Well-defined instructions that describe computations from their initial state to their final state.

always-on VPN   A method of VPN where the user can always access the connection without the need to periodically disconnect and reconnect. It often uses SSL/TLS for encrypted connections instead of PPTP or L2TP.

anomaly-based monitoring   Also known as statistical anomaly-based monitoring, establishes a performance baseline based on a set of normal network traffic evaluations.

AP isolation   Each client connected to the AP will not be able to communicate with each other, but they can each still access the Internet.

application blacklisting   A method of disallowing one or more applications from use.

application containerization   A virtualization method that allows an organization to run applications without launching an entire virtual machine. Also known simply as *containerization*.

application firewall   A firewall that can control the traffic associated with specific applications. Works all the way up to the application layer of the OSI model.

application-level gateway (ALG)   Applies security mechanisms to specific applications, such as FTP and/or BitTorrent. It supports address and port translation and checks whether the type of application traffic is allowed.

application whitelisting   A method of restricting users to specific applications.

ARP poisoning   An attack that exploits Ethernet networks and may enable an attacker to sniff frames of information, modify that information, or stop it from getting to its intended destination.

asymmetric key algorithm   A type of cipher that uses a pair of different keys to encrypt and decrypt data.

attack vector   The path or means by which an attacker gains access to a computer.

attestation   The act of verifying whether a process is secure, for example, the secure boot process of a UEFI-based system.

attribute-based access control (ABAC)   An access model that is dynamic and context-aware and uses IF-THEN statements and a combination of policies to control access to resources.

audit trail   Record or log that shows the tracked actions of users, regardless of whether the users successfully completed the actions.

authentication   When a person's identity is confirmed. Authentication is the *verification* of a person's identity.

authorization   When a user is granted access to specific resources after authentication is complete.

availability   Data is obtainable regardless of how information is stored, accessed, or protected.

backdoors   Used in computer programs to bypass normal authentication and other security mechanisms in place.

back-to-back perimeter   A type of DMZ that is located between the LAN and the Internet.

backup generator   Part of an emergency power system used when there is an outage of regular electric grid power.

baiting   When a malicious individual leaves malware-infected removable media, such as a USB drive or optical disc, lying around in plain view.

banner grabbing   A technique used to gain information about servers and take inventory of systems and services. It can be used legitimately by network administrators or illegitimately by attackers to grab information such as HTTP headers.

baseline reporting   Identification of the security posture of an application, system, or network.

baselining   The process of measuring changes in networking, hardware, software, and so on.

behavior-based monitoring   A monitoring system that looks at the previous behavior of applications, executables, and/or the operating system and compares that to current activity on the system.

biometrics   The science of recognizing humans based on one or more physical characteristics.

birthday attack   An attack on a hashing system that attempts to send two different messages with the same hash function, causing a collision.

black-box testing   When people test a system but have no specific knowledge of the system code involved with the system.

black hat   A hacker that breaks into computer systems without permission, with the express purpose of theft, piracy, credit card fraud, or other illegal activities.

blackout   When a total loss of power for a prolonged period occurs.

block cipher   A type of algorithm that encrypts a number of bits as individual units known as blocks.

Blowfish   A 64-bit block cipher designed by Bruce Schneier as an alternative to DES.

bluejacking   The sending of unsolicited messages to Bluetooth-enabled devices such as mobile phones and tablets.

bluesnarfing   The unauthorized access of information from a wireless device through a Bluetooth connection.

botnet   A group of compromised computers used to distribute malware across the Internet; the members are referred to as "bots" and are usually zombies.

broadcast storm   When there is an accumulation of broadcast and multicast packet traffic on the LAN coming from one or more network interfaces.

brownout   When the voltage drops to such an extent that it typically causes the lights to dim and causes computers to shut off.

brute-force attack   A password attack where every possible password is attempted.

buffer overflow   When a process stores data outside the memory that the developer intended to be used for storage. This could cause erratic behavior in the application, especially if the memory already had other data in it.

business impact analysis (BIA)   The examination of critical versus noncritical functions; part of a business continuity plan (BCP).

butt set   A device that looks similar to a phone but has alligator clips that can connect to the various terminals used by phone equipment, enabling a person to listen in to a conversation. Also called a lineman's handset.

CAM table   The Content Addressable Memory table, a table that is in a switch's memory that contains ports and their corresponding MAC addresses.

CAPTCHA   A type of challenge-response mechanism used primarily in websites to tell whether or not the user is human. Stands for Completely Automated Public Turing test to tell Computers and Humans Apart.

certificate   Digitally signed electronic document that binds a public key with a user identity.

certificate authority (CA)   The entity (usually a server) that issues digital certificates to users.

certificate revocation list (CRL)   A list of certificates no longer valid or that have been revoked by the issuer.

chain of custody   Documents who had custody of evidence all the way up to litigation or a court trial (if necessary) and verifies that the evidence has not been modified.

Challenge Handshake Authentication Protocol (CHAP)   An authentication scheme used by the Point-to-Point Protocol (PPP) that is the standard for dial-up connections.

change management   A structured way of changing the state of a computer system, network, or IT procedure.

chromatic dispersion   The refraction of light as in a rainbow. If light is refracted in such a manner on fiber-optic cables, the signal cannot be read by the receiver.

cipher   An algorithm that can perform encryption or decryption.

circuit-level gateway   Works at the session layer of the OSI model and applies security mechanisms when a TCP or UDP connection is established; acts as a go-between for the transport and application layers in TCP/IP.

closed-circuit television (CCTV)   A video system (often used for surveillance) that makes use of traditional coaxial-based video components, but is used privately, within a building or campus.

cloud computing   A way of offering on-demand services that extend the capabilities of a person's computer or an organization's network.

cluster   Two or more servers that work with each other.

cold site   A site that has tables, chairs, bathrooms, and possibly some technical setup (for example, basic phone, data, and electric lines), but will require days if not weeks to set up properly.

collision   When two different files end up using the same hash, which is possible with less secure hashing algorithms.

Common Vulnerabilities and Exposures (CVE)   An online list of known vulnerabilities (and patches) to software, especially web servers. It is maintained by the MITRE Corporation.

computer security audits   Technical assessments made of applications, systems, or networks.

confidentiality   Preventing the disclosure of information to unauthorized persons.

content filters   Individual computer programs that block external files that use JavaScript or images from loading into the browser.

context-aware authentication   An adaptive way of authenticating users based on their usage of resources, and the confidence that the system has in the user.

Controller Area Network (CAN)   A multimaster serial bus that allows connectivity between the various microcontrollers in an automobile.

cookies   Text files placed on the client computer that store information about it, which could include your computer's browsing habits and credentials. Tracking cookies are used by spyware to collect information about a web user's activities. Session cookies are used by attackers in an attempt to hijack a session.

crossover error rate (CER)   The collective analysis and comparison of the false acceptance rate (FAR) and false rejection rate (FRR). It is also known as equal error rate.

cross-site request forgery (XSRF)   An attack that exploits the trust a website has in a user's browser in an attempt to transmit unauthorized commands to the website.

cross-site scripting (XSS)   A type of vulnerability found in web applications used with session hijacking. XSS enables an attacker to inject client-side scripts into web pages.

crosstalk   When a signal transmitted on one copper wire creates an undesired effect on another wire; the signal "bleeds" over, so to speak.

cryptanalysis attack   A password attack that uses a considerable set of precalculated encrypted passwords located in a lookup table.

cryptographic hash functions   Hash functions based on block ciphers.

cryptography   The practice and study of hiding information.

data emanation   Also known as signal emanation, the electromagnetic field generated by a network cable or network device, which can be manipulated to eavesdrop on conversations or to steal data.

Data Encryption Standard (DES)   An older type of block cipher selected by the U.S. federal government back in the 1970s as its encryption standard; due to its weak key, it is now considered deprecated.

data loss prevention (DLP)   Systems that are designed to protect data by way of content inspection. They are meant to stop the leakage of confidential data, often concentrating on communications.

data at rest   Inactive data that is archived.

data in transit   Data that crosses the network or data that resides in computer memory.

data in use   Data that is undergoing constant change.

default account   An account installed by default on a device or within an operating system with a default set of user credentials that are usually insecure.

defense in depth   The building up and layering of security measures that protect data from inception, on through storage and network transfer, and lastly to final disposal.

demilitarized zone (DMZ)   A special area of the network (sometimes referred to as a subnetwork) that houses servers that host information accessed by clients or other networks on the Internet.

denial-of-service (DoS)   A broad term given to many different types of network attacks that attempt to make computer resources unavailable.

dictionary attack   A password attack that uses a prearranged list of likely words, trying each of them one at a time.

differential backup   Type of backup that backs up only the contents of a folder that have changed since the last full backup.

Diffie-Hellman key exchange   Invented in the 1970s, the first practical method for establishing a shared secret key over an unprotected communications channel.

digital signature   A signature that authenticates a document through math, letting the recipient know that the document was created and sent by the actual sender and not someone else.

directory traversal   Also known as the ../ (dot dot slash) attack, a method of accessing unauthorized parent directories.

disaster recovery plan (DRP)   A plan that details the policies and procedures concerning the recovery and/or continuation of an organization's technology infrastructure.

discretionary access control (DAC)   An access control policy generally determined by the owner.

disk duplexing   When each disk is connected to a separate controller.

distributed denial-of-service (DDoS)   An attack in which a group of compromised systems attacks a single target, causing a DoS to occur at that host, usually using a botnet.

diversion theft   When a thief attempts to take responsibility for a shipment by diverting the delivery to a nearby location.

DNS amplification attack   An attack that initiates a DNS request with a spoofed source address. Responses (which are larger than the request) are sent to the victim server in an attempt to flood it.

DNS poisoning   The modification of name resolution information that should be in a DNS server's cache.

domain name kiting   The process of deleting a domain name during the five-day grace period (known as the add grace period, or AGP) and immediately reregistering it for another five-day period to keep a domain name indefinitely and for free.

downgrade attack   When a protocol (such as TLS or SSL) is downgraded from the current version to a previous version, exploiting backward compatibility.

due care   The mitigation action that an organization takes to defend against the risks that have been uncovered during due diligence.

due diligence   Ensuring that IT infrastructure risks are known and managed.

due process   The principle that an organization must respect and safeguard personnel's rights.

dumpster diving   When a person literally scavenges for private information in garbage and recycling containers.

eavesdropping   When a person uses direct observation to "listen" in to a conversation.

electromagnetic interference (EMI)   A disturbance that can affect electrical circuits, devices, and cables due to electromagnetic conduction or radiation.

elliptic curve cryptography (ECC)   A type of public key cryptography based on the structure of an elliptic curve.

Elliptic Curve Diffie-Hellman Ephemeral (ECDHE)   An asymmetric algorithm created by Diffie and Hellman that is based on elliptic curve cryptography and runs in ephemeral mode.

encryption   The process of changing information using an algorithm (or cipher) into another form that is unreadable by others—unless they possess the key to that data.

ethical hacker   An expert at breaking into systems and can attack systems on behalf of the system's owner and with the owner's consent.

evil twin   A rogue wireless access point that uses the same SSID as a nearby legitimate access point.

explicit allow   When an administrator sets a rule that allows a specific type of traffic through a firewall, often within an ACL.

explicit deny   When an administrator sets a rule that denies a specific type of traffic access through a firewall, often within an ACL.

Extensible Authentication Protocol (EAP)   Not an authentication mechanism in itself but instead defines message formats. 802.1X would be the authentication mechanism and defines how EAP is encapsulated within messages.

fail-open mode   When a switch broadcasts data on all ports the way a hub does.

failover clusters   Also known as high-availability clusters, these are designed so that a secondary server can take over in the case that the primary one fails, with limited or no downtime.

false acceptance   When a biometric system authenticates a user who should *not* be allowed access to the system. It is analyzed with the false acceptance rate (FAR).

false negative   Speaking in terms of intrusion monitoring, this is when an IDS/IPS fails to block an attack, thinking it is legitimate traffic.

false positive   Speaking in terms of intrusion monitoring, this is when an IDS/IPS blocks legitimate traffic from passing on to the network.

false rejection   When a biometric system fails to recognize an authorized person and doesn't allow that person access. It is analyzed with the false rejection rate (FRR).

Faraday cage   An enclosure formed by conducting material or by a mesh of such material; it blocks out external static electric fields and can stop emanations from cell phones and other devices within the cage from leaking out.

federated identity management (FIM)   When a user's identity is shared across multiple identity management systems.

fire suppression   The process of controlling and/or extinguishing fires to protect people and an organization's data and equipment.

firewall   A part of a computer system or network designed to block unauthorized access while permitting authorized communications. It is a device or set of devices configured to permit or deny computer applications based on a set of rules and other criteria.

first responders   People who perform preliminary analysis of the incident data and determine whether the incident is an incident or just an event, and the criticality of the incident.

flood guard   Security feature implemented on some firewalls to protect against SYN floods and other flooding attacks. Also known as an attack guard.

fork bomb   An attack that works by creating a large number of processes quickly to saturate the available processing space in the computer's operating system. It is a type of wabbit.

Fraggle   A type of DoS similar to the Smurf attack, but the traffic sent is UDP echo traffic as opposed to ICMP echo traffic.

full backup   Type of backup where all the contents of a folder are backed up.

fuzz testing   Also called fuzzing, a type of test in which random data is inputted into a computer program in an attempt to find vulnerabilities.

GNU Privacy Guard (GPG)   A free alternative to PGP that is compliant with OpenPGP.

grandfather-father-son   A backup rotation scheme in which three sets of backup tapes must be defined—usually they are daily, weekly, and monthly, which correspond to son, father, and grandfather.

grayware   A general term used to describe applications that are behaving improperly but without serious consequences; often describes types of spyware.

Group Policy   Used in Microsoft environments to govern user and computer accounts through a set of rules.

hacktivist   An attacker who has an agenda that may or may not be benign.

hardening   The act of configuring an OS securely, updating it, creating rules and policies to help govern the system in a secure manner, and removing unnecessary applications and services.

hardware security module (HSM)   A physical device that deals with the encryption of authentication processes, digital signings, and payment processes.

hash   A summary of a file or message. It is generated to verify the integrity of the file or message.

hash function   A mathematical procedure that converts a variable-sized amount of data into a smaller block of data.

high availability   When a system or component (such as a RAID array) is continuously operational for an extended period of time. The component should have an average 99.9% uptime or higher.

hoax   The attempt at deceiving people into believing something that is false.

honeynet   One or more computers or servers, or an area of a network, used to attract and trap potential attackers to counteract any attempts at unauthorized access of the network.

honeypot   Generally is a single computer but could also be a file, group of files, or an area of unused IP address space used to attract and trap potential attackers to counteract any attempts at unauthorized access of the network.

host-based intrusion detection system (HIDS)   A type of system loaded on an individual computer that analyzes and monitors what happens inside that computer—for example, if any changes have been made to file integrity.

hot and cold aisles   The aisles in a server room or data center that circulate cold air into the systems and hot air out of them. Usually, the systems and cabinets are supported by a raised floor.

hot site   A near duplicate of the original site of the organization, complete with phones, computers, networking devices, and full backups.

hotfix   Originally defined as a patch to an individual OS or application to fix a single problem, installed live while the system was up and running, and without a reboot necessary. However, this term has changed over time and varies from vendor to vendor.

HTTP proxy (web proxy)   Caches web pages from servers on the Internet for a set amount of time.

hypervisor   The portion of virtual machine software that allows multiple virtual operating systems (guests) to run at the same time on a single computer.

identification   When a person is in a state of being identified. It can also be described as something that identifies a person such as an ID card.

identity proofing   An initial validation of an identity.

implicit deny   Denies all traffic to a resource unless the users generating that traffic are specifically granted access to the resource. For example, when a device denies all traffic unless a rule is made to open the port associated with the type of traffic desired to be let through.

incident management   The monitoring and detection of security events on a computer network and the execution of proper responses to those security events.

incident response   A set of procedures that an investigator follows when examining a computer security incident.

incremental backup   Type of backup that backs up only the contents of a folder that have changed since the last full backup or the last incremental backup.

information assurance (IA)   The practice of managing risks that are related to computer hardware and software systems.

information security   The act of protecting information from unauthorized access. It usually includes an in-depth plan on how to secure data, computers, and networks.

infrastructure as a service (IaaS)   A cloud computing service that offers computer networking, storage, load balancing, routing, and VM hosting.

input validation   Also called data validation, a process that ensures the correct usage of data.

integer overflow   When arithmetic operations attempt to create a numeric value that is too big for the available memory space.

integrity   Ensuring that data can be modified only by those authorized to do so.

interconnection security agreement (ISA)   An agreement that is established between two (or more) organizations that own and operate connected IT systems and data; it specifically documents the technical and security requirements of the interconnection between the organizations.

Internet content filter   A filter that is usually applied as software at the application layer and can filter out various types of Internet activities such as websites accessed, e-mail, instant messaging, and more. It is used most often to disallow access to inappropriate web material.

Internet Protocol Security (IPsec)   A TCP/IP protocol that authenticates and encrypts IP packets, effectively securing communications between computers and devices using the protocol.

IP proxy   Secures a network by keeping machines behind it anonymous; it does this through the use of NAT.

IV attack   A type of related-key attack based on the initialization vector of wireless network communications, where an attacker observes the operation of a cipher using several different keys and finds a mathematical relationship between them, allowing the attacker to ultimately decipher data.

job rotation   When users are cycled through various assignments.

Kerberos   An authentication protocol that enables computers to prove their identity to each other in a secure manner.

key   The essential piece of information that determines the output of a cipher.

key escrow   When certificate keys are held in case third parties, such as government or other organizations, need access to encrypted communications.

key recovery agent   Software that can be used to archive and restore keys if necessary.

key stretching   Takes a weak key, processes it, and outputs an enhanced and more powerful key, usually increasing key size to 128 bits.

LANMAN hash   The original hash used to store Windows passwords, known as LM hash, based off the DES algorithm.

Layer 2 Tunneling Protocol (L2TP)   A tunneling protocol used to connect virtual private networks. It does not include confidentiality or encryption on its own. It uses port 1701 and can be more secure than PPTP if used in conjunction with IPsec.

least functionality   When a computer is configured to only allow required functions, applications, services, ports, and protocols.

least privilege   When a user is given only the amount of privileges needed to do his or her job.

Lightweight Directory Access Protocol (LDAP)   An application layer protocol used for accessing and modifying directory services data.

load-balancing clusters   When multiple computers are connected in an attempt to share resources such as CPU, RAM, and hard disks.

locally shared objects (LSOs)   Also known as Flash cookies, files stored on users' computers that allow websites to collect information about visitors. Also referred to as "local shared objects."

logic bomb   Code that has, in some way, been inserted into software; it is meant to initiate some type of malicious function when specific criteria are met.

MAC filtering   A method used to filter out which computers can access the wireless network; the WAP does this by consulting a list of MAC addresses that have been previously entered.

MAC flooding   An attack that sends numerous packets to a switch, each of which has a different source MAC address, in an attempt to use up the memory on the switch. If this is successful, the switch will change state to fail-open mode.

MAC spoofing   An attack where the attacker masks the MAC address of the computer's network adapter. Can be enhanced by a DHCP starvation attack.

malware   Software designed to infiltrate a computer system and possibly damage it without the user's knowledge or consent.

mandatory access control (MAC)   An access control policy determined by a computer system, not by a user or owner, as it is in DAC.

mandatory vacations   When an organization requires that employees take a certain number of days of vacation consecutively, helping to detect potential malicious activity such as fraud or embezzlement.

man-in-the-browser (MITB)   Infects a vulnerable web browser and modifies online transactions. Similar to MITM.

man-in-the-middle (MITM)   A form of eavesdropping that intercepts all data between a client and a server, relaying that information back and forth.

mantrap   An area between two doorways, meant to hold people until they are identified and authenticated.

many-to-one mapping   When multiple certificates are mapped to a single recipient.

mean time between failures (MTBF)   Defines the average number of failures per million hours for a product in question.

measured boot   Takes measurements of the secure boot process, signs those results with a TPM, and reports those measurements to a trusted third party such as a remote attestation service.

memorandum of understanding (MoU)   A letter of intent between two entities (such as government agencies) concerning SLAs and BPAs.

memory leak   When a program allocates memory but does not free it up properly after the process using it has completed.

Message-Digest algorithm 5 (MD5)   A 128-bit key hash used to provide integrity of files and messages.

mobile device management (MDM)   A centralized software solution that allows for the control and configuration of mobile devices.

multifactor authentication (MFA)   When two or more types of authentication are used when dealing with user access control.

mutual authentication   When two computers (for example, a client and a server) verify each other's identity.

network access control (NAC)   Sets the rules by which connections to a network are governed.

network address translation (NAT)   The process of changing an IP address while it is in transit across a router. This is usually implemented so that one larger address space (private) can be remapped to another address space, or single IP address (public).

network intrusion detection system (NIDS)   A type of IDS that attempts to detect malicious network activities—for example, port scans and DoS attacks—by constantly monitoring network traffic.

network intrusion prevention system (NIPS)   Designed to inspect traffic and, based on its configuration or security policy, remove, detain, or redirect malicious traffic.

Network Management System (NMS)   The software run on one or more servers that controls the monitoring of network-attached devices and computers.

network mapping   The study of physical and logical connectivity of networks.

network perimeter   The border of a computer network, commonly secured by devices such as firewalls and NIDS/NIPS solutions.

null pointer dereference   A memory dereference that can result in a memory fault error.

null session   A connection to the Windows interprocess communications share (IPC$) that can be exploited by a null session attack, which makes unauthenticated NetBIOS connections to a target computer.

nonce   A random number issued by an authentication protocol that can only be used once.

non-promiscuous mode   When a network adapter captures only the packets that are addressed to it.

non-repudiation   The idea of ensuring that a person or group cannot refute the validity of your proof against them.

NTLM hash   Successor to the LM hash. A more advanced hash used to store Windows passwords, based off the RC4 algorithm.

NTLMv2 hash   Successor to the NTLM hash. Based off the MD5 hashing algorithm.

null session   When used by an attacker, a malicious connection to the Windows interprocess communications share (IPC$).

onboarding   When a new employee is added to an organization, and to its identity and access management system.

one-time pad   A cipher that encrypts plaintext with a secret random key that is the same length as the plaintext.

one-to-one mapping   When an individual certificate is mapped to a single recipient.

one-way function   A hash that is easy to compute when generated but difficult (or impossible) to compute in reverse.

Online Certificate Status Protocol (OCSP)   An alternative to using a certificate revocation list (CRL). It contains less information than a CRL does, and does not require encryption.

open mail relay   Also known as an SMTP open relay, enables anyone on the Internet to send e-mail through an SMTP server.

Open Vulnerability and Assessment Language (OVAL)   A standard and a programming language designed to standardize the transfer of secure public information across networks and the Internet utilizing any security tools and services available.

organized crime   A criminal enterprise run by well-funded and sophisticated people motivated mainly by money, using computer systems and hacking techniques to gain access to company information and secrets.

packet filtering   In the context of firewalls, inspects each packet passing through the firewall and accepts or rejects it based on rules. Two types of packet filtering include stateless packet filters and stateful packet inspection (SPI).

pass the hash   An attack where password hashes are obtained from a server and reused in an attempt to trick the server's authentication system.

passive reconnaissance   Gaining information about a target system without engaging the system.

password cracker   Software tool used to recover passwords from hosts or to discover weak passwords.

patch   An update to a system. Patches generally carry the connotation of a small fix in the mind of the user or system administrator, so larger patches often are referred to as software updates, service packs, or something similar.

patch management   The planning, testing, implementing, and auditing of patches.

PBKDF2   A type of key stretching software that incorporates salting for additional security, usually in password hashing.

ponotration tocting   Also called pen testing, a method of evaluating the security of a system by simulating one or more attacks on that system.

permanent DoS (PDoS) attack   Generally consists of an attacker's exploiting security flaws in routers and other networking hardware by flashing the firmware of the device and replacing it with a modified image.

permissions   Control which file system resources a person can access on the network.

personal firewall   An application that protects an individual computer from unwanted Internet traffic; it does so by way of a set of rules and policies.

personally identifiable information (PII)   Information used to uniquely identify, contact, or locate a person.

pharming   When an attacker redirects one website's traffic to another bogus and possibly malicious website by modifying a DNS server or hosts file.

phishing   The criminally fraudulent process of attempting to acquire sensitive information such as usernames, passwords, and credit card details by masquerading as a trustworthy entity in an electronic communication.

piggybacking   When an unauthorized person tags along with an authorized person to gain entry to a restricted area.

ping flood   When an attacker attempts to send many ICMP echo request packets (pings) to a host in an attempt to use up all available bandwidth. Also known as an ICMP flood attack.

Ping of Death (POD)   A type of DoS that sends an oversized and/or malformed packet to another computer.

pivot   A technique used to gain access to other systems or other parts of the network after an initial system has been exploited.

platform as a service (PaaS)   A cloud computing service that provides various software solutions to organizations, especially the ability to develop applications without the cost or administration of a physical platform.

Point-to-Point Tunneling Protocol (PPTP)   A tunneling protocol used to support VPNs. Generally includes security mechanisms, and no additional software or protocols need to be loaded. A VPN device or server must have inbound port 1723 open to enable incoming PPTP connections.

policy   Rules or guidelines used to guide decisions and achieve outcomes. They can be written or configured on a computer.

pop-up blocker   An application or add-on to a web browser that blocks pop-up windows that usually contain advertisements.

port address translation (PAT)   Like NAT, but it translates both IP addresses and port numbers.

port mirroring   When you configure one or more ports on a switch to forward all packets to another port. Often used when capturing packets.

port scanner   Software used to decipher which ports are open on a host.

pre-action sprinkler system   Similar to a dry pipe system, but there are requirements for it to be set off such as heat or smoke.

pre-shared key   A key based on a generated (or selected) passphrase that is used to enable connectivity between wireless clients and an access point.

pretexting   When a person invents a scenario, or pretext, in the hope of persuading a victim to divulge information.

Pretty Good Privacy (PGP)   An encryption program used primarily for signing, encrypting, and decrypting e-mails in an attempt to increase the security of e-mail communications.

private key   A type of key that is known only to a specific user or users who keep the key a secret.

privilege escalation   The act of exploiting a bug or design flaw in a software or firmware application to gain access to resources that normally would've been protected from an application or user.

promiscuous mode   When the network adapter captures all frames/packets that it has access to regardless of the destination for those packets.

protected distribution system   Security system implemented to protect unencrypted data transfer over wired networks.

Protected Extensible Authentication Protocol (PEAP)   Protocol used to encapsulate EAP packets within encrypted and authenticated tunnels.

protocol analyzer   Software tool used to capture and analyze packets.

proxy auto-configuration (PAC)   A file in web browsers that automatically chooses an appropriate proxy server.

proxy server   Acts as an intermediary between clients, usually located on a LAN, and the servers that they want to access, usually located on the Internet.

pseudorandom number generator (PRNG)   Used by cryptographic applications that require unpredictable output. Example: SHA2PRNG. Threat: random number generator attack. Prevention: additional randomness, AES, SHA256 or higher, and physical control of the system.

public key   A type of key that is known to all parties involved in encrypted transactions within a given group.

public key cryptography   Uses asymmetric keys alone or in addition to symmetric keys. The asymmetric key algorithm creates a secret private key and a published public key.

public key infrastructure (PKI)   An entire system of hardware and software, policies and procedures, and people, used to create, distribute, manage, store, and revoke digital certificates.

qualitative risk assessment   An assessment that assigns numeric values to the probability of a risk and the impact it can have on the system or network.

quantitative risk assessment   An assessment that measures risk by using exact monetary values.

race condition   An exploitable situation that happens when a system or application is performing two tasks and the time between them can be exploited to gain access to the program, change a file, or gain access to a resource.

radio frequency interference (RFI)   Interference that can come from AM/FM transmissions and cell towers.

RAID 1   Mirroring. Data is copied to two identical drives. If one drive fails, the other continues to operate.

RAID 10   Combining the advantages of RAID 1 and 0, normally two sets of RAID 1 mirrors (minimum) that are then striped.

RAID 5   Striping with parity. Data is striped across multiple drives; fault-tolerant parity data is also written to each drive.

RAID 6   Striping with double parity. Four drives minimum.

rainbow table   In password cracking, a set of precalculated encrypted passwords located in a lookup table.

ransomware   A type of malware that restricts access to a computer system and demands a ransom be paid to restore access.

recovery point objective (RPO)   In business impact analysis, the acceptable latency of data.

recovery time objective (RTO)   In business impact analysis, the acceptable amount of time to restore a function.

redundant ISP   Secondary connections to another ISP; for example, a backup T-1 line.

redundant power supply   An enclosure that contains two complete power supplies, the second of which turns on when the first fails.

registration authority (RA)   Used to verify requests for certificates.

Remote Access Service (RAS)   A networking service that allows incoming connections from remote dial-in clients. It is also used with VPNs.

remote access Trojan (RAT)   A type of Trojan used to gain back-end access to a server, taking control of it, often for malicious purposes.

Remote Authentication Dial-In User Service (RADIUS)   Used to provide centralized administration of dial-up, VPN, and wireless authentication.

remote code execution (RCE)   When an attacker acquires control of a remote computer through a code vulnerability. Also known as arbitrary code execution. Attackers often use a web browser's URL field or a tool such as Netcat to accomplish this.

removable media controls   Security controls put in place to protect the data residing on USB flash drives and other removable media, and to protect the systems that they connect to.

replay attack   An attack in which valid data transmission is maliciously or fraudulently repeated or delayed.

residual risk   The risk that is left over after a security plan and a disaster recovery plan have been implemented.

risk   The possibility of a malicious attack or other threat causing damage or downtime to a computer system.

risk acceptance   The amount of risk an organization is willing to accept. Also known as risk retention.

risk assessment   The attempt to determine the number of threats or hazards that could possibly occur in a given amount of time to your computers and networks.

risk avoidance   When an organization avoids risk because the risk factor is too great.

risk management   The identification, assessment, and prioritization of risks, and the mitigation and monitoring of those risks.

risk mitigation   When a risk is reduced or eliminated altogether.

risk reduction   When an organization mitigates risk to an acceptable level.

risk register   Helps to track issues and address problems as they occur. Also known as a risk log.

risk transference   The transfer or outsourcing of risk to a third party. Also known as risk sharing.

rogue access point   An unauthorized wireless access point/router that allows access to secure networks. Also, rogue AP.

role-based access control (RBAC)   An access model that works with sets of permissions, instead of individual permissions that are label-based, so roles are created for various job functions in an organization.

root of trust (RoT)   A set of code and functions, usually embedded into a trusted platform module, that allows or denies tasks such as booting and drive encryption.

rootkit   A type of software designed to gain administrator-level control over a computer system without being detected.

RSA   A public key cryptography algorithm created by Rivest, Shamir, Adleman. It is commonly used in e-commerce.

sag   An unexpected decrease in the amount of voltage provided.

salting   The randomization of the hashing process to defend against cryptanalysis password attacks and rainbow tables.

sandbox   When a web script runs in its own environment for the express purpose of not interfering with other processes, possibly for testing.

script kiddie   An individual with little technical skill that reuses code and scripts that are freely available on the Internet.

secure code review   An in-depth code inspection procedure.

secure coding concepts   The best practices used during the life cycle of software development.

Secure Hash Algorithm (SHA)   A group of hash functions designed by the NSA and published by the NIST, widely used in government. The most common currently is SHA-1.

Secure/Multipurpose Internet Mail Extensions (S/MIME)   An IETF standard that provides cryptographic security for electronic messaging such as e-mail.

Secure Shell (SSH)   A protocol that can create a secure channel between two computers or network devices.

Secure Sockets Layer (SSL)   A cryptographic protocol that provides secure Internet communications such as web browsing, instant messaging, e-mail, and VoIP.

security as a service (SECaaS)   A cloud computing service where a large service provider integrates its security services into the customer's infrastructure.

security log files   Files that log activity of users. They show who did what and when, plus whether they succeeded or failed in their attempt.

security posture   The risk level to which a system, or other technology element, is exposed.

security posture assessment (SPA)   An assessment that uses baseline reporting and other analyses to discover vulnerabilities and weaknesses in systems and networks.

security template   Groups of policies that can be loaded in one procedure.

security tokens   Physical devices given to authorized users to help with authentication. These devices might be attached to a keychain or might be part of a card system.

self-encrypting drive (SED)   Hard drives that encrypt all of the contents held within using encryption keys that are maintained independently from the CPU of the housing computer.

separation of duties (SoD)   This is when more than one person is required to complete a particular task or operation.

service-level agreement (SLA)   Part of a service contract where the level of service is formally defined.

service pack (SP)   A group of updates, bug fixes, updated drivers, and security fixes that is installed from one downloadable package or from one disc.

service set identifier (SSID)   The name of a wireless access point (or network) to which network clients will connect; it is broadcast through the air.

shoulder surfing   When a person uses direct observation to find out a target's password, PIN, or other such authentication information.

sideloading   The loading of third-party apps from a location outside of the official application store for that device. Can occur either by direct Internet connection (usually disabled by default), by connecting to a second mobile device via USB OTG or Bluetooth, or by copying apps directly from a microSD card.

signature-based monitoring   Frames and packets of network traffic are analyzed for predetermined attack patterns. These attack patterns are known as signatures.

Simple Network Management Protocol (SNMP)   A TCP/IP protocol that monitors network-attached devices and computers. It's usually incorporated as part of a network management system.

single point of failure   An element, object, or part of a system that, if it fails, will cause the whole system to fail.

single sign-on (SSO)   When a user can log in once but gain access to multiple systems without being asked to log in again.

Smurf attack   A type of DoS that sends large amounts of ICMP echoes, broadcasting the ICMP echo requests to every computer on its network or subnetwork. The header of the ICMP echo requests will have a spoofed IP address. That IP address is the target of the Smurf attack. Every computer that replies to the ICMP echo requests will do so to the spoofed IP.

snapshot backup   A type of backup primarily associated with operating system imaging, but could also be used for applications or individual drives.

SNMP agent   Software deployed by the network management system that is loaded on managed devices. The software redirects the information that the NMS needs to monitor the remote managed devices.

software as a service (SaaS)   A cloud computing service where users access applications over the Internet that are provided by a third party.

software development life cycle (SDLC)   The process of creating systems and applications, and the methodologies used to do so. Also known as *systems development life cycle*.

spam   The abuse of electronic messaging systems such as e-mail, broadcast media, and instant messaging.

Spanning Tree Protocol (STP)   A networking protocol that automatically creates a loop-free topology of Ethernet switches. Prevents looping that can occur when connecting both ends of a patch cable to ports on one switch.

spear phishing   A type of phishing attack that targets particular individuals.

special hazard protection system   A clean agent sprinkler system such as FM-200 used in server rooms.

spike   A short transient in voltage that can be due to a short circuit, tripped circuit breaker, power outage, or lightning strike.

spim   The abuse of instant messaging systems, a derivative of spam.

spoofing   When an attacker masquerades as another person by falsifying information.

spyware   A type of malicious software either downloaded unwittingly from a website or installed along with some other third-party software.

standby generator   Systems that turn on automatically within seconds of a power outage.

stateful packet inspection (SPI)   Type of packet inspection that keeps track of network connections by examining the header in each packet.

static NAT   When a single private IP address translates to a single public IP address. This is also called one-to-one mapping.

steganography   The science (and art) of writing hidden messages; it is a form of security through obscurity.

storage segmentation   A clear separation of organizational and personal information, applications, and other content.

stream cipher   A type of algorithm that encrypts each byte in a message one at a time.

structured exception handling (SEH)   A way of handling exceptions generated by errors, such as ones that can be initiated by diving by zero.

subject alternative name(SAN)   A field (or fields) in PKI certificates that allows an organization to specify additional hostnames, domain names, and so on.

supervisory control and data acquisition (SCADA)   System of hardware and software that controls and monitors industrial systems such as HVAC.

surge   An unexpected increase in the amount of voltage provided.

symmetric key algorithm   A class of cipher that uses identical or closely related keys for encryption and decryption.

SYN flood   A type of DoS where an attacker sends a large amount of SYN request packets to a server in an attempt to deny service.

tailgating   A type of piggybacking where an unauthorized person follows an authorized person into a secure area, without the authorized person's consent.

TCP reset attack   Sets the reset flag in a TCP header to 1, telling the respective computer to kill the TCP session immediately.

TCP/IP hijacking   When a hacker takes over a TCP session between two computers without the need of a cookie or any other type of host access.

teardrop attack   A type of DoS that sends mangled IP fragments with overlapping and oversized payloads to the target machine.

TEMPEST   Refers to the investigations of conducted emissions from electrical and mechanical devices, which could be compromising to an organization.

Temporal Key Integrity Protocol (TKIP)   An algorithm used to secure wireless computer networks; meant as a replacement for WEP.

Terminal Access Controller Access-Control System Plus (TACACS+)   A remote authentication protocol similar to RADIUS used in Cisco networks.

threat modeling   A way of prioritizing threats to an application.

threat vector   The method a threat uses to gain access to a target computer.

tickets   Part of the authentication process used by Kerberos.

time bomb   A Trojan programmed to set off on a certain date.

time of day restriction   When a user's logon hours are configured to restrict access to the network during certain times of the day and week.

Towers of Hanoi   A backup rotation scheme based on the mathematics of the Towers of Hanoi puzzle. Uses three backup sets. For example, the first tape is used every second day, the second tape is used every fourth day, and the third tape is used every eighth day.

transitive trust   When two or more networks have a relationship where users from one network can gain access to resources on the other.

Transport Layer Security (TLS)   The successor to SSL, provides secure Internet communications. This is shown in a browser as HTTPS.

Triple DES (3DES)   Similar to DES but applies the cipher algorithm three times to each cipher block.

Trojan horse   An application that appears to perform desired functions but is actually performing malicious functions behind the scenes.

Trusted Computer System Evaluation Criteria (TCSEC)   A DoD standard that sets basic requirements for assessing the effectiveness of computer security access policies. Also known as The Orange Book.

Trusted Operating System (TOS)   A system that adheres to criteria for multilevel security and meets government regulations.

Twofish   A 128-bit block cipher designed by Bruce Schneier and based on Feistel.

typosquatting   Also called URL hijacking, a method used by attackers that takes advantage of user typos when accessing websites. Instead of the expected website, the user ends up at a website with a similar name but often malicious content.

UDP flood attack   A similar attack to the Fraggle. It uses the connectionless User Datagram Protocol. It is enticing to attackers because it does not require a synchronization process.

unified threat management (UTM)   A security product that evolved from the firewall and also includes IDS/IPS, antivirus, VPN, content filtering, DLP, and load balancing, among other technologies.

uninterruptible power supply (UPS)   Takes the functionality of a surge suppressor and combines that with a battery backup, protecting computers not only from surges and spikes, but also from sags, brownouts, and blackouts.

User Account Control (UAC)   A security component of Windows that keeps every user (besides the actual Administrator account) in standard user mode instead of as an administrator with full administrative rights—even if they are a member of the administrators group.

vampire tap   A device used to add computers to a 10BASE5 network. It pierces the copper conductor of a coaxial cable and can also be used for malicious purposes.

virtual machine (VM)   An operating system (or application) created by virtual machine software that runs within a hosting operating system.

virtual machine escape (VM)   When a user (or malware) is able to break out of a VM's isolation (or lack thereof) and gain access to the hosting computer.

virtual private network (VPN)   A connection between two or more computers or devices that are not on the same private network.

virtualization   The creation of a virtual entity, as opposed to a true or actual entity.

virtualization sprawl   Also known as VM sprawl, when there are too many VMs for an administrator to manage effectively.

virus   Code that runs on a computer without the user's knowledge; it infects the computer when the code is accessed and executed.

vishing   A type of phishing attack that makes use of telephones and VoIP.

VLAN hopping   The act of gaining access to traffic on other VLANs that would not normally be accessible by jumping from one VLAN to another.

VPN concentrator   A hardware appliance that allows hundreds of users to connect to the network from remote locations via a VPN.

vulnerability   Weaknesses in your computer network design and individual host configuration.

vulnerability assessment   Baselining of the network to assess the current security state of computers, servers, network devices, and the entire network in general.

vulnerability management   The practice of finding and mitigating software vulnerabilities in computers and networks.

vulnerability scanning   The act of scanning for weaknesses and susceptibilities in the network and on individual systems.

war-chalking   The act of physically drawing symbols in public places that denote open, closed, or protected wireless networks.

war-dialing   The act of scanning telephone numbers by dialing them one at a time and adding them to a list, in an attempt to gain access to computer networks.

war-driving   The act of searching for wireless networks by a person in a vehicle through the use of a device with a wireless antenna, often a particularly strong antenna.

warm site   A site that has computers, phones, and servers, but they might require some configuration before users can start using them.

waterfall model   An SDLC model divided into sequential phases such as planning, design, implementation, testing, integration, deployment, and maintenance. *See* software development life cycle (SDLC).

watering hole attack   An attack where the attacker profiles which websites a user accesses and installs malware to those sites that either infects the user's computer or redirects the user to other websites.

web application firewall (WAF)   An application firewall used to protect servers (and their client sessions) from XSS and SQL injection, among other attacks, during HTTP sessions.

web of trust   A decentralized model used for sharing certificates without the need for a centralized CA.

web security gateway   An intermediary that can scan for viruses and filter Internet content.

wet pipe sprinkler system   Consists of a pressurized water supply system that can deliver a high quantity of water to an entire building via a piping distribution system.

whaling A phishing attack that targets senior executives.

white-box testing A method of testing applications or systems where the tester is given access to the internal workings of the system.

white hat A type of hacker that is contracted to break into a company's system.

Wi-Fi disassociation attack Also known as Wi-Fi deauthentication attack, when an attacker targets a user's Wi-Fi-connected system, deauthenticates it using special software, and then reauthenticates it to find out SSID and WPA handshake information.

Wi-Fi Protected Access (WPA) A security protocol created by the Wi-Fi Alliance to secure wireless computer networks; more secure than WEP.

Wi-Fi Protected Setup (WPS) A simplified way of connecting to wireless networks using an eight-digit code. It is now deprecated due to its insecure nature and should be disabled if currently used.

wildcard certificate A single public key certificate that can be used by multiple sub-domains (or all subdomains) of a single domain; for example, *.davidlprowse.com.

Wired Equivalent Privacy (WEP) A deprecated wireless network security standard, less secure than WPA.

Wireless Transport Layer Security (WTLS) A protocol that is part of the Wireless Application Protocol (WAP) stack used by mobile devices. It enables secure user sessions.

wiretapping Tapping into a network cable in an attempt to eavesdrop on a conversation or steal data.

worm Code that runs on a computer without the user's knowledge; a worm self-replicates, whereas a virus does not.

X.509 A common PKI standard developed by the ITU-T that incorporates the single sign-on authentication method.

zero day attack An attack that is executed on a vulnerability in software before that vulnerability is known to the creator of the software.

zombie An individual compromised computer in a botnet.

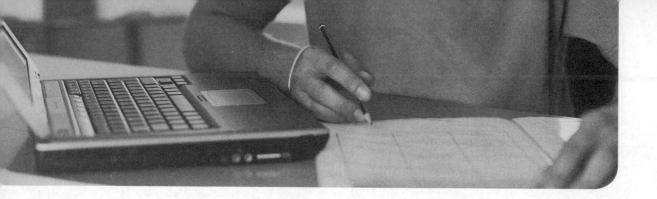

Index

O

Q - R

verifying identification. *See* authentication

vetting, 592

UTM (Unified Threat Management), 272

UTP (Unshielded Twisted-Pair) cabling, 292

V

V-shaped model (SDLC), 145

V2 cards, SIM cloning, 69

vacations (mandatory), 620-622

validation

CA, 525

certificates, 525

DV certificates, 522

EV certificates, 522

identity validation, 322

input validation, 150-151

OV certificates, 522

vehicles, facilities security

air gaps, 600-601

CAN, 600

drones, 601

locking systems, 601

UAV, 601

Wi-Fi, 601

vendor policies

BPA, 623-624

ISA, 624

MoU, 624

SLA, 623-624

verifying

attestation, BIOS, 62

certificates with RA, 527

user identity. *See* authentication

VeriSign certificates, 72, 525

Verisys, 57

Vernam ciphers. *See* **one-time pads**

vertical privilege escalation, 288

vetting employees, 592

video

exam preparation, 648

incident response procedures, 631

record time offset, 631

video surveillance, physical security, 323

virtualization. *See also* **VM (Virtual Machines)**

application containerization, 112

definition of, 109

emulators, 111

hardware, disabling, 115

Hyper-V, 114

hypervisors, 111-112

network security, 115

updates, 115

virtual appliances, 111

virtual escape protection, 115

virtualization sprawl, 114

viruses

armored viruses, 21

boot sector viruses, 20, 34

definition of, 25

encrypted viruses, 20

Love Bug virus, 25

macro viruses, 20

metamorphic viruses, 21

multipartite viruses, 21

polymorphic viruses, 20

preventing/troubleshooting, 41

antivirus software, 31, 34

encryption, 33

Linux-based tools, 35

Windows Firewall, 31

Windows Update, 31

program viruses, 20

stealth viruses, 21

symptoms of, 33-34

virus hoaxes, 21

vishing, 586, 590

To receive your 10% off Exam Voucher, register your product at:

www.pearsonitcertification.com/register

and follow the instructions.